TEXAS
HANDBOOK

SECOND EDITION

TEXAS HANDBOOK

SECOND EDITION

JOE CUMMINGS

MOON
PUBLICATIONS, INC.

TEXAS HANDBOOK

Published by
Moon Publications, Inc.
722 Wall Street
Chico, California 95928 USA

Please send all comments,
corrections, additions,
amendments, and critiques to:

**JOE CUMMINGS
c/o MOON PUBLICATIONS, INC.
722 WALL STREET
CHICO, CA 95928, USA**

Printed by
Colorcraft, Ltd.

Printing History
1st edition—August 1990
2nd edition—September 1992

Library of Congress Cataloging in Publication Data

Cummings, Joe
        Texas handbook / Joe Cummings. -- 2nd Ed.
            p.   cm.
        Includes bibliographical references and index.
        ISBN 0-918373-86-7 : $13.95
        1. Texas--Guidebooks.   I. Title
F384.3.C86   1992
917.6404'63--dc20

92-19879
CIP

Editor: Beth Rhudy
Copy Editors: Asha Johnson, Mark Arends
Production & Design: David Hurst, Carey Wilson
Cartographers: Bob Race, Brian Bardwell, Anne Hikido
Index: Mark Arends

All photos by Joe Cummings unless otherwise noted.

Printed in Hong Kong

Dedicated to my parents,
Will Joe & Mary Cummings

ABBREVIATIONS

a/c–air conditioned
B&B–bed and breakfast
d–double occupancy
I–interstate highway
mph–miles per hour
OW–one way

pp–per person
RT–roundtrip
RV–recreation vehicle
s–single occupancy
t–triple occupancy
w/e–water and electricity

CONTENTS

MAPS

MAP SYMBOLS

FREEWAY

MAIN HIGHWAY

SECONDARY ROAD

UNPAVED RD.

FOOT TRAIL

TUNNEL

RAILROAD

BRIDGE

REGIONAL BORDER

COUNTY BORDER

STATE BORDER

INTERNATIONAL BORDER

N.R.A. NATIONAL RECREATION AREA

S.R.A. STATE RECREATION AREA

N.W.R. NATIONAL WILDLIFE REFUGE

N.P. NATIONAL PARK

INTERSTATE HIGHWAY

U.S. HIGHWAY

STATE HIGHWAY

OTHER NUMBERED ROAD

MEXICAN HIGHWAY

O   LARGE CITY

o   TOWN

■   POINT OF INTEREST

⌐L GATE

WATER

▲   MOUNTAIN

CHARTS

ACKNOWLEDGEMENTS

During the updating process for the second edition of *Texas Handbook*, a legion of Texans gave generously of their time and energy.

First and foremost, thanks to Texas PR wrangler Jim Battersby, who offered invaluable logistical assistance before and during my road trip through the central and southwestern portions of the state. As usual, visitors bureaus and chambers of commerce throughout Texas were extremely helpful (most of them anyway) with the gathering of the latest information. Specific individuals and institutions who deserve mention include Homer O. Blair, Marion Szurek Bottomley, Jerry Brite, Terri Bortness, Sudie Burditt, Judith M. Bureske, Cathy Cabler, June Causey, Pete Danko, Milton Evans, Fiesta Texas, Orren Gaspard, Angela Gonzalez, Annetta Gray, Debbie Studer Green, Barbara Grove, La Mansón del Rio, Ernest Loeffler, Jr., April MacDowell, Shirley Milam, National Park Concessions, John Neilson, Kimberly Parsons, Diane Probst, Ramada Inn-Del Rio, Judy Ramos, Gail Rankin, Rondell G. Sanders, Jane Satel, Southwest Airlines, Judy Stone, Ronald Switzer, Lana Tolleson, Deborah Washington, Kathryn Fuller, and Ruth Wilson.

Thanks also to my parents, Will Joe and Mary Cummings, who provided ongoing research assistance and whose home served as "mission control Texas."

IS THIS BOOK OUT OF DATE?

Between the time this book went to press and the time it got onto the shelves, motels have closed, restaurants have changed hands, and prices have probably gone up. Because of this, all prices herein should be regarded as approximations and are not guaranteed by the publisher or author. Because keeping this book accurate and timely means second and later editions, we would appreciate hearing about any errors or omissions you may encounter in *Texas Handbook*. Also, if you have any noteworthy experiences (good or bad) with establishments listed in this book, please pass it along to us. If an attraction is out of place on a map, tell us; if the best restaurant in town is not included, we'd like to know. All contributions will be deeply appreciated and properly acknowledged. Address your letters to:

Joe Cummings
c/o Moon Publications
722 Wall St., Chico, CA 95928

BOB RACE

INTRODUCTION

Texas *is* big. And along with its awe-inspiring size comes an incomparable diversity of people, flora, fauna, arts, and cultures. In no other state can you experience as much change, both geographic and cultural, as when you travel from one end of Texas to another. Despite the homogenizing in-

fluences of TV and chain restaurants, which threaten to create a unified American way of life throughout the U.S., Texas remains a proudly different state, an area with strong roots and uncommon perspective.

THE LAND

Naturalist Richard Phelan has noted that Texas is blessed with "nearly every kind of land except tundra and tropical rainforest." In Texas you can't separate the land from the culture, especially when there is so much more land than people. The state is 267,300 square miles of faults, folds, extrusions, intrusions, high and low plains, canyons, mountains, valleys, forests, islands, rivers, lakes, and bayous—a lot for a geographer to work with. A drive from Laredo on the Mexican border to Wichita Falls on the Oklahoma border will take you through four or five obviously different terrains. Texans are fond of mentioning that it's farther from Texarkana to El Paso than it is from Chicago to New York (or from El Paso to Los

Angeles). But few people today recall that when the government of the Republic of Texas signed the treaty annexing their sovereign nation to the United States in 1845, they reserved the right in perpetuity to subdivide the new state into as many as five smaller states. Few Texans have advocated such a course of action in recent years, but in topographical variety as well as size, Texas easily lends itself to this kind of thinking.

Talk to six different Texana experts about how best to divide the state into physiographic regions and you'll get six different plans. Geography forms climate, and climate in turn influences wildlife and the human population, which make their own contributions to ongoing topographical

TEXAS ORIENTATION

changes. The task of classification is especially difficult in Texas, which forms the intersection of four major American physiographic regions—the Great Plains, the Interior Lowlands, the Rocky Mountain System, and the Basin and Range Province. But if you synthesize descriptions of Texas from the fields of geology, biology, and meteorology, you'll find they agree on eight basic geographic sections: the **Llano Estacado** (also called High Plains), the **Prairies and Cross Timbers** (or Low Plains), the **Trans-Pecos**, the **Edwards Plateau**, the **Llano Uplift**, the **Rio Grande Plain**, the **Gulf Coast**, and the **East Texas Forests**.

Llano Estacado

One of the myths about Texas is that it is flat and dry. The flat part of the myth has most likely been propagated by people who have driven cross-country via Interstate 40, which cuts across the Texas Panhandle through Amarillo and miles of seemingly unending flat territory. Spanish explorers called it the Llano Estacado, or "Staked Plain," but no one is sure why. Maybe it was because they had to drive stakes in the earth for navigation since there were few natural landmarks. Or perhaps it was because the western edge (in New Mexico) and eastern edge (in Texas) dropped so suddenly, like a stockade wall (*estacado* can also mean "stockaded").

Geographically speaking, this area is the southernmost tip of the Great Plains, which stretch from the Panhandle all the way north to Canada. In Texas, the Llano Estacado covers mostly the western part of the Panhandle as far south as Odessa. A few miles east of Lubbock, it is separated from the Low Plains by the Caprock Escarpment, where the hard layer of caliche, marl, chalk, and gravel that underlies the Llano (the Caprock) crumbles away. Caliche is a cement-like substance that forms when water evaporates from limestone mixed with soil, leaving behind a calcified "hardpan." You don't see that much caliche naturally exposed on the High Plains, but once you descend the Caprock Escarpment, it becomes a fairly common feature of Central Texas. When Texans say they live "up on the Caprock," they mean in the Llano Estacado area of the Panhandle.

The Caprock slows the erosion of topsoil from the High Plains, and this vast layer of topsoil at one time supported uninterrupted grasslands throughout the Plains. Huge herds of buffalo once grazed here, and the Comanche Indians who lived off the herds managed to keep European settlers out of the Llano Estacado until the late 19th century. While neither the Texas Rangers nor the U.S. Army could defeat the Comanches in battle, Indians as well as white buffalo hunters (often supplied with ammunition by the Army) managed to deplete the buffalo herds to such an extent that many of the Comanches simply moved on to Oklahoma. At that point cattle ranchers from farther south in Texas moved in and overstocked the land, destroying the natural grasslands in less than a hundred years.

Today, the grasslands have returned to some degree in the form of large grain farms that grow oats, corn, and sorghum. Many of these farms are irrigated by windmills that pump water from deep below the Caprock. The windmill has become a symbol of Texas farming and on the Llano Estacado many families erect mock Texas windmills in front of their homes, one for each child. The last remaining American windmill manufacturer is in San Angelo, Texas, at the southernmost edge of the Llano. Ironically, the larger cattle ranches, such as the XIT in Lubbock, have split up and ranchers must now grow (or purchase) their own feed to supplement grazing.

The table-top flatness of the Llano Estacado is interrupted by two rivers. The Canadian runs east to west across the top portion of the Panhandle, cutting a 20-mile-wide trough known as The Breaks. The Breaks expose layers of gypsum, petrified wood, and a type of flint that was once

© MOON PUBLICATIONS, INC.

highly prized by North American Indians. On a bluff near what is today Lake Meredith are the remains of the Alibates Flint Quarries, where 12,000 years ago Indians obtained flint for spear points and arrowheads that were traded throughout the Plains. The Canadian is also known for its quicksand areas and was thus one of the trickier rivers to cross in the days when cattlemen drove stock north to Kansas.

The Prairie Dog Town Fork of the Red River and smaller tributaries have formed technicolor Palo Duro Canyon south of Amarillo. Charles Goodnight established the first ranch on the Llano in 1876 right in Palo Duro Canyon; he stayed for 53 years. For more details, see "Palo Duro Canyon," p. 159.

Trans-Pecos

For many people, the Trans-Pecos region is the most compellingly beautiful of Texas landscapes, an inspiring combination of mountains, desert, mesas, and endless blue skies—in short, what most people think of as classic Southwestern scenery. This area is part of a geologic phenomenon called the Basin and Range Province. Centered in Nevada, it encompasses the Colorado Plateau to include parts of Colorado and Utah, and extends across New Mexico and into Texas for thousands of square miles before butting up against the Texas High Plains. Trans-Pecos means, of course, "across the Pecos River," but in Texas the area actually begins a bit northeast of the Pecos River at the southwestern edge of the High Plains.

The 70-foot sand dunes of the Monahans Sandhills in the eastern Trans-Pecos were once part of the floor of a Permian sea. Although they shimmer in the midday summer heat, at night the dunes make a good campsite—as long as you stay within sight of a road or other stationary landmarks. Smaller dunes feature shinnery oaks, which are only about three feet high but have a root system that reaches as far as 90 feet underground. Mesquite, hardy grasses, and wildflowers also appear occasionally to interrupt the sandy landscape. The lower part of the Trans-Pecos belongs to the great Chihuahuan Desert, which stretches far south into the Mexican state of Chihuahua, from which it gets its name.

Dividing the Mexican part of the desert from the American is, of course, the Rio Grande, which has its source in Colorado, flows north-south through New Mexico, then along the Texas-Mexico border until it empties into the Gulf of Mexico. The Upper Rio Grande Valley near El Paso is the oldest irrigated region in the state and the oldest continually cultivated area in the country. Water from the river is so heavily diverted for agricultural use here that the Rio Grande just about comes to a halt until it is joined farther down by Mexico's Rio Conchos at Presidio, Texas. Then for 100 miles or so, the Rio Grande follows the southern boundary of Big Bend National Park, flowing through three successive canyons: the Santa Elena, the Mariscal, and the Boquillas.

Texans like saying that their state has 90 mountains over a mile high, but they seldom mention that every one of them is located in the Trans-Pecos area. Thirty mountain ranges here have been named, and all are "fault-block" ranges, large chunks of the earth's crust that have broken loose and tilted like a broken sidewalk. All of the mountain ranges of the Basin and Range Province, including the Rockies, are of this type. The Guadalupe Mountains, straddling the New Mexican border, are the state's highest range (Guadalupe Peak, 8,749 feet), followed by the Davis Mountains (Mount Livermore, 8,206 feet), and the Chisos Mountains of Big Bend (Mount Emory, 7,825 feet).

In places, the Trans-Pecos mountain ranges surround large drainage basins called *bolsones,* Spanish for "bags" or "large purses." These basins hold rainwater that flows down the sides of the mountains; during times of sparse precip-

itation, this is the only source of surface water. Since the Trans-Pecos only receives about nine inches of rain per annum, yet averages nine *feet* of evaporation in that same time period, minerals distilled from the water tend to collect in the lowest points of a *bolson.* Salt is one of the primary distillates, so salt flats (locally called *playas)* are common among the basin areas, especially at the base of the Guadalupe Mountains. Until quite recently, commercial salt was collected from the *playas* in the Diablo Plateau area.

When rain falls into these basins, it forms lakes and pools of extremely salty water, which compounds the problem of scarce drinking water for humans, animals, and plants. Fortunately for animate life, natural cisterns called *huecos* (Spanish for "hole") occur in rock formations throughout certain parts of the Trans-Pecos, some of which shelter pools of pure rainwater year-round. Hueco Tanks State Park, 32 miles east of El Paso, features a high concentration of these pools and is the site of one of the state's largest collections of Indian pictographs. Apaches, Comanches, and Kiowas made Hueco Tanks a regular stop in their travels through West Texas, as did the Butterfield Overland Mail stagecoach line.

Big Bend country, where the Rio Grande forms a deep loop through the Chisos Mountains, is one of the more spectacular places in the Trans-Pecos, or indeed in the entire United States. Big Bend National Park itself is the best-preserved portion of the Chihuahuan Desert in either the U.S. or Mexico. See "Big Bend National Park," p. 114, for a complete description.

Edwards Plateau

Just south of Abilene is the Callahan Divide, a series of gaps where the Texas High Plains give way to the lower Edwards Plateau. It was through these gaps that herds of buffalo once migrated to warmer and greener pastures during harsh winters. But the soil of the Edwards Plateau is much thinner than that of the High Plains, and grasslands here were overgrazed by cattle ranching even more quickly than on the Llano Estacado.

Below the thin layer of topsoil is a giant slab of limestone that reaches a thickness of 10,000 feet in places. Many old homes, courthouses, and banks in this region are made from blocks of this limestone, locally called tufa limestone. Unpaved roads in Central Texas are usually laid with caliche, a limestone gravel that resists water-soaking. Domesticated animals far outnumber the people in this area and many counties have only one town, the county seat.

Deer and other cloven-hoofed creatures thrive on the rocky terrain, and the Edwards Plateau happens to be the world's leading area for the raising of Angora goats for mohair. Even cattle ranchers on the Plateau breed goats and sheep to supplement their income from cattle auctions. In many ways the terrain strongly resembles the high plains of East Africa, and a few ranches here specialize in exotic breeds from Asia and Africa,

including giraffe, rhinoceros, and wildebeest.

The Plateau stands 1,500 to 3,000 feet above sea level and stretches southward from the Callahan Divide until it begins to crumble away into the Rio Grande and Gulf Coast Plains at a large fault zone called the Balcones Escarpment. The Balcones, so named by Spanish settlers because of its resemblance to a series of balconies when viewed from the plains below, cuts a steep curve east from Del Rio over to San Antonio and then northeast from there past San Marcos, New Braunfels, Austin, and farther northward to Waco.

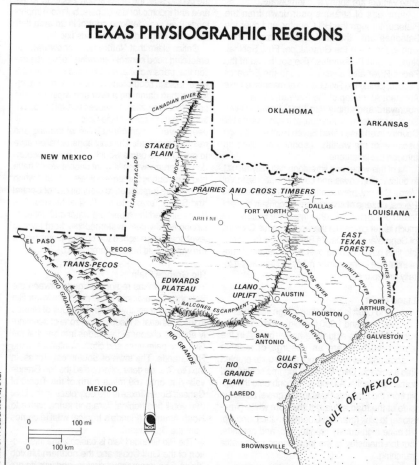

TEXAS PHYSIOGRAPHIC REGIONS

© MOON PUBLICATIONS, INC.

Cracks in the limestone shell allow water to spring forth from underground aquifers all along the fault, forming streams and rivers. All of these towns developed along the fault zone because of the easy access to water. Today, Interstate 35 runs parallel to the Balcones Escarpment from town to town.

The area of the Edwards Plateau along the fault zone is usually called the Hill Country and is highly prized as a recreation area because of its mild climate and abundant streams. During the height of the summer, nights are dry, cool, and often breezy, while winters are sunny and temperate.

Hundreds of streams pour down from the Plateau, through the Hill Country, and over the Balcones onto the Gulf Coast Plains. Chief among them are the Guadalupe, Frio, Sabinal, Nueces, and Pedernales. The south end of the Pecos River also passes through the Edwards Plateau, joining the Rio Grande at manmade Lake Amistad. At the top of the Plateau, streams run northward and empty into the Colorado River. South of the town of Junction, at the foot of the Hill Country, is an area called Seven Hundred Springs because of the wealth of springs bubbling up through the limestone.

All of this water and limestone naturally results in outstanding caves and cave formations. In Val Verde County, between the Rio Grande and the Pecos, dozens of shallow caves contain ancient Indian pictographs. Farther inside the Plateau are much larger caves like the world-famous Caverns of Sonora and the Devil's Sinkhole. So far, speleologists have counted over 2,000 caves of substantial size in the vicinity, many of them as yet totally unexplored.

Llano Uplift

The Llano Uplift is a very large, high valley, about 70 miles wide and 1,000 feet high, surrounded by rugged hills. It's actually a huge "bump" in the earth's crust where an upsurge of magma pushed against the crust but never quite erupted into a volcano. Over time, the magma cooled and turned to granite. As you drive north onto the Uplift from the Edwards Plateau, the gravel along the side of the road actually turns from white (limestone) to pink (granite)! Quarries in the Llano Uplift mine high-quality granite, talc, and graphite, but the mainstay of the local economy is cattle ranching.

The area is named for the Llano River, which runs off the Edwards Plateau from Junction to the town of Llano, and from there to a string of lakes northwest of Austin that were once part of the Colorado River. Called the Highland Lakes, they were created by damming the Colorado River in several places.

The area surrounding the lakes is fast becoming a resort area for Central Texas residents. The recent transformation has been great for Central Texans, but not so good for the (former) wildlife and plants of the Colorado River floodplains. On the people side, the dams supply electricity to the area and income for developers, but more importantly they provide flood control in an area that was once plagued by disastrous floods.

Critics claim that Nature has her own way of practicing flood control—growing heavy vegetation that traps water and allows it to soak into the water table in flood-prone areas—that is more effective than damming a river and wiping out the protective vegetation. However, natural flood control along this section of the Colorado had already been severely hampered by local farming and ranching practices. The only apparent alternative to erecting the dams would have been to abandon the area—which is what people would have had to do during the torrential rains of 1957 when floodwaters threatened to carry off half of Central and South Texas into the Gulf of Mexico. The dams allowed the municipal water authorities to siphon floodwaters systematically from level to level until they reached the coastal plains where the water could be accommodated.

Rio Grande Plain

The South Texas region wedged between the Balcones Escarpment to the north, the lower Rio Grande to the southwest, and the Gulf of Mexico to the southeast is a subtropical zone of seemingly endless chaparral that fades into sand at the Gulf, and palm trees and citrus plantations at the Rio Grande. The town of Southmost, Texas, in the Rio Grande delta (often called the Rio Grande valley) is only 169 miles north of the Tropic of Cancer. South Texas is the only place in the U.S. that you'll find tropical flora and fauna native to North America (Florida's tropical wildlife comes from the Caribbean).

The Rio Grande Plain is basically the intersection of the Gulf Coast and the northern Mexico plains. The geography, climate, and wildlife are relatively similar from San Antonio all the way to Mexico's Sierra Madre Oriental beyond Monterrey. Much of it consists of the famous "Brush Country" of South Texas and northern Mexico. Brush or chaparral is rather a recent phenomenon, a natural result of the overgrazing of cattle that occurred throughout the Great Plains. At one time this area featured extensive savannah or grasslands, but as the grass thinned, the brush took over.

"Brush" is a mixture of tenacious plants, mostly thorny ones: cactus, mesquite, dwarf oak, black bush, yucca, huisache, huajillo, and other wild shrubs. Often it grows in tangled clumps, some of them up to 20 feet in height. Spanish *vaqueros* taught their Anglo counterparts the skill of "brush-popping," or riding through the brush at top speed in pursuit of stray cattle. This kind of riding required special leather leggings *(chaparrera)* for protection from the brush. Texas cowboys or "buckaroos" (from *vaqueros*) called them "chaps"—a shortening of *chaparrera*.

Cattle ranching is still big on the Rio Grande Plain (this is where it started), but as on the Edwards Plateau, many ranchers now raise sheep and goats as well. Cloven-hoofed animals like deer, sheep, and goats do well in brush country, since they "browse" rather than graze—they prefer twigs and leaves to grass. A few South Texas ranches stock Australian and African breeds like ostrich and rhinoceros. Down toward the Rio Grande delta, vegetable and citrus cultivation are important industries.

Gulf Coast

The Texas Gulf coast is an extension of the coastal plains that reach all the way from the Atlantic Ocean to the Rio Grande. They are bounded at the northwest by the Balcones Escarpment, at the north by the East Texas Forests, and on the southwest by the Rio Grande Plains. The Gulf of Mexico coast, of course, is the southeast boundary, stretching for over 600 miles. The Gulf, the world's largest body of water by that name, is really a tropical sea in itself, with coral reefs, underwater mountains, and submarine canyons. The well-known Gulf Stream runs clockwise around the Gulf (the "Loop Current") and then into the Atlantic, where it warms East Coast beaches. Near Texas, the water temperature varies from 52° to 85°, depending on the time of year.

Parallel to the coastline are the long, sandy barrier islands of North and South Padre, Mustang, and Matagordas, as well as the vibrant salt marshes of Galveston Island and the Bolivar Peninsula. Salt marshes produce the greatest biomass of any environment on the planet, that is, the highest concentration of living organisms per square mile. In the Bolivar Peninsula's salt marshes you'll see everything from gnats to alligators.

A large underground supply of geothermal energy lies untapped beneath the Texas coast in the form of very hot (320°) water. Geothermal engineers are still deliberating on how best to utilize the energy. The water is fresh, not salty, which also makes it a potential source of drinking water once it's cooled.

East Texas Forests

The East Texas Forests are the westernmost extension of the Southern Appalachian Woodland. If the Trans-Pecos belongs to the American Southwest, East Texas belongs to the American Southeast. The forests here can be divided into the Pine Belt (farthest east), the Big Thicket (south of the Pine Belt), and the Post Oak Belt (west of both).

Timber has been the main long-term industry in the Pine Belt. In addition to pine, hundreds of other tree species grow in the Pine Belt. Because of heavy annual rainfall (up to 60 inches a year), growth is profuse and forest fires are rarely a problem. High humidity and the morning fog that is common throughout the East Texas woodlands keep the woods moist. Huge oil fields have also yielded local revenue over the years. Cotton and cattle have become increasingly important in the region as well.

Before the 1800s, most of East Texas was almost entirely virgin forest inhabited only by a small group of Caddo Indians. Farming and cattle ranching later turned vast tracts of land into prairie, but the establishment of four national forests as well as a national reserve has offered some protection to over 700,000 acres of woodlands.

One of these, Big Thicket National Preserve, is said to be among the most magnificent and complex forests remaining in the world. Part of the reason for this is that it is not far from the Gulf coast and has a thick layer of sand just under the topsoil. Roots flourish in the sand, penetrating deeply and easily; sand is also an efficient water repository. This sandy layer, together with the mild combination of subtropic and temperate climates and the lack of forest fires, means that trees grow to great size and age. For more detail on this forest wonder, see "Big Thicket National Preserve," p. 451.

The only natural lake of any size in Texas is Caddo Lake, which straddles the Texas-Louisiana border near Shreveport. Between Caddo Lake and the Sabine River to the south are several classic bayous. The Sabine River flows into the Toledo Bend Reservoir, also on the Louisiana border. If this lake were entirely within Texas, it would be the largest body of water in the state.

The Piney Woods begin to fade out as they move west into the Post Oak Belt. The tall pines give way to sturdy post oaks, which have become fewer and farther between since there are no national forests here to preserve them from farming and ranching interests. Clay, lignite, and other minerals in this area are mined for commercial use. Though based on the same kind of sandy soil, the Post Oak Belt is very much a transition area between the East Texas Forests and the Prairies and Cross Timbers farther west.

Prairies And Cross Timbers

Between the Caprock Escarpment just east of Abilene and the Post Oak Belt east of Dallas are the Prairies and Cross Timbers, an area made up of smaller plains, prairies, and former woodlands running in north-south strips toward the Colorado River. Proceeding east to west, they include the Blackland Prairie, the Eastern Cross Timbers, the Grand Prairie, the Western Cross Timbers, and the Rolling Plains. In the same direction, the underlying geology alternates sand, limestone, and red Permian to account for these differing topographies.

The Chisholm Cattle Trail, the Western (Dodge City) Cattle Trail, and the Butterfield Overland Mail stagecoach line all intersected in this part of Texas, which makes up about a quarter of the state. As the cities of Dallas, Ft. Worth, Wichita Falls, and Austin grew up along these 19th-century routes (and today along Interstates 35 and 20), intensive land use blurred the lines between discrete geological entities to form more or less one topographical region: a patchwork of fairly similar-looking farms, cities, towns, and suburbs.

If you look closely, though, as you drive from Dallas to Abilene, you'll notice some variation. The Grand Prairie is dairy country, still rolling and grassy. Add the occasional tree to this scene and you've got the Blackland Prairie, which is one of the most agriculturally rich areas in the state. Toward Abilene, wayward mesas begin to crop up among the gently rolling hills, signaling the crumbly red earth of the Permian Basin. The Rolling Plains near Abilene are the last land contours to be seen before they are literally rolled up in the Great Plains of the Panhandle.

THE TRANS-PECOS

The Pecos River is the nominal eastern boundary for the Trans-Pecos region, but geographically this area also includes the Monahan Sandhills, northeast of the Pecos. For many people, the Trans-Pecos region is the most compellingly beautiful of Texas landscapes, with its deep canyons, orange-tinged mesas, flowering cacti, and sparkling arroyos.

The Trans-Pecos once presented a set of formidable barriers to riders, drovers, or wagon trains seeking to travel due west from Central Texas. First, there was the Pecos River itself, with its sheer chasms and turbulent waters. Then came the long stretches of alluring but unforgiving Chihuahuan Desert, broken only by the equally formidable Glass, Davis, and Guadalupe mountains.

In the 1850s, the U.S. Army imported camels from the Middle East and maintained a Camel Corps for the exploration of the Trans-Pecos. Even until fairly recently, most people drove through the Trans-Pecos with canvas water bags strapped to their radiators. Today Interstate 10 provides a relatively safe and speedy transit across this part of West Texas, if getting to El Paso as quickly as possible is your objective. But a sparse network of good U.S. highways, state highways, and farm/ranch roads makes it fairly easy to explore the scenic Upper Rio Grande, the sandhills, the major mountain ranges, and stunning Big Bend National Park.

When people speak today of the old "Law West of the Pecos," they tend to forget that this referred not simply to the vast remoteness of the area, but to mark it as the most lawless area of what was generally known as a lawless state. In the 19th and early 20th centuries, you had to be rough to get here, and you had to be rough to survive. Even today, law enforcement is scarce between Del Rio and El Paso; local residents claim they like it that way, that they prefer to take care of disputes on their own.

CLIMATE

Meteorologists love Texas weather because the state has so much of it. A saying goes that if you don't like the weather in Texas, stick around a couple of minutes and it'll change. While this isn't always so, it's worth noting that if you don't like the weather in one part of the state, you can always drive to another part and get an entirely different climate.

WET AND DRY

Texas rainfall varies mostly from east to west rather than north to south, though North Central Texas does get a few more inches of rain than South Texas each year. The driest part of Texas is the Trans-Pecos region between Big Bend and El Paso, where the average annual precipitation is 9 to 12 inches. The Davis Mountains of the Trans-Pecos get a bit more, up to 18 inches a year.

The wettest places are in East Texas, ranging from 52 inches a year in the Houston area to 56 inches a year on the lower Louisiana border. In areas between Far West Texas and Far East Texas, rainfall averages 25-28 inches a year.

Time of year is just as important to average precipitation as longitude. The Trans-Pecos receives more rainfall in summer and fall rather than in winter or spring. In East Texas, on the other hand, it rains most in the spring, followed by the fall months. For Central Texas, the fall months definitely bring the most rain.

HOT AND COLD

Several factors affect the state's average temperatures: latitude, longitude, elevation, and proximity to the Gulf of Mexico. As in most of the U.S., the lowest average temperatures occur between December and February, the highest between June and August.

In January, the average low temperatures vary from 28° F in Wichita Falls to 51° F in Brownsville. The average highs in January for these same cities are 52° F and 70° F respectively.

August temperatures range from average lows of 65° F in Amarillo and 75° F in Corpus Christi to average highs of 87° F in El Paso and 98° F in Laredo.

But averages are only averages and actual temperatures may zoom up and down the thermometer. Furthermore, perceived temperatures can diverge from actual temperatures due to wind velocity and humidity. Eighty-five degrees Fahrenheit is perceived as only 80° F at 0% humidity, 86° F at 50% humidity, and 101° at 100% humidity. While the Texas coast is more humid than most inland areas, breezes off the Gulf keep temperatures lower. South Central and East Texas, however, are humid year-round, ranging from 52% to 93% depending on the time of day—mornings and evenings are the most humid.

In general, the hottest days during the summer months are in the upper Rio Grande plains. The small town of Presidio, for example, often records daily high temperatures in excess of 100° F during June, July, and August. Because of the desert climate, however, nighttime temperatures at Presidio average a relatively cool 70-72° F during these same months. In the mountains of West Texas, temperatures are much more moderate during the summer, e.g., at Chisos Basin the daily average high is 63-73° F.

One climate feature of note is what Texans call a "norther," a cold front that moves in suddenly from a northerly direction. In the fall and winter months, these can arrive so rapidly that temperatures can drop as much as 50 degrees Fahrenheit in a half-hour. Sometimes you can actually see the cold front on the distant northern horizon—a steel-blue bank of high clouds floating over clear blue skies. Texans call this a "blue norther," a front that tends to come in fast and hard.

BEST SEASONS FOR TRAVEL

For statewide travel, the overall best months in Texas are usually late fall (late October through November), early spring (March and April), and early summer (late May and early June). A pan-Texas tour during these periods would avoid the

AVERAGE ANNUAL RAINFALL (IN INCHES)

© MOON PUBLICATIONS, INC.

AMARILLO
16
20
24 28 32 36 40 44
ABILENE DALLAS 46 48
10 12 SAN NACOGDOCHES 52
EL PASO ANGELO 56
8 FT. DAVIS AUSTIN PORT
14 16 ARTHUR
10 18 20 HOUSTON
TERLINGUA 12 DEL RIO 32 44
16 SAN 52
ANTONIO 44
LAREDO 22 40
28 36
24 CORPUS CHRISTI

0   200 mi
0   200 km

BROWNSVILLE

state's highest and lowest average temperatures as well as the highest rainfall. Of course not every year is the same.

Texas has no real peak tourist periods; the state as a whole tends to get roughly the same numbers of visitors year-round (though South Texas is more heavily traveled in the winter due to the influx of "Winter Texans" from the upper midwestern United States).

For regional travel, optimum months vary according to Texas geography.

South And South Central Texas

South Texas is fairly seasonable year-round, though temperatures in the high 90s are common June to August. High temperatures coupled with high humidity make parts of South Central Texas quite sticky in the daytime during these months.

Near the Mexican border, however, the humidity is significantly lower, so some people find the lower Rio Grande more comfortable than South Central Texas (Austin and San Antonio) during the summer, in spite of slightly higher temperatures. The Hill Country makes a good escape from San Antonio or Austin when temperature and humidity get to be too much. Temperatures tend to be four or five degrees lower and because of the elevation, the air is drier and there is usually a breeze.

During the winter, the weather in the lower Rio Grande valley is prime—as evidenced by all the "snowbirds" who drive down here from the midwestern U.S. to get away from plunging temperatures.

Trans-Pecos And Big Bend

October to December and March to May are generally good weather months in the Trans-Pecos and Big Bend area. January and February here may be a bit chilly for some, but just fine for others. The summer months, June-August, are usually too hot for the average visitor—daytime temperatures reach the high 90s and low 100s (although the mountains are quite temperate this time of year—just stay away from desert hikes). For Rio Grande river running, the fall is best for water action while the spring is best for birdwatching and wildflowers.

North Central Texas

The area around Dallas, Ft. Worth, and Waco features a climate that's sort of a cross between East Texas and South Central Texas weather. Heavy rains and the occasional tornado come in the late spring (April-May), but the rest of the year the weather is fairly moderate. Summers are hot, but not as hot as farther south or east.

East Texas

East Texas is best visited in the fall, when temperatures and rainfall are moderate. During the summer months, high temperatures and humidity slow most visitors down. Spring in East Texas is also comfortable if you can put up with occasional thundershowers.

Northwest Texas

Upper West Texas and the Panhandle can be rather blustery during the winter months and hot during the summer. Since rainfall is moderate year-round, these areas are well visited in both the spring and the fall.

HEAVY WEATHER

Tornadoes

Texas is famous for tornadoes, and, to a much lesser extent, hurricanes. Tornadoes (often called "twisters" in Texas) evolve from large, heavy thunderstorms in which a combination of atmospheric

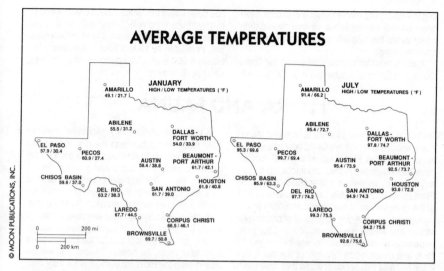

AVERAGE TEMPERATURES

JANUARY HIGH / LOW TEMPERATURES (°F)

AMARILLO 49.1 / 21.7

ABILENE 55.5 / 31.2

EL PASO 57.9 / 30.4

PECOS 60.9 / 27.4

DALLAS - FORT WORTH 54.0 / 33.9

AUSTIN 59.4 / 38.8

BEAUMONT - PORT ARTHUR 61.7 / 42.1

CHISOS BASIN 59.6 / 37.0

DEL RIO 63.2 / 38.3

SAN ANTONIO 61.7 / 39.0

HOUSTON 61.9 / 40.8

LAREDO 67.7 / 44.5

CORPUS CHRISTI 66.5 / 46.1

BROWNSVILLE 69.7 / 50.8

0   200 mi
0   200 km

JULY HIGH / LOW TEMPERATURES (°F)

AMARILLO 91.4 / 66.2

ABILENE 95.4 / 72.7

EL PASO 95.3 / 69.6

PECOS 99.7 / 69.4

DALLAS - FORT WORTH 97.8 / 74.7

AUSTIN 95.4 / 73.9

BEAUMONT - PORT ARTHUR 92.5 / 73.7

CHISOS BASIN 85.9 / 63.3

DEL RIO 97.7 / 74.2

SAN ANTONIO 94.9 / 74.3

HOUSTON 93.6 / 72.5

LAREDO 99.3 / 75.5

CORPUS CHRISTI 94.2 / 75.6

BROWNSVILLE 92.6 / 75.6

© MOON PUBLICATIONS, INC.

conditions produces a not-yet-understood set of spinning air currents. These currents spin faster and faster as they move toward the center, much as skaters spin more rapidly as they draw in their arms.

Texas reports an average of just over 100 tornadoes a year, most of which occur during the tornado season, March to May. Most of the tornadoes occur in a north-south corridor called "Tornado Alley," which stretches from the North Texas plains through Oklahoma, Kansas, and Nebraska (Oklahoma actually averages more tornadoes per year than any other state). Tornado warnings are fairly common during the tornado season as national and state meteorologists keep a close watch on storms and air currents that show twister potential.

It's highly unlikely that you'll be faced with a twister unless you happen to be traveling through Tornado Alley during peak season. If one is headed your way (you'll know if you see a dark funnel cloud undulating on the horizon), get to the lowest place you can find. A cellar or basement of a building is best, but if you're caught outdoors, look for a ditch or any depression in the ground—twisters tend to "skip" over low spots such as these. Don't try to outrun a tornado by car or on foot; experts say, in fact, that you'll fare better outside of a vehicle, lying flat on the ground if necessary, rather than sitting in an exposed car. Wind speeds at the rotating center of a tornado have been clocked at 280 miles per hour, and tornadoes have been known to lift entire cars and houses dozens of feet into the air before they come crashing to the ground.

Hurricanes

Hurricanes are fairly common on the Gulf of Mexico in August and September, less frequently in June, July, and October. The name comes from the Spanish for tropical cyclone, *huracán,* which is itself a corruption of the Mayan word for their storm god, Hunraken or Huraken. By definition, a hurricane or tropical cyclone is a "highly advanced tropical storm"; the effective difference between a tropical storm and a hurricane is force and potential for damage.

Between 1871 and 1982, an average of 41 hurricanes a year entered the state of Texas, most of them directly from the Gulf with a few from Mexico or Louisiana. The vast majority of reported hurricanes, however, cause little or no damage to either the coastal or inland areas of the state. Cities and towns always take the precaution of alerting residents and evacuating areas in advance of a storm's arrival when deemed necessary. Oftentimes a hurricane will lose momentum or change direction before hitting the coast, even when severe warnings have been issued. Nonetheless, visitors should definitely avoid the sea whenever there's a hurricane warning.

Texas's most famous hurricane was the Great Galveston Storm of September 8-9, 1900, which has been called the "worst natural disaster in U.S. history." Peak wind velocity was estimated at 120 miles per hour and the entire island of Galveston was inundated by 15-foot tides. Somewhere between 6,000 and 8,000 people lost their lives, most by drowning.

FLORA AND FAUNA

Texas has a fascinating variety of flora and fauna, many species of which are found nowhere else in the United States. Five hundred forty bird species have been identified in the state (including migratory species), as well as 142 species of animals. Plant species are virtually uncountable because of the wide variety of geographical niches found throughout Texas. A certain amount of native vegetation and wildlife is easily visible along the wide expanses of rural Texas, accessible by public farm and ranch roads throughout the state. But there are also thousands of acres that have been set aside by the U.S. and by the state of Texas especially for the preservation of Texas plants and animals. Most of these admit human visitors as well.

Besides some of the better city zoos in the nation, botanical gardens, and other manmade venues for the viewing of plant and animal life, Texas has 12 National Park Service facilities, 133 state parks, four national forests, 13 national wildlife refuges (more than any other state in the Southwest), and 28 state wildlife areas. Many of these are listed in this book by destination.

Below are names of some of the more common and more notable native flora and fauna.

VEGETATION

Physiographically, the vegetational zones of Texas cover the gamut from both the arid and humid lower Sonoran Zones to Canadian Zones. Before the arrival of European settlers, Texas was about 80% grasslands. The remaining 20% consisted of the deserts and mountains of the Trans-Pecos region and the forests of East Texas. Cattle were introduced to the region in the 17th and 18th centuries by the Spanish, and by the middle of the 19th century, overgrazing was beginning to take its toll on Texas grasslands.

A U.S. Department of Agriculture report in 1898 recorded a cattlemen's meeting at which an attending botanist tried to explain the complex relationship between grazers and grasses. Before the botanist completed his explanation, a rancher had interrupted with the following resolution, which was unanimously adopted by the cattlemen: "Resolved, that none of us know, or care to know, anything about grasses, native or otherwise, outside of the fact that for the present there are lots of them, the best on record, and we are after getting the most out of them while they last."

century plant

LOUISE FOOTE

Although this conspicuously ignorant attitude resulted in the thinning or elimination of grasslands throughout Texas (and in the Plains states from Kansas to Montana, too, where the same attitude prevailed), the benefit to nature-lovers was that this process allowed many other species to develop and proliferate. The complex "brush" that is considered a nuisance by ranchers has developed a fascinating ecosystem all its own (see "Mesquite," below.

Over 100 million acres of Texas land is still considered "range," or land most suitable for grazing, which remains the single-largest land use in the state. Range lands are a vital part of the regional ecosystem; they provide watershed for springs, streams, and lakes, food and shelter for wildlife, and forage for domestic livestock, as well as resources for human recreation—not to mention their prominent role in Texas mythology. The one native grass that still appears throughout most of the state is **sideoats grama,** identifiable by its scimitar-shaped seed tops. **Buffalo grass, Texas grama,** and **Indian grass** are also common across several zones.

Texas in the post-Cattle Kingdom era can be divided into 10 vegetational zones. The following describes each zone:

Trans-Pecos, Mountains And Basins

In spite of the fact that this area receives an average of less than 10 inches of rain a year, Far West Texas has perhaps the most interesting flora in the state. Texas boasts 106 species of cacti, more than the other 49 states combined, and most of them can be found in this area. The flowering **prickly pear cactus** alone comes in a splendid variety of shapes, sizes, colors, and number of spines. **Agave, yucca,** and **sotol** are also ubiquitous here. **Peyote,** a hallucinogenic cactus that is sought after by certain Indian groups for religious purposes, is native to the Big Bend area but is difficult to spot because it grows so low to the ground.

Other common plants are the **cenizo bush** (also called purple sage), the **creosote bush** (which emits a bittersweet "desert" smell after a rain), and the slender **ocotillo** (or coachwhip). In the Big Bend area, the **candelilla** is collected illegally by Mexicans who render wax from the plant. The **guayule** or rubber plant is found in the extreme west part of the Trans-Pecos.

On the mountain slopes, you'll find Rocky Mountain grasses not native to Texas as well as the native **ponderosa pine, madrone, juniper,** and **piñon pine.**

Wildflowers appear occasionally in basin areas where there is enough water. In the basins of the Chisos Mountains, the **Chisos bluebonnet,** which is actually larger than the state flower (the Texas bluebonnet), flourishes. Mexicans call this plant *el conejo,* the rabbit, because of the white tip's resemblance to a rabbit's tail.

High Plains

Just about the only vegetation native to the High Plains is a variety of grasses. With the thinning of the grasslands, "brush" moved in—**mesquite, sagebrush, yucca,** and others—plants which are common throughout much of Texas. Most of the trees you may see in the High Plains have been introduced by Texas residents, though the native **cottonwood** grows in the Palo Duro Canyon, and **sand shinnery oak** can be seen in many places.

On the "sandyland" parts of the High Plains (where the soil is sandy), **little bluestem, switch grass, Indian grass,** and **western wheatgrass** are the principal grasses. On the "hardlands" (clay-based soil), **buffalo grass** and **blue grama** are common, both excellent for grazing.

Rolling Plains

This area has the same grasses as the High Plains, with the addition of **red love grass, tumble grass, Texas winter grass, sideoats, wild ryes, big** and **sand bluestems,** and **tobosa grass.**

Mesquite woodlands now make up about half of the Rolling Plains, and are considered a big problem by local ranchers. As fast as they can chop it up and send it to Southwestern grills and barbecue houses, the tenacious mesquite grows back!

Edwards Plateau

Sturdy trees have colonized the rocky Edwards Plateau area from the Hill Country on the Balcones Escarpment to the Stockton Plateau, adjacent to the Trans-Pecos. The **bald cypress** is isolated from its native habitat, the bayous of Deep East Texas and southwestern Louisiana, but grows quite well along streams in the Hill

MESQUITE

Texas ranchers often consider the mesquite tree to be "brush"—problematic vegetation that encroaches on grasslands when native grasses have become depleted. They commonly believe that there is more mesquite in Texas now than a hundred years ago, and that it has "migrated" from Mexico. In actual fact, the mesquite tree is native to Texas and northern Mexico; in centuries past there were many more of these trees than now, in large mesquite woodlands throughout sections of the state. Much of the original mesquite was cut down by settlers in the 19th century and is only now coming back due to an overall decline in the use of mesquite as a source of lumber and everyday fuel.

The name for the tree comes from the Aztec *mizquitl,* and the Aztecs and other Indian groups have used the trunk, roots, leaves, beans, and bark for hundreds of years for a variety of purposes. The Aztecs combined ground mesquite leaves and water to form a balm for sore eyes—a remedy still used by *curanderos* in rural Mexico today. Comanches chewed the leaves to relieve toothaches. Mesquite gum has also been used by various tribes as a balm for wounds, a ceramic glue, a dye, and a digestive.

Indians used the mesquite beans—which grow from mesquite branches in long slender pods—as a source of nutrition as well. A ripe bean pod grows as long as nine inches, contains roughly 30% glucose, and is high in protein. Many animals and birds savor the beans (horses will eat them until they're sick if allowed). Rural Mexicans grind the dried pods into a flour with which they make bread and a kind of beer. Today many people in Texas and Mexico enjoy the bean pods straight from the tree, or boiled, dried, and crushed to make jellies, wine, and bread.

Early Texas ranchers used mesquite wood for fence posts, wagon wheels, fuel, and furniture. Before the Aztec name for the tree became popular, it was known as "Texas ironwood." San Antonio's Houston Street was once entirely paved with mesquite blocks, as were early streets in Brownsville. Mesquite makes an excellent woodcrafting material since it's extremely durable and resistant to rot. Woodworkers in the Southwest have rediscovered the pleasures and profits of working with mesquite—a finely crafted mesquite rocking chair fetches as much as $2500 in Texas today.

But mesquite's most famous use nowadays is as a fuel for barbecue pits and grills as well as for smoking meat, poultry, and fish. The wood is especially well suited to cooking because it yields a hot flame when burned; smoke is sparse and aromatic, imparting a savory flavor to foods cooked over it. Even coffee brewed over a mesquite fire is said to taste better.

A tip: to give mesquite-grilled foods an even more pronounced mesquite flavor, throw a few mesquite pods on the coals before cooking.

LOUISE FOOTE

Country. Hanging in the cypress is the occasional **ball moss,** a close relative of the Spanish moss commonly seen on cypress and oaks of Deep East Texas. Actually, neither of these species is a true moss—they're flowering plants of the bromeliad family—and contrary to myth, they aren't parasitic.

Common trees throughout the Edwards Plateau include the omnipresent **mesquite, shinnery oak, pecan,** and **live oak,** as well as **mountain cedar,** a tree that gives the Hill Country its characteristic fragrance. Along the Bal-

cones Escarpment a thorny shrub called **huajillo** (also guajillo) is common, especially in the Uvalde area. The white flowers of the huajillo produce Uvalde honey, which honey connoisseurs claim is among the world's best.

Between the trees and brush, the Plateau sprouts many of the same grasses as the High and Rolling plains northward.

South Texas Plains
The area south of San Antonio is a subtropical dryland zone in which smaller trees, shrubs, cacti,

and hardy grasses thrive—a mixture of vegetation usually called "brush" or "chaparral." Since this zone has many plants in common with the chaparral of northern Mexico, Spanish names are common. Parts of the South Texas plains are said to resemble Africa's Zambezi Valley, and at least one ranch here is successfully breeding rhinoceros, which thrive on the omnipresent **huisache** shrub, a close relative of the African acacia.

The most typical brush country inhabitants are **small live oak, mesquite, post oak, prickly pear cactus, catclaw, rat-tail cactus, black chaparral** (black bush), **acacia, granjeno, retama, yucca, cenizo, huisache,** and **huajillo.** Beneath the brush canopy are what remains of the original **bunch grasses,** plus **Arizona cottontop, curly mesquite, buffalo grass,** and various Texas **gramas.**

Toward the Gulf coast, the sandy soils produce **tanglehead, sandbur, windmill grass, seacoast bluestem, bristle grass,** and **paspalum.** Where the soil is particularly saline, **seashore salt grass, gulf cord grass,** and **alkali sacaton** are the dominant grasses. Along the coast in the Rockport/Fulton area are striking **coastal oaks,** with windswept branches all pointing inland.

At the southernmost reaches of the Rio Grande plains grow the only tropical species in the U.S. that are native to North America. Of the many palm trees growing in the area, most are imported royal and California palms, but one is Texas's own: the *Sabal texana* or **Texas palm** (look for a straight trunk crowned by palm leaves that extend in all directions, like a sphere rather than an umbrella). The fruit of the Texas palm is edible and is occasionally sold in Brownsville and Matamoros markets. The Sabal Palm Grove Sanctuary, a preserve on the Rio Grande near Brownsville, protects a small but significant part of the native palm forest which was once common throughout the lower Rio Grande delta.

Citrus plantations are now common in tropical South Texas, but the species cultivated here were introduced from other climes.

Prairies And Cross Timbers

This area is a mixture of small woodlands alternating with prairies in North Central Texas. Trees that are native to the area include **post, live, shinnery,** and **blackjack oak.** Mesquite and juniper are present as well, having moved in as the grasses were depleted by grazing. Prairie grasses here are similar to those in the westward High and Rolling plains—various **gramas, bluestems, Indian grass,** and **buffalo grass.**

Blackland Prairie

The narrow Blackland Prairie extends for some 400 miles from the Red River south to near San Antonio and has the most fertile topsoil in Texas. The rich, black soil runs deep and Blackland farms are coveted like gold mines. Hence, most of the land here is under cultivation.

Some of the classic Texas trees are found in the Blacklands. Although farming interests have cleared much of the timberland that once existed here, various species still stand untouched along rivers and streams. A variety of oaks predominate, along with **pecan, elm,** and **bois d'arc** (horse-apple). The bois d'arc was a favorite tree for Indian bow-makers in East Texas.

Post Oak Savannah

As its name suggests, this was originally grassland with a canopy of hardwoods, predominantly **post oaks.** Post oaks are still characteristic of the area, along with **blackjack oak, pecan, walnut,** and **elm** trees.

Native grasses include the usual gramas, bluestems, switch grass, and Indian grass, plus **longleaf wood oats, spike wood oats,** and **red love grass.** As elsewhere in the state, brush has entered the savannah—**mesquite, oak brush, greenbriar,** and **yaupon** are typical of the area.

Piney Woods

In the space available here, it would be impossible to do justice to the wide variety of vegetation in the East Texas Forests collectively called the Piney Woods. In the Big Thicket alone (often considered separate from the Piney Woods), there are six forest layers (most woodlands have only three) and eight separate plant communities extending from the upland forests to the cypress bogs. Plant species you'd never expect to find in Texas, including 40 species of wild orchids and nine carnivorous plants, grow in abundance.

Common trees in the Big Thicket include **loblolly pine, beech, hornbeam, magnolia, sweet gum, black gum, walnut, hickory, white oak, red oak, ash, tupelo, dogwood, hawthorn,** and **mulberry.** Along the forest floor are various ferns and mosses, **partridgeberry, Vir-**

ginia willow, corkwood, blueberry, holly, and swamp honeysuckle.

The four national forests north of the Big Thicket (sometimes the term "Piney Woods" refers only to these) contain a predominance of pines, plus maples, oaks, beeches, gums, and bois d'arc. Many smaller trees used by the Caddo Indians for food and medicine are also common in the Piney Woods: persimmon, chinquapin, pawpaw, witch hazel, and sassafras.

On sandier soils toward the coast grow palmettos, a small semitropical shrub that resembles a dwarf palm tree.

Gulf Marshes And Coast

Most of the existing Gulf Marshes are located along the inside of the Gulf coast barrier islands and Bolivar Peninsula, facing tidal basins. (At one time there were many marshes at river mouths on the mainland shore but a good number have been dredged, filled, or destroyed by dams upriver that have deprived them of fresh water and minerals.) In certain spots along the Bolivar Peninsula and Galveston Island, thriving marshes extend completely across the islands to face the Gulf.

Marshlands vary from wet to dry and fresh to salty, depending on the level of the underlying land and proximity to river mouths. Plants and animals that live in marshes have adapted to various combinations along these continuums, so there is great variety. Because of this extensive variation, salt marshes represent the most concentrated biomass on the planet (exceeding even tropical rainforests), especially as environments for birds and animals (see "Wildlife" below).

The tall grasses growing over the marshlands are generally called "salt grass," though there are actually several different species present. Some grow as high as eight feet, swallowing the flat-bottomed boats that scoot along canals which are the main avenues of transport in the marshes. Other vegetation in the Gulf Marshes include bullrush, sedge, smooth and marshhay cord grasses, maidencane, and marsh millet. On sandy beach areas, a few grasses resistant to saline environments, such as seashore salt grass, may be seen.

One of the more interesting plants that is occasionally seen along Gulf coast beaches is the sargassum weed. Sargassum doesn't grow on the coast, nor does it grow on the sea bottom like other seaweeds. Instead, it floats along on top of the sea, supported by a system of air bladders. A specially adapted group of tiny animals live in sargassum weed and depend on it for food and as their nesting area (some can't swim, and if they lose their hold on sargassum they sink and die). Sargassum is not very common along the Gulf coast except when severe tropical storms force it to wash onto shore. Then it not only litters the beach but after a while begins to stink—the smell comes from the dying organisms clinging to the sargassum.

WILDLIFE

The animals and birds of Texas cannot be as easily confined to geographic areas as Texas plants. While there are definite favored habitats, there's no stopping most critters when they decide to fly, walk, run, hop, or crawl across, say, the Balcones Escarpment.

While Texas wildlife can easily be seen in the national and state parks, forests, and recreation areas, the highest populations are naturally in the 13 national wildlife refuges and 28 state wildlife areas. These areas are devoted to the preservation of wildlife, but most are open to nature study, hiking, and camping.

In addition, most of the state wildlife areas are open to hunting and fishing during regulated seasons. The State Parks and Wildlife Department issues state hunting and fishing licenses (see "Hunting," p. 56, and "Fishing," p. 57 for more information).

The descriptions below fall into four basic categories: mammals, reptiles, birds, and fish.

Mammals

Probably the most famous Texas animal is the armadillo, which can be found virtually all over the state. The standard Texas issue is the nine-banded armadillo (Dasypus novemcinctus linnaeus), an armored relative of the opossum. Mesoamerica's Mayans believed that when vultures died they shed their wings and metamorphosed into 'dillos. During the Depression they became a popular food supplement, and Texans called them "Texas turkeys" or "Hoover hogs." Stuffed armadillos and armadillo shells are favored curios among residents and visitors alike. Armadillo chili is supposed to be good. It is illegal to harm one, however; only 'dillos that have died of natural causes (this includes auto collisions—a common cause of death) can be taken.

In the caves of Central Texas, the **Brazilian bat** and the **cave myotis bat** are fairly common. The **black bear** was once common throughout the state but is now confined to the mountains of the Trans-Pecos and riverbottoms of East Texas. **Cougars** (also known as mountain lions, panthers, or pumas) are still fairly common in places on the Edwards Plateau, in the Trans-Pecos, and in the brush country of South Texas. The **ocelot** and **jaguarundi,** once common throughout South Texas, are now mostly confined to the Laguna Atascosa and Santa Ana national wildlife refuges and along the Rio Grande. Smaller cats such as the **bobcat** are common throughout the state. **Coyotes,** the scourge of small livestock, are found all over Texas, but especially in the brush country of South Texas. They are also a protected species on the Muleshoe National Wildlife Refuge in the Panhandle.

Deer are prolific in Texas and are estimated to number above three million. The most common is the **white-tailed deer,** which thrives in the Hill Country and Edwards Plateau. The largest Texas deer is the **mule deer,** which is found in the Trans-Pecos, the Llano Estacado, and to a lesser extent in South Texas. The elegant **pronghorn,** a type of antelope, lives primarily on the Texas plains in the Panhandle and in the Trans-Pecos Region. The **Texas bighorn** mountain sheep is native to the Trans-Pecos but is increasingly hard to find. Many non-native varieties of deer, antelope, mountain sheep, goats, and even giraffes have been introduced to "exotic game ranches" on the Edwards Plateau with great success.

The **javelina** or **collared peccary** (or, occasionally, "muskhog") is a wild, tusked creature similar to a pig (but zoologically unrelated) common in South Texas's brush country. Another strange creature in the brush country is the **coatimundi** (also called coati), an acrobatic relative of the raccoon.

The Trans-Pecos area is about the only place you'll find the famed **kangaroo rat.** If you're lucky, you'll see one hopping across your headlight beams while driving at night—they're rarely seen during the day.

The **black-tailed prairie dog** was once ubiquitous throughout the plains and prairies of Texas but has been so nearly eradicated that you now have to go out of your way to see one. Two "prairie dog towns" (colonies of prairie dogs) have been preserved in the Panhandle—one at Mackenzie State Park in Lubbock and the other at the Muleshoe National Wildlife Refuge.

At one time there were many types of wolves in Texas, but ranchers just about exterminated them in retaliation for livestock attacks. One type which definitely survives is the handsome **red wolf,** whose primary habitat now is the Anahuac National Wildlife Refuge on the Texas coast. There may be a few **gray wolves** left in the mountains of the Trans-Pecos as well.

Texas claims a couple of water-borne mammals, the **bottlenose dolphin** and the **manatee**. Both are native to the Gulf, but the manatee is occasionally seen in Texas bays and rivers. During the winter, they migrate south toward Mexico's Yucatan Peninsula.

Reptiles

The largest reptile in Texas is the **American alligator,** which is common in the bayous of East Texas and in the salt marshes along the Gulf coast.

Then there are the snakes of Texas. Over a hundred species of snakes call Texas their home, but only 15 species and subspecies are considered poisonous to humans. Of these, three are **copperheads**—the Trans-Pecos (found in the Big Bend area), the broadbanded (North and South Central Texas), and the southern (East Texas). The Trans-Pecos copperhead is fairly rare, so hikers in Big Bend country should consider the risk of encounter very low.

Only one water snake in Texas is poisonous, the **western cottonmouth.** The cottonmouth is actually semiaquatic and lives in a variety of habitats near water. Its domain covers the entire eastern half of the state, starting as far west as the Hill

Texas horned lizard

LOUISE FOOTE

SNAKEBITE PREVENTION AND TREATMENT

The overall risk of being bitten by a poisonous snake while in Texas is quite low, but it is often exaggerated by Texans who are proud of their snake population. According to Texas Department of Health statistics covering a 10-year period between 1968 and 1978, there were only 2.7 deaths per year attributable to snakebite. Compare this with 5.7 for venomous arthropods (insect stings), 8.1 for lightning strikes, 10.1 for hunting accidents, 518.5 for drowning, and 3,511 for auto accidents. Most of the unfortunate who are bitten by snakes in Texas are farmers and small children.

Nonetheless, anyone spending time in the Texas outdoors, including campers and hikers, would be well advised to follow a few simple precautions.

Prevention

First of all, use caution when placing hands or feet in areas where snakes may lie. These primarily include rocky ledges, holes, and fallen logs. Always look first, and if you must move a rock or log, use a long stick or other instrument. Wear sturdy footwear when walking in possible snake habitats. High-top leather shoes or boots are best.

coral snake

Most snakes strike only when they feel threatened. Naturally, if you step on or next to a snake, it is likely to strike. If you see a venomous snake (or hear one, in the case of a rattlesnake), remain still until the snake moves away. Sudden movements may cause a snake to strike; they rarely strike a stationary target. Also, none of the venomous snakes found in Texas can strike a target that is farther away than three-fourths of its body length. Use this rough measure to judge when it may be safe to move away from a snake, leaving plenty of room for error.

If you'll be hiking in wilderness areas far from professional medical treatment, by all means carry an elastic bandage or two, the type used for sprains. The old "slice and suck" method of treating snakebite has been discredited by most medical experts.

Treatment

If bitten by a snake, it is important that you remain calm in order to slow the spread of venom in your body and so that you can follow the necessary steps for treatment in a cool-headed manner.

First, immediately following the bite, try to identify the snake (see "Reptiles" on pp. 17 and 19 for a de-

scription of venomous snakes in Texas). At the very least, memorize the markings and physical characteristics so that a physician can administer the most appropriate antivenin. If you can kill the snake and bring it to the nearest treatment center, all the better, but this could expose you or your fellow hikers to the risk of another bite.

Second, examine the bite for teeth marks. A successful bite by a poisonous pit viper (copperhead, cottonmouth, or rattlesnake) will have one or two large fang punctures in addition to smaller teeth marks, while a bite by a nonpoisonous snake will not feature fang punctures. A coral snake bite will usually feature a series of small, closely spaced punctures made by the "chewing" motion of smaller fangs (coral snakes have to chew or bite their victims' flesh repeatedly in order to inject sufficient quantities of venom). In general, nonpoisonous bites cause relatively small, shallow marks or scratches.

If it's suspected that the bite is poisonous, *immobilize the affected limb and wrap tightly in an elastic bandage.* This will slow the spread of venom through the lymphatic system and mitigate swelling. Be careful that the bandage isn't wrapped so tightly that it cuts off circulation—you should be able to insert a finger under it without difficulty. Keep the arm or leg below the level of the heart. The victim should avoid all physical activity if possible since increased circulation will accelerate the absorption of the venom. For this same reason, aspirin, sedatives, and alcohol should be avoided. Do not apply cold therapy—ice packs, cold compresses, and so on—to the bite area or to any other part of the victim's body.

Get the victim to a hospital or physician if possible. Where feasible, carry the victim to restrict physical exertion. Even when wrapping the limb appears successful in preventing symptoms, the bite will need medical attention and a physician may decide that antivenin treatment is necessary. (However, it's possible for a poisonous snake to bite without injecting any venom—up to 20% of reported bites are "dry bites" like these.) Snakebite victims who require antivenin treatment will usually receive the broad-spectrum North American Antisnakebite Serum for pit viper poisoning (rattlesnakes, copperheads, and cottonmouths) or a special coral snake antivenin for coral snake poisoning.

Country. The cottonmouth is most common, however, in the coastal marshes of Southeast Texas and along the streams and rivers of East Texas.

Ten kinds of **rattlesnakes** live in Texas—the western and desert massasauga (found on low plains throughout most of the state), the western pygmy (East Texas), the western diamondback (throughout the state except East Texas), the Mojave (Far West Texas), the canebrake (East Texas), the mottled rock and banded rock (mountains of the Trans-Pecos), the black-tailed (Central and West Texas), and prairie (West Texas). Of these, the western diamondback and the Mojave rattlesnakes are the most dangerous, the Mojave because it has the most potent venom of any North American snake, and the diamondback because it is the second most venomous snake in North America and the most common rattlesnake in Texas.

Finally, Texas boasts one **coral snake,** aptly named the Texas coral snake. It is found in a variety of habitats throughout Central, South, and East Texas. For important information on how to avoid snakebite, see "Snakebite Prevention And Treatment," opposite.

Lizards are common throughout the lower half of the state, especially **geckos** and the large **Texas horned lizards** (often called "horny toads"). The horned lizard can shoot a stream of blood from its eyes to distances as great as four feet, but no one knows why.

Five of the world's nine species of sea turtle are occasionally seen along the Texas coast. Largest is the **giant leatherback turtle,** which reaches six to seven feet in length and dives as deeply as 3,900 feet (deepest of all air-breathing animals). Other sea turtles occasionally seen

Texas tortoise

along the Texas coast include the **loggerhead, hawksbill, green sea turtle,** and **Kemp's ridley**.

Birds

Texas harbors more species of birds than any other state, mainly because birds find it a comfortable winter home. The best areas for Texas birdwatching are along the Gulf coast or just a bit inland. Every spring, accommodations along the coast fill up with bird aficionados who come from all over the U.S. to view the variety of birds in this area. Late fall is also a popular time for birders. The salt marshes make especially good hunting grounds for large birds like **egrets, cranes, terns, ducks, geese,** and **herons.**

Perhaps the most famous part-time bird resident in Texas is the **whooping crane,** which commonly has a wingspan of 7 1/2 feet. In 1941, this huge white bird was on the brink of extinction—only 15 whooping cranes remained in the wild. By 1989, their numbers had swelled to over 100, all of which were spending their winters at the Aransas National Wildlife Refuge on the Texas coast. From November to April, local boats offer cruises devoted to the viewing of the crane.

Another winter resident is the **snow goose,** which nests in salt marshes along the coast. **Canada geese** are also common among the marshes, as are **blue geese, mottled ducks,** and ibises.

Also on the coast are a variety of **pelicans, gulls, sandpipers, loons,** and **marsh hawks.** The magnificent and ever present **white pelican** attains wingspans of up to nine feet, and the occasional **frigate bird** reaches seven to eight feet. The pink-feathered **roseate spoonbill** is another impressive coastal bird, often mistaken for a flamingo. .

The Muleshoe National Wildlife Refuge in the Panhandle is home to as many as 100,000 **sandhill cranes.** Also in this area are a few remaining **golden eagles.**

The Big Thicket and Piney Woods forests of East Texas are a natural attraction for woodpeckers and there are several different kinds thriving among the tall pines and oaks. Most impressive is the large, red-crested **pileated woodpecker**—it's not only the largest but is the loudest of the woodpeckers (sometimes called "peckerwoods" by East Texans).

In the Rio Grande plains of South Texas, espe-

whooping crane

cially around the Santa Ana National Wildlife Refuge, is the squawking **chachalaca** (sometimes called the Mexican turkey), a pheasant-like cross between a wild turkey and a chicken. In brush country throughout South Texas, you'll find lots of **wild turkey, quail, doves,** and **roadrunners.** The roadrunner, as its name suggests, prefers to run rather than fly and has been clocked at 15 miles per hour. The roadrunner goes by several other names as well—chaparral and paisano are two local names you might hear. The endangered **peregrine falcon** and **bald eagle** nest at nearby Laguna Atascosa National Wildlife Refuge.

Fish

Guadalupe bass (the official state fish), **striped bass, spotted bass, largemouth bass, white bass, sunfish, crappie,** and various kinds of **catfish** (channel, blue, and flathead) are freshwater fish of note which are native to Texas. Various other bass have been introduced to lakes and streams with much success, as well as **rainbow trout** and the **saltwater red drum,** which has adapted to freshwater habitats. **Crayfish** (more commonly called crawfish) thrive in the bayous of East Texas.

The Gulf of Mexico is rich with sealife in spite of oil shipping and the commercial fishing industry. Sportfishing is very big in Texas and fishing enthusiasts are part of the conservation effort in the area, as ironic as that might sound. Among large Gulf fish are 30 species of **shark,** including the great white shark (which reaches weights of up to 8,000 pounds). Also common are **yellowfin tuna, blue marlin, sailfish, wahoo,** and **tarpon.** At the other end of the yardstick are the various kinds of shellfish, including **shrimp, crabs, clams, oysters,** and **mussels.**

Commercial fishing is big business along the 640-mile Texas coast. Fleets net mostly shrimp (82% of the weight landed), crabs, and oysters—shellfish, in fact, account for more than 30 times the amount of finfish taken. Among Gulf finfish, the commercial catch (in descending order) includes **black drum, flounder, sheepshead,** and **red snapper.** All of these are commonly taken by amateur anglers as well. See the "Gulf Coast" chapter for more information on Gulf sportfishing.

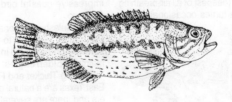

spotted bass

BOB RACE

LOUISE FOOTE / 2

HISTORY

PREHISTORY

Most of the earliest evidence of human habitation in Texas dates back 10,000-13,000 years. Grinding stones, beads, human skeletons, and pictographs found in several places throughout inland Texas date to this period. These Paleo-Indians were no doubt descendants of Asian groups that are known to have migrated across the Bering Strait to North America from the Asian continent some 50,000 years ago.

Artifacts spread across the state indicate that the Paleo-Indian groups in Texas were nomadic and small in number. They hunted prehistoric bison (today's bison are descendants of these beasts, looming seven feet high) and small horses (which later became extinct in North America, only to be replaced by a later version of the horse imported by the Spanish in the 16th century). Bison were brought down by flint-headed spears or were driven over cliffs—hunting techniques that persisted through thousands of years of Amerindian history. The first Clovis points were discovered near the Colorado River in Texas in 1924, but weren't named until similar points were found and dated near Clovis, New Mexico, in 1936.

When the Ice Age ended around 5000 B.C., the human population in Texas (by this time in the Archaic Indian stage of development) expanded the hunting cycle to include small as well as large animals. Their expanding tool kit included implements for working stone, bone, and wood. They harvested fruits and nuts from the land, and freshwater fish from streams and rivers. Limited trade with other Indian groups was carried on throughout the area, with flint extracted from the Alibates quarry in the Texas Panhandle as a prime unit of barter.

Around the beginning of the 1st century A.D., a Woodland Indian culture developed in East Texas. Pre-Caddoan groups established permanent settlements, erected burial mounds, and made pottery. By the end of the first millennium, a neo-American or late-prehistoric Indian emerged, characterized by a complex culture. The creation of food surpluses by the Caddo Indians of East Texas allowed them to develop social stratification. In addition to hunters and farmers, there were chiefs, priests, and artisans. A certain gender equality must have existed, since Caddo women as well as men belonged to these latter groups.

Prior to European contact with Texas in the 16th century, what is considered "confirmed evidence" about Texas prehistory is rather limited.

PERIODS OF HUMAN HABITATION IN THE AMERICAN SOUTHWEST

(B.P. = YEARS BEFORE PRESENT)

12,500 B.P	8,500 B.P	2,000 B.P
Paleo-Indian	Archaic	Ceramic
(Clovis-Folsom-		500 B.P
Plainview-Firstview)		Protohistoric
		350 B.P
		Historic

A number of mysteries remain which have led to some interesting speculations. A series of horizontal and vertical lines engraved on a West Central Texas hillside are said to be ancient Celtic line writing representative of a Celtiberian language. Epigraphist Barry Fell postulates that these inscriptions are travel instructions left by Celtic explorers who traded in the area long before the arrival of Columbus or the Vikings.

In Big Bend, a plaque bearing an inscription in archaic Libyan was found in the early 1960s. Unfortunately, the plaque was not dated and later was lost. Photos of the undeciphered plaque remain, however, and it has been suggested that Africans may have traded some with this part of the New World in ancient times. Additional support for this suggestion is available in the Olmec and Toltec statuary of early Mexico, some of which bears Negroid features.

Probably most mystifying of Texas's prehistoric anomalies are the Malakoff-Trinidad heads. These stone carvings in the shape of human heads were found in Henderson County within an eight-year period overlapping the 1920s and '30s. They were found at the bottom of a gravel bed that dates 40,000-50,000 years ago. Assuming they were originally deposited in the stratum in which they were found, this marks a local culture that was considerably more advanced than that which crossed the Bering Strait at about the same time.

EUROPEAN CONTACT

Spanish Exploration Of The New World

Following 700 years of conflict with the Moors over control of the Iberian Peninsula, Spain in the 15th century emerged as the most powerful nation in Europe. Convinced that a Roman Catholic God was destined to rule the world with Spain as His emissary, the Spanish monarchy sent Christopher Columbus in search of a new route to the Far East. His mission was to establish contact with a mythical "Great Khan" in order to develop an alternate trade route with the Orient, since Arabs controlled the overland route through the Middle East. Along the way as many pagans as possible were to be converted to Christianity. Once the Arab trade monopoly was broken, the Holy Land would be returned to Christian control.

Pope Alexander VI presented Spain with a papal bull in 1493 which gave the Spanish the rights to any new land discovered west of the Azores, as long as the Spanish made "God's name known there." Hence, the Spanish conquest of the New World started as a roundabout extension of the Holy Crusades.

Columbus's "discovery" of the West Indies was followed by a succession of Spanish expeditions into the Caribbean and Gulf of Mexico. The conquest of Mexico and Central America was rapidly achieved. Hernán Cortez subdued the Valley of Mexico Aztecs in three years, and the allegiance of other Aztecs and Mayans followed. At first the Indians were enslaved, but another papal bull issued in 1537 by Pope Paul III discouraged slavery. Spain's policy changed from "conquest" to "pacification"—a policy all too often open to interpretation.

Spanish missionaries debated the best way to effect conversion in conformity with this vaguely worded new policy. A Dominican missionary named Bartoleme de las Casas urged a paternal attitude toward native populations, and from his ideas the mission system was developed. Basically, it worked like this: traveling missionaries (Franciscan, Dominican, or Jesuit) offered Indians the protection of the Spanish armies in return for a willingness to undergo religious instruction. Those natives who agreed were congregated at a suitable spot and directed to build a mission. The mission in turn became a refuge for the Indians and a place for them to learn European farming and other trades, as well as Catholic ways. Once pacification was complete, the mission became a secularized church community and the missionaries moved on to new areas. The system worked well among the docile Indians of Central Mexico.

The Spanish Push Into Texas

As the missions moved north pacification became increasingly difficult. The nomadic Indians of the north, called norteños by the Spanish, were no more susceptible to Spanish rule than they had been to Aztec rule. The Spanish were intrigued by this new territory, but proceeded cautiously. In 1519, a Spanish captain mapped the coast of Texas under orders from the governor of Jamaica. Two Cortez expeditions also slipped across the Rio Grande in 1528, but returned to

Rio Panuco in Mexico that same year.

Then in the 1530s, Alvar Nunez Cabeza de Vaca, two other Spanish explorers, and a famous Moorish slave named Esteban (considered the first black to arrive in Texas) came from Cuba to explore the Gulf coast. They were shipwrecked somewhere near present-day Galveston and ended up living among a variety of Indian tribes in West Texas and farther west for a number of years. Cabeza de Vaca developed a reputation among Texas Indians as a healer, and in his travels he kept hearing tales of great wealth in the "Seven Golden Cities of Cibola" somewhere to the north.

Esteban stayed on with the Indians, but in 1536 Cabeza de Vaca rejoined his compatriots in Mexico. Tantalized by his stories of gold, the colonial government commissioned Francisco Vasquez de Coronado to explore the Southwest. In the New Mexico area, Pueblo Indians fed Coronado a story about a place with greater riches than even Cibola, called Gran Quivera. Not knowing that accounts of mythical golden cities were just a way for the Indians to lead the Spanish away from their homelands, Coronado embarked on a search for gold throughout the Texas Panhandle, Oklahoma, and Kansas. He never found any, but along the way he left missionaries in the upper Rio Grande valley to "pacify" the Indians.

The Pueblo Indians of the upper Rio Grande eventually rebelled against the Spanish settlers, so the missionaries retreated to the El Paso area. El Paso del Norte was an opening in the mountains that allowed a trade route to extend between Santa Barbara in Chihuahua and the northern colony. Here the Spanish established the missions of Ysleta del Sur and Socorro del Sur in 1681. Ysleta became part of Texas when the course of the Rio Grande changed and is now the oldest European settlement in the state.

Conflict With The French

Meanwhile the French were conducting their own expeditions in the area. They didn't like the Spanish claims to such a large portion of the New World and in 1682 they sent Rene Robert Cavalier, Sieur de la Salle (nowadays shortened to LaSalle) to explore the Mississippi delta area. He claimed the Gulf coast for France, returned home, and then set sail again for the New World with four ships full of potential colonists. On the way he lost two of the ships, and finally came ashore at Lavaca Bay (about halfway between today's Galveston and Corpus Christi) to establish Fort Saint Louis. From here, LaSalle made three exploratory expeditions in the area but was killed by one of his men while en route to other French colonies along the Mississippi.

In spite of the fact that Fort Saint Louis was subsequently abandoned, France claimed the Rio Grande as the western boundary of the Louisiana Territory. This infuriated the Spanish, who sent five sea expeditions and six land expeditions to explore the Texas coast and interior in order to learn more about the area and to check French influence.

The Spanish established two unsuccessful missions in East Texas, but these expeditions would not be of historic interest except for the contact the Spanish made with the Caddo Indians. The Caddo were part of a sophisticated native culture that had a loose federation of settlements throughout East Texas, Arkansas, Oklahoma, and Louisiana. They were anxious to form an alliance with the Spanish when they found out that the Spanish were enemies of the French, who were trading partners with Indian enemies of the Caddo.

They greeted the Spanish missionaries with the Caddo word *Taysha* ("Friend"), which the Spanish took to be either the name of the tribe or the name of the territory. Thereafter, the Spanish colonists often referred to the area north of the Rio Grande as *Tejas* or *Texas,* Spanish corruptions of Taysha. Unfortunately, the Spanish missionaries brought with them European diseases which largely decimated the peaceful Caddo. The remaining Caddo blamed the priests' holy water for the fatal illnesses and returned to their traditional religion.

So the missionaries moved out of East Texas and in 1718 established what became the most famous mission in the Southwest, San Antonio de Valero (later nicknamed the Alamo when it was taken over by the military in 1800). Over the next 13 years, five more missions were established in the San Antonio area.

In 1720, the French diverted their attention from the American colonies to their crumbling economy in France. Trade with the Indians slackened and in response the Indians began attacking French settlements in the Mississippi area. The Spanish took the opportunity to slip into the French territory through the back door, establishing a mission and presidio at Los Adaes, Louisiana. Los Adaes became the capital of the Spanish colonial province of Texas for the next 50 years.

Spanish Expansion In Texas

But in the heart of Texas, the San Antonio area missions were having a hard time with the pesky Apaches. In fact, the whole area of South Texas right on down to the Sierra Madre Oriental in central Mexico was barely under Spanish control. Few settlers dared to make a go of it here and it became a haven for renegade Indians and marauders.

Spain conducted a seven-year search for the "right colonizer" to tame the area. "Good Indians" were brought in from southern Mexico and Central America to serve as role models for the "wayward natives." Colonial descendants from the Canary Islands came in 1731 and set up the first civil jurisdiction in San Antonio, the Villa de San Fernando de Bexar. Finally in 1746, Jose de Escandon, a highly regarded military officer and colonial administrator, received the assignment to survey the area from Mexico's Rio Panuco north to the Nueces River in Texas. The width of the area he surveyed extended from the Gulf coast to the mountains. In 1747, Escandon began sending colonists into the area and named it the State of Nuevo Santander, after his home province in Spain. By 1753, Texas's first cattle ranch was established on 433,800 acres of land granted to Jose Vasquez Borrego in what is today Zapata County in South Texas. Many of the wealthy Hispanic landowners living along the Rio Grande today are heirs of these original Spanish land grants.

Although the Spanish colonists had met with hostile Indians from time to time, the Indian population wasn't a major problem until the Spanish introduced horses to the Comanches. With the increased mobility, the Comanches had begun moving southward onto the Great Plains from the Rocky Mountains in the 17th century. They displaced the Apaches, who moved to the lower Texas plains, displacing in turn the Jumano and Coahuiltecan tribes. The Jumano and Coahuiltecan both pleaded for help from the Spanish, who turned a deaf ear. The Apaches wreaked havoc throughout the Texas plains and then laid siege to Spanish missions in the El Paso area. But the

Spaniards were able to defeat the Apaches on several occasions.

Squeezed between the fierce Comanches to the northwest and the Spanish to the south, the Apaches made peace with the colonizers in the San Antonio area but couldn't gain acceptance in the missions—the other Indians feared and distrusted the warlike Apaches. The mission of San Saba de la Santa Cruz was established in 1757 in an area about 200 miles northwest of San Antonio (present-day Menard County), but two years later the Comanches destroyed the mission, killing both priests and Indians. A major battle ensued with the Comanches and their Plains Indian allies on one side and the Spanish, Apaches, and various Mexican Indians on the other. The Comanches, using French rifles and field tactics, soundly defeated the Spanish.

The defeat was the most humiliating loss the Spanish had ever suffered against the northern Indians. The more sedentary Indians of Mexico and Central America had been relatively easy to subjugate, but the Plains Indians were a new breed of warrior for the Spanish. Spain's control of the province of Texas began slipping, compounded by France's cession of the Louisiana Territory in 1762 to Spain. This considerably enlarged the Spanish territory and lent a false sense of security to the Spanish colonial administration. The entire province was reorganized to leave East Texas without a defense (no longer needed, it was thought, in the absence of westward pressure from the French). East Texas missions and presidios were closed again and moved to Central Texas to defend the area against Indian attacks. For a while this reorganization worked well for the Spanish, and the area from San Antonio west to El Paso was pacified for the last 20 years of the 18th century.

ANGLO-AMERICAN MIGRATION AND MEXICAN RULE

Blurred Borders

By 1803, Spain had returned the Louisiana Territory to France after an alliance with the losing sides in the French Revolution and the Napoleonic wars. Although Napoleon had promised not to turn the territory over to any other power, he sold it to the United States.

U.S. President Thomas Jefferson at first claimed all of the territory extending to the Rio Grande as part of the Louisiana Purchase (based on LaSalle's expeditions). Almost immediately, Anglo-Americans began looking toward the undeveloped regions of Texas. Spain had a strict immigration policy that barred all non-Hispanics from settling in Texas, but because France and Spain had never agreed on the boundaries between Louisiana and Texas, a sprinkling of Anglo-Americans had been settling in East Texas since the 1760s. Without any presidios in East Texas, Spain could hardly enforce its policy. But when Zebulon Pike, commissioned by President Jefferson, arrived in the Spanish-settled upper Rio Grande valley with a survey team, he was arrested by the Spanish and sent back to Washington.

Realizing that they were going to have to develop Texas in order to strengthen their claim to it and to keep the Americans out, the Spanish began making plans to send colonists to East Texas, the area receiving the most westward pressure. They offered huge land grants to *empresarios* who would take on the task of settling large numbers of families in the Texas interior.

Mexican Independence
And The New *Empresarios*

By this time, Mexican-born Spanish colonists in Mexico were getting fed up with the machinations of Spanish rule. In 1810, a revolutionary group of Mexican-born Spanish, *mestizos* (Mexican-Indians), and Indians declared Mexico an independent nation and began 10 years of battle against Spain.

In 1811, Mexican revolutionaries sent an emissary, Jose Bernardo Gutierrez, to Washington to try to gain support for their cause. The U.S. gave him a cordial reception but offered no official recognition of the provisional revolutionary government and no weapons for their armies. What happened next may have seemed odd for the time, but set the trend for U.S.-Mexico-Central America intrigue for the next century. Gutierrez rode to Nachtitoches, Louisiana, and was met there by U.S. agents. Under the leadership of West Point graduate Augustus Magee, they formed a "Republican Army of the North," which entered Texas in August 1812. After taking Nacogdoches and La Bahia, they occupied San Antonio and declared the "Republic of Texas" in April 1813. The republic was never recognized by

any foreign government, however, and a few months later the Spanish reconquered San Antonio at the Battle of Medina River and over 300 Texas republicans were executed.

Meanwhile, Spain's Ferdinand VII tried to regain control over Mexico and negotiated a border between Texas and Louisiana with the United States. An attempted punitive invasion of Mexico failed, however, and Spain finally relinquished Mexico in 1821.

In spite of the new Texas-Louisiana border, Anglo-Americans continued to filter across into East Texas, motivated by an unstable economy in the United States. Mexico didn't have the forces necessary to prevent the unregulated and illegal immigration of the Anglos (and Indians, too, who began arriving in some numbers after being pushed out of the southeastern U.S.). So instead they tried to pursue a policy that encouraged Mexicans and Europeans to settle in Texas. The idea was to get the Anglos to settle in the interior, with the non-Anglos around the perimeter as a form of containment.

But Europeans and Mexicans didn't seem interested in settling in the remote Texas area, which was part of Coahuila y Texas, the poorest state in Mexico, and few came. The plan to dilute the Anglo presence suffered another blow when Mexico decided to recognize an 1821 land grant that Spain had given an Anglo-American named Moses Austin. Austin, under the *empresario* plan, had been given the right to settle 300 families in the area between the Brazos and Colorado rivers. Originally Mexico refused to honor the grant, but after Austin spent a year lobbying for the grant in Mexico City, they conceded on conditions that Mexican law be strictly adhered to by the new colonists.

Austin turned out to be a successful administrator and he scrupulously followed the terms of the Spanish grant as well as Mexican policy. The Mexican government remained distrustful of Anglo intentions overall but admitted that Austin's efforts were contributing to the development of Texas. The desire to develop Texas as quickly as possible was great, since Mexican leaders wanted a buffer zone between northern Mexico and the U.S. (as well as the Plains Indians). In 1825, Mexico authorized Austin to bring 900 more families into Texas, and in 1831 he was contracted to bring in 800 European and Mexican families. By the end of 1831, Austin was responsible for a population of 5,665 among his Texas colonies. Other *empresarios,* both Anglo-American and Mexican, were successful in settling new towns as well, though none brought in as many immigrants as Austin.

The new colonists concentrated on establishing themselves throughout the early 19th century. Anglos that settled in Central and North Texas tended to come from Missouri, Kentucky, and Tennessee, while those in East Texas usually immigrated from Mississippi, Louisiana, Arkansas, and Alabama. Mexicans gravitated toward South Texas. Cotton farming was the main economic activity, along with the raising of corn and livestock. But distrust between the Mexican government and their Anglo subjects never subsided, and a series of events in the early 1800s caused a growing resentment among the settlers.

Anglo-Mexican Friction
First, the Mexican bank in Texas (Banco Nacional de Texas, in San Antonio) failed because the Mexican government issued Texas bank notes and then refused to redeem them at full face value. Problems with land titles also emerged, mostly due to miscommunication as a result of the Anglo settlers' lack of Spanish proficiency.

One disgruntled Anglo who lost land because of this organized a group of like-minded individuals and forced Mexican soldiers out of a part of East Texas. They declared a "Republic of Fredonia" and made a pact with the Cherokees to split sovereignty over Texas in return for Cherokee support in battle. The Mexican army, assisted by Anglo colonists who didn't support the "Fredonians," quickly quelled the rebellion.

The failed Fredonian experiment had an immediate effect on Mexican immigration policy. The Mexican government became more anxious than ever about the Anglo presence in Texas and passed a law in 1829 that effectively barred further Anglo-American immigration. The Mexican army then reinforced garrisons in San Antonio, Nacogdoches, La Bahia, and Velasco, and established five new forts elsewhere in the territory. These measures further alienated the Anglos, who began to feel like they were under martial law.

Adding to the friction between the two cultures was the lack of religious freedom in Texas (all colonists were required to embrace Roman Catholicism) and the Mexican ban on slavery. Anglo settlers had easily been able to ignore these policies before additional armed forces arrived. With the new military presence, religious constraints were still difficult to enforce, but many Texans were worried that slavery would be eliminated. Even non-slaveholders, who constituted the majority of Anglo Texans, supported the right of their fellow colonists (mostly cotton farmers in East Texas who had migrated from the South) to use slaves on their farms, since it was legal where they had come from.

But the final disillusionment with Mexican rule came about two years after the Mexican election of 1828, when a democratically elected president was overthrown by a losing candidate and Mexico descended into a governmental chaos that lasted beyond the remainder of the century. A cycle of coups d'état was putting a new president in office an average of every 7 1/2 months.

THE TEXAN REVOLUTION

Texans Petition Mexico
Although most Texas immigrants arrived with the intention of pledging allegiance to Mexico, they did so with the understanding that they would be living under a republican form of government as outlined in the Constitution of 1824. With the overthrow of President Guerrero in 1830 and the installment of dictator Gen. Anastasio Bustamante, the future of republicanism in Mexico looked grim. So the Texans cheered Gen. Antonio Lopez de Santa Anna in Veracruz when he fomented an army revolt in the name of the republican cause and installed himself as president.

Encouraged by Santa Anna's successes, the Texans held a convention in San Felipe to prepare a petition which they hoped to present to the Mexican government. The petition contained requests for several reforms, including the establishment of Texas as a separate Mexican state (apart from Coahuila), a halt to Mexican encroachment on Indian lands, religious freedom, and donation of land for public schools. Mexican officials at the Coahuila y Texas state level condemned the convention and would not accept the petition.

The Texan response to the government's condemnation was to hold another convention at San Felipe. This time the meeting was led by a more radical faction, though the content of the second petition was essentially the same as in the first. A former U.S. senator and Tennessee governor, Sam Houston, chaired the committee that prepared a sample state constitution based on the then-current constitution of Massachusetts in the United States.

Stephen Austin went to Mexico City in 1833 and presented the petition to President Santa Anna. Santa Anna agreed with most of the reforms except for the separation of Coahuila y Texas and the donation of land for schools. Unfortunately, while traveling back to Texas, Austin was arrested in Saltillo for having written a letter from Mexico City to officials in San Antonio (before meeting with Santa Anna) requesting that they set up a separate Texas state government. The rhetoric contained in the letter was considered treasonous in nature and Austin was sent to prison in Mexico City.

While Austin lay in prison, the Coahuila y Texas state government faithfully began instituting reforms in Texas. Religious freedom was declared, the English language was allowed for official purposes, and a Texas appellate court was established. This seemed promising to the colonists until Santa Anna suddenly exiled his vice president, dissolved the federalist government, repealed the Constitution of 1824, and instituted one-man rule. Soon the Coahuila y Texas government was sapped of all authority and reforms were halted.

Armed Resistance

In 1835, Austin was released from prison and returned to Texas. He no longer counseled patience in dealing with the Mexican government, and called for an armed struggle to regain the rights which Texans had enjoyed under the Mexican Constitution of 1824 and later state reforms. At a convention at Washington-on-the-Brazos, Texans formed a provisional state government with Henry Smith as governor and Austin as commander in chief of the state militia.

The first shots in what was to become the Texan Revolution were fired when the Mexican army demanded the return of a six-pound cannon given to the colonists in Gonzales, Texas, for defense against Indian attacks. The Gonzales colonists refused and issued a call for volunteers to help defend the cannon. On October 2, 1835,

they flew the famous "Come And Take It" flag over the cannon and repelled a small unit of Mexican troops sent to retrieve it.

The Mexican unit retreated to San Antonio with the Texas volunteers in pursuit. More volunteers joined them and together they laid siege to San Antonio. After five days, the Mexican forces surrendered and the Texans released the survivors after the Mexicans pledged never to fight against the Constitution of 1824 again. Texans were also able to gain control of garrisons at Nacogdoches, Goliad, and Anahuac.

By the end of 1835, the Mexican military had been expelled from Texas and the colonists felt they had won back their rights. The victors were divided, however, about how to use their new-found power. A minority, led by Governor Henry Smith, was in favor of outright independence from Mexico. But most of the state council wanted to throw their support behind Mexican liberals in the restoration of a constitutional Mexican government. Meanwhile, they had to assemble some sort of defense in the event that a non-republican Mexican army tried to retake Texas. Only about 750 men made up the Texan army, nearly all of them volunteers. Four hundred men were stationed at San Antonio and the rest were scattered among the other garrisons throughout the state.

President Santa Anna not only ordered the Mexican army to march on Texas, he led them himself. A force of approximately 6,000 troops left Mexico City in February 1835. At first, the Texans assumed that the Mexican army would bypass San Antonio to hit the center of the Anglo colonies in San Felipe. When scouts spotted Santa Anna's front guard and realized that San Antonio was going to be the target, it was really too late to mount an effective defense.

The legendary battle of the Alamo lasted 12 days. James Bowie of "Bowie knife" fame was supposed to lead the defense but fell ill the day after the Mexican army lay siege to the Alamo, so William Travis took command. Santa Anna flew a red flag, the Mexican symbol for "no quarter, no mercy, no surrender" while the colonists flew the Mexican flag to which they had added the numeral "1824," the date of the Mexican constitution (the flying of the Mexican flag by the Alamo defenders has naturally been hotly disputed by loyal Texans ever since). Although the defenders (many of whom were of Mexican descent) were outnumbered 40 to 1, the superior marksmanship of the frontiersmen inside the Alamo held off the Mexican troops without a single Texan death until the walls were finally breached on March 6. The Mexican troops killed every one of the defenders and lost about a third of their own.

Independence

Before the Alamo siege had ended, however, the state council had convened at Washington-on-the-Brazos and on March 2 had declared Texas an independent republic. Of the 59 delegates who signed the Texas Declaration, only two were actually born in the state, Jose Antonio Navarro and Francisco Ruiz. Fifty-three were former U.S. citizens and the remaining four were born in Canada, Scotland, Ireland, and England.

After their victory at the Alamo, Santa Anna's forces regrouped and plunged northward. The remainder of the Texan volunteer army under the command of Sam Houston began retreating in the same direction. Along the way they picked up additional volunteers, including a company of Mexican Texans. No one today seems to know what Houston's intended destination was, but he may well have been heading for Louisiana to seek U.S.

assistance. However, Santa Anna's remaining force of 1,100-1,300 somehow got ahead of Houston's battalion on April 21, and while the Mexican troops were having an afternoon siesta at San Jacinto, 800 Texans charged. In less than 20 minutes, the Mexican army surrendered.

Although Santa Anna had escaped during the San Jacinto battle, he was captured the next day and held prisoner until he signed treaties which guaranteed the withdrawal of all Mexican troops from Texas and which recognized the new Republic of Texas.

THE REPUBLIC OF TEXAS AND U.S. ANNEXATION

The republic lasted 10 years, and throughout its short history was plagued by difficulties. Most of these difficulties no doubt stemmed from the fact that Texans could not govern themselves very well. Perhaps they had been rebellious citizens of Spain and Mexico too long and couldn't stomach their own authority, or perhaps they were simply disorganized. There were many other pressures on the new nation as well: a suffering economy, aggressive Indians, lack of foreign relations, and an unstable government on the southern border.

Sam Houston

Sam Houston, a leading figure before, during, and after the Texas Republican period, came forward to guide the fledgling republic. In 1836, he was elected president of the republic and, along with his vice president Lorenzo de Zavala (born in Yucatán, Mexico), enacted a voter-ratified constitution. Voters also came out overwhelmingly in favor of annexation to the United States. Houston made a formal request for annexation in 1837, but withdrew it when U.S. abolitionists argued against the idea. U.S. President Andrew Jackson formally recognized the republic later that year, just before leaving office.

Under Houston, the Republic of Texas initially enacted humane Indian policies. Houston had grown up with the neighboring Cherokees in his native Tennessee and had in fact been adopted by a Cherokee tribe as a child. He was also married to a full-blooded Cherokee woman. Long before he arrived in Texas, Houston had been an advocate of Indian rights as governor of Tennessee. As president of Texas, his policy toward Texas Indians

Sam Houston

was peaceful coexistence wherever possible and he gave land to Indian refugees fleeing persecution in the eastern United States. He was in the process of making peace with the Comanches on Texas's western frontier when his two-year term ended. Under the then-current constitution, he could not run for a second consecutive term.

The Lamar Presidency

Mirabeau Lamar succeeded Houston and almost immediately began reversing Houston's Indian policies. In 1838, he forcibly expelled the Cherokees from their new lands in East Texas and killed Cherokee chief Philip Bowles, a close friend of Houston's. Equally disastrous was his 1840 invitation to 12 Comanche chiefs to meet in San Antonio and exchange war prisoners. The Comanches only brought one white prisoner with them, so Texas commissioners tried to hold the chiefs captive until more prisoners were brought. The so-called Council House Fight resulted, in which many Indian warriors and chiefs were killed. When the Comanches found out about the treachery, they began a series of raids on Anglo settlements that lasted 35 years.

Texas didn't have the militia (or the budget to create such a militia) to defend western settlements from Indian raids. Instead, ranchers and local communities hired "rangering companies" to patrol their interests. The most famous of these were the Texas Rangers. They became known for their skill in fighting the Plains Indians (aided by Samuel Colt's patented six-shot revolver) and were paid very well for doing so. Eventually they became a public menace and had to be dissolved as an independent entity, but in the early years of their existence the Rangers played an important role in defending the frontier.

President Lamar fared better in foreign affairs, compelling France to recognize the Republic of Texas in 1839. Holland, Belgium, and Great Britain soon followed. But the economy was on the verge of collapse, so the Texan government reinstated the *empresario* program used by the Mexicans to attract more immigrants. The colonization bill of 1842 allowed Europeans to be awarded substantial land grants in return for bringing large groups of settlers to Texas. Frenchman Henri Castro brought 600 Alsatians to Texas and his settlement in Central Texas later was named Castroville. Many Germans came over as a result of these land grants as well.

Overtures To Annexation

When Lamar's term ended, Sam Houston was re-elected. Houston immediately took measures to try to offset the huge budget deficit created by Lamar. He also attempted to bring peace to the Indian frontiers by reopening negotiations with the Comanches and establishing trading posts along the frontier.

But Texas soon had major difficulties with Mexico. In 1842, the Mexican army broke the independence treaty of 1836 and launched guerrilla

Texas Rangers on Texas-Mexico border

raids against San Antonio, Goliad, and Victoria. Fourteen hundred Mexican troops occupied San Antonio and declared the reconquest of Texas. The Texas Rangers and a group of 600 Texan volunteers, under the leadership of Capt. Jack Hays, were able to expel the Mexicans. Houston was under extreme popular pressure to "punish" Mexico for the assault, but would not order troops to invade Mexico, an act which would surely have led to a military disaster. The attacks ceased.

Toward the end of Houston's second term as president of the Republic of Texas, the U.S. began making overtures toward Texas annexation. U.S. leaders were worried that Texas was getting too intimate with European nations, especially Great Britain. Americans were afraid that Texas might become part of the British empire. Already trade between Texas and the U.S. was decreasing while trade with Britain was on the rise. In order to get trade concessions from Britain, Texas had banned the further importation of slaves. Slavery was a major issue in American politics by this time, and southern Americans were anxious about the future of slavery in Texas.

In 1844, Texas and the U.S. signed a tentative annexation treaty in which Texas was to become a U.S. territory, not a state. However, the treaty was voted down in the U.S. Senate by an unintentional alliance between parties on both sides of the slavery issue. Southern senators who feared the demise of slavery (because of the treaty with Britain) as well as northerners who feared its expansion (because of the reality of slaveholdings in Texas) came out against annexation.

Houston swore he'd never court annexation again. But later that same year, James Polk ran for the U.S. presidency on a Democratic platform of westward expansion, which included the annexation of Texas and occupation of Oregon. Meanwhile, France and Great Britain put pressure on Mexico to lay aside all claims to Texas in hopes that an acquiescent Mexico would strengthen Texas independence. They didn't want to see Texas become part of the U.S. and figured that official Mexican recognition (the treaties previously signed by Santa Anna were considered void) would make Texans feel more secure in their status as an independent nation. And so began a short tug-of-war between Europe and the U.S., only a year after the U.S. Congress had refused to ratify annexation.

Polk won the election, but U.S. leadership was so worried about Mexico's decision that before Polk was even inaugurated, the incumbent President Tyler pushed an annexation bill through Congress in February 1845 that offered Texas status as a full-fledged state. Great Britain countered by urging the Texans to delay acceptance of statehood for at least 90 days while they continued negotiations with Mexico for recognition of the Texas republic. But the Texas government decided in favor of annexation and submitted a state constitution that was approved by Congress in December 1845.

STATEHOOD, SECESSION, AND CIVIL WAR

War With Mexico
Texas's annexation to the U.S. sparked the war with Mexico. Mexico hadn't officially recognized Texas as a republic and was slow to accept it as part of the United States. Mexico particularly didn't want to concede the area between the Nueces River and the Rio Grande, in spite of the fact that the Mexican military hadn't occupied that territory for many years. The U.S. considered the Rio Grande to be the southern boundary of Texas, just as the Republic of Texas had prior to annexation. When the U.S. Army moved into the area, Mexico retaliated.

After a series of skirmishes along the Rio Grande, President Polk ordered the Army to invade Mexico. Mexico City fell to U.S. forces in March 1847 and Mexico signed the Treaty of Guadalupe Hidalgo. In the treaty, Mexico conceded not only the Rio Grande area but all of what was to become the American Southwest for a payment of $25 million ($10 million for South Texas and $15 million for New Mexico, Arizona, and California). In retrospect, it is likely that the annexation of Texas was part of a U.S. plan to provoke Mexico into declaring war so that the U.S. could gain the entire Southwest.

Population Growth
Texas's population began expanding in the middle of the 19th century as new immigrants arrived to take advantage of cheap Texas land. But most of the settlement took place east of the Balcones Escarpment, since the Edwards Plateau and

Llano Estacado areas of the Texas High Plains were considered uninhabitable due to the presence of hostile Indians. The U.S. Army established forts along this line but was unable to push the Indians back—no Army unit, whether infantry or cavalry, was a match for mounted Comanches.

John Meusebach led a group of 140 German immigrants onto the edge of the Edwards Plateau, however, and established the town of Fredericksburg in May 1846. Meusebach negotiated a mutually favorable treaty with the Comanches on the San Saba River. This treaty was never broken by either side and gained the distinction of becoming the only successful treaty between whites and any group of Indians in Texas history. Other Germans moved into the area beyond the Balcones, the only immigrant nationality that was able to do so, and by 1850 German Texans outnumbered Mexican Texans.

Between 1850 and 1860 Texas's population exceeded 600,000, nearly triple what it had been 10 years earlier. Although only about a third of Texas farmers at this time held slaves, they were generally the wealthiest and most influential individuals. By 1860, half of those holding office at the state and local levels were slaveholders, and Texas became increasingly drawn into the national debate on slavery.

Secession

States-rights advocate and Democrat Hardin Runnels was elected governor in 1857 and openly called for the reinstitution of the slave trade, which was still illegal in Texas. There was talk of joining the growing movement among slave states toward secession from the United States. But Texans had mixed feelings about supporting secession, and when Sam Houston ran again on a strong Unionist platform, he was reelected. Texas also chose two Unionist senators to represent the state in Washington. For the time being, Texas took the Union side against the secessionists.

But in 1860, John Brown's raid on Harper's Ferry, Virginia, and the capture of Brownsville on the Rio Grande by Mexican bandit Juan Cortina changed Texas popular opinion. Secessionists used these incidents as proof of an abolitionist conspiracy to violate state rights and impose authoritarian rule. A siege mentality soon developed and secessionists called for a convention to pass a secession ordinance. Houston maintained his

Union stance and refused to approve the convention, so secessionist leaders convened on their own. The ordinance was drafted and issued to Texas counties for a vote. Only 13% of the population participated in the vote; of these, 76% percent (only 61,000, or roughly 10% of the total population) voted for secession.

Houston declared the ordinance unconstitutional since it annexed Texas to a foreign government, the Confederacy. He argued that if Texas were going to secede from the Union, it ought to return to its status as an independent republic. But the secessionists held forth the voter mandate and on March 2, 1861, Texas became a Confederate state.

In a letter to Governor Houston, U.S. President Abraham Lincoln offered to send 50,000 federal troops to aid Houston and the Unionists in putting down the rebellion. But Houston declined, and wrote back saying, "I love Texas too well to bring strife and bloodshed upon her." When he refused to swear allegiance to the Confederacy, Houston was deposed from the governorship.

The Civil War

The interior of Texas saw virtually no action during the Civil War and hence did not suffer the widespread destruction that occurred in the South. The state's main role in the confrontation was as a supplier of cloth and ammunition to the rest of the Confederacy. Eventually, the Union navy barricaded the Gulf coast to halt the flow of supplies by that route. But shipping continued from the mouth of the Rio Grande since the Union could not block international waters without taking on Mexico again. Many of the ships carrying Texas supplies flew under Mexican flags from the Mexican port of Matamoros.

A very few Civil War battles were fought at the perimeters of Texas, most of them at the Louisiana border. But probably the most decisive battle involving Texas occurred at Glorieta Pass, New Mexico, where a Texas supply train was captured on its way to California. Southern California industrial interests supported the Confederacy and had agreed to send gold and lumber to Texas for Confederate use. Once Union soldiers discovered the supply route, however, they occupied El Paso for the remainder of the war. Had the supply route to California remained open, the Civil War might have taken a completely different turn.

By the beginning of 1865, Texan morale was very low. Non-slaveholders, the majority of the state, began to resent the sacrifices they were making on behalf of the wealthy cotton producers (especially when they learned that slaveholders were often exempted from military service). Texan forces rebelled against the Confederacy and raided the state treasury for $5000 in gold. By the time the Confederate army had surrendered at Appomattox in April 1865, the Texas Confederates had disbanded.

The Union occupation of Texas began on June 19, 1865, with the arrival of 1,800 Union soldiers at the port of Galveston. Union Gen. Gordon Granger announced the emancipation of all Texas slaves that same day. June 19 (Emancipation Day) became an annual statewide holiday in Texas and is now an occasion for "Juneteenth" festivals in black communities throughout the state.

TEXAS IN TRANSITION

Reconstruction And Frontier Justice

Immediately following the end of the Civil War, Texas entered a period of lawlessness. Local militia were banned by the U.S. as part of "Reconstruction" and the Indian frontier was left defenseless. Federal troops occupied the state but were concentrated along the Rio Grande, so it was difficult to enforce state laws elsewhere in the state. Indian raids increased, gun-dueling became commonplace, and banditry went unchecked. State records registered 1,035 murders between 1865 and 1868, and it is this era in Texas history that earned the state its Wild West reputation. Texas well deserved the distinction: you had to be rough, tough, and quick with a gun to contemplate living on the Texas frontiers. But in the interior towns east of the Balcones Escarpment and north of the Nueces River, life continued as usual.

At first the cotton industry, once the backbone of the Texas economy, suffered a severe labor shortage when the slaves were freed. Some blacks elected to stay on as paid laborers or tenant farmers, but most migrated elsewhere. While the East Texas economy declined, the cattle industry in South and West Texas began to develop quickly. During the Civil War, unbranded cattle had proliferated throughout South and West Texas and were available to anyone who took the trouble to round them up. Cattle drives moved hundreds of thousands of cattle northward to Kansas and Missouri, often braving Indian attacks (in West Texas) and bandits (in South Texas) to do so.

The greatest trail drive in history moved 700,000 head of cattle from Texas to Kansas in 1871. This helped to offset losses in East Texas and, by 1873, Texas was shipping large amounts of cotton again as new immigration eased the labor shortage. The development of railroads across Texas made it easier to move agricultural products out of state and contributed to a fast-growing economy. Texans contemplated a bright future for themselves and their state.

But the problem of lawlessness remained. In 1874 the state government recommissioned the Texas Rangers to patrol Texas borders. Major L.H. McNelly led a special force of 40 Rangers that patrolled the Rio Grande while Major John Jones was given charge of six units of 75 men each for the Indian frontier. McNelly's brand of ruthless frontier justice soon "pacified" the lower Rio Grande valley, and he moved up the river to Eagle Pass to concentrate on an area plagued by American bandits. An 1876 Texas Ranger report on a cattle thief read "Mean as hell. Had to kill him."

Meanwhile, Rangers on the Indian frontier had their hands full. Spaniards, Mexicans, Texans, and the U.S. Army had spent a century trying to push the Plains Indians out of northwestern Texas, and their efforts had met with overwhelming failure. Some Texas histories claim that Major Jones's battalion of Texas Rangers finally accomplished what the rest could not. They fought what is generally considered to be the last Indian battle on the Texas Plains when they cornered a band of 100 Comanches at Lost Valley in June 1875. The U.S. Cavalry arrived to help the Rangers finish the fight, and from then on the Texas Plains were considered "safe" from Indians. But the truth is that 100 Comanches wouldn't have made a bit of difference to the area even 50 years earlier. The Plains Indians had already begun leaving northwest Texas by the latter half of the 19th century because of the lack of buffalo that they depended on for survival. White and Indian buffalo hunters, not the Texas Rangers, drove the Comanches away by so depleting the migratory herds that the Indians had no choice but to move on in search of better hunting grounds.

The Fencing Of The Cattle Kingdom

Cattlemen soon moved onto the West Texas plains

to take advantage of the grasslands and established huge cattle ranches. They practiced the Spanish tradition of open grazing, wherein cattle were allowed to roam freely most of the time and were rounded up twice a year for branding or trail drives. The subsequent introduction of barbed wire revolutionized the cattle industry and divided ranchers into two camps, fencers and open-rangers.

Ranchers who used fences were better able to control the quality of their herds. Farmers (called "nesters" by ranchers) also used barbed wire to keep cattle from trampling their fields. But a "Don't Fence Me In" mentality developed among the open-rangers and feelings on both sides provoked a series of small range wars. (In the 20th century, this became a common premise for B-grade Hollywood Westerns.) Fence-cutting became a favorite activity among the open-rangers while fencers would string barbed wire across public roads. In 1883 the state Legislature made it illegal to fence public lands or to cut fences other than your own, thus ending the range wars. The barbed wire legacy remains: in West Texas today, often the only sign of human presence on vast tracts of land is a barbed wire fence. Plaques that exhibit varieties of Texas barbed wire adorn the walls of West Texas living rooms.

With railroads established, the frontiers tamed, and the cotton and cattle industries booming,

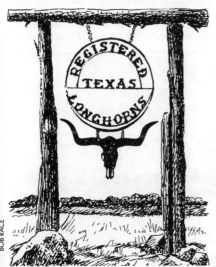

Texas by the end of the century was a U.S. leader in commercial agriculture. The standard of living for the average Texan was quite low, however, as most of the money was made by cattle and cotton brokers, not by ranch hands and farmers. Railroad monopolies skimmed huge sums of money from the state treasury as well, until in 1893 the Texas Legislature empowered a public railroad commission to review rates and stock revenues for the first time.

OIL

Long before Europeans arrived, Indians in East Texas had found oil seeping from the ground and used petroleum for medicinal purposes. Survivors of the DeSoto expedition in 1543 used it to caulk boats near the Sabine Pass. But the first oil well wasn't drilled in Texas until 1866, when Lyne Barret in Nacogdoches County devised the first rotary drill. Oil had only a few uses, though—as a lubricant, in road construction (to settle dust), and as a rather expensive cooking or heating fuel. Barret's well, and others that were drilled in Bexar and Brown counties, yielded modest productions.

In 1894, a larger oil reservoir was discovered by accident in Corsicana and the first commercial refinery in Texas was established. The Corsicana refinery developed a locomotive fuel and people became more interested in oil. Yet it was still more expensive than other kinds of fuel available at the time such as coal and wood.

At the beginning of the 20th century, the Corsicana oil field, at 500,000 barrels a year, was Texas's biggest producer. Then an oil strike at Spindletop, near Beaumont, in 1901 set Texas on its way to becoming the oil capital of the United States. In its first year of production, Spindletop yielded over three million barrels of oil and in 1902 the per annum output climbed beyond 17 million.

Naturally, the price of oil bottomed out, but this made petroleum the cheapest fuel available and new markets soon opened up. Railroads and steamship lines converted from coal to oil and the petroleum industry developed practically overnight. Texaco, Gulf, and Mobil are three present-day oil companies that got their start at Spindletop.

East and Southeast Texas turned out to be good sources for other large oil deposits because of the presence of huge salt domes below the earth's surface that created perfect conditions for oil "pooling." Subterranean oil doesn't actually collect in pools but permeates sandstone layers which absorb it like a sponge. Water below the sandstone layers exerts upward pressure on the oil while a thick layer of impermeable Austin chalk above the sandstone holds the oil back. Equally impermeable salt domes form containers around such layers, resulting in higher concentrations of oil. When a drill pierces the layer of Austin chalk that holds the oil back, it spurts forth.

An even bigger oil reservoir than the one at Spindletop was discovered near Kilgore in East Texas in 1930. The East Texas Oil Field covered 200 square miles and yielded 100 million barrels in its first year. Following the East Texas strike, Texas gained a production lead over Oklahoma and California, its previous rivals, and has remained the top U.S. oil producer ever since. Many more large fields have been discovered in Texas since (particularly in the Permian Basin of West Texas), but none were ever as big as the East Texas Oil Field.

INTO THE TWENTIETH CENTURY

Revolution In Mexico

In the early 1900s, Texas was settling down and becoming somewhat civilized. Most of the Rio Grande area had been secured by Texas Rangers, though there were brief skirmishes with bandit-revolutionaries during the Mexican rebellion against a succession of corrupt Mexican presidents between 1911 and 1916. The revolutionaries were initially led by Francisco Madero, an opposition leader who had been imprisoned by President Porfirio Diaz. Madero fled to Texas and proclaimed himself president of Mexico. His opposition group planned the overthrow of Diaz from San Antonio and Dallas. From their tactical headquarters in El Paso and Juarez, they soon gained control of the northern Mexican states of Sonora and Chihuahua. Thousands of Mexican refugees fled across the border into Texas to escape the violence of the revolution, however.

Pancho Villa, a cattle rustler and bandit, became an important figure in the Chihuahua takeover and other battles. At first, the U.S. public was so enamored of his escapades that Hollywood film crews would accompany Villa on his raids against local Mexican militia. After he was defeated three times in 1915, however, he turned his attention to border raids on villages in Texas and New Mexico. Whether the raids were a return to his old livelihood or an attempt to draw U.S. forces into military action against Mexico is a matter for continuing debate. At any rate, U.S. President Wilson responded by stationing 100,000 National Guard troops along the border and sent Gen. John Pershing into Mexico in pursuit of Villa in 1916.

Pershing failed to capture Villa, and when the U.S. became involved in World War I in 1917, the Mexican border immediately became a low priority. By 1935, Mexico had steadied its presidential merry-go-round. But the colorful Villa is still re-

San Antonio Plaza, late 1800s

membered by elderly residents in West Texas who love to talk about his movements in Texas—where he had his saddles made, his favorite cantinas, and so on.

A 1919 investigation into the border problems revealed that the Texas Rangers played a role in fanning the flames through their vigilante behavior, especially along the lower Rio Grande. The Rangers were immediately reduced in number from 1,000 men to 76, and their activities were more closely monitored. One of the last famous Ranger actions was the pursuit and killing of Texas bank robbers Bonnie Parker and Clyde Barrow in the late '20s. Eventually, the Rangers were absorbed by the state highway patrol under the Department of Public Safety.

The Depression And World War II

During the Depression years of the early '30s, Texas managed fairly well, buoyed by the oil boom. Farmers were hit hardest, especially in cotton-growing East Texas where cotton prices bottomed out. New Deal policies eventually pumped $1.5 billion into the Texas economy and revived the agricultural sector. By the end of the decade the economy was back on track and growing at a rate of about 4% per annum.

The World War II years were especially good to the Texas industrial sector. Shipbuilding and aircraft manufacturing became important new industries and the petroleum companies expanded as fuel demands increased. Between 1940 and 1955, economic growth exceeded 9% per annum and many Texans moved into urban areas. The development of plastics further fueled the oil boom.

POSTWAR TEXAS

Texas's industrial base diversified throughout the '50s and '60s as manufacturing companies moved to the state to take advantage of inexpensive electricity and land. In 1959, Jack Kilby of Texas Instruments developed the first silicon microchip, which put Texas on the "high-tech" road.

Petroleum continued as the state's principal income-earner and was given a major boost following the OPEC (Organization of Petroleum Exporting Countries) embargo of the United States market. American oil now had no competition from foreign suppliers so Texas fields went into full production. Oil exploration and speculation moved forward unchecked and Texas soon became the U.S. millionaires capital, ushering in the privileged lifestyle (for a privileged minority) depicted in the world-popular soap opera "Dallas."

Over the next decade, Texas prospered and was able to upgrade the state university system, sponsor new arts programs, and attract Americans from around the country who were seeking to benefit from the boomtown atmosphere. But in the mid-1980s, the economy suffered a shock when oil prices dropped because of disagreements on production quotas among OPEC members. For Texas oil interests, this meant that it was no longer profitable to pump oil fields at 100% capacity and petroleum exploration slowed to a near halt.

Cities that were oil-dependent, like Houston, suffered the most, turning into partial ghost towns virtually overnight. But the entire state had to face the reality of the situation and admit that the economy needed further diversification. Texans have also begun to realize that even if oil prices rise again (as they did in the late '80s), petroleum reserves are running low. Even newly discovered oil fields will probably not be sufficient to compensate for the overall decline in reserves.

Texas has been working vigorously to attract more high-tech interests and to expand the service sector of the economy, including tourism. So far the state has been fairly successful in bringing in new light industries which benefit from the lower cost of production in Texas (lower wages, energy costs, and real estate). But Texans will probably have to accept the fact that the accelerated boom of the '70s is now characteristic of their history, not their future.

GOVERNMENT

Texas gained its current status as an American state when the Texas Constitution was approved by the U.S. Congress on February 15, 1876 (an earlier 1845 constitution had been accepted but nullified by secession in 1860). Amendments to the state constitution are enacted by a two-thirds majority vote in the state Legislature, followed by a simple majority of Texas voters at large. The Texas governor does not have veto power over constitutional amendments.

Like the U.S. Congress, the Texas Legislature is bicameral—divided into the Senate, consisting of 31 members, and the House of Representatives, with 150 members. At the national level, Texas has two U.S. Senators and 27 members of the U.S. House of Representatives.

Traditionally, Texas has been a bastion of the Democratic Party at both state and national lev-els. During the past two decades, however, the Republicans have been gaining strength rapidly. In 1978, William P. Clements Jr. became the first Republican candidate to win the state governorship. He lost to Democrat Mark White Jr. in 1982 but won again in 1986. In 1990 the state elected Austin Democrat Ann W. Richards (former state treasurer) as governor, the third time in the state's history a woman had been selected for this office. So far the statewide consensus seems to be that Richards has performed competently; her victory may signal a return to Democratic Party ascendancy in the state.

The state is divided into 254 county jurisdictions with an average county size of 1,000 square miles. Brewster County in West Texas is the largest, with an area of 6,169 square miles (but a population density of only 1.3 persons per square mile).

ECONOMY

Contrary to popular belief, petroleum is not the state's number-one source of revenue. The value of manufactured goods produced in Texas in 1988 totaled a whopping $149 billion, making manufacturing by far the state's most important income-earner. The next most important contributor to the state's GDP is travel and tourism, which accounted for $17.3 billion in 1986 (last available figures). Crude oil squeezes in at third place, taking in $15 billion for 1990. In production terms, about 200,000 oil wells in 12,228 fields pumped 672 million barrels of crude during that year, or about 25% of total U.S. oil production. Obviously, fairly small changes in oil prices can significantly affect oil's rank in the state's economy. Natural gas is also an important product, earning just over $8 bil-lion in '89. Minerals (crushed stone, sulfur, gypsum, talc, and salt) were valued at $1.4 billion that same year.

Texas is the nation's leader in livestock production. In fact, livestock far outnumber the people in Texas. At the beginning of 1990, the state's ranches harbored 13.5 million cattle, 2.5 million sheep, 2.1 million goats, 580,000 hogs, and over 18 million chickens! Ranching receipts for 1987 totaled $6.1 billion, more than any other state. Farming follows ranching with a 1987 income of $3 billion. The leading crop is cotton, followed by grains (grain sorghum, rice, wheat, corn, barley), vegetables, pecans, peanuts, citrus, and other fruits. Texas leads the nation in cotton and rice production.

THE PEOPLE

POPULATION

In 1990, the U.S. census estimated the population of Texas to be 16,986,500, with an average population growth of 1.9% per annum. This growth is due mostly to net in-migration from other states, and the population most likely exceeds 17 million at this writing. Like other states in the "Sun Belt," Texas is benefiting (or suffering, depending on your point of view) from the gradual exodus of Americans from the colder and more industrialized northern states. Texas is now the United States's third-most populous state, after California and New York. By the middle of the 1990s, it will probably have overtaken New York for second place.

No other state has as many Metropolitan Statistical Areas (28) as Texas. The state's four primary metropolitan areas have populations exceeding one million each: Houston (3,301,900), Dallas (2,553,400), San Antonio (1,302,100), and Fort Worth-Arlington (1,332,000). Dallas and Fort Worth can also be combined as a federally defined Consolidated Metropolitan Statistical Area (CMSA) of 3,885,400; by the same reckoning, the Houston-Galveston-Brazoria CMSA has a population of 3,711,000. When Houston and Dallas residents argue over which city is bigger, they often confuse these two different ways of counting the population. However you slice it, Texas has three of the country's largest 10 cities.

Seven metropolitan areas in the state have populations between 250,000 and one million: Austin, Beaumont-Port Arthur, Brownsville-Harlingen, Corpus Christi, El Paso, Killeen-Temple, and McAllen-Edinburg-Mission. The remaining 19 MSAs have populations ranging from 75,000 to 250,000.

Texas also has hundreds of tiny towns with minute populations. Driving along out-of-the-way farm and ranch roads you might come across places like Acme (pop. 14), Airville (pop. 10), Babyhead (pop. 20), Bug Tussle (pop. 15), Eolian (pop. 9), Grit (pop. 30), Nickel Creek (pop. 16), Rio Frio (pop. 50), or Zorn (pop. 26).

Age

Texas is a young state, demographically speaking. The 1988 U.S. census shows that of the 10 most populous states in the U.S., Texas has the largest percentage (40.6%) of residents under 25 years of age. Of these 10 states, Texas also has the smallest share of those over 45 years.

BREAKDOWN

Since the mid-19th century, the majority of Texans have been of European descent. At present, roughly two-thirds of the population is of Anglo or northern European ancestry. About one-fourth is Hispanic, that is, of Spanish, Mexican, or *mestizo* (Mexican-Indian) descent. The third-largest ethnic group, Afro-Americans, make up about 12% of the state's residents. Of these three groups, the Hispanic populace is increasing the most rapidly and is expected to constitute about one-third of the state by the year 2000. This disproportionate increase is due to a higher overall birthrate along with a steady stream of Mexican immigration.

In the major urban areas, there are many other ethnic groups represented as well. Asians are one of the newer immigrant groups to make Texas their home and are especially prominent in the Houston and Beaumont-Port Arthur areas.

Although many have tried to define a "Texan character" or personality, it never really works. This is mainly because Texans are such a diverse people, both historically and presently. In spite of the Anglo majority, cross-influences from many different cultures—Amerindian, European, African, and Hispanic—have made it impossible to identify Texan culture with any one ethnicity. The most that can be said for a traditional "Texas spirit" is that perhaps there is a shared attitude of tenacity in the face of adversity—a "do or die" temperament that is both courageous and stubborn. This attitude was typical of early residents in many other western and southwestern states, but seems to have been best preserved in only a very few—besides Texas, perhaps Montana, Wyoming, and Alaska.

Amerindians

Unfortunately, the "frontier spirit" that is so noble in many ways has been responsible for the almost complete demise of the great Indian cultures that existed throughout North America before European immigration began 500 years ago. It would be unethical and dishonest for any writer to ignore this basic and unchangeable fact of history.

To be fair, however, it must be noted that when the Spanish first arrived in what is now Texas, the Indian population was fairly small and consisted of mainly nomadic tribes whose residency was somewhat sporadic or seasonal. Later, the Indian population in Texas grew concurrent with Anglo-American immigration, as many of the new Indian arrivals were themselves immigrants fleeing persecution in the eastern states. The Plains Indians that we see in American "Cowboy-and-Indian" movies were not native to Texas but came down from the Rocky Mountains and the Great Plains following the first European settlements in the 17th century.

The groups that can be considered most "native" to Texas—the Caddos (actually a sophisticated confederation of around 25 tribes) of East Texas, the Tonkawas of Central Texas, the Coahuiltecans and Jumanos of South and Southwest Texas, and the Karankawa Indians of the Gulf coast—are gone today and were all but gone before the Anglo-American push westward. Most died at the hands of the Spanish and French (either by disease or in battle), and the rest were later absorbed by the Mexican colonial population or killed by the more aggressive Plains Indians. By the mid-19th century, virtually all of the Indian tribes in Texas were originally from elsewhere —the Plains Indians (Comanche, Apache, Kiowa) from the Rocky Mountains and Great Plains, and the Five Civilized Tribes (Choctaw, Chickasaw, Cherokee, Creek, and Seminole) from the eastern United States.

From the start, the source of friction between the Europeans and Indians was essentially cultural, resting primarily on differing concepts of property—the Europeans believed in the ownership of land, the Indians didn't. Perceiving that Indians didn't lay personal claims to land, Europeans took it, and were then surprised when the Indians reacted. This is, admittedly, a gross simplification, since behavior among all groups concerned varied tremendously. But in the end it came down to the fact that the Europeans had more firepower than the Indians, and so their culture prevailed. By the end of the 19th century, most of the Indians living in Texas had been exterminated or assimilated, had left on their own, or had been forced out of the state, in the same way that Indians were "removed" by other U.S. states.

Today, there are only two officially recognized tribes (the Tiguas and the Alabama-Coushattas) living in Texas year-round, plus one migratory tribe (the Kickapoos) of seasonal residents. The Tiguas, a Pueblo Indian group, can be considered neo-native to Texas, having moved into the El Paso area around 1680. Residing in Ysleta del Sur Pueblo, just outside of El Paso, the Tiguas are descendants of an original Spanish mission community. Their most important festival takes place every June 13, the feast day of their patron saint, Saint Anthony.

The only other permanent Indian group maintaining a tribal tradition in Texas are the Alabama-Coushattas, a mix of two closely related Creek Indian tribes originally from Mississippi and Alabama. The Alabama-Coushatta reservation is located in the Big Thicket area of East Texas, on lands given to them by Sam Houston in the 19th century in return for their assistance during the Texan Revolution. The reservation is fairly large and is the site of a yearly national powwow. (For more information on these two tribes, see "Alabama-Coushatta Indian Reservation," p. 455.)

During certain times of the year, the Kickapoo Indians migrate from their home in El Nacimiento, Mexico, to a 125-acre residential site on the Rio Grande near Eagle Pass. A U.S.-Mexican agreement gives them the right to travel freely between the two countries and reside in either.

The largest Amerindian populations in Texas now are actually in Dallas and Houston, and consist mainly of Cherokees from Oklahoma and Navajos from New Mexico who have come in recent years to take advantage of the state's relatively superior economy. These newcomers do not live along tribal lines, but many participate in intertribal community activities.

In spite of the low numbers of Amerindians residing in Texas, an Indian influence on Texas remains in the language (place names, geographical terms, camping terms), cuisine (much of what is called "Mexican" or "Tex-Mex" cuisine was developed from Indian cookery), and folklore of Texas.

Western Europeans

Most of the **Anglos** or English-speaking immigrants who came to Spanish and later Mexican Texas in the 19th century were former U.S. citizens seeking new opportunities. They largely set the tone for Texas settlement and took up positions of leadership in the political events which led to independence and later U.S. annexation. They were joined by small groups of Anglo Europeans (generally Scotch and Irish) who were often fleeing religious or political persecution in their homelands.

Texans of **German** descent make up the state's fourth-largest ethnic group, behind Anglos, Hispanics, and Afro-Americans. Early German immigrants settled mostly in Central Texas, bringing with them the customs, dialects, and social organization of village Germany. In 1842, a group of Germans residing on the Rhine formed the Mainzer Adelsverein, a "Society for the Protection of German Immigrants to Texas." This organization worked with Texas land-grant *empresarios* to facilitate German immigration. The Germans were the first immigrant group to successfully settle along the Indian frontiers in Texas.

Today, German-style beer halls are fairly common in Central Texas, as is the tradition of German sausage-making. Around 17 German "singing societies" are still active in the state, getting together for regular *Sängerfests* or song festivals. Few German descendants in Texas, however, speak German as their mother tongue, and even during the famous *wurstfests* of Fredericksburg and New Braunfels, the festivities feature rather trivialized representations of German culture, though they're still great fun.

People of **French** ancestry occupy fifth place among the ethnic groups in Texas if one includes the Acadian French (or Cajuns) living in Southeast Texas. The first French settlement in Texas was LaSalle's Fort Saint Louis at Matagorda Bay, which lasted from 1685 to 1689 before succumbing to famine, disease, and Indian attacks. In 1817, the famous French buccaneer Jean Lafitte established Campeachy, a colony of 1,000 assorted pirates and privateers on Galveston Island, but in 1821 the U.S. Navy forced them to leave the vicinity.

The first established French colony came about when Henri Castro received a land grant in 1842 to settle 600 families along the Medina River near San Antonio. By 1848, Castro had brought Texas more than 2,000 French immigrants, most from the province of Alsace. Today, many of the citizens of Castroville, Quihi, Vandenburg, and D'Hanis are descendants of these first colonists. The local language, food, and architecture continue to reflect Alsatian French heritage.

Other French immigrants came in smaller groups in the late 19th century, settled around the state, and were eventually assimilated. The discovery of oil in the early 20th century, however, brought thousands of French-speaking Cajuns and Creoles from Louisiana, most of whom settled in Southeast Texas. Cajuns are descendants of a French-Canadian group from Nova Scotia (also known as Acadia) who were forced by the

the San Antonio
Gun Club, early
1900s

BARKER TEXAS HISTORICAL CENTER

British to leave Canada in the 18th century because they had refused to swear allegiance to the British Crown. The Acadians, or Cajuns as they came to be known by Anglos, brought their unique culture with them and have made the Port Arthur-Beaumont-Orange area (sometimes called the Cajun Triangle) a center for Cajun music and food, cultural hallmarks which are enjoyed by many non-French Texans.

The Creoles are most often said to be of mixed Afro-American and French descent or *mulâtre*. Actually, many Creoles are non-*mulâtre* descendants of either the slaves of French planters in Louisiana and Haiti or *gens libres de couleur* ("free people of color") from the French Caribbean. (In New Orleans, people of mixed French and Spanish descent often call themselves Creoles—the term can be applied quite loosely.)

Creoles have emigrated in large numbers to the Houston-Galveston area. Fewer Creoles speak French than do the Cajuns nowadays, and they have been to a large extent assimilated by other black populations in Texas (though they still carry on a unique musical tradition—see "Arts And Entertainment," p. 42).

Central Europeans

Slavic immigration has also made its mark on Texas culture. Communities of Poles, Czechs, and Wends dot Central and East Texas, with Czechs the most numerous group. Thousands of Czechs immigrated to Texas from Bohemia and Moravia in the late 19th and early 20th centuries. Currently, the largest rural populations of Czechs in North America are found in Texas.

In the towns of Praha, Fayetteville, and Halletsville, Czech is still a first language for many residents. Almost every small-town bakery in Texas sells *kolaches,* a traditional Czech pastry. Country and western music owes a large debt to the polkas and waltzes of Moravia and Bohemia, and the Texas-style dance hall was actually introduced by the Czechs. Moreover, the accordions used in Tex-Mex *conjunto* bands, as well as in the Creole zydeco music of East Texas and southern Louisiana, were introduced by early Czech immigrant musicians (Germans played accordions as well, but not in the style that was adopted by Mexicans and Creoles).

The town of Panna Maria (population 96) in Karnes County was founded by Poles in 1854 and is the oldest Polish settlement in the United States.

Afro-Americans

Texas's black residents live mostly in East Texas, particularly in the Houston-Galveston and Port Arthur-Beaumont areas. For many of their ancestors, immigration to Texas was not voluntary, since they came as slaves or indentured servants. Once slavery was abolished in Texas following the Civil War, many former slaves migrated to urban centers outside of Texas. Some remained, however, and took advantage of the situation as best they could (as elsewhere in America, blacks didn't receive full civil rights by federal law until the 1960s). The numerous Creoles (see above) of Southeast Texas constitute one Afro-American group that immigrated to the area voluntarily, either in flight from French plantations in Louisiana and Haiti in the 18th century, or in search of better economic circumstances later in the 19th and 20th centuries.

Black Texans played an important role in Texas history when they served as the U.S. vanguard during the Indian wars of the late 19th century, in several all-black infantry and cavalry units. The Comanches called them "buffalo soldiers," and the famous 9th and 10th cavalries adopted the buffalo as their coat of arms. Black cowboys were fairly common throughout the Cattle Kingdom era, and there is still a strong black cowboy tradition in East Texas. Beaumont is the annual venue for the well-attended Bill Pickett Invitational Rodeo, an all-black event.

Afro-Americans have also made undeniably strong contributions to a collective Texan culture, particularly to Texas music (see "Arts And Entertainment," p. 42). Their influence is present in Texas cuisine as well, especially throughout East Texas, where "home-style" or "southern" cooking predominates. Even Texas barbecue aficionados are divided between those who favor the "western" style developed by white and Hispanic chuck wagon cooks and those who prefer the "soul" style developed by blacks in East Texas.

Hispanics

Although Hispanics haven't always been as numerous in Texas as they are at the present time, historically they have had more influence than any other group besides the Anglo-Americans. The Hispanic influence began, of course, with the arrival of the Spanish in the 16th and 17th centuries (see "History," p. 21-36) and continued through the period when Texas was a Mexican territory (first Nuevo Santander and later part of Coahuila y Texas). Altogether, Texas was under Spanish or Mexican rule for around 150 years, from the first Spanish colony at Ysleta in 1681 until Texas independence from Mexico in 1836.

The Hispanic influences on many phases of Texan life (language, food, architecture, music, and fashion, to name a few) are so ubiquitous that it would take a thick tome to enumerate and describe them even briefly. Some influences are so deeply woven into the Texan fabric that their origins are virtually indiscernible from what is assumed by the unaware to be Anglo-American culture.

Practically the entire Texas cowboy mythology, for example, is based on the Spanish *vaquero* tradition, which developed when Spaniards brought cattle to the New World in the 16th century. Many of the words associated with "western" life come from the Spanish language—ranch (rancho), buckaroo (vaquero), rodeo, lariat (la reata), corral, chaps (chaparreras), bronco, and posse are a few well-known borrowings.

Texas architecture is another area that has borrowed much from Spanish and Mexican heritage. In addition to the Spanish cathedrals, missions, and presidios that remain standing in West and South Texas, modern interpretations of these early buildings continue to evolve and provide the state with a distinguishable regional style of architecture.

From margaritas to fajitas, Texas food wouldn't be Texan without the Spanish-Indian influence that is responsible for many of its tastiest dishes. Almost every Texan has his or her favorite Mexican or Tex-Mex restaurant and is quick to claim that Texas Mexican is better than Arizona or California Mexican. In the "nouvelle Tex" or "southwestern" cuisines of Dallas and Houston restaurants, the Hispanic influence is always part of the presentation, whether it's a touch of cumin and lime or paste of ancho chilies. (See "Food And Drink," pp. 62-63, for more details on Tex-Mex eating.)

A few descendants of the original Spanish colonists still live along the Rio Grande and in San Antonio, but for the most part, the Hispanics living in Texas now are of Mexican or Mexican-American ancestry. Mexicans continue to migrate to Texas from Mexico, some legally and others as so-called "wetbacks" who cross the border illegally. It's ironic that the illegal Mexican immigrants have arrived in an area that 150 years ago belonged to Mexico and doubly ironic that many

Anglo-Americans were themselves illegal aliens in Texas at that time.

LANGUAGE

Since Texas's annexation to the U.S. in 1845, English has become the most widely spoken language in the state, with Spanish a distant second. Ironically enough, one of the issues that provoked the Texan rebellion against Mexican rule was the Anglo-Americans' desire for English to be allowed as an official language alongside the majority language, Spanish; these days, Chicanos are struggling for a similar recognition of Spanish.

But the majority of Texans, whatever their ethnic background, speak a unique style of English that sets them apart from the residents of other states in the South and Southwest. Stephen Brook, British author of the insightful *Honkytonk Gelato*, enthused thusly about Texas speech:

What nourishing mouthfuls of language, flush with redundancy, one can hear in Texas, words stumbling over each other, vowels endlessly elongated into diphthongs like verbal rainbows, containing elements and ghosts of every vowel sound known to the human race, including a few that, like the Big Bend mosquitofish, are unique to Texas.

In the cities, the language is diluted by cosmopolitan populations into something approximating Standard American English, but in rural areas, the ripe Texas sound is usually quite prominent. Texan English also varies from one part of the state to another, especially from east (very slow rhythms) to west (linguistic minimalism, punctuated by long squints at the horizon).

Texas vocabulary can also vary significantly from Standard American English. For example, the three meals of the day are usually breakfast, dinner, and supper, rather than breakfast, lunch, and dinner. In small towns, people may say a cinema has "refrigerated air" rather than air-conditioning. Many rural Texans like to use two words when one would suffice, as in "big ole" for "big" and "little bitty" (or even "itty bitty") for "little" (in West Texas, you might also hear "t-niny" for "tiny"). And, of course, Texans are well known for hyperbole; when talking about their state, it's always "biggest," "best," or "most" (only true about half the time).

In South and Southwest Texas, Texas-born residents of Mexican descent often speak a unique mixture of Spanish and English that non-Hispanics may call Spanglish or Tex-Mex. It's especially distinctive among older and rural Chicanos who mix a Texas drawl with Spanish vocabulary. Nowadays, many younger, urban Chicanos speak a blend common throughout the Southwest and California, a symbol of the pan-Hispanic social movement among Hispanic Americans. Listen to the local radio stations of Corpus Christi, Brownsville, and Laredo and you'll hear bilingual disk jockeys switching back and forth between Spanish and English as they play an exciting mixture of Tex-Mex conjunto, salsa, and swamp music.

Anglos throughout Texas pepper their language with Spanish words and phrases like *arroyo* (dry stream bed) or *Quien sabe?* (Who knows?). The pronunciation of these is very Texan however.

Most Spanish words ending in "o" will get an "a" sound instead; likewise an "e" ending is pronounced like a "y" or "i." Pecos becomes Pay-kas, Amarillo is Am-a-rill-a, arroyo is a-roy-a, and Rio Grande is Rio Grand-y.

In a few small towns in Central Texas, European languages are still spoken, most notably Czech, German, Polish, and Alsatian or Belgian French. In Southeast Texas, primarily in the Port Arthur-Beaumont-Orange triangle but also in Houston and Galveston, approximately 50,000 residents speak Cajun or Creole French as a first language. In Port Arthur, about 10% of the population is Vietnamese, so dialects of the Vietnamese language are commonly spoken (see "Port Arthur," p. 444, for more on the large Vietnamese community there).

Body language in Texas can differ significantly from other states as well. West of the Sabine River, men may emphasize a point by grabbing a listener's shoulder briefly or with a quick slap on the back. In South Texas, the *abrazo* (a friendly embrace) is common, even among non-Hispanics.

ARTS AND ENTERTAINMENT

Texas has become a very entertaining place in the 20th century. In fact, during most of the year and in most of the state (sparsely populated West Texas is the exception), you'd be hard pressed to drive more than 20 miles without coming across a festival, honky-tonk, party, concert, rodeo, or outdoor dance. And that's just a few of the different kinds of entertainment available.

If you're looking for something to do in Texas but don't know where to find it, a good place to start is the local newspaper. Don't worry about the general lack of high-quality journalism (with few exceptions, Texas newspapers aren't known for their excellence)—most publish an informative "datebook" or "calendar" on Fridays, Saturdays, or Sundays which lists local events and ongoing exhibits. Independent arts-oriented weeklies (modeled after San Francisco's *Bay Guardian* and similar weeklies in other large American cities) in San Antonio *(Current* and *SA News)*, Austin *(Austin Chronicle)*, Houston *(Houston Press)*, and Dallas *(Dallas Observer)* contain fairly comprehensive activities calendars that are generally superior to the daily papers and are distributed around town for free. These weeklies

cover not only the cities in which they're published, but also the surrounding towns.

City Texans are amazingly diverse in their interests, perhaps even more so than their counterparts in other U.S. capitals. Young folks in Texas think nothing of hitting a blues bar on Friday night, a polka festival Saturday afternoon, followed by Saturday night sushi and cowboy punk.

Museum and classical music enthusiasts needn't feel left out either. As an obvious consequence of big oil money, some of the most well-endowed public and private museums in the U.S. are located in Texas. Most are in the large urban centers of Dallas, Houston, and San Antonio, but Texas travelers shouldn't neglect the smaller out-of-the-way places like the Cowboy Artists Museum in Kerrville or the Museum of the Pacific War in Fredericksburg.

All the major cities have their own symphonies and dance companies, and some of them are very good. In addition, there are several prestigious music festivals in the state, including the acclaimed San Antonio Festival, the Van Cliburn International Piano Competition (in Dallas), and the Round Top Music Festival.

TEXAS MUSIC

The classical music in Texas is fine, but where the state really excels is in American roots music. You can hear good Beethoven in New York or Minneapolis, but Texas offers a combination of uniquely American musical styles, most of which developed in Texas, that no other state can approach.

The main reason for the heavy proliferation of musical styles in the state is simple geography—Texas occupies a position in the nation that is impossible to avoid or breeze through quickly when traveling east to west along the southern half of the United States. Plus it has the longest international border of any state and curves right up into the Mississippi delta, the birthplace of American music as distinct from European music. A color-coded map of the U.S., in which different colors represent different musical influences, turns Texas into a patchwork quilt.

Scores of bands throughout the state continue to experiment with the many musical styles available, forging new sounds and garnering critical praise. In *Musician* magazine's nationwide 1990 "Best Unsigned Bands" contest, four out of the 12 winning bands were from Texas (no other state on the award list had more than one winner).

There's only one place where you can hear "Texas radio and the big beat" (Jim Morrison), and that's "down in Texas where the guitars grow" (Steve Miller). It's worth going to Texas to hear roots music if for no other reason—but you have to know where to look for the best.

Blues And Rhythm And Blues

Blues music is probably the oldest popular music form in Texas. The blues developed during the post-Civil War years in an area that stretched from Texas to Alabama, sung by freed black slaves. Records show that collectors were transcribing blues lyrics in Texas as early as 1890. The singing style originated from "field hollers" or "shouts," that is, a capella work songs, but evolved into a troubadour tradition in the late 19th and early 20th centuries, in which wandering musicians accompanied themselves on guitar or fiddle. Musically, the obvious origins of blues-style melodies and rhythms are African; but lyrically, early black Americans developed their own topics based on the suf-

Blind Lemon Jefferson

fering they had experienced first as slaves and later in the post-emancipation South.

Wandering musicians were drawn to developing urban areas in the South and Southwest, and Dallas and Houston quickly became blues centers because of their large black migrant populations. The Deep Ellum area of Dallas (at the east end of Elm Street where it meets Central Avenue) was a favorite venue for legendary blues guitarists and singers like Blind Lemon Jefferson (1897-1929) and Huddie Ledbetter ("Leadbelly," 1889-1949) in the 1910s and 1920s. Virtually all blues players today can trace their roots back to Blind Lemon, whose mid-1920s recording of "Black Snake Moan" made him the first popular blues performer in the United States. *Jefferson,* a leading European blues magazine published in Sweden, is named after him. Other famous blues musicians who came out of the Deep Ellum tradition include Lonnie Johnson, Texas Alexander, Sam Price, and Mance Lipscomb (who didn't perform there but created his style from watching Blind Lemon play in Deep Ellum).

The electric guitar was invented by San Marcos-Dallas blues and jazz guitarist Eddie Durham (1906-87) when he devised a microphone from radio and phonograph amplifiers that fit into the body of his guitar (earlier he had developed the first acoustic guitar resonator from a tin plate, and later a vibrato arm from a clothes hanger). When the D'Armand Company developed a factory-built guitar pickup, Durham was among the first to use it. Jazz guitar legend and fellow Texan Charlie Christian learned about the pickup from Durham and also copied Durham's legato playing style. Christian was later hailed as the father of jazz guitar.

Probably the second-most influential blues artist in American music, after Blind Lemon Jefferson, is T-Bone Walker. T-Bone was born in Linden, Texas, but moved to Dallas while he was still a boy. There he befriended Jefferson and was introduced to the electric guitar by Charlie Christian. He made his first blues recording in Dallas in 1929 and eventually revolutionized the way the electric guitar was played by bending strings to get a "vocal" sound, thus establishing the guitar as a lead instrument for the first time. His influence on the entire blues idiom was tremendous and he is credited with developing the style known as "Texas shuffle blues" or "jump blues," an up-tempo form with links to early swing jazz. Out of Texas shuffle evolved early **rock and roll** as composed and performed by Chuck Berry, Jerry Lee Lewis, Elvis Presley, and others.

Houston's blues tradition goes back at least as far as Dallas's, but the city didn't develop a blues recording industry until the late '40s. Lightnin' Hopkins (1901-82) is the earliest blues musician of note who performed regularly in Houston. His style was basically an idiosyncratic interpretation of Jefferson's. From 1947 to 1949, he recorded what are today considered his greatest performances on Houston's Gold Star label. He was a major influence on such famous rock guitarists as Billy Gibbons (of ZZ Top)

and Jimi Hendrix, as well as on developers of the blues-tinged "swamp sound" like Credence Clearwater Revival and later Omar and the Howlers.

Houston's post-Lightnin' Hopkins blues style includes not only the up-tempo Texas shuffle originally popular in Dallas and Fort Worth but also a slow-to-medium blues with the 6/8 tempo popularized by Junior Parker and Bobby Blue Bland. Besides Parker and Bland, other Houston-based blues performers who have achieved international status include Sippie Wallace, Charles "Gatemouth" Brown, Big Mama Thornton, Juke Boy Bonner, and more recently, Johnny Guitar Watson, B.B. King, Johnny Copeland, and Albert Collins.

By the '60s, blues music was commonly played by non-black as well as black musicians (although whites have been playing blues since the late 19th century when black fiddlers and white guitarists played together at white dances, and throughout the '30s and '40s many white swing bands played blues tunes). Blues purists complain that white players watered down the blues during the heyday of white guitar blues in

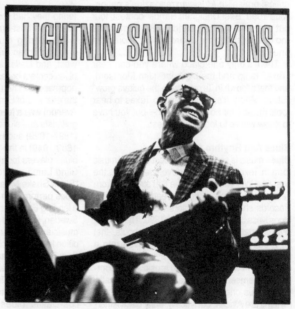

Lightnin' Hopkins

ARHOOLIE PHOTO ARCHIVES

the '60s and '70s, but the fact is that most blues musicians (black and white) were branching out into other musical areas at that time, including **rhythm and blues** ("soul music") and rock. White Texas artists such as Doug Sahm, Johnny Winter, Janis Joplin, Steve Miller, Boz Scaggs, and Stevie Ray Vaughan, and Texas bands like ZZ Top and the Fabulous Thunderbirds vary in their devotion to the blues, but all are blues-inspired. What promoted the blues most during this period may have been the British blues experiments of groups like the Rolling Stones, Cream, and Led Zeppelin. For most of the British bands at the time, however, playing the blues was just a passing fad and by the mid-'70s the "blues experiment" had ended.

In the '80s, a blues revival spread across the U.S. and more Texas bands than ever were swearing their allegiance. Dallas's Deep Ellum district is currently undergoing a musical resurrection that includes all types of popular music; you can also hear new and "revived" Texas blues and R&B artists in clubs in Austin, Fort Worth, San Antonio, Beaumont, and Houston, as well as in various honky-tonks, roadhouses, and cafes in more rural areas. Zu Zu Bollins, a resident of Dallas and one of T-Bone's main disciples, is playing again in Texas, as are a number of devoted younger musicians who have picked up the blues torch, like Anson Funderburgh and the Rockets, Marcia Ball, Angela Strehli, the Juke Jumpers, Jesse Taylor and Tornado Alley, Mannish Boys, Steve James, and The Westside Sound. San Antonio's Doug Sahm travels the U.S. with the house band from Antone's (a popular Austin club devoted to American roots music) and other Texas musicians, playing an assortment of Texas music that includes blues tunes originally performed by T-Bone Walker, Junior Parker, and Bobby Blue Bland.

California cinematographer Les Blank has directed two definitive films about Texas blues men, *The Blues Accordin' to Lightnin' Hopkins* and *A Well Spent Life* (about Mance Lipscomb). These are frequently shown at university campuses and art cinemas around the U.S. and Europe and are available on video from Flower Films & Video (tel. 510-525-0942), 10341 San Pablo Ave., El Cerrito, CA 94530. Both are worth seeing before you come to Texas, if you get the chance (the Lipscomb film is the better of the two).

Country And Western

The style of country and western music most associated with Texas essentially developed out of a meeting between the Anglo-Irish-Scottish fiddle traditions and folk ballads of British descendants and the polkas and dance music of central and eastern Europe (principally Germany, Poland, Bohemia, and Moravia). That's about the extent to which you can generalize about Texas C&W, however, since it covers such a myriad assortment of styles, from the range songs of Gene Autry to the rockabilly of Buddy Holly.

You might say that Texas put the "western" in "country and western." The early country music of Kentucky and Tennessee is traditionally more bluegrass or mountain music oriented, featuring fiddle and banjo as prominent instruments, while Texas country is traditionally supported by fiddle and guitar. In the 1920s, Texas fiddler A.C. Robertson made what is considered the first recording of American country music, "Sally Gooden."

Texas C&W also borrowed a great deal from outside the classic Appalachian sound, starting with the electric instrumentation and jazz stylings that created honky-tonk and western swing. Ernest Tubb, "the Texas Troubadour," developed the guitar-based honky-tonk tradition that drew heavily from jazz arrangements, most notably in the walking bass lines; Hank Williams continued the tradition. The most famous western swing outfit was Bob Wills and His Texas Playboys, a band which assembled in the 1920s and continued to perform into the 1970s.

Today, Asleep at the Wheel of Austin and San Antonio's George Strait carry on the tradition of western swing while relative newcomer Lyle Lovett updates it with a style that's part western swing, part rhythm and blues. Texas C&W has also brought in Mexican border influences from *norteño* or Tex-Mex music that now seem right at home in Austin or Nashville.

In the '60s and '70s, the difference between the Austin and Nashville sounds was less a musical split than one of attitude toward the music business—"outlaw" artists versus "commercial" artists. Austin performers Willie Nelson, Waylon Jennings, and Jerry Jeff Walker were the embodiment of outlaw country and influenced changes throughout the C&W scene. They claimed the right to inject modern C&W with nontraditional song topics, and to dress in more "expressive" styles, but the music they played was essentially the same. A strong sense of Texas geography was often present as well, as in Waylon and Willie's "Luckenbach, Texas."

Today, Texas C&W continues to borrow from other sources, most prominently rock and roll. Joe Ely of Lubbock and Steve Earle of San Antonio are two musicians who are pursuing a raw, more elemental sound that attracts listeners from disparate audiences nationwide. Other songwriters who are creating an updated Texas music style (using Austin and Lubbock as main centers) include Butch Hancock, Jimmie Dale Gilmore, Robert Earl Keen, Jr., James McMurtry, Nanci Griffith, and Hal Michael Ketchum. As in the old days, Texas country song lyrics express working-class angst, covering the classic themes of lost love, unemployment, travel (trains, trucks, and horses), drinking, and loneliness. A strong sense of place remains (e.g., George Strait's "All My Ex's Live in Texas").

Authentic Texas country and western of various styles can be heard in clubs and concert halls in the state's major cities, but is probably best enjoyed in the dance halls, honky-tonks, and roadhouses of small-town Texas. In general, there are more live music venues in South and West Texas than in the "dry" counties (where liquor isn't sold) of the north and east. If you draw a line extending from El Paso in the west to Orange in the southeast, you can figure it's honky-tonk territory below the line and churches above (with Lubbock and Amarillo as notable exceptions). The Hill Country between Austin and San Antonio is an especially good area, with venues like Gruene Hall in Gruene, Floores Country Store in Helotes, the Leon Springs Cafe in Leon Springs, or the Blue Bonnet Palace on the outskirts of San Antonio, to name a few.

Flaco Jimenez

ARHOOLIE PHOTO ARCHIVES

Tex-Mex *(Conjunto)*

Texas-Mexican border music is perhaps the most interesting of all Texas music with regard to the mixture of influences that created it. Because it hasn't received as much nationwide commercial attention as other Texan forms, no record industry publicist has yet written a definitive history for border music, thus leaving it open to much speculation among aficionados. They can't even agree on the best name for the music, which has been called border music, *norteño, tejano, conjunto,* and Tex-Mex. Texas-Mexican border music and *conjunto* seem to be the terms in current vogue, with "Tex-Mex" receiving the widest publication in English-language media. Hispanics in Texas generally prefer the term "*conjunto* music," while *norteño* is used more by border musicians in northern Mexico.

The Tex-Mex or *conjunto* sound has been an acknowledged influence for a number of non-Texas performers, including Paul Simon, Ry Cooder, Tom Waits, Los Lobos, and the Talking Heads. Through these and other international recording artists, more and more music listeners are turning an ear toward San Antonio and the Rio Grande.

Actually, the most descriptive term for this music might be Czech-Mex, since *conjunto* originally developed from accordion music (primarily the waltz, polka, schottische, and mazurka) introduced to Hispanics in South Texas and northern Mexico by Czech (Bohemian or Moravian) and German immigrants in the late 19th and early 20th centuries. While the Spanish word *conjunto* refers to any musical group, along the Texas-Mexico border (which was very fluid prior to the 1920s) it has always (in this century) referred to an ensemble led by an accordion and *bajo sexto*, a large Mexican 12-string guitar. Originally, these two instruments were supported by a string bass and trap drum set only; later, electric bass and guitar were occasionally added, along with alto sax and keyboards (though most *conjunto* bands maintain the traditional accordion, *bajo sexto*, bass, and drums line-up).

The first known *conjunto* recording was made in 1935 by Narciso Martinez of San Benito, Texas (also the birthplace of Baldermar Huerta, better known as Freddy Fender), and the music became extremely popular on both sides of the border in the '40s and '50s. The early 1960s saw a decline in the popularity and performance of *conjunto*, but by the late '60s it was on a roll again and has remained popular ever since. Typical performances by Chicanos (Mexican-Americans) today present a range of songs sung in Spanish that include primarily polkas, *rancheras* (similar to C&W), and *corridos* (Mexican ballads) as well as modern Latin forms like *cumbias* and salsa. Current Texas *conjunto* stars include accordionists Ramon Ayala, Valerio Longoria, Flaco Jimenez, and Esteban (Steve) Jordan. Jordan (sometimes nicknamed "El Parche" for the eye patch he wears) is a particularly hot player who blends *conjunto*, salsa, jazz, and blues into a passionate whole.

But border music has long been popular with Anglo-Texans as well as Hispanics, as performed by enduring Texas artists like Doug Sahm, Augie Meyers, Joe "King" Carrasco, and the Brave Combo, all of whom often sing in a mixture of English and Spanish (predominantly English) and who perform other styles of Texas music along with Tex-Mex. Augie Meyers prefers to call his brand of border music "Mexican rock and roll."

Austin's Brave Combo performs an especially engaging mixture of Tex-Mex, polka, and Latin music that explores both the Czech and Latin roots of *conjunto*.

Conjunto-style performances can be heard throughout Texas, but particularly in the South Texas border towns between Brownsville and Laredo and in San Antonio, which has a population that is around 55% Mexican and Chicano (see "San Antonio," p. 294, for further details).

Not surprisingly, Les Blank, along with Arhoolie Records' Chris Strachwitz, has directed a film on Tex-Mex music called *Chulas Fronteras,* available on video from Flower Films & Video (tel. 415-525-0942), 10341 San Pablo Ave., El Cerrito, CA 94530. The film is a great introduction not only to the music but to the *frontera* (border) culture of South Texas.

Joey Records (tel. 512-432-7893, 6707 W. Commerce St., San Antonio TX 78227) is the granddaddy of Texas *conjunto* labels, with releases by Valerio Longoria, Flaco Jimenez, Los Tigres del Norte, Los Alegres, and others.

San Antonio's Martín Macías created the modern *bajo sexto* in the '40s by extending the traditional fingerboard onto the body, adding a neck cutaway, rococo strike plates, and the checkerboard binding now standard on every *bajo*. He also makes a 10-string *bajo quinto* (a smaller version of the *bajo sexto*) and custom string sets for *bajos*. For further information, contact Macías Musical Instruments (tel. 512-923-0563), 1130 Division Ave., San Antonio, TX 78225.

Cajun And Zydeco

The Louisiana-born Cajun and Texas-born Zydeco musical genres (sometimes called "French music" because the lyrics are usually sung in Cajun or Creole French) are very popular in Southeast Texas, particularly in Houston, Galveston, and in the Beaumont-Port Arthur-Orange area (or "Cajun Triangle"). About 150,000 Cajuns and Creoles live in this part of the state, at least 50,000 of whom speak Acadian or Creole French as a first language. Texans of non-French descent tend to confuse the two distinct musics, however, misled by newer bands that play both types.

Cajuns are whites of French descent (see "The People," p. 37) and the typical Cajun ensemble features fiddle, guitar, and button accordion. Cajun music is basically a cross between traditional Acadian dance music and Texas-style country music (it was Hank Williams's hit song "Jambalaya" that brought Cajun music to national attention). Traveling to Texas in search of a better life is a common theme in Cajun song lyrics. Port Arthur is one of the better places to hear Cajun music in Texas today, as hundreds of Cajuns work at the oil refineries in the Port Arthur area. In spite of the fact that many of the most well-known Cajun bands come from Louisiana, Port Arthur is the site of the annual Cajun Music Awards in May.

Zydeco music is most often played by Creoles (see "The People" p. 40), people of mixed Afro-American and French heritage. The name "zydeco" is a Creole French pronunciation of *les haricots,* "the snapbeans," from the song "Les Haricots Sont Pas Salés" ("The Snapbeans Aren't Salted"). The song was first recorded by the legendary Clifton Chenier (1925-1987), who was born in southwestern Louisiana but who performed often in Southeast Texas, where this style of music originated. Before Chenier popularized the name zydeco, the music was known as "la la" (slang for *la musique Creole*), among other terms.

Zydeco (occasionally spelled "zydico" or "zodico") is essentially a fusion of Afro-Caribbean rhythms, blues, and traditional Cajun song forms that was created by Creoles living in Houston, Galveston, and Port Arthur during World War II. The pre-zydeco music or "la la" was played originally in southwestern Louisiana by Creole ensembles that featured button accordion, fiddle, *frottoir* or rub board (a corrugated metal slab used for washing clothes), and "iron angle" (triangle). But in the World War II and postwar era, modern rhythm and blues became an important influence as well, as Creoles moved to the urban areas of Texas and were exposed to R&B for the first time. To accommodate these new influences, the button accordion was replaced by the larger piano accordion, the fiddle and triangle were lost, and in-

Clifton Chenier

ARHOOLIE PHOTO ARCHIVES

struments typical of urban R&B bands, such as electric guitars, bass, keyboards, and horns, were added (but the *frottoir* remains).

Today the biggest zydeco centers are Lake Charles, Louisiana, and Houston, Texas—although Galveston, Beaumont, Port Arthur, and Corpus Christi also support plenty of zydeco bands. Catholic churches in Houston frequently hold zydeco dances and several Houston clubs (e.g., the Continental Club, the Silver Slipper Club, and the Zydeco Cha-Cha Lounge) feature zydeco music on a regular basis. The word zydeco, in fact, is often used to refer to social gatherings where this type of music is played.

Zydeco players worth looking for in Southeast Texas include old-timers like Fernest Arceneaux, L. C. Donatello, Anderson Moss, Boozoo Chavis, and Vincent Frank, as well as relative new-timers Paul Richard and Jabo. Clifton Chenier's heir apparent to the zydeco throne, Stanley "Buckwheat" Dural (based in Louisiana), often plays clubs elsewhere in Texas as well, such as Antone's in Austin. The city of Beaumont holds an annual Zydeco Creole Dust Festival as part of the local

Juneteenth celebration, where you can hear the best in down-home zydeco from Texas and southwestern Louisiana.

Les Blank's (see "Blues And Rhythm And Blues" and "Tex-Mex" above) film about the late Clifton Chenier, *Hot Pepper,* is a good aural primer for the music.

Texas Music Sources
Two stores that carry large selections of LP, cassette tape, and compact disc recordings of Texas roots music are Antone's Record Store (tel. 512-322-0660), 2928 Guadalupe, Austin, TX 78705, and Roots And Rhythm Music (tel. 510-525-1494), 10341 San Pablo Ave., El Cerrito, CA 94530. Both can handle mail and telephone orders.

Another mail-order house specializing in Texas roots music is Home Cooking Records, P.O. Box 980454, Houston, 77098.

For a live compendium of Texas music styles, catch a performance by the recently formed Texas Tornadoes, a band consisting of blues/rock/country/Tex-Mex legends Doug Sahm, Freddy Fender, Flaco Jimenez, and Augie Meyers. All four hail from South Texas, so a Tex-Mex flavor holds the edge; their second album, *Zone of Their Own,* earned a 1991 Grammy for Best Mexican-American performance.

San Angelo stockyards

RODEO

Rodeo is a huge year-round sport in Texas. A recent *Rodeo Times Calendar* for the month of May alone (not even the height of the rodeo season) listed nearly a hundred rodeo events around the state, from goat roping to full open rodeos. First prize for any single event at a professional rodeo can be as high as $50,000, which makes up a huge purse when you consider that most rodeo events are over in well under a minute.

Professional rodeo began in the 1800s with impromptu roping and riding contests between cowboys, whether on ranches or on the trail. The oldest rodeo in the U.S. is the annual Pecos Rodeo in Pecos, Texas, which began as an open invitational competition in 1883 and is still held every July 4th.

Nowadays, the Professional Rodeo Cowboys Association sets the standards for competition, from the various professional levels on down to amateur youth, civic, high school, and college rodeo. These standards provide systematic and exacting methods for judging rodeo events, monitoring rodeo safety, and for the welfare of livestock used in competition, as well as regulating cowboy tack (equipment used in the rodeo, such as bronc saddles, spurs, bull rope, and bareback rigging). Rodeo is part of the curriculum at many Texas colleges and universities; Sul Ross University in Alpine, West Texas, is reputed to have the top rodeo school in the nation.

The rodeo world comes with its own language: *hooey* (a half-hitch knot used in calf roping); *pullin' leather* (also "grabbin' the apple," touching any part of the saddle with the free hand during the saddle bronc riding event—immediate grounds for disqualification); *lap and tap* (a cattle- roping event in which cattle are not given the usual 10- to 30-foot head start—used in small arenas); *piggin' string* (a six-foot length of soft rope used in calf roping); *honda* (the eye in the end of a rope). To fully appreciate Texas rodeo (as with any sport), it helps to know a bit of the jargon that's commonly used by announcers and spectators in order to understand the fundamentals of the action.

The roughstock events are the most well-known events in rodeo and also the most dangerous. The basic objective for these three events, **saddle bronc riding, bareback riding,** and **bull riding,** is the same: the rider must stay atop the animal for at least eight seconds, using only one hand to hold on. Additional rules govern recoveries from near falls and spurring (no rowels or spiked wheels are allowed, only certain areas of the animal can be spurred), with the rules slanted in favor of the animal. Points are scored for the ride as a whole, with half of the potential points allotted to the animal and half for the rider.

Rodeo "roughstock" is livestock that is considered untrainable. The bucking broncs you see in the arena are not wild in the sense of being born away from human society, but are horses that refuse any kind of domestication, and cannot be used in ranching, pleasure riding, racing, or even as pack horses. Owners of such animals approach rodeo stock contractors who give them a try-out to see if they're truly untrainable. Most of the time these ill-tempered animals only buck a few times out of the chute, and then calm down in the hands of professional riders. Only a small percentage of horses are accepted as prorodeo broncs (from the Spanish *bronco*, "rough") and prices can go into five figures; a genuine bronc will perform well for up to 20 years.

The harder a horse or bull is to stay on, the more points it scores toward the ride. Bareback broncs are small and quick, and the saddle rigging used in this event has no stirrups, making the bareback event somewhat more difficult than saddle-bronc riding. Bull riding takes exceptional balance and control because of the sheer power a bull brings to the event. Once a year the top 30 prorodeo cowboys select three animals as "bucking stock of the year" for their outstanding performances. In spite of the violent appearance of roughstock events, a cowboy's riding finesse is much more important than strength since it's simply not possible for a 200-pound rider to overpower bucking animals that weigh anywhere from 1,000 pounds to a ton.

Another common rodeo event is **barrel racing,** which involves a slalom-type horseback race through a triangle of three equidistant barrels. Times are measured in hundredths of seconds.

In the **steer wrestling** event, a cowboy rides alongside a running steer, slides from the horse onto the steer, and wrestles it to the ground by a skillful turning of the horns. As in the roughstock events, technique and timing are more important than strength.

Roping competitions are popular among amateur rodeo cowboys because they don't require the apparent daredevil attitude that roughstock and steer wrestling events do. In **calf roping** the rider must chase a running calf, lassoing the animal, and then dropping to the ground to tie the calf's legs together quickly with a soft rope. **Team roping** requires two riders, a "header" and a "heeler," to chase a steer given a head start and then rope the horns (the header) and hind legs (the heeler). The rider's end of the rope must be given a couple of "dallies" (turns) around the saddle horn as part of the action—a thumb or finger that gets caught between horn and rope is instantly lost.

Less common events may supplement the standard six rodeo events. Goat roping or tying, similar to calf roping, is fairly commonplace in Texas, especially at rodeos in the Edwards Plateau where goats and sheep are raised. The World Championship Goat Roping contest takes place every June in San Angelo. Women compete in rodeos too, and the Panhandle's Hereford is the site of a National Cowgirl Hall of Fame as well as an annual All Girl Rodeo.

In South Texas, Mexican rodeos or *charreadas* are an exciting alternative to the usual fare. Rules and events for the *charreada* differ from American rodeo significantly and are generally festive occasions as well. Brownsville on the Texas-Mexico border holds *charreadas* during the last week of February every year, and there are several in San Antonio throughout the year.

The best source of information on Texas rodeo events is the *Rodeo Times,* a monthly newspaper published in San Antonio (2823 Hillcrest, San Antonio, TX 78201, $25 a year)—it's given out free at rodeos and at many western-wear stores. Texas travelers who don't have time to seek out periodic local or state rodeos might try the weekly Mesquite Rodeo near·Dallas. This professional rodeo in the town of Mesquite, just west of Dallas, has been a weekly event from April to September for over 30 years. Events are held in the Mesquite Arena every Friday and Saturday night from 8-10 p.m.; the entry fee is $7 for adults, $3 for children.

HOLIDAYS AND EVENTS

Perhaps due to the cross-cultural blend of peoples and its proximity to Mexico, Texas is an unusually festive state. Besides the usual national and state holidays there's a full range of activities that celebrate ethnic heritage, folklore, ranching, farming, and Texas cuisines. The Tourism Division of the State Department of Commerce publishes a yearly calendar of events that lists and describes such activities across the state (see "Services and Information," p. 69 for the address). Even more comprehensive is the Department of Highways' quarterly "Texas Events Calendar," which can be obtained free by writing to Texas Events Calendar, P.O. Box 5064, Austin, TX 78763.

NATIONAL HOLIDAYS

Government offices and some businesses may close on the following national holidays (when they fall on weekdays). These closings are not always mentioned in the text, so you may want to call ahead to make sure.

New Year's Day: January 1
Civil Rights Day (Martin Luther King Jr.'s Birthday): January 15; usually observed the third Monday in January
Presidents Day: third Monday in February
Easter Sunday: late March or early April
Memorial Day: last Monday in May
American Independence Day: July 4
Labor Day: first Monday in September
Columbus Day: second Monday in October
Veterans Day: November 11
Thanksgiving Day: fourth Thursday in November
Christmas Day: December 25

STATE EVENTS

Some of the more memorable yearly events around the state are highlighted below according to month. Some of the festivals and events listed here are in towns that aren't described elsewhere in the text—these are places that are only worth going to during a particular festival! Actual dates may vary from year to year, so be sure to check the Texas Highways Department calendar in advance.

January
Cotton Bowl Football Game and Parade, Dallas; first Monday in January. A football classic in which the champion college team of the Southwest Conference plays another regional winner.
Southwestern Exposition Stock Show and Rodeo, Forth Worth; usually the last week of the month. Began in 1917 as the world's first indoor rodeo and has expanded to become one of the largest livestock expositions in the United States.

February
Mardi Gras, Galveston; early February. Several Southeast Texas towns with large Creole and Cajun populations celebrate Mardi Gras, but Galveston started theirs in 1867; it's now the state's biggest, with masked balls, coronations, parades, Cajun and Creole cook-offs, and jazz performances that last 10 days. For many people, Galveston's Mardi Gras is a satisfying alternative to New Orleans's currently overcrowded festivities.
Southwestern Livestock Show and Rodeo, El Paso; first week of February. The largest livestock exposition in West Texas since 1931.

Shakespeare Festival, Odessa; every weekend from mid-February through mid-March. The state's oldest Shakespeare festival, staged at a faithful replica of the original Globe Theatre.

Charro Days, Brownsville, late February. Four days of Mexican rodeo **(charreada)**, balls, street dances, and parades in the Mexican fiesta tradition.

George Washington's Birthday, Laredo; third week in February. As unlikely as it may sound, Laredo celebrate's George Washington's Birthday and the signing of the U.S. Constitution in a big way (even though George Washington's birthday has been subsumed under "Presidents Day" on the national level). This is one of the best times to be in Laredo; beauty contest ("Princess Pocahantas"), tejano music festival, jalapeño-eating contest, parades, dancing, Mexican food competitions.

March
South by Southwest Music and Media Confer-

COWBOY POLO

If you've never heard of cowboy polo, don't worry—neither have most Americans. Only nine states have member teams in the National Cowboy Polo Association (NCPA)—Texas, California, Colorado, Alabama, New Mexico, Washington, Oregon, Montana, and Arizona. The NCPA was formed in 1959 when cowboy polo split off from its American predecessor, palmetto polo (still played in Florida).

If cowboy polo differs from palmetto polo, it's a world away from English polo, though all three sports involve horses, mallets, and balls. To begin with, the playing atmospheres and social backgrounds of English and cowboy polo are very different. While English polo is generally a game of the aristocracy, cowboy polo is a rough-and-tumble working-class game. As one player described the difference: "English polo is tea and crumpets. We're beer and hamburgers."

A cowboy playing field is more compact than the English field, 300 feet by 120 feet. Teams field five players who remain in designated zones, which makes it more difficult to move downfield without a constant jostling for control of the ball. The ball used in cowboy polo is made of rubber and is 13 inches in diameter; the English ball is small and wooden, more like a croquet ball (admittedly, this is one area in which English polo seems more macho than cowboy polo).

Until the '70s the only acceptable headgear was a cowboy hat. These days many NCPA players wear helmets of their own choice, including football helmets and construction hardhats with a heavy wire grill rigged across the face, though rules don't require them. NCPA rules require jeans and western-style shirts, and of course only western saddles are allowed (none of these cowboys would be caught dead on an English saddle anyway). Players wear padded chaps as shin guards.

At the moment, the best team in the NCPA is a Texas club from San Jacinto. The Boston Celtics of cowboy polo, San Jacinto has won the national title 12 times in the last 14 years. Also tops is the San Angelo team from West Texas. Their main rivals are the Colorado and Cal-Zona (a California/Arizona team) clubs, but competition is always hot, regardless of the teams involved. The cowboy polo season starts in March and ends in August with the national title series. Most matches are held in rodeo arenas, sometimes in conjunction with professional rodeos.

ence, Austin; second week of March. Over 300 musical groups from throughout the state and beyond perform in some 25 clubs and other venues around town in hopes of being noticed by members of the music industry and press. Other activities include music workshops and award presentations. In recent years, this has become one of the most important pop music events in the United States.

Rio Grande Valley Livestock Show and Rodeo, Mercedes; third week of March. The Valley's largest event, with all the usual activities.

April

Hill Country Wine and Food Festival, Austin and Lake Buchanan; first week in April. Winetastings, seminars, vintner demonstrations, eating, and more eating. Typically features wines of foods of Texas, California, and France.

Fiesta San Antonio, San Antonio; third week in April. A celebration of the city's Hispanic heritage and one of Texas's most impressive festivals. The Fiesta features *charreada,* street food, *conjunto* and mariachi performances, country and western dances, parades, art shows, fashion shows, and lots of flowers.

Buccaneer Days, Corpus Christi; 10 consecutive days in mid-April. Celebrates Alonzo Alvarez Piñeda's landing in Corpus Christi Bay in 1519 with sailing regattas, a music festival, a coronation ball, and fireworks.

May

Polka Festival, Ennis; first full weekend in May. One of the state's premier Czech polka fests, with plenty of dance performances, costumes, and traditional Czech food.

Cinco de Mayo, San Antonio and other towns with significant Hispanic populations; first week in May. This festival commemorates the defeat of an attempted French invasion at Pueblo de los Angelos, Mexico, during the American Civil War. Mexican music, dance, food, and other cultural events.

Texas Wine Country Chili Cookoff, Lakeside or another location near Dallas/Fort Worth; second weekend in May. A North Texas winetasting and chili competition. The morning after could be deadly.

Old Fiddlers Reunion, Athens; last weekend in May. A reputable and enduring fiddlers festival sponsored by the Texas Fiddlers Association. The program most prominently features the unique Texas fiddle tradition, but also attracts fiddlers from around the country who play different kinds of American and Irish-Scottish fiddle music and compete for cash prizes. A must for people who like to fiddle around.

Van Cliburn International Piano Competition, Fort Worth; every four years during late May and early June (last competition was in 1989). The most prestigious piano competition in the United States, held in honor of Fort Worth native Van Cliburn. Thirty-five of the world's most gifted pianists are invited to compete.

June

Lone Star Outdoor Drama, Galveston; from June through Labor Day (September). A historical drama written by Pulitzer Prize-winning author Paul Green which recounts the events of the Texan Revolution. The show actually alternates nights with a different contemporary Broadway show every year.

Texas: A Historical Musical Drama, Palo Duro Canyon State Park; summer. Another outdoor musical penned by Paul Green, *Texas* has run for over 25 years and puts the awesome canyon setting to good use in enacting the highlights of Texas history. It's a slanted perspective for sure, but the cast of 80 actors and actresses, plus props that include a real, working train, make an enjoyable show.

Fiesta del Noche, San Antonio; every Tuesday, Friday, and Saturday from June through Labor Day (September). A variety of Hispanic cultural performances held at the outdoor Arneson River Theater on the San Antonio River.

Chisholm Trail Roundup, Fort Worth; second week in June. Commemorates Fort Worth as the last stop on the Chisholm Trail. Includes traditional trail rides, chili cook-offs, Indian dance competition, street dances, rodeos, and shoot-outs. Most activities are centered in the Stockyards district.

Texas Water Safari, San Marcos and Seadrift; second weekend in June. A grueling, four-day, 260-mile boat race along the San Marcos and Guadalupe rivers.

Round Top Music Festival, Round Top; mid-June through mid-July. Features high-quality classical musical performances from a variety of repertoires and periods.

Juneteenth (Emancipation Day), statewide; week of June 19th. A commemoration of the announcement in Galveston that Texas slaves were freed following the War Between the States. Black civic organizations throughout the state hold festivals of various lengths featuring music, dancing, and food. The biggest Juneteenth festival (on two consecutive weekends) is in Houston, site of the **Juneteenth Blues and Gospel Festivals,** which feature local and national talent. The city of Beaumont holds the rockin' **Zydeco Creole Dust Festival** and the **Bill Picket Invitational Rodeo** as well.

Watermelon Thump Festival, Luling; last weekend in June. One of the oldest fruit-growing festivals in the state, the Watermelon Thump stages several different kinds of competitions involving watermelons—largest melon, tastiest melon, a seed-spitting contest, a melon-eating contest, and so on. There is also the coronation of the Watermelon Thump Queen, and lots of barbecue, since Luling is the acclaimed capital of Central Texas-style barbecue.

July

Texas Cowboy Reunion, Stamford; week of July 4th. Texas's biggest amateur rodeo—only real working cowboys and cowgirls can participate, no rodeo pros allowed.

Pecos Rodeo, Pecos; week of July 4th. The oldest ongoing professional rodeo in the country; always features top prorodeo champs.

Texas Jazz Festival, Corpus Christi; first weekend in July. Jazz performances at Bayfront Park, plus free jazz workshops, jazz cruises in the Gulf, and jazz films.

The Great Texas Mosquito Festival, Clute; last weekend in July. Inane, but true, the little town of Clute pays tribute to the Texas mosquito. Features a mosquito legs look-alike contest, a mosquito-calling contest, as well as other excuses for a good time.

August

XIT Rodeo and Reunion, Dalhart; first weekend in August. An annual homecoming for the remaining XIT ranch hands (the XIT was once the largest ranch in Texas). In addition to the rodeo, activities include dances, pony express races, parades, and storytelling.

Texas Folklife Festival, San Antonio; first weekend in August. A well-attended celebration of the state's ethnic diversity that exhibits a compendium of arts, crafts, music, folklore, and foods from around the world.

All Girl Rodeo, Hereford; second week in August. An all-female professional rodeo with all the familiar events.

Prazka Pout, Praha; August 15. Czech homecoming centered around an English and Czech mass at St. Mary's Church. A Czech country bazaar includes traditional Czech games, food, music, and dancing.

Saint Louis Day, Castroville; August 20. An Alsatian and Belgian festival held at Koenig Park on Medina River, celebrating Castroville's Alsatian/ Belgian heritage with music, dance, crafts, and food. The food alone is worth a trip from San Antonio.

September

Westfest, West; Labor Day. A Czech and Slavic festival with traditional street dances, costumes, Sokol gymnastics, folk dancing, and a Miss Westfest contest.

National Championship Pow-Wow, Grand Prairie; first weekend after Labor Day. A large Amerindian gathering that draws participants from throughout the Southwest and the Dakotas, sponsored by the Dallas-Fort Worth Intertribal Association. Indian dancing competitions, arts and crafts shows, and food booths are some of the festivities.

Republic of Texas Chilympiad, San Marcos; third weekend in September. Reputedly the largest "bowl o' red" cook-off in the country. Sponsored by the Chili Appreciation Society International (CASI).

Texas International Wine Classic, Lubbock; last weekend in September. The most prestigious of the state's wine festivals, featuring seminars, tastings, and gourmet dinners. Texas's best wineries are in this area and will be open for tours.

October

Heart O' Texas Fair and Rodeo, Waco; first weekend in October. One of the largest fairs in Texas (average attendance of 300,000), featuring livestock exhibits and a professional rodeo.

Oktoberfest, Fredericksburg; first full weekend in October. Many Central Texas towns hold Oktoberfest celebrations in recognition of the early German immigration to Texas. Since this is the oldest and largest of the early German colonies, the celebration is especially hearty. *Bierhalle*-style

entertainment, dance contests, costumes, and lots of sausage and beer.

Texas State Fair, Dallas; second two weeks in October. The largest state fair in the United States, a virtual "mega-fair." Rodeos, football games (University of Texas versus the University of Oklahoma is the "big game"), livestock shows, theater, and other events.

Texas Rose Festival, Tyler; mid-October. A tribute to the unofficial state flower—the bluebonnet is official but probably not as readily identified with Texas as the rose—and the state's rose capital (over half the roses commercially grown in the U.S. are grown here). Rose shows, Rose Parade (with rose-decorated floats), local garden tours, and the coronation of the Rose Queen.

Czhilispiel, Flatonia; third weekend in October. A Czech-German heritage festival and the second-largest chili cook-off in Texas.

November

World Championship Chili Cookoff, Terlingua; first Saturday in November. Texas' first and most famous chili contest, also called the "Original Frank X. Tolbert/Wick Fowler Memorial Championship Cookoff." The original cook-off has split into two events. See "Terlingua," p.135, for more details.

Wurstfest, New Braunfels; first full week of November. The state's largest German festival, with sausage-making demonstrations, German music, singing, and dancing, contests, and other activities. The best of the "wurst."

December

Candlelight Tour, Jefferson; first weekend in December. Historic homes in Jefferson open their doors to Christmas carolers and out-of-town visitors. Free choral concerts and other Christmas shows.

Dickens Evening on the Strand, Galveston; first weekend in December. Galveston's historic Strand district is transformed into a century-old English street scene a la Dickens. Participants dress in period costume and present street performances, and there are Dickens shows on local stages as well.

Christmas at Old Fort Concho, San Angelo; first weekend in December. This four-day celebration centers on the restored frontier garrison of Fort Concho, which is decorated especially for the occasion. Activities vary from year to year but usually include a historical pageant, caroling, dancing, an "Old Fashioned Melodrama" in a tent on the parade grounds, culminating on Sunday with a cowboy church service.

Las Posadas, San Antonio; second week in December. Dance, drama, music, food, and piñata parties culminating in a candlelight procession along the Paseo del Rio in commemoration of the Holy Family's search for lodging. Laredo holds a similar celebration.

OUTDOOR RECREATION

ON LAND

National Parks, Forests, Recreation Areas, And Preserves

Texas has some of the largest and least crowded national outdoor recreation facilities in the United States. The U.S. National Parks Service manages Big Bend National Park, Guadalupe Mountains National Park, Padre Island National Seashore, Rio Grande Wild and Scenic River, Lake Meredith National Recreation Area, Amistad National Recreation Area, and Big Thicket National Preserve. Each of these is described in some detail elsewhere in this book, including addresses and phone numbers. Depending on the park, preserve, or recreation area, a range of outdoor activities is available, from wilderness hiking and backcountry camping to boating and fishing.

In addition, Texas has several Park Service-operated national monuments, historical sites, and historical parks: Alibates Flint National Monument, Chamizal National Monument, Fort Davis National Historical Site, Lyndon Baines Johnson National Historical Park, Palo Alto Battlefield National Historical Site, and San Antonio Missions National Historical Parks. None of these feature camping or hiking facilities, but are interesting outdoor attractions nonetheless.

Some NPS-administered sites in Texas charge nominal entry fees—usually $1-3 per person or $3-10 per vehicle. The NPS offers several entrance passes that can reduce total fee expenditures for visitors who plan to visit several NPS sites. Each is available at any fee-operated national site. A **Golden Eagle Pass** costs $25 and allows unlimited admission to all federally operated outdoor recreation areas (including national parks, forests, recreation areas, and wildlife areas) for one calendar year. Senior citizens age 62 and over are entitled to a **Golden Age Passport** which allows free lifetime entry to all of the same facilities. The **Golden Access Passport,** for blind and disabled persons, carries all the same benefits as the Golden Age Passport. Finally, a **Park Pass** can be purchased from specific NPS-administered sites for $10-15 and allows unlimited entry to that site for one calendar year. For general information on national parks, preserves, recreation areas, and monuments in Texas, write the National Park Service, Southwest Region, Box 728, Santa Fe, NM 87102.

State Parks

The Texas Parks and Wildlife Department operates 105 state park and recreation areas, over half of which have camping areas. More parks and camping facilities are being added all the time; the state's objective of having a state park within a two-hour drive of every metropolitan area in Texas has nearly been reached.

Most state parks charge entry fees—usually $3 per vehicle or $1 per individual on bicycle, foot, or boat. A $25 Conservation Passport that allows unlimited admission into all fee-entry state parks can be purchased by mail from the Texas Parks and Wildlife Department (see below) or in person at any fee-entry state park. The Conservation Passport also provides a $1 discount on overnight facility use fees and allows access to certain park areas (e.g., Big Bend Ranch State Natural Area) closed to non-Passport holders, and it allows for participation in periodic guided tours (e.g., Matagorda Island State Park). Senior Citizens (65 years or older) can obtain a State Parklands Permit that exempts them from all entry fees.

Not every state park and recreation area is covered in this book. The State Department of Highways Official Highway Travel Map (obtainable from the Texas Department of Highways or from the Texas Tourism Division; see "Services and Information," p. 69) marks every one of them, however, or for a complete list, contact: Texas Parks and Wildlife Department (tel. 800-792-1112 within Texas, 512-389-4890 elsewhere), 4200 Smith School Rd., Austin, TX 78744.

Hiking

From desert basins to mountaintops, from salt marshes to hardwood forests, from creeks to canyons, Texas offers an unsurpassed variety of hiking trails. The state's hundreds of designated trails can be divided into three basic categories: **nature trails,** which are generally short (one to two hours walk) and require little preparation; **day-hiking trails,** which can be completed in a day or less and which call for some planning in the way of water, food, clothing, and footwear; and **backpacking trails,** which cover distances that require overnight camping and careful preparation with regard to camping equipment, food supplies, and clothing. Several parks in Texas also have horse trails for use with private and/or hired mounts.

Longer trails can, of course, be broken up into a series of shorter hikes. Few people, for example, have hiked the entire length of the 140-mile Lone Star Trail through Sam Houston National Forest. Instead, hikers and backpackers tend to tackle the trail a few days at a time.

Descriptions and maps of state and national park trails can be obtained from individual park offices. Maps of the 14 Woodland Trails in the Piney Woods region of East Texas can be ordered by calling or writing the Texas Forestry Association (tel. 409-632-TREE), Box 1488, Lufkin, TX 75901. Maps of the Lone Star Trail are distributed by the Forest Supervisor (tel. 409-639-8501), 701 N. First St., Lufkin, TX 75901.

Private Recreation Areas

Besides the large, privately owned Texas amusement parks like Six Flags Over Texas and Astroworld, a variety of active outdoor possibilities are offered around the state by private individuals, families, and small companies.

In the Hill Country and to a lesser extent in West Texas are a number of popular "dude ranches." A dude ranch offers city people and other non-ranchers an opportunity to experience ranch life for a few days or weeks at a time. Typical activities include trail rides, outdoor ranch-style dances, fishing, river rafting, barbecues, and nature tours. Dude ranches vary from inexpensive, family-oriented affairs to higher-priced working ranches oriented toward equestrians and sometimes hunters (these don't like to be called "dude ranches," but still cater mainly to city folks).

Private campgrounds occasionally offer outdoor activities in conjunction with basic camping facilities. This is especially true for those camping areas located near streams and rivers, where tubing, rafting, canoeing, and fishing gear can often be rented or where guided trips are provided. See "On Water" and "Guided Trips" below, as well as "Camping," p. 60.

Private recreation areas of note are described throughout this book.

Hunting

Hunting is popular in Texas among men and women of all ages. Many state wildlife management areas allow regulated hunting in season, as do licensed private game ranches.

The ethics of hunting for sport is a controversial topic to say the least (the author is not a hunter), but it must be recognized that Texas hunters, as a group, are largely responsible (but not solely responsible, as many like to think) for wildlife conservation efforts in the state. Several introduced species that are now extinct in Asia and Africa are maintained on Texas game ranches, for example; these same ranches have been known to send U.S.-born animals to their native habitats for breeding in countries where they have been eliminated through excessive hunting.

Whether on state or private grounds, hunting regulations that include bag (size and number) limits are strictly enforced. White-tail deer, mule deer, and wild turkey are by far the most popular game animals, followed by javelina (collared peccary) and smaller game birds. The best hunting in the state is said to be in South Texas and on the Edwards Plateau, which is also where most game ranches are located. The Texas Parks and Wildlife Department issues 12 different types of licenses, ranging from resident and nonresident basic seasonal hunting licenses ($13-300) to alligator hunters' ($35) and trappers' ($15) licenses. For detailed information on licenses, seasons, and regulations, write or call the Texas Parks and Wildlife Department (tel. 512-389-4890), 4200 Smith School Rd., Austin, Texas 78744.

ON WATER

One of the common myths about Texas is that the entire state is bone-dry. The Trans-Pecos area of Far West Texas (less than 20% of the total land area) is mostly desert; but elsewhere in the state, the facts quickly dispel the myth. According to the 1987 U.S. Statistical Abstract, Texas is second only to Minnesota in the amount of inland water area within her borders, including over three million acres (or 5,175 square miles) of lakes, streams, rivers, and springs. Then, of course, the Texas Gulf coast is the third-longest shoreline in the continental U.S., over 600 miles long. Finally, the legendary Rio Grande (second longest river in the U.S., after the Mississippi) runs for 1,200 miles along the Texas-Mexico border. East Texas is the wettest part of Texas, since well over 50 inches of yearly rainfall keep the water level high in lakes, rivers, and bayous.

Thirteen major rivers and over 11,000 named streams, creeks, and bayous run across Texas, mostly in a Gulf-ward direction. Many of them were first explored by Spanish colonists and hence have Spanish names. Besides the Rio Grande, some of the more popular rivers for water recreation (canoeing, kayaking, whitewater rafting, fishing, and swimming) include the Nueces, the Guadalupe, the Colorado, the Canadian, the San Antonio, the Brazos, the Neches, the Sabine, and the Red rivers.

Over 150 lakes and reservoirs dot the state,

most of them created by the damming of inland waterways in order to provide drinking water, agricultural irrigation, and hydroelectric power. Virtually all of the state's lakes and reservoirs are open to recreational activities like sailing, canoeing, swimming, and fishing. Many of the larger lakes are suitable for water-skiing and scuba diving as well. Major bodies of water (each over 20,000 acres in surface area) include Amistad Reservoir, Lake Buchanan, Calaveras Lake, Cedar Creek Reservoir, Choke Canyon Reservoir, Lake Conroe, Falcon Reservoir, Lake Fork Reservoir, Livingston Lake, Lake Palestine, Lake Ray Hubbard, Richland Creek Reservoir, Sam Rayburn Reservoir, Lake Tawakoni, Toledo Bend Reservoir (the largest, with a surface area of 181,000 acres), and Lake Wichita.

Fishing

Sportfishing is popular all over the state, from the Red River in the Panhandle to the Gulf coast. Deep-sea fishing in the Gulf of Mexico is one of the state's most important tourist industries. Surf fishing and flats fishing (in the shallow waters of lagoons created by barrier islands) are also quite popular. You'll find sportfishing outfits that rent equipment, charter boats, or lead small-group

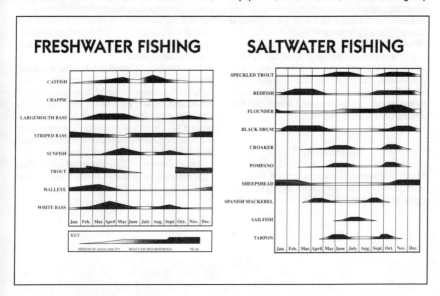

fishing trips from the ports of Galveston, Port Aransas, Port Arthur, Corpus Christi, and Port Isabel as well as a few smaller port towns. Bass fishing is excellent on many Texas lakes.

As of 1991, the Texas coast led the nation in International Game Fish Association (IGFA) records, with 141 of the largest saltwater and 42 of the largest freshwater species caught. Florida is a distant second with 73 and 25 respectively.

As with hunting (see "On Land" above), the Texas Parks and Wildlife Department regulates type, size, and number of game fish that can be taken from Texas waters. Fishing equipment also comes under detailed regulation (types of lines, traps, and nets that can be used, for example). But unlike hunting, fishing regs aren't strictly enforced, simply because it's virtually impossible to patrol all the inland and coastal waterways. Nonetheless, fishing licenses are fairly inexpensive and it's best for future sportfishers and fish if everyone cooperates with state efforts to preserve the decreasing marine population.

Sportfishing licenses vary from $13 for a year-long resident license to $20 for a five-day nonresident license (either is good for all freshwater fishing), plus $7 for a saltwater sportfishing stamp. Special licenses are needed to take shellfish such as shrimp, oyster, clams, and mussels. Crab has no season or number limit, though it is unlawful to take egg-bearing females or crabs less than five inches in body width.

For detailed information on sportfishing regulations and licenses, write or call the Texas Parks and Wildlife Department (tel. 512-389-4890, 4200 Smith School Rd., Austin, TX 78744). Specific information on local fishing spots is included with destinations listed in this book.

GUIDED TRIPS

Many different organizations around the state offer guided outdoor recreation, ranging from trail rides to canoeing and backcountry camping.

Guided trips like these are a great way for novices to learn outdoor skills under the supervision of experienced guides. For experts they're a good way to meet folks interested in the same kinds of activities as yourself.

The best places to contact guides are in the vicinity of recreational areas. Near Big Bend National Park, for example, several companies lead raft trips through the canyons of the Rio Grande. Along sections of other rivers in the state that are popular for rafting or canoeing are outfits that rent equipment and/or provide guided trips.

Wherever there are horse trails in national or state parks, you'll find a stable or two nearby that offer guided trail rides. Outdoor societies such as the Sierra Club arrange regular hiking and camping trips around the state. Some clubs concentrate on a particular kind of activity, such as rock-climbing or canoeing.

Along the coast are dozens of places that lead fishing trips (see "Fishing" above). In many of the same ports are dive shops that organize scuba trips to the Flower Gardens reefs in the Gulf. Inland dive shops also lead dives at Texas quarries, lakes, and reservoirs.

Perhaps one of the best places to find a wide selection of outdoor trips is on Texas college and university campuses. Many schools have established outdoor programs that run year-round, but most are active primarily in the summer months. Most activities are open to the public and costs are very reasonable.

The University of Texas at Austin, for example, offers a week-long canoe trip on the Rio Grande for $250 that covers transport, food, group camping equipment, and a guide. UT also has a regular program of one-day nature hikes that run around $7. University programs like these offer the best bargains in the state for guided outdoor trips. For a current schedule of UT-sponsored activities, call or write UT Recreational Sports Outdoor Program (tel. 512-471-1093), Gregory Gym 31, Austin, TX 78712.

ACCOMMODATIONS

Accommodations are available in Texas for every budget and proclivity, including hostels, historic inns, bed and breakfasts, swank international-class hotels, dude ranches, and campgrounds.

HOTELS AND MOTELS

Budget

Hotels and motels in Texas are, generally speaking, reasonably priced when compared with average hotel rates across the United States. In smaller towns, they can be downright bargains, averaging about $30 a night for the best place in town (which may be the only place in town—and definitely not a Hilton). In mid-sized and larger towns, your best bets are the bargain chains like Motel 6 or Day's Inn. Except in South and West Texas you won't find many places anywhere under $20, so if you want to keep accommodation expenses lower than this, see "Hostels" and "Camping."

Medium-priced

In the $40-65 range, you'll find a wide choice of chain hotels like Best Western, Ramada, and Holiday Inn (though not all Holiday Inns will be this low—the newer ones are moving upscale). Near urban centers like Houston, Dallas, San Antonio, Beaumont, and Austin, the interstate highways are lined with hotels and motels like these, as well as a few independents in this price category.

Deluxe

Generally speaking, you'll only find truly deluxe accommodation in Dallas, Houston, El Paso, and San Antonio. Here again, Texas is good value. For a room that would cost $200 in New York or San Francisco, you can get away with paying about $125. In any of these cities, you can also find several high-quality hotels in the $75-100 range.

Historic Inns

With hundreds of 19th-century hostelries still standing throughout the state, the restoration of historic hotels and inns has become a popular Texas undertaking. Historic inns range from the three-room Lickskillet Inn in Fayetteville to the 310-room Warwick in Houston. Those in smaller towns are usually medium-priced, while those in larger cities are mostly in the deluxe category. The deluxe historic inns can further be divided into the ones that have attempted a faithful reproduction of the original interiors (e.g., The Driskell in Austin) and those which have historic exteriors and lobbies, but whose rooms are rather the same as any other hotel's in this price range (e.g., Hotel Galvez in Galveston).

If you plan to stay in hotels while traveling in Texas, you really owe it to yourself to stay in at least one historic place. Usually the attention to restorative detail carries over to attentive guest service as well, and the traditional Texas architecture, whether it's Mission style (e.g., the San Juan Hotel in San Juan), Alsatian (the Landmark Inn in Castroville), classic Richardson-Romanesque (The Driskell), or Queen Anne Victorian (the Woodbine Hotel in Madisonville), makes the travel experience so much more satisfying than staying in another nondescript Sheraton or Holiday Inn.

Historic inns of note are mentioned throughout the text. Another source of information is the Historic Hotel Association, which has a membership roster of 59 hotels and inns throughout the state. Their membership by no means includes all of the historic inns in Texas, but does include places that more appropriately belong in the bed and breakfast category (see below); their brochure is a fair starting point for those interested in seeking out such places. For information on this organization, call or write O'Reilly Advertising (tel. 214-828-0100), 3600 Commerce, Suite C, Dallas, TX 75226.

A good source of background information on historic inns is Ann Ruff's *A Guide to Historic Texas Inns and Hotels* (Houston: Gulf Publishing, 1985). The book gives a fairly comprehensive, if somewhat dated, account of historic accommodations in Texas, including brief histories and descriptions of each place.

BED AND BREAKFASTS

The bed and breakfast concept has taken full root in Texas. As elsewhere in the U.S. and Europe,

Texas bed and breakfast establishments are basically private homes with a few rooms for rent at modest rates. Rates always include some kind of breakfast and often much more—complimentary tea or coffee in the afternoon, possibly wine in the evening, reading material, attentive service, and sightseeing tips. Bed and breakfast rates in Texas are very reasonable, starting at around $20 for more modest establishments.

In historic districts or towns, the line between "bed and breakfast" and "historic inn" often blurs. Hence, bed and breakfast rates at a home that is a registered state or national landmark may run as much as $100. Old Victorians in historic Galveston or Jefferson are in this higher range as well, due to simple supply and demand; Houston and Dallas residents keep them booked most weekends. Most bed and breakfast inns of this nature, however, will have discounted rates for weekday guests.

An organization called Bed & Breakfast Texas Style (tel. 214-298-8585 or 298-5433), 4224 W. Red Bird Lane, Dallas, TX 75237, handles information requests and bookings for many Texas B&Bs, but their listing does not cover every single place in the state. Many towns with several bed and breakfasts have their own B&B associations, and these are usually better sources of information than Bed & Breakfast Texas Style. Occasionally, in towns with only a few B&Bs, you'll have to book directly through the proprietors.

Names and addresses of individual bed and breakfast inns (except in cases where they only take bookings through a registry and don't want their addresses published) as well as local B&B associations (where they exist) are listed in the "Accommodations" section for each destination throughout this book. Individual chambers of commerce around the state can usually provide you with the updated B&B information as well.

HOSTELS

American Youth Hostels have member hostels in Austin, Houston, San Antonio, El Paso, and Dallas/Irving. In spite of the name, youth hostels are open to people of all ages, and staying at hostels is a good way to cut costs no matter what your income is. Conditions vary from hostel to hostel, but generally you can expect clean, quiet accommodations. Regulations include the mandatory use of a sleeping sheet (a regular sheet folded in half and sewn to form a bag; they can be purchased or rented at most hostels for a nominal cost), a curfew of 11 p.m. (though keys for later entry can usually be rented), and minimal participation in hostel maintenance—usually sweeping or dishwashing. Males and females sleep in separate rooms or dormitories (this applies to couples, too).

The rates at Texas hostels vary from $10 a night in Austin to $12.62 in San Antonio. Advance reservations are not usually necessary (El Paso and San Antonio are exceptions), but are accepted with one night's deposit. To stay at a hostel, you must be a member of either the International Youth Hostel Federation (IYHF) or American Youth Hostels (AYH). A 12-month membership costs $25 for adults (age 18-54), $10 for youths (age 17 and under), and $15 for senior citizens (age 55+). There are also special family memberships—write or call AYH for details. A temporary AYH membership, good for one night only, may be purchased for $3 at any hostel. The cost of temporary membership can be applied toward a full membership later if desired.

The address and nightly rate of each Texas hostel are listed in the text under the corresponding destination. For further information on American hosteling, call or write American Youth Hostels (tel. 202-783-6161), Box 37613, Washington, D.C. 20013-7613.

CAMPING

Sleeping outdoors is one of the best ways to experience the Texan wilderness, while cutting accommodation costs dramatically. With over 200 state- or federally owned and privately owned public campgrounds throughout Texas, there is someplace to camp near virtually every destination worth visiting.

Federal Campgrounds

These include not only campgrounds in Park Service-operated national parks, recreation areas, and forests, but those along the 20 plus lakes administered by the U.S. Army Corps of Engineers. As with all federal, state, and private campgrounds, fee schedules and regulations vary from one site to another, depending on facilities and user demand. For details on campground fees and regulations, refer to individual destinations in the text.

Persons 62 years and older can obtain a free, lifetime Golden Age Passport at any national park, forest, or recreation area or by writing or calling the National Park Service. This permit exempts them from all entry fees and provides a 50% discount on all other federal user fees, including campground fees. The Golden Access Passport offers the same benefits to blind and disabled persons. For more information write the National Park Service, Southwest Region, Box 728, Santa Fe, NM 87504.

State Park Campgrounds

Texas's extensive state park system manages nearly 70 parks and recreation areas that permit camping. These parks offer a range of amenities from camping areas where facilities are as yet undeveloped (Brazos Island, Bryan Beach, and Matagordas Island), to parks with full trailer hookups, campsites, and barbecue grills. Nearly all of the state parks that permit camping have, at minimum, graded campsites, water, cooking areas, and rest rooms, while many also have electrical hookups. Forty-one state parks also have cabins or screened shelters suitable for overnight stays.

The rates for state park camping vary according to campsite facilities and whether your stay is on the weekend (Fri. or Sat. nights) or during the week. A primitive site without water but suitable for tent camping costs $4-7. With running water the rate goes to $6-9; add electrical outlets and it's $9-12; finally, with electrical and sewage hookups (for trailers and other recreational vehicles) it's $10-14. Screened shelters, available at a few parks, cost $15-18 a night, depending on the park. One vehicle per campsite is admitted free; additional vehicles (small utility or boat trailers don't count) are charged a $2 parking fee each. Reservations for campsites or shelters can be made by phone, mail, or in person at any state park up to 90 days in advance, but reservations made more than 10 days in advance require a deposit equal to one day's campsite/shelter fee.

Most state parks have a camping limit of 14 days; some limit stays to seven days. The Texas Department of Highways and Transportation issues a handy booklet called *Texas Public Campgrounds*, which lists all state and national parks with campgrounds and/or trailer facilities, including a list of the facilities at each, stay limits, and auto directions. Each entry in the booklet is keyed by number to the Department's "Official Highway Travel Map"; armed with map and booklet, you'll never have to sleep indoors while in Texas. These free publications may be obtained by writing to the Travel and Information Division, State Department of Highways and Transportation, P.O. Box 5064, Austin, TX 78763.

Private Campgrounds

Roughly half of the total number of campgrounds in Texas are privately owned but open to the paying public. Some belong to campground chains like KOA Kampgrounds or Good Sampark. Nearly all private campgrounds cater to RV (recreational vehicle) campers as well as tent campers, and many rent tents as well. Campground facilities range from basic drive-through campsites to trailer parks with spas and shuffleboard rooms.

Private campgrounds tend to be found: clustered around major cities; on the outskirts of larger state and national parks; along the Gulf Coast and on the shores of popular lakes, reservoirs, and rivers; and in the "snowbird" retreat area between Brownsville and McAllen (the "Rio Grande Valley") in South Texas, near the Mexican border, where retirees from the colder midwestern states migrate during winter.

Rates vary from $5 to $15 a night, depending on facilities and location. Some private campgrounds have lower weekly and monthly rates as well. The best list available of private campgrounds is the free "RV and Camping Guide to Texas," issued annually by the Texas Association of Campground Owners (tel. 409-886-4082), 6900 Oak Leaf Dr., Orange, TX 77630. TACO is an affiliate of the National Campground Owners Association (NCOA).

Another source of information for RV owners is the Texas Recreational Vehicle Association (tel. 512-327-4514), 3355 Bee Cave Rd., Austin, TX 78746. TRVA will provide a free list of RV parks in Texas upon request.

FOOD AND DRINK

EATING

Texans love life and they love food. In the cities, you'll find all the latest culinary trends from Thai to West Coast nouvelle to mesquite-grilled nuevo Southwest, as well as American fast-food chains like McDonald's, Pizza Hut, and Kentucky Fried Chicken. In the smaller towns and hamlets, you can forget about trendy haute cuisine, it's down to two basic choices: the local Dairy Queen or real Texas food.

Real Texas food comes in different varieties, depending on what part of the state you're in (certain Texas foods may be found almost anywhere in the state but are differentiated by local recipe twists). To appreciate all the subtle variations, you might need several years of eating and travel. But by the time you're an expert, you'll have gained more than several pounds, as real Texas food is not your typical health food. In fact, it should be taken in measured quantities in order to stave off a premature heart attack (some say that Texas has more opportunities for indigestion than any other state). Wise Texans vary their diet in order to live long and fruitful lives.

Barbecue Pits And Bierhalles

Basically, what you'll find in Texas are five different styles of regional cooking. In West Texas, the accent is on barbecued brisket, sirloin steaks, spit-roasted chicken, ranch-style salads, barbecue beans, and dessert cobblers. An authentic Texas-style barbecue establishment has oak or mesquite logs piled out back and serves a choice of brisket, ribs, sausage, and either chicken or turkey. In Central Texas, barbecued meats and poultry are also popular but are prepared with different marinades than in West Texas. Also common in Central Texas are "chicken-fried" steak (fried breaded beef or veal with a cream-style gravy), Polish and German sausages, standard Tex-Mex fare like tacos and enchiladas, beans, pickled vegetables, and Dutch apple pie.

Down-home

Over in East Texas are two major culinary divisions. Northeast Texas is known for "down-home," "home-style," or "southern" cooking, which includes dishes like fried catfish, cornbread, fried chicken, roast ham, cream gravy and biscuits, boiled cabbage, poke salad, and vinegar pie. In Southeast Texas, which has a higher black and Cajun population than the rest of the state, you'll find "soul food" like barbecued ribs, chitterlings (fried tripe), boiled collard greens, candied sweet potatoes, rice, and cornbread, as well as Cajun and Creole dishes like shrimp gumbo, crawfish etouffé, boudain (a rice and pork sausage), French-style rolls, and potato pie.

Tex-Mex

South Texas is the bastion of true Tex-Mex food as well as a few Mexican dishes of more remote origins that Texans refer to as "interior cooking" (as differentiated from "border cooking"). Almost all Mexican foods are, of course, a blend of Indian and Spanish influences. But most Americans are familiar with a kind of chain restaurant-style Mexican food that bears little relation to what you'll find in the *frontera* cuisine of South Texas, except for the shared names of some dishes.

Tex-Mex cooking, like Tex-Mex music, is a regional style that is found across a broad area from San Antonio and El Paso to Torreon and Monterrey, Mexico. Tacos and enchiladas are the most common dishes, both made with corn tortillas and filled with various meats and cheeses. Wheat flour tortillas are most often eaten on the side as an accompanying bread in Texas and northern Mexico, rather than as burritos, which are more typical of Arizona and California Mexican.

One Tex-Mex dish that has rather recently become a favorite addition to Mexican menus across the U.S. is fajitas (pronounced fa-HEE-tas), which started out as street vendors fare—strips of inexpensive skirt steak marinated in lime juice and spices, then grilled over a hot fire and served with flour tortillas and *pico de gallo,* a freshly made salsa (sauce) of tomatoes, onions, and hot chilies. Other typical grilled meats like *cabrito* (roast kid) are also common, served with plenty of tortillas, salsa, and beans—either pinto beans or black beans. *Carne asada* is the Mexican equivalent of barbecue, while a *barbacoa* is a more elaborate Mexican smorgasbord featuring several dishes. Most Tex-Mex dishes are not inherently hot and chile-laden—individual diners devise their own degree of spiciness at the table by adding from a variety of salsas.

Another typical Tex-Mex dish is the tamal (plural tamales), shredded pork or chicken that is mixed with Mexican spices, rolled in a thick corn meal dough, wrapped in a corn husk, and steamed. Most Mexican cafes in South Texas also serve mouthwatering breakfasts like *migas,* eggs scrambled with onions, chiles, and corn tortilla strips, *chilaquiles,* similar to *migas* but with cheese, or *huevos mexicanos,* eggs fried with tomatoes, onions, and chiles.

A word about "nachos," the tortilla-chip appetizers that are commonplace all over the U.S.: in most border towns between Del Rio and Brownsville, "nachos" refers to one arrangement only— cheese melted over tortilla chips (with sliced jalapeños on the side). If you add beans to the dish, it becomes *cincos*; add guacamole and it's *pericos* (not "bean nachos" or "guacamole nachos"). In Laredo, they also have *ponchos,* nachos with beef.

In general, the most typical and most inexpensive Mexican restaurants in Texas are those with "Bakery" or "Cafe" in the name. "Restaurants" are a bit pricier (though usually quite moderate by restaurant standards) and tend to alter time-tried recipes in search of either middle-America-style Mexican for tourists or "nouvelle Tex-Mex" for Dallas and Houston urbanites. Noteworthy Texas restaurants and cafes are mentioned throughout the text. If you want to get a lively conversation going among a small crowd of Texans, ask one or both of the following questions: Where's the best barbecue in town? or Where's the best Tex-Mex around these parts?

If you're drooling over the prospect of dining on Tex-Mex right away, drive straight to Texas to whichever of the following is nearest your starting point: Mi Tierra Bakery and Cafe, 218 Produce Row, San Antonio; Avila's, 6232 N. Mesa, El Paso; or Joe T. Garcia Mexican Bakery, 2201 N. Commerce, Fort Worth—three of the most dependable and authentic Tex-Mex eateries in the state (but not necessarily the best—the best are the little discoveries you make on your own in small out-of-the-way towns in South and West Texas).

Chili

You don't have to think twice to guess what Texas's "state dish" is. Chili, from the Texan pronunciation of *chile* (Spanish for the pepper of the Capsicum family; originally from the Nahuatl word *chilli),* is a thoroughly Texan food and is found on menus throughout the state (and yes, elsewhere in the U.S.—but often in name only).

Traditional Texas chili is a meat stew in a fiery sauce of chiles, onions, and various Tex-Mex spices. Beef is the customary meat employed in chili, though virtually every other kind of meat appears in modern variations, from venison to armadillo. Texas chili aficionados eschew beans as an ingredient, though they can be served on the side (as the saying goes, "If you know beans about chili, you know chili has no beans").

No one knows for sure when it was created, but mid-1800 accounts of Texas street life seldom fail to mention the "chili queens" of San Antonio, women who sold bowls of chili from impromptu street stands. The dish seems to have been conceived by Texas cowboys (and embellished upon later by trail cooks) in the 1840s, when they began pounding tough, stringy beef with chilipequins and ground spices into compressed bricks. The bricks were later boiled in pots along the trail to make a stew; the peppers and spices helped preserve the meat and also masked the taste when it began to go bad.

BOB RACE

Somewhere along the middle of the 20th century, chili developed into a Texas cultural symbol. The Chili Appreciation Society International (CASI) was founded by chili fanatics in 1951 and has chapters ("pods") all over the world which indulge in collective chili appreciation. Will Rogers called it "a bowl of blessedness" and Elizabeth Taylor had chili flown to Rome during the filming of *Cleopatra*. Many chili-eaters consider it a potent aphrodisiac; chili is obviously a popular excuse for shedding one's inhibitions, as attendance at any major Texas chili cook-off will surely demonstrate.

Entire books have been written about this humble dish, most notably *A Bowl of Red* by the late *Dallas Morning News* food columnist Frank X. Tolbert. Tolbert organized the first chili cook-off, "The Great Chili Confrontation," between Texas chili cook Wick Fowler and New York journalist H. Allen Smith, who claimed he could prepare better chili than anyone in Texas. The standoff took place at high noon on an October day in 1967, in the abandoned mining town of Terlingua in West Texas. No one won, since the judges declared that their taste buds had become paralyzed (some say it was the beans in the New York chili; others say it was the peppers in Wick's), but the cook-off became an annual event in Terlingua and chili cook-offs are now part of Texas festival life (see "Terlingua," p. 135, for more information on the annual World Championship Chili Cookoff).

One monthly periodical maintains a running schedule of virtually all Texas chili events: the *Goat Gap Gazette* ("Clarion of the Chili World"), tel. 713-667-4652, 5110 Bayard Ln. #2, Houston, TX 77006.

Sweets

Texas desserts aren't fancy. Pie is the state favorite, especially pecan pie (pecan trees thrive in most of the state) and buttermilk pie. In Central Texas, German and Czech pastries are common, especially the *kolache,* a fluffy star-shaped pastry similar to what most Americans call a "Danish," but not as sweet and sticky.

Ice-cream connoisseurs shouldn't miss tasting the Texas-made Blue Bell brand. This ice cream is made in Brenham and distributed throughout the state—you can only get it in Texas (an occasional shipment makes it as far as Oklahoma

City). *Time* magazine recently stated that Blue Bell is the best ice cream in America.

Pecan pralines, a chewy concoction of buttery caramel and pecans, are another Texan specialty. These vary incredibly from recipe to recipe, but the most savory are Lamme's Texas Chewies made in Austin. Texans must like sweetened nuts: besides pecan pralines and pecan pie, practically every Texas schoolkid knows the trick of buying a bag of salted peanuts and adding them to a bottle of Dr. Pepper (a soft drink named for the Waco father of the inventor's girlfriend).

DRINKING

Texas has liquor laws that make travel there a bit like traveling in India. Eighty-four of the state's 254 counties are "dry," which means no beer, wine, or liquor at all is permitted to be sold within county boundaries. Thirty-five are "wet," which means any alcoholic beverage can be sold. The remaining 135 counties vary in local restrictions; some sell only beer or beer and wine, others sell liquor in bars but not at liquor stores. A legislative "local option" allows counties to have both wet and dry areas within the same jurisdiction—upscale North Dallas, for example, is dry, while other areas of the city are wet.

In actual practice, however, booze is everywhere in Texas, since no dry area is ever very far from a wet one.

Beer

Of the several brands of beer brewed in Texas, three are famous as Texas beers: Pearl, Lone Star, and Shiner. Just as Texans argue about the best barbecue and best Tex-Mex food in the state, they differ on which Texas beer is best. All three taste as typically bland as most mass-produced American beer, but every Texan agrees that the best container from which to consume the foamy stuff is the longneck bottle. In fact, in Texas, "longneck" is practically synonymous with "beer."

One Texas brew that does stand out from the rest is Shiner Bock, a dark variety produced from toasted barley. In many urban Texas bars nowadays, this is the only Shiner offered, either on tap or in longnecks. A few microbreweries in Texas are cashing in on the national trend toward pricey "handmade" beer, but so far none has distinguished itself.

Wine

Fifteen years ago, wine made in Texas was strictly a curiosity that was best left on the shelf as a conversation piece. In fact, in 1975 there existed only one commercial vintner in the state, Del Rio's Val Verde Winery, originally founded in 1883. Today the state claims around 7,000 acres of vineyards, which supply 26 bonded wineries. Some of them produce very good wines, on a par with certain of the better California vintages. The retail value of Texas wines produced in 1990 was over $30 million, which makes it fifth or sixth among wine-producing states.

Until Prohibition, Texas was a leader in North American viticulture. The first vinifera (wine grapes) were planted in 1662 by Franciscan padres in the El Paso area, a century before Junipero Serra began cultivating California's first vines. By the early 1900s, Texas had as many commercial wineries as it does now, but Prohibition forced them all to close. Unlike in California, where wine-making took off in the early '60s, a Texas viticultural renaissance didn't occur until the late '70s.

Outside of California's Napa and Sonoma valleys, some areas of Texas probably have the best wine-producing conditions in the United States. In fact, there are more naturally present grape species in Texas than anywhere else in the world,

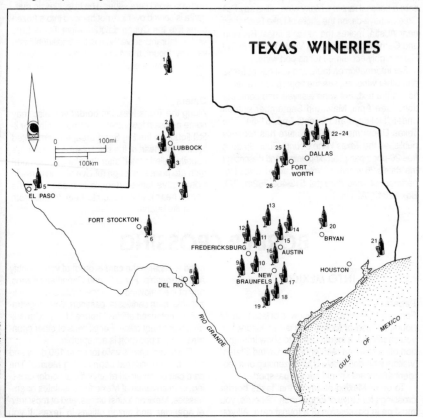

TEXAS WINERIES

according to recognized wine authority Leon Adams. Texas wine country can be divided into four small areas: on the Llano Estacado near Lubbock; just east and north of the Dallas/Fort Worth area; in the Trans-Pecos region near mountainous areas and in the Hill Country near Austin and San Antonio. There are also a few scattered wineries in East Texas, but this area is really too humid and too rainy to produce a world-class or even nationally ranked wine.

The top labels in the state are in the Lubbock area: Llano Estacado Winery, Pheasant Ridge Winery, and the newer Teysha Cellars. Llano Estacado and Pheasant Ridge have won awards in state and national wine competitions, and Teysha, a personal favorite, will probably soon earn a national ranking. Many wine critics say Fall Creek Vineyards, on the shore of Lake Buchanan near Austin, makes the nation's finest Riesling and Carnelian varietals. Val Verde Winery in Del Rio is highly acclaimed for its port wine.

For information on tours and tastings at these and other wineries, see the appropriate destination in the text. For wine festivals and competitions, see April, May, and September entries under "Holidays and Events," pp. 51-54. The Texas Department of Agriculture has recently published the *Texas Wine Country Tour Guide,* a free 20-page pamphlet pinpointing and describing the state's 26 wineries. Write or call the Texas Department of Agriculture (tel. 512-463-7624), P.O. Box 12847, Austin, TX 78711.

Tequila
This well-known product of the agave cactus is not made in Texas, at least not legally (Jalisco state in Mexico is the only place that produces real tequila). But tequila is probably the most popular alcoholic beverage in the state after beer. The authentic, Mexican way to drink tequila is straight up, chased with water or beer. A popular alternative is to lick a few grains of salt from the back of your hand, down a shot glass of the fiery liquid, and then bite into a wedge of lime and suck out the juice. Ay caramba!

The margarita, a potent concoction of tequila, lime juice, and triple sec served in a salt-rimmed glass, was invented on the Texas border, but no one remembers which side. Drink a few of these and you won't care either. The true, classic margarita is served over ice, not blended into a frozen drink like the Cuban daiquiri. Most Texas bars and restaurants serve them in the traditional fashion only, though those oriented toward the tourist trade will offer a choice between frozen and "on the rocks."

Others
Along the Texas-Mexican border you also may come across a few varieties of "moonshine" or illicit liquor. In the Big Bend area, the fermented juice of the heart of the sotol plant is popular (it's usually called "sotol" after the plant). Less common are pulque, a rough relative of tequila made from agave leaves (tequila is made from the agave heart), and mesquite beer (made from mesquite beans).

BORDER CROSSING

INTO MEXICO

Papers
For visits to Mexican border towns of less than 72 hours, no visa or tourist card is necessary, but you should have identification to show immigration officers when reentering the United States. Visitors who don't have U.S. citizenship or a resident alien card should carry a passport.

To enter Mexico at any of the Texas border crossings for stays of longer than 72 hours, you must be in possession of a tourist card. All you

need to receive the card is proof of your identity and citizenship. For U.S. and Canadian citizens, any of the following are acceptable proof of citizenship: birth certificate, passport, voter registration, or notarized affidavit from a U.S. or Canadian government office. For citizens of other countries, only a passport is acceptable.

The tourist card is valid for up to 180 days and must be surrendered upon exiting Mexico. The card can be obtained at any official border crossing, or in advance at Mexican consulates or embassies, Mexican tourist offices, and at most travel agencies and airline offices in Texas. If you drive a vehicle into Mexico, you will be given a free auto permit at the border after your tourist card is stamped, but only if you present proof of ownership (a photocopy of the title will do) and an American insurance policy valid for at least two months after the date of entry. Keep both handy if you're driving, as the Mexican police will demand them if you're stopped (and 12 miles into Mexico, every vehicle without Mexico tags is stopped at border patrol checkpoints).

Mexican auto insurance is required for all vehicles entering Mexico—U.S. insurance is not valid in Mexico, no matter what your insurance company may tell you. Several agencies have offices at the border where this can be arranged for a few dollars. Sanborn's is a reliable American company that specializes in providing valid Mexican auto insurance for short-term visitors to Mexico; they have offices in all of the larger border towns as well as in San Antonio.

U.S. Customs

Upon returning from Mexico, you're allowed a $400 exemption on customs duties every 30 days. For tobacco, this includes 100 cigars and 200 cigarettes; for alcoholic beverages, one liter of wine, beer, or liquor.

MONEY, MEASUREMENTS, AND COMMUNICATIONS

In general, prices in Texas are a bit lower than the U.S. average due to an overall deflationary state economy, which makes it an excellent American travel bargain. Gasoline (petrol) is less expensive than in most states, hotel rates in Texas cities are lower than in other U.S. cities of comparable size, and food, both in grocery stores and in restaurants, is also noticeably cheaper. Most other consumer items cost about the same as in other parts of the continental United States.

Any prices mentioned in this book were current at press time, but prices do change. All Mexican border towns will take U.S. currency. Texas has a 6.25% sales tax on merchandise as well as a 6% hotel tax. With the addition of city/county levies, these figures can increase to as high as 8.25% and 15% respectively.

INTO THE U.S.

Overseas visitors need a passport and visa to enter the United States. Except for diplomats, students, or refugees, this means a non-immigrant visitor's visa, which must be obtained in advance at a U.S. consulate or embassy abroad. Residents of Western European and Commonwealth countries are usually issued these readily; residents of other countries may have to provide the consulate with proof of "sufficient personal funds" before the visa will be issued.

Upon arrival in the U.S., an immigration inspector will decide on the time validity of the visa—the maximum for a temporary visitor's visa (B-1 or B-2) is six months. If you visit Mexico from Texas (or from anywhere else in the U.S.) for stays of 30 days or less, you can reenter the U.S. with the same visa, provided the visa is still valid, by presenting your stamped arrival/departure card (INS form I-94) and passport to a U.S. immigration inspector. If your U.S. visa has expired, you can still enter the country for a stay of 29 days or less on a transit visa—issued at the border—but you may be required to show proof of onward travel (an air ticket or ship travel voucher).

COMMUNICATIONS

Time Zones

Most of Texas is in the U.S. Central Time Zone, which is six hours earlier than Greenwich Mean Time. The exception is the El Paso area, which is on Mountain Time (the same time zone as New Mexico and the Rocky Mountain states), seven hours ahead of Greenwich Time . From the last Sunday in April until the last Sunday in October, Texas, like the rest of the U.S., goes on Daylight-Saving Time, which advances the clock one hour across all American time zones.

Voltage

Power outlets in the U.S. run on a 117-volt AC system, which means that only appliances of that

TEXAS AREA CODES

AMARILLO
806

WICHITA FALLS
LUBBOCK   TEXARKANA
ABILENE   FORT WORTH 214
817   DALLAS
903
NACOGDOCHES
EL PASO   ODESSA   WACO
PECOS
915   409
FORT DAVIS
AUSTIN   BEAUMONT
PRESIDIO   DEL RIO   HOUSTON   PORT
512   ARTHUR
SAN ANTONIO   GALVESTON
210
512
CORPUS CHRISTI
LAREDO
713
BROWNSVILLE

0   200 mi
0   200 km

© MOON PUBLICATIONS, INC.

approximate voltage will run as manufactured. If you bring along a hair-dryer or another small appliance that runs on 200 or 220 volts, you'll have to use a transformer or it won't work properly. Transformers, as well as adaptors (to make the prongs on foreign appliances fit American outlets), are available in most larger American hardware stores and in many electronic supplies stores. Department stores such as J.C. Penney or Sears also carry such equipment.

Modern hotels in the larger Texas cities may have switchable power outlets in the bathroom which will allow for the use of 200/220 volt appliances, but carrying your own transformer is safer than relying on these (they aren't always there and, when they are, may not work properly).

Postal Service

General U.S. Postal Service (USPS) hours are Monday to Friday, 8:30 a.m. to 5:30 p.m. Many post offices also open for a few hours on Saturday mornings, usually 8:30 a.m.-noon. The main post offices in larger cities often have longer weekday hours (a select few are open as late as 10 p.m.)—call ahead to find out.

Visitors can have mail sent to them at any town in Texas c/o General Delivery. A General Delivery letter will only be held by the post office for 10 days before being returned to sender. You can also rent a post office box in any town where they are available (almost all of them) for around $6 a month.

Various privately owned and operated establishments also handle mail, most prominently a nationwide company called Mail Boxes, Etc. These places generally stay open longer hours than USPS offices and handle telegram, facsimile, and UPS parcel services as well. If you need to mail something and can't find an open post office, check the local phone book for one of these private services.

Telephone Services

Texas has seven different area codes (see the map on this page for area code locations). Most telephone systems in the U.S. require that you dial a "1" before dialing a long-distance number. For directory assistance within the area code from which you're calling, dial 411; between different area codes, dial the area code plus 555-1212 (e.g., calling from Houston for a number in San Antonio, dial 1-512-555-1212). Many businesses have toll-free (no charge) long-distance numbers; these are always preceded by "800" rather than an area code.

Business Hours

Most businesses in Texas are open Monday through Friday from 8 or 9 a.m. until 5 or 5:30 p.m. Small shops may close for lunch from noon to 1 p.m. or thereabouts. Retail shops usually don't open until 10 or 11 a.m., and close their doors at 5 or 6 p.m. The exception for retail shops is in large shopping malls, where they'll often stay open until 8, 9, or 10 p.m.

Restaurants and cafes vary widely in the hours they choose to open their doors. It isn't uncommon for restaurants in small and medium-sized towns to close on Sundays; some close on Mondays or Tuesdays as well. Trying to find a non-chain restaurant that's open on Sunday in a small Texas town is often futile; your only choice may be the Dairy Queen or the grocery store (and sometimes the grocery stores are closed on Sunday). In general, small-town restaurants close by 9 or 10 p.m. (sometimes a bit earlier). In Dallas, Houston, and San Antonio, however, there is always someplace to eat or drink—any time of day or night.

Banks and museums are among the most restrictive places when it comes to getting inside their doors. Public banking hours are usually confined to a short period between 9-10 a.m. and 3-

4 p.m., weekdays only. Many museums are open Wednesday through Saturday only, including even big ones like the Amon Carter in Fort Worth.

Mondays and Tuesdays, then, are good days to visit parks and outdoor attractions, since many urban attractions may be closed on these days. Also, you'll have almost exclusive use of such facilities since local weekend tourists won't be around.

SERVICES AND INFORMATION

Emergency Services

Emergency medical and police assistance can usually be summoned by dialing 911 from any phone, whether public or private (no charge for the call). If you get no response dialing 911, try the operator (dial "0"). Virtually every town of any size in Texas has a hospital or clinic that provides 24-hour emergency service.

Tourist Information

Texas has an excellent Tourism Division, administered under the State Department of Commerce, which provides fairly extensive information on standard Texas travel. To request information, call or write the Tourism Division (tel. 512-462-9191), Texas Department of Commerce, P.O. Box 12728, Austin, TX 78711.

Another good source of information is the State Department of Highways and Transportation. The department's "Official Highway Travel Map" seems quite accurate and up-to-date, and marks the location of every state and national park, forest, preserve, recreation area, monument, and wildlife refuge. The department also operates 12 tourist bureaus around the state, mostly in state and international border areas. The bureaus are conveniently located off interstate and U.S. highways (plus one in the state capitol in Austin). Their map is available free of charge at these bureaus, or by mail from the Tourism Division (see above) or directly from the department. For further information or to request a map, contact the State Department of Highways and Transportation, P.O. Box 5064, Austin, TX 78763.

The State Department of Highways also issues a free quarterly Texas Events Calendar that provides up-to-date details on virtually every celebration, from chili cook-offs to jazz festivals, in the state. Each calendar covers only three months and is usually very accurate. They're available from the State Tourist Bureaus described above or by writing "Texas Events Calendar" at the above address.

Many Texas towns also have their own local tourist offices—sometimes as part of convention and visitors bureaus (CVBs)—which are usually headquartered in the local chamber of commerce or very nearby. When a town doesn't have a CVB, you can always get information at the chamber of commerce—every Texas town (well, almost) has something it's proud of, even if this author hasn't yet discovered it!

Weather Information

If you have any intimation that catastrophic weather (e.g., tornadoes or hurricanes) may be in your vicinity or headed your way, by all means tune in to one of the following AM radio frequencies to receive a continuous state forecast: 162.550 KHz, 162.400 KHz, or 162.475 KHz. Different parts of the state broadcast via one of these three (e.g., Dallas is 162.400 while nearby Fort Worth uses 162.550), but all you have to do is head for 162.4 KHz on the AM range and make minor adjustments to get the proper frequency.

Magazines

Of the several Texas magazines with statewide coverage, the best for travel information are *Texas Monthly* (P.O. Box 1569, Austin, TX 78767-1569, tel. 800-759-2000) and *Texas Highways* (P.O. Box 5016, Austin, TX 78763-5016, tel. 512-483-3689). The award-winning *Texas Monthly* offers a variety of well-researched, well-edited features on political and social trends in the state, along with regular columns on music, art, cuisine, sports, and Texana.

Texas Highways, published by the State Department of Highways and Transportation, carries detailed articles on destinations, festivals, people, and cultural events throughout the state, accompanied by mouth-watering photos taken by the state's top shooters. Readers interested in Texas flora and fauna may want to subscribe to *Texas*

Parks & Wildlife magazine (4200 Smith School Rd., Austin, TX 78744), which has a format similar to that of *Texas Highways* (excellent photography, detailed travel information) with an emphasis on wildlife.

TRANSPORTATION

BY AIR

Texas claims over 1,600 airports, three of which are classified international (Dallas/Fort Worth, Houston, and San Antonio). Several airports in South and West Texas (e.g., El Paso, Harlingen, Corpus Christi, and Laredo) can also be considered international since they have flights to and from Mexico. You should have no trouble at all finding flights in, out, or around the Lone Star State, since Texas is second only to California in the number of commercial aircraft arrivals/departures per year in the United States.

About 50 air carriers operate out of Texas, including at least 17 commuter airlines (defined as 60 seats or less per plane). The commuter lines are constantly jockeying for a greater share of the market, keeping intrastate fares relatively low. Though it's always worth checking around for the bottom fare, Southwest Airlines seems to do the best job of keeping fares at a consistently reasonable level. Southwest's "fun fares" are one of the best deals going—with an advance booking of seven days, you can get a flight between San Antonio and New Orleans, for example, for as little as $19.

BY LAND

Driving

For most people, the best way to get around Texas is by car. The state has an excellent highway system, with 300,000 miles of roadway—the most extensive road network in the nation. The best thing about driving in Texas is that—anywhere in the state outside of Dallas, San Antonio, and Houston—traffic is relatively light. In West Texas, you can drive for half an hour or more without seeing another vehicle. The longest highway in Texas (and the longest in any state in the U.S.) is US 83, which runs 903 miles from Perryton on the Oklahoma border to Brownsville on the Rio Grande.

Always keep an eye on your fuel gauge when traveling long distances in rural areas (particularly West Texas), as gas stations may be few and far between on some stretches of road.

When driving in the West Texas desert during the summer months, always carry several gallons of water for radiator mishaps or for drinking should you become stranded. If you do become stranded on a desert road, it's best to stay with the vehicle until a highway patrol car or good Samaritan happens along. If you decide to leave your vehicle to seek assistance elsewhere, leave a note on the vehicle indicating your route and departure time.

The state highway department maintains over a thousand roadside rest stops, some with picnic tables, drinking water and restrooms, some with tables only (scenic overlooks may just have a turnaround area). While camping per se is prohibited at these rest stops, vehicles are allowed to park for rest purposes for periods up to 24 hours—as long as you don't pitch a tent or go over the time limit, you're welcome to sleep in your car, truck, van, or RV at any rest stop.

Auto Rental

All the major American auto rental agencies have offices in Texas, and most have airport locations so that it's easy to get off a plane and pick up a rental car. The most economic way to rent a vehicle is on a weekly or monthly basis. Most agencies also have special weekend deals where you get three days rental for the price of two. Some agencies give an extra discount to customers who reserve cars at least a week in advance. With planning, a small car can be rented for as little as $20 a day (24-hour basis) or $105 a week.

Motorcycles

Texas is a great state for motorcycle touring—lots of room to stretch out on the highway and few bothersome cars and trucks. The mountainous parts of the Trans-Pecos, the Hill Country in Central Texas, and the Piney Woods area of East

Texas are probably the best areas overall for motorcycle touring.

Only about a third of the Gulf coast really has a road that parallels the shore. This begins in the Brazosport Area at Surfside Beach, then proceeds northeast over Follets Island, by toll bridge to Galveston Island, by ferry to the Bolivar Peninsula, and a final straight shot along the Gulf to Sabine Pass and the Louisiana border.

Other good rides are along the Rio Grande between Eagle Pass and Langtry via State 277 and State 90, between Lajitas and Presidio on Ranch Road 170, and in the Davis Mountains along State 118 and State 166.

Roadways

For the most part, you'll find four different types of roadways in Texas. You can identify the kind of road you're on by the symbol that encloses the highway number on roadside signs.

Biggest and best maintained are the interstate highways, which are indicated by a blue shield. As elsewhere in the U.S., two-digit, even-numbered interstates (e.g., I-10, I-20) run in an east-west direction, while odd-numbered interstates (I-35, I-45) run north-south. This is the way they're designed, anyway; some parts of an interstate may run in a different direction for a number of miles, but the overall direction will conform to the odd-even system of numbering. It helps to know this if you get lost somewhere in the middle of East Texas and are trying to figure out which interstate to take. A three-digit interstate is merely a "beltway" or "loop" (Texans prefer the latter term) that runs around major cities (San Antonio, Dallas, Fort Worth, and Houston), e.g., Loop 410 in San Antonio.

The interstates are almost always the fastest way to get from one point to another (provided an interstate goes where you're going, or nearby), but they're not always the most scenic. And they're definitely not the type of road to take if you want to stop in small towns along the way. No sir, if you want to see the Heart of Texas, you'll have to slow down a bit and take the lowlier U.S. highways (red shield), state highways (black circle), or farm/ranch roads (white silhouette of Texas with a black background).

The farm and ranch roads will take you to some of the most inspiring places in Texas. These are rural roads that were developed by the state beginning early this century to enable ranchers and farmers to get their livestock or crops to town markets. Hence, their full classification is "Farm-to-Market" or "Ranch-to-Market," which is why the road signs read "FM" or "RM" before the route number (it's surprising how few Texans know what these initials stand for). There's no difference between them except that ranch roads are in areas that are traditional ranch territory while farm roads are in farming areas. In West Texas, you'll occasionally see "RR," which stands for "Ranch Road"—they link ranch areas rather than ranch and urban areas.

Regulations

The maximum speed limit in Texas is 65 miles per hour on interstates in rural parts of the state. Near towns and cities, the interstate speed limit is 55 miles per hour. On state highways, the police sometimes enforce speed limits strictly, especially on the outskirts of small towns where speeding fines may be an important source of municipal funds. A state highway can drop from a 55-mph limit to 25 mph in a very short road span.

Texas has the following seat-belt laws: All front-seat occupants of cars and trucks must wear safety belts. Children aged two to four must wear belts no matter where in a vehicle they're sitting, and infants under two must ride in a federally approved child safety seat. Most rental car agencies will supply customers with a safety seat when requested.

You are permitted to turn right at a red light after coming to a full stop, unless a road sign says otherwise.

LOUISE FOOTE

Driving Etiquette

Texas drivers are generally courteous. On rural state highways and farm/ranch roads, most Texans will automatically pull onto the shoulder of the road when approached from behind by a faster vehicle. You should do the same if a faster vehicle approaches you from behind. In sparsely populated areas, don't be surprised on a two-lane road if the driver of a vehicle coming toward you from the opposite direction raises a hand or waves. Folks that live hundreds of miles apart in these areas may consider each other neighbors. Wave back, you might need that rancher's help down the road.

Although you won't find much traffic in rural Texas, you're likely to encounter various animals on the road, from armadillos to mule deer. In some areas, carcasses are so common that people make "road kill chili," in which the meat is whatever got run over in the road that day. There's even a line of Texas arts and crafts called Road Kill, which designs pieces from bone and feather found at the roadside. Do keep an eye out for such creatures so that they're less likely to end up in a chili bowl or as a wall hanging.

Buses

Various regional bus companies connect virtually all the towns in Texas. Larger cities are also linked by Greyhound-Trailways Bus Lines, as part of their nationwide networks. All inter-city buses are air-conditioned and have restrooms. Because of the state's size, if you plan to travel by bus, a bus pass may be more economical than buying single-journey tickets. Outside North America, a Greyhound-Trailways *Ameripass,* which allows unlimited bus travel within specified dates, can be purchased from travel agencies at a discount (e.g., a seven-day pass bought outside the U.S. costs $99; in the U.S., $125).

Within large towns and cities, local bus systems serve the downtown areas and, to a lesser extent, the suburbs. Houston, Dallas, Fort Worth, Austin, Corpus Christi, and San Antonio all have special downtown lines for visitors and shoppers that are handy on weekends, when many bus services are otherwise curtailed.

Trains

Rail is an excellent, if somewhat costly way to travel to Texas. The old regional railways have been replaced by Amtrak, a nationwide passenger service. Two Amtrak lines run through Texas, the *Eagle* and the *Sunset Limited,* both of which run between Los Angeles and Chicago along different routes. Between the two of these lines, Amtrak stops at the following 18 passenger terminals: Alpine, Austin, Beaumont, Cleburne, Dallas, Del Rio, El Paso, Fort Worth, Houston, Longview, Marshall, McGregor, San Antonio, Sanderson, San Marcos, Taylor, Temple, and Texarkana.

Amtrak has special one-way, roundtrip, or excursion fares on occasion—always ask before booking.

Outside North America, a **USA Railpass** can be purchased (from travel agencies) which allows unlimited rail travel within specified dates. For schedule information or bookings inside the U.S., call (800) 872-7245 (800-USA-RAIL). A rail pass called **All Aboard America** is sold inside the country at slightly higher prices.

Within Texas, there are few non-Amtrak alternatives. A steam train, the Texas State Railroad, runs weekend tourist excursions through the Piney Woods between Rusk and Palestine. It's the only state historical park in the nation that's a railway.

The recently established Texas High Speed Rail Authority is developing plans for a 185-mph bullet train that will link San Antonio, Dallas, Fort Worth, and Houston, with stops in San Marcos, Austin, and Waco. The first phase of the proposed $4.4 billion rail system is expected to be completed by 1998 and will link Houston, Dallas, and Fort Worth. San Antonio and Austin will be added by 2003, and the other cities by 2008. The completed "Texas Triangle" will extend a total of 618 miles.

Bicycles

Texas is a good state for cycling, since the variance in elevation for most of the state is not great. Of course, distances are long, but serious touring cyclists won't find that much of a deterrent.

One of the best areas for cycling is the Hill Country, since it is fairly compact (by Texas standards), most of the roads have wide shoulders, and the many small towns are nicely spaced (not so far apart that total self-sufficiency is necessary, nor so close together that one has to keep constant watch for cars or pedestrians). Because of all the university students, Austin is

GEOCULTURAL DIVISIONS

© MOON PUBLICATIONS, INC.

definitely the state cycling capital and is hence the best place to seek out bicycle supplies or tricky repairs.

A decent, lightweight touring bike is best for the kind of terrain most of Texas offers. A mountain bike might be better, however, if you plan to do a lot of cycling in Big Bend country, the Davis Mountains, or the Guadalupe Mountains (inside the national parks, of course, no off-road cycling is allowed). If you enjoy cycling competitions and/or group touring, check with any Texas bicycle shop for a schedule of current events. Cycling is very popular in the state and there's almost always a cycling event going on.

BY SEA

You can also sail in and out of one of the Gulf coast's 27 ports. In fact, you could sail all the way from Florida and down the Texas coast without actually braving Gulf currents if you wanted to, by following the Gulf Intracoastal Waterway, which is part manmade canal, part natural waterway formed by barrier islands. You'll have to bring your own boat, however, since there are no commercial passenger lines between Texas and other states (there are leisure cruises from Texas into the Gulf, however; see "Port Isabel," p. 410).

BOB RACE

WEST TEXAS
EL PASO

To people who haven't been there, the name El Paso evokes images of the quintessential Old West town. The reality is that El Paso has a heady mixture of identities that makes it difficult to classify. Imagine a place caught in a cultural twilight zone between American, Mexican, Indian, Texan, and New Mexican cultures and you'll begin to get an idea of what it's really like.

The dominant cultural presence is Mexican, simply because it is joined by the Rio Grande to Mexico's fourth-largest city, Juarez (about 1.2 million people). The Tigua Pueblo Indians who live in greater El Paso's Ysleta, the oldest settlement in Texas, have also brought their influence to bear on modern El Paso. The *maquiladora* or "twin plant" industry, which takes advantage of Third World labor costs and First World management, has brought in people from all over the world, thus adding a small but growing cosmopolitan veneer. Tourism also adds to the mix, by drawing people to El Paso for shopping and gambling in Juarez or simply for the abundant sunshine that bakes this desert town year-round.

El Paso is the largest city on the U.S.-Mexico border and the fourth-largest city in Texas, with a booming population of half a million. It's the unofficial capital of *la frontera,* the unique third nation created by the meeting of Mexico and the United States that extends from the Gulf of Mexico to the Pacific Ocean. But sitting out on the edge of the Chihuahuan Desert, El Paso is practically in the middle of nowhere. It's just barely in Texas, in fact, tucked away in a remote pocket where Texas, Mexico, and New Mexico meet (the nearest American town to El Paso is Las Cruces, New Mexico). Thus, it's closer to three other state capitals (Santa Fe, Phoenix, and Chihuahua City) than it is to Austin, and it's closer to Los Angeles than it is to Houston. And unlike the rest of Texas, El Paso is in the Mountain Time Zone.

CLIMATE

El Paso is at an elevation of 3,762 feet and has a desert climate. The average annual rainfall is only

7.7 inches and the air is extremely dry most of the time. The city records maximum temperatures above 90° F an average of 104 days a year, most of which fall between May and September. Because of the desert environment, nights around El Paso are usually cool, even during the summer (the average low temperature between June and August—the hottest months—is 67-69° F). As long as the temperature isn't greater than 96° or so, summer days are tolerable because of the relatively low humidity. But don't let anyone lead you too far astray on this humidity business; a hundred degrees in the desert feels hot. And, unfortunately, air pollution from the nearby maquiladoras sometimes becomes compressed by convection layers over the city, and this phenomenon is the worst during the summer months.

Freezing temperatures occur an average of 65 days a year, mostly between November and February (average low temperature during these months is 32° F). Climate-wise, the best months to visit El Paso are March, April, October, and early November, when the temperatures are neither too hot nor too cold and the air is usually clear.

HISTORY

The Pass Of The North

The first Europeans "discovered" El Paso del Norte (The Pass of the North) during the Rodriguez-Chamuscado expedition of 1581. The discovery was considered significant because the pass provided access to the north for the Spanish colonists in Mexico. Later opportunists coming from the east used the pass to continue westward.

In 1598, Don Juan de Oñate led a group of several hundred conquistadors from Santa Barbara, Mexico across the Chihuahuan Desert to the pass. They were lured by Indian stories of gold in the mountains of New Mexico and Far West Texas. Most historians say the Spanish never found any substantial gold deposits, but one commonly recited legend says that Juan de Oñate cached a vast treasure of gold, silver, and jewels in the Lost Padre Mine somewhere in the Franklin Mountains, on the northern outskirts of El Paso.

Sixty-one years after Don Juan came north, the first Spanish mission was established in what is now Juarez. The mission was named Nuestra Señora de Guadalupe, and the village that grew up around it was called El Paso del Norte. This settlement became an important stop on the Camino Real or "Royal Road" which extended between Chihuahua City and Santa Fe (and later became known as the Chihuahua-Santa Fe Trail), the first road in North America.

Anglo-American Settlement

In 1680, El Paso del Norte received an influx of Spanish and Indian (Tigua and Piro) refugees from the Pueblo Indian Revolt in Ysleta, New Mexico. They called their new home Ysleta del Sur ("The Islet of the South") and the Spanish-Indian settlements thrived for a time. In 1780 the Spanish military garrison of San Elizario was founded near Ysleta del Sur. The first Anglo-Americans began arriving in 1827 and by the late 1840s there were five Anglo settlements north of the Rio Grande. Although Juan Maria Ponce de Leon built a hacienda in what is now downtown El Paso, it was the Anglo settlement of Franklin (named for one of the principal settlers) that provided the political anchor for what later became The Texas Republic's El Paso.

The U.S. Army established Fort Bliss in 1848 to defend the area against Apache attacks. When the California Gold Rush of 1849 suddenly increased east-west traffic through the pass, two stagecoach lines were established, including the famous Butterfield Overland Mail (the first Butterfield Overland coach arrived in El Paso in 1858). During the Civil War, Fort Bliss briefly fell into the hands of the Confederacy, but Union troops from California regained control and so it remained a Federal post throughout most of the war.

During this same period, the French invaded Mexico and crowned Maximilian as emperor of Mexico. Mexican President Benito Juarez established a revolutionary government at El Paso del Norte and following the Mexican defeat of the French in 1866, the city was renamed Juarez in his honor.

Wild West Era

The Southern Pacific railroad finally reached El Paso from California in 1881. The Santa Fe and Mexican Central railroads soon followed suit and El Paso was opened to the world at large. For the next 40 years or so, gunfighters, soldiers of fortune, Texas Rangers, cattle rustlers, banditos,

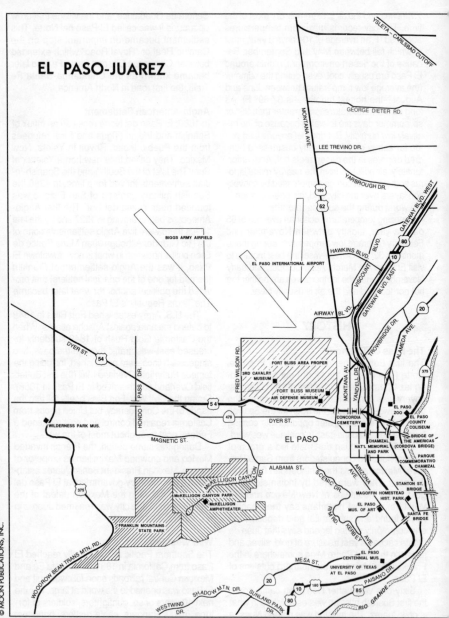

EL PASO-JUAREZ

BIGGS ARMY AIRFIELD

YSLETA - CARLSBAD CUTOFF

MONTANA AVE.

GEORGE DIETER RD.

LEE TREVINO DR.

YARBROUGH DR.

180
62

HAWKINS BLVD.

GATEWAY BLVD WEST

80
10

EL PASO INTERNATIONAL AIRPORT

VISCOUNT BLVD.

GATEWAY BLVD EAST

AIRWAY BLVD.

TROWBRIDGE DR.

ALAMEDA AVE.

20

375

DYER ST.

54

PASS DR.

HONDO

FRED WILSON RD.

FORT BLISS AREA PROPER

3RD CAVALRY MUSEUM

FORT BLISS MUSEUM
AIR DEFENSE MUSEUM

MONTANA AV.

YANDELL DR.

EL PASO ZOO

EL PASO COUNTY COLISEUM

54

478

DYER ST.

CONCORDIA CEMETERY

CHAMIZAL NAT'L MEMORIAL AND PARK

BRIDGE OF THE AMERICAS (CORDOVA BRIDGE)

PARQUE COMMEMORATIVO CHAMIZAL

WILDERNESS PARK MUS.

MAGNETIC ST.

EL PASO

375

McKELLIGON CANYON RD.

ALABAMA ST.

SCENIC DR.

ARIZONA AVE.

MAGOFFIN HOMESTEAD HIST. PARK

STANTON ST. BRIDGE

McKELLIGON CANYON PARK

McKELLIGON AMPHITHEATER

EL PASO MUS. OF ART

SANTA FE BRIDGE

RIM RD.

KERBEY AVE.

FRANKLIN MOUNTAINS STATE PARK

EL PASO CENTENNIAL MUS.

UNIVERSITY OF TEXAS AT EL PASO

MESA ST.

PAISANO DR.

WOODROW BEAN TRANS MTN. RD.

20

SHADOW MTN. DR.

SUNLAND PARK DR.

180

10

80

85

RIO GRANDE

WESTWIND DR.

© MOON PUBLICATIONS, INC.

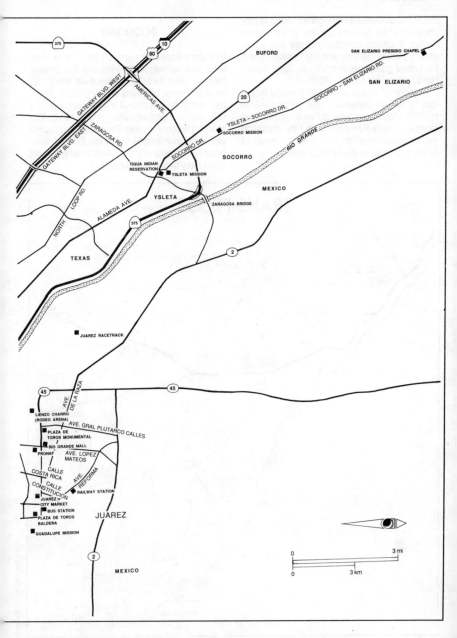

and Mexican revolutionaries gave El Paso its reputation as "Six-Shooter Capital" of the United States. Famous marshalls came and went, among them Wyatt Earp and Bat Masterson, and the fastest gunslinger in the West, John Wesley Hardin, was shot here in 1895.

The end of an era came with General Blackjack Pershing's expedition against Pancho Villa in 1916, which was based at Fort Bliss. Pershing failed to capture Pancho Villa, but the expanded military presence at Fort Bliss brought a measure of law and order to the El Paso area.

ECONOMY

El Paso's economy rests on agriculture, Fort Bliss, and the *maquiladora* industry. The famous Mesilla Valley chiles are grown here, along with abundant crops of onions and long-staple Egyptian cotton (this is one of the only areas in the U.S. where Egyptian cotton is cultivated). The growing number of *maquiladoras* on the Juarez side of the river infuses capital into El Paso, while bestowing Juarez with the lowest unemployment rate of any large city in Mexico.

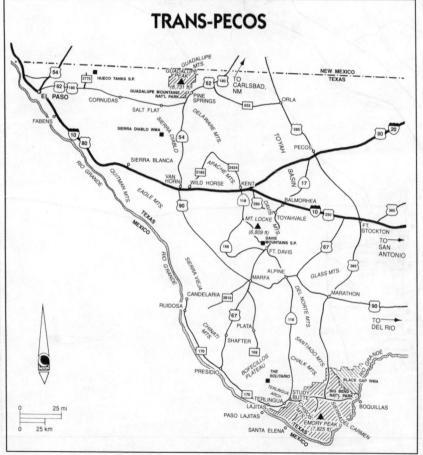

TRANS-PECOS

© MOON PUBLICATIONS, INC.

One of the city's more infamous industries is GuyRex Associates, America's "queenmakers." Rex Holt and Richard Guy are the state directors for the Miss El Paso and Miss Texas beauty pageants, but they not only handle the pageants, they groom the winners for higher accomplishments. For the last five years in a row, their Miss Texas clients have been crowned Miss U.S.A.

SIGHTS

The Mission Trail

The oldest settlements in Texas grew up around Spanish missions and presidios established along the Rio Grande and the Camino Real near what are today El Paso and Juarez. The old Camino Real is now divided into State 20 (Alameda Ave.) and FM 258 (Socorro Dr.). The Mission Trail is marked by signs with mission symbols and mileage between missions, beginning at the Zaragosa exit off I-10, southeast of downtown El Paso, and ending at FM 1110 (Clint-San Elizario Rd.).

A leisurely drive along the eight-mile trail (tourist brochures often say it's 12 miles, but this includes San Lorenzo Church in Clint, which was neither a mission nor a presidio) is definitely an El Paso must. As these are the earliest Spanish-Indian monuments in North America, they show more Indian influence than do the missions and presidios of Spanish California or Central Texas. Besides leading to the missions of Ysleta and Socorro and the presidio of San Elizario, the Mission Trail runs through El Paso's oldest Mexican and Indian districts, and there are several good restaurants, craft shops, and antique stores along the way. The Ysleta-Socorro area (unlike most of El Paso) is blessed with lots of trees.

None of the mission or presidio chapels charge admission fees, but donations for continued restoration are always welcome—there is usually a collection box near the entrance.

Tigua Indian Arts And Crafts Center

Two miles along the Mission Trail you'll enter the Tigua Indian Reservation (Ysleta del Sur Pueblo). The focus of the Tigua community for visitors is the Arts and Crafts Center, which is situated in a living replica of a Tigua pueblo. This is the only part of the reservation open to the public and includes pottery, jewelry, woodcarving and weaving

TIGUA INDIANS

The Tigua Indians are the oldest identifiable ethnic group in Texas, having lived in Ysleta del Sur (now simply called Ysleta) since 1680. They're a "displaced portion" of the Tiwa Pueblo Indians of New Mexico, and have chosen the Spanish spelling ("Tigua") to distinguish themselves from that group. The original Tiguas were converted to Christianity by Spanish missionaries and took St. Anthony as their patron saint. When a number of them fled the Pueblo Indian Revolt of 1680, they brought their patron saint with them, thus differentiating them from the Tiwas who remained behind. The Tiguas, along with a number of Piro Indians (whose community no longer survives), built the Ysleta del Sur mission in 1681 near the banks of the Rio Grande.

In spite of their devotion to St. Anthony, today's Tiguas still practice many of the traditional Pueblo customs that were practiced before the Spanish came, including a basic form of tribal government, some of the original ceremonial dances, the use of traditional herbal medicine, and the pueblo-style living arrangement. Until recently, only tribal elders maintained the Tigua language, but efforts are now being made among the young people to revive Tigua as a means of tribal communication.

The Tiguas were not officially recognized as an Indian tribe by state and federal authorities until the mid-1960s. This came in the nick of time, since many Tigua Indian homelands were being foreclosed and their sense of identity was eroding. A Tribal Roll was established to which Tiguas make voluntary application for tribal membership. Membership must be approved by the Tribal Junta or their representatives, the Tribal Council, after verification of blood lines and blood quantum.

A Tribal Junta is a public meeting that settles all important tribal matters by consensus without any formal constitution or by-laws. The Junta selects members of the Tribal Council, which consists of a *cacique* (generally the oldest man in the tribe, who looks after ceremonial affairs), a war chief (assistant to the *cacique),* a governor and lieutenant governor (administrators), and the *alguacil,* plus two members at large from the tribal community. The Council is authorized to represent the Tigua Indian tribe in dealings with the Texas Indian Commission. Today there are around 600 Tigua Indians living on or near the 37-acre urban reservation.

workshops, outdoor bread-baking in traditional hive-shaped adobe ovens, and a dance plaza where a variety of Pueblo social dances are performed for the public. The Tigua bread is baked in the morning, so if you want to buy it fresh ($1.75 a loaf), that's the best time to go. The traditional Tigua dances are performed according to the following schedule: (in winter) Sat. 11 a.m., 1 p.m., and 3 p.m., and Sun. at 10:30 a.m., 1 p.m., and 3 p.m.; (in summer) Wed.-Sat. at 11 a.m., 1 p.m., and 3 p.m., and Sun. at 10:30 a.m., 1 p.m., and 3 p.m.

The pueblo has two excellent restaurants that are quite popular with local El Pasoans, the **Tigua Restaurant** (open daily from 8 a.m.-4:30 p.m., except Sunday when it closes at 3:30 p.m.) and **Wyngs** (open 3:30-10 p.m. daily). For more information on these eateries, see "Food," pp. 87-88.

Ysleta Mission

The original 1681 foundation and some of the original adobe walls form part of the current mission chapel, which is adjacent to the Tigua Indian Arts and Crafts Center. Much of the mission was destroyed by a flooded Rio Grande in 1740 and again by a fire in 1907. Originally christened as

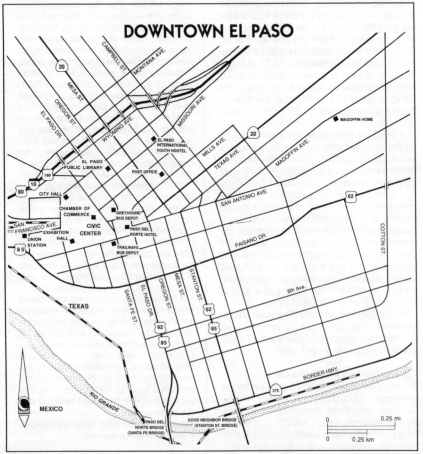

DOWNTOWN EL PASO

© MOON PUBLICATIONS, INC.

Misión Santisma Sacramento and dedicated to St. Anthony, after it was rebuilt in 1908 the name was changed to Our Lady of Mount Carmel. In a niche over the entrance is a statue of St. Anthony. Next to the altar is a Santo Enterrio or Christ-in-a-coffin dating from 1722 which is used for Easter processions.

Socorro Mission

This mission is two miles east of Ysleta on FM 258 (Socorro Rd.). It's one day younger than Ysleta and was originally built by Piro Indians (like the Tiguas, refugees from the Pueblo Indian Revolt) as Nuestra Señora de los Piros del Socorro. An 1829 flood destroyed the original building and the site was moved to higher ground in 1840.

The Socorro chapel embodies probably the most uniquely Indian mission architecture in the country. The shape of the chapel facade is said to represent the Piro rainstorm deity. Inside, the distinctive hand-carved vigas or roof-beams are the handiwork of the Piros, salvaged from the original chapel. The vigas support latias or lattices of sotol, a desert shrub.

Next to the altar is a hand-carved wooden statue of San Miguel (St. Michael) with a legend attached to it. The story goes that in 1845 it was being transported by cart from Mexico to a church in New Mexico, but the cart miraculously became too heavy to move as it passed Socorro. So the Socorro parish took the statue for their own.

Although the Ysleta mission is one day older, the Socorro parish is considered the oldest active parish in the U.S. since Ysleta was apparently abandoned for a period of time during the 19th century.

San Elizario Presidio Chapel

Six miles east of Socorro is the site of an old Spanish presidio or garrison. The San Elizario Presidio was originally established in 1774 at a nearby site and was moved to the current site at Hacienda de los Tiburcios in 1780. Following a flood, the chapel had to be reconstructed in 1877.

In front of the chapel are five state historical markers which detail Spanish expeditions to the area in 1581, 1582-83, and 1598. The impressive bell tower over the chapel supports four bells, and to the left of the entrance is a Virgin Mary shrine. The inside of this still-active chapel is striking, with a painted tin ceiling, stained glass windows, hand-carved wooden pews, and an ancient wooden confessional.

Museums

El Pasoans take great pride in their museums. While there's nothing here to compare with the museums of Dallas and Houston, for a city of half a million they fare pretty well. Entry to all those listed below is free of charge.

The **El Paso Museum of Art** (tel. 541-4040) is in the 1910 home of former Senator W.W. Turney, at 1211 Montana Avenue. The west wing of the museum contains the permanent Kress Collection, which encompasses 59 paintings and sculptures by various European masters. The works of art are displayed in three galleries corresponding to the three classic periods of European art history. In the east wing are two galleries in which 15 to 20 temporary exhibits are presented. The EPMA also offers art classes, free tours, and a reference library for art historians and working artists. Hours are Tues.-Sat. 10-5 and Sun. 1-5., p.m.

The **Americana/Southwestern Museum of Cultural History** (tel. 542-0394) is located in the Convention and Performing Arts Center on Santa Fe Street. Exhibits in this small museum display Pan-American and pre-Columbian art, especially ceramics, in a chronological fashion in order to recount the cultural history of the Southwest. Hours are Tues.-Sat. 10-5, p.m.

Better is the **El Paso Centennial Museum** (tel. 747-5565) on the University of Texas at El Paso (UTEP) campus. The museum was established in 1936 during the state's centennial celebration and exhibits focus on the human and natural history of the region surrounding El Paso. Indian pottery, prehistoric tools, dinosaur remains, as well as local folk art and historical photographs from the late 19th century, are some of the more interesting displays. Open Tues.-Fri. 10-4:30, Sat.-Sun. 1-5.

The **El Paso Museum of History** exhibits dioramas and period rooms that depict historical life in the El Paso area since the days of Spanish exploration. It was once the Cavalry Museum, so most displays are keyed to "man on horseback" —Indians, conquistadors, vaqueros, cowboys, and U.S. cavalrymen. The museum is about 15 miles east of downtown off I-10 at the Americas Ave. exit. Open Tues.-Sat. 10-4.

The **Wilderness Park Museum** is an indoor-outdoor museum situated on 17 acres at the eastern edge of the Franklin Mountains. It's dedicated to natural and Indian history of the El Paso region, from the Paleo-Indian era to the present. A mile-long nature trail leads visitors through replicas of a Pueblo ruin, kiva (Indian meeting house), and pithouse. Inside the Diorama Hall are life-size dioramas that depict various scenes from Indian life. The Wilderness Park Museum is at 2000 Transmountain Rd. and is open Tues.-Sun. 9-5.

Magoffin Homestead Historic Site
This adobe hacienda was built by El Paso pioneer Joseph Magoffin (this part of El Paso was once known as Magoffinville) in 1875 and is a splendid example of the Southwest Territorial architecture that flourished between 1865 and 1880. The four-foot-thick adobe walls are composed of hand-made, sun-dried brick that is plastered and scored to make the house look as if it were built of stone. All of the hand-hewn flooring and woodwork was brought from mountainous Mescalero, a hundred miles distant. The house is decorated in authentic period furnishings and accessories, much of which belonged to the original owners.

Six of the 19 rooms in the Magoffin Homestead are open to the public at 1120 Magoffin Ave. (from I-10 take the Cotton St. exit and follow Cotton St. south to Magoffin Ave.). Hours are Wed.-Sun. 9-4; admission is $1 adults, 50 cents for children (under six, no charge) and includes a guided tour.

Concordia Cemetery
This famous cemetery was named for the early 1840s settlement of Concordia that was established here by Chihuahua trader Hugh Stephenson. When his wife died in 1856, Stephenson buried her here, and it slowly became the cemetery for all El Paso. It was divided into different sections according to various ethnic, religious, or civic divisions, and if you wander around you'll begin to discern how Chinese, Catholic, Jewish, Masonic, military, and other formal designations are clustered together. Many of the town's pioneering families are buried here.

But Concordia's most famous resident is John Wesley Hardin, who is said to have been the fastest gun in the West. Legend has it that he won 40 gun duels before being shot in the head by lawman John Selman (who is also buried here). There are no signposts to Hardin's grave. To find it look for the entrance to the walled Chinese section of the cemetery; the gunfighter's headstone is just a little northwest of the west entrance to the Chinese section, in the undistinguished "Boot Hill" area (for desperadoes who died with their boots on). The stone merely reads "John Wesley Hardin, 1853-1895."

The cemetery is just north of I-10 at the Gateway North and US 54 interchange, which locals call the "spaghetti bowl"—you'll know why if you try to get here directly from the freeway. The easiest access to the cemetery is from Yandell Dr., which runs parallel to I-10 (coming west on I-10, take the Copia St. exit, make a right on Stevens and another right on Yandell).

Fort Bliss
The small frontier fort of the 1840s has grown into a 1.2-million-acre facility that is the largest air-defense establishment in the Western world and headquarters for the U.S. Army Air Defense, 11th Brigade. Well over 20,000 American troops are stationed here (including the only stateside armored cavalry regiment) along with uncounted military personnel from 25 different nations who come to the Air Defense School for training.

Fort Bliss is open to the public and has four museums. The museum of most general interest is the **Fort Bliss Museum** at Pershing and Pleasanton, which consists of a group of adobe buildings that are exact replicas of the original fort as it appeared between 1848 and 1868. A three-star American flag (representing the 30 U.S. states of the period) flies over the museum, the only such flag authorized for public display in the country. Three of the buildings contain displays that chronicle the 100-year history of Fort Bliss from 1848 to 1948—the fort actually had five different locations in and around El Paso. The museum is open daily 8:30-4:30 and admission is free.

Of interest to military history buffs are these museums: the **Air Defense Artillery Museum** (Building 5000, Pleasanton Rd., open daily 9-4:30), which includes an outdoor display of anti-aircraft weapons from around the world; the **Cavalry Museum** (Building 2407, at Forest and Chaffee roads, open Mon.-Fri. 9-4:30), which chronicles the history of the U.S. Cavalry since 1856 with photos, paintings, armored vehicle displays, and other artifacts; and the **Museum of the Noncommissioned Officer** (Building 11331, 5th and Barksdale, Biggs Army Airfield, open Mon.-Fri. 9-4 and Sat.-Sun. noon-4), which pays tribute to the evolutionary development of the NCO since the Civil War (Fort Bliss is the home of the U.S. Army Sergeant Majors Academy). Admission to all of these museums is free of charge.

Chamizal National Memorial

The Chamizal plains area along the Rio Grande that is now Chamizal National Memorial was once a serious bone of contention between the U.S. and Mexican governments. Because the river occasionally changed course, neither side was able to establish a mutually agreed-upon border. Finally, in 1963, the two governments agreed to build a concrete channel from which the river could not stray. At the time the agreement was reached, this meant an 823-acre gain for Mexico.

Both sides chose to develop their portions of the Chamizal as national parks. The American side encompasses 55 acres, including a visitors center that contains a border history museum, information desk, art gallery, and 500-seat theater. The grounds are used for picnicking and outdoor performances during the spring, summer, and early fall. The Border Folk Festival is held here in October, and the Siglo de Oro Drama Festival in March (see "Events" for more information).

The entrance to the park is off Paisano Dr. (US 62) on San Marcial Street. Hours are daily 8-5, year-round; on days when there are outdoor performances, it's open till 11 p.m. Admission is free (but theater performances may occasionally have admission fees).

The Mexican side, Parque Commemorativo Chamizal, encompasses 700 acres of well-landscaped grounds, botanical gardens, and an archaeological museum. Access is from Avenida de las Americas, via the Bridge of the Americas (also called Cordova Bridge) from I-10 on the El Paso side.

Paso Del Norte Hotel

Now owned by the Westin chain (the new name is the Westin Paso del Norte), this historic hotel was erected between 1908 and 1912 by an architect who was inspired by the great hotels of San Francisco. Pancho Villa, President Taft, and General Blackjack Pershing have all been guests here, and President Johnson and Mexican President Diaz-Ordas signed the Chamizal agreement in the hotel. During downtown El Paso's postwar

decline (due mostly to the national transition from rail to highway travel), the hotel closed for a time and was eventually sold to Mexican interests for $1 million in 1972. The Mexicans weren't able to turn a profit running the hotel, so they sold it to Westin in 1981 for $2 million. Westin undertook an extensive renovation and today the place probably looks better than when it first opened.

Even if you're not staying here (rates are high), you can get a taste of history by visiting the hotel's Dome Bar, which was the original lobby. A Tiffany dome overhangs the round, marble-topped bar and has been insured by Lloyd's of London for a reputed $1.2 million. An incredible array of marble walls, columns, and flooring surround the bar—in cherrystone, black, and pink marble. The building has earned a listing with the U.S. Department of Interior's National Register of Historic Places.

The Westin Paso del Norte is located at the junction of Santa Fe, El Paso, San Francisco, and Santa Fe streets downtown. For information on rates, see "El Paso Accommodations."

Sierra Del Cristo Rey

At the junction of Texas, New Mexico, and Mexico, atop a 4,756-foot peak, a Cristo Rey or "Christ the King" statue overlooks El Paso (it's visible from I-10 as you drive west into New Mexico). Sculptor Urbici Soler carved the figure out of Cordova cream limestone in 1938 and it is identical in style and scale to the Christ on the Cross that overlooks Rio de Janeiro in Brazil.

On the last Sunday of October, Sierra del Cristo Rey is the site of an annual procession in which hundreds of worshipers climb two and a half miles along a winding footpath to reach the top via the 14 Stations of the Cross. Hiking to the shrine alone is not advisable due to the potential for robbery in this remote area. Wait for the annual pageant or get a small group together.

University Of Texas At El Paso

UTEP was originally the Texas State School of Mines and Metallurgy, founded in 1913. It became Texas Western College in 1949 and was finally brought into the University of Texas system in 1967. The school's strongest departments are still geology and metallurgy, but the curriculum has broadened to include the liberal arts, of which international relations (especially inter-American relations) and Spanish linguistics enjoy good reputations. Student enrollment averages around 14,000 a year and includes more Mexican students than any other university in the United States.

The most outstanding visual feature of the university is its resemblance to a Himalayan lamasery. The original buildings were designed in this style back in 1914 after the first dean's wife saw pictures of Bhutanese lamaseries in an issue of *National Geographic*. The mountain setting of the pictures reminded her of El Paso, so she convinced her husband to have the university follow a similar architectural style. The original theme has been preserved in newer buildings as well.

UTEP's Sun Bowl Stadium is the venue for the John Hancock Sun Bowl, a post-season college football match held in December.

Viewpoints

You can get panoramic views of El Paso and Juarez from aptly named Scenic Drive. Scenic Drive skirts the southern edge of the Franklin Mountains and passes tiny Murchison Park, which has a parking lot and the best view of the area.

The Transmountain Rd. cuts through the Franklin Mountains from west to east and affords impressive views at several points. Most of the road is actually a four-lane highway, with plenty of space to pull off to the side along the way. To get there from the west, take the Transmountain Rd. exit off I-10 at Canutillo; from the east, access it from the North-South Freeway (US 54).

JUAREZ

Ciudad Juarez is the largest city in the Mexican state of Chihuahua, the fourth-largest city in Mexico, and probably the largest border city in the world. If you make it to El Paso, a visit to Juarez is a must. Besides the tourist strips along Avenida Juarez and Avenida Lincoln, the city offers a historic plaza with a classic cathedral and 17th-century mission (Misión Nuestra Señora de Guadalupe, built in 1668), great Mexican restaurants, bullfighting, *charreada* (Mexican rodeo), and bargains on handmade goods such as boots and weavings, as well as tobacco and liquor. For further information see "Entertainment" and "Shopping."

Getting There

If you're driving, the best way to get to Juarez is via the Cordova Bridge (Bridge of the Americas) of I-10. This takes you past Parque Commemorativo Chamizal and toward Avenida Lincoln, where PRONAF and the Centro Artesanal are located (see "Shopping"). To get to the more interesting plaza area of town, you must turn right at Avenida 16 de Septiembre and proceed 15 blocks or so till you reach Avenida Juarez—then pray for a parking spot!

A much better way to visit Juarez on day trips is to walk 10 minutes across the Santa Fe Street Bridge (also called Paso del Norte Bridge) from downtown El Paso. You can also drive across this bridge, but the traffic scene is intense. There are several parking lots near the El Paso side of the bridge. The toll for crossing this bridge is 10 cents for pedestrians, 25 cents for cars. To return to El Paso from this part of Juarez, you must take the parallel Stanton Bridge. You can also take a cab in either direction for about $13.

Yet a fourth bridge crossing is via Zaragosa St. off I-10, near Ysleta. After crossing the bridge, Zaragosa St. meets Federal Mexico Hwy. 2, which, if you turn right, becomes Avenida 16 de Septiembre.

The new El Paso-Juarez Trolley Co. (tel. 544-0061) operates trolley-style buses between downtown El Paso and Juarez. The trolley departs from the El Paso Civic Center and makes eight stops along a circular route via the Cordova Bridge, the PRONAF shopping area, various large restaurants, and Mercado Juarez (City Market) before returning to El Paso via the Santa Fe St. Bridge. The fare is $5 per person roundtrip; trolleys leave hourly 9 a.m.-4 p.m. from Nov. through March, 10 a.m.-5 p.m. April through October. A free shuttle service to the Civic Center terminal is available from the following hotels: Westin Paso Del Norte, Holiday Inn (Sunland Park), Airport Hilton, Howard Johnson, Rodeway Inn, Embassy Suites, Radisson Suite Inn.

EL PASO ACCOMMODATIONS

Hotel And Motels

El Paso has hundreds of rooms ranging from around $18 to $130 a night. Most hotels and mo-

EL PASO HOTELS AND MOTELS

Add 14% hotel tax to all rates. Area code: 915

NAME	ADDRESS	PHONE	RATES	FEATURES
DOWNTOWN				
Cliff Inn	1600 Cliff Dr.	533-6700	$62	pool, tennis, kitchenettes
Park Place	325 N. Kansas	533-8241	$89	pool, airport shuttle
Travelodge City Center	409 E. Missouri	544-3333 or (800) 654-2000	$55	heated pool, airport shuttle
Travelodge El Paso del Norte	101 S. El Paso	534-3000 or (800) 228-3000	$69-135	health club, historic, 50% weekend discount, senior discount
AIRPORT/MID-CITY				
Best Western Airport Inn	7144 Gateway E	779-7700 or (800) 528-1234	$41-64	heated pool, airport shuttle
Coral Motel	6420 Montana Ave.	772-3263	$30-38	pool, senior discount
Econo Lodge	6363 Montana Ave.	778-1097	$32-36	small pool, weekly rates, airport shuttle
El Parador	6400 Montana Ave.	772-4231	$34-40	pool, airport shuttle
El Paso Airport Hilton	2027 Airway Blvd.	778-4241 or (800) HILTONS	$85-95	health club, airport shuttle
El Paso Marriott	1600 Airway Blvd.	779-3300 or (800) 228-9290	$64-114	pools, airport shuttle weekend discounts
Holiday Inn–Airport	I-10 & Airway Blvd.	778-6411 or(800) HOLIDAY	$59-64	pool, airport shuttle
Holiday Inn Sunland Park	900 Sunland Park Dr.	833-2900 or (800) HOLIDAY	$63-72	pool, monthly rates
La Quinta	7550 Gateway E	778-9312 or (800) 531-5900	$49-63	heated pool, airport shuttle
WEST				
Executive Inn	500 E. Executive Center Blvd.	532-8981 or (800) 234-8981	$42-47	pool, senior and weekend discount, complimentary continental breakfast, airport shuttle
La Quinta	7550 Remcon Circle	833-2522 or (800) 531-5900	$49-63	pool
Motel 6	7840 N. Mesa	584-2129	$24.95 + $6 ea. add.	pool
Warren Inn	4748 N. Mesa	544-4494	$28-35	pool, kitchenettes, senior discount

EL PASO HOTELS AND MOTELS

Add 14% hotel tax to all rates. Area code: 915

NAME	ADDRESS	PHONE	RATES	FEATURES
EAST				
Comfort Inn	900 Yarbrough	594-9111 or (800) 226-5150	$40-44	pool, airport shuttle
Howard Johnson Lodge	8887 Gateway W	591-9471	$43-50	pool, airport shuttle senior discount
Motel 6	11049 Gateway W	594-8533	$24.95 + $6 ea. add.	pool

tels in the city are clustered in the airport/mid-city area and east of town along I-10. To a lesser extent, there are also choices downtown and west of the city. Any location in the city is convenient if you have a car; for those relying on foot and public transit, a downtown location is the most convenient (you can walk to Juarez from downtown).

The chart on the following pages is meant to be representative of the kinds of places available and also lists some of the choicest spots (like the Westin Paso del Norte). The El Paso Convention and Visitors Bureau publishes an *Accommodations and Dining Guide* that lists most of the hotels and motels in El Paso (unfortunately, rates aren't listed); it's available at their office (One Civic Center Plaza) or at Texas Dept. of Highway Tourist Bureaus around the state.

Youth Hostel

The **El Paso International Youth Hostel** (tel. 532-3661) is located in the former Gardner Hotel at 311 E. Franklin Ave. in downtown El Paso. The building is on the El Paso Historic Register and John Dillinger purportedly stayed here just before he was captured in Tucson. The location is good; it's a mile from Juarez, and five to six blocks from the Greyhound-Trailways bus depot.

Room rates are the same for AYH or IHYF members and non-members: $17 s, 24 d for a room with bath in the hall, $24 s, $26 d for rooms with shared bath, and $26 s, $30 d for rooms with private bath. They offer discounts for weekly and monthly stays. Dorm rooms are $11 for members, $13 for non-members (see "Hostels" on p. 60 for membership details).

Camping

The nearest state park campground is Hueco Tanks State Park, 32 miles east of downtown El Paso along US 62/180 and RM 2775. During the week, the park is virtually deserted (except during rock-climbing season, late October through February), so there are almost always campsites available then. For information on camping facilities, see "Hueco Tanks State Park," p. 98.

RV Parks

Four RV parks can be found about 10-15 miles east of El Paso, off I-10 or US 62/180. All charge around $15 a night for full hookups, with discounts for long-term stays. **Roadrunner Travel\ Trailer Park** (tel. 598-4469) is at 1212 Lafayette, about 10 miles east off I-10. **Western Horizon Campground** (tel. 852-3388) and **Samson RV Park** (tel. 859-8383) are both just off I-10 at the Horizon exit. **Cotton Valley RV Park** (tel. 851-2137) is eight miles east of the city at the Clint exit. **Desert Oasis Park** (tel. 855-3366) is 16 miles east of town on US 62/180, convenient to El Paso and Hueco Tanks.

There's also one RV park that's just northeast of town near the east edge of the Franklin Mountains—**Starlight Mobile Home Park** (tel. 755-5768) at Dyer (US 54) and Transmountain Road.

FOOD

El Paso fancies itself the Mexican food capital of Texas ("of the world" if you ask some of the

Mission Espada, San Antonio (Joe Cummings)

1. Mission Concepcion, San Antonio; 2. the Alamo (photos by Joe Cummings)

more ambitious residents) and there is indeed a good variety of Mexican restaurants, most of them serving good ol' Tex-Mex. The El Paso Convention and Visitors Bureau's *Accommodations and Dining Guide* contains a comprehensive list of reliable eateries, with price ranges. Restaurants across the river in Juarez are especially good value.

Dress for almost all restaurants in El Paso is casual (more so than Dallas, Houston, or even San Antonio). The more expensive places often require reservations, however, so be sure to call ahead if dining in the upper price ranges (also, call ahead to make sure they're open, as restaurant hours change frequently in Texas's fluctuating economy). The following restaurants have either been duly tested by the author or have solid reputations among El Pasoans. Per person price ranges (excluding beverages) are marked $ for inexpensive (under $8); $$ for moderate ($8-15); $$$ for expensive (over $15).

Barbecue

El Paso, like most sizable Texas towns, has plenty of barbecue joints. In El Paso, they're mostly Central and West Texas style, and none of them really stand out.

$ to $$ **Buck's Bar-B-Que:** All the usual— brisket, links, and ribs, plus chicken. At 9496 Dyer (tel. 755-1356). Open daily for breakfast, lunch, and dinner.

$ to $$ **The State Line:** This one's part of a statewide Texas barbecue chain that started in Austin. The quality is consistent and they bake their own bread (homemade ice cream, too). In addition to the usual barbecue setup, they also serve steaks. At 1222 Sunland Park Dr. (tel. 581-3371). Open daily for lunch and dinner.

Burgers

El Paso has all the usual American franchises like McDonald's, Dairy Queen, and so on, but with El Paso twists like green chile cheeseburgers, tacos, and gorditas. Two more unusual places for burgers, fries, and shakes are:

$ to $$ **El Paso Surf Club:** This is a student hangout across from UTEP with a bar, dining room, and outdoor patio. The logo depicts a surfboard propped against a cactus.

$ **Hudson's Grill:** The theme here is 1950s Americana. In addition to the usual burger and

fries selection is a daily "blue plate special" that might include chicken-fried steak or other Texas favorites. At 1770 Lee Trevino (tel. 595-2769). Open daily for lunch and dinner.

Cajun/Creole

$ to $$ **Louisiana Kitchens:** El Paso's only eatery devoted to Cajun and Creole food at 508 N. Stanton (tel. 532-6411). Open daily for lunch and dinner.

$ to $$ **Miguel's Central Cafe:** In addition to Mexican and American dishes, this downtown restaurant serves good Cajun food.

European

El Paso's not exactly a mecca for connoisseurs of continental cuisine, but there are a handful of restaurants that specialize in European food.

$-$$ **Bella Napoli:** Typical middle-America Italian, with Chianti-bottle candleholders on checkered tablecloths. Good, mostly Neapolitan menu. At 6331 N. Mesa (tel. 584-3321). Open Tues.-Sun. for lunch and dinner.

$$$ **The Dome Grill:** One of El Paso's most refined dining venues, in the historic Westin Paso del Norte hotel. The kitchen specializes in continental dishes with a sometimes nouvelle approach. Steak and seafood are also available. At 101 S. El Paso (tel. 534-3010). Open Mon.-Sat. for lunch and dinner.

$$ **Günther's Edelweiss:** Good Bavarian cuisine in a kitschy German decor. At 11055 Gateway W. (tel. 592-1084). Open Tues.-Sun. for lunch and dinner.

Mexican

$ **Avila's:** This is probably El Paso's most well-known Mexican restaurant, and deservedly so. The extensive menu is classic Tex-Mex, with no orange cheese, and features unique dishes such as tri-color enchiladas, chile relleno burritos, chilaquiles, plus an endless assortment of combination plates. All meals are served with fresh sopapillas and/or tortillas. There are two locations, one on the east side and one on the west side (only the east side restaurant serves margaritas; both serve beer). The westside Avila's is at 6232 N. Mesa (tel. 584-3621). Their east side location is at 10600 Montana (tel. 598-3333). They're open daily for lunch and dinner.

$ **Forti's Mexican Elder:** Forti's is another

long-time El Paso favorite. The specialties here include fajitas and tacos al carbon. Forti's is at 321 Chelsea, at the Paisano exit off I-10 (tel. 772-0066). Open daily for lunch and dinner.

$ to $$ **Griggs:** (Sometimes called Señor Juan's Griggs.) The food here is New Mexican or Santa Fe style, that is, not as fiery as Tex-Mex (but still tasty). At 9007 Montana on the west side (tel. 598-3451). Open daily for lunch and dinner.

$ **La Hacienda:** This inexpensive Mexican restaurant is in an 1880s building that was part of one of Fort Bliss's former locations, right near the Rio Grande. Combination plates are huge. At 1720 W. Paisano, under the Yandell overpass (tel. 546-9197) Open Tues.-Sun. for lunch and dinner.

$ **Ysleta del Sur Restaurant** and **Wyngs 'n Spirit:** The menus here mainly feature Mexican-Indian food, but burgers and steaks are also available. The tortilla soup, fajitas, and chile verde con carne (very hot) are specialties of the house, along with fresh Tigua adobe bread. Located in the Tigua Indian Reservation's Arts and Crafts Center at 122 S. Pueblo Rd. (tel. 859-3916). The Tigua Restaurant is open Mon.-Sat. 8-4:30 and Sun. till 3:30 p.m.; Wyngs, next door, is open daily 3:30-10, p.m.

$ **Julio's Cafe Corona:** Long-touted as Juarez's best Mexican eatery, Julio's now has an El Paso location as well. Tlapeño, a spicy chicken-avocado soup, and Veracruz bass are among the highlights here. In Juarez, they're at the intersection of Avenida de las Americas and Avenida 16 de Septiembre (tel. 13-33-97). In El Paso, they're at 8050 Gateway E. (tel. 591-7676). Open daily for lunch and dinner.

$ **Leo's:** Very similar to Avila's but a tad cheaper. El Pasoans argue about which is better. The four locations are at 2285 Trawood (tel. 591-2511); 5315 Hondo Pass (tel. 757-0505); 5103 Montana (tel. 566-4972); and 7872 N. Loop (tel. 593-9025).

Steak

$$ **Cattleman's Steakhouse at Indian Cliffs Ranch:** This one's 33 miles southwest of the I-10/US 54 interchange in El Paso, near Fabens, but is always cited by El Pasoans as the best steak around (*People* magazine even called it the best steak in the U.S.). Indian Cliffs Ranch is a

good place to take children, as there are all kinds of recreational opportunities (a small children's zoo, a playground, "Fort Apache," etc.) and if you get a window table the desert sunset is beautiful. Take I-10 west to the Fabens exit (28 miles), then north for five miles on FM 793. Open Mon.-Sat. 4-10, Sun. 12-9.

Oriental

Several Chinese and Japanese restaurants are located on the east side of town, between I-10 and Montana. They're all okay, but the following have the best reputation.

$ to $$ **Shangri-La:** An old, established Cantonese restaurant in Juarez owned by Paco Wong (many Chinese settled in the El Paso area in the late 1800s after working as coolies on the railroads). The menu is extensive and consistent. At 133 Avenida de las Americas (tel. 546-3837, or in Juarez 13-00-33). Open daily for lunch and dinner.

$-$$ **Asia Garden:** The emphasis here is on Cantonese. At 4410 N. Mesa (tel. 594-0290); open daily for lunch and dinner.

$-$$ **Delhi Palace:** A good spot for North Indian dishes. The weekday lunch buffet is a bargain. Near the airport at 1160 Airway (tel. 772-9334); open daily for lunch and dinner.

Seafood

El Paso and Juarez are a good distance from both oceans and the Gulf, so seafood is not one of the area's strong suits. Best to stick with freshwater fish (e.g., black bass) caught in nearby lakes or streams.

$$ **Martino's:** As with Chinese food, Juarez is the place to go for the best seafood in the area. Extensive menu. At 412 Avenida Juarez (tel. 14-33-70), within walking distance of downtown El Paso. Open daily for lunch and dinner.

$$ **Miguel's Central Cafe:** Miguel's has good seafood prepared in Mexican and Cajun styles. See "Cajun/Creole" above for address and hours.

$$ to $$$ **Pelican's:** This one has a good local reputation on the El Paso side. Two locations, on the west side at 130 Shadow Mountain (tel. 581-1392) and on the east side at 9077 Gateway W. (tel. 591-8139). Open Tues.-Sun. for dinner only.

$ to $$$ **Seafood Galley:** One of the first seafood places ever established in El Paso. Standard American seafood selection, specializing in fried dishes (fresh oysters are available here). At 1130 Geronimo (tel. 779-8388).

ENTERTAINMENT

Clubs And Bars

Three of El Paso's classic dance halls (Caravan East, Bronco Ballroom, and El Palomino) have bit the dust since the last edition. The hot spots for C&W dancing are now **McGee's** (tel. 592-995) at 8750 E. Gateway and **Dallas** (tel. 598-1309) at 1840 Lee Trevino. Both are open nightly but charge $3 cover only on weekends; McGee's also advertises 15 minutes of rock music every evening.

For rock and Top 40, the **Surf Club** (tel. 544-7873) at 2500 N. Mesa is popular. DJs handle the Sun.-Wed. program while live bands perform Thurs.-Sat, when there's a $2 cover charge. **Club 101** (tel. 544-2101) is the center for El Paso's alternative music scene; on most nights there's recorded dance music but occasional live acts perform as well.

The classiest disco in town is **Uptown** in the Paso del Norte Hotel. A $3 cover is collected on weekends.

Avenida Juarez in Juarez is lined with bars and small discos, but none of them really lives up to the town's former wild reputation since they started closing everything down at midnight (purportedly to curb teenage alcoholism in Juarez). A few of the classic bars still hang on, including the **Kentucky Club**, at 629 Avenida Juarez, and the amazing **Cavern of Music** (also called Las Glutas Bar) near the intersection of Avenida Juarez and Ignacio Mejia. The women's room at Las Glutas has a famous statuette of Adam with movable fig leaf (lift the leaf and flashing lights go on in the bar). Behind the plaza area (in perfect irony, not far from the cathedral), is "Boy's Town," which is Juarez's red-light district. Warning: a sign that reads "ladies bar" doesn't mean it's a bar for ladies; on the contrary, it's a bar for men looking for ladies.

The two most popular Juarez discos for visitors from across the border are in the Avenida Lincoln/PRONAF area of town. **Sesto Senso** is on Avenida Lincoln just after it splits from Avenida de las Americas; **Amadeus** is in the PRONAF complex.

Radio

The liveliest FM radio station in El Paso is KBNA ("K-Buena") at 97.4 megahertz. Bilingual DJs on KBNA play a great mix of *conjunto,* South Texas R&B, soul, and other jumpin' music. For more salsa, listen to Juarez's XEWR-AM 1110, where you can hear tunes by Mexican bands like Los Teen Tops and Rebeldes de Rock. The University of Texas at El Paso's FM station (KTEP 88.5) is also quite good and plays a variety of non-commercial music. El Paso's most popular C&W station is KHEY FM 96.

Viva! El Paso Outdoor Pageant

This outdoor musical drama (or "pageant") pays tribute to the area's 400-year history. It's held from the last week of June through the last week of August at McKelligon Canyon Amphitheater (on McKelligon Canyon off Alabama), Wed.-Sat. at 8:30 p.m. Tickets are $3-6. Call 565-6900 for more information.

Racetracks

The **Juarez Racetrack** (tel. 542-1942) is located off Avenida Vicente Guerrero to the east of PRONAF. It's primarily a *galgodromo* (dog track) and features greyhound racing Wed.-Sat. at 7 p.m. year-round; horse races are occasionally held during the summer. Admission is 50 cents.

Sunland Park Racetrack is across the state border in New Mexico, about five miles west of El Paso via I-10. Thoroughbred and quarter-horse racing takes place Fri.-Sun. between October and May.

Off-track betting for major U.S. horse races is offered at the Juarez Racetrack (see above) and also at the **Juarez Turf Club** on Avenida Juarez, a block south of the Santa Fe bridge. Televised coverage of the races is broadcast live at both places.

Bullfights

Each summer, four bullfights are held in Juarez at the **Plaza de Toros Monumental** on Avenida 16 de Septiembre, beside Rio Grande Mall (a bit east of PRONAF). The first *corrida de toros* takes place around Easter and then three more *corridas* are held on four Sundays before Labor Day (it varies from year to year). Check with the Mexico Tourist Information Center (tel. 534-0536 in El Paso or 01231 in Juarez) for the latest scheduling.

The Plaza de Toros Monumental is on the professional *corridas* circuit in Mexico, which means these are real Spanish-style bullfights in which the bull may be killed by the matador (but not always). For amateur, bloodless bullfighting, check the old bullring (Plaza de Toros Baldera) between Avenida Juarez and Avenida Lerdo, off Calle Gonzales.

Mexican Rodeos (Charreadas)

Charros or Mexican rodeo cowboys are quite active in the El Paso-Juarez area. In Juarez, you can attend *charreadas* at the Lienzo Charro Adolfo López Mateos, which is about a half mile past the Plaza de Toros Monumental off Avenida de 16 Septiembre (which at this point has become the Pan-American Hwy.) on Avenida del Charro. Mexican rodeos are held here most Sundays between April and October at 4 p.m. or so. Admission is about $4.

On the El Paso side, the Emiliano Zapata Charro Association holds *charreadas* most Sunday afternoons at their arena on North Loop (FM 76), about two miles east of Horizon Blvd. in southeast El Paso (between Buford and Clint). *Charreadas* are also held at Chamizal Memorial Park during the Border Folk Festival in October and sometimes during other celebrations.

EVENTS

February

Southwestern Livestock Show and Rodeo, El Paso County Coliseum, 4200 E. Paisano. This 10-day event is reported to be the oldest livestock show and rodeo in the Southwest. Over 2,800 animals are entered in the show by nearly 1,500 contestants. The rodeo is PRCA-sponsored and features top rodeo performers from all over the U.S. and Canada.

March

Transmountain Run, Transmountain Rd., Franklin Mountains. A 10-mile foot race sponsored by the American Heart Association. **Siglo de Oro Drama Festival,** Chamizal National Memorial Theater. Siglo de Oro roughly translates as "Golden Age" and refers to the zenith of Hispanic drama and literature between the 16th and 18th centuries. Troupes from all over the Hispanic world and the U.S. meet at this festival to perform dramas by Miguel de Cervantes and other Spanish master playwrights.

May

International Balloon Festival. On Memorial Day weekend, hot-air balloonists from around the U.S. and Mexico meet for a border crossing in their balloons. Also features music, dancing, food vendors, and fireworks.

June

Feast of St. Anthony, Ysleta Mission, Tigua Indian Reservation. June 13 is St. Anthony's Day, the most important religious holiday for Ysleta's Tigua Indians. The celebration starts with various ceremonies at the mission, followed by feasting and dancing later in the day. Visitors are welcome

Don Gay, bull rider

to attend the festivities. **El Paso Street Festival,** El Paso Civic Center Grounds, downtown. A major downtown festival that celebrates the founding of El Paso for a week with live music, dancing, food concessions, and other events.

July
Viva! El Paso Outdoor Pageant, McKelligon Amphitheater. Continues through Labor Day. See "Entertainment" above. **Festival de la Zarazuela El Paso/Ciudad Juarez,** Chamizal National Memorial. Another Spanish drama festival with performing troupes from all over the Hispanic world. This one focuses on Spanish folk opera. For information on scheduled events, call 534-2900.

September
Dies y Seis, various locations in El Paso and Juarez. The 16th *(dies y seis)* of September is the day Mexico celebrates independence from Spain. Festivities begin on the 15th at Chamizal National Memorial in El Paso with music and a *charreada.* A colorful parade and other events are held in downtown Juarez on the 16th.

October
Amigo Airshow, Biggs Army Airfield. A major regional airshow that features fancy formation flying, weapons displays, skydiving, and so on. Held the second weekend in October. During the same weekend is the **Kermezaar Arts and Crafts Festival** at El Paso Convention and Performing Arts Center, which emphasizes Southwestern art and is attended by artisans from all over the Southwest and northern Mexico. **Border Folk Festival,** Chamizal National Memorial. Usually held the first weekend of October, this cross-cultural celebration features music and dance from the Anglo and Hispanic worlds, craft show, ethnic food, and a *charreada.*

November
Coors World Finals Rodeo, El Paso County Coliseum. This event is the grand finale of the North American Rodeo Commission's rodeo season. The NARC is the largest international rodeo association in the world, and this event brings contestants from the U.S., Canada, Mexico, and Australia. The event's location used to rotate from year to year but seems to have found a permanent home in El Paso. **Sun Carnival Parade,**

Thanksgiving Day. This parade kicks off a series of sports-related events (plus a Coronation and Ball) leading to the John Hancock Sun Bowl on Christmas Day.

December
John Hancock Sun Bowl Football Classic, Sun Bowl, UTEP. A post-season college bowl game.

RECREATION

Amusement Parks
The **Magic Landing Amusement Park** (tel. 858-3100) has is a medium-sized theme park with all the usual American rides. It's about 18 miles east of downtown El Paso off I-10—you can't miss it. Admission in $11 per person on weekends, $9 weekdays. **Western Playland** (tel. 772-3914) at Ascarate Park (intersection of Alameda and Delta) is similar but has a western theme. Admission is $11 pp.

Indian Cliffs Ranch (tel. 544-3200) is 33 miles from downtown El Paso but has more of a sense of place then either of the aforementioned amusement parks. It's not an amusement park in the traditional sense, but is rather a sort of daytime dude ranch for families. The ranch actually covers 23,000 acres of desert with the main facilities set on a hill. Activities include free hayrides, trail rides, a children's petting zoo, exotic animals (emus, Barbados sheep, African goats, Belgian horses), and a mock frontier fort. Overnight hayrides to the fort can be arranged in advance by groups. Admission to the ranch is free as long as you eat in the restaurant (see "Cattleman's Steakhouse" under "Food" above).

El Paso Zoo
This small, five-acre zoo has about 200 creatures on display in natural settings, including elephants, bears, large African cats, amphibians, birds, and reptiles. It's located at Evergreen and Paisano, across from the El Paso County Coliseum. Hours are Mon.-Fri. 9:30-4:15, Sat.-Sun. and holidays 10-5. Adult admission is $1.50, children 3-11 get in for 75 cents, infants under three and senior citizens are admitted free.

Golf
El Paso has two 18-hole golf courses open to the

public, and Juarez has one. Lowest green fees in El Paso are at the county course in **Ascarate Park** (tel. 772-7381)—only $7 weekdays, $10 weekends. The **Cielo Vista Municipal Golf Course** (tel. 591-4927) is at 1510 Hawkins and charges $10.28 weekdays, $12.45 weekends.

Across the border, the **Campestre Golf Course** at the Juarez Country Club (tel. 70806 in Juarez, 011-52-16-173732 from El Paso) has green fees of $5-10, slightly more on weekends. The Campestre course uses caddies—no golf carts—but caddy fees are quite low.

Hiking In The Franklin Mountains

The Franklin Mountains are honeycombed with narrow, faded footpaths—probably worn by people looking for the Lost Padre Mine where Don Juan de Oñate is supposed to have hidden a fortune in gold, silver, and jewelry. **Franklin Mountains State Park** covers a 16,108-acre portion of the mountains; the park is undeveloped and so far only day use is permitted (no overnight camping). Big Bend it's not, but hardy hikers may want to give the Franklins a try for a taste of desert hiking.

The only formally constructed trail in the park is the Ron Coleman Trail. It's unmarked but fairly easy to follow (other trails in the Franklins may require some orienteering skills). The trail starts at Smuggler's Pass, which is off Transmountain Rd. (Loop 375) 5.3 miles west of the North-South Freeway (US 54). If you're coming from the west side of the mountains, Smuggler's Pass is about six miles east of the Canutillo exit off I-10. There is a turnaround at the side of the road where hikers usually park their cars or have accomplices retrieve them. The trailhead is on the south side of the road and is marked by a ruined stone gate. Alternatively, the hike can be done from the south end in McKelligon Canyon—just follow the directions backward.

The trail from Smuggler's Pass to McKelligon Canyon is about 3 1/2 miles. For the seven-mile roundtrip hike you must figure on about four to five hours' hiking time with an elevation change from 5,400 (Smuggler's Pass) to 6,700 (ridge along South Franklin Mountain) to 4,880 feet (McKelligon Canyon). The going is fairly strenuous in the steep parts, but there are also long stretches of easy walking.

About 300 yards down the trail from Smuggler's Pass, you'll come to an old road on the right, which you'll take for another 160 yards or so till the trail branches left. From here, the trail reaches the crest of a ridge and follows it for another 0.6 mile. When the path seems to fade or branch off, look ahead for where it picks up along the ridge crest. Three FAA radio towers can be seen from here—you should be heading in that direction. As you approach the towers, the trail drops to the left below the jagged crest to the south. At mile 1.6 you'll come to a level area with a good view where the trail forks into three. Two of the trails go left (east) to the radio towers and the summit of South Franklin Mountain (elev. 6,764 feet) while the one on the right continues south along the Ron Coleman Trail.

From here, the trail is fairly easy to follow as it skirts a small canyon and comes to a meadow at mile 1.8, a good spot for a picnic. Beyond the meadow, the trail drops quickly to the right (west) of the ridge till it arrives at a three-by-five foot hole in the ridge known as the Keyhole. After this, the trail drops and dissolves across an area of loose rock for 50 yards or so—take care on the descent. Keep the top of the ridge in sight so you can pick up the trail again when it crosses over onto the other side of the ridge at mile 2.2.

By this time, you should be able to see a paved, circular road in McKelligon Canyon ahead—a good landmark to keep in view as you try to pick out the main trail since it's crisscrossed by several side trails. The trail ends at the parking area off McKelligon Canyon Road. You are now in McKelligon Canyon Municipal Park. If you started from this end, you're finished; if you started at Smuggler's Pass, it's more strenuous on the return since you have to ascend at the Keyhole.

SHOPPING

El Paso-Juarez is the regional trade center for the Southwest and literally hundreds of manufacturers and importers are headquartered here. Hence, selection and bargains abound if you know where to look. Among the better buys are Tarahumara Indian blankets, Casa Grande pottery, Pueblo Indian jewelry, and cowboy boots. Rustic Southwestern-style furniture made of mission oak and/or ponderosa pine is good value as well. There's also a lot of junk for sale, so it pays to shop around before spending your money.

BOOTS AND BOOTMAKERS

Western-wear shops are popular destinations for many Texas visitors. Cowboy hats, yoked western shirts with mother-of-pearl buttons, and bolos (rawhide Mexican ties) are all favorite purchases. But of all classic cowboy gear, boots probably hold the most allure for Texans and non-Texans alike.

A century ago, an estimated 600 bootmakers plied their craft in Texas. Now there are only 60 or 70, and the best are descendants of Mexican craftsmen who inherited their trade from the Spanish. The best-quality boots are totally handmade, which means they're handcut and handstitched in small shops.

When boots became a popular part of mass American culture in the 1960s, many bootmakers had to begin using machines to keep up with the demand. Older cowboy boots (pre-1970) generally feature the favored "X-toe," a sharply pointed toe, rather than a rounded toe. The rounded toe can be stitched by machine; the X-toe cannot.

The classic cowboy boot is designed for western riding and ranching (not for propping up on guitar cases). The pointed toe makes it easy to slip the front of the boot through the stirrup while the arch and heel hold it in place. The tall sleeve or upper part of the boot protects the wearer from brush, snakes, and the friction of the stirrup strap.

The Justin Boot Company of Fort Worth was the first bootmaker to use lasts (forms in the shape of the foot) on which to craft their boots; they also introduced the steel shank between the heel and sole, which adds a large degree of support and comfort to bootwear. The company no longer makes boots by hand, but they offer a good quality off-the-shelf Texas boot, as do Tony Lama of El Paso and Lucchese of San Antonio. Of the three, Lucchese probably makes the best-looking boot.

For the ultimate, you have to go to a bootmaker who will measure your feet, create custom-made lasts, and then cut and sew a pair of boots by hand. Handmade boots will have small wooden pegs holding the outer sole to the shank, rather than nails. Nails rust and fall out while pegs hold their position until removed by a bootmaker or repairman. A good boot, in fact, will last a lifetime with periodic resoling. Although custom-made boots start at a rock-bottom $175-300 a pair (some bootmakers start as high as $600), you can sometimes find good used boots in pawn shops or shoe and boot repair shops around the state for as little as $30-50. Cadillac Jack in Austin (6623 N. Lamar, tel. 512-452-4428) is one shop that specializes in used boots and other western wear.

Austin has become something of a Texas boot capital because of the local music industry. Austin's most famous bootmaker, Charlie Dunn, is retired now, but a former apprentice of his, Lee Miller (tel. 512-443-4447, by appointment only), designs boots in the Charlie Dunn tradition. Another highly reputable bootmaker in Austin is Noel Escobar Jr. of Texas Custom Boots (6616 Hwy. 290 West, tel. 512-892-6321).

Some of the best bootmakers live in South Texas, near the Mexican border, and carry on the Mexican tradition of fine bootmaking. Armando Duarte has a shop in Raymondville called Armando's Boot Company (tel. 512-689-3521). Raymondville has a couple of other custom-boot shops, as does nearby Mercedes.

Other well-known bootmakers to look up in Texas include the M.L. Leddy Company and Mercer's Boot Shop, both in San Angelo (West Texas), Henry Leopold in Garland (north of Dallas), and Dave Little in San Antonio.

Whether you buy a pair of boots off the shelf or have them custom-made, here are a few pointers in assuring a good fit. 1) **Heel:** The heel of a new boot should slip a bit. This is because the sole is still stiff; once the ball of your foot wears in the boot enough that the sole flexes normally, heel slippage will disappear. No heel slippage in a new boot means it's too tight and will cause blisters and other foot problems. 2) **Instep:** Should be fairly snug, even hard to slip on at first. If the instep is loose or the boot goes on easily, the instep is probably too large and you should try for a narrower size. 3) **Ball and Toe:** The widest part of the boot should line up with the ball of the foot. If the ball of your foot sits forward of the widest part, it's too small (and the toes will be crammed into the toe box); if the ball sits much behind the widest part of the boot, the boot is too large and will chafe your foot mercilessly when you walk. 4) **Arch:** The boot shank should be wide enough and long enough to cover your entire arch.

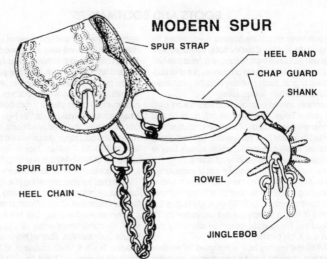

MODERN SPUR

SPUR STRAP

HEEL BAND

CHAP GUARD

SHANK

SPUR BUTTON

ROWEL

HEEL CHAIN

JINGLEBOB

LOUISE FOOTE

Skip the big shopping malls like Cielo Vista unless you want to go to the movies.

El Paso Saddleblanket
This is a huge store with Southwestern pottery, hand-woven blankets, leather goods, local antiques, furniture, and just about anything else of Mexican or Indian origin that you might expect to find in the El Paso-Juarez area. Most everything comes from Mexico, and while it's more fun to ferret this stuff out in Juarez on your own (at lower prices), if you're short on time and bargaining skills this is a reasonable proxy. As the name suggests, they're strong on blankets and have probably the largest selection of Indian blankets in the country. It's at 601 N. Oregon downtown next to the Ramada Inn; open Mon.-Fri. 9-5 and Sat. 10-4.

Ysleta And Socorro
The Mission Trail through Ysleta and Socorro is lined with arts and crafts and antique shops that specialize in Mexican and Southwestern goods—most are open only on weekends. In Socorro, the **Bosque Trading Post,** at 10167 Socorro Rd. (open Fri.-Sun. 10-5:30), **El Mercadito,** at 10189 (Wed.-Sun. 10-5:30), and the **Riverside Trading Post,** at 10300 (Thurs.-Sun. 10-5:30) are three of the larger places, all ensconced in 19th-century pueblo-style houses near the river. The jewelry shops here have good selections. The **Tigua In-**dian Reservation Arts and Crafts Center specializes, naturally, in Tigua Indian art. Tigua pottery, which features very bold designs, is a definite highlight here.

Boots And Western Wear
All of the major Texas bootmakers have factory outlets in El Paso. Prices are usually about 20-40% lower than retail, sometimes more on selected boots. Boots on display at these outlets, however, tend to be either "seconds" with flaws or outrageous styles that they haven't been able to sell in their regular retail stores (e.g., pink ostrich-skin boots). Because of this, the range of sizes available also varies erratically—but there's always a chance you'll stumble onto something you like that actually fits. These are the bootmakers with outlets: **Justin,** 7100 Gateway E, tel. 779-5465; **Tony Lama,** 7176 Gateway E, tel. 772-4327; **Dan Post and Lucchese,** 6601 Montana, tel. 778-8060.

For a slightly higher investment, you can order a pair of custom-made boots from Vick (former bootmaker for Tony Lama) at **Plainsman Boots** (tel. 544-1831), at 1425 E. Missouri. Vick's prices are very reasonable for custom work.

Over in Juarez, you might try **Botas Santa Fe** at 738 Avenida de las Americas, near PRONAF and Avenida Lincoln, for custom-made boots. Santa Fe specializes in exotic skins like python, armadillo, and ostrich. **Botas Arizona** is similar but perhaps lower priced (bargain at either place for the best prices), and is on Avenida 16 de Septiembre across from the City Market. There's also **Botas Herradero** at Avenida Insurgentes and Saltillo, a little more off the tourist track. At any of these three, you should be able to get a pair of custom-made leather (cowhide) boots for under $100, which is quite low compared to stateside prices. For exotics, you'll have to pay $100-300, depending on the critter who gave up his life for stylish walking.

Morris Saddlery (tel. 859-6705) at 10949 E. Burt sells custom- and ready-made saddles, Western and English riding gear, and Western wear. **Farah** has a factory outlet in El Paso at 8889 Gateway E, but, as all Texans know, real cowboys and cowgirls wear Wrangler Cowboy Cut jeans (get 'em at Morris Saddlery).

Downtown Juarez

Two sections of town are the focal points of tourist shopping, one that caters to auto traffic (**Avenida Lincoln** and the PRONAF/Centro Artesanal complex) and one for pedestrians (**Avenida Juarez**). Both areas carry the same basic variety of arts and crafts, but quality and prices are a bit higher along Avenida Lincoln. Avenida Juarez is mostly Mexican kitsch, but there are bargains to be found here and there, especially in the side-street stores that are primarily for Mexican shoppers. Untaxed liquor and cigarettes are always reliable deals in either area.

The U.S. dollar is acceptable currency throughout Juarez. Many shops (as well as hotels and restaurants) quote dollar prices. If you want to change dollars for Mexican pesos, there are plenty of moneychangers on either side of all four bridges over the Rio Grande.

Recorded Music

Music collectors should not miss **Nostalgia Records, Tapes, and CDs** (tel. 594-9900) at 1360 N. Lee Trevino, two blocks north of I-10 in Sunpointe Centre. Nostalgia sells collector recordings, imports, pop, C&W, Tejano, rock, and just about any other kind of roots music of the region you can name, plus books and other materials for music collectors. Open Mon.-Sat. 10-9, Sun. noon-6.

EL PASO INFORMATION

Tourist Offices

Out on I-10 at the Texas-New Mexico state line is one of the Texas Dept. of Highways' 12 information centers, where you can get information about El Paso as well as about the rest of Texas. Better for information specific to the El Paso area are the two **El Paso Tourist Information Centers**; one is in Civic Center Plaza downtown (tel. 534-0653); another is at El Paso International Airport. The two in town are open Mon.-Fri. 8-4:30, while the airport counter is open daily 10-6. The staffs are very helpful and they give out maps, brochures, and other free publications that can assist in finding out more about the El Paso area.

The **El Paso Convention and Visitors Bureau,** also located in Civic Center Plaza, is oriented mostly toward arranging for group tourism and conventions.

In Juarez, there's a **Mexico Tourist Information Center** (El Paso, tel. 534-0536) in the Municipal Building at Avenida Malecon and Francisco Villa near the Juarez side of the Stanton Street Bridge. The staff speak English and they distribute travel information regarding Juarez and Mexico. They can also assist if you have a problem, such as theft, while in Juarez. Their El Paso office, in the chamber of commerce, is open Mon.-Fri. 9-11 a.m.

Publications

Periodicals: The two main English-language dailies in El Paso are the *El Paso Times* (issued in the morning) and the *El Paso Herald Post* (afternoon). Either is worth reading for the latest information on local cinema and events. Two Spanish-language dailies are also distributed in El Paso, the long-established *El Continental* and the *Diario de Juarez,* which covers Juarez, El Paso, and Las Cruces, New Mexico.

Probably the most helpful local publication for visitors is the bilingual (Spanish and English) *Southwest Guide,* which is published quarterly. In it you'll find the most current information about various local attractions and events—information even the tourist offices in El Paso and Juarez don't seem to know. The freely distributed *Southwest Guide* can be found in most hotel and motel lobbies, at the airport, and at the various tourist offices.

TELEPHONE AND EMERGENCY INFORMATION

Emergency (police, fire, medical)	911
Crisis Help Line	779-1800
Fort Bliss Information	568-2121
Telephone Directory Assistance	411
U.S. Customs	541-6794
Weather Service	778-9343

Maps: Continental Maps' *El Paso* is widely available at El Paso grocery stores and at the tourist offices. Better is the AAA (American Automobile Association) El Paso map, which is available from most AAA offices in Texas. The El Paso AAA office at 1201 Airway Blvd. (tel. 778-9521), near the airport, is open Mon.-Fri. 8:30-5. Both maps show portions of Juarez as well.

Mexican Consulate General
The Mexican Consulate in El Paso is located at 910 E. San Antonio (tel. 533-4082). If you're a U.S. citizen planning to enter Mexico as a tourist, without a private vehicle, for less than 180 days, you don't need to come here at all. Citizens of other countries may need to apply in advance for a visa to enter Mexico (see "Border Crossing," p. 66 for more details). Any non-Mexican citizen who intends to take a car, motorcycle, or other vehicle across the border must apply for the necessary papers at the Consulate, or at a travel agency that handles vehicle permits (check the yellow pages in the El Paso telephone book).

Telephone Service
The area code for El Paso is 915; when calling El Paso, remember that it's in the Mountain Time Zone, unlike most of the rest of Texas (which is in the Central Time Zone). The area code for Juarez is 16. If you're dialing a Juarez number from the U.S. you must precede the area code and phone number with 011-52. Juarez phone numbers should have six digits; if a Juarez listing only shows five digits, add a "1" to the number (most phone numbers in Juarez begin with a "1," so it's often left off in the listings). For example, if you've located a number for someplace in Juarez that reads 53342 and you're dialing from El Paso, you should dial 011-52-16-15-33-42.

TRANSPORT

City Buses
Sun Metro is the name of the city bus line, which only operates during the day and is really only convenient for the downtown area. Call 533-3333 for schedule information.

Taxi
Two companies operate reliable taxi services in El Paso, **Checker** (tel. 532-2626) and **Yellow Cab** (tel. 533-3433). Fares are comparable to taxi services in other American cities. At either side of the several bridges that cross the Rio Grande are a fleet of private taxis that take passengers back and forth between El Paso and Juarez—the average gringo fare is $13-20. Along the river, you may notice the "human taxis" that wade back and forth with passengers astride their shoulders. For Mexicans, the fare is only about 25 cents, but it is doubtful they would carry a gringo across.

Tours
Three companies in El Paso conduct bus tours of the area that include half- or full-day sightseeing tours, shopping tours, and tours to the Juarez Racetrack or bullring. Most motels and hotels can arrange the tours, or you can contact them directly: **Fantastic Tours,** tel. 859-4261; **Golden Tours,** tel. 779-0555; and **Tourific Tours,** tel. 595-2205.

HUECO TANKS STATE PARK

History
Hueco Tanks is a unique complex of huge syenite (a granite-like rock) masses in the middle of the Chihuahuan Desert. The formations, created 34 million years ago, are named for the myriad huecos (pronounced WAY-kos) or hollows that are scattered across the rock surfaces, some large, most of them the size of a fist. Geologists disagree on how the huecos were formed, but most likely they're the result of some as yet undocumented weathering process. Most significantly, the huecos are a source of stored rainwater, a scarce commodity in the desert. Because of this natural capacity to collect and store water, the area became an important habitat for semi-nomadic Indian tribes as far back as 10,000 years

ago. Evidence of an early Paleo-Indian culture has been found at Hueco Tanks in the form of flint tips called Folsom points.

Later, during the Desert Archaic period, the first rock art appeared in the form of pictographs drawn by hunter-gatherers with paints made of ground stone. These groups were succeeded by the Jornada branch of the Mogollon Culture (A.D. 1000-1500), who added classic Pueblo motifs to the growing collection of rock art. In the 19th century, the Apaches, Kiowas, and Comanches created the bulk of the dynamic pictographs and petroglyphs (rock carvings) that are still visible.

From 1858 to 1859, Hueco Tanks was an important stop for the famous Butterfield Overland Mail, and Butterfield built a stone and adobe stagecoach station here. When an alternate route through Fort Davis offered protection from Indians and highwaymen, the Hueco Tanks station was abandoned; the ruins can still be seen near the entrance of the park.

The latest group to take a liking to Hueco Tanks has been the rock climbers, both technical climbers and scramblers, who have made the park something of an international rock-climbing mecca over the last few years. The large pocked boulders offer some of the most exciting bouldering in the world, complete with sets of complex "problems" that climbers must work out step by step.

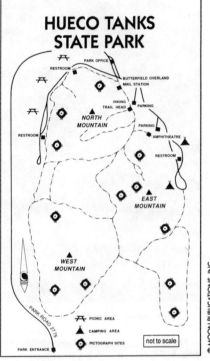

Wildlife

Hueco Tanks State Park encompasses 860 acres, most of which is covered by the three main syenite mountains, interspersed with desert scrub and the park's own unique ecosystem. The huecos and tinajas (small desert springs) attract an unusually rich combination of flora and fauna, including over 190 verified species of birds (turkey vultures, red-tailed hawks, golden eagles, prairie falcons, cliff swallows, to name a memorable few) as well as bobcats, gray foxes, and the occasional cougar. The best time for birdwatching is late October through early March, when the native species are supplemented by migrational species. Animals are attracted not only by the water but by the varieties of shrimp (tadpole shrimp, fairy shrimp, and clam shrimp) found in water-filled huecos.

Besides the usual Chihuahuan Desert scrub like creosote, mesquite, yucca, agave, and var-ious desert acacias, the areas between the syenite masses support a variety of grasses, sotol, ocotillo, and small trees like the Mexican buckeye, juniper, Arizona oak, hackberry, and Texas mulberry. Wildflowers come out after the late summer rains and as many as 10 species of ferns can be found in wet years.

Rock Climbing

While a number of the estimated 5,000 Indian pictographs at Hueco Tanks can be viewed from park trails, the best way to see them is to do some bouldering. The rangers at the park office at the entrance to the park can be quite helpful in suggesting simple hiking and climbing routes. Climbers are allowed to climb anywhere they like except on rock art. However, no bolts, pitons, or other equipment with a potential for damaging rock face are allowed.

rock climbing, Hueco Tanks State Park

The main season for rock climbing is late October to February, though any time of year other than Jun.-Aug. is good. During the summer months the boulders really get too hot to handle (this capacity to store and reflect heat is a definite asset during cold weather, however).

Experienced rock climbers will want to have a look at the booklet *Indian Heights: A Climber's Guide to Hueco Tanks* by Crump, Head, and Head (El Paso: Yahoo Publications, 1985) that is tethered to the information counter in the park office. Unfortunately, it's out of print at the moment so is difficult to find in any bookstore or library. The authors say they're in the process of revising it and that it will be published again in the near future—inquire at the park office.

Better yet, talk to the climbers who hang out at Pete's (Hueco Tanks Country Store), the Quonset hut on the left side of RR 2775 as you approach the park. Pete's is owned and operated for the primary benefit of rock climbers by Pete Zavala and his wife Queta, who treat climbers like part of

the family. Besides providing climbers with a cheap place to stay, Pete sells food, beer, and chalk (to enhance a climber's hand grip), and also keeps a dog-eared notebook entitled "New Routes and Register" in which climbers write tips and tales of rock climbing. As you'll soon see from scanning this notebook or the *Indian Heights* guide, Hueco Tanks has an incredible variety of potential climbs that range in difficulty from "Looking For Mars Bars" (5.5 on the Yosemite Decimal System, suitable for accomplished novices) to "The Gunfighter" (5.13, the most difficult).

Other routes have equally creative names like "Do Fries Go With That Shake?" and "Dark Heart." "Center El Murray" on Mushroom Boulder is said to be Hueco Tanks's greatest problem climb (only one climber has accomplished it). Hueco Tanks has even added a term to the climber's technical vocabulary—"hueco pulling."

Facilities And Services
The park provides 20 drive-in campsites with electricity and water, a trailer dump station, showers, and rest rooms. There are also some 58 picnic sites scattered about the park. Camping fees are $9 for sites with water, $12 with water and electricity. For day use, there's a $3 per vehicle ($1 for pedestrians and cyclists) entry fee. Most of the year the park is very uncrowded although summer weekends see a lot of local families; during the climbing season (late October to February), climbers make their presence known but never really take the place over.

From June through August, park rangers offer guided tours of Hueco Tanks rock art and on Friday and Saturday evenings there are slide shows. The park gates open at 8 a.m. and close at sunset to all except campers. The park office is open daily 8-5. For further information on the park or campsite reservations, contact the Superintendent (tel. 915-857-1135), Hueco Tanks State Park, Rural Route 3, Box 1, El Paso, TX 79935.

Outside The Park
Many climbers don't stay in the park but elect instead to crash at **Pete's** (otherwise known as Hueco Tanks Country Store, tel. 915-857-1095, Rural Route 3, 611 Hueco Tanks Rd., El Paso, TX 79936), which is on RR 2775 on the way to the park from US 62/180. Pete charges $1.75 a night for floor space in the upstairs portion of his

large Quonset hut (see "Rock Climbing" above for more on "Pete's").

Getting There
To get to Hueco Tanks State Park from El Paso, drive or hitch 26 miles east on US 62/180 till you see the sign for the park, then head north on RR 2775 for another six miles till you come to the park entrance. Buses between El Paso and Carlsbad, New Mexico, will let passengers off at the entrance to RR 2775 (make arrangements with the driver in advance), from where you can either walk or hike the six miles to the park.

GUADALUPE MOUNTAINS

INTRODUCTION

The Guadalupe Mountain range lies astride the Texas-New Mexico border, rising high above the Chihuahuan Desert that surrounds it. The north end of the range opens up like the top of a V and descends gradually into New Mexico's Carlsbad Plains, while in the south the range ends abruptly at precipitous cliffs over a huge salt basin in Texas. The Guadalupes' craggy peaks can be seen from at least 50 miles away in any direction, yet the area has long been virtually ignored by the nation that grew up around it. Many cross-country tourists find their way to Carlsbad Caverns on the New Mexico side, but few venture farther south to the 76,000-plus acres of magnificent highlands and canyons over the Texas line that make up Guadalupe Mountains National Park (only 200,000 visitors in 1991, compared with over 800,000 next door at Carlsbad Caverns National Park). Fewer still backpack into the 46,850 acres (around 60% of the park) set aside as wilderness, making this one of the least crowded national parks in the United States.

It isn't likely that the Guadalupe Mountains will ever get the crowds typical of many other national parks in the west because of a conscious effort on the part of the National Park Service and the locals to keep it as pristine a wilderness as possible. This is partially because the main attractions of the park's interior are simply inaccessible by road, but the policy extends even beyond park boundaries. No hotels or lodges have been allowed to be built in or near the park (the nearest motel is in White's City, New Mexico, 35 miles north). And neither of the two drive-in campgrounds in the park have RV hookups (though RVs are allowed to park in spaces provided). For a true Southwestern wilderness experience, this national park is unparalleled.

History
The Guadalupe Mountains began forming some 250 million years ago when an immense tropical ocean, teeming with life, covered much of what is today Texas and New Mexico. Calcium compounds secreted by marine organisms and precipitated from the ocean water gradually formed a 400-mile horseshoe-shaped reef, later named Capitan Reef by geologists in honor of the peak called El Capitan at the southern tip of the Guadalupe range. Eventually the sea evaporated, leaving a thick sediment that buried the reef for millions of years until lateral compression forced it upward through the sediment, thus exposing what was to become known as the Guadalupe Mountains, part of the world's largest fossil reef. Two other exposed portions make up the Apache Mountains near Van Horn and the Glass Mountains near Alpine.

Archaeological evidence (pictographs, firepits, stone tool remnants) suggests that humans first occupied the Guadalupes' McKittrick Canyon some 12,000 years ago. In recorded history, the first reference to Indian habitation in the Guadalupes was made by Spanish conquistadors who passed through in the 16th century (Coronado in 1541, Espejo in 1583) during their search for gold in the New World. At that time, these mountains were the exclusive domain of the Mescalero Apaches, and they remained so until the mid-1800s. The Mescaleros used the canyons as shelter from their enemies as well as from the harsh desert climate and lived on native agave, sotol, deer, elk, rabbit, and bison. They also believed that their sacred fire god dwelt on Guadalupe Peak (8,749 feet), the tallest mountain in Texas.

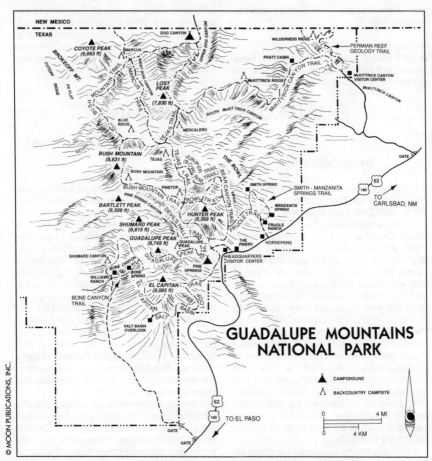

GUADALUPE MOUNTAINS
NATIONAL PARK

▲ CAMPGROUND

△ BACKCOUNTRY CAMPSITE

0   4 MI

0   4 KM

TO EL PASO

© MOON PUBLICATIONS, INC.

Following the 1849 California gold rush, the Butterfield Overland Mail established a stage station called the Pinery along the St. Louis-San Francisco route (now US 62/180), the ruins of which can still be seen near the Pine Springs Campground. In 1858 the first meeting of transcontinental stagecoaches occurred just west of Guadalupe Pass.

By the 1880s, the Mescaleros had been driven out of the mountains by the U.S. Army and a few ranchers (cattle and sheep) and miners (copper and bat guano) moved into the area. Stories of vast deposits or caches of gold in the Guad-

alupes have been around since the era of the Spanish conquistadors. Even the Apache chief Geronimo claimed that somewhere in the mountains was the greatest gold mine on earth.

One famous prospector, William Sublette, used to ride into West Texas towns with moneybelts full of gold dust and nuggets, and claim that he'd gotten it in the Guadalupes. When Sublette ran out of gold, he went back for more, often with would-be miners in pursuit (stories say he knew the mountains so well that he always lost his pursuers). Sublette died in 1892 without ever giving up the secret source of his wealth, and no one ever found the cache. It has been theorized that he may have stumbled onto a cave that concealed gold taken in a Butterfield stage robbery. This is quite plausible, as Butterfield stagecoaches were held up several times in this area before the route was diverted along the safer Fort Davis route.

In the early 1930s, petroleum geologist William Pratt established a ranch in McKittrick Canyon (named for an earlier canyon resident who lived in a dugout house) that eventually spread for 16,000 acres. In the '50s, Pratt began donating parts of his ranch to the U.S. government for use as a national park and by 1959 he'd given it all away. Pratt's original stone cabin has been preserved in McKittrick Canyon. Additional land (70,000 acres) was later purchased from the J.C. Hunter Ranch and Guadalupe Mountains National Park was officially opened in 1972.

Flora

The Guadalupe Mountains stretch from the southeastern limit of the Rocky Mountains to the northern limit of the Chihuahuan Desert. Because of the rare interaction of desert, canyon, and highland biotic communities, the Guadalupes support an unusually diverse community of plant and animal species.

Along the desert surrounding the Guadalupes and on the floors of the lower canyons are typical Chihuahuan Desert plants and succulents like agave, prickly pear, creosote bush, lechuguilla, yucca, and sotol. With elevation gains, one encounters ponderosa pine, Douglas fir, quaking aspen, chokecherry, and piñon. In sheltered canyons, add big-tooth maple, walnut, chinquapin oak, alligator junipers, and various ferns.

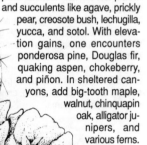

Engelmann prickly pear

LOUISE FOOTE

MESCAL

The Mescalero Apaches got their name from their most important food source in the Guadalupe Mountains area, mescal. Mescal is the heart of the agave or "century plant," which was so called because it seemed that the plant sent out only one bloom every 100 years. Actually, the plant sends up its single reproductive stalk (which reaches heights of 10-15 feet) after about 20 years of normal growth, and then dies. During that 20-year span, the agave stores high concentrations of carbohydrates in its center. The Mescaleros discovered this and harvested the plants just before they bloomed. They then roasted the hearts in special mescal pits dug into the ground.

The agave was considered so important to survival that mescal pits were sacred. A new pit was always consecrated before sunrise and during the 24-36 hours required to roast mescal, the Mescaleros chanted and performed rituals specific to the preparation of mescal. Remains of Apache mescal pits can still be seen near the Pine Springs Campground, by the Mescalero Campsite, and near the junction of the Bush Mountain and Tejas hiking trails. Three species of agave still flourish in the Guadalupes, *A. neomexicana, A. lechugilla,* and *A. gracilipes.*

One of the most beautiful and most rare of trees found in the canyons is the Texas madrone *(Arbutus texana),* which grows only in the mountains of West Texas and on the Edwards Plateau. Outside of the Guadalupes and Big Bend, its numbers are fast dwindling since it thrives only in the wild. The madrone is identifiable by its smooth, reddish bark and by thick, deep-green oval leaves. The leaves don't drop off in the winter, and clusters of small white flowers appear in the spring. In the fall, bright red berries sprout and are an important food source for birds and other native wildlife.

Mammals

Around 58 species of mammals make the Guadalupe Mountains their home. Among the smaller varmints are 14 species of bats (including two free-tail species) and three species of rabbits. Javelinas or collared peccaries, an introduced species, are occasionally seen.

Pronghorn, mule deer, bison, and bighorn

sheep were once native to the area but all except the mule deer had disappeared by the turn of the century. Mule deer are commonly seen throughout the canyons and highlands. Merriam's elk *(Cervus canadensis merriami)* are native to the Guadalupes, but the closely related species seen here now are descendants of a herd of Rocky Mountain elk *(Cervus canadensis)* from South Dakota that J.C. Hunter introduced to the mountains in 1928. About 50 of them wander all parts of the park and are frequently spotted by hikers.

Other mammals commonly seen include gray foxes, coyotes, raccoons, and porcupines. At night, you can often hear a chorus of coyotes singing the high desert blues. Less common are black bears, bobcats, and mountain lions.

The estimated mountain lion population in the park is 50-60 individuals. Like most felines, lions are nocturnal creatures so your chances of encountering one are very slim unless you like to hike at night. The National Park Service offers these simple suggestions for how to behave if you meet one: 1) Give a surprised lion ample escape opportunity; 2) Do not turn your back on a lion, crouch, or run from it; 3) Do not approach a lion, especially one that is feeding; 4) Do not make direct eye contact, as mountain lions may perceive it as a threat.

Birds

The number and variety of bird species in the Guadalupes is fairly remarkable. At last count, 255 species in 44 bird families had been spotted in the park. Among the birds seen year-round are wild turkeys, roadrunners, doves, woodpeckers, Montezuma and scaled quail, killdeer, and various hawks (sharp-shinned, Cooper's, red-tailed).

Bald eagles occasionally breed here in the summer and may appear in the spring or fall as migrant species. The golden eagle can be seen all year-round but is most frequently spotted in the winter. Four species of falcon frequent the park, the American kestrel, the merlin, the peregrine, and the prairie. And hummingbird fanciers can thrill to no less than six species, most commonly the magnificent hummingbird, the black-chinned hummingbird, and the broad-tailed hummingbird.

Amphibians And Reptiles

Now for the creepy-crawly things. Eight amphibs

(frogs, toads, and salamanders) and 42 reptile species (including 19 kinds of lizards and 23 species of snakes) are known to inhabit the Guadalupes. Of the 23 snake species, six are rattlesnakes, which are venomous.

The most commonly encountered rattlesnake in the park is the northern blacktail *(Crotalus molossus),* which is gray-brown or green in color with irregular blotches along its back and is 2 1/2 to 4 feet long. The western diamondback *(crotalus atrox),* 2 1/2 to 6 feet long with diamond-shaped markings, is also fairly common. Both rattlers prefer rocky areas like dry stream beds—never reach or step into a pile of rocks without lifting them first with a stick (better yet, avoid rockpiles altogether). The other four rattlesnake species in the park are rarely spotted by humans.

Climate

Temperatures in the Guadalupe Mountains vary from an average high/low of 53°/30° F in January to an average high/low of 88°/63° F in July. High winds can be expected between late fall and late spring (in the highlands, 60-mile-an-hour winds are not uncommon, and velocities in excess of 100 mph have been recorded). Average precipitation is highest in August (3.77 inches) and September (5.22 inches), but it can rain anytime—backpackers shouldn't consider camping in the Guadalupes without a tent. The driest months are November, December, March, and April. Snow is not unusual in the high country during the winter.

October and April are probably the best times to visit the Guadalupes, considering all weather factors. These months are also peak tourist season for the area, but except for the last weekend in October (when hundreds of people come to see the fall change of colors), crowding doesn't seem to be a problem.

LOUISE FOOTE

Visiting The Park

The **Headquarters Visitor Center** is off US 62/180 east of Guadalupe Pass and is open daily 8-4:30 (Mountain Time). Besides restrooms and drinking water, the visitor center offers free park brochures and maps, a slide program, various exhibits, and a schedule of ranger-guided walking tours through the park. A ranger on duty will be glad to assist with planning your visit, whether you're a wilderness backpacker or a day hiker. The center also sells books with extensive historical and natural information about the area as well as topographic maps for backpackers.

Information on the park can be obtained in advance by calling or writing Guadalupe Mountains National Park (tel. 915-828-3251), HC 60, Box 400, Salt Flat, Texas 79847-9400.

Hiking

It's impossible to appreciate the beauty and grandeur of Guadalupe Mountains National Park without hiking into the interior. Unlike other national parks such as Yosemite or Big Bend, you can't drive through the park and stop at scenic overlooks. In fact, none of the canyons or highlands is accessible by car (there is now a parking lot at the mouth of McKittrick Canyon—but visitors must still walk a minimum of 2.3 miles to really get into the canyon). Fortunately, the park offers 80 miles of trails that extend through the length and breadth of the canyons and high country, ranging from the 2.3-mile Devil's Hall Trail (from Pine Springs Campground) to the 12.3-mile Bush Mountain Trail (from the Tejas Trail Junction). If you can spare the time and stamina required for hikes into the interior, you'll be greatly rewarded by eye-popping vistas as well as a rich pageant of natural history.

Most of the hikes in the park involve some elevation gain—anywhere from 400 feet to 3,000 feet. Inquire at the Frijole Visitor Center if you have any doubt about your abilities to accomplish a particular trail. You should figure on spending about one hour per mile of hiking, taking into consideration elevation changes and rest stops. Sturdy shoes or hiking boots are a must. Since temperature and precipitation can vary widely from place to place within the park, it's essential that you be prepared for possible weather changes. In the summer, a hat, sunglasses, sunscreen, and light rain gear are essential; in the winter,

wear warm, layered clothing.

The only sources of drinking water in the park are at Frijole Visitor Center, McKittrick Canyon Visitor Center, Pine Springs Campground, and Dog Canyon Campground—you can't count on finding spring water, even in the highlands. Hikers should carry at least a half gallon of water on day hikes (more on hot days); overnight hikes require a minimum of one gallon of water per person.

Backpacking

Two of the park's campgrounds are accessible by car, Pine Springs and Dog Canyon (see relevant sections below for more detail on these sites). Beyond these drive-in campgrounds, farther into the interior of the park, are nine designated wilderness camping sites that can only be reached on foot. Backcountry camping in the Guadalupes requires careful preparation because of the water situation and because of the changeable weather patterns that occur. A no-fee Backcountry Use Permit is also required and can be obtained from the visitor center or at Dog Canyon Campground.

Backpacking essentials include a compass, map, first-aid kit (with an elastic bandage for sprains or snakebite—see "Snakebite Prevention and Treatment," p. 18), waterproof matches, knife, flashlight with extra batteries, foul-weather gear, tent or sleeping shelter, a signal device (mirror or whistle), and, of course, ample food and water.

For extensive backpacking trips, a topographic map is highly recommended. A waterproof topographic map of the park, published by Trails Illustrated, is available at the visitor center for $5. This detailed map marks the backcountry campsites, established hiking trails as well as primitive hiking trails, equestrian trails, all trail distances, unpaved roads, intermittent streams, wooded areas, springs, and contour differentials. (The giveaway National Park Service map is also quite good, but lacks contour lines, trail distances, and many of the intermittent streams.) Remember, however, that you can't count on any of the springs or streams as dependable sources of water—during dry spells, the flow retreats beneath ground level. Another good source of information for backpackers is the booklet *Trails of the Guadalupes* by Goran and Kurtz (Champaign: Environmental Associates, 1986), which is sold at the visitors center for $3. This 55-page publication contains a history of the area and detailed descriptions of many park trails, plus essays on the Guadalupe environment. The maps included are not as detailed as the Trails Illustrated topo map, however.

The usual minimum-impact camping ethics apply for the Guadalupes: pack out all trash, bury human waste four to six inches down, and build no open fires (if you plan to cook, bring a backpacking stove). For the sake of historical preservation, please don't disturb Indian mescal pits or pictographs. Special cave entry permits are required for hikers who wish to explore caves within the park boundaries—apply at the visitor center.

Horseback Riding
Approximately 80% of the park trail system is open to equestrian use, mostly along the north-south ridges that run through the center of the park. Neither the Park Service nor anyone nearby has horses for hire, so all saddle stock must be brought to the park for riding. Riding is not permitted on the following trails: McKittrick Canyon (between McKittrick Ridge Campsite and the visitor center), Bear Canyon, the Bowl Loop, Devil's Hall, Smith-Manzanita Spring, and Permian Reef Geology. Riders must obtain a free Backcountry Use Permit from the visitor center before taking their horses on any park trail. During periods of wet weather, trails may be closed to horses until dry enough to prevent tread damage.

You'll find horse pens near Frijole Ranch about a mile east of the Headquarters Visitor Center (maximum 24 horses) and a corral at Dog Canyon (maximum 10 horses). Both corrals have water for horses. Riders must stop by one of the visitor centers for a permit before using either facility.

A free "Saddle Stock Access Guide" for the park is available at the visitor center. This guide rates 16 different trail sections according to difficulty, using a three-point scale: 1 = easy, 2 = moderate, 3 = difficult (El Capitan and Frijole, for example, are rated 1-2 while most of Bush Mountain is rated 3). None of the trails in Guadalupe Mountains National Park are suitable for novice riders or for horses that aren't conditioned to mountain trail riding.

MCKITTRICK CANYON

Often called "the most beautiful spot in Texas," McKittrick Canyon is also the most popular destination for visitors to Guadalupe Mountains National Park. Of all the canyons in the park, McKittrick has the greatest variety of foliage and is particularly colorful from late October to mid-November when the leaves of chinquapin oak, big-tooth maple, and walnut trees change color. William Pratt, the geologist who donated his ranch to the Park Service, constructed a cabin of local limestone in 1929 at the west end of the canyon where it splits into North and South McKittrick canyons. The Pratt Cabin still stands and there is now a picnic area nearby.

Next to the parking area at the canyon mouth is the McKittrick Canyon Visitor Center, which features interpretive exhibits, restrooms, and a picnic area. A 0.8-mile interpretive nature trail starts next to the visitor center, for those who want a quick education in native vegetation. You can also get water here before starting out on the McKittrick Canyon Trail. No camping is allowed in McKittrick, but there are backcountry camping sites at McKittrick Ridge (7.4 miles from the visitor center) and at Wilderness Ridge (4.1 miles from the visitor center). The canyon is open to visitors daily 8-6 in the summer and 8-4:30 during the winter. Backpackers are permitted to leave their vehicles in the McKittrick parking area overnight while hiking.

Vehicle access to the McKittrick Canyon Visitor Center and trailhead is via a five-mile road off US 62/180 that begins about seven miles northeast of Pine Springs.

Trails In McKittrick Canyon
McKittrick Canyon Trail (10.9 miles): This trail begins at the McKittrick Canyon Visitor Center and proceeds 2.3 miles along the canyon floor to the Pratt Cabin, where there's a picnic area. From here, it's another 1.1 miles to the Grotto Picnic Area, one of the most scenic areas in the McKittrick Canyon proper. To get a good view of the canyon and encompassing ridges, continue four more miles to McKittrick Ridge. This section of the trail involves an elevation gain of about 2,300 feet and is fairly demanding. A roundtrip hike to McKittrick Ridge from the trailhead can be done

in a full day but is better done as an overnight.

The trail continues on another 3.5 miles along the McKittrick Ridge above South McKittrick Canyon, affording good views of Hunter Peak, the Bowl, and the Blue Ridge to the southwest. The McKittrick Canyon Trail ends at a T-junction with the Tejas Trail.

Permian Reef Geology Trail (4.7 miles): This trail begins a few hundred feet from the McKittrick Canyon Visitor Center and forks north along the northern edge of the canyon and then west along Wilderness Ridge. Elevation gain is about 2,000 feet with views all the way into South McKittrick Canyon. The trail skirts McKittrick Peak (7,064 feet) before reaching the Wilderness Ridge Campsite at mile 4.1. From here the trail veers north again and after 0.6 miles ends at the New Mexico state line. At this point, the established trail gives way to a primitive trail that continues north into New Mexico's Lincoln National Forest. A map of Lincoln National Forest trails can be purchased at any of the visitor centers in Guadalupe Mountains National Park or at the Lincoln National Forest Office in Carlsbad, New Mexico.

At points along the Permian Reef Geology Trail, hikers can see fossil-ridden segments of the Permian Reef as well as fore-reef and back-reef marine deposits.

PINE SPRINGS

The park's Pine Springs area, just off US 62/180 at Guadalupe Pass, has a long history of human habitation since water was easily available from Lower Pine Spring (the spring was buried following a 1931 earthquake). Numerous mescal pits near the Pine Springs Campground show that Mescalero Apaches occupied the spot at times. Before and after the Civil War, the U.S. Army camped here during Indian campaigns, and in the 1850s the Butterfield Overland Mail established a stage station at Pine Springs called the Pinery.

Pine Springs Campground

This is the larger of the two drive-in campgrounds in the park, with 19 tentsites and 29 RV sites. Water, restrooms, and tables are available. There are no RV hookups or dump stations and the Park Service has no plans to provide them in the future. Wood or charcoal fires are not permitted for environmental reasons.

Camper registration at Pine Springs is mandatory and "self-service," via the registration board near the restrooms. Camping fees are $6 per site per night and are collected daily from the fee deposit tube near the registration board. Golden Age and Golden Access Passport holders pay only $2.50. During the summer, park rangers present interpretive programs every evening at the campground; during the rest of the year such programs are scheduled less regularly. Campground restrooms and campsite #25 are wheelchair accessible.

The Pinery

The original Butterfield Overland Mail came through Guadalupe Pass and stopped at the Pinery Station, one of 200 stage stations between St. Louis and San Francisco. The Pinery was the only inhabited spot for the 458-mile stretch between Fort Chadborne and El Paso and had the distinction of being the highest stage station (5,543 feet) along the 2,800-mile route.

The station consisted of high limestone walls that enclosed a wagon repair shop, a blacksmith shop, a corral for replacement horses, and three mud-roofed rooms where passengers and crew could rest while coach and team were being tended to. Stagecoaches arrived at the Pinery four times a week, but the station was open for business 24 hours a day since it also handled express riders, mule trains, and road crews.

The first Butterfield coach arrived at the Pinery in September 1858 and the last in August 1859, when the Guadalupe route was abandoned for a better-protected route that served Fort Stockton and Fort Davis. Long after the Pinery was abandoned, however, it continued to play host to passing emigrants, desperadoes, and cattle drovers. The ruins of the Pinery Station are the best preserved of any Butterfield station close to a major U.S. highway—in this case, US 62/180, which began as the original Butterfield mail route. (The new route became the basis for I-10 farther south.) The Pinery ruins are just off the road that leads to Pine Springs Campground.

Pine Springs Trails

Tejas Trail (11.9 miles): The Tejas Trail extends the length of the park between Pine Springs and Dog Canyon and is one of the main access routes to the high country. The first section of the trail climbs for 3.8 miles along the base of Pine

Springs Canyon and then along a series of steep switchbacks to the top of the north canyon wall, for an elevation gain of about 2,000 feet. The ascent is fairly difficult but affords excellent views of the canyon below as well as the Guadalupe, Bartlett, and Shumard peaks. This section makes an excellent day hike for hikers who wish to return to the Pine Springs Campground before evening. Hikers who wish to continue on from this escarpment can choose to change over to the Bush Mountain or Hunter Peak trails; 0.2 miles west along Bush Mountain Trail is Pine Top Campsite.

For those staying with the Tejas Trail, the next section descends north along a short ridge into a stand of pine and Douglas fir. About 1.5 miles from the escarpment, the trail cross, the junction for the Bowl Rim Trail to the east, which leads into the Bowl (see "The Bowl"). After another 1.1 miles, the Tejas Trail meets the **Blue Ridge Trail,** which leads west to the Marcus Trail junction and to Blue Ridge Campsite, then on to another section of the Bush Mountain Trail.

From the Blue Ridge Trail junction, the Tejas Trail continues north above the west end of South McKittrick Canyon to Mescalero Campsite with little elevation change. From here, the trail starts climbing to the McKittrick Ridge, meeting the terminus of McKittrick Canyon Trail 1.5 miles after the Blue Ridge Trail junction. The trail continues to climb as it crosses the slopes of Lost Peak (7,830 feet), where a side trail leads to the summit and views of the overall reef structure to the north.

After Lost Peak, the Tejas Trail begins descending toward Dog Canyon along an old wagon track. West of the trail are the remains of a 1930s cabin built by a copper miner who worked the Texas Calumet Mine nearby. The woods of Dog Canyon are a refreshing sight, and hikers finally reach Dog Canyon Campground 5.5 miles past the Blue Ridge Trail junction.

Guadalupe Peak Trail (4.4 miles): This trail leads to the highest point in Texas, Guadalupe Peak (8,749 feet). This steady upward hike along a well-maintained trail is not as difficult as the peak's elevation might suggest. It's best not to stray from the path, however, since limestone cliffs easily crumble underfoot.

Naturally, the views from Guadalupe Peak are outstanding. To the north are the park's second and third-highest points, Bush Mountain and Shumard Peak. To the immediate south is El Capitan, the point of the wedge formed by the Guadalu-

pes, and beyond are vast expanses of the Chihuahuan Desert.

About a mile before the summit is Guadalupe Peak Campsite. In spite of the pine and juniper trees that surround it, this campsite is subject to high winds.

El Capitan Trail (9.4 miles): El Capitan is the very impressive cliff peak one sees upon approaching the Guadalupes from the south on US 62/180. This trail doesn't lead to the summit of El Capitan as the name suggests (it would be quite dangerous to attempt such an ascent), but skirts the base and leads to the west side of the Guadalupe Escarpment, then on to the Williams Ranch. The hike all the way to the ranch is rigorous, in spite of the relative lack of elevation change, mainly due to exposure to southwesterly winds and lack of water at the other end. Most visitors who want to visit the Williams Ranch area (see "Williams Ranch" below) come by four-wheel drive along the unpaved road from US 62/180. Backpackers can also camp at Shumard Canyon Campsite, which is 0.3 mile north of Williams Ranch.

Hiking the first 3.4 miles of the El Capitan Trail to Guadalupe Canyon or continuing on a bit to the Salt Basin Overlook Trail is perhaps more rewarding than hiking the trail's entire length. This section breaks off from the Guadalupe Peak Trail a short distance from Pine Springs Campground and proceeds through desert savanna, then gradually climbs along the base of El Capitan. At 3.4 miles the trail descends into Guadalupe Canyon and meets a junction where hikers can choose to go south along the Salt Basin Overlook Trail (a loop), or north along the west side of the escarpment on the main trail. The main trail can be followed along the base of the escarpment until it meets the west junction of the Salt Basin loop at 4.3 miles. At this point the views of the cliffs and of the huge salt flat below begin to open up. It's another 5.1 miles to the Williams Ranch (4.8 to the Shumard Canyon Campsite).

Salt Basin Overlook Trail (3.5 miles): This trail begins in Guadalupe Canyon as described above and goes south into the canyon, then up along steep cliffs till it rejoins the El Capitan Trail. About a half mile before the loop rejoins the El Capitan Trail, a short path leads to the Salt Basin Overlook, which provides an excellent view of the bolsones (salt lakes) below. The smooth-surfaced Salt Basin extends for 90 miles along a northwest-southeast axis between the Permian Front Ranges (Guadalupe, Delaware, and Apache mountains) to the east and the Diablo Plateau to the west—and this is one of the best vantage points for appreciating its grand scale. Along the way are several views of El Capitan as well.

If one hikes El Capitan to the first junction with the Salt Basin loop, hikes the loop, then exits at the west junction and returns to the Pine Spring Campgrounds via El Capitan, the entire hike is 11.2 miles.

Bear Canyon Trail (3.3 miles): This trail goes east from the Tejas Trail just beyond the Guadalupe Peak Trail junction, and then north into the high country via Upper Pine Spring. The ascent to the top of Bear Canyon is very steep, so this trail is most often used to descend from the high country. The trail was once part of the Hunter Ranch and was used to maintain a pipeline system that pumped water from Upper Pine Spring until 1967. The trail passes just above Upper Pine Spring about 1.5 miles from the trailhead. The water source has created an oasis for maple, ash, oak, and madrone in the immediate area.

Just beyond Upper Pine Spring, the Frijole Trail branches off to the east and hooks up with Smith-Manzanita Spring Trail after 1.2 miles. The Bear Canyon Trail continues north along its steepest incline for 1.8 miles until it ends at the Bowl Rim Trail. Just before it ends, it passes a junction for the Hunter Peak Trail to the west.

Hunter Peak Trail (0.9 miles): The Bear Canyon and Bowl trails are joined by Hunter Peak Trail, which extends east-west between them via Hunter Peak (8,368 feet). From Hunter Peak, there are good views into Pine Springs Canyon as well as across the entire reef structure.

Devil's Hall Trail (2.3 miles): This trails leads to the upper end of Hiker's Staircase, a canyon formed by Pine Springs. Devil's Hall refers to the narrow, stratified walls at this end. Because of the pools of water that usually collect in the canyon, this is a good hike for viewing wildlife and vegetation. It is also a relatively cool hike on hot days, since the narrow canyon walls shade much of the trail. The trailhead is reached via the Guadalupe Peak Horse Trail (mileage quoted above is from Pine Springs Campground).

Frijole And Smith-Manzanita Springs Trails: The Frijole Trail connects the Bear Canyon Trail at Upper Pine Spring with the Smith-Manzanita Springs Trail and is not very exciting in itself. The Smith-Manzanita Springs Trail can more easily

be hiked from the **Frijole Ranch,** about a mile north of the Frijole Visitor Center. The Frijole Ranch was built in 1876 and was supposedly the first permanent residence in the park (guess the Mescaleros weren't permanent). It is now a ranger residence.

The Smith-Manzanita Springs Trail forms an easy 2.3-mile loop and the trailhead is near the ranch. If you take the east fork, you'll come to Manzanita Spring after 0.3 mile. This spot was inhabited by Mescaleros until they were routed out by the U.S. Cavalry in 1878. From here it's another 0.9 mile with a gradual ascent along Smith Canyon to Smith Spring, an oasis for madrone, maple, and juniper. Taking the west half of the loop for the return, hikers will pass the Frijole Trail junction at 0.9 mile from Smith Spring; from there it's 0.2 mile back to the trailhead at Frijole Ranch.

THE BOWL

This large depression in the high country contains a dense Douglas fir and pine forest and is an important source of water for wildlife. Two trails lead into the Bowl, the Bowl Trail and the Bowl Rim Trail (the latter is called the Juniper Trail on the Trails Illustrated topographic map).

The 0.9-mile **Bowl Trail** connects the Hunter Peak Trail with the Bowl Rim. The **Bowl Rim Trail** links the Tejas and Bear Canyon trails and passes through the center of the Bowl for a total distance of 2.8 miles (the topo map marks two miles of this as the Juniper Trail). The nearest campsites for Bowl explorations are Pine Top (0.7 mile from the Bowl Trail) and Mescalero (0.8 mile from the Juniper/Bowl Rim Trail).

DOG CANYON

This canyon in the north of the park receives run-off from ridges leading to Lost Peak, water that supports a variety of deciduous trees and wildlife. This means that Dog Canyon, like McKittrick Canyon, is a good viewing spot for fall foliage. Rocky Mountain elk and mule deer often browse in the canyon as well. Two major trailheads are located near Dog Canyon Campground, the Tejas Trail (described above under "Pine Springs") and the Bush Mountain Trail.

Dog Canyon Campground

This is the second drive-in camping facility in Guadalupe Mountains National Park. Because of its 6,300-foot elevation, temperatures tend to be a bit cooler than at the Pine Springs Campground to the south. Since Dog Canyon is also less dry than Pine Springs, cooking grills are provided for charcoal fires. Open fires are not permitted.

Camping facilities include 18 walk-in tentsites and five RV parking spaces. As at Pine Springs, there are not RV hookups or dump stations. A ranger station, picnic area, restrooms, and horse corrals are close at hand. Drinking water for hikers is available.

Vehicle access to Dog Canyon Campground is via New Mexico State 137, which runs south off US 285 about 12 miles north of Carlsbad. From this junction it's around 59 miles to the Dog Canyon Campground through private lands and Lincoln National Forest.

Bush Mountain Trail (12.3 miles): This is the park's longest single trail, running vaguely parallel to the Tejas Trail from Dog Canyon Campground to the top of Pine Springs Canyon. It also takes you as far west into the Guadalupes as you can go on established trails, following the western escarpment over Bush Mountain, the second highest peak in the park. The trail could be hiked starting from either end; the following description begins in Dog Canyon.

The first section of the trail takes you west from the canyon floor, up and over a ridge into West Dog Canyon, and then meets the **Marcus Trail** junction at 3.5 miles. The Marcus Trail heads directly south along West Dog Canyon and terminates at the Blue Ridge Trail after 3.8 miles. North of Marcus-Bush Mountain Trail junction about 200 yards is the Marcus Campsite.

From the Marcus Trail junction, the Bush Mountain Trail veers southwest and climbs past Cox Tank (part of a former ranch water system) toward Blue Ridge. Once Blue Ridge is attained, hikers can see the Chihuahuan Desert thousands of feet below to the west, as well as Lost Peak to the east. After 7.4 miles from Dog Canyon Campground (3.9 miles from the Marcus Trail junction in West Dog Canyon), the trail meets the west terminus of Blue Ridge Trail, which leads east to the Blue Ridge Campsite (a half mile away) and connects the Bush Mountain Trail with the central section of the Tejas Trail.

On the ascent toward Bush Mountain, one can look west and spot the lush green fields of Dell City, Texas, 20 miles away. About two miles south of the Blue Ridge Trail junction, the trail passes over the slopes of Bush Mountain (8,631 feet) and then descends to the Bush Mountain Campsite. From here the trail twists east above the upper reaches of Pine Springs Canyon, providing excellent views of the canyon below, Bartlett Peak (8,508 feet) on the other side of the canyon, and Shumard Peak (8,615 feet) to the south. The Bush Mountain Trail terminates at the Tejas Trail, 2.9 miles from the Bush Mountain Campsite.

WILLIAMS RANCH

The Williams Ranch lies to the west of the Guadalupe Escarpment amidst a classic shrub desert biome. Originally built in 1900 by Henry Belcher as a longhorn cattle ranch, it was bought by James Adolphus Williams in 1915 and converted to a sheep ranch. A mile east of the ranch house is Bone Canyon, which exposes the oldest layer of limestone reef in the park. Because the west side of the Guadalupes gets the least amount of average precipitation, Bone Canyon is nearly bone-dry, but there is a grassy area near the source of Bone Spring. El Capitan towers above.

The Williams Ranch area can be reached by horse or on foot via El Capitan Trail from Pine Springs Campground, 9.4 miles away (see description of El Capitan Trail above), or by four-wheel drive via an eight-mile unpaved road off US 62/180, about 8.5 miles south of Guadalupe Pass.

GUADALUPE AREA ACCOMMODATIONS AND FOOD

Guadalupe Mountains National Park has no lodging facilities other than campgrounds, nor are there any grocery stores or gas stations in the park. The nearest tourist motels are in White's City, New Mexico, 35 miles north on US 62/180, but rates are higher than usual; better value accommodations are available in Carlsbad, New Mexico, 20 miles past White's City. The nearest Texas motels are in Van Horn, 75 miles south of the park at I-10 and State 54.

Across US 62/180 from the Pine Springs Campground is the ancient **Pine Springs Cafe,** which sells gas and minimal groceries (in spite of the name, they don't prepare food). The Park Service tried to bulldoze the cafe recently, but the family who run it called the TV networks and forced the Park Service to back off, at least for the time being (after all, the cafe has been there longer than the Park Service).

Thirteen miles west of the park on US 62/180, just before the near-ghost town of Salt Flat, is a no-name diner with gas pumps out front that has the best food between Cornudas (another 17 miles further east) and White's City. The woman who does the cooking serves tasty Filipino chicken with rice (is this really West Texas?) and "Shanghai coffee." Cowboys ride in from local cattle drives for the burgers here.

In Salt Flat, another couple of miles east, the **Salt Flat Cafe** serves standard diner fare and

has gasoline. The **Cornudas Cafe** in tiny Cornudas, 32 miles west of the park, is reputed to serve the best green chile burgers in a 100-mile radius. Next to the cafe is a truckers motel that is sometimes open, sometimes not.

TRANSPORT

Guadalupe Mountains National Park is 110 miles east of El Paso, 75 miles north of Van Horn, and 55 miles southwest of Carlsbad, New Mexico. Regional Texas and New Mexico bus lines pass the park en route between El Paso and Carlsbad and between Carlsbad and Fort Stockton. Since there's no official bus stop at the park, you must make advance arrangements with the bus driver to get off at the park; call (806) 765-6641 for more information.

DAVIS MOUNTAINS

The Davis Mountains are unique among West Texas mountain ranges in that they are for the most part smooth-topped and grassy. These mountains constitute the northern end of the Tertiary Volcanic Region that lies between the Western Front Ranges (Malone, Quitman, Eagle, and Indio mountains) and the Eastern Front Ranges (Sierra del Carmen, Santiago, Del Norte, and Altuda mountains). The Tertiary Volcanic Region (formed by thick accumulations of lava flow) extends from the Davis Mountains in the north to the Bofecillos Mountains on the Texas-Mexico border to the south, just west of Big Bend National Park. The state's fifth-highest peak, **Mt. Livermore** (8,382 feet), is in the southeastern section of the Davis Mountains, in the middle of a loop formed by Texas Highways 166 and 118.

It's no secret in Texas that this area has what many argue is the best year-round climate in the state—cool summers and mild winters—mostly because of the elevation, which averages around 5,000-6,000 feet. Also, unlike most of the Trans-Pecos, the Davis Mountains average over 20 inches of rain a year, more than enough to support wooded grasslands. The air is so clear that when the University of Texas decided to build an observatory, the Davis Mountains were the natural choice (see "McDonald Observatory" p. 111).

DAVIS MOUNTAINS STATE PARK

About six miles west of Fort Davis off State 118, this 1,869-acre park is centered around a canyon formed by Limpia Creek. The park features easy to moderate hiking trails, a longhorn herd, a scenic drive with overlooks, and an interpretive center. A trail that starts at the interpretive center proceeds east 4.5 miles to Fort Davis National Historical Site (see "Fort Davis" below). Between June and August, rangers conduct campfire programs. Fishing and swimming are permitted in Limpia Creek.

Facilities
Separate camping areas feature sites with water only ($6 weekdays, $8 weekends), water and electricity ($9/11), and full RV hookups ($10/12). All sites have tables and cooking grills as well. Hot showers, restrooms, and a trailer dump site are available. For campsite reservations, contact the Superintendent (tel. 915-426-3337), Davis Mountains State Park, Box 786, Fort Davis, TX 79734.

The **Indian Lodge** is a 39-room pueblo-style motel in the park that was built by the Civilian Conservation Corps in the 1930s. The adobe walls of the lodge are 18 inches thick and many of the interior furnishings are original. Rooms are basic, but all have TV and air-conditioning. The lodge has a good restaurant (open daily 7:30 a.m.-9 p.m. except when the lodge is closed) and heated swimming pool. The Indian Lodge is open year-round except for two weeks beginning on the second Monday of January, when it's closed for general repairs. Room rates are $40-50 per night. For further information and reservations (accepted up to a year in advance), contact the Indian Lodge Manager (tel. 915-426-3254), Box 786, Fort Davis, TX 79734.

FORT DAVIS

The town of Fort Davis (pop. 1200) is named for a frontier fort that was founded in 1854 near the intersection of the Chihuahua Trail and the San Antonio-El Paso Trail (which later became part of the Butterfield Overland Mail Route). The fort closed in 1891 (see "Fort Davis National Historical Site" below for details) but the town managed to hang on as county seat of Presidio County and then later Jeff Davis County. Today its economy for the most part depends on serving visitors to the Davis Mountains and Fort Davis National Historical Site.

Fort Davis is at an elevation of 5,050 feet, making it the highest town in the state (about the same elevation as Denver, Colorado). Temperatures in the summer are a pleasant 70-80° F while in the winter it's in the 30s and 40s.

Fort Davis's main street has a couple of historic inns (see "Accommodations") and buildings (Fort Davis State Bank, Jeff Davis County Courthouse), and a few tourist-oriented shops. To get an idea of the town's real charm, walk or drive the unpaved back streets, with their cozy adobe, wood-frame houses, and little country churches.

FORT DAVIS SIGHTS

Fort Davis National Historical Site

History: Fort Davis was originally established by the U.S. Army to protect travelers and freight along the San Antonio-El Paso Trail from Apache and Comanche Indian attacks. The first garrison buildings were built in 1854 of pine slabs with thatched roofs and named for then Secretary of War Jefferson Davis. When the Civil War broke out, the Union army abandoned the fort and it was taken over by Confederate troops in 1861. The Confederates held Fort Davis for less than a year; when Union troops took El Paso, the Confederates at Fort Davis joined other Confederate troops along the West Texas frontier in a general retreat to San Antonio.

The fort lay abandoned for five years and was burned to the ground by the Mescalero Apaches. Two years after the end of the Civil War, in 1867, the U.S. Army returned and rebuilt the fort, this time of stone and adobe. Fort Davis became the headquarters for the 9th U.S. Cavalry, one of two black cavalry regiments that earned the nickname "Buffalo Soldiers" from Indians who encountered them in the ensuing Indian Wars. The fort's military function evolved from one of frontier defense to one of outright assault upon Apache tribes in the area. The last Apache battle in Texas was fought by black soldiers from Fort Davis along the Mexican border in 1880. In 1885, the Buffalo Soldiers were transferred to Arizona Territory, where they obtained Geronimo's surrender in the following year. When there were no Indians left to fight, the fort closed in 1891.

The National Park Service took over the site in 1961 and eventually restored half of the original 50 structures.

Facilities: The restored site features a visitors center (in a former company barrack) with slide and audio programs, a small museum that chronicles the 1854-91 history of the fort, and a self-guiding tour year-round. During the summer, the park staff and volunteers dress in period costume and give free guided tours. An 1875 vintage Retreat Parade is also reenacted with sound effects (bugles and cavalry hoofbeats) daily at 11 a.m. and 4 p.m. during the summer.

Behind the officers' quarters is the trailhead for the **Tall Grass Nature Trail,** a 1.2-mile loop that takes hikers to a viewpoint in the hills over the site.

The fort is located at the north end of the town of Fort Davis, off State 17. Admission is $1 per person. Persons under age 16 or over age 62 are admitted free. For additional information, contact the Superintendent (tel. 915-426-3225), Fort Davis National Historical Site, P.O. Box 1456, Fort Davis, TX 79734.

107-inch telescope, McDonald Observatory

McDonald Observatory

High atop Mount Locke at 6,800 feet, this University of Texas astronomy research center is one of the top-10 observatories in the world. When it wast built in 1938, its 82-inch telescope was the second largest in existence. In 1969, the observatory added a 107-inch telescope under joint contract between the university and NASA. This scope is in heavy demand by research astronomers from around the country for all kinds of research but is best suited for spectroscopic analysis of the light from planets, satellites, stars, and quasars.

McDonald is also the site of a 16-foot millimeter-wave dish for studying gas clouds and particles in the Milky Way, a 30-inch scope responsible for over half of the world's records on lunar occultations (which occur when the moon passes in front of a star), and a laser-ranging telescope that is used for precise lunar calculations (orbit and distance). In a valley below the peak is the Harvard Radio Astronomy Center, which harbors a radio telescope that's part of a worldwide system called Very Long Base Array (VLBA). Radio scopes in this system, which is a joint University of California-University of Texas-Harvard University project, measure continental drift by base-line vectoring.

The Davis Mountains are a particularly good location for astronomical viewing because of the lack of light pollution from nearby artificial light sources, the high annual number of cloudless nights, and the concentration of native plants and trees in the vicinity that filter dust and radiation.

The observatory complex is 19 miles northwest of Fort Davis via State 118 and Spur 78.

Visitors Center: A few hundred yards below the peak is the W.L. Moody, Jr. Visitors' Information Center, where visitors are asked to check in before proceeding on to the observatory complex. The exhibits here are quite good and the gift shop carries star charts and other astronomy-related items. Don't miss the Gravity Well. The center is open daily 9-5 except for Thanksgiving, Christmas, and New Year's Day.

Visitor Activities: Only the dome that contains the 107-inch scope is open to the public. Guided tours of the dome and the immediate grounds are conducted daily at 2 p.m. year-round and, from June through August, at 9:30 a.m. as well. The tours are excellent and last about an hour, but if you miss the appointed starting times, you can take a self-guided walking tour of the facility. The Moody Center distributes maps with step-by-step instructions for the self-guided tour. There is no charge for either type of tour but donations are accepted in the 107-inch telescope dome.

Once a month the observatory allows visitors to view the sky through the big scope—this is the only major observatory in North America with such a program. Admission is $5 for adults, $4 for students and seniors, or $2.59 for children under 12. Tickets and a schedule of the public viewing nights are available from the W.L. Moody, Jr. Visitors' Information Center.

Every Tues., Fri., and Sun. evening, the Moody Center puts on a "Star Party," in which a docent presents a visual tour of the constellations as well as a chance to view heavenly bodies through eight- and 14-inch telescopes. Star parties are free of charge and begin just after sunset outside the center, weather permitting.

Daily at 11 a.m., the center holds solar viewing sessions in which active sunspots are viewed through a filtered telescope. Lunar spying is also a possibility during these sessions on days when the moon rises early or sets late. For more information call or write McDonald Observatory (tel. 915-426-3640), P.O. Box 1337, Fort Davis, TX 79734.

Chihuahuan Desert Research Institute

Founded in 1974 by Sul Ross University for the scientific study of the Chihuahuan Desert and for public education, the institute covers 580 acres that include a botanical garden (with over 500 regional species), an arboretum, and nature trails. They also have native plants for sale (largest selection is around the last week of April during the institute's annual Native Plant Sale). The visitor center is 3.5 miles south of Fort Davis on State 118. Open weekdays 1-5 p.m. and weekends 9-6, May through Labor Day. No admission charge. Call (915) 837-8370 for information.

Scenic Loop

State Highways 166 and 118 form a 74-mile loop through the lower third of the Davis Mountains, circling Mount Livermore and passing Madera Canyon, Mount Locke, and Davis Mountains State Park. Driving west from Fort Davis, the mountains look their prettiest at sunrise or from the east, at sunset.

FORT DAVIS PRACTICALITIES

Hotels And Motels

The **Old Texas Inn** (tel. 915-426-3118; P.O. Box 785, Fort Davis, TX 79734) above Fort Davis Drug on the town's main drag has six rooms, decorated with country antiques, for $40-55. Discounts are available for longer stays and the entire Inn can be rented for $200 a night. The **Limpia Hotel** (tel. 800-662-5517, P.O. Box 822, Fort Davis, TX 79734) across the street was originally built in 1912 but was restored in 1978 with nine rooms on the upper floor and eight across the street in "Limpia West." There are also three suites in the old wing that sleep four to eight. Rates are $59 s, 62 d, $68+ (triple), or add $5 for suites. During the winter months, Sun.-Thurs. rates are approximately $10 lower;

year round there's a 10% senior discount (62 years and over).

The **Stone Village Motel** (tel. 426-3941) is the closest lodging to Fort Davis National Historic Site. Simple but well-kept rooms cost $29-41 a night, the best value in town. The nearby **Butterfield's** (tel. 426-3252) has four cottages with Jacuzzis and fireplaces for $60 a night. Off the main road in town are a couple of bed-and-breakfasts, **Wayside Inn** (tel. 426-3535) for $45 a night and Victorian-style **Neill Doll Museum** (tel. 426-3969) for $50-60. The doll museum displays over 400 antique dolls.

The **Prude Ranch** (tel. 426-3202, P.O. Box 1431, Fort Davis, TX 79734), 6.5 miles northwest of town off State 118, is a tourist attraction in itself. It started out in 1898 as a cattle ranch and then in the '30s cabins were erected on the ranch for workers who were building the McDonald Observatory. Currently, it's a combination dude ranch (offering trail rides, country dances, etc.), mountain resort (with tennis, indoor swimming pool, hot tub), RV park, and campground. Cabins run $27-$42, motel rooms are $37-52, RV hookups are $11, and tentsites are $8 with water and electricity, $6 without. Weekly rates are lower.

Food

Good food is available at **Fort Davis Drug** on the town square (downstairs from the Old Texas Inn), but it's only open for breakfast and lunch during the week, for breakfast, lunch, and dinner on Friday and Saturday. It's no longer a pharmacy, although the original soda fountain has been preserved and they still offer hand-mixed Cokes and ice-cream floats.

Across the street, the **Hotel Limpia Dining Room** serves good country-style fare for breakfast, lunch, and dinner daily. Farther north along the main street are several other possibilities, including the popular **Cueva de Leon**, a Tex-Mex place open Tues.-Sun. for lunch and dinner. The nearby **Desert Rose** offers a simple menu of Texas dishes daily for breakfast, lunch, and dinner. Further north, **Poco Mexico** is an inexpensive choice for Mexican lunches (open 11 a.m.-2 p.m. only, closed Thursday).

Shopping

Several shops in town sell West Texas souvenirs, including one attached to the Hotel Limpia Dining

Room. This shop also carries a good selection of books on Texas.

Fort Davis Astronomical Supply, next to the Stone Village Motel, sells everything for the amateur astronomer including large backyard scopes.

VICINITY OF FORT DAVIS

Balmorhea
Pronounced Bal-mo-ray (and named for three early residents—Balcom, Morrow, and Rhea), this small farming community of 568 is irrigated by San Solomon Springs, an old watering place along the San Antonio-El Paso Trail. The springs pump 26 million gallons of water a day onto 14,000 acres and flow into the country's largest spring-fed swimming pool at Balmorhea State Recreation Area (see below).

Lake Balmorhea, three miles south of town off US 290, is an impoundment of Sandia Creek that covers nearly 600 acres. The lake is stocked with catfish, stripers, bass, and crappie and fishing is permitted on the lake for $2 a day. RV hookups are available for $7 a night.

Highway 17 between Balmorhea and Fort Davis winds through scenic, mostly unpopulated Davis Mountains countryside, passing several cool running streams, interesting rock formations, and lots of potential picnic spots.

Balmorhea State Recreation Area
Four miles southwest of Balmorhea off US 290, near the minuscule town of Toyahvale (pop. 60), is a state park whose claim to fame is a spring-fed pool with a 68,000-square-foot surface. In some places the pool is 30 feet deep, so this is a scuba diving center for much of West Texas. The bottom of the pool is a mixture of rock and sand, interspersed with native aquatic plants. The water is Caribbean clear (the constant flow from San Solomon Springs changes the entire pool volume

every six hours) and maintains a constant temperature of 72-76° Fahrenheit. Freshwater fish inhabit the pool, including catfish, crayfish, perch, and two rare species, the Comanche Springs pupfish and the Pecos mosquitofish. The pool is open from Memorial Day through Labor Day but scuba diving is restricted to mornings from 8:30 to 11. The non-diving public can stay until sunset when the park closes. The rest of the park is open year-round.

Facilities: The park has 28 campsites with water ($7 weekdays, $9 weekends) and six with water and electricity ($10/12). No RV hookups are available but there's a dump station, a picnic area with grills, restrooms, showers, and, in the summer only, a snack bar and bathhouse. Rooms at the rustic **San Solomon Springs Court** cost $35 s, plus $5 for each additional adult. Children ages 6-12 are $2 each; add $5 for rooms with kitchen units. For more information contact the Superintendent (tel. 915-375-2370), Balmorhea State Recreation Area, Box 15, Toyahvale, TX 79786.

Valentine
Valentine is one of two towns along US 90 (the other is Lobo) that were practically killed off when the construction of I-10 diverted traffic away from the lovely valley between the Sierra Vieja and Davis Mountains. If you happen to be passing through Valentine before Feb. 14, you can stop off here and mail a bundle of Valentine's Day cards from the post office (you can't miss it, there's only one). Why? So your cards will receive postmarks from Valentine, Texas. This post office has a unique service in which the postmaster holds cards so designated until just before February 14, then franks the stamps with a special Valentine's Day cancellation. (You can actually get this done from anywhere in the U.S. by sending your bundle of cards in a large envelope, before Feb. 10, to Postmaster, Valentine, TX 79854.)

BIG BEND NATIONAL PARK

INTRODUCTION

Big Bend is a corner of Texas where the Rio Grande bends its mighty elbow around an area of extreme geologic confusion. Indians say the Great Spirit placed all the leftover rocks here after creating the Earth. In spite of this massive detour, in which the river interrupts its northwest-southeast flow to go southwest-northeast, the Rio Grande must cut through three Big Bend mountain ranges, thus creating the Bend's most striking canyons.

The Chihuahuan Desert, resting between the "mother ranges" of the Sierra Madre Oriental and the Sierra Madre Occidental, is the backdrop for a national park that covers nearly a million acres (larger than the state of Rhode Island) and administers 234 miles of the Rio Grande for recreational and educational use. The park in fact encompasses the best-preserved example of native Chihuahuan Desert in the U.S. or Mexico. The desert covers parts of six states—Texas and New Mexico in the U.S., plus Chihuahua, Coahuila, Durango, and Zacatecas in Mexico. This is one of North America's greatest national parks—one that most park aficionados would place in their top five. Yet it receives far fewer visitors than any of its rivals, and is thus one of the least-crowded national parks in the United States. (For comparison: in 1991 Big Bend National Park received 296,000 visitors, Arizona's Grand Canyon National Park saw 3.9 million, California's Yosemite National Park endured 3.4 million, and Montana's Glacier National Park took in 2.1 million.)

But it's not all desert. Besides the very non-desert-like Rio Grande environment that runs along the base of the park through brakes of river cane and cedar, there are mountain oases where conifer forests and shaded springs provide startling biotic contrasts—like ferns and cacti living side by side. Unique plant and animal communities thrive on these mountain islands cast in a desert sea, several species of which are found only in the Big Bend area. This uniqueness led UNESCO in 1976 to designate Big Bend as an International Biosphere Reserve, one of only 250 sites in the world whose particularly well-preserved ecosystems are thus listed.

One of the best descriptions of Big Bend was offered by an unidentified Mexican vaquero over a hundred years ago: "Where the rainbows wait for the rain, and the big river is kept in a stone box, and water runs uphill and mountains float in the air, except at night when they go away to play with other mountains . . ."

The Land

Film buffs might say it's classic Sergio Leone country, but geologists classify Big Bend as part of the Eastern Volcanic Area of the state's Tertiary Volcanic Region. This area extends from the Bofecillos Mountains just west of the park to the Sierra del Carmen along the park's eastern border, and as far north as the Santiago Mountains. The dominant range within the park (and within the entire Eastern Volcanic Area) is the **Chisos Mountains,** a collection of exposed intrusive lava masses and peaks that reach up to 7,835 feet (Emory Peak, the park's highest). Other volcanic ranges in the park include the Sierra de Santa Eleña and the Rosillos mountains (which became part of the park in 1989), as well as many singular peaks like Burro Mesa, Tule Mountain, Talley Mountain, Chilicotal Mountain, and Mariscal Mountain.

The volcanos that erupted in this area probably did so around the time the dinosaurs disappeared and the American Southwest was pushing its way up through tropical seas (50-75 million years ago). At least eight calderas (volcanic craters) have been identified in Big Bend, whose output of lava, volcanic ash, and other debris covered an area of nearly 10,000 square miles with a thickness of about a mile and a half. In the intervening eons, erosion carved peaks and canyons out of the layers of volcanic detritus to create Big Bend's topographical majesty.

Over its half-century history, the park's ecosystem has continued to flourish, coming ever closer to its original state before humans intervened (i.e., the Comanches, who trampled it underfoot and beneath the feet of captured slaves and livestock by making Big Bend the main intersection for the Comanche War Trail; the Mexicans, who over-

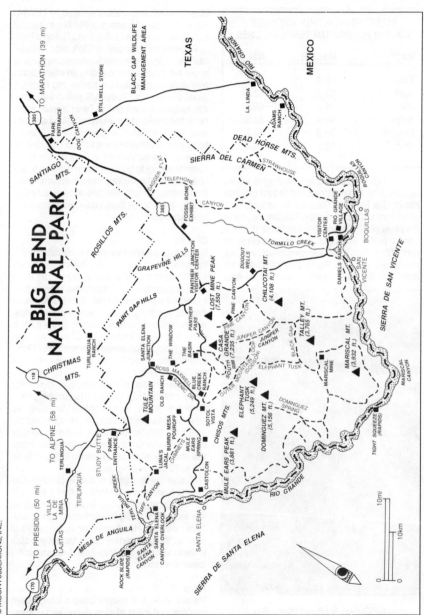

© MOON PUBLICATIONS, INC.

SELECTED MONTHLY AVERAGE MAXIMUM/MINIMUM TEMPERATURES

Month	Max. (°F)	Min. (°F)
Feb.	66.2	37.8
April	80.7	52.3
June	94.2	65.5
Aug.	91.1	68.3
Oct.	78.8	52.7
Dec.	62.2	36.4

farmed and overgrazed it, and the Anglos, whose ranches and mines threatened to turn the area into another El Paso. Recently the park has benefited from the addition of the Rosillos Mountains Preserve (90,000 acres transferred to the Park Service by the Texas Nature Conservancy) to the north, Black Gap Wildlife Management Area (administered by Texas Parks and Wildlife) to the east, and Big Bend Ranch State Natural Area

Tuff Canyon, Big Bend National Park

(over 215,000 acres, also managed by TPW) to the west. These areas provide large, natural buffers for the biomes in Big Bend National Park.

Recently national park officials have entered into discussions with their Mexican counterparts about the possibility of creating an international park extending across the border into Mexico's Sierra del Carmen. On the U.S. side of the border this range is known as the Dead Horse Mountains; the peaks rise in elevation along a southeast axis from Boquillas Canyon. If the international park is established, it will join Glacier-Waterton International Peace Park on the U.S.-Canada border to become North America's second cross-border nature preserve. In preparation, the Mexican government has already set aside 37,000 acres of the Sierra del Carmen as a nature reserve.

Climate

Because of the great variation in elevation within the park (1,800 feet at the Rio Grande to over 7,800 feet in the Chisos Mountains), Big Bend harbors a number of microclimates, ranging from furnace-like summer temperatures at Mesa de Anguila (on the park's extreme western edge) and in the Dead Horse Mountains (in the east) to short-lived winter snow in the Chisos. Average annual precipitation varies from five to eight inches along the desert floor to 15 inches or more in the Chisos. Most of the year, visitors can count on a high percentage of sunshine, even during the wetter months (July to Oct.). The following chart shows average temperatures for selected months, measured at Panther Junction near the park's center. Temperatures in the mountains may run five to 10 degrees Fahrenheit lower than this average, while along the river they may be five to 10 degrees higher.

Overall, the best times to visit Big Bend are October to November and March to April. Fall is best for river running (with water levels reaching about four feet), while spring is best for birding and wildflower viewing. However, even in the height of summer the park can be comfortable if you stick to the mountains, or in the winter if you stay in the lower elevations.

Flora

People who have never visited a living desert imagine vast tracts of sand dunes with vultures circling above. As they first enter the Chihuahuan Desert, they're awed to see just how beautiful the arid landscape is. The subtle tapestry of desert plants yields hues of purple, brown, blue, orange, yellow, and green that change with the seasons (not the uniform khaki of cartoon deserts).

One of the most characteristic Big Bend desert plants is the **creosote bush,** a short evergreen with a taproot that goes down as far as 30 feet to obtain underground water. In the spring, after a good rain, it blooms with yellow flowers. After any rainfall, it emits the creosote aroma for which it is named—the smell of the desert. Another common Chihuahuan Desert plant is the **ocotillo** or coachwhip, so called because it looks like a bunch of coach whips stuck in the ground. After a rain it bursts with tiny green leaves and during dry spells looks almost dead with just the bare brown stems waving in the arid breeze.

The "indicator" plant for the Chihuahuan Desert is the **lechuguilla** (Spanish for "little lettuce"), a unique succulent which grows only in this desert. The lechuguilla belongs to the genus *Agave* (from the Greek word for "noble") and as such blooms only once in its lifetime of 10-15 years, when it shoots up a 15-foot stalk and then dies. Unlike more typical broad-leaved agaves, the lechuguilla produces clusters of narrow, spiked blades that are a menace to hikers, horses, and deer but perfect for making strong twine (locally called istle or tampico fiber) used in weaving mats, ropes, bags, and other household items. The tradition of istle-making has not been lost in Big Bend (outside the park, where the plant is not protected) and you can buy items made from lechuguilla— rope, donkey bridles, cordage, brooms, and sandals—at the Lajitas Trading Co. (see "Lajitas") just west of the park.

If you've come to Big Bend to see cacti you won't be disappointed. No other national park has so many species of cacti, over 70 at last count, nor as many unique species. In the spring, usually in early to mid-April, many cacti produce splendid

Cane Cholla

flowers. They come in two basic groups, those with glochids (the tiny barbed hairs or bristles that sprout around the same areole from which cactus spines emerge) and those without glochids. Most common among the first group (all of which belong to the genus *Opuntia)* are the **chollas** and **prickly pears.** Chollas have cylindrical stems that branch out and may be anywhere from a few inches to over five feet tall, while prickly pears produce flattened pads that also branch out but stay closer to the ground, usually under three feet.

Cane cholla is one of the most common chollas in Big Bend—it's the one that looks like twisted rope standing on end. Prickly pears occur in nine commonly seen varieties, including the **blind prickly pear,** which has no spines, the **Chisos prickly pear** with yellow spines and glochids, and the **purple-tinged prickly pear,** which has purplish pads (most pronounced in the winter) and very long spines. The prickly pear cactus is often eaten locally, especially before Christian lent (look for *nopales* or *nopalitos* on menus).

The non-glochid cacti belong to seven different genera, *Echinocactus, Echinocereus, Cereus, Ariocarpus, Mamillaria,* and *Epithelantha,* all of which produce spines, and *Lophophora,* which does not have spines. Some of the most striking include the **southwestern barrel cactus,** with a globular, ribbed stem and hooked spines, and **devil's claw** or "horse crippler," which is a barrel cactus that grows low to the ground but has thick, heavy spines. One of the most common cacti in Big Bend is the **strawberry cactus,** which forms stem mounds around three feet high and four feet wide, is covered with a profusion of spines, and produces bright red flowers and fruit in the spring and summer. The fruit may be eaten like strawberries (it's especially tasty with honey and milk or cream), hence its name.

The most famous of the non-glochids in Big Bend is **peyote** *(Lophophora williamsii),* also called "mescal" or "dry whiskey," a cactus that contains a variety of psychoactive alkaloids, principally mescaline. The dried "buttons" of the peyote cactus have been used by various Indian tribes as a hallucinogenic sacrament in important religious ceremonies since pre-Columbian days. Peyote came to prominence among non-Indians in the 1960s and early '70s along with a series of books by Latin American writer Carlos Castañeda, who supposedly ate peyote in northern Mexico under the tutelage of a Yaqui sorcerer named Don Juan. This cactus is actually very difficult to find, since it grows in small clumps very close to the ground, disappearing beneath the ground altogether during dry periods. After spring and summer rains, small pink flowers appear in the center of the spineless stem. Peyote cacti are now rather rare within the park boundaries, in part because so many would-be Don Juans have dug them up over the years. Remember that it is illegal to remove or cut any part of any plant in the park, and that possession of peyote, classified as a harmful drug by most state governments, is illegal in Texas.

In the highlands you'll find thick conifer forests mixed with high desert scrub. The typical Chisos Mountain woodlands are dominated by **piñon, oak,** and **juniper.** Outside of Mexico, **drooping juniper** (so called because the tree's foliage appears to sag or droop, even after a good rain) is only found in the Chisos Mountains. Other trees not normally found outside Mexico are the **chinquapin oak** and the **Coahuila scrub oak.** Also growing in the Chisos are **ponderosa pine, Arizona cypress, Douglas fir, bigtooth maple,** and **quaking aspen,** all of which are at the southern or western extremes of their normal ranges. The rare **Texas madrone,** with its shiny evergreen leaves and brilliant red berries, is seen in the Big Bend high country as well. Highland vegetation that is found only in the park, and nowhere else in the world, includes the **Chisos oak** (seen only in Blue Creek Canyon) and the **Chisos agave.**

The banks of the Rio Grande comprise their own vegetational zone, what might be termed desert riparian. Subtropical river cane grows thickly in many places and is still used locally for ramadas (shade porches) and simple roofing. Salt cedar also grows in some abundance along the river.

Fauna

Mammals: At least 75 species of mammals make Big Bend their habitat. Among the larger mammals are two species of deer **(Sierra del Carmen whitetail,** generally found above 5,000 feet and **mule deer,** usually below 5,000 feet), two foxes (the **kit fox** above 5,000 feet, and, more commonly, the **gray fox), Barbary sheep, pronghorn** (on the increase in the park), the **coyote,** the **gray wolf,** the **black bear** (rare, but there were 29 sightings in 1990), and the **mountain lion** (a nocturnal animal, also called cougar, panther, or puma). Of these, only the mountain lion has been known to attack humans, and then only rarely (there have been only two attacks since 1984; in both cases the attacking lions were killed by park rangers).

Another nocturnal creature is the **javelina** or collared peccary. Although the javelina looks like a wild pig, it's actually a member of a very small family of mammals called Tayassuidae, and is more closely related to tapirs and horses than to pigs of any kind. They're not uncommon in Big Bend, and if you spend any time along Grapevine Hills Rd. or in Panther or Ash canyons, you're quite likely to see one or even a small herd when they feed in the early morning or late evening. They're also commonly seen near the Chisos Mountain Lodge. Because they're very nearsighted and naturally curious, javelinas will occasion-

LION ENCOUNTERS

About 95% of all mountain lion sightings since the 1950s have been along park roads, rather than on hiking trails. Furthermore, lions are nocturnal animals, so you're not likely to see them unless you hike at night. At last estimate about two dozen lions were living in the park, most often seen in the Chisos. If you encounter a lion while hiking in the park, the Park Service advises you to "convince the lion that you are not prey and that you may be dangerous yourself." The way to make your case for this is, first, do not run from the lion. Do not try to hide or crouch down either, since the lion will have seen you long before you've seen it. If you hold your ground, shout, and wave your hands, the lion will most likely leave the vicinity; if the lion behaves aggressively, throw stones. If you're hiking with children, it's best to pick them up so that you look larger to the lion.

1. Monahans Sandhills, West Texas; **2.** ocotillo, Big Bend
(photos by Joe Cummings)

1. Palo Duro Canyon; **2.** volcanic formations, Big Bend; **3.** Santa Elena Canyon, Big Bend
(photos by Joe Cummings)

javelina

ally approach people for a few sniffs, but there's no need to be alarmed unless young peccaries are present (that's when the mothers may act unpredictably).

A host of smaller mammals live in the park, including various rabbits, squirrels, bats, raccoons, skunks, badgers, and mice. Of these, perhaps the most distinctive are the huge **black-tailed jack rabbit** and the **kangaroo rat.** Both are uniquely adapted to desert life. The long, upright ears of the jack rabbit enable it to hear sounds from quite a distance, a necessity for an animal that is prey for practically every larger animal (including coyotes, eagles, and bobcats) in the park. The ears also act as radiators on hot desert days, allowing the jack rabbit to release excess body heat into the air. The kangaroo rat, which you may see hopping in front of your headlights at night, is built so that it doesn't need to drink water, ever. It derives moisture from seeds that it eats, from the air deep inside its burrows where the relative humidity is 30-50%, and from condensation in its nasal passages (its nostrils are much cooler than the rest of its body). Its efficient kidneys excrete uric acid in a concentrated paste, rather than in liquid form.

Birds: Big Bend is a mecca for birders since it's at the southern end of the central flyway and because there is such a diversity of habitats for birds to choose from. Well over 400 species of birds have been recorded here, more than any other national park in the U.S. or Canada. Several bird species appear only in Big Bend, specifically in the Chisos Mountains. Others are native to Mexico and Central America and Big Bend is the northern limit of their habitat. Most famous is the **Colima warbler,** a small yellow-and-gray warbler that nests in Boot Canyon and in Laguna Meadow (most commonly seen May to July). The **Lucifer hummingbird** is another whose only American habitat is Big Bend (very common around blooming agave plants in the summer). Other birds found in Big Bend include **great blue herons, Mexican mallards, roadrunners** (usually called paisano locally), **golden eagles, bald eagles, red-tailed hawks, American kestrels, peregrine falcons, great horned owls, screechowls, white-throated swifts,** and **cactus wrens** (which build their nests in cacti). To learn the best seasons to spot these and other species, get the *Bird Checklist* published by the Big Bend Natural History Association and distributed by the National Park Service.

Reptiles and Amphibians: Big Bend's herpetofauna includes 10 species of amphibians and 56 species of reptiles (30 snake species, 22 lizard species, and four turtle species). Look for the **Rio Grande leopard frog,** a slim, slimy, spotted green frog found in pools alongside the river and occasionally in springs and tinajas, or the uncommon **spiny softshell turtle,** found only in the Rio Grande. Naturally the park has horned lizards ("horny toads") in abundance (two species: the **Texas horned lizard,** found in grassy areas of the park's northernmost parts, and the **round-tailed horned lizard,** found in sparse desert flats, often near ant mounds).

Probably the most commonly seen snake is the harmless **coachwhip,** a long pink snake that slithers along very quickly. Most of the other 29 species found in the park are on the shy and secretive side, so you won't see many of them. Five are venomous: the **Trans-Pecos copperhead,** which is nocturnal and lives in cane patches along the river, occasionally seen in canyons; the mostly nocturnal, agressive **western diamondback rattlesnake,** frequents dry riverbeds, desert flats, grasslands, canyons—just about any rocky place below 4,500 feet; the **mottled rock rattlesnake,** which looks like mottled rock and prefers rocky terrain but is somewhat uncommon; the agressive **Mojave rattlesnake,** also rather uncommon, frequents hot desert flats, especially around creosote bush; and the most common Big Bend rattler, the black-tailed rattlesnake, found throughout the park but mostly in the Chisos Mountains and surrounding foothills. Visitors are very unlikely to be bitten by one of these venomous snakes, but the usual precautions should be followed (see "Snakebite Prevention and Treatment," p. 18).

Fish: Rio Grande fishing is said to be good, especially for anglers who like tasty **blue, channel,** and **flathead catfish.** Other fish large enough for the hook include **longnose gar, carp, smallmouth buffalo, river carpsucker,** and **freshwater drum.** Most other fish species in the Rio Grande and in river pools are minnow-like; some of the more Big Bend-specific fishes are the **Mexican stoneroller,** known only in this park and in Arizona's Rucker Canyon, the **Chihuahua shiner,** found only in the park and in a few locations in the Mexican state of Chihuahua, and the **Big Bend gambusia,** which is found only in a certain pond in the park's Rio Grande Village.

Insects and Arachnids: Yes, the park has **tarantulas,** commonly seen on roadways in the late summer and fall. These large, hirsute spiders have quite a movie reputation for mayhem but are not dangerous to humans in the least. If handled roughly, they may bite in self-defense, but they aren't poisonous. The **giant desert centipede** is another formidable-looking creature and is worth avoiding. Its poisonous bite is quite painful to humans but not lethal. This centipede

prefers darkness and is not commonly seen in daylight. **Millipedes** are often mistaken for centipedes, but their legs are more numerous and they are generally smaller than centipedes. They aren't poisonous and they don't bite. Big Bend harbors around a dozen species of **scorpions,** which inject venom by means of a stinger in their tails. None of the scorpions found in the park carry a sting that's lethal to humans (unless you happen to be allergic to scorpion stings). "Whip scorpions" or **vinegaroons** (named for the vinegar-like odor they emit as a defense mechanism) can reach six inches in length—they look nasty and their pinchers are larger than those of the scorpion, but they have no stinger. The vinegaroon is strictly nonpoisonous.

History

Prehistoric Inhabitants: Seventy-five million years ago Big Bend was inhabited only by dinosaurs, including the recently discovered petrosaur, a flying reptile with a 36-foot wingspan (greater than that of a small jet). Human habitation in the Big Bend area goes back about 12,000 years, starting with big-game hunters who preyed on mastodon, bison, camels, pronghorns, and horses. During this period, at the end of the Ice Age, the Big Bend country was lush with vegetation that thrived on the volcanic soils. As the Earth warmed and the glaciers receded, Big Bend began to dry up, the big-game species perished, and the hunters disappeared.

They were followed around 8,000 years ago by groups of nomadic Indians who were hunter-gatherers. Anthropological evidence shows that they hunted desert animals for meat and hides and ate all the classic desert plant foods—yucca, agave hearts, mesquite beans, and prickly pear cactus. They also crafted baskets, mats, sandals, and nets from desert plant fibers, particularly lechuguilla, just as the local Mexicans do today. These nomads later either disappeared or were supplanted by Patarabueyes Indians who built pueblos and farmed the alluvial plains to the west, near present-day Presidio, beginning around A.D. 1200.

Chisos and Chisos Apaches: These Puebloans were in the area when the Spanish arrived in the 1500s and named them La Junta Indians because the center of their culture was at the meeting *(la junta)* of the Rio Conchos and the Rio Grande. But neither the Spanish nor the La Junta had much interest in rugged Big Bend, which they called El Despoblado (The Unpeopled or Uninhabited). So the area was vacant when an Indian tribe from northcentral Mexico began spending their summers in Big Bend a few years later. These were the Chisos, who gave their name to Big Bend's highest mountain range (Chiso is derived from the Apache word *chishe,* which means "people of the forest"). The Spanish conquistadors eventually began kidnapping the Chisos and forcing them to work as slaves in their copper and silver mines, but the Chisos gathered their forces and were able to keep the Spaniards away from Big Bend following a great 1644 battle.

When the Comanches began persecuting the Apaches on the Great Plains to the north, groups of Apaches were forced into Texas. Like dominoes falling, many of the Chisos were then forced out of the Big Bend area by the Apaches. This was the same group of Apaches that came to be known as Mescaleros for their ritual and nutritional dependence on agave hearts or "mescal," but in this area they became known as Chisos Apaches (not to be confused with their predecessors, the Chisos). In their new West Texas homelands, the Mescaleros became fierce guerrilla fighters and supreme desert dwellers, holding off all intruders throughout the 18th century. That is, until the Comanches came to Texas on Spanish horses.

The greatest horsemen the world has ever known, the Comanches reigned over the south plains from Oklahoma to Texas like Hell's Angels on hooves and turned Big Bend into a crossroads for the notorious Comanche War Trail. For over a century they came down from the Llano Estacado through Persimmon Gap (now the park's north entrance) every September during the full moon, on their way to Mexico. They forded the Rio Grande at Paso Lajitas and then pillaged every village between there and Durango for whatever they needed. On the way back, they brought captive slaves and livestock northward through the Paso de Chisos, just west of Mariscal Canyon. This put them farther away from the Spanish garrison at Presidio to the east of Big Bend, which was an important consideration during the return trip when they were loaded down with slaves and pillaged goods. For decades after the last Comanches left Big Bend, their War Trail left a mile-wide scar on the land, scraped bare by horses' hooves. People who live in the area still call the September full moon a "Comanche Moon."

The Comanches forced the remaining Chisos Apaches deep into Big Bend's interior. In the late 1800s, the westward expansion of Anglo-American settlements put pressure on the Comanches and the raids stopped. The Chisos Apaches were invited to sign a peace treaty with the Mexican government. But when the last Chisos chief, Alsate, took his braves across the river for the signing of the treaty, the Mexicans got them drunk, manacled them, and forced them to march to Chihuahua, where some were killed and some were distributed among the Mexican *rurales* (roughly equivalent to the Texas Rangers) as household slaves. Mexican villagers say that Alsate's ghost still appears in the Sierra del Carmen on the Mexican side of Big Bend from time to time; others identify the mysterious Marfa lights with the last band of Chisos Apaches.

adobe ruins

BOB RACE

Cinnabar and Candlewax: With the Indian threat removed, Anglos finally began moving into the Big Bend area at the turn of the century. At first their only enterprises were sheep and cattle ranches, but when a red ore called "cinnabar" was discovered (it had long been used for pictographs and for war paint by the Indians), Big Bend changed almost overnight. When cinnabar is heated, it produces "quicksilver" or mercury vapor, which can be condensed and collected as liquid mercury. The towns of Terlingua and Study Butte grew up around the cinnabar mines, which were mostly owned by the Chisos Mining Company. For a time this outfit had the second-largest cinnabar mine in the world, producing 100,000 flasks over a 40-year period. Eventually the ore veins were exhausted and the 2,000 workers who lived in Terlingua and Study Butte drifted away around the start of WW II, leaving ghost towns behind.

Another local industry that was big for a while was the rendering of wax from the candelilla plant (a Big Bend succulent that coats itself with hard wax during the dry season). Candelilla wax was used in the U.S. for the production of candles, phonograph records, chewing gum, and polishes during the first half of the 20th century (in Mexico it still is). As the plant became scarcer because of all the wax factories at McKinney Springs and Glenn Springs, and as other methods of wax manufacture became more cost-effective, the candelilla industry waned. Today there are still a few Mexican wax camps along the Rio Grande where candelilla is processed using traditional methods (some of the plants used are gathered illegally in the park). But since the industry is now small-scale and rangers patrol the park for *candelilleras* (wax-makers) during the dry seasons, the plant is flourishing once again.

Park Establishment: Everett E. Townsend, a U.S. Customs inspector, Texas Ranger, and Brewster County Sheriff in the early 1900s, lobbied to set aside part of the Big Bend region as a park. The Texas Legislature responded to public pressure by establishing a Texas Canyons State Park in May 1933 which included the Santa Elena, Mariscal, and Boquillas canyons. A few months later, the Chisos Basin was added and the name was changed to Big Bend State Park. The Civilian Conservation Corps (CCC) developed trails and built stone cabins during the late '30s and early '40s. Meanwhile, concerned Texans began applying pressure in Washington to change Big Bend over to national park status. After the state agreed to donate another 286,000 hectares of land for the prospective park, the federal government made Big Bend the country's 27th national park in June 1944.

Park Access

Two highways lead into the park: US 385 from Marathon through Persimmon Gap to the north (along the old Comanche War Trail) and State 118 from Alpine, through Study Butte to the west. You can also drive to Big Bend via Marfa and Presidio on US 67 and FM 170, a particularly scenic drive; FM 170 then connects with State 118 at Study Butte. There is no public transport into the park, but buses are available between Alpine and Study Butte, at the west entrance; call (915) 424-3471 for current schedule and fare information.

The park headquarters is at Panther Junction in the north-central area of the park. The main visitor center is here, but there are also ranger stations at Castolon Valley in the southwest quarter of the park, at the Chisos Basin in the center, and at Rio Grande Village in the southeast. The visitor center is open daily 8-5. The park entrance fee is $5 per vehicle or $2 per person for cyclists and pedestrians. At the moment, this fee is collected only at Panther Junction, but there is a possibility that collection kiosks will be installed at the north and west entrances eventually (currently, local residents often drive through the park without paying). Payment of the entrance fee is valid for one week's visit.

U.S. residents who are 62 years or older are admitted free with a Golden Age Passport (which can be issued on the spot). Disabled U.S. residents can receive the same benefits with the Golden Access Passport. Children under 16 are also admitted free. Adults can purchase a Big Bend Park Pass for $15 that allows unlimited entry into the park for one calendar year.

BIG BEND ACCOMMODATIONS

Chisos Mountains Lodge

The park's only indoor accommodation originated as cabins for CCC workers in the '30s and early '40s. The lodge complex, located in the Chisos

Basin at 5,400 feet, now consists of a motel unit, a lodge, and several stone cabins, for a total of 34 guest rooms. Rooms in the lodge and motel units are $57 s, $62 d, while the stone cabins sleep three to six persons for $50 to $66. Reservations must be made well ahead of time and require payment for one night's lodging in advance. The Lodge Dining Room and Coffee Shop serve a variety of American and Mexican food and are open 7 a.m.-7:30 p.m. in the winter, 7 a.m.-8 p.m. in the summer. Lunch and dinner run $5-12, breakfast less.

For reservations, contact National Parks Concession, Inc. (tel. 915-477-2291), Chisos Mountains Lodge, Big Bend National Park, TX 79834.

Camping

There are three drive-in camping areas in the park. The **Chisos Basin Campground,** in The Basin a few hundred feet below the Chisos Mountains Lodge, has 63 sites suitable for tents and campers under 24 feet, along with flush toilets, running water, dump station, tables, and cooking grills. The fee is $5 per night per site.

Rio Grande Village in the park's southeast corner on the river has a 25-site RV park with full hookups (the only hookups in the park). A space costs $12 a night per vehicle with two persons, plus $1 for each additional person. Also at Rio Grande Village is a "Class A" campground with 100 sites, flush toilets, running water, tables, and grills ($5 per night per site). A "Class B" campground with pit toilets only (no tables or grills) is open only when the Class A campsites are full (Thanksgiving, Christmas, and spring break) and cost only $3 a night.

The **Cottonwood Campground** in Castolon Valley along the Rio Grande has 35 sites, pit toilets, water, tables, and grills; $3 per site per night.

Backcountry campsites are scattered throughout the park and offer no facilities other than a flat area for pitching tents. Backcountry permits are required for use of these sites and are available free from any ranger station.

Between Feb. 1 and April 15, a 14-day camping limit is in effect for the developed campgrounds (and RV park) at The Basin, Rio Grande Village, and Cottonwood Campgrounds. During the remainder of the year you may stay beyond 14 days with the day-to-day approval of park authorities.

All campgrounds and campsites in the park are assigned on a first-come, first-served basis. Outside the park, there are also campgrounds and RV parks in Terlingua, Study Butte, and Lajitas. See "Vicinity of Big Bend" for more information.

SUPPLIES AND SERVICES

The most complete facilities are to be found in The Basin, where there is a well-stocked grocery and sundries store (open 9-8:45 May 1-Oct. 1 or 9-5:30 Nov. 1-April 30), a gift shop with photographic supplies, crafts, postcards, and souvenirs, a restaurant, a post office, and a Western Union office (incoming wires only). The post office (open same hours as grocery store) will take poste restante letters under visitors' names addressed to Big Bend National Park, TX 79834.

A service station at Panther Junction offers gasoline, auto parts, and minor automotive repairs (open 7:30 a.m.-7 p.m. May 1-Oct. 31, 8-6 Nov. 1-April 30). Gas and oil are also sold at stores in Castolon (open 10-6) and Rio Grande Village (9-6 June 1-Feb. 28, 9-8 March 1-May 31), but not at The Basin. The nearest diesel pump is in Study Butte, 26 miles west of Panther Junction on State 118. The stores in Panther Junction, Castolon, and Rio Grande Village also sell groceries, ice, and camping supplies.

Hot showers and a coin-operated laundromat are available at Rio Grande Village. See "Vicinity of Big Bend" for facilities outside the park.

DRIVING IN THE PARK

The park has three kinds of roads suitable for motorcycles, automobiles, and trucks: paved roads, improved dirt roads, and backcountry dirt roads. An ordinary passenger car can handle the first two except during heavy rains when even improved dirt roads may turn to mud (in which case the park staff will close them to all traffic). The backcountry dirt roads are only suitable for high-clearance vehicles (four-wheel drive isn't necessarily required, but the vehicle chassis must be high enough to avoid the large rocks that are common along these roads). No off-road travel is allowed anywhere in the park, even on motorcycles. The maximum speed limit in the park is 45 mph, though on some roads it's much lower.

Most RVs can handle the paved and improved dirt roads, except that vehicles over 24 feet long should not use Basin Dr. due to tight switchbacks.

Scenic Drives

Recommended drives for the typical passenger car include the **Ross Maxwell Scenic Drive** (22 miles from Santa Elena Junction), **Rio Grande Village Drive** (20 miles from Panther Junction), **Maverick Drive** (13 miles from Santa Elena Junction), and **Basin Drive** (nine miles from Panther Junction). If you don't have time for all of these, the Ross Maxwell Scenic Dr., which leads west along the Chisos to the historic farming settlement of **Castolon Valley** and to the mouth of **Santa Elena Canyon** is the most scenic, offering plenty of mountain, canyon, and desert vistas along the way. Drive-in campgrounds are avail-

able at the ends of the Ross Maxwell Scenic Dr. (Cottonwood Campground), Rio Grande Village Dr. (Rio Grande Village Campground), and Basin Dr. (Basin Campground). Recreational vehicles over 24 feet long or autos towing trailers over 20 feet should not attempt to reach the Chisos Basin because of the steep and winding nature of Basin Drive.

High-clearance vehicles have an additional choice of four backcountry dirt roads: Old Ore Rd. (26.4 miles), Glenn Spring Rd. (15.6 miles), River Rd. (50.6 miles), and Paint Gap Rd. (3.9 miles). River Rd. is the most scenic, beginning at Castolon and proceeding along the bottom edge of the park to the Rio Grande Village Visitor Center. Along the way, you'll pass river vistas (though most of the road is a distance from the river), old ranches and mining camps, Mariscal Mountain,

arroyos, and salt cedar brakes, as well as 14 different designated backcountry campsites.

The *Road Guide to Paved and Improved Dirt Roads* and the *Road Guide to Backcountry Dirt Roads* are available at Panther Junction Park Headquarters. Each contains detailed route descriptions as well as suggested side trips.

Vehicle Precautions

Whatever type of vehicle you're driving, always be sure to start a drive off with a full tank of gas, since gas is only available at three widely separated points in the park: Panther Junction, Rio Grande Village, and Castolon (for more information, see "Supplies and Services" above). Also make sure to travel with a spare tire, jack, and plenty of water—for yourself as well as for the vehicle's radiator (if it has one), especially during the summer. For primitive road travel, you should also carry a tire pump, extra fan belts and radiator hoses, and a first-aid kit.

If you get stuck in sand, don't spin the wheels—this will only bury them more deeply. Instead, get out and deflate the tires to around 15 psi and then slowly accelerate out of the sand. If the vehicle breaks down or gets stuck so badly that you're unable to extricate it, stay with it until a park ranger or another traveler comes along. If you're anywhere near a telephone, call 477-2291 for towing service.

The park staff recommends that you always lock your vehicle when hiking and that you not leave valuables in sight; petty theft is a problem in the park, particularly along isolated dirt roads near the river.

BIG BEND HIKING AND BACKPACKING

Over 200 miles of developed trails are accessible in the park, with designated lengths from 50 yards to 33 miles, and a range of elevation from 1,800 feet (Boquillas Canyon) to 7,835 feet (Emory Peak in the Chisos). The highly informative *Hiker's Guide to Trails in Big Bend National Park*, published by the Big Bend Natural History Association and available at all visitor centers within the park, has details on 36 separate hikes. These are divided into eight self-guiding trails, 11 developed trails (including the High Chisos Complex,

which actually consists of six additional shorter routes), and 17 primitive routes. Each trail is further classified according to difficulty (easy walking, medium difficulty, strenuous day hike, and strenuous—backpackers only).

Prerequisites

Always carry plenty of water—a minimum of one gallon per person per full day of walking during hot weather, slightly less in winter. Although there are a few springs and tinajas in the park, the water level varies considerably and you shouldn't count on finding sources of water along the way. If you need drinking water from one of these sources, always boil it first for at least 10 minutes or treat it with iodine tablets or solution. Bring enough food for the duration of your hike.

Some of the shorter, easier hikes can be done in sneakers or street shoes, but for any serious hiking wear sturdy hiking boots. Lug soles are preferable, as they provide protection from sharp rocks and desert plants. Bring along a first-aid kit that includes an elastic bandage for sprains and snakebite treatment (see "Snakebite Prevention and Treatment" on p. 18 for more detail) and a pair of tweezers for removing thorns and cactus spines. Also bring a flashlight, compass, and for long hikes on primitive routes, a topographic map (available at the park headquarters).

Recommended Day Hikes

Santa Elena Canyon Trail (1.7 miles roundtrip): This trail begins where the Ross Maxwell Scenic Dr. ends at the junction of the Rio Grande and Terlingua Creek. To start the trail, you must wade across the creek (during periods of heavy rain, it may be too swift and too deep to cross). On the other side is a section of concrete steps that will take you up and over a rocky point and into the mouth of the canyon. From here the trail winds around several huge boulders until the canyon wall veers right into the Rio Grande. Though quite short, the canyon scenery is quite impressive, especially since this is one of the narrowest sections of Santa Elena Canyon. Easy, but some climbing involved.

Window Trail (5.6 miles roundtrip): Many repeat visitors say this is their favorite Big Bend hike because it covers such a variety of terrain and affords great valley and desert views. Starting at the Basin trailhead, the first section involves a rapid descent with distant views of "the Window" —a cleft in the mountain peaks surrounding Chisos Basin. As the trail drops from subalpine topography to canyon floor, piñon pines, oaks, sotol, and grasses give way to oaks, mesquite, prickly pear, and agave. After passing though wooded, spring-fed idylls the trail ends at a clearing where trail riders tie their horses, but you can continue hiking along rock steps to the Window itself. From the Window, a waterfall drops 200 feet to the desert floor below; a second cleft rock formation opposite the Window is known as "the Gunsight," and beyond to the west are the Christmas Mountains. This hike takes three to four hours roundtrip depending on pace and number of stops. The same trail can be done on horseback through the Chisos Remuda (see "Trail Riding" below).

Lost Mine Trail (4.6 miles roundtrip): This is an interpretative trail that heads west from Panther Pass, off Basin Drive. Elevation gain on the trail is about 1,250 feet, as it proceeds along the northern slope of Casa Grande, a volcanic block, to a ridge that divides the Pine and Juniper canyons. A good, fairly short trail for viewing typical Chisos Mountains flora and fauna—figure on about four hours roundtrip. A self-guiding booklet is available at the Panther Pass trailhead. Medium difficulty.

Pine Canyon Trail (4 miles round trip): This trail begins at the end of Pine Canyon Rd., a dirt road off Glenn Spring Rd., which is itself a dirt road off the paved Rio Grande Village Dr., about 10 miles from Panther Junction. Winding up through Pine Canyon, the trail is one of the park's prettiest, with stands of Mexican piñon, juniper, and oak. Higher up come ponderosa pine, bigtooth maple, Emory and Graves oaks, and Texas madrone. The trail ends at the bottom of a 200-foot cliff that supports a waterfall during the rainy season (July-September). There's a backcountry campsite near the mouth of the canyon. Medium difficulty.

South Rim Loop (13-14.5 miles roundtrip): South Rim refers to the southwestern edge of the Chisos Mountains, about 2,500 feet above the desert. This loop within the High Chisos Complex offers some of the most stupendous mountain views in the park, but you'll have to earn them through fairly challenging hiking. It can be done as a strenuous day hike, starting and finishing at

the Basin Trailhead, or you can take your time and camp along the way (there are 13 backcountry campsites along the South Rim alone, and over two dozen more throughout the Chisos trail complex). On the way up you can choose between the Pinnacles Trail (6.4 miles one way) or the Laguna Meadow Trail (6.5 miles one way). Pinnacles is the steeper of the two, so it is usually used for the descent from South Rim. Once you make the South Rim, you'll be able to see Mexican peaks that are 80 miles away or more, plus Emory Peak (the Chisoses' highest) and Santa Elena Canyon. To the east is the Sierra del Carmen range, which starts at the top of the park and crosses some 50 miles into Mexico. Take care descending on scenic Pinnacles, as it's easy to lose traction on the loose rubble. The High Chisos Complex connects with the Juniper Canyon Trail at Boot Canyon (4.5 miles from the Basin Trailhead) and there are backcountry campsites at the intersection of this trail and Outer Mountain Loop, 6.2 miles from Boot Canyon.

Emory Peak Trail (one mile from Pinnacles Pass or 4.5 miles from the Basin Trailhead): This one runs west off the Pinnacles Trail just beyond Pinnacles Pass. Not very difficult, except for the last 15-foot scramble up a sheer rock face. Naturally a great view, since this is the highest point in the park (elev. 7,835 feet). The equipment at the summit is part of Big Bend's solar-powered two-way radio system.

Blue Creek Trail (5.5 miles one way from the South Rim or 9 miles from the Basin Trailhead): Can be done from the Blue Creek Ranch Overlook, near Sotol Vista on the Ross Maxwell Scenic Dr. but that means a constant ascent for 5.5 miles. The least strenuous way to do (it's a strenuous hike either way) is to arrange to leave a vehicle parked at the Blue Creek Ranch Overlook and hike down to it from the South Rim. You'll pass through several different terrains, from high woodlands to sotol grasslands, oak and juniper canyon floor, and desert savanna. The desert part of the trail meanders through some of the park's most colorful volcanic formations (these could also be seen by hiking from the Blue Creek Ranch Overlook just 2.5 miles along the trail toward the Chisos). Originally developed as a sheepherding trail.

Chimneys Trail (4.8 miles roundtrip): This one

starts from the west side of Ross Maxwell Scenic Dr. about 1.2 miles south of the turnoff for Burro Mesa. It follows an old dirt track to a series of high rock outcroppings ("chimneys") to the west of Kit Mountain. Rare Indian petroglyphs (rock carvings) can be seen on the southernmost chimney. This track continues eastward another 4.6 miles past Peña Spring to the Chimneys West backcountry campsite at the base of Peña Mountain.

Backpacking

Preparation: To stay overnight at a backcountry campsite, you must obtain a Backcountry Use Permit in advance from one of the ranger stations or visitor center. If you're backpacking alone, you should fill out a Solo Hiker Form so that the rangers will know where to look if you don't come back when you predict you will. Topographic maps are highly recommended for backcountry hikes and can be purchased at the Panther Junction Visitor Center. During the colder months, a tent is a good idea. Other essential gear includes a compass, flashlight, knife, and first-aid kit. No open fires are allowed in the park, so bring a backpacking stove if you plan to cook. Pack out all trash (including cigarette butts—they take 10-12 years to decompose), bury human waste six inches down, and don't use soap in streams or springs.

Desert Sports (tel. 915-424-3366 or 800-523-8170), at Lajitas On The Rio Grande outside the park, sells camping, hiking, and back packing gear. Minimal camping supplies are also available at the Chisos Basin store.

Backcountry Trails

The following hikes involve primitive trails that either require overnight stops or aren't easily reached by the day hiker.

Cross Canyon Trail (14 miles from the Solis backcountry campsite): Solis is a put-in point for river runners below Mariscal Canyon. The trail starts west of the Solis campsite and leads west over limestone ridges and flats toward the eastern cliffs of Mariscal Mountain. At the cliffs, the trail climbs up and through a break, then follows along the summit ridge until it heads south into Mariscal Canyon, ending at the edge of the river. Directly across the river, you can see a Mexican wax camp. Out in the river is a set of boulders known as Tight Squeeze because of the difficulty boaters have navigating between them.

Outer Mountain Loop (31.6 miles): This loop comprises parts of the Dodson, Juniper Canyon, Pinnacles, Laguna Meadows, and Blue Creek trails. The trail can be done clockwise or counterclockwise beginning at any of three trailheads—the Blue Creek Ranch Overlook, The Basin, or Juniper Canyon. However you decide to go, this loop will take you through more different kinds of Big Bend terrain and biotic communities than any other hike. The route with the fewest elevation changes is from The Basin up to Laguna Meadow and the South Rim, then down Blue Creek Canyon Trail until it meets the Dodson Trail, then east on the Dodson to the Juniper Canyon Trail and up to Boot Spring, where you get the Pinnacles Trail down to The Basin. The Pinnacle-South Rim-Laguna Meadow sections of the loop are covered above under "Recommended Day Hikes."

The **Dodson Trail** itself is 11.5 miles long and crosses very rugged terrain with lots of ups and downs. The trail is not always distinct, so a 7.5-minute topo map is necessary if you're not familiar with the trail. From the Blue Creek Trail junction, the Dodson Trail is fairly easy to follow until you reach the junction for the Elephant Tusk Trail, about halfway. Keep an eye out for cairns that point the way, since several drainages break up the trail. At around mile 6 you should reach the remains of the Dodson Place, a ranch that operated between 1919 and 1943. A spring near the old ranch usually has water, but don't count on it and treat the water before drinking if you do find the spring flowing. After the Dodson Place, follow the trail as it parallels an old fence to the south. If you keep the fence on your right, you won't lose the trail as it intersects with several smaller trails. There are also rock cairns along this part of the trail.

The **Juniper Canyon Trail** is 6.2 miles from the Dodson Trail junction to Boot Canyon. There are two primitive campsites at the Dodson-Juniper Canyon Trail junction, as well as a primitive dirt road (Juniper Canyon Rd.) that leads southeast to the Glenn Spring Road. The trail is fairly level through Juniper Canyon until you reach Upper Juniper Spring where it climbs up and over a ridge into Boot Canyon.

Trail Riding

Only one outfit in the park is licensed to lead horseback trail rides through Big Bend National Park, **Chisos Remuda Saddle Horses.** They operate out of The Basin and lead trail rides through Oak Creek Canyon to the Window (three trips daily at 8 a.m., 1 p.m., and 4 p.m., $20 per person) and along the South Rim (one trip daily, leaving at 8 a.m. and returning at 4 p.m., $45 per person). Chisos Remuda provides horses, saddle equipment, and guides; you must bring your own food and water. In February, they lead the annual Big Bend Trail Ride, a four-day trip in which horses, tack, food, and wranglers are provided (personal saddle stock may also be brought along). This ride costs $300 if you bring your own beast, $400 if you ride one of theirs. For detailed information or reservations (required for all trail rides), call Lynn Carter at (915) 477-2374 or write Chisos Remuda, Big Bend National Park, TX 79834.

RIVER RUNNING

The segment of the Rio Grande that wraps around Big Bend wasn't successfully navigated until rather late in the 19th century, compared with other great western rivers, because it was initially considered impassable. Unlike the upper reaches of the Rio Grande near El Paso, which are fairly tame waters, the river here has gained volume and momentum after being joined by Mexico's Rio Conchos near Presidio, 55 miles west of the park. By the time the Rio Grande reaches the canyons of Big Bend, its currents are strong and deep. The Apaches especially feared the high narrow walls of Santa Elena Canyon, believing

that anyone who entered would never be seen again. In 1852, the Chandler-Green expedition released an empty boat at the entrance of Santa Elena; at the other end, nothing but splinters emerged. Several other adventurers tried to float the river in the latter half of the 19th century to no avail. Finally, in 1899, a well-equipped Dr. Robert Hill, with the aid of a local trapper who knew the canyons, completed a successful Rio Grande journey from Presidio to the mouth of the Pecos near Langtry (it took him a month).

Now, nearly a century later, anyone with determination and the assistance of local experts can float down 245 miles of well-preserved Rio Grande wilderness in a couple of weeks. The river forms the southern boundary of Big Bend National Park (as well as the international border between the U.S. and Mexico) for 118 miles, running through three major canyons—the Santa Elena, Mariscal, and Boquillas. The Park Service also has jurisdiction over an additional 127 miles of the river downstream from Boquillas designated as the **Rio Grande Wild and Scenic River.** This section runs through an area called the Lower Canyons that is popular among serious river runners (there are few take-outs along the 83 miles of canyons, so a week is usually necessary to complete this run). Above the park is the Colorado Canyon, with numerous, moderately easy rapids. Because of the impressive scenery and whitewater runs they offer, the individual canyons are the focus for most river trips, rather than the entire stretch.

Rio Grande rafting,
Big Bend National Park

Equipment

The Rio Grande can be navigated by canoe, kayak, or inflatable raft. Canoes should not be taken into the Colorado, Santa Elena, or Lower canyons, however, because they're unlikely to hold up in collisions with boulders and canyon walls. A sturdy inflatable raft, on the other hand, will bounce off walls and boulders and will stay afloat even if filled with water. Rafts should be made of heavy-duty neoprene or rubberized canvas. Whatever the craft, park regulations require that river runners carry one USCG-approved life jacket per person, one extra paddle or oar per boat, a boat-patching kit, a pump (for inflatable rafts and kayaks), a bailing bucket, and a campstove or fire pan if cooking is planned. Without these items, the park staff won't issue a river-use permit (free from ranger stations at Persimmon Gap, Panther Junction, Rio Grande Village, and in Lajitas at the Lajitas Museum). Additional gear recommended by the Park Service includes a throw line (a 60-foot length is suggested), cords for lashing gear to the craft, a bow or stern line (40-foot recommended), first-aid kit, tarp, trash bags, signal mirror, and flashlight. Plus enough food and water for the planned trip, of course, and some extra provisions for unplanned trip extensions.

Rafting equipment can be rented and supplies purchased at Lajitas Trading Post outside the park above Santa Elena in Lajitas (open 8 a.m.-9 p.m. daily, tel. 915-424-3234), or at Desert Sports (tel. 424-3366) at Lajitas On The Rio Grande. Motors may not be operated on most stretches of the river which are administered by the park. To learn the exact locations of these zones, and for further information on river-use regulations, call the clearing- house number for the Rio Grande Wild and Scenic River, tel. (915) 477-2251.

Other Considerations

When you pick up a river-use permit at one of the ranger stations, the rangers will apprise you of river conditions and can help with route planning if this is your first Big Bend river trip. For the novice river runner, water levels between one and four feet (measured in Boquillas Canyon) are navigable with the proper equipment, generally speaking. Levels over four or five feet shouldn't be attempted except by experienced whitewater rafters. During the rainy season, July to October, the river level can be quite high following heavy

rains—it's best to wait a few days until the level recedes to a depth you're capable of handling.

If you plan an overnight river run, be sure to set up camp well above the high-water mark due to the possibility of flash floods at any time of year. Stow gear that needs to remain dry (cameras, food, etc.) in watertight containers—ice chests work nicely. Don't attempt the challenging Santa Elena Canyon or Lower Canyons until you've successfully navigated Mariscal or Boquillas or both. If you see a section of white water or tight boulders ahead that look like more than you can handle, by all means carry the craft around if possible or lead it through from shore with a line.

One major logistical problem that must be worked out in advance is how you will get back to your vehicle once you reach the end of the run. It's best to have a companion drop you off at the start of the run and meet you at the take-out at a designated time. Or use two vehicles, one parked at the put-in and one at the take-out (keep in mind that theft is common along the river—leave no valuables in the vehicles). It's also possible to pay someone in Lajitas, Terlingua, or Study Butte to shuttle you back to your put-in—ask around (don't pay until they've picked you up, of course). **Big Bend Shuttle Service** (tel. 915-371-2523) in Terlingua is reliable.

If you are running the canyons for the first time, it's essential that you purchase the relevant copy or copies of the *River Guide* series from one of the ranger stations in the park. These thoroughly researched booklets contain detailed topographic maps that indicate river mileage, whitewater areas, navigation tips, and points of interest along the way.

Colorado Canyon

This canyon is actually west of the park boundary but is often run as a day trip because of its short duration and ease of navigation. Most people do a 10-mile run from the Rancheras Canyon put-in to the Teepees Roadside Park take-out (look for the picnic shelters built to resemble Indian teepees), which is near the boundary of Big Bend Ranch Natural Area—both are off FM 170 and easily reached by car.

The Colorado Canyon walls are of interest because they're entirely volcanic (unlike the three major park canyons, which contain layers of limestone). The Rancheras Rapids at the very beginning of the run in Rancheras Canyon are Class II rapids (easy rapids with waves up to three feet and wide clear channels) on the AWA's International Scale of Difficulty, as are the Closed Canyon, Quarter-Mile, and Panther rapids further on before the Teepees take-out. You could float all the way to Lajitas, a 21-mile trip, but once you're out of the Colorado Canyon the waters aren't very challenging until you reach the mouth of Fresno Creek (15 miles from Rancheras Canyon), where there are Class III rapids with high, irregular waves capable of swamping a canoe—it's a good idea to scout these from shore first.

Santa Elena Canyon

This is the classic Big Bend river run, and the most popular run among visitors who choose to take guided trips (see "Guided Raft Trips" below). However you go, once you're in this high-walled box, there's no turning back. The scenery is stupendous, ranging from feather-leafed salt cedar and river cane along sandy banks to 1,500-foot-high stone walls. For dedicated river runners, Santa Elena boasts the infamous Rock Slide, a series of swirling Class IV rapids that sling boats between, around, and against house-sized boulders. Not a canyon for novices.

The only put-in for Santa Elena is near where FM 170 breaks west from Lajitas on the way to Presidio. The put-in is directly opposite Paso Lajitas, a village on the Mexican side of the river. The usual take-out is 20 miles downriver at the mouth of the canyon, just past where Terlingua Creek feeds into the river. The run can be done in a day, but is perhaps better as an overnight trip. The first 11 miles pass through occasional minor rapids until the canyon entrance is reached, where a set of stiff rapids cuts back and forth with the river—kayakers have been known to get caught in rock undercuts along the base of the wall when the river level is down. Most overnighters camp on the left bank just before the river enters the canyon, since this is the approximate halfway point (this also gives you a whole day to run the canyon itself, in case you experience difficulties).

Two miles downstream from the entrance is the Rock Slide, with its tight squeezes, suck-holes, and Class IV rapids. The Rock Slide in Santa Elena has been responsible for more deaths, injuries, and other boating mishaps than any other feature in the Big Bend section of the river. So by all means pull over to the side and take some time

to scout the rapids first. If it looks too rough, you can skirt around them on the Texas side by portage and line, or, during times of extremely high water when the lower Texas side is flooded, portage over the higher Mexican side. If you decide to go for it, make sure your gear is tightly secured.

Two to three miles past the Rock Slide are two side canyons on the Mexican side of the river, Arch and Fern canyons. Organized raft trips sometimes stop for a short hike into narrow Fern Canyon, with its clear spring and atypical ferns growing from crevices. Another mile down on the right is a large dome-like cave variously known as Smuggler's, Sheep, or Cow cave. The canyon ends after another mile at Terlingua Creek.

Mariscal Canyon

The straight Mariscal Canyon run from the Talley put-in to the Solis take-out is only 10 miles, an easy day trip. Mariscal features the Rock Pile (not to be confused with Santa Elena's Rock Slide), about 100 yards from the canyon entrance, with Class II and III rapids. In another half mile or so is the Tight Squeeze, with Class III rapids that should be scouted first by first-timers (there is room for a landing on the right just before the rapids). Just over a mile later is another chute of Class II rapids. The rest of the canyon is peaceful floating, with good canyon scenery—look for great horned owls, canyon wrens, falcons.

The Mariscal run can be combined with the Vicente and Hot Springs Canyon downriver for a 32-mile desert and canyon trip that takes three or more days. There are virtually no rapids in these canyons but in between you'll pass Mexican villages and Tornillo Creek, site of the old Boquillas Hot Springs Resort.

Boquillas Canyon

The usual run through Boquillas Canyon is 33 miles between the put-in near Rio Grande Village and the take-out at La Linda, Mexico (the Mexican authorities allow river runners to drive vehicles across the bridge here for boat pick-ups and launches). Except for one chute at Arroyo del Veinte (Class II-III) about 3.5 miles before La Linda, there's usually no whitewater, but the scenery is quite good. Boquillas is more eroded than the other park canyons, so colors and shapes of rock formations are more complex. This trip takes at least two days—there are plenty of landings along the way for camping.

Lower Canyons

This trip is absolutely *not* for novice river runners, mainly because it's remote, long (83 miles), and requires extensive preparation. Even seasoned river rats should do this one first with someone who's done the Lower Canyons before. Or consider going with one of the river outfitters (see below). All of the land along this section of the river is privately owned—you're allowed to camp anywhere along the floodplain but go beyond and you're trespassing. The canyons and scenery are quite rugged (that's why it's called the Rio Grande Wild and Scenic River) and you're virtually guaranteed not to see other humans anywhere along the way.

The usual put-in is at La Linda (same as the take-out for the Boquillas Canyon run described above). Boats can be taken out at Dryden Crossing (a five-day trip), or, to run the total length of the Lower Canyons, you can float all the way to Foster's Ranch or Langtry, which will add two or three days to the trip. From La Linda, the Lower Canyons don't really begin for 29 miles; there are several springs near the riverbanks along this first stretch, including a couple of thermal springs, where you can collect drinking water. Just before the mouth of the first canyon (Big Canyon) is a set of Class II rapids. Once you pass through this entrance, you're walled in for the next 43 miles. At 41 miles (from La Linda) you'll hit Hot Springs Rapids (Class III-IV). After another seven miles are the Palmas Canyon Rapids (Class II-III). Then it's another four miles to the small Complejo del Caballo Rapids, and five more until the Class IV Upper Madison Falls, the most exciting of the Lower Canyons trip. Lower Madison Falls, two miles downriver, are Class III, followed by the Panther Rapids (Class II-III), the San Francisco Rapids (Class II-III), the Sanderson Rapids (Class I-II), and finally, just before Dryden Crossing, the anticlimactic Class II Agua Verde Rapids.

Guided Raft Trips

Visitors without previous whitewater rafting experience, and even experienced river runners who haven't done the Big Bend canyons before, might want to consider participating in a guided raft trip. Going with a licensed, experienced outfitter is safer the first time out since the pilots are expert navigators and know practically every inch of these canyons. They can also offer informed commentary about the environment along the

Fern Canyon, Big Bend National Park

way and answer questions about the river and about rafting techniques specific to Big Bend. An added advantage is that you can concentrate on enjoying the trip and let the outfitters worry about equipment details and navigation.

The longest-running outfitter is **Far Flung Adventures** (tel. 915-371-2489, Box 31, Terlingua, TX 79852) in Terlingua, to the west of the park off FM 170. They offer 11 different trips in all the canyons, ranging from a one-day Colorado Canyon trip for $65 per person to a seven-day Lower Canyons trip for $600. A two-day Santa Elena trip is $180 per person. FFA also runs occasional specialty raft trips that focus on music, gourmet cooking, photography, or whitewater rafting instruction. Groups of six or more can charter a raft and guide for nonscheduled trips. One-day trips include lunch, overnighters include all meals beginning with lunch on the first day through lunch on the last day. All gear except sleeping bags is provided, including watertight metal boxes for cameras and personal effects.

Another established local company is **Big Bend River Tours** (tel. 800-545-4240, Box 317, Lajitas, TX 79852), headquartered at the Lajitas On The Rio Grande complex in Lajitas. Their itineraries and rates are about the same as those of Far Flung Adventures.

MEXICAN BORDER VILLAGES

Two Mexican villages can easily be visited from the park or while river rafting, **Santa Eleña,** across the river from Castolon, and **Boquillas,** across from Rio Grande Village. Both are fairly typical representations of rural, rustic Mexico, with border overtones (neither has electricity, though Boquillas may soon be receiving power lines from the U.S. side). Rowboats ferry residents and visitors back and forth across the Rio Grande for $2 roundtrip (pay on the way back).

Boquillas is the most picturesque, with the Sierra del Carmen range as a backdrop. When you land on the Mexican side of the river, the locals will try to sell you a burro ride into the village, saying it's too far to walk, but it's really less than a mile (if you've never ridden a burro, though, here's your chance). Less expensive is the pick-up "taxi" service which costs $2 per person roundtrip. The main activity is sitting on the front porch of José Falcón's store, drinking cold *cerveza* with hot burritos. If you happen to be in the park on Christmas Eve, cross over to Boquillas to watch Las Posadas, a candlelight procession in which Mexican Catholics commemorate Joseph and Mary's search for lodging. The candles are made locally from the rendered wax of the *candelilla* plant.

Santa Elena is slightly larger than Boquillas and features a small town plaza, a schoolhouse, and a couple of churches. Two restaurants, **Enedinas** and **Maria Elena's,** serve simple border-style food. Mexican crafts can be purchased at either village.

A third village, Paso Lajitas, is easily reached from Lajitas on the U.S. side, just beyond the park's southwestern perimeter (see "Lajitas" below for details on this crossing). Another village farther into northern Mexico (about 17 miles south of the Rio Grande) that gringos sometimes visit is San Carlos. An island in the desert, San Carlos sits 2,000 feet above the Rio Grande in a green, spring-fed arroyo; temperatures tend to run 15 degrees cooler than the temps in Lajitas. Local guide Kiko Garcia leads all-day GMC Suburban trips to San Carlos from the Lajitas Trading Post for $50 per person (20% discount for seniors) including lunch every Sat., Sun., and Mon. at 10 a.m., returning at 6:30 p.m. In addition to cruising the town, Kiko leads a hike through Cañon de San Carlos that takes in a hot springs, a wax factory, and a 150-year-old aqueduct. After lunch the group goes to Cañon de las Pilas to cool off in a waterfall.

PARK INFORMATION

Naturalist Activities
The park staff at Big Bend arrange daily activities that include guided interpretive walks, slide presentations, and occasional special lectures. An up-to-date Naturalist Schedule is posted at all campground bulletin boards and is also available at ranger stations.

Seminars
The Big Bend Natural History Association sponsors annual seminars in the park from mid-April through late August on topics as varied as Trans-Pecos archaeology, mountain lion behavior and ecology, the history of early Big Bend river settlements, wildlife photography, and oil painting. Depending on the seminar, each of which generally lasts two to four days, class meetings may be held at campground amphitheaters, the Panther Junction Park Headquarters, or in the wilderness. Varying fees are charged for each seminar, but they include free camping at groups sites. For the latest schedule, write to the Seminar Coordinator, Big Bend Natural History Association, Box 68, Big Bend National Park, TX 79834.

Events
The parks sponsor an International Good Neighbor Day Festival during the third week of October. The festival is held at Rio Grande Village and features Mexican folk dance performances, Texas country dances, and *conjunto* music.

Publications
El Paisano, the "Official Big Bend National Park Newspaper," comes out quarterly and contains 12 pages of information on currently scheduled park

events, special naturalist features, general park information, and park news. It's distributed free at various points throughout the park. *Big Bend, Handbook No. 119* is a Park Service publication that serves as a combination guidebook and natural history text for the park (available for $5.95 at the Panther Junction Visitor Center). The Big Bend Natural History Association publishes a dozen or more free handouts on separate park topics, from mountain lions to wildflowers, that are available at any ranger station or at the visitor center.

General Information

For further information on park features, regulations, or activities, contact the Superintendent (tel. 915-477-2251), Big Bend National Park, TX 79834. The Big Bend Natural History Association, which produces most Big Bend National Park publications and organizes park seminars, can be contacted at Box 68, BBNP, TX 89834 (tel. 915-477-2236).

VICINITY OF BIG BEND NATIONAL PARK

The four counties in the crux of Big Bend's elbow— Brewster, Presidio, Jeff Davis, and Pecos—are known in Texas as "Big Bend Country." Geologically speaking, only Presidio, Jeff Davis, and the southern portion of Brewster share the Tertiary Volcanic Region that characterizes Big Bend National Park. The topography of north Brewster (including the Glass, Wood Hollow, and Tinaja mountains) and west Pecos (below the Stockton Plateau) are defined by the Marathon Uplift, an area of limestone and sandstone formations.

All four counties are sparsely populated. Brewster County is the largest in the state (6,169 square miles, larger than Connecticut and Rhode Island combined) but only has five towns and a total population of 8,681—a density of one person per square mile! Tourism, ranching, and farming are the main sources of income in Big Bend Country.

A good source of current information on Big Bend Country is the *Big Bend Quarterly* (published four times a year by Trans-Pecos Productions, Box 4124, Dallas, TX 79735, tel. 214-942-4905), which also carries features on the history and folklore of the region. The *BBQ* is distributed free at various locations throughout Big Bend or you can get a year's subscription for $8 by writing the above address.

LAJITAS

At the extreme southwest corner of Brewster County, wedged between the Presidio-Brewster county line and Big Bend National Park, is the ghost-town-turned-desert-resort of Lajitas. In the 18th and 19th centuries, the Rio Grande crossing here was popular among Indians and traders. In the early 1900s, Gen. "Blackjack" Pershing established a cavalry outpost to deal with bandito-revolutionary Pancho Villa, who used this crossing for raids on local villages.

Lajitas Trading Post

Since the 1880s, the social center for Lajitas has been the Lajitas Trading Post, which still operates out of the same adobe building but is now somewhat dwarfed by the Lajitas On The Rio Grande resort that has grown around it. For such a small establishment, the trading post sells an amazing variety of farm and ranch supplies, food, and recreational gear. A goat pen out front contains Clay Henry, the famous beer-drinking goat (several other goats in the pen have taken up the custom as well). Mexicans still cross the river from nearby Paso Lajitas to trade here. Occasionally the store holds *conjunto* dances on Saturday nights.

Lajitas On The Rio Grande

This desert resort started out as the Cavalry Post Motel (built on the foundations of Pershing's former post) and has grown to include additional lodgings, tennis courts, a nine-hole golf course, a 4,700-foot airstrip, and various other enterprises catering to Big Bend tourists (gift shops, Big Bend River Tours, Desert Sports, and Lajitas Stables). Staying here is not for everyone, as it's really a pre-fab Big Bend experience, but some people may prefer the resort to "roughing it" in the park itself.

A real estate office in the complex is busy buying up the surrounding desert and reselling it at a premium (most of the resort is owned by

Houstonian Walter Mischer and his Mischer Corporation).

Barton Warnock Environmental Education Center

Near the entrance to Lajitas on FM 170, toward Terlingua, is a hacienda-style building that contains a regional museum. Exhibits include archaeological and geological displays, photography, and local natural history. The building also houses a gift shop with books and souvenirs, and a small research library. Outside is a four-acre desert garden that showcases Chihuahuan Desert flora as well as fauna (javelinas, burros, tortoises). The facility is open daily 8-5. Admission is $2.50 for adults, $1.50 for children under 12, free for children under six. The Center also provides information as well as permits for Big Bend Ranch State Natural Area.

Paso Lajitas

Just across the Rio Grande from Lajitas is the Mexican village of Paso Lajitas. Boatmen waiting at the shore will take visitors across for $1 roundtrip (you pay on the way back). There's not much to do in Paso Lajitas except drink beer and eat good border-style food at **Garcia's** or **Dos Amigos**.

Accommodations And Food

Lajitas On The Rio Grande (tel. 915-424-3471, 800-527-4078) offers four basic lodging choices, the **Badlands Hotel** (17 rooms, old west theme), **La Cuesta** (18 rooms, mission style), **Officers Quarters** (20 rooms, frontier fort theme), and the original **Cavalry Post** (26 rooms, early American). Rates are the same in all four hotels/motels—from $59 s, $65 d. Condos are also available at $100 for a one-bedroom, $158 for a two-bedroom.

Also on the grounds is the **Lajitas RV Park** which offers full hookups for $11 a night. Tentsites are available for $8 a night. Discounts for weekly and monthly stays.

The restaurant in the Lajitas resort is not bad and is moderately priced. You can buy homemade tamales at Lajitas Trading Post, as well as a few grocery items.

Events

Comanche Moon, the September full moon when the Comanches used to ride down the War Trail through Lajitas into Mexico, is celebrated with some fervor in these parts. Check the *Lajitas Sun,* published monthly and distributed free in Lajitas, Terlingua, and in Big Bend National Park, for scheduled activities.

The **Chihuahuan Desert Challenge**, an international-class, off-road bicycle race, is held yearly in mid-February. The race's 34- and 70-mile loops are usually charted in the Big Bend Ranch State Natural Area. For information contact Desert Sports (P.O. Box 584, Terlingua, TX 79852, tel. 915-424-3366 or 800-523-8170) in Lajitas.

Recreation

Lajitas On The Rio Grande has tennis courts and a golf course available to non-guests for user

---

TEXAS MOUNTAIN RANGES

Texas has 18 major mountain ranges, all of them found in the Basin and Range region of West Texas. They can be divided into four main groups: the Permian Ranges, the Western Front Ranges, the Eastern Front Ranges, and the Volcanic Region. The list below enumerates the highest peaks in each range.

Permian Ranges
Guadalupe Peak 8,751 feet: Guadalupe Mtns.
North Franklin Peak 7,192 feet: Franklin Mtns.
San Antonio 7,031 feet: Cornudas Mtns.
Cerro Alto 6,717 feet: Hueco Mtns.

Western Front Ranges
Eagle Peak, 7,496 feet: Eagle Mtns.
Quitman Peak, 6,505 feet: Quitman Mtns.
High Lonesome, 5,612 feet: Van Horn Mtns.
Squaw Peak, 5,435 feet: Indio Mtns.

Eastern Front Ranges
Bird Peak 6,140 feet: Altuda Mtns.
Cathedral Peak 5,938 feet: Glass Mtns.
Sue Peak 5,854 feet: Sierra del Carmen
Cupola 3,988 feet: Serrania Highlands

Volcanic Region
Emory Peak 7,835 feet: Chisos Mtns.
Chinati Peak 7,721 feet: Chinati Mtns.
Sawtooth 7,719 feet: Davis Mtns.
Capote Peak 6,208 feet: Sierra Vieja
Needle Peak 5,193 feet: Solitario Mtns.
La Mota 5,037 feet: Bofecillos Plateau

Rio Grande rapids,
Santa Elena Canyon

fees. The **Lajitas Stables** (tel. 915-424-3238), across from the Lajitas Airfield, offers trail rides that vary in length from one hour ($14) to all day ($60). Those who don't like to straddle horses but who would like to see the desert can take buck-board rides ($7 one hour, $12 two hours, $20 four hours) instead. Overnight trips can also be ar-ranged.

Big Bend River Tours tel. (800-545-4240) is a licensed river outfitter that does raft trips along the Rio Grande through the canyons of Big Bend National Park and beyond. See "Guided Raft Trips," p. 130 for more information.

Desert Sports (tel. 915-424-3366), also in the LOTRG complex, rents mountain bikes ($15 half day, $25 all day) and canoes ($40-45 a day). This shop sells an array of backpacking, biking, and river-running gear, and is affiliated with the Chihuahuan Desert Challenge mountain-bike race. They also offer mountain bike tours to San Carlos, Mexico, sometimes combined with river rafting.

Desert Walker (tel. 371-2533) is a small outfit that leads Big Bend hikes that emphasize the natural and human history of the area. Rates average $45 for a half-day hike, $75 for a full day, but discounts are available for groups.

TERLINGUA

Terlingua, a few miles west of Big Bend on FM 170, was the center of the Big Bend quicksilver mining industry between the late 1800s and mid-

1900s. When the cinnabar ore was played out around the start of WW II, the miners' adobe shacks were abandoned and Terlingua became a ghost town almost overnight. It's still called a ghost town by the media, but the truth is that a small number of people began living and working here again in the 1960s, drawn this time by the beauty of the Chihuahuan Desert and the thrills of river running.

The official year-round population here is only 25 (but they have their own post office); that num-ber swells to over 7,000 during the Terlingua Chili Cook-offs in November (see "Events" below). The nonprofit Terlingua Foundation is trying to preserve a bit of Terlingua's history and has re-stored some of the old miners' shacks and the original storefronts.

Accommodations And Food

Terlingua has nothing on quite so grand a scale as Lajitas On The Rio Grande (yet), but it does offer a couple of choices: **Easter Egg Valley Motel** (tel. 915-371-2430) and **Terlingua Ranch** (tel. 371-2416) have basic rooms for $40-50 a night.

Big Bend Travel Park (tel. 371-2250), next to the famous La Kiva restaurant/bar, has 50 RV spaces with full hookups for $10 a night. Tentsites are also available here for $2 per person. **BJ's RV Park** (tel. 371-2259) nearby on FM 170 is similar.

Terlingua has only two eateries. **La Kiva** (tel. 371-2250) is more of a nightspot, with excellent margaritas, barbecued chicken, steak, and plenty of atmosphere—it's built into the side of a hill and the bar stools are tree trunks. **Desert Deli & Diner** (tel. 371-2305), off FM 170 next to Terlingua Trading Co. and Far Flung Adventures, is good any time of day, but especially for breakfast and lunch—breakfast burritos, frito pie, and chili are house specialties, with "blue-plate specials" at night. Prices are low, and the picture window at one end provides a Chisos view. Best of all, they open at 7 a.m. (Tue.-Sat.), so you can have breakfast here before starting on a Santa Elena Canyon raft trip from Lajitas.

Events

If you've ever heard of Terlingua before, it's probably because of the annual **World Championship Chili Cook-off** that was first held here in 1967. Frank X. Tolbert and Wick Fowler, two renowned Texas chili experts, competed that year against a New England journalist who claimed he could make better chili than any Texan (and since chili is the national dish of Texas, the challenge had to be met). No one won that first competition, but every year since then chili chefs, chili-eaters, spectators, and assorted hell-raisers from around the world have gathered here to practice chili voodoo.

Several years ago, Fowler and Tolbert had a difference of opinion with the Chili Appreciation Society International (CASI) regarding commercial sponsorship. Tolbert, the purist, stayed in Terlingua in behind the Terlingua Store off FM 170, and that event is officially called **Viva Terlingua.** Viva Terlingua attracts fewer chili chefs than **Arriba Terlingua,** which is the CASI wing that took its cook-off down the road to Villa de la Mina (a large property-owners development). The Arriba event attracts more tourists. Both events can get pretty rowdy, but Arriba has the rowdier edge.

Both cook-offs are held the first weekend in November. It's best to arrive a few days early since campgrounds and motels in Terlingua, Lajitas, and Study Butte fill up fast that weekend. If you want to avoid the crowds altogether, leave town before that weekend (as many locals do).

On the first weekend of February, local residents have their own "Cookie Chill-Off" to lampoon the chili cook-offs and to raise money for the Terlingua Foundation. It's a semi-serious contest, though—a no-bake dessert competition held in the old ghost town area off FM 170.

Recreation

Far Flung Adventures (tel. 915-371-2489) is the oldest, most established river outfitter in the Big Bend area. They organize raft trips down the Rio Grande (see "Guided Raft Trips," p. 131 for details) as well as in Arizona, New Mexico, Colorado, and Mexico. Their head office is located next to Terlingua Trading Co., just north of FM 170. The hand-drawn map of the Rio Grande on one of the office walls is worth a special trip for those seeking detailed rafting info—it's the best around.

Far Flung also arranges monthly pack-horse trips into Mexico's unspoiled Sierra del Carmen with local outfitter and BBNP river ranger Marcos Paredes. The five-day trip climbs to nearly 10,000 feet with stops at various canyons and mountain ridges along the way. The cost is $600 per person including transport, saddle stock, pack animals, meals, and guide services. Call or write Far Flung for their current schedule; the Sierra del Carmen trips don't operate Dec.-Feb. because of the risk of snowstorms.

Guided Hikes

An outfit called **Desert Walker** (tel. 915-371-2364 or 800-545-4240) in Terlingua offers half-day and full-day guided hikes for individuals and groups. Rates vary from $25 per person for a half-day hike (five-person minimum) to $225 per person (up to seven persons) for a two-day, one-night trip that includes a hike over Mesa de Anguila and a raft trip through Santa Elena Canyon (see "River Running," p. 128 for more on raft trips).

Shopping

The **Terlingua Trading Co.** (tel. 371-2234) , in the original Chisos Mining Co. building off FM 170, sells souvenirs and crafts. In the back of the store is **Quicksilver Jewelry Gallery,** which offers better-than-average Indian and Mexican jewelry. Another room off the main store contains an excellent selection of books on Texana, Mexican, and Southwestern cooking, geology, geography, natural and regional history, Native American and Mexican cultures, and art.

Entertainment

Next to Far Flung Adventures and the Terlingua Trading Co., the recently restored **Starlight Theater** hosts live music on weekends. The Desert

Deli and Diner also has a tiny stage where local musicians sometimes perform.

Post Office

Outside of Big Bend's Chisos Basin, the only post office for at least 50 miles in any direction (there are no post offices in Study Butte or Lajitas) is in Terlingua, right on FM 170. Hours are Mon.-Fri. 8-1 and 2-4:30.

STUDY BUTTE

Pronounced Stoody Beaut, since the man it's named for was miner Will Study and that's how he said his name, this former ghost town is located at the junction of State 118 and FM 170, near the west entrance to Big Bend National Park. The town (just a group of buildings without a post office) is well-located for park visits, but traffic in and out of the park detracts.

Accommodations And Food

Big Bend Motor Inn (915-371-2218) on State 118 at the FM 170 junction is a modern sort of place with rooms for $58 s, $63 d; efficiencies cost $65 s, $70 d.. They've also got an RV park. A bit farther north on State 118 is the lower-priced **Mission Lodge** (tel. 371-2555, under the same management as Big Bend Motor Inn), where rooms are $47 s, $53 d a night. The Study Butte Store sells groceries (as well as gasoline, diesel, and propane). **Boatman's Bar And Grill** on State 118 near the park entrance, is a small, quirky place that's open daily 5 p.m.-midnight and offers burgers, chili, and occasional live music.

BIG BEND RANCH STATE NATURAL AREA

This recent acquisition (1989) by the Texas Parks and Wildlife Dept. has doubled the size of the state park system. Those who have seen it say it rivals Big Bend National Park for raw scenery and has several geographical features that the national park doesn't have. One is the **Solitario,** a huge laccolith with a diameter of nine miles. It was formed by a subterranean magma fount that lifted the limestone bedrock like a giant blister and then collapsed, leaving a ragged series of concentric circular mountain ranges. From the air, the Solitario looks like a pond that froze just as a thrown

stone sent ripples through the water.

The other principal feature of the 265,000-acre park is the **Bofecillos Mountains,** a result of the same volcanic forces that shaped the Chisos and the Davis mountains. The Bofecillos top out at about 5,000 feet and are honeycombed with canyons and caves. Fresno Canyon's Arroyo Segundo contains the 100-foot Mexicano Falls, one of the three highest in the state. The second highest, the Madrid Falls, is also in Fresno Canyon, at Arroyo Primero. Many of the caves feature Indian pictographs, as well as a diversity of bat species that is reportedly unparalleled anywhere in the world.

Until it was sold to the TP&W Dept., Big Bend Ranch was operated by the Diamond A Cattle Co. and was owned by the chairman of the Atlantic Richfield oil company. For more information, contact Texas Parks and Wildlife Dept. (tel. 512-389-4890), 4200 Smith School Road, Austin, TX 78744.

Planned recreational use at BBRSNA is still under state review. At present, several kinds of visitor activities are permitted in the area, including rafting, hiking, camping, and bus tours. A drive along the River Road from Lajitas to Presidio, which requires no special permits or fees (see "Presidio" below), is probably the best introduction to the area's stunning topography. Primitive camping is permitted at Madera Canyon on the Rio Grande, and rafts or canoes can put in at three points along the river for the Colorado Canyon run.

Hikers can choose among three trails open to the public: the Rancherías Loop Trail (21 miles, overnight camping permitted); Rancherías Canyon Trail (9.5 miles); and Closed Canyon Trail (0.7 mile). All are accessible from FM 170; hikers must possess valid backcountry use permits ($2 per person for 24 hours), available at Fort Leaton (Presidio) or the Barton Warnock Environmental Education Center (Lajitas). You can also obtain a good topographical map–along with a compass, a necessity for hiking the longer trails–at these facilities.

Park and Wildlife officials lead twice-monthly interpretive bus tours of BBRSNA. On the first Saturday of the month, the bus leaves from Fort Leaton (tel. 915-229-3613) at 8 a.m., returning at 5 p.m., and on the third Saturday it leaves from the Warnock Center (tel. 424-3327) at 8 a.m., returning at 5:30 p.m. The bus route extends well into the interior of the park, stopping at the Fresno

Canyon Overlook for a view of Solitario. The cost is $30 per person, which includes roundtrip transport from Fort Leaton or the Warnock Center, guide service, and a chuckwagon lunch at the Saucedo Complex (a visitor center in the center of the park). To qualify for the tour, however, you must hold a Conservation Passport, issued by the Texas Parks and Wildlife for $25 per year and available at any state park facility. These tours are very popular, so reservations should be made far in advance; for a current schedule, write or call Big Bend Ranch State Natural Area, HCR 70, Box 375, Terlingua, TX 79853 (tel. 915-424-3327)

PRESIDIO

Unless you were a frontier fort or La Junta aficionado (see "Fort Leaton State Historic Site" below), the only reason to come to Presidio in the past was to drive the spectacular **River Road** along the Rio Grande between Lajitas and Presidio. Now that the state has established the Big

Fort Leaton, Presidio

Bend Ranch State Natural Area (see above), the Lajitas-Presidio trip is likely to become more alluring to travelers.

The town itself is over 300 years old, having been founded (along with Ojinaga across the river in Mexico) by the Spanish in the 1600s. The original name for the settlement was Nuevo Real Presidio de Nuestra Señora de Betleña y Santiago de Las Amarillas de La Junta de Los Rios Norte y Conchos—"New Royal Presidio [Garrison] of Our Lady of Bethlehem and St. James on the Banks of the Junction of the Rios Grande and Conchos." On the American side, this was later shortened to Presidio del Norte and finally Presidio.

The surrounding floodplains are extremely fertile and are the oldest continually cultivated farmlands in North America. The Patarabueyes Indians, about whom little is known except that they seem to have been a Pueblo Indian group, farmed this land as long ago as A.D. 1200. When the Spanish arrived here in the early 1500s, they were astonished by these "advanced" Indians who lived in adobe houses and cultivated their own food. By the late 1600s, the Patarabueyes had been missionized and, due to Spanish mistreatment and Mescalero Apache pressure, they disappeared by the 19th century.

Today Presidio is primarily known as the hottest town in Texas. Visit in midsummer, and you'll be able to confirm this (the *average* high temperature in June is 103° F—and it's sometimes hotter). The population of 1,800 are predominantly Mexicans and Chicanos who speak a Chihuahuan-inflected Spanish; the town newspaper *(Presidio Paper)* is bilingual and is priced in both US cents and Mexican pesos. The surrounding area is famed for its sweet onions and cantaloupes. A sign on the eastern outskirts of town reads "Welcome to the Presidio—Gateway to the Interior of Mexico and Onion Capital of the World." Local *botánicas* sell traditional herbal medicine made from desert plants.

Fort Leaton State Historic Site

Fort Leaton started out as a trading post for trader Ben Leaton, an American who had formerly been employed as an Indian scalp hunter for the Mexican government. Leaton built his private adobe fortress in 1848 on the site of an earlier Spanish settlement, El Fortín de San José, that had been built in the 1770s and abandoned in 1810. In

BIG BEND RANCH
STATE NATURAL AREA

© MOON PUBLICATIONS, INC.

spite of his former occupation, Leaton traded with the local Apaches and Comanches and is said to have encouraged Indian raids on Mexican villages (which is why local Hispanic residents still refuse to call the settlement Fort Leaton, referring to it instead as El Fortín). His business also benefited from being on the San Antonio-Chihuahua Trail, which extended 800 miles from Chihuahua, Mexico, to Indianola on the Texas Gulf Coast.

Leaton died in 1851, the adobe fort passed through various hands, and the Texas Parks and Wildlife Dept. acquired the property in 1968. It has been fully restored and now contains excellent exhibits on the area's history, including displays concerning the Patarabueyes Indians. A shaded, sometimes breezy picnic area adjoins the grounds. Open daily 8-4:30. Admission is $1 for adults, 50 cents children.

El Camino Del Rio (River Road)

Farm Road 170 between Presidio and Lajitas (50 miles) parallels a trail used by Spanish explorers over three centuries ago. The San Antonio-Chihuahua Trail passed along here as well until the railroads came through in the 1880s; in the early 1900s Pancho Villa reactivated the trail for his mule trains during the Mexican Revolution. During this era, the road earned the name Muerte del Burro ("Donkey's Death"); only paved 35 years ago, the road still boasts a couple of 15% grades. The scenery along the eastern half of the road is excellent, as the road winds up, down, and around the volcanic and limestone rock formations of the Bofecillos Mountains, with views of the Rio Grande below. West of the mountains, the road passes through the farming community of **Redford** (pop. 107), a collection of adobe houses, a church, and two stores (the Madrid Store and Cordera), where gas and food are available.

Ojinaga

This Mexican city of 45,000 people is only 142 miles from Chihuahua, capital of the Mexican state of the same name. Although there's not much to do in Ojinaga, it makes a convenient gateway for trips on the famous Chihuahua al Pacifico train, a spur of which runs between Ojinaga and Chihuahua. The Ojinaga train takes eight hours to reach Chihuahua, however, and the scenery along that section is rather monotonous—better to take the bus to Chihuahua (three hours), then the main trunk line to Los Mochis. This section runs through the scenic Copper Canyon area (home of the Tarahumara Indians) on the way southwest to the Pacific coast, an overnight trip.

Accommodations And Food

Balia Inn (tel. 915-229-3611) is on the north edge of Presidio off US 67 on the way to Marfa. Clean, basic rooms are $22. The Balia Inn has a popular coffee shop that serves steaks and good Tex-Mex food. In the center of town off FM 170 is **La Pampas,** a Mexican restaurant that also serves a few Argentine dishes. **La Frontera** is also good for Mexican.

Transport

A group of Big Bend and Dallas investors recently bought the rights to a railway route that runs from Dallas's Union Station to Presidio via Fort Stockton and Alpine. They've also purchased several Pullman cars and have plans to launch a regular passenger service within the next two years. If the project reaches fruition, this will not only provide a transport alternative between the Dallas-Fort Worth and Big Bend areas, it will also create an important U.S. rail link with the Copper Canyon train from Chihuahua, Mexico.

MARFA

This is the Presidio County seat (pop. 2,466) but for most Texans it's famous for just two things: the filming of the James Dean, Elizabeth Taylor, Rock Hudson epic *Giant* and the Marfa Lights (nine times out of 10 when you read about the Marfa Lights in the press, it's "the mysterious Marfa Lights"). The town is the second highest in the state (after Fort Davis), with an elevation of 4,688 feet, and is a mecca for glider pilots since the air currents are perfect for long sailplane flights.

The local economy rests on cattle, goat, and sheep ranching, so Marfa (named for a heroine in a Russian novel) has a real "ranch town" feel. Wander some of the side streets for a look at the tidy adobe and wood-frame houses.

Downtown

Highland Ave. is Marfa's main thoroughfare, where you'll find the **El Paisano Hotel,** a refurbished 1929 hotel listed on the National Register of Historic Places. El Paisano has become something of a shrine for James Dean fanatics, not because he stayed here (he didn't) during the filming of his last movie, *Giant,* but because a glass case in the lobby contains autographed pictures of each of the major cast members (including Dennis Hopper, Carroll Baker, and Chill Wills) and newspaper clippings about the production. The 1955 movie was actually filmed on a ranch west of Marfa. The crew stayed at El Paisano, but Jimmy, Rock, and Liz stayed at rented private homes in town. Tangentially, Marfa was the script setting for the 1983 motion picture *Come Back to the Five and Dime, Jimmy Dean, Jimmy Dean* (starring Sandy Dennis, Karen Black, and Cher), a movie about the effect the *Giant* production had on a group of Marfa residents.

More architecturally impressive is the 1886 Presidio County Courthouse at the end of Highland Avenue. There's a good view of the surrounding countryside from its Renaissance-style dome (open to the public during office hours).

Marfa Lights

Nobody can figure out the source of these lights (theories include UFOs, Indian ghosts, atmospheric reflections), but most nights you can easily see them from the Official Marfa Lights Viewing Site (complete with bronze state plaque) off US 90, nine miles east of town. The first historic reports of the "ghost lights" began in the 1800s, which is why some people dismiss the common theory that they're headlights from vehicles farther down US 90 or nearby US 67 that are reflected off atmospheric inversion layers.

A 50-page booklet on the phenomena, *Marfa Lights,* can be ordered from Ocotillo Enterprises, P.O. Box 195, Alpine, TX, 79831.

The Chinati Foundation

The Chinati Foundation is a nonprofit organization centered in Marfa that sponsors Big Bend Country artists. Exhibits are on display in a former mohair and wool warehouse on Highland St., including a permanent exhibit of John Chamberlain sculpture. At the site of now-defunct Fort Russell, south of Marfa off US 67 near Border Patrol

Headquarters, is a collection of concrete sculpture by renowned sculptor Donald Judd. Additional aluminum pieces can be seen in the former gun sheds at the old fort.

Accommodations And Food

Not many people elect to stay the night in Marfa, since it's so close to the Davis Mountains to the north and Big Bend to the south, the usual destinations for visitors to this part of Texas. The **Lash-Up Bed & Breakfast** (tel. 915-729-4487) at 215 N. Austin, a block from the County Courthouse, is a two-story 1909-vintage house with four country-decorated bedrooms for $50 per room per night, including a full breakfast (lunch and dinner available on request). **El Paisano Hotel** is used as a time-share now, but when suites are unoccupied they will occasionally take walk-in guests. The **Thunderbird Hotel** and **Holiday Capri Inn** (tel. 729-4391) on W. US 90 share the same management and offer basic motel rooms for $33 s, $39 d.

Apache Pines RV Park (tel. 729-4326, W. US 90), **Corder Trailer Park** (tel. 729-4576, 816 N. Hill), and **Marfa Overnight Trailer Park** (tel. 729-4405, S. US 67) have trailer slots for $10-12 a night.

Mando's on W. US 90 just outside Marfa is famed for miles around for its enchiladas. Beer can be consumed on the premises if you bring your own.

Outside Marfa

Ranch Road 2810 south from Marfa to Riudosa on the Mexican border passes through secluded ranch country with glimpses of burgeoning pronghorn antelope and mule deer herds. While there's nothing to see in Riudosa, this road connects with FM 170 to Presidio and Lajitas.

ALPINE

Alpine is the Brewster County seat and the largest town in the tri-county area (pop. 5,637). At an elevation of 4,481 feet, it's not exactly in the mountains but is set in a geological cul-de-sac formed by the Altuda Mountains and the Paisano Plateau. The town developed as the intersection between two rail lines, the Southern Pacific and the Atchison, Topeka, and Santa Fe. More important nowadays is the fact that it's the home of Sul Ross State University, the only institute of higher education in Big Bend Country.

Sul Ross State University

Located on US 90 east of town, Sul Ross is reputed to have one of the best range science departments in the country; even the liberal arts departments specialize in what might be termed "West Texas Studies." The National Intercollegiate Rodeo Association (NIRA) was founded at Sul Ross in 1948 and the university rodeo team is one of the nation's top collegiate competitors. The NIRA championship is held in the Sul Ross Range Science Arena each October.

Also on campus is the **Museum of the Big Bend** (tel. 915-837-8143), which features exhibits that chronicle Big Bend history from the early Indian settlements and Spanish exploration through the development of American ranching in the area. Open Tues.-Sat. 9-5, Sun. 1-5, free admission.

In March, the university sponsors a Cowboy Poetry Gathering in which cowboy poets from California to New York (and some from Canada, too) meet for a long weekend of lectures and readings. Cowboy poetry was a dying art, but a recent revival of interest in western lyricism has brought it back from the brink of extinction.

Woodward Agate Ranch

This 4,000-acre ranch is a favorite haunt for rockhunters. For 35 cents a gram, you can collect all the rock specimens you can carry (over 70 varieties are available, including pom pom agate, red plume, opal, and amethyst). The ranch also has a store where rocks can be purchased for $1.25 a gram.

The ranch, about 15 miles south off State 118 toward Big Bend, is always open since there're also a campground and RV park here. Call (915) 364-2271 for more information.

Hotels And Food

As with Marfa, most visitors to Big Bend Country pass through Alpine with plans to stay somewhere in the Davis Mountains or closer to Big Bend National Park. The **Highland Inn** (tel. 915-837-5811) costs $31 s, $33 d per night and has a pool. Other motels in Alpine include the **Bien Venido** (tel. 837-3454), **Comfort Inn** (tel. 837-3417), **Siesta Motel** (tel. 837-2503), and **Sunday**

House Motor Inn (tel. 827-3363), all with rooms in the $25-35 range.

About 65 miles south of Alpine (18 miles northwest of Big Bend National Park) on State 118 is the new **Longhorn Ranch Motel** (tel. 371-2541, fax 371-2540), where rooms cost $40 a night. The Longhorn has a pool and is the first motel in the area to receive AAA approval.

Gallegos Mexican Restaurant (tel. 837-2416) at 110 E. Holland is open daily except Sunday and features a popular all-you-can-eat buffet 11:30-1:30. For steak and barbecue, **Longhorn Cattle Company** (tel. 837-3692), 801 N. 5th St. (State 118), is the eatery of choice, open for lunch and dinner daily except Sunday. **Alpine Bakery**, at 302 E. Holland, is a good spot for an early breakfast of coffee and pastries.

RV Parks
Just outside Alpine are three RV parks in the $12-15 a night range with full hookups: **Alpine Pecan Grove RV Park** (tel. 915-837-7175, US 90 west), **Danny Boy Camper Park** (tel. 837-7135, US 90 east), and **La Vista 5400 RV Resort** (tel. 364-2293, State 118 south). La Vista has 50-amp electrical service.

Shopping
Hook or Crook Books (tel. 915-837-3128), 110 N. 6th St., specializes in new, used, and rare books on West Texas. **Ocotillo Enterprises** (tel. 837-5353), 205 N. 5th St., carries books, magazines, craft supplies, music cassettes, and rocks. **Big Bend Saddlery**, off US 67 at the north entrance to Alpine, crafts custom leather gear primarily for working cowboys in the tri-county area, plus cowboys as far away as New Mexico, England, and Japan. They also sell belts, belt buckles, boots, hats, bandanas, and other western wear as well as books on ranching and western lore. The **Apache Trading Post,** in a log cabin off US 90 about a mile west of town, carries souvenirs, Indian crafts (including a good selection of silver and turquoise jewelry), Mexican Indian pottery, books, and a variety of regional maps.

Transport
Lone Star Airlines, a Fort Worth-based commuter airline, may soon begin biweekly flights between Dallas-Fort Worth and Alpine with a stop in Austin. Currently, Lone Star is trying to convince Big Bend area businesses to establish a fund that would guarantee revenue for 13 seats per flight. If the agreement comes through, regular service should begin by 1993. Air service to Alpine would be a great boon to business and tourism in the Big Bend area; at present the nearest airport is in Midland, over 170 miles north of Alpine. For the latest information, call Lone Star Airlines at (817) 626-2932 or 625-7050.

MARATHON

A retired sea captain who had sailed the Aegean Sea gave this town its name because the area reminded him of Marathon, Greece. If you're driving to Big Bend from Fort Stockton or Del Rio, you'll pass through Marathon and if it's been a long drive, you might consider dining or staying the night at the historic Gage Hotel. Otherwise, there's little else to see or do in Marathon itself, though the Gage Hotel operates jeep, horseback, and rafting trips in the Big Bend area (including Big Bend National Park and the Black Gap Wildlife Management Area).

The Marathon Chamber of Commerce distributes an annotated walking tour map of the town that leads visitors to a couple of old churches, the original railroad depot, and various other historic buildings. This map can be picked up in the lobby of the Gage Hotel.

Gage Hotel
Alfred Gage, a banker and cattle baron who once owned a half-million-acre ranch in the area, built this hotel in 1927 to house business acquaintances. He died the year after the hotel opened, but it became a popular resting place for ranchers and cattlemen from all over Texas. In 1978 a Houston interest bought the yellow-brick property and skillfully refurbished it. The bedrooms and common rooms are tastefully decorated with West Texas antiques and artifacts, including a Yaqui Indian altar and a Chusa game (a sort of Mexican roulette that rolls several white marbles on a cowhide board) from Chihuahua in the bar and Tarahumara pottery in the lobby. Guest rooms upstairs are furnished with Mexican colonial and 19th-centuryTexas ranch furniture, each with a separate theme (e.g., the "Dagger Mesa" room is decorated with Spanish daggers).

the Gage Hotel

Rates are $52 per room with private bath, $38 with shared bath. A new adobe wing of the hotel has rooms with fireplace and private bath for $85, without fireplace for $75, plus a swimming pool. The restaurant (tel. 915-386-4205) open daily for breakfast, lunch, and dinner, specializes in Southwestern and Mexican cuisine (moderately priced, but not cheap). Located right on US 90 at Avenue C.

Other Accommodations
Marathon Motel & RV Park (tel. 915-386-4241) on W. US 90 has motel rooms for $28 a night and full RV hookups for $10. RVers can also find full hookups for $10 at **Southern Route RV Park & Cafe** (tel. 386-4512) on E. US 90.

Stillwell Store & RV Park (tel. 915-376-2244), 46 miles southeast of Marathon off US 385 on FM 2627 (near Black Gap Wildlife Management Area), has RV sites with full hookups for $11.50, tent/camper sites with water and electricity for $10.50, and primitive tent sites for $3.50 a night. There is hiking in the immediate area; the Stillwell outfit can also arrange jeep tours of Maravillas Canyon and shuttle service for river trips.

Black Gap Wildlife Management Area
This 100,000-acre preserve is not open to the general public for recreational use except during state-designated fishing and hunting seasons, nor are there any hiking or camping facilities. State 2627 passes through the area, however, and visitors are permitted to take "driving nature tours" along this road. Located 55 miles south of Marathon off US 385 (and adjacent to Big Bend National Park), it's the largest WMA in Texas and comprises mostly shrub desert plus 25 miles of the Rio Grande. Principal game species include mule deer, javelina, quail, and dove. For Black Gap hunting information, contact Texas Parks and Wildlife, 3407 S. Chadbourne, San Angelo, TX 76904.

FORT STOCKTON

Pecos County seat and home to about 9,000 West Texans, Fort Stockton started out as a Spanish mission called St. Gall in the 18th century. The Spanish left when the Comanches came down this far to water at what later became known as Comanche Springs (the springs were pumped dry in the 1950s following a long drought and never returned). In 1840 the U.S. Army established Camp Stockton at the intersection of the San Antonio-Chihuahua Trail and the Comanche War Trail to protect settlers from Indian attacks. The camp closed at the outbreak of the Civil War, but reopened as Fort Stockton in 1867. The Army left again in 1886 but the town retained the name and developed into a prosperous ranching and farming community. When oil and natural gas deposits were discovered in nearby fields in the '20s, the local economy shifted toward the energy industry.

The first thing visitors see when entering Fort Stockton from I-10/US 67 is the Paisano Pete statue, "the world's largest roadrunner." It's 10 feet tall and 22 feet long.

Annie Riggs Museum

A striking example of "frontier Victorian" adobe architecture, this building was originally a hotel that catered to passengers on the Butterfield Overland Mail coaches. The 14 rooms now contain exhibits that display historical artifacts from the frontier era and local fossils, including the tusks and other remains of a 22,000-year-old mastodon. At 301 S. Main St. (tel. 336-2167); open Mon.-Sat. 10-noon and 1-5 p.m., Sun. 1:30-5 p.m. between September and May, or Mon.-Sat. 9-8, Sun. 1:30-8 p.m. June through August. Admission is $1 adults, 50 cents children.

Between June and August, the museum presents **Summer on the Patio**—four evenings of live music.

Downtown Historical Tour

This is a self-guided driving tour through town past 16 historical sites—follow the orange arrow. A free map of the route is available at the Annie Riggs Museum. The Old Fort Stockton part of the route can be done as a walking tour, starting at the Guardhouse between 3rd and 4th streets off Rooney Drive. Three of the original 1867-70 Officers Row buildings remain standing near the intersection of 5th and Rooney. A bit north of Officers Row, off Water St., is the old fort cemetery. A look at the headstones shows that most people died by the age of 40. Sheriff A.J. Royal, who terrorized Pecos County in the late 1800s with his ruthless six-shooter justice, is also buried here. Local citizens drew beans to see who would assassinate him, and that's how the headstone reads—"assassinated."

Other notable sights along the route include the **Grey Mule Saloon,** originally built and operated by the infamous Sheriff Royal, the 1885 **county jail,** and the 1875 **St. Joseph's Church.**

Butterfield Overland Mail Stop

A stagecoach "remount stand" has been reconstructed 20 miles east of town at a highway rest stop on I-10/US 290. It was moved here stone by stone from its original location at Tunis Springs (a mile and a half southwest) during the 1936 Texas Centennial to make it more accessible to modern travelers.

Ste. Genevieve Winery

This winery has 7,000 acres of vineyards under cultivation and is a cooperative effort between the University of Texas (which owns the land) and France's Domain Cordier (which supplied the technology and expertise). Almost all of the equipment is of French manufacture and French viticulturalists work on site—unusual for an American winery. The Ft. Stockton Chamber of Commerce (tel. 915-336-2264) sponsors tours of the winery and vineyards every Saturday at 10 a.m. for $5 per person, which includes winetasting. Tours leave from the chamber of commerce office at 222 W. Dickinson Boulevard.

Accommodations

Most Ft. Stockton accommodations are on Dickinson Blvd., which is the same as US 67/290, just off I-10. Cheapest motels in town are the **Motel 6** (tel. 915-336-9737, 3001 W. Dickinson Blvd., I-10 exit 256 or 257), with rooms at $23 s, additional adults $6 each, and the **Sands Motor Inn** (tel. 336-2274, 1801 W. Dickinson Blvd., junction US 285 and US 67/290) with rooms for $25 s, $28 d. Near the Motel Six is the **Sunset Inn** (tel. 336-9781, 2601 I-10, exit 257) with $30-36 rooms. All three motels have small pools. Moving up in price, the **Best Western Sunday House** (tel. 336-8521, 3200 W. Dickinson Blvd., I-10 exit 257) has nicer rooms for $36-54 a night.

The **Econo Lodge** (tel. 915-336-9711) at 800 W. Dickenson Blvd. has satellite TV and a pool for $32-46 a night. Several other small motels along Dickenson Blvd. offer basic but serviceable rooms for only $15-17 a night, including **Comanche Motel** (E. Dickenson and Gatlin), **El Rancho Motel** (opposite Econo Lodge), **Silver Saddle Lodge** (next to El Rancho), **Deluxe Motor Inn** (opposite the Silver Saddle), **Gateway Lodge, Rio Conchos Motel**, and **Town and Country Motel**.

The **KOA Fort Stockton** (tel. 915-395-2494), 3.5 miles east of town off I-10 has what may be the best commercial RV park and campground in West Texas. It features a well-stocked store (with gas, ice, groceries), a cafe, a cactus garden, a pool, and 80 acres to wander around. Rates are $15.50 for a tent/camper site with w/e, $17.50 for a full RV hookup, or $24 for a cabin. **Comanche Land RV Park** (tel. 336-7112), near the I-10 junction, has full-hookups for only $4.95 a night.

Food

The **Comanche Tortilla Factory** (tel. 915-336-3245, 107 S. Nelson), run by the Gallegos family and open Mon. through Fri., makes a good take-out food stop if you're continuing east- or westward through Fort Stockton. A dozen homemade, jumbo tamales are under $5; they also have fresh tortillas and tostados. Go south on Nelson off Dickinson Blvd. at the Big A Auto sign to find this little adobe across from Sarah's. **Sarah's Cafe** (tel. 336-7124, 106 S. Nelson) is the oldest and most famous Mexican restaurant in town. It's open Mon.-Sat. for lunch and dinner (the enchiladas and chile con queso are recommended).

Events

The three-day **Pecos County Fair** is held annually in mid-October at the Fort Stockton Civic Center (Pecos Hwy., near I-10), featuring arts and crafts exhibits, food vendors, games, and a fiddler's competition.

TOYAH-PERMIAN BASINS

"Basin" is a fancy geological term for a low, flat place, and that's about all you've got between the Delaware, Apache, and Davis mountains to the west and the edge of the High Plains to the northeast—a wide, low, flat place. The Toyah Basin is just within the northern perimeter of the Chihuahuan Desert, as it slopes down to meet the Pecos River, which cuts the basin in half along a northwest-southeast axis. The alluvial plains of the Pecos River are remarkably fertile considering the overall geographic context, and with canal irrigation the Pecos River Plains have become an important agricultural area.

East of the Pecos River the desert landscape expires in a beautiful series of sand dunes known as the Monahans Sandhills. Beyond the Sandhills begins the Permian Basin, layers of lower Permian strata that contain the largest oil and natural gas deposits in Texas. The towns and counties of the Permian Basin developed along with the petroleum industry beginning in the '20s and have watched their fortunes grow and shrink with the vacillations of the petrol market ever since.

PECOS

One of Pecos's main claims to fame is that it was the roughest frontier town in the Old West—a short period of time between the 1880s and the early 1900s. Back then, the town's name could be used as a verb; to "pecos" somebody was to shoot him and dump his body in the Pecos River. All that remains of this legacy is the West of the Pecos Museum.

Another claim is that the first American rodeo was held here, motivated by a saloon argument between cowhands from several local ranches about riding and roping skills. To decide who were the best steer ropers and saddle-bronc riders among them, they held a competition on July 4, 1883, next to the courthouse. The purse was $40 and a thousand spectators showed up to watch the event. The West of the Pecos Rodeo has been held every year since.

The third claim is that Pecos cantaloupes are the sweetest in Texas. If you come through Pecos between July and August, cantaloupe season, you'll see 'loupe vendors all along US 285 and elsewhere around town. The surrounding county is also a major producer of watermelons, cotton, onions, alfalfa, and bell peppers.

West Of The Pecos Museum

At Cedar St. (US 285) and 1st St., the museum occupies a former saloon, built in 1896, and 30 rooms of the adjacent Orient Hotel, which was added in 1904. At one time this hotel was the classiest hostelry between El Paso and Fort Worth but it stopped taking guests in the mid '50s and was converted into a museum in the early '60s. The rooms contain a variety of exhibits with a local history focus (railroad, Indians, ranching), plus one exhibit in the large room downstairs (to the left of the lobby) that is state-funded and presents a good geocultural history of the region. The saloon has been restored to its original appearance and features bronze plaques that mark the spots where two men fell dead in a gun duel with one Barney Riggs, a Pecos man, in 1896.

In back of the museum is a collection of local atifacts commemorating Pecos's Wild West reputation: a hanging tree, a replica of Judge Roy Bean's saloon-courthouse (the original was in Langtry), a jail, and the grave of Clay Allison, "The Gentleman Gunfighter."

The museum is open Mon.-Sat. 9-5, Sun. 2-5 (2-6 in the summer); admission is adults $2, senior citizens $1, children under 12 free.

Accommodations

Pecos is blessed with a **Motel 6** (tel. 915-445-9034) where single rooms are only $20.95, plus $6 for each additional person. It's at 3002 S. Cedar (US 285), just north of I-20. **Laura Lodge** (tel. 445-4924) at 1000 E. US 80 (3rd St.) has about the same rates, but is located on Pecos's honky-tonk strip. Also inexpensive is the **American Motor Inn** (tel. 445-5431) on State 17 north of I-20, where rates are $23-30. The **Best Western Sunday House** (tel. 447-2215) at 900 W. Palmer, east of the State 17 and I-20 junction, is the nicest place in town and costs $34-48 a night.

Food

Pecos farms hire Mexican migrant labor, so there are plenty of Tex-Mex restaurants in town, especially along 3rd St. (US 80). **La Norteña Tortilla Factory**, on 3rd St. across from La Norteña Ball-

room, has inexpensive Tex-Mex food to go. **Ben's Spanish Inn,** also on 3rd St., is a 40-year old Pecos institution that serves American as well as Tex-Mex dishes. For a quick breakfast or coffee-and-donut fix, stop by **Ma Wilson's Texas-Sized Donuts** on Cedar St. (US 285), about midway between 1st St. and I-20. A classic car hop on W. 3rd, **Sonic,** does burgers and other fast food. There's also a **Pizza Hut** on Cedar St. near the 3rd St. intersection.

Entertainment And Events

The **West of the Pecos Rodeo** is held annually for four days around the 4th of July at the Pecos Rodeo Arena. The main rodeo events start nightly at 8 p.m. and tickets are $4-7. Other events during the day include rodeo parades, an Old West Pageant (with the coronation of the latest Golden Girl), a western art show, and the Sheriff's Posse Bar-B-Q. For information on current scheduling, call the Pecos Chamber of Commerce at (915) 445-2406.

Along 3rd St. (US 80) are several honky-tonks and Mexican dance halls, including the **Oasis Lounge** and **La Norteña Ballroom.**

Shopping

The **Pecos Saddle Shop** (tel. 915-445-3125) at 123 S. Oak is a custom saddlery that makes all kinds of leather cowboy gear.

MONAHANS SANDHILLS
STATE PARK

About halfway between Pecos and Odessa, off I-20, this 3,840-acre park protects a huge complex of sand dunes, some of which reach 70 feet high. The entire dune field stretches for some 200 miles northwest into New Mexico. Many of the dunes are still active, that is drifting, while some are stabilized by rooted vegetation such as the **shin oak** (*Quercus havardii,* also known as the dwarf shinnery oak or Havard oak) which at full maturity reaches only four feet. The shin oak produces an abundance of acorns, which various nomadic Indian groups used as an important food source. The shin oaks also signal as to where to find water among the dunes, and the Apaches and Comanches often battled here over water and acorns. But they weren't the first to know of

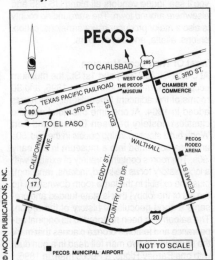

PECOS

TO CARLSBAD

285

WEST OF THE PECOS MUSEUM

E. 3RD ST.

CHAMBER OF COMMERCE

TEXAS PACIFIC RAILROAD

80 W. 3RD ST.

TO EL PASO

EDDY ST.

WALTHALL

PECOS RODEO ARENA

CALIFORNIA AVE.

17

EDDY ST.

COUNTRY CLUB DR.

CEDAR ST.

20

© MOON PUBLICATIONS, INC.

PECOS MUNICIPAL AIRPORT

NOT TO SCALE

ROBERT CLAY ALLISON
1840 — 1887

HE NEVER KILLED A MAN
THAT DID NOT NEED KILLING

Clay Allison's headstone, Pecos

the dunes; the Spanish explorer Cabeza de Vaca encountered Jumano Indians here in 1535.

Other vegetation that grows among the dunes includes tasajilla or "Christmas cactus," mesquite, yucca, prickly pear, sand sagebrush, and several varieties of "desert morning glory," including the white-flowered **bindweed.** The dunes form pristine hills and valleys of sand that can be explored for hours (hiking is permitted throughout the park). The park office rents out sandsurfing discs for 80 cents to use for sliding down the dune slopes. The dunes are highest in the summer.

Facilities

The park visitor center contains interpretive exhibits that explain the geological, historical, and botanical features of the sandhills. Next to the center is a quarter-mile nature trail where examples of native vegetation are on display. During the summer, a concession stand is open in a former railroad section house near the campground.

The park has 24 tent/camper sites, 19 of which offer w/e for $9 a night; the remaining five have water nearby and are $6 a night. A dump station is available, as are flush toilets, showers, grills, and tables. The park entry fee is the standard $3 per vehicle, $1 for cyclists and pedestrians. For further information, contact the Superintendent (tel. 915-943-2092), Monahans Sandhills State Park, Box 1738, Monahans, TX 79756.

ODESSA

Originally Odessa was merely a way station on the Texas-Pacific Railroad (est. 1881), named by Russian rail workers for its resemblance to the Ukrainian town of the same name (it's as flat as the Steppes). After the large Permian Basin oil and gas discoveries in the late '20s, however, it became an oil town practically overnight. Neither Odessa nor its next-door neighbor Midland are places you'd want to drive out of your way to see (Odessa made Rand McNally's list of the 10 worst places to live in the U.S.), but if you happen to stop here on a cross-Texas trip via I-20, you'll find a city of around 100,000 and the nation's largest inland petrochemical complex.

In an all-out effort to make the town more attractive to visitors and potential residents, civic leaders have promoted the establishment of several cultural and performing arts centers (see below), so visiting Odessa doesn't have to be as bleak as the barren landscape might suggest. The second-largest meteor crater in the U.S., the sixth largest in the world, is just southwest of the city.

Odessa Meteor Crater

A large nickel-iron meteorite shower made a series of craters over a two-square-mile area here 20,000 years ago. One particularly large meteor (estimated to weigh 1,000 tons) penetrated deep into the surrounding bedrock and exploded, leaving a crater 550 feet in diameter. Smaller craters in the area have diameters of 15-70 feet. Over the eons, the largest crater has filled to within six feet of its top with accumulated sediments, so what remains is not dramatically deep. Exploratory trenches and shafts (which are still in place) were dug into the main crater in the late '30s and early '40s, and have brought to the surface portions of "rock flour," an extremely fine, powdered rock that was formed by shock waves through the bedrock below the earth's surface. A nature trail leads across the center of the crater and along one side of the crater rim.

To get to the Odessa Meteor Crater, drive west from Odessa on US 80/I-20 until you see signs for the crater about 5½ miles from town. An access road goes south for two miles to the crater. Admission is free.

The Globe Theatre
(Globe Of The Great Southwest)

This is a replica of England's Globe Theatre, and like the original it's designed specifically for performances of William Shakespeare's dramas. A Shakespeare Festival is held here annually February-March, and during the rest of the year there are other theatrical performances. The Globe is on the Odessa College campus on Shakespeare Rd., just west of US 385 (Andrews Highway). Free tours of the theater are offered

ODESSA

PACIFIC LOOP

385

52nd ST.

42nd ST.

ANDREWS HWY.

GRANDVIEW AVE.

UNIVERSITY OF TEXAS AT THE PERMIAN BASIN

PACIFIC LOOP

302

GLOBE THEATRE ■ UNIVERSITY BLVD.

UNIVERSITY BLVD. EAST

WASHINGTON AVE.

GRANT AVE.

DIXIE

7th ST.

PARKWAY BLVD.

8th ST.

HILLCREST AVE.

4th ST.

80

2nd ST.

SOUTH GRANT AVE.

20

TO MIDLAND, BIG SPRING

TO PECOS

NOT TO SCALE

© MOON PUBLICATIONS, INC.

Mon.-Fri. 9-5. For performance schedules and other information, call (915) 332-1586.

Presidential Museum

A museum dedicated to the office of the U.S. presidency, with campaign memorabilia, presidential medals, inaugural gowns, and other relics. Fascinating to some, the height of boredom for others. Located at 622 N. Lee at 7th Street. Open Tues.-Sat. 10-5; free admission.

Art Institute Of The Permian Basin

The three galleries contain all the art that oil money can buy, with an emphasis on contemporary artists. The institute also offers a varied series of films and concerts. At 4909 E. University between Loop 338 and Parkway Blvd., not far from the Odessa Hilton. Open Tues.-Sat. 10-5, Sun. 2-5; free admission.

Accommodations

The **Villa West Inn** (tel. 915-335-5055) on I-20 at exit 116 has rooms for $19-28. **Motel 6** has two locations, one at exit 116 (tel. 333-4025) and one at 2925 E. 2nd St. (tel. 332-2600); room rates at both are $19.95 s, $6 for each additional adult.

Nearby **Lexington Hotel Suites** (tel. 333-9678), 3031 E. 2nd, has rooms with kitchenettes at a reasonable $28-40. **La Quinta Motor Inn** (tel. 333-2850) at 5001 E. 2nd (exit 116 off I-20) has well-kept rooms for $48 s, $55 d. Top digs in Odessa is the **Odessa Hilton** (tel. 268-5885) at 5200 E. University. Rooms at the Hilton start at $58 s, $68 d.

Food

The **Barn Door** (tel. 915-332-3512) at 2140 Grant St. (Andrews Hwy.) is a moderately priced local favorite for steaks, seafood, and Tex-Mex. Open Mon.-Sat. for lunch and dinner. Next door is the **Pecos Depot Lounge,** an 1892 train depot that was moved here from Pecos. Along Andrews Hwy. are tons of other restaurants, mostly fast-food places (including all the usual chain restaurants). Odessa's oldest restaurant is **Manuel's** (tel. 333-2751) at 1404 E. 2nd, which started out as a tortilla factory but now serves a full range of Mexican, steak, chicken, and seafood dishes (the tortillas now come from down the street). Open Tues.-Sun. for lunch and dinner.

For inexpensive, buffet-style Tex-Mex, **Rosa's Café and Tortilla Factory** (tel. 915-332-6648) at 1810 E. 8th St. can't be beat. Tortillas are made fresh here throughout the day and their salsa bar has an extensive selection. Open daily for lunch and dinner. **Dumplin's Home Cookin'** at US 385 (Andrews Hwy.) and W. 46th specializes in down-home breakfasts and homemade pies—great breakfast place, open daily for breakfast, lunch, and dinner.

Entertainment

Dena's (tel. 335-8839) at 8th and Grandview Ave. is an urban country dance hall that's open Mon.-Sat. till 2 a.m. They also have a happy hour buffet Mon.-Fri. 4-8, when free food goes with the drinks.

MIDLAND

Midland (pop. 97,000) got its name because it was midway between Fort Worth and El Paso on the Texas-Pacific Railroad line in the 1880s. It was just a small farming community until the Permian Basin oil discoveries of the '20s. Even though Midland County itself wasn't a site for major oil strikes, the town somehow maneuvered itself into becoming the West Texas capital for petrobusiness (which means that, like its neighbor Odessa, the local economy swings up and down with international oil prices).

Permian Basin Petroleum Museum

Everything you ever wanted to know about the history of oil exploration and oil technology is covered in this museum, probably the largest in the world devoted exclusively to the petroleum industry. It's all very well executed, with many audio-visual and hands-on exhibits (a "Time Trip" tunnel-like diorama takes visitors through a facsimile of the reef bottom of the 230-million-year-old Permian Ocean, for example). Antique drilling machinery is displayed outside in the "Oil Patch." Open Mon.-Sat. 9-5, Sun. 2-5. Admission is $2 adults, $1 for children 6-11, under 6 free. Wheelchairs and baby strollers are available. Off I-20 at State 349.

Museum Of The Southwest

This museum houses permanent and rotating collections of Southwestern art as well as archaeological artifacts in a 1934 mansion designed by Anton Korn. One of the permanent exhibits is the Hogan Collection, which includes works by the founding members of the Taos Society of Artists. The mansion itself covers an entire city block, with an interior of carved wooden friezes and hand-painted tilework. At 1705 W. Missouri at J St. (a block south of US 80).

Confederate Air Force And American Airpower Flying Museum

The Confederate Air Force (tel. 915-563-1000) is a nonprofit organization, headquartered at Valley International Airport, whose members collect and

nose art, Confederate Air Force Museum

restore military aircraft used during WW II (1939-45). The CAF now has over 140 craft representing 61 different models from the U.S. Army Air Force, Royal Air Force, German Luftwaffe, and Imperial Japanese Navy. Many are the only flyable planes of their kind in existence (e.g., the A-20 Havoc, A6M2 Zero, SB2C Helldiver, F-82 Twin Mustang, and B-29 Superfortress). Members of the CAF are called "colonels," and there are CAF "wings" and "squadrons" in 25 countries (neither a pilot's license nor veteran status is required for membership). They even have an "officers' club" on site. Ask a member why it's called the "Confederate" Air Force and you'll get a funny look. Every October there's a four-day air show featuring the "Ghost Squadron."

Visitors may view about a third of the planes on the CAF ramp or in the hangar at any given time—other aircraft may be on tour to air shows or other CAF wings/squadrons, or may be being used in a current Hollywood film production. On the interior walls of the hangar is a collection of classic nose art—pinup-style paintings of scantily clad sirens with labels like "Night Mission," "Flamin' Mamie," and "Miss Yourlovin'." An indoor museum contains detailed exhibits which display the uniforms of the Allied and Axis powers, WW II memorabilia, propaganda posters, and various bits of war machinery. A rather moldy but informative 30-minute movie at the officers' club chronicles the history of the Ghost Squadron. At the entrance to the museum is a souvenir shop that sells historic military patches and flight jackets (including exact reproductions of the classic Cooper B-2 USAAF leather jacket).

The CAF Flying Museum is open Mon.-Sat. 9-5, Sun. and holidays 12-5. Admission is $4 adults, $3 teens and seniors, $2 children 6-12.

Accommodations And Food

Most hotels and motels in Midland are clustered around the intersection of Midkiff and Wall St. off I-20 (exit 134). **Motel 6** (tel. 915-697-3197) at 1000 S. Midkiff (between I-20 and W. Wall St.) has singles for $19.95, plus $6 for each additional adult. Nearby **Lexington Hotel Suites** (tel. 687-3155) at 1003 S. Midkiff has rooms with kitchenettes for $30-36. **La Quinta Motor Inn** (tel. 697-9900) at 4130 W. Wall St. has comfortable rooms for $48-61.

A step up is the **Ramada Hotel** (tel. 915-699-

4144), 3100 W. Wall St., where rooms run $42-56. At the top is the **Midland Hilton** (tel. 683-6131), downtown at Wall and Lorraine, with rooms for $78-108.

For campers, there's the **Midessa KOA** (tel. 915-563-2368) off I-20 at exit 126, between Odessa and Midland. Tentsites with w/e are $15, full hookups are $18, and Kamping Kabins are $22 d ($2 for additional persons).

Midland restaurants are a little more upscale than those in Odessa. **Luigi's** (tel. 915-683-6363) at 111 N. Big Spring (at W. Wall St.) is a small, moderately priced trattoria that's been serving reputable Italian food for over 25 years. Open Mon.-Sat. for lunch and dinner, Sun. for dinner only. The **Wall Street Bar & Grill** (tel. 684-8686) downtown at 115 E. Wall St. has a grand 1867 bar and embossed tin ceiling, and specializes in seafood and steaks. Open Mon.-Sat. for lunch and dinner, Sun. for brunch only.

Entertainment

The **Granada Club** (tel. 915-697-4138) at 3312 W. Wall St. is a venerable country dance hall that's open every night except Sunday. No cover charge.

BIG SPRING

Big Spring sits on the southern edge of the Cap Rock Escarpment as it gives way to the Edwards Plateau below. This geological intersection brought significant springs to the surface in several areas, which is how the town got its name. The Comanches and Shawnees used to fight over the water, travelers stopped here to fill their water containers, and finally in 1881 the railroad came through. Still, Big Spring wasn't much of a town until oil was discovered nearby. Cotton is also big in these parts so you'll see large cotton fields along the highway. During the fall harvest, huge container-sized bales of harvested cotton sit in the fields waiting to be picked up.

The downtown area has a few historic buildings and the hilly environment lends some charm to the town that is absent from most stopovers along I-20. The **Heritage Museum** at S. Scurry and W. 5th St. contains collections of pioneer and Indian artifacts from the area. Open Tues.-Fri. 9-5, Sat. 10-5; free admission. The **Potton House** at 2nd and Gregg streets is a 1901 sandstone Victorian listed with the National Register of Historic Places. Tours are free but by appointment only (call the chamber of commerce at 915-263-7641).

Record collectors should not miss **The Record Shop** at 211 Main St., which has been in continuous operation since 1934 and offers around 8,000 vintage 33s, 45s, and 78s (some of the 78s go back to the early 1900s) as well as new titles.

Accommodations And Food
There's a **Motel 6** (tel. 915-267-1695) just off I-20 at US 87, with rooms at the typical $21.95 single rate, plus $6 for each additional adult. Very nearby (same exit) is the **Best Western Mid-Continent Inn** (tel. 267-1601) with room rates at $36-44. The **Ponderosa Motor Inn** (tel. 267-5237) at 27000 S. Gregg (US 87) has rooms for $23-30.

Tent/camper/RV sites are $9-12 a night at the **Whip In Campground** (tel. 915-393-5242), seven miles east of town at the junction of I-20 and Moss Lake Road.

La Posada at 206 W. 3rd serves fresh tortillas and Tex-Mex Tues.-Sun. for lunch and dinner. **Big John's Feed Lot** (tel. 915-263-3178) at 802 W. 3rd is a rustic barbecue place with the menus written on paper sacks. Open Mon.-Sat. for lunch only. For steaks **K-C Steakhouse** (tel. 263-1651), on a hillside off I-20 (exit 176), is the top choice. It's open Mon.-Sat. for dinner only.

Events
Big Spring is the site for the annual **Rattlesnake Roundup** held in the Howard County Fairgrounds every March. A ton and a half of rattlesnakes are rounded up for the occasion, and then they're milked, skinned, eaten, and made into belts and hatbands. Whether it's herpetophobia or herpetophilia, it's definitely a one-of-a-kind event.

AMARILLO

Amarillo is the unofficial Panhandle capital by simple virtue of being the largest city (pop. 162,000) and because it's an important transshipment point for goods carried by truck across the southern half of the nation. It started out as a buffalo-hide-tent camp for railroad workers in 1887 and within a few years was the nation's largest shipping point for northward-bound cattle. Early this century, natural gas and petroleum were discovered in the area. In 1929, helium was extracted from gas in Amarillo for the first time and the area is now the source for 90% of the world's helium (used in aerospace technology, welding, cryogenics, and as a prime leak detector).

CLIMATE

Summers in Amarillo are warm during the day, cool at night. Late fall, winter, and early spring are blustery. Because of the mostly flat terrain, winds can sweep across the plains with considerable momentum, so wind chill often alters perceived temperature. Rainfall averages 20 inches a year, with the rainiest months being May, June, and August (around three inches a month during each). During the winter, snow is not uncommon.

SIGHTS

Amarillo Livestock Auction
Every Tuesday beginning at 9 a.m., what may be the world's largest weekly cattle auction is held at Amarillo's Western Stockyards (S. Manhattan at 3rd St.). Annually, the stockyards sell off around a half-million head of cattle. Visitors are welcome to attend, with no obligation to bid on livestock (and no admission charge). On other days of the week, there are also occasional smaller, special auctions. Call (806) 373-7464 for more information or look for the *Amarillo Livestock Reporter,* a weekly that features livestock industry news.

SELECTED MONTHLY AVERAGE MAXIMUM/MINIMUM TEMPERATURES

Month	Max. (°F)	Min. (°F)
Jan.	50	24
March	62	33
May	80	53
July	94	67
Sept.	85	58
Nov.	60	32

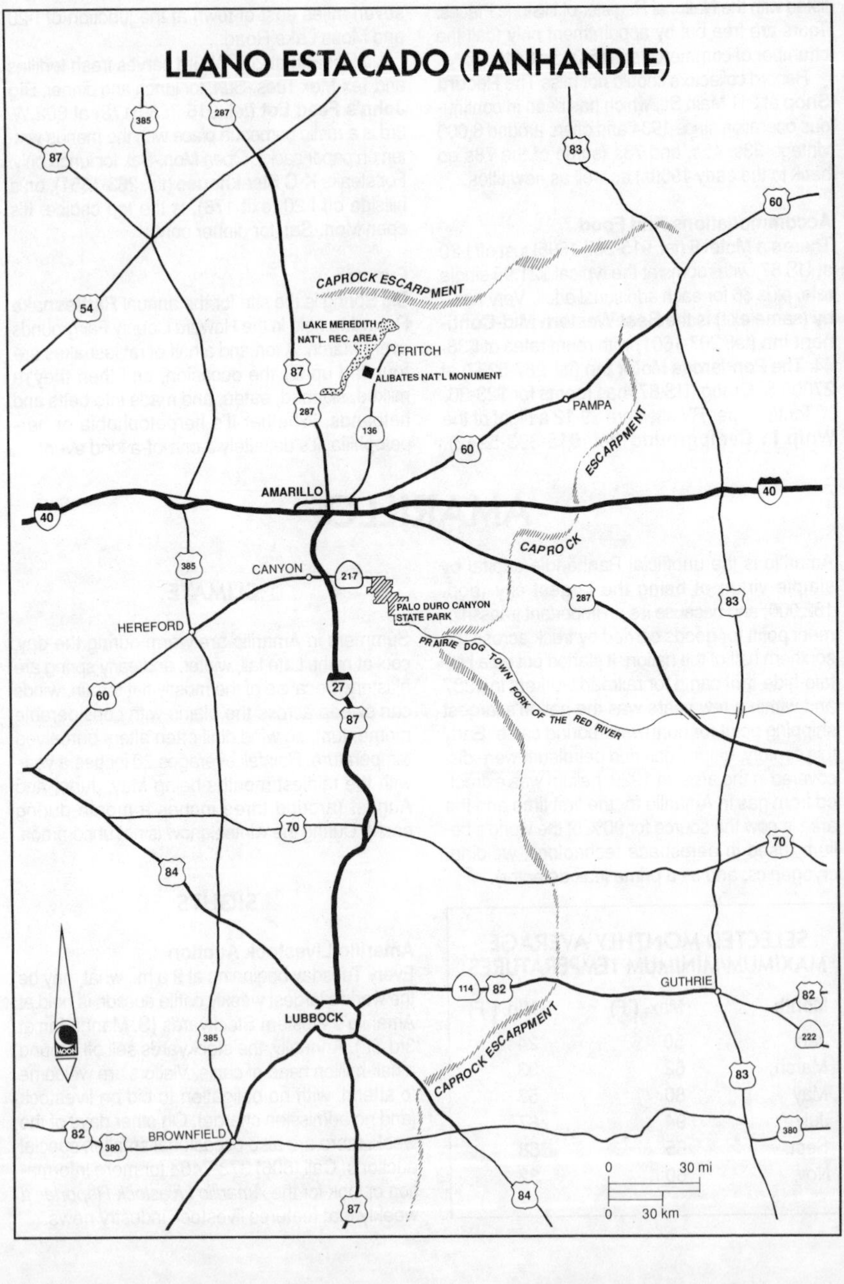

LLANO ESTACADO (PANHANDLE)

CAPROCK ESCARPMENT

LAKE MEREDITH NAT'L. REC. AREA

FRITCH

ALIBATES NAT'L MONUMENT

PAMPA

ESCARPMENT

AMARILLO

CAPROCK

CANYON

PALO DURO CANYON STATE PARK

HEREFORD

PRAIRIE DOG TOWN FORK OF THE RED RIVER

LUBBOCK

GUTHRIE

BROWNFIELD

0   30 mi

0   30 km

MOON

© MOON PUBLICATIONS, INC.

LLANO ESTACADO
(THE PANHANDLE)

The "Staked Plain" or Llano (pronounced YAH-no) Estacado is the southernmost extension of the Great Plains, a broad, flat area of limestone caprock that finally gives way at the Cap Rock Escarpment at Big Spring. Texans sometimes call it "the Panhandle" because most of the Llano Estacado juts above the rest of Texas on U.S. maps, like the handle of a pan. The term "panhandle" is terribly imprecise, though, and people argue over where the handle ends and the pan begins.

It's not entirely flat, either. The flatness is interrupted in several places by low hills and by deep canyons, most notably Palo Duro Canyon just below Amarillo. But the mostly flat plain is the most memorable feature of the Llano Estacado; when George Lucas sought a perfectly flat landscape for the final scenes of the film *Indiana Jones and the Last Crusade*, he chose a ranch at the edge of Palo Duro.

Oil and helium are the big income earners, along with ranching and agriculture (cotton, wheat, sorghum, vegetables, and sunflowers). Of late, wineries in the Lubbock area have gained international attention because of the excellent wines they've produced.

Amarillo Art Center

This three-building complex, designed by architect Edward Stone (who also designed Washington, D.C.'s Kennedy Center), and serves as the cultural and fine arts center for West Texas. The permanent collection focuses on 20th-century art, including works by Georgia O'Keeffe, Fritz Scholder, Franz Kline, Jack Boynton, Elaine de Koonig, and others. Rotating exhibits bring in everything from cowboy art to Rembrandt. In addition to the six galleries, there is also a theater, a sculpture court, an outdoor amphitheater, and several rooms for art classes, seminars, and other periodic cultural events. Located on the main campus of Amarillo College, 2200 S. Van Buren. Galleries are open Tues.-Fri. 10-5, Sat.-Sun. 1-5, plus Wed. evenings 7-9:30 p.m. Free admission (donations accepted).

Cadillac Ranch

Ten Cadillacs (1949-63 models) buried nose-down in a field at the same angle used for the Cheops pyramids—what could it mean? Could be a tribute to the time when Route 66 reigned supreme as the country's main east-west artery (now I-40) and fins were hot; could be a poke at the Texas oilman's proclivity for Cadillacs; or it could be a simple testament to the eccentricity of helium tycoon Stanley Marsh III, who put them here (his ranch bears the very un-Texan name of "Toad Hall"). It's worth the short drive west of Amarillo just to check out the graffiti on these rusting hulks. To get here, drive west on I-40 about five miles; take the Hope Rd. exit, then turn onto the frontage road that heads east back toward Amarillo (like most frontage roads in Texas, it's one-way); Cadillac Ranch will be on your right before the Soncy Rd.

Cadillac Ranch,
Amarillo

on-ramp. A worn path in the field leads straight to the old Caddies for a closer look.

FOOD

Since Amarillo is a livestock center, the local emphasis is on steak. But there are also barbecue, Tex-Mex, down-home, Oriental, continental, and nouvelle restaurants in town. And all along I-40 through town is a string of the usual fast-food and chain restaurants if you're looking for a quick, cheap meal. For one-of-a-kind eating, try the following.

Artsy
In its own category, the **OHMS (On Her Majesty's Service) Gallery Café,** is both a power-lunch scene and a place where Amarillo's artists and musicians hang out. Paintings by local artists decorate the walls, while folksingers, cowboy poets, and bongo players do their thing— when it's open (Mon.-Fri. 10-4 only, unfortunately). Food is served cafeteria style and ranges from American to Mexican to Italian. Prices are moderate. At 619 S. Tyler in the Atrium (806-373-3233).

Barbecue
$ to $$ **Sutphen's:** This is the traditional Amarillo favorite, and they cater the *Texas* outdoor drama at Palo Duro in the summer. There are two locations, one at 620 W. 16th (tel. 806-373-0726) and one at 4100 S. Georgia (tel. 359-9369). Both are open daily for lunch and dinner. Expect to wait for a table during peak dining hours.

$ to $$ **Cattle Call:** This newer establishment is preferred by younger Amarilloans (if for no other reason than to avoid the long lines at Sutphen's, which, some say, is resting on its laurels). At Westgate Mall, off I-40 W (tel. 806-353-1227); open Mon.-Sat. 11-9.

$ **Van Dyke's Bar-B-Q:** More than a barbecue place, though they do serve the usual brisket and links. Country-style breakfasts are huge, and come with their famous sourdough biscuits (available with lunch as well). Lunch features ham and beef stew as well as barbecue. Customers order at the counter and bus their own tables. At 210 W. 6th (tel. 806-373-1441); open for breakfast and lunch daily except Sunday.

Burgers
$ **Doodles:** The best burger joint in town because they let you make them yourself. Great fries and dessert cobbler. There are two locations, one at 3701 Olsen Blvd. (tel. 355-0064), the other at 2105 S. Grand (tel. 806-374-0717).

European
$ to $$ **Nick's:** For Greek and Italian, this is a long-time Amarillo favorite. Specialties include moussaka, dolmades, gyro sandwiches, spaghetti, and lasagna. At 3420 I-40 W (tel. 806-353-2976).

$$ to $$$ **Maison Blanche:** Serves French dishes in an elegant atmosphere at 2740 Westgate Village (Georgia and 34th, tel. 806-353-3523).

Mexican
$ **The Plaza:** This is a large, airy place with a fountain in the middle of the dining room. Plates are huge and come with tortillas or sopapillas, El Paso-style. Extensive menu. Located in a shopping center at 3415 Bell St. (tel. 806-358-4897); open daily for lunch and dinner.

$ to $$ **Restaurant Los Insurgentes:** The real thing, including interior cooking like *mole poblano* as well as classic Tex-Mex dishes like fajitas, *cabrito,* and menudo. At 3521 W. 15th (tel. 353-5361); open daily except Sunday for lunch and dinner.

Oriental
$ **Blackstone Café:** An unpretentious diner that's open only weekdays for breakfast and lunch. Breakfast is American, but lunch features unique Thai and Chinese dishes. At 202 W. 10th St. downtown (tel. 806-372-0753).

$ **Hong Kong Restaurant:** Out on Amarillo's honkytonk strip is this classic American-Cantonese joint with great egg rolls and egg fu yung. At 3011 E. Amarillo Blvd. (tel. 383-4304); open daily for lunch and dinner.

Seafood
$ to $$ **Seafood Galley:** Amarillo's not exactly an ideal location for seafood, but this one beats the Red Lobster. In addition to a repertoire of fried, boiled, and broiled marine creatures, Seafood Galley has homemade pies. Also a take-out window for eaters on the move. At 2721 S. Virginia (tel. 806-355-8171); open daily for lunch and dinner.

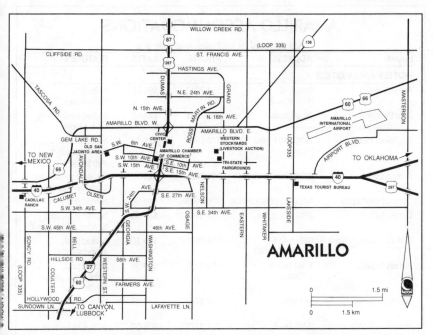

Map labels:
WILLOW CREEK RD. — 87 — (LOOP 335) — 136 — CLIFFSIDE RD. — ST. FRANCIS AVE. — 287 — HASTINGS AVE. — TASCOSA RD. — DUMAS — N.E. 24th AVE. — GRAND — 60 — 66 — MASTERSON — N. 15th AVE. — MARTIN RD. — N. 16th AVE. — AMARILLO BLVD. W. — AMARILLO INTERNATIONAL AIRPORT — CIVIC CENTER — ROSS — AMARILLO BLVD. E. — GEM LAKE RD. — S.W. 6th AVE. — WESTERN STOCKYARDS (LIVESTOCK AUCTION) — OLD SAN JACINTO AREA — AMARILLO CHAMBER OF COMMERCE — AIRPORT BLVD. — TO NEW MEXICO — 66 — AVONDALE — S.W. 10th AVE. — S.E. 10th AVE. — TRI-STATE FAIRGROUNDS — TO OKLAHOMA — S.W. 15th AVE. — S.E. 15th AVE. — LOOP 335 — 287 — AVE. — NELSON — 40 — TEXAS TOURIST BUREAU — 40 — CADILLAC RANCH — CALUMET — OLSEN — 24th — S.E. 27th AVE. — M S. — LAKESIDE — WHITAKER — EASTERN — OSAGE — S.W. 34th AVE. — S.E. 34th AVE. — S.W. 45th AVE. — GEORGIA — 46th AVE. — WASHINGTON — **AMARILLO** — SONCY RD. — (LOOP 335) — BELL — HILLSIDE RD. — WESTERN ST. — 58th AVE. — 27 — COULTER — 60 — FARMERS AVE. — 1.5 mi — HOLLYWOOD RD. — SUNDOWN LN. — TO CANYON, LUBBOCK — LAFAYETTE LN. — 1.5 km — MOON

Steak

$ to $$$ The Big Texan: Could also be called "The Big Tourist Trap" (except that even the locals like to come here once in a while). You can't miss the billboards on all highways leading to Amarillo that advertise a free 72-oz. steak (4.5 pounds) if you can eat the entire thing; what they don't mention is that you have to eat all the side dishes as well—shrimp cocktail, baked potato, salad, and roll—and eat it all within one hour. If you don't make it, the price of the meal is $30. Over 200,000 have tried and about 20% of these have succeeded. They also have smaller steaks, barbecue, chicken, seafood, and such West Texas specialties as jackrabbit, rattlesnake, buffalo burgers, and calf fries (bovine testicles). Off I-40E (tel. 372-7000); open daily 10:30 a.m.-midnight.

$$ Iron Horse Café: Formerly the Stockyards Café before it burnt down and was rebuilt, this location in the Old Santa Fe Depot, near the stockyards, has served cowboys and livestock auctiongoers since 1945. Besides club steaks, chicken-fried steak, and "Republican steaks with the Democratic flavor," they also serve broiled chick-en. At 401 S. Grant (tel. 373-1591); open Mon.-Sat. for lunch and dinner.

ENTERTAINMENT AND ACTIVITIES

Clubs

Caravan East (tel. 806-359-5436) is one of five huge country dance clubs by the same name in Texas and New Mexico. Men must check cowboy hats at the door. At 3601 Olsen Blvd.; open every night. **Sneakers** (tel. 355-0811), at 2600 Paramount, is the type of country rock club that's mainly found only in the Panhandle—for urban cowboys who like their country music with some extra sizzle. More rock bands are playing here these days. The **Western Horseman Club** (tel. 379-6555), at the Fifth Season Inn off I-40 (Nelson St. exit), caters to an older country disco crowd. For more of a honky-tonk atmosphere, try the **Rodeo** at 2700 S. Georgia. The *real* honky-tonk strip is E. Amarillo Blvd., along former Route 66, where cross-country truckers hang out (if you've never been honky-tonkin' before, this ain't the place to start).

AMARILLO ACCOMMODATIONS

Add 13% hotel tax to all rates. Area code: 806

NAME	ADDRESS	PHONE	RATES	FEATURES
HOTELS AND MOTELS				
AmeriSuites	6800 I-40 (Bell St. exit)	358-7943	$50-58	heated pool, kitchenettes
Best Western Amarillo Inn	1610 Coulter	358-7861	$44-55	heated pool coin laundry
Big Texan Motel	7701 I-40 E (exit 75)	372-5000	$35-43	heated pool, Old-West decor, coin laundry
Bronco Lodge	6005 Amarillo Blvd. W	355-3521	$25-32	heated pool, refrigerators on request
Comfort Inn-Airport	I-40 (Ross-Osage exit)	376-9993	$40-56	heated pool
Comfort Inn	2100 S. Coulter	358-6141	$36-50	heated pool, coin laundry, refrigerators
Fifth Season Inn-West	6801 I-40 E (Coulter St. exit)	358-7881	$50-150	heated pool, airport shuttle
Harvey Hotel	3100 I-40 W at Georgia	358-6161	$49-99	heated pool, health club, airport shuttle
Holiday Inn I-40	I-40 at Ross	372-8741	$70-80	heated pool, airport shuttle
Howard Johnson Lodge Lodge-East	3205 I-4- E	372-8171	$36-52	pool, coin laundry
La Quinta Inn	1708 I-40 E (Ross-Osage exit)	373-7486	$48-52	heated pool
Motel 6 (Central)	2032 Paramount (I-40 exit 68-A)	355-6554	$21.95 + $6 ea. add.	small pool
Motel 6 (East)	3930 I-40 (exit 72-B)	374-6444	$21.95 + $6 ea. add.	small pool
Travelodge Amarillo	2801 I-40 W	355-9171	$34-44	pool
BED AND BREAKFASTS				
Galbraith House	1710 S. Polk	374-0237	$60-75	1912 house, 5 rooms, private bath, full breakfast
Parkview House	1311 S. Jefferson	373-9464	$40-55	1909 house, 3 rooms, shared bath, cont. breakfast
CAMPGROUNDS				
Amarillo KOA	off US 60 3 miles east of town	335-1792	$13 tents, $16-18 RVs, $24 cabins	
Overnight Trailer Inn	off I-40 east	373-1431	$15 RVs	

Amarillo has its share of rock music clubs, too, but they're notoriously temporary. **S.R.O. Club** (tel. 806-358-8163) at 34371 I-40 W tends toward "modern rock" sounds (used to be called new wave, remember?) while **Smitty's** (tel. 383-8455) is more of a rock 'n' roll honky-tonk.

Amusement Parks

Kids will like **Wonderland Park,** with the Texas Tornado, a double-loop roller coaster, and the Rattlesnake River Raft Ride. It's in Thompson Park, north of town off US 87/287 and is open from 1 p.m. weekends mid-March through September; May through Labor Day it's also open weekdays from 7 p.m. Admission is 50 cents per person plus separate fees per ride.

EVENTS

June Through August

The **Texas Outdoor Musical Drama** is held in Palo Duro Canyon. See "Palo Duro Canyon State Park" below for details.

September

The **Tri-State Fair** attracts participants from New Mexico, Texas, and Oklahoma for a week-long series of activities including the usual farming and ranching exhibits, arts and crafts vendors, rodeo and livestock competitions, and a carnival. Held at the fairgrounds, Bell and 10th St.; usually begins the third Monday in September.

November

The **National Old-Timers Rodeo** is the U.S. finals competition for rodeo cowboys over the age of 40. Usually held four days in early November at the Civic Center, Buchanan and 3rd Street.

Tours

Old West Tours, in conjunction with the Amarillo Convention and Visitors Bureau, offers a range of tours of Amarillo and the vicinity for individuals as well as groups. A guided city tour costs $20 an hour.

The most popular tour is **Cowboy Morning** at Tom Christian's Figure 3 Ranch on the rim of Palo Duro Canyon. Visitors ride in a mule-drawn wagon to a canyon overlook and then eat a huge "cowboy breakfast" that includes cowboy coffee,

scrambled eggs, country sausage, and sourdough biscuits served from the chuck wagon. Breakfast is followed by roping and branding demonstrations. To join the Cowboy Morning tour, you must drive 27 miles to the ranch (take I-40 east to the Pullman Rd. exit, then south on FM 1258 to the Figure 3 Ranch) or cadge a ride from the Amarillo CVB (possible if they have a tour group going). This activity costs $19 for adults, $14.50 for children. Reservations must be made in advance by contacting Old West Tours, Box 9480, Amarillo, TX 79105, tel. (800) 692-1338 in Texas, (800) 654-1902 outside Texas or by contacting the Figure 3 Ranch directly at 944-5562 (call after 5 p.m. or on weekends only).

SHOPPING

Old San Jacinto

Along W. 6th St. between Western and Georgia in what used to be a streetcar suburb is a string of antique and craft shops. Some specialize in furniture and accessories, others sell records, coins, used books, and just about any other aged item. **Precision Gunsmithing** still does custom gunsmithing and repairs. The unique **Tecovas Creek Traders** deals in historical frontier clothing and accessories.

Old Santa Fe Depot

This former railway station (built in 1910) now houses three shops in addition to the acclaimed Iron Horse Café (see "Food" above). **Texas Express** is devoted to train memorabilia and nostalgic toys. **Hobos on the Patio** offers gourmet desserts, fresh roasted coffee, and spices. The **Boxcar Gallery** displays the work of local artists.

Boot And Saddle Shops

Hilltop Boot and Saddle (tel. 806-383-0501), at 4624 River Rd., north of Thompson Park off US 87/287, offers custom-made boots (prices start at around $300), belts, wallets, and other leather work. Their saddles are ready-mades. **Bob Marrs Stockman's Saddle Shop** (tel. 372-8439), at 2710 E. 3rd at Nelson, near the stockyards, makes saddles for working cowboys throughout the country, also leather tack and chaps. Marrs's work is in high demand—you may have to wait as long as a year for a custom-made saddle. **Oliver Bros. Saddle Shop** (tel. 372-7562), at 3016 Plains, between Western and Georgia, also does custom saddle and leather work, and their customers include prorodeo cowboys and other professional equestrians in addition to working cowboys. They make English as well as Western gear and have one of the largest selections of tack in the state.

Western Wear

Several shops and department stores in Amarillo offer western wear, but the best prices and selection are found at **Boots 'n' Jeans** (tel. 806-353-4368) at 2225 S. Georgia downtown. A pair of Wrangler Prorodeo 13 MWZ Cowboy Cut Jeans is a bargain $14 here. Boots start at around $50 for ropers.

AMARILLO INFORMATION

Tourist Offices

The **Amarillo Convention and Visitors Bureau** (tel. 806-374-1497 or 800-654-1902) is headquartered in the historic Bivins Home at 1000 S. Polk downtown (zip code 79101). The staff is happy to assist individuals or groups and can provide all manner of brochures and maps on the city and area, as well as information on Old West Tours (see under "Events" above). Open Mon.-Fri. 8-5. The city also maintains an information booth at Amarillo International Airport.

There's a **Texas Information Center** (tel. 335-1179) just off I-40 at the Airport exit where you can get information on Amarillo as well as the rest of the state. Open daily 8-5.

Publications

Accent West Amarillo is a monthly magazine that covers local events and culture (available at newsstands and bookstores). The Amarillo CVB issues a bimonthly *Amarillo Entertainment Guide* that contains a comprehensive, up-to-date calendar of events for each two-month period (available at the CVB—see address above under Tourist Offices).

Detailed maps of the city are available free from any of the three tourist offices mentioned above.

TELEPHONE AND EMERGENCY INFORMATION

Emergency (police, fire, medical)	911
Telephone Directory Assistance	411
Weather Service	335-1684
AAA Emergency Road Service	376-5821
Texas State Highway Patrol	359-4751
Road Conditions	358-6300

Telephone And Post

The area code for Amarillo and vicinity is 806. Like most of Texas, Amarillo is in the Central Time Zone. The main post office is at 2300 Ross St., Amarillo, TX 79120. Western Union has an office at 2403 W. 3rd. Supplementary mail services, including packing and shipping, are available at **The Mail Man,** 5701 S.W. 45th and at **Pack-N-Mail,** 2514 Paramount.

TRANSPORT

Buses

For city bus information, call **Amarillo City Transit** at tel. (806) 378-3094. The **Greyhound Trailways** bus terminal, for long-distance buses, is centrally located at 700 S. Tyler. Regional bus lines to New Mexico and Oklahoma stop at 117 S. Johnson. Shuttles to the Texas Outdoor Musical Drama at Palo Duro (see "Vicinity of Amarillo," below) are available through **Amarillo Tours,** tel. 655-9637.

Taxis

Three cab companies do business in Amarillo: Bob's Taxi Service (tel. 806-373-1171), Checker Cab (tel. 376-8211), and Dependable Cab (tel. 372-5500).

Amarillo International Airport

Four airlines use the Amarillo airport: American (tel. 806-373-4490), Continental (tel. 525-0280), Delta (tel. 374-6481), and Southwest (tel. 374-1221). The airport information number is 335-1671.

VICINITY OF AMARILLO

PALO DURO CANYON STATE PARK

This is the gem of the Texas state park system, a 120-mile-long canyon that drops 1,200 feet from rim to floor. You can drive past millions of years of geologic time on a park road that winds through the canyon along the Prairie Dog Fork of the Red River. Other activities include camping, hiking, horseback riding, picnicking, riding the Sad Monkey Railroad, and, in the summer, watching the outdoor historical-musical drama *Texas*. The park is 22 miles southeast of Amarillo, via I-27 South and State 217 East.

History

Four major geologic periods are exposed by the canyon walls. The lowermost strata are from the Permian Period (230-250 million years ago) when this area was under the Permian Sea. The layers left behind consist of dark red shale and mudstone with veins of white gypsum. Next up are the red, gray, yellow, and lavender shales and sandstones of the Triassic Period, which form blocky ledges and cliffs undercut by erosion. Fossils found in this layer show that the area was once covered by swamp and inhabited by 12-foot-long, crocodile-like amphibians. The Triassic layers are topped by the pink and tan Ogallala caliche of the Tertiary Period, which is in turn covered by the Pleistocene sands and pond deposits of the Quaternary Period.

Because of the shelter provided by the canyon walls and the availability of water from springs and perennial waterways, the canyon vegetation is quite lush in places, especially in comparison with the surrounding plains. Rocky Mountain and juniper woodlands along the canyon floor gave Palo Duro its name (Palo Duro is Spanish for "hard wood"), and riparian species thrive along the Prairie Dog Fork of the Red River. Even the upper parts of the canyon display brush-covered slopes and grasslands.

Humans apparently didn't make use of this plains oasis until 10,000-12,000 years ago when Folsom and Clovis man hunted mastodon and giant bison in the area, using flint weapons that were quarried at nearby Alibates (see "Lake Meredith," p. 163). Later came the hunting and foraging Archaic Indians (8,000-10,000 years ago) who utilized the plants and animals of the canyon environment to support minor settlements. They were followed by a High Plains pueblo culture in the 13th-15th centuries A.D.

The first Europeans to set eyes on the canyon were Spanish conquistador Francisco Coronado and his men, who found winter shelter here in 1541 while searching for the Seven Cities of Cibola. Over the next two centuries, several Plains Indian tribes, including the Apache, Cheyenne, Arapaho, and Kiowa, began using the canyon intermittently as shelter from the fierce High Plains winters and to take advantage of the abundance of game. As elsewhere in the Southwest, they displaced the more peaceful Pueblo Indians that they encountered. But by the beginning of the 19th century, Comanches, the most aggressive of Plains Indians, dominated the canyon.

As the 19th century came to a close, Palo Duro Canyon was the last Texas holdout for the Comanches until they were driven out in the 1874 Battle of Palo Duro when a unit of Texas Rangers cornered them in the canyon and captured their horses. The Comanches retreated to Oklahoma on foot and never came back. Two years later, ex-Texas Ranger Charles Goodnight (who scouted for the Rangers during the Civil War years so was not involved in the 1874 battle) started the first commercial ranch in the Panhandle when he drove 1,600 head of cattle into the canyon. He and his English partner John Adair established the J.A. Ranch in the canyon, which grew to nearly a million acres of land and 100,000 head of cattle at its peak. In 1933, 16,000 acres of the canyon were acquired by Texas Parks and Wildlife for development into a state park.

Texas: A Musical Romance Of Panhandle History

From mid-June through late August every year since 1966, a cast of 80 has performed this musical drama at the outdoor Pioneer Amphitheater, with 600-foot canyon cliffs as a backdrop. The

Prairie Dog Fork of
the Red River,
Palo Duro Canyon

drama was penned by Pulitzer Prize-winner Paul Green (a native of North Carolina who also wrote *The Lost Colony)* and although it sounds very hokey, the whole performance actually succeeds as a heart-warming piece of Americana. The story centers on seven main characters who collaborate to establish a railroad through the Panhandle and eventually develop the first Panhandle town.

The show starts at 8 p.m., Mon.-Saturday. Tickets cost $6-10 for adults, $3-10 for children, depending on seating, and are available by mail from TEXAS, Box 268, Canyon, TX 79015, or at the Pioneer Amphitheater box office between 6 and 7 p.m. Telephone reservations are accepted at (806) 655-2181, Mon.-Sat. 8:30-4:30.

Parking for the performance is free. An added bonus: if you enter Palo Duro Canyon after 5:30 p.m., you don't have to pay the $2 park admission. Come early and watch the sun set over the canyon. Sutphen's Barbecue of Amarillo caters a barbecue meal in the park starting at 6:30 p.m. (about $5 a plate). Shuttle buses to the performance are available from virtually any hotel or motel in Amarillo for a nominal cost.

Visitor Center

About a quarter mile past the park entrance is the visitor center, where interpretative exhibits explain the area's geology, history, flora, and fauna. An overlook next to the center affords a good view of the widest part of the canyon. A trail next to the parking lot leads to lower sets of cliffs where side canyons can be viewed.

Sad Monkey Train

If you don't plan to hike along the canyon floor, the miniature Sad Monkey Railroad is a good way to get closer to some of the canyon's colorful rock formations, since the park road only passes a few. The two-mile train ride lasts about 20 minutes. A guide gives an ongoing narrative of the history and geology of the canyon as the train passes the formations of Santana's Face, Triassic Peak, Sad Monkey Rock, Spanish Skirts, and Catarina Cave, as well as Indian petroglyphs. Fare is $2.50 per person, kids under six free.

Trails

The park has few developed trails, but visitors are free to wander anywhere along the Prairie Dog Fork of the Red River, which is particularly scenic in late October when the leaves are turning or in April when the wildflowers are out. The other option is to explore the side canyons (the widest portions of the canyon floor are privately owned), which can be quite challenging since a bit of rock climbing is usually called for. Don't get too close to cliff edges, as the limestone, mudstone, and sandstone can easily crumble. An official hiking and equestrian trail (the "Lighthouse Trail") leads south from where the park road forks and into Sunday Canyon, past a promontory called Sleeping Indian, and then ends at the foot of Lighthouse Peak, the rock and mudstone tower that is the "symbol" of Palo Duro; it's about three miles roundtrip (allow

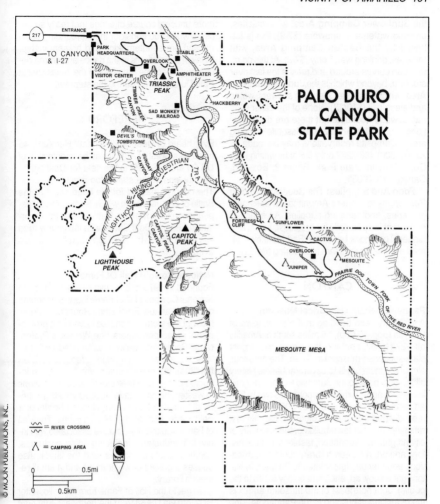

PALO DURO CANYON STATE PARK

= RIVER CROSSING

∧ = CAMPING AREA

0   0.5mi

0   0.5km

© MOON PUBLICATIONS, INC.

three hours on foot). During periods of heavy rain (rare) the trail may be closed because of the danger of flash floods.

Horses and riding equipment can be hired at the park stables, located next to Goodnight Trading Post.

Facilities
Camping: The park has six camping areas, with a total of 116 sites. Each camping area is off the main park road, which crosses the river six times (during high-water periods, some areas may be temporarily closed). The first sites you come to as you enter the lower canyon are part of the **Hackberry Camping Area,** which has multi-use sites with drinking water, showers, and electricity ($10 weekdays, $12 weekends). About a half mile further, the road splits; the left fork leads to the **Fortress Cliff Camping Area,** which has are tentsites with drinking water only ($7/9). Next is

the **Sunflower Camping Area,** with tentsites, drinking water, and showers ($7/9); this is followed by the **Cactus Camping Area,** with tentsites, drinking water only ($7/9). At this point, the road curves around and makes the last river crossing, beyond which is the **Juniper Camping Area,** which has trailer sites with showers, water, and electricity ($10/12). None of the trailer sites has sewage hookups, but there are dump stations near the Hackberry and Mesquite camping areas. Campsite reservations may be made by calling (806) 488-2227 daily 8-5 or by writing Palo Duro Canyon State Park, Route 2, Box 285, Canyon, TX 79051.

Food And Supplies: The Goodnight Trading Post opposite Pioneer Amphitheater sells gas, groceries, and camping supplies. An attached restaurant is open daily for breakfast, lunch, and dinner. The snack bar at the Sad Monkey Railroad terminal serves fast food during the day.

CANYON

Panhandle-Plains Historical Museum

A 1933 art-deco building in the small town of Canyon (pop. 12,000), 15 miles south of Amarillo off I-27/US 87, contains the oldest and largest state-supported museum in Texas. The ambitious aim of the museum is to cover Panhandle history all the way back to the Jurassic Period (160 million years ago). Exhibits encompass two million artifacts that are spread over 300,000 square feet, divided into paleontology, Indian history, ranching, pioneer town-building, the discovery of oil and gas, transportation, fashions, natural history, and art. A research library contains publications and manuscripts related to Panhandle history, genealogy, art, and archaeology (open to the public). Just northeast of the museum annex is the oldest intact building in the Panhandle—the former headquarters of the T Anchor Ranch, built in 1877.

The museum (tel. 806-656-2244) is open Mon.-Sat. 9-6 (Sept.-May till 5 p.m.) and Sun. 2-6. No admission charge (donations requested).

West Texas State University

This 6,500-student campus supports six schools and colleges in the arts and sciences, fine arts, agriculture, business, and education. Among the more unusual course offerings (not really so unusual when you consider the surrounding community) are saddlemaking and horsemanship. Many of the students in the dance and drama departments become members of the *Texas* cast at Palo Duro Canyon during the summer.

HEREFORD

Ever heard of Deaf Smith wheat? Hereford, 45 miles southwest of Amarillo at the intersection of US 60 and US 385, is the seat for Deaf Smith County, one of the state's top grain producers. The county's named for the head scout at the Battle of San Jacinto, in which Texas gained independence from Mexico. Cattle is also an important industry in Deaf Smith, with the county feed lots servicing nearly a million head per year on average.

National Cowgirl Hall Of Fame

Founded in 1975, the female counterpart to the National Cowboy Hall of Fame inducts honorees during the annual Rhinestone Roundup in June. Most of the women honored have been professional rodeo performers (the Women's Professional Rodeo Association was founded in the mid '40s, though women rode in rodeos as early as the '20s), but other women who have been inducted because of their significant contributions to western heritage have included yodeling country singer Patsy Montana, Nocona bootmaker Enid Justin, and rancher Mamie Burns. The Hall of Fame displays memorabilia associated with individual inductees, including riding costumes, saddles, photos, trophies, and the like; it also houses a gallery of western art and a small research library.

To get to the Hall of Fame from Amarillo, enter Hereford via US 60 from the northeast, turn right on US 85 to the north, then right on 15th Street. The Hall of Fame is about a half mile down 15th Street. Open Mon.-Fri. 9-5. Admission is free. For information, call (806) 364-5252.

All Girl Rodeo

The National Cowgirl Hall of Fame sponsors this rodeo every August. One of the largest women's rodeos in the country, it lasts for several days and includes bareback bronc riding, calf roping, barrel racing, goat tying, bull riding, and team roping. It's held at the Riders Club Arena on US 60, southeast of town. Call the Hall of Fame (telephone number above) or the Hereford Chamber of Commerce (806-364-3333) for current information.

FRITCH (LAKE MEREDITH)

This town of 2,000, 38 miles northeast of Amarillo via State 136, is the gateway for Lake Meredith and the Alibates Flint Quarries National Monument.

Lake Meredith National Recreation Area
The only lake in the Panhandle didn't exist until 1964 when the Canadian River was dammed. Now it draws over a million visitors a year in search of water recreation. The nonstop Panhandle winds in particular attract sailors and windsurfers. In the summer there are at least six sailboat regattas, and both the Lake Meredith Yacht Club and the Amarillo Yacht Club are quite active on the lake. Fishing is also big, since the lake is stocked with walleye, smallmouth bass, largemouth bass, yellow perch, blue, channel, and flathead catfish, crappie, bluegill, carp, and sunfish. A Walleye Tournament is held each Memorial Day. In season, Lake Meredith opens public hunting land with white-tailed and mule deer, wild turkey, quail, dove, geese, and ducks.

The National Park Service administers eight public-use areas around the lake that make up the Lake Meredith National Recreation Area. Facilities at these shore areas include picnic tables, grills, restrooms, undeveloped campgrounds (seven in all, no fee), and boat launches. There are also a few commercial facilities, like the **Lake Meredith Marina,** just west of the dam (which offers 212 boat slips for rent), a ship's store (with gas and bait as well as sailing gear), a heated fish house, and a fishing pier.

Information
The Park Service headquarters (tel. 857-3151) is at 419 E. Broadway (State 136) in Fritch. *The Lake Meredith Press,* a quarterly newspaper that's available free in Amarillo and in Fritch, covers lake events and contains a map of the lake.

Alibates Flint Quarries National Monument
About six miles south of Fritch off State 136 is an 800-acre area protected by the National Park Service that features a series of ancient Indian flint quarries. Over thousands of years, from the time of the prehistoric game hunters until iron was introduced to the Plains Indians in the 19th century, Indian groups mined flint here. Alibates flint (named for Ali Bates, a cowboy who once lived here) is equal in hardness to the hardest of steels and was highly valued because of its brilliant color variations. One Indian tribe (possibly Pawnees) settled in the area for 250 years, trading the flint with other Indians far and wide; tools made of Alibates flint have been found throughout the U.S. as a result.

The Park Service leads free 1.5-mile tours through the quarries and Indian ruins daily during the summer at 10 and 2, on weekends only in spring and fall. The tour ends with a flint-chipping demonstration. During the winter, tours can be arranged by calling the local Park Service office at (806) 857-3151.

LUBBOCK

Lubbock was established in 1890 as a ranching center for the South Plains area of the Panhandle. Some of the state's largest ranches developed in north Lubbock County, including the three-million-acre XIT. By the early 1920s, farming began competing with the livestock industry and today agriculture is the second-greatest economic producer locally (primarily cotton, grain sorghum, and wheat). Number one is Texas Tech University (and the Texas Tech Health Sciences Center), one of the state's four major universities, which makes Lubbock very much a university town (about 13% of the city's 190,000 population consists of TTU students). Nearby Reese Air Force Base, a training center for jet pilots, is the third most important economic force in Lubbock. Lubbock area vineyards have also achieved some esteem due to the award-winning efforts of three local vintners (see "Wineries" below).

Buddy Holly statue, Lubbock

One aspect of Lubbock's heritage, however, seemingly overshadows all the others. It's world famous as the birthplace of singer-songwriter Buddy Holly, a major figure in the early development of rock 'n' roll. Fans from all over the world come to Lubbock to pay homage to Holly at his memorial statue and grave. Lubbock is still very much a music town, though it seems that the most talented local musicians end up going elsewhere to "make it."

SIGHTS

Buddy Holly Monuments

Holly was born in Lubbock in 1936 and became an international star when his song "That'll Be the Day" broke in 1957. In February 1959 he died in a plane crash in Iowa along with singers Ritchie Valens and The Big Bopper (J.P. Richardson). His rockabilly-style music lived on and has been an acknowledged major influence on many noted performers, including the Beatles (whose name paid tribute to Holly's band, the Crickets), Linda Ronstadt, Marshall Crenshaw, Elvis Costello, and others.

In 1979, Holly's hometown unveiled a **Buddy Holly statue** to coincide with the release of the motion picture *The Buddy Holly Story*. The 8 1/2-foot bronze statue stands at the corner of 8th and Ave. Q near the Lubbock Civic Center. A **Walk of Fame** has been established around the base of the statue to honor other Lubbock area musicians that have succeeded in the music business, with bronze plaques commemorating Sonny Curtis (one of the original Crickets), Roy Orbison, Waylon Jennings, Mac Davis, Bobby Keys, Joe Ely, and others. Each year another plaque is added during the Lubbock Music Festival in August.

Buddy Holly's grave is in the Lubbock Cemetery at the east end of 31st Street. After entering the cemetery, take the right fork and you'll find the grave on the left not far from the entrance. The original headstone was stolen and has been replaced by a new one, with engraved guitar and musical notes. You may notice triangular pieces of plastic on the grave—along with flowers, fans often leave guitar picks.

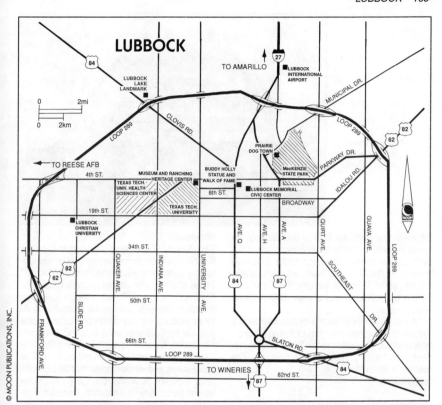

Texas Tech University

Yes, the official name is Texas Tech University, or Texas Tech for short (or locally, just Tech). The university was chartered in 1923 and now has over 23,000 students in seven colleges (covering 115 majors), a graduate school (with 104 majors), and a law school. TTU shares an attractive 1,800-acre campus in the center of town with the Texas Tech University Health Sciences Center, which includes one of the state's major schools of medicine.

One of Tech's most outstanding features is **The Museum of Texas Tech University,** which includes the main museum, the Ranching Heritage Center, the Moody Planetarium, the Lubbock Lake Landmark, and two research-oriented museums (not open to the general public): the Natural Science Research Center and the Val Verde County Research Site.

The Museum: The main museum building at Texas Tech is located on campus at 4th and Indiana. Temporary and permanent exhibits cover various topics in the natural and social sciences as well as the visual arts. Permanent exhibits worth seeing include the Heritage of the Llano Estacado, the Taos/Southwest Art Gallery, and the Early Texas Cultures Hall. Open Tues.-Sat. 10-5 (Thurs. till 8:30) and Sun. 1-5. Admission is free. For further information, call (806) 742-2490.

Ranching Heritage Center: This is a mostly outdoor attraction, consisting of 33 ranching structures that have been relocated to the center from around the state. The 14-acre grounds are adjacent to the main museum building on the Texas Tech campus; a free map guides visitors along a trail throughout the center. Among the most interesting structures are four different kinds

*1909 ranch house,
Ranching Heritage
Center*

of windmills from the turn of the century, an 1838 log cabin, a 1918 railway depot (complete with steam locomotive and cattle shipping pens), an 1877 horse barn, an 1880 bunkhouse, an 1886 house from the XIT Ranch, an 1890s schoolhouse, and a huge 1909 Victorian ranch house.

An indoor portion of the center contains a gallery that displays ranching tools and other artifacts of Southwestern ranch life, including collections of spurs, saddles, and firearms. The center is open Mon.-Sat. 10-5, Sun. 1-5. Free admission.

Lubbock Lake Landmark
State Historical Park

A watering place for humans and animals for at least 12,000 years, Lubbock Lake has yielded a cultural and geologic record of the Clovis period (North America's earliest human culture), plus evidence of archaic, ceramic, proto-historic and historic occupation of the area. The Nash Interpretive Center on the site contains exhibits on the discoveries and work of the archaeologists as well as a children's educational center and a gift shop. There is also a picnic area and self-guided interpretive trail.

The park is located at the northwest edge of the city; from the junction of US 84 and Loop 289 follow the signs to Landmark Drive. It's open Tues.-Sat. 9-5, Sun. 1-5; admission is $2 adults, $1 children and seniors. For more information, call (806) 741-0306.

Wineries

Viticulture has become so important to Lubbock that the chamber of commerce city logo now features a bunch of grapes dangling across the "O." Three of the major vintners, Llano Estacado, Teysha Cellars, and Pheasant Ridge, have won awards in statewide and national competitions. All three produce the standard appellations made popular by California wine-makers: Cabernet Sauvignon, Chardonnay, Johannisberg Riesling, Chenin Blanc, and Gewürztraminer, as well as various red and white blends. For all Lubbock area wineries, however, the Gewürztraminer seems particularly well-suited to the soil and climate. Two of these wineries are open daily for free tours and tasting and are close enough together that they can be visited in an afternoon.

Llano Estacado: This winery has the best overall reputation and distribution in Texas and was the first "modern" (Napa Valley-style) vintner in Texas, founded in 1976. Its 1984 Chardonnay took a Double Gold Award at the 1986 San Francisco Fair. In addition to the wines listed above, Llano Estacado produces a Fumé Blanc as well as red and white table wines. The winery gift shops sells wines and wine-serving paraphernalia. To get there, drive south of Lubbock on US 87 to FM 1585 (about four miles south of Loop 289) and then east 3.2 miles. The winery is open for tours and tasting Mon.-Sat. 10-5 and Sun. noon-5.

Teysha Cellars: This state-of-the-art winery was opened in 1988; at a cost of $6 million, it's the most expensive wine-making facility ever built. The main building, which contains the tasting room, is a striking example of new Southwestern architecture. In 1989, Teysha's outstanding 1988 Gewürztraminer won medals at the San Francisco National Wine Competition, the Santa Fe Sixth Annual Southwestern Competition, and the National Orange Show in Orange County, California. Their Chenin Blanc and Johannisberg Riesling are also quite good. The winery is open for tours and tasting Mon.-Sat. 10-5, Sun. noon-5.

Prairie Dog Town

This is one of only two prairie dog towns left in the state since these rodents proved such pests early this century that farmers practically wiped them out. They look like giant, tan squirrels without tails; it's hard to believe that the little retaining wall around this colony actually keeps them from colonizing local fields. If you have binoculars, bring them, as the prairie dogs stay close to their burrows and don't often come near the wall (visitors aren't allowed inside). It's in MacKenzie State Park in the northeast corner of Lubbock; the entrance is at Ave. A and E. Broadway. Free.

FOOD

American

The Depot: A 1928 railroad depot converted to a very popular restaurant that specializes in prime rib, steak, and seafood. Has an outdoor beer garden. At 19th and Ave. G (tel. 806-747-1646); open Mon.-Sat. for lunch and dinner.

The Greenery: Offers a wide variety of American dishes, but is especially good for daily breakfasts and Sunday brunch, when they serve made-to-order omelets and cheese blintzes. At 801 Ave. Q. Open daily 6 a.m.-10 p.m. (Sunday brunch served 10-2).

$ to $$ **Schlotzky's:** Part of a Texas chain that serves good deli-style sandwiches. Four locations: 3719 19th St. (tel. 806-793-5542), 5204 Slide Rd. (tel. 793-1233), 8101 Indiana Ave. (tel. 792-3396), and 120 Main St. (tel. 744-3803). Open daily for lunch and dinner.

Barbecue

$ to $$ **Bigham's Smokehouse:** The local favorite, at three locations: 3306 4th St. (tel. 806-

762-8782), 3310 82nd St. (tel. 797-9241), and 2318 50th St. (tel. 793-3346). Open daily for lunch and dinner.

$ to $$ **The County Line:** Part of a statewide chain that started in Austin; always reliable, basic menu of ribs, brisket, sausage, and chicken, served with cole slaw, potato salad, and beans. Occasional "blue plate specials" include smoked duck, grilled fish, and other non-typical selections. The Lubbock branch (tel. 806-763-6001) is situated next to a stream frequented by ducks, on FM 2641 (half mile west of I-27/US 87 north). Open daily for dinner.

$ **Mesquite's BBQ & Steaks:** Besides barbecue, specialities here include homemade onion rings and Mexican food. Two locations: 2419 Broadway (tel. 763-1159) and 7202 Indiana (tel. 792-0441). Both locations are open daily for breakfast, lunch, and dinner.

Health Food

$ **Well Body Natural Foods:** The eclectic, health-oriented menu features dishes like spinach lasagna and walnut broccoli stir-fry (but also offers chicken and seafood dishes), cooked with light oils and using all-natural ingredients. No smoking is allowed in the dining room—unusual for Texas. At 3651 34th (tel. 793-1015); open Mon.-Sat. 11-8.

Italian

$$ **Olive Garden Restaurant:** This local favorite specializes in traditional Italian cuisine. Near South Plains Mall at 5702 Slide Rd. (tel. 806-791-3575). Open daily for lunch and dinner.

$-$$ **Orlando's:** Features huge portions of pasta, veal dishes, pizza, and other Italian meals. At 2402 Ave. Q (tel. 747-5998) and 5404 4th St. (tel. 796-2333); open Mon.-Sat. for lunch and dinner, Sun. dinner only.

Mexican

$ **Jimenez Bakery and Restaurant:** Classic Tex-Mex and Mexican pastries at 1219 Ave. G (tel. 806-744-2685). Open daily except Tues. for breakfast and lunch only.

$$ **Santa Fe:** Southwestern-style Mexican along with a few down-home dishes like chicken-fried steak. At 4th and Ave. Q. Open daily for lunch and dinner.

$$ **Texas Café and Bar:** Specializes in Tex-Mex, but also serves steak, barbecue, and down-home

dishes. At 3604 50th St. (tel. 762-8544); open daily for lunch and dinner.

Oriental

$-$$ Great Wall: Features Hunan and Szechwan cuisine, plus all-you-can-eat Mongolian barbecue. At 1625 University Ave. (tel. 806-747-1264); open Sun.-Fri. for lunch and dinner, Sat. dinner only.

$ Thai Thai Restaurant: Good selection of curries, noodles, and Thai-style salads *(yam)* at low prices. Could be called Tex-Thai, since the Thai food here accommodates local tastes without losing its essential Thainess (the innovative *Thai Thai* is a chicken-potato eggroll). At 5105 Quaker Ave. (tel 791-0024); open daily 11:30-9.

Seafood

$$ Lone Star Oyster Bar: A popular seafood place that specializes in fresh oysters (on the half shell, baked, or fried), gumbo, and catfish. Two locations: 34th and Flint (tel. 806-796-0101); 59th and Slide (tel. 797-3773). Open daily for lunch and dinner.

ENTERTAINMENT

Lubbock, like Amarillo, is a town where live bands tend to play a mixture of rock and country tunes, in the spirit of Buddy Holly. Local groups like The Convertibles and the Maines Brothers Band perform original as well as cover tunes, and singer-songwriters are plentiful. If you're lucky, you may get to see Jimmie Dale Gilmore, Butch Hancock, or Jesse Taylor perform here in their hometown, although they usually stay close to Austin these days, where the recording studios are. Cover charges are quite reasonable at Lubbock clubs, usually under $5.

The **Texas Café and Bar** (see "Food" above) brings in progressive country (or as some call it locally, "aggressive country") and western swing. More traditional C&W can be heard at the **Westernaire Club** (tel. 806-747-5763, 4801 Ave. Q.), a longtime favorite of the western swing crowd. The **Villa Club** (tel. 744-8026, 5401 Ave. Q) is another established country dance hall. For more of a honky-tonk atmosphere, try **Midnight Rodeo** (tel. 745-2813, 7301 University Ave.). **Jiggers Up** (tel. 744-5061, 4802 Ave. Q) hosts country jam sessions on Sunday evenings, as does the **Silver Bullet** (799-9166, 5145 Aberdeen).

The **Main Street Saloon** (tel. 762-0940, 2417 Main St.) showcases live rock 'n' roll and blues bands; on Sunday nights they host an open jam session.

For disco and modern rock, the popular places are **West LA** (tel. 797-0220, 5203 34th St.), **Studio C** (tel. 744-2582, 1928 Ave. H), and **Depot 10th Street Warehouse** (tel. 747-6156, 1824 Ave. G).

South of town at US 87 and FM 1585 (near Llano Estacado Winery) is a real Texas roadhouse, the **Yellow Rose** (tel. 806-745-9875), which features live hard-core country and rock 'n' roll.

EVENTS

All the major events in Lubbock seem to take place in September and October (too hot in the summer, too cold in the winter, and spring is tornado season in the Panhandle).

Fiestas Del Llano

This is the local version of Dies y Seis, Mexican independence day. Held at the Lubbock Memorial Civic Center (6th St.) for three days around September 16, the celebration features plenty of Mexican food, music, and dancing.

Buddy Holly's Birthday

Holly was born September 7, 1936, so this event is held the first week of September. The main purpose of the celebration is to display, trade, buy, and sell Buddy Holly memorabilia—records, autographs, musical instruments—from local and international collections. For information on location and scheduling, call Bill Griggs at (806) 799-4299.

Texas International Wine Classic

An event that takes place one weekend in late September or early October, the Wine Classic features tastings and competition among local, national, and international wines, plus wine seminars, lectures, and gourmet meals. Held in the Lubbock Memorial Civic Center. Call (806) 763-4666 for details.

Panhandle South Plains Fair

Held in late September or early October at the Fair Park and Fair Park Coliseum, 105 E. Broadway. Includes all the usual fair events: carnival

LUBBOCK HOTELS AND MOTELS

Add 13% hotel tax to all rates. Area code: 806

NAME	ADDRESS	PHONE	RATES	FEATURES
Astro Motel	501 Ave. Q	762-8726	$30-55	pool
Barcelona Ct.	5215 S. Loop 289	794-5353	$70-100	heated pool, kitchens, coin laundry, airport shuttle, senior discount
Coronado Inn	501 Amarillo Hwy.	763-6441	$20-32	pool, kitchenette
Days Inn	2401 4th	747-7111	$35-50	pool
El Tehas Motel	1000 N. Ave. Q	763-9343	$18-24	pool
Holiday Inn Civic Center	801 Ave. Q	763-1200	$65-90	heated pool, coin laundry, refrigerators available, airport shuttle
Holiday Inn South	6624 Ave. H	745-2208	$55-88	heated pool, coin laundry, airport shuttle
KoKo Inn	5201 Ave. Q	747-2591	$37-46	heated pool, airport shuttle
La Quinta Motor Inn	601 Ave. Q	763-9441	$49-63	pool, airport shuttle
Lubbock Inn	3901 19th St.	792-5181 or 800-545-8226	$44-66	pool, airport shuttle
Lubbock Plaza	3201 S. Loop 289	797	$67-80	heated pool, airport shuttle
Motel 6	909 66th	745-5541	$25- +6 ea. add.	small pool
Paragon Hotel	4115 Brownfield Hwy.	792-0065 or 800-333-1146	$44-50	pool, refrigerators available
Residence Inn	251 S. Loop 289	745-1963	$80-100	heated pool, fireplace, kitchens, coin laundry
Sheraton Inn Lubbock	505 Ave. Q	747-0171	$62-82	heated pool, airport shuttle
Stadium Motel	405 University	763-5779	$18-38	—
Village Inn	4925 Brownfield Hwy.	795-5821	$30-38	heated pool, coin laundry, senior discount

midway, horse and livestock shows, agricultural and industrial exhibits, contests, games, and music by top country performers.

SHOPPING

Lubbock has the usual malls and chain department stores. One unique spot is the **Antique Mall** at 7907 W. 19th St. (about three miles west of Loop 289), where around 50 antique and collectibles dealers rent booths. A map of the mall is available from the Lubbock Convention and Visitors Bureau (see "Lubbock Information" below). Another is **Cactus Alley** at 2600 Salem, where shops around a courtyard are devoted to such whimsical items as balloons, spices, clocks, stuffed bears, costumes, and art (one store specializes in eggshell art and items shaped like eggs).

LUBBOCK INFORMATION

Tourist Office
The **Lubbock Convention and Visitors Bureau** is oriented toward group tourism and conventions but the staff are happy to answer questions from individuals. They distribute a number of helpful maps and brochures that may be of interest to the casual visitor. At Ave. K and 14th St., tel. (806) 763-4666 or (800) 692-4035.

TELEPHONE AND EMERGENCY INFORMATION

Emergency (police, fire, medical)	911
Telephone Directory Assistance	411
Weather Service	762-0141
Texas Tech University	742-3610
Chamber of Commerce	763-4666

TRANSPORT

Buses
For city bus information, call **Citibus** at (806) 762-0111. The bus terminal for the **Texas, New Mexico, and Oklahoma** line, a subsidiary of Greyhound, is at 1313 13th St. (southeast corner of 13th and Ave. M) downtown. Call 765-6644 for TNM&O information.

Taxis
There are two cab companies in Lubbock: **City Cab** (tel. 806-765-7474) and **Yellow Cab** (tel. 765-7777).

Lubbock International Airport
The four commercial passenger airlines that fly into Lubbock are America West (tel. 800-247-5692, in Texas), American (tel. 806-763-0675 or, in Texas, 800-334-7400), Delta (tel. 762-6150), and Southwest (tel. 762-8881).

THE PRAIRIES

Wedged between Oklahoma to the north, the Llano Estacado to the west, the Edwards Plateau to the south, and the Cross Timbers to the east is an area of rolling, grassy hills known as the Prairies. Because there are only two cities of size here, Abilene and Wichita Falls, the area is often lumped together with the Panhandle.

The area was a favorite buffalo-hunting ground for the nomadic South Plains Indians during the winter, when buffalo herds migrated here to avoid colder weather on the High Plains. Buffalo Gap, near present-day Abilene, was one of the first areas on the Prairies to be settled; white and Creek Indian buffalo hunters began coming here in the 1870s when they discovered what the Plains Indians knew all along—that huge buffalo herds always used this gap in the Callahan Divide on their way south in the late fall and north in the early spring. As the demand for buffalo hide increased in the eastern U.S., a wholesale slaughter ensued: buffalo hunters shot hundreds of animals daily, followed by skinners who skinned the buffalo where they fell and stacked the hides on the ground to be collected later by traders, which forced the Comanches, who depended on the buffalo as a source of food, clothing, household tools, and shelter, to move on. This left the area open for farms, ranches, and railroads.

ABILENE

Once the Comanches were out of the area, the Texas & Pacific Railroad established a railhead at milepost 407 along the telegraph line between Marshall and El Paso in 1881. The town founders named it after Abilene, Kansas, in hopes that the new town would soon become as prosperous as its namesake.

Abilene's economy rests on ranching, agriculture, oil, and the military (Dyess Air Force Base). Early on, the town became a stronghold for Christian fundamentalists and has been called "the buckle of the Bible Belt." The two universities and one college here are religious institutions: Abilene Christian University (Church of Christ, est. 1906, 4,600 students), Hardins-Simmons University (Baptist, est. 1891, 2,000 stu-

Buffalo Gap
Historic Village

ABILENE CONVENTION & VISITORS BUREAU

Fort Phantom Hill, Abilene

ABILENE CONVENTION & VISITORS BUREAU

dents), and McMurray University (Methodist, est. 1923, 1,600 students). It's a conservative town so don't go looking for honky-tonks—the nightlife is virtually nil.

Buffalo Gap

Ten miles southwest of Abilene off FM 89 (Buffalo Gap Rd.) is a little town that's hardly changed since the turn of the century except that now it caters to tourists rather than frontierspeople. Most of the 397 residents are ranchers; the Buffalo Gap Volunteer Fire Dept. has an all-woman staff since most men are out riding herd during the day. The main tourist attraction is **Buffalo Gap Historic Village,** a collection of hundred-year-old buildings. The original Taylor County Courthouse and Jail, built in 1879 of sandstone blocks and Civil War cannonballs, still stands solidly. The building now houses a museum with local artifacts from that era. Other buildings include a chapel, a railroad depot, a print shop, a post office, a wagon barn, and several mercantile stores. It's open to visitors daily 10-7 March 15 to Nov. 15, or on weekends 10-6 Nov. 16 to March 14. Admission is $4 adults, seniors $3, children $1.75.

Several small country restaurants and cafés in Buffalo Gap include the **Bar-B-Que Barn, Judy's Gathering Place**, and **Perini Ranch.**

Abilene Zoo

This 13-acre zoo is the only zoo between Fort Worth and El Paso. It's divided into three habitats, the Texas Plains, the African Veldt, and the Herpetarium. The Texas Plains exhibit is of particular note since it houses animals native to upper West Texas that you might not otherwise get a chance to see, including bison, pronghorn, javelina, coyote, wild turkey, prairie dogs, and roadrunners.

The zoo's 10,300-square-foot **Discovery Center** is a self-contained facility consisting of four climatized biomes that compare habitats in the American Southwest and Mexico with similar areas in East Africa and Madagascar. The "Aquatic Adventure" section, for example, draws parallels between Texas' Lake Amistad and Africa's Lake Tanganyika, as well as the Rio Grande and the Zambesi River. The zoo is located in Nelson Park, off US 80 just inside Loop 322. From Memorial Day to Labor Day, hours are weekdays 9-5, weekends and holidays 9-7, and the rest of the year daily 9-5. Admission is $2 adults, $1 seniors and children. Call (915) 672-9771 for further information.

Fort Phantom Hill

This was one of four U.S. Army infantry forts established in the early 1850s (along with Fort McKavett, Fort Belknap, and Fort Chadbourne) to protect the westward-expanding Texas frontier. It was never officially named, however, and was known only as the Post on the Clear Fork of the Brazos. The five infantry companies based here were of little use against the mounted Comanches. The current name probably originated after the fort closed in 1854, either in reference to its abandoned condition or because the hill that it rests on seems to recede as one approaches it. In 1858 it was turned into a way station (No. 54) for the Butterfield Overland Mail, but was again abandoned upon the outbreak of the Civil War. During the war, a Confederate Frontier Battalion occasionally used the abandoned fort as a base, and in the 1870s it became a sub-post for nearby Fort Griffin which was used in the last of the Indian Wars.

The ruins consist of three half-standing buildings and over a dozen chimneys, all made of locally quarried stone. They're on privately owned land 14 miles north of Abilene on FM 600, but are open to the public (no charge).

Four miles south of the ruins is **Lake Fort**

Phantom Hill, a 4,200-acre reservoir that's a popular local fishing spot for walleye and crappie. Lake facilities include marinas, public boat ramps, free campsites, and picnic areas.

Abilene State Recreation Area

Once a Comanche rest stop, this scenic, 500-acre park runs along Cedar Creek near Lake Abilene. A spring-fed swimming pool is open to the public daily noon-9 p.m. between Memorial Day and Labor Day. There are also nature trails, picnic areas, campsites ($6 with water or $9 with w/e), and screened shelters ($12). To get there from Abilene, take FM 89 southeast 14.5 miles to Park Rd. 32. Admission is $2 per vehicle or 50 cents per person for pedestrians and cyclists.

Dyess Air Force Base

Abilene AFB (changed to Dyess AFB in 1956) was established as a Strategic Air Command (SAC) base during the Korean War in 1952. Today the base is the headquarters for the 96th

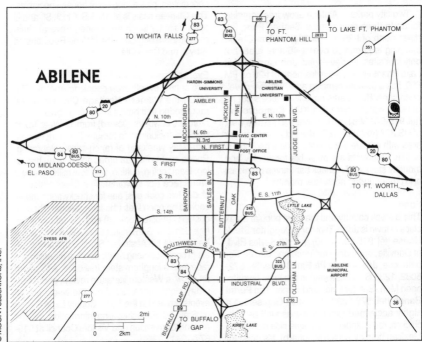

Strategic Bombardment Wing, which trains B1-B combat crews. A collection of 25 restored military aircraft from WW II and the Korean and Vietnam wars is on display at the Linear Air Park on base. Admission is free; stop at the main base entrance for a pass.

Accommodations

Rooms at Abilene's **Motel 6** (tel. 915-672-8462, 4951 W. Stamford St., exit 282 off I-20) are $20.95 a night, plus $6 for each additional adult. Cheaper for two or more people is the **Family Motor Inn** (tel. 677-2935) at 1633 W. Stamford (exit 285), where rooms are $18 s, $22-25 d. The **Kiva Inn** (tel. 695-2150), 5403 S. 1st, is good middle-range value, with well-kept rooms for $39 s, $46 d—and it has a heated indoor pool, whirlpool, and saunas. The **Embassy Suites Hotel** (tel. 698-1234), at 4250 Ridgemont Dr., across from the Mall of Abilene, has efficiencies for $74-84 during the week—it's $5-14 cheaper on weekends and there are senior discounts anytime.

Two city parks in Abilene allow free camping for up to three days. One is **Seabee Park,** 3.2 miles north of I-20 on FM 600, on Elm Creek; camping is permitted over a 40-acre area, but only four sites are developed. **Johnson Park** at Lake Phantom Hill, 6.6 miles north of I-20 on FM 600, has a 37-acre camping area, with five developed sites. Both parks have flush toilets but no drinking water. There is a **KOA Kampground** (tel. 915-672-3681) off I-20 West, a half mile west of US 277 (exit 282 for Shirley Rd.). Tent/camper sites with w/e are $15 a night while a full hookup is $18. Discounts are available for weekly and monthly stays and a snack bar serves breakfast and dinner during nonwinter months.

Food

This is steak country and the most popular steak place in town is **John Zentner's Daughter Steak House** (tel. 915-695-4290) at 4358 Sayles Blvd. at Danville; open daily for lunch and dinner. For barbecue, **Joe Allen's Pit Bar-B-Que** (tel. 672-6082, 1233 S. Treadaway) is the local favorite; open Mon.-Sat. for lunch and dinner. The **Perini Ranch** (tel. 572-3339) in Buffalo Gap serves a highly acclaimed ranch roast as well as ribs, chicken, red snapper, and unique side dishes like Mexican hominy (which is superb). It's open for

dinner every day except Monday and Tuesday. **Judy's Gathering Place** (tel. 572-3731) in Buffalo Gap specializes in New Mexican-style Mexican for lunch daily except Monday.

Back in town are two inexpensive Mexican places: the **Monterrey** (tel. 915-673-1711) at 3310 N. 10th St. (open daily from 7 a.m., specializing in Tex-Mex) and **Dos Amigos** (tel. 672-2992) at 3650 N. 6th St. (open Mon.-Sat. for lunch and dinner, specializing in Sonoran dishes). Dos Amigos also has cantina dancing in the evenings—one of the few dance venues in town. For fresh take-out tamales, **Pompa's** at 1326 Butternut can't be beat—it's been supplying Abilene with fresh tortillas since 1954. A more upscale Mexican atmosphere is available at **Macario's** (tel. 915-672-3071), at 602 S. Treadaway, which features fajitas and carne guisada. Open daily for lunch and dinner.

House of Hunan (tel. 695-9282) has a menu that goes on forever and includes rice dishes, noodles, seafood, all the usual beef, poultry, and pork dishes, plus a long list of house specialties. This Chinese oasis is at 3106 S. Clack St. and is open daily for lunch and dinner. Several chain restaurants along Clack St. include Red Lobster, Arby's, and Casa Olé.

Events

Two annual events draw people to Abilene. The first is the **Western Heritage Classic,** a real ranch rodeo that brings in working cowboys (no prorodeo cowboys allowed) from 12 West Texas ranches, including the famous Pitchfork Ranch, for a May weekend of ranch-style celebrating. Rodeo events include bronc riding, team branding, team roping, cutting, wild cow milking, and a barrel race (for cowgirls). The Classic also includes two cook-offs, one for chuckwagon meals cooked on open fires (the International Championship Campfire Cook-off) and one for barbecue (the Son-of-a-Gun Brisket Cook-off). Other activities include the Australian Shepherd Working Trials (a contest among ranch dogs), a mounted parade, and a longhorn steer trail drive. A Western art show, a Western literature review, and a Saturday night dance round out the weekend. All events are held in the Taylor County Expo Center on State 36. For scheduling information, call the Abilene Convention and Visitors Council at 915-677-7241.

A smaller, more local event is the **Chile Super-bowl** that's held each Labor Day weekend at the Perini Ranch in Buffalo Gap. All proceeds from this event benefit the Ben Richey Boys Ranch. Call the Perini Ranch (see "Food" above) for more information.

Shopping

Two shops in Abilene specialize in outfitting working cowboys with handmade goods. **James Leddy Boots** (tel. 677-7811) at 926 Ambler is a member of the famous bootmaking Leddy family; his custom-made boots start at $300 for basic cowhide and go over $2000 for something in exotic skins with extra hand-tooling. Leddy accepts visitors who just want to look around the shop. At nearby **Art Reed Custom Saddles** (tel. 677-4572), 904 Ambler, Art Reed makes saddles, tack, chaps, and belts. Reed even makes his own saddle trees (the wooden frame the saddle is sewn onto), a rare skill among custom saddle-makers these days.

WICHITA FALLS

Like Abilene, Wichita Falls grew up around a rail stop in the 1880s, but somehow the circuit preachers that came through town didn't stay on as they did in Abilene. Instead of churches, Wichita Falls raised saloons and soon became known as "Whiskeytaw Falls." Today you can still get a "red draw" (a local invention consisting of beer and tomato juice) at any drinking establishment in town. The Wichita Falls economy is based on oil, wheat, and manufacturing, with the accent on oil.

There isn't much to see in Wichita Falls itself; for most Texas visitors, it's just a brief stop upon entering the state via I-44 from Oklahoma City. The waterfall that gave the town its name was destroyed by an 1886 flood, but in 1987 an artificial waterfall was constructed along the Wichita River to take its place (too many visitors were asking "Where's the falls?"). The new falls are 54 feet high, supposedly 10 times taller than the original.

Lake Arrowhead State Park

Lake Arrowhead is a Little Wichita River impoundment that covers 16,000 acres of what used to be an oil field. Folks around here like the oil business so much they've left oil derricks in the middle of the lake as ornamentation (anglers also say the fishing is best around the old derricks). Boating, swimming, water-skiing, picnicking, and camping are popular activities in the park, and there are a few nature trails as well. Campsites with water and electricity (total of 48) are $9 a night; sites with water only (19 sites) are $6 a night. Entry fee is $3 for vehicles, $1 for pedestrians and cyclists. Call (817) 528-2211 for campsite reservations or information.

Events

Two large events held every August are the **Hotter 'n Hell One Hundred**, the largest 100-mile bicycle race in the U.S., and the **Texas Ranch Roundup**, in which ranch hands from around the state compete in events that display working-ranch skills, including saddle-bronc riding, horseshoeing, chuckwagon cooking, even fiddling and guitar-picking. The ranch team that accumulates the most points is awarded the title "Best Ranch in Texas."

Accommodations And Food

The **Best Western Towne Crest Inn** (tel. 817-322-1182), 1601 8th St. (two blocks west of US 82 S), has rooms for $30 s, $35 d. The trusty **Motel 6** (tel. 322-8817) is off I-44 at 1812 Maurine St. (Maurine exit) and costs $26 s, plus $6 per additional adult. The nearby **Days Inn** (tel. 723-5541, 1211 Central Fwy., Maurine exit I-44) has rooms for $36 s, 42-48 d. Also on Central Fwy., at No. 100 (Texas Tourist Bureau exit off I-44) is the **Wichita Falls Sheraton** (tel. 761-6000), where rooms are $60-70, the most expensive in town (senior discounts available).

There's a **KOA Kampground** 15 miles north of town off I-44 (E. 3rd St. exit) where tent/camper sites are $12 a night, full hookups $14.

All the usual fast-food joints abound along I-44. **Hacienda Hernandez** (tel. 817-767-5932, 1105 Broadway) serves inexpensive Tex-Mex and American; open Mon.-Sat. for lunch and dinner. The **McBride Land & Cattle Co.** (tel. 692-2462, 501 Scott) has mesquite-grilled steaks and frog legs at moderate prices; open weekdays for lunch and dinner, weekends dinner only. **Wichita Bend RV Park** (tel. 761-7490), north of the Sheraton off I-44, offers two-way hookups (dump station available) for only $5 a night. **Shady Park RV**

And Travel (tel. 723-1532), 2944 5th St. (off US 277 west), has shaded spaces with full hookups and cable TV for $12-14 a night.

Information

The Wichita County Heritage Society (tel. 817-723-0623, 900 Bluff St.) distributes "A Drive Through History," an annotated map of historical landmarks in the city that includes many buildings built around the turn of the century.

One of the Texas Highway Dept.'s 12 tourist bureaus is on I-44 at the edge of town. A wealth of maps, brochures, newspapers, and information on Texas travel is available here seven days a week, 8-5.

SAN ANGELO

INTRODUCTION

One might think that a town of 90,000 out in the middle of central West Texas wouldn't have much to offer. But it's almost a secret that San Angelo (pronounced "sin-EN-jala" in local dialect) is in fact one of the most inhabitable towns north of the Davis Mountains. Unlike its counterparts to the southwest (Odessa and Midland) and to the north (Abilene and Wichita Falls), it's a fairly vibrant city, mainly due to the fact that the local economy isn't oil dependent. Geography has been San Angelo's main savior; while some oil has been discovered in the area, the rocky Edwards Plateau environment is perfect for raising goats and sheep and the town has become the U.S. wool and mohair capital. Four scenic rivers join here, the Main Concho, the North Concho, the South Concho, and the Middle Concho, and lakes are on three sides of the city. The locals almost regard themselves as living on an island, not because of the surrounding rivers and lakes but because this is the only town of any size between Lubbock and San Antonio, a distance of 400 miles.

Anyone cutting diagonally across the state on US 87, which extends over 600 miles from Amarillo to the Gulf coast, might consider spending a night or two here. Western history buffs shouldn't miss old Fort Concho, said to be the most well-preserved Western fort in the U.S., and Paint Rock, the country's largest Indian pictograph site. The city is also famous for Concho River pearls, striking natural pearls found in mussels that live in the Concho River.

Climate

San Angelo has hot summers and short, fairly mild winters. June and July are the hottest months, with daytime high temperatures in the 90s and occasionally over 100 degrees. From December to February, average low temperatures are in the 30s and 40s (with an average of 42 days a year below freezing), average highs in the 50s and 60s. Precipitation averages 24 inches per year, with showers most frequently occurring in the spring and late summer. As a San Angelo Convention and Visitors Bureau brochure states, "Contrary to fact, not all of West Texas is dry."

History

Although El Paso's Ysleta district is considered the oldest continually inhabited European settlement in Texas, Spanish missionaries were in San Angelo first. Franciscans established a Jumano Indian mission along the Main Concho River in 1632, but it lasted only six months. In 1650 the Spanish explorers Hernan Martin and Diego del Castillo traded with local Indians for Concho River pearls, some of which eventually found their way

San Angelo Cowboys, 1887

FORT CONCHO HISTORICAL LANDMARK

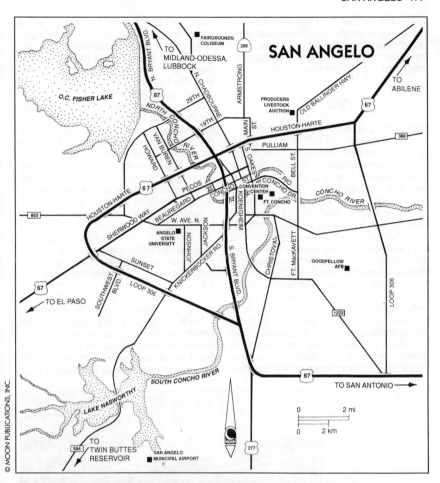

into the crown jewels of Spain. (The name for the river, in fact, comes from the Spanish for "shell," *concho.*) In the 18th century, Plains Indians came down from the north and made this part of the Edwards Plateau uninhabitable for Europeans until Fort Concho arrived on the scene in 1867. The fort was built at the junction of the Concho and Middle Concho rivers to protect mail routes and to escort cattle drives.

The first sheep ranchers arrived in the area in 1877 and found the fort to be a ready market for wool. Around this time, pioneer Bart DeWitt

planned a town to service the comings and goings of the military. The town, which DeWitt apparently named after his deceased wife Angela de la Garza, grew up across the North Concho from the fort. (Records disagree as to whether it was originally called Saint Angela or Santa Angela but somehow people started calling the town San Angela; in the 1880s, postal authorities objected to the Spanish gender clash and changed the name to San Angelo.) In 1882 the U.S. Army's 16th Infantry headquarters were moved to Fort Concho, further increasing the fort's significance, and by 1884 there was a local building boom. Five years later, Fort Concho was abandoned as the Indian Wars came to a close, but by then San Angelo was well-established as a rough-and-ready ranching town.

SIGHTS

Fort Concho National Historic Landmark

An active frontier fort from 1867 to 1889, Fort Concho housed eight companies in 40 buildings made of locally quarried limestone. Though abandoned over a century ago, the fort is still very much a center of San Angelo life. The townspeople have been painstakingly restoring the fort ever since the 1930s, and at this writing at least 25 buildings have been restored. Members of the Fort Concho Museum Association hold on-site events throughout the year and publish the monthly *Fort Concho Members' Dispatch* as well as the *Concho River Review,* a journal of Texas and Southwestern literature, and the *Fort Concho and the South Plains Journal,* a historical journal and update of the national landmark's master plan.

Visitor facilities at the 20-acre fort (between Dugan and Burgess streets, and avenues C and D) include the **San Angelo Museum of Fine Arts,** housed in the former quartermaster storehouse. The museum features rotating exhibits of historic and contemporary works of art, a lecture series, and a museum shop that sells crafts, books, cards, and unique children's toys. The museum is open Tues.-Sat. 10-4 and Sun. 1-4. Admission is 75 cents adults, 25 cents children six to 17, free for children under six. For more information, call (915) 658-4084.

In Officers' Quarters No. 4, the new **E.H. Danner Museum of Telephony** contains a display of early telephones and telephone directories that chronicle the history of the telephone. Included in the collection are New York's first Bell Telephone list of subscribers (only one-page long) and one of only two examples in existence of the original five models of the Gallows Frame Telephone designed by Alexander Graham Bell. The museum is open Tues.-Sat. 10-5 and Sun. 1-5; closed Monday. Admission is free.

Other buildings open to the public are collectively known as the **Fort Concho Museum** and include a restored infantry barracks, officers' quarters, a hospital, and mess hall. Open Tues.-Sat. 10-5, Sun. 1-5; admission is $1.25 adults, 75 cents for active military and students, free for children under six. For more information, call (915) 657-4444.

The **Fort Concho Living History Program** has enlisted around 60 San Angelo volunteers who recreate frontier military life at Fort Concho events as well as elsewhere in the state. The 60 men belong to four historic Fort Concho units:

Fort Concho

FORT CONCHO HISTORICAL LANDMARK

Paint Rock pictographs

the 11th and 16th Infantry Regiments, the 4th Cavalry Regiment, and the Buffalo Soldiers or 10th Cavalry Regiment, an all-black unit. The program is dedicated to an authentic appearance, including uniforms and gear as well as training maneuvers.

Yearly Fort Concho events include Black History Month (Feb.); Sabers, Saddles, and Spurs (April); Frontier Day (part of Fiesta del Concho in June); U.S. Independence Day (July 4); Fiestas Patrias (Mexican Independence Day, Sept. 16); and Christmas at Old Fort Concho (Dec.).

Miss Hattie's Bordello Museum
Around the turn of the century, Concho St. was a strip of saloons and bordellos or "parlor houses." Miss Hattie's was established in 1896 and stayed in business until 1946 when Texas Rangers shut it down. During its time, Miss Hattie's was one of many bordellos in San Angelo, but was considered the most elegant. Miss Mona's Chicken Ranch in La Grange (East Texas), immortalized as "The Best Little Whorehouse in Texas," wasn't nearly as swank an establishment—Miss Hattie's even had an underground tunnel to the bank next door. Once the place closed, it was boarded up and abandoned until a local woman bought the building in 1976 and found that all the period furnishings were still there. It's now a museum where you can wander through the front parlor of velvet and lace and into the 10 bedrooms where the women plied their trade amidst oak-and-brass beds, satin sheets, and Oriental rugs. The largest room belonged to a blonde prostitute named Goldie, who was the highest draw and charged a steep $2. Miss Hattie herself lived on in San Angelo until she passed away in 1982 at the age of 104.

The museum at 18 E. Concho and is open Tues.-Sat. 9:30-4. Admission is $2 for adults, free for children.

Concho River Walk
A well-maintained, four-mile walking/jogging trail parallels the Concho River and passes by several hotels, the convention center, the River Stage, and Sunken Garden Park, a small botanical garden. The highlight of the River Walk is a 1.5-mile section between Concho St. and the 1st St. dam, where there's a series of brick plazas, fountains, falls, and walkways that incorporate native stone. A few fortunate residents have large, historic houses overlooking the river—all future residential construction has been banned.

Producers Livestock Auction
San Angelo has the second-largest cattle auction in Texas and the largest sheep and goat auction in the United States. Sheep and goats are auctioned weekly Tues. and Wed. starting around 9 a.m., while cattle sales take place Thurs. and Fri. at the same time. Visitors are welcome to sit at the indoor auction ring and watch, or to walk along the catwalks above the outdoor pens. The stockyards are at the north end of Bell St. just

after it forks left from Old Ballinger Highway.

Aermotor Windmill

San Angelo is the home of the last American windmill manufacturer, Aermotor (and there aren't more than three windmill manufacturers left in the world). The first Aermotor windmill was the final result of over 5,000 steel windmill experiments conducted by Thomas Perry in Chicago in the 1880s. His wheel was 87% more efficient than the best wooden wheels in use at that time, but he only sold 45 units in 1888, the first year it was on the market. By 1892, the Aermotor was the definitive "mathematical windmill," as windmills became a popular way to pump water on farms and ranches all over the United States and elsewhere in the world. The company made a considerable fortune until the 1960s when windmills fell out of fashion, so in 1969 the company moved to Argentina, where demand remained high. Ten years later it was purchased by another company and moved to Arkansas, where it stayed until 1986 when another group of investors bought the company and moved the factory to San Angelo. Aermotor now makes six sizes of windmills, ranging in diameter from six to 16 feet. The plant is located at 3015 N. Bryant; visitors are welcome to tour the plant if they call ahead (tel. 915-658-2795).

Paint Rock

Thirty miles west of San Angelo, close to the north banks of the Concho River, is a long set of limestone cliffs that are a virtual Indian art gallery. The site was a favorite camping area for nomadic tribes for thousands of years, since the river provided water, game was plentiful, and the cliffs could be used not only as shelter but as a bison run-off (in which Indians would chase herds of bison over the cliffs). The cliffs also provided the perfect stone canvas for Indian pictographs as well as the materials for making paint. Their palette consisted of red, made from a mixture of bear or buffalo fat and powdered hematite, yellow, from geodes and ochers, and black, from charcoal and manganese oxide. An estimated 1,500 images decorate the site, including such standouts as winged serpents, Indian shields, shamanic figures, comets, a propellered sun, running bison, and Spanish missionaries.

The land surrounding the pictograph site is owned by Kay Campbell, whose grandparents set-

tled at Paint Rock in the 1880s. Her small tour operation, **Paint Rock Excursions,** has an office in the little town of Paint Rock, at the intersection of FM 380/180 and US 83. To view the pictographs, you must take a guided tour with her or a member of her family. The tour takes about an hour and proceeds along a trail about 50 feet below the bluff (in the summer, a pontoon raft carries visitors down the river to the trail). Kay usually gives a paint-making demonstration before or after the tour, in which she grinds hematite to a powder with flint and then mixes it with oil in an Indian paint pot (river stones with eroded depressions or holes). Tours are available during the summer Mon.-Sat. 9-4, Sun. 1-5, on weekends only from April to May and Labor Day to Thanksgiving (same times). For information or reservations, call (915) 732-4418 on weekends, 655-4434 on weekdays.

Angelo State University

Around 6,400 students are enrolled in the undergraduate and graduate programs here. ASU was listed in *US News and World Report*'s 1991 guide to the country's best colleges as one of a few "up and comers." The planetarium is said to be one of the best in the state. Off Ave. N between Johnson and Rosemont.

Goodfellow Air Force Base

Southeast of town, Goodfellow is headquarters for U.S. Air Force Intelligence, a training site for other military espionage branches, and a major local employer. Not open to the public (naturally).

ACCOMMODATIONS

Hotels And Motels

Four places near the river include: the **Motel 6** (tel. 915-658-8061, 311 N. Bryant Blvd.), $22 s, $6 each additional adult; the **Days Inn** (tel. 655-8151, 333 Rio Concho Dr.), $42-50; the **Best Western Inn of the West** (tel. 653-2995, 415 W. Beauregard), $32-44, and the **Holiday Inn Convention Center** (tel. 658-2828, 441 Rio Concho Dr.), $45-62. The clean and comfortable **El Patio Motel** (tel. 655-5711), at 1901 W. Beauregard, has rooms for $31 s, $34 d.

Bed And Breakfasts

Two moderately priced B&Bs in the Paint Rock

area offer rooms for $35-45 a night including breakfasts. **Chaparral Ranch Bed & Breakfast** (tel. 915-732-4225, RR 1, Box 20) is near the Concho River and two creeks; rooms are in a large ranch house with a fireplace and rock floor. **Lipan Ranch Bed & Breakfast** (tel. 468-2571, RR 1, Box 21C) is similar but offers TV and non-smoking rooms.

Camping
Twin Buttes Marina (tel. 915-949-7187), four miles west of town off US 67, has a campground where full hookups are $10, sites with w/e are $8, and dry campsites are $4. **Spring Creek Marina** (tel. 944-3850) at 45 Fisherman's Rd. on Lake Nasworthy has full hookups plus cable TV for $12 a night. The San Angelo **KOA Kampground** (tel. 949-3242) is off Knickerbocker Rd. (FM 584) three miles west of Loop 306. Tentsites are $11, RV sites are $12 without hookups, $14.50 with w/e, $15.50 with full hookup.

FOOD

Like most of upper West Texas, steak is king in San Angelo. Locals say the best steak is served at **Twin Mountain Steakhouse** (tel. 915-949-4239), two miles west of town on US 67 (Mertzon Hwy.). The specialty here is "scraps" (called "tenders" on the menu), small choice cuts of steak. They also have chicken and seafood. Open for dinner nightly except Sunday. A competitor for best local steakhouse is **Zentner's Daughter Steak House** (tel. 949-2821) at 1901 Knickerbocker across from the San Angelo Stadium. They're open daily for lunch and dinner.

The hot spot for Tex-Mex is the inexpensive **Mejor Que Nada** ("Better Than Nothing") at 1911 S. Bryant (tel. 915-655-3553), in a former gas station. Open daily except Sun. for lunch and dinner. A personal favorite, and even cheaper, is **Los Dos Hermanos**, at 1406 S. Chadbourne, open daily 7 a.m.-10 p.m.—great *desayuno* (Mexican breakfast) for under $3. On Sundays they serve *caldo* and menudo.

Mexican and steaks are what San Angelo restaurants do best, but there is also an excellent down-home-style place near the Producers Livestock Auction called **Dun Bar East** (tel. 915-655-8780), 1728 Pilliam. Catfish, chicken-fried steak,

and liver and onions are the specialties of the house, along with delicious homemade pies and cornbread. Open Tues.-Sun. 6 a.m.-10 p.m.; on auction days the lunch crowd gets pretty thick.

A Taste of Italy (tel. 944-3290, 3520 Knickerbocker, Southwest Plaza) serves good Italian food weekdays for lunch and dinner, Saturday dinner only (closed Sunday).

ENTERTAINMENT

For over a hundred years, San Angelo has had a reputation as a wide-open town; an early sheepman once wrote that it was "overrun with drink saloons, gambling dens, and dance houses of the lowest class." It still has an unusually large number of clubs for a town of its size, from little honky-tonk bars to huge dance halls. The big rockin' cowboy spots are **Texas** at 4611 S. Jackson and the **Little River Club** at 2502 Loop 306. These two feature mostly "aggressive country" crossover bands. **Finnegan's**, usually just called "The Fin," is in the Southwest Plaza shopping center and features live comedy and various types of live music, including a regular jam session on Tuesday nights. **Caraway's**, in "Block One" on historic E. Concho St., is a popular piano bar that's not as formal as the term implies—it's more New Orleans than New York. It's housed in the former San Angelo National Bank building (the bank that had the tunnel to Miss Hattie's bordello).

The biweekly *City Lites Entertainment Guide* keeps up with local entertainment events and is distributed free at many clubs and restaurants in town.

RECREATION

The main sources of outdoor activity in San Angelo are the three lakes within 30 minutes' drive of town. **O.C. Fisher Reservoir** (tel. 915-949-4757) is three miles northwest of town off FM 2288 (Mercedes St.) and is sometimes called Lake San Angelo or North Concho Lake. It's a 12,700-acre impoundment of the North Concho River, built and maintained by the U.S. Army Corps of Engineers. There are 20 boat launches along the south shore and the lake is well-fished for walleye, crappie, sunfish, white and black bass, smallmouth, and channel, flathead, and yellow catfish. Swimming, picnicking, and horseback riding are also popular activities in the warmer months. There are four camping areas around the lake at Dry Creek Park ($7 tent, $9 w/e), Grandview Park (primitive, free), Highland Range Park (primitive, free), and Red Arroyo Park ($7 tent, $9 w/e). All campsites have a 14-day limit.

Lake Nasworthy (tel. 944-3850) is six miles southwest of town off FM 584 (Knickerbocker Rd.) and covers 1,500 acres, fed by the South Concho River. The black bass fishing here is very good. Two camping areas: Spring Creek Marina Park (full hookups available, $12) and Middle Concho (primitive sites, no fee).

Twin Buttes Reservoir is actually two lakes (total of 10,000 acres) connected by a canal, just south of Lake Nasworthy off US 67. The larger northern section is fed by Spring Creek and the Middle Concho River while the smaller southern section is fed by the South Concho River. Hybrid striped bass and blue catfish are big here. Recreational facilities are more developed than at either of the other two area lakes. Primitive tentsites are $2 a night, $5 with electricity. See "Accommodations" above for details on the Twin Buttes Marina campground.

EVENTS

March
The **San Angelo Stock Show and Rodeo** features a PRCA-sponsored rodeo, livestock shows, country music, arts and crafts at the Coliseum Fairgrounds (tel. 915-942-1900).

April
World Championship Goat Roping Invitational: The only rodeo in the country devoted solely to goat roping. At the Coliseum Fairgrounds (tel. 915-942-1900); dates vary from year to year—call the Convention and Visitors Bureau (tel. 653-1206) for current scheduling.

Sabers, Saddles, and Spurs: An event that focuses on the Fort Concho Equestrian Review, featuring polo, cavalry drills, and displays of horsemanship. The San Angelo Saddle Club has one of the best polo teams in the state. Held on the Fort Concho parade grounds (tel. 915-658-4084).

May
Fiesta del Concho: This is the city's biggest festival and is centered on the Concho River. Kicks off with a hot-air balloon race on the second weekend in June and continues through the third weekend, featuring barge rides, arts and crafts, food vendors, armadillo races, a parade, and a western dance. On the second Saturday, Frontier Day is held at Fort Concho with the Living History Program in full swing. Call (915) 655-4136 for more information.

September
Fiestas Patrias: A celebration of Mexican independence held the second week of September at Fort Concho. Parades, Mexican food, music, dance, and the coronation of La Perla, "The Pearl."

December
Christmas at Old Fort Concho: A community-wide effort that always takes place the first weekend in December. The officers' quarters are decorated according to themes in Fort Concho's cultural history, e.g., Victorian House, Early Texas House, Mexican House, German House, Czech House, Arc Light Saloon, and an "Officer's Christmas." Each house is candlelit and staffed by volunteers in period costume; food is served, too, with the Czech House usually providing the greatest bounty. Other events include a children's tea party, a "Christmas Comida," caroling, a historical pageant on the parade grounds, a melodrama matinee, a live nativity, and Sunday Christmas dinner. A huge tent is erected on the parade grounds for the weekend to house craft demonstrations and food vendors. Mostly free, except for food.

SHOPPING

Concho Pearls
The rare Concho pearl is found only in the Concho River complex of West Texas, most especially in the "sweetwater" vicinity of San Angelo. It's a product of a native river mussel that was once an Indian food staple; however, there are 12 or more mussel species in the Concho system and only one, *Cyrtonaias tampicoenis*, produces pearls. In the 17th century, Spanish explorers traded with local Indians for the Concho pearls, which vary in color from a soft pink to a deep lavender. Today's Texans find the huge, leathery

*R.E. Donaho
saddle shop*

mussels unpalatable but the pearls are more highly prized than ever. Size varies from a couple of millimeters to around 6.5 mm. Several jewelry shops in town carry the pearls loose, in strands, and in gold settings. One shop that specializes in Concho pearls is **Bart Mann Originals** (tel. 915-653-2902) at 105 S. Irving. All their jewelry is designed and crafted on the premises.

Hats
The **Hatatorium** (tel. 915-655-9191) has been making all manner of hats since 1948. Their most famous model is the "Angelo," which is popular throughout the state. They also carry fedoras, Panamas, and other non-cowboy styles, which can be custom-sized if necessary. At 25 N. Chadbourne.

Boots
Famous bootmaker M.L. Leddy came to San Angelo in 1936, purchased Mercer Boot Co., and enjoyed much local success. Generations later, there are three bootshops that claim to be direct descendants of the original: **M.L. Leddy Boots & Saddles** (tel. 915-942-7655, 2200 W. Beauregard, in the Village Shopping Center), **J.L. Mercer & Son Boots** (658-7634, 224 S. Chadbourne), and **Franklin Mercer Boot Co.** (tel. 655-7784, 3275 Arden Rd.). All make custom boots that start at around $350.

Saddles And Saddleblankets
M.L. Leddy makes custom saddles that start at the customary $1000. The most venerable saddlery in town is the **R.E. Donaho Saddle Shop** (tel. 915-655-3270), which has been doing a steady business since 1890. (Pancho Villa had his saddle work done here.) Their most famous model is the Concho Saddle, a cross between Mexican and Western styles. Prices start at $1000 for a basic working saddle. At 8 E. Concho, near Miss Hattie's.

Since San Angelo is a wool center, saddleblankets are a popular item. Probably the best selection is at **Ingrid's** (tel. 915-732-4370 or 800-752-8004) in Paint Rock at the intersection of FM 380/180 and US 83. They make custom floor rugs and wall-hangings as well.

Antiques
Most of the town's antiques stores are clustered on E. Concho, including **Adobe Red Antiques** at No. 33, and **Concho Confetti** (also a tea room) at No. 42. North Chadbourne St. is another area of antique shops, with **Sunshine Place** at No. 226, **Doris' Den of Antiquities** at No. 1901, **Concho Rarities** at No. 1911, **The White Elephant** at No. 2613, and **S&R Trading Post** at No. 4736.

Art
The **Chicken Farm Art Center** (tel. 915-653-4936) is a chicken farm that's been converted into artists' studios and galleries. Visitors are welcome to watch local artists at work or peruse works of art for sale. At 2505 Martin Luther King off US 87

CAVERNS OF SONORA

N (take 23rd St. east to Martin Luther King).

SAN ANGELO INFORMATION

Tourist Office

The **San Angelo Convention and Visitors Bureau** (tel. 915-655-1206 or 800-375-1206) is at 500 Rio Concho Dr. and is open Mon.-Fri. 8:30-5. They hand out plenty of free brochures and maps for visitors and can also arrange tours. The **San Angelo Chamber of Commerce** office is in the same building. On weekends, visitor information is available at the Fort Concho Museum.

Telephone

San Angelo has a 915 area code.

VICINITY OF SAN ANGELO

Fort McKavett State Historic Site

Old Fort McKavett is about 75 miles southeast of San Angelo in Menard County. The fort was established in 1852 as the "Camp on the San Saba" by five companies of the 8th Infantry but was soon named in honor of an 8th Infantry colonel who was killed in the War with Mexico's Battle of Monterrey. As with Fort Concho and other West Texas forts, Fort McKavett served as a first line of defense against Indian raids along the Texas frontier and provided protection for travelers along the Upper San Antonio-El Paso Trail. Later in the 1850s, the 8th Infantry was joined by the 2nd

TELEPHONE AND EMERGENCY INFORMATION

Emergency (police, fire, medical)	911
Telephone Directory Assistance	411
Weather Service	655-0212
Crisis Intervention Hotline	653-5933
Texas State Highway Patrol	655-7359

Dragoons and the 1st Infantry, but when area Indian activity declined, the fort was temporarily abandoned in 1859.

In 1868 the post was reestablished by the 4th Cavalry after local residents lobbied for Army protection against renewed Indian attacks. The 4th Cavalry was soon replaced by a company of black troops, the 38th Infantry, and out of that unit and the 41st, the famous 24th Infantry was organized at McKavett in 1869. All four of the Army's black units, who came to be known as "Buffalo Soldiers" by the Indians, eventually served at McKavett, including the 9th and 10th cavalries. Of all the frontier forts, McKavett is said to have had the best site—built high on a hill on the banks of the San Saba River in the shade of oak and pecan groves. Soldiers were able to supplement the basic Army diet of beans and salt pork by fishing in the river and cultivating vegetables in the river's floodplain. As at Fort Concho, a settlement of camp followers established itself on the opposite bank of the river (known at Fort McKavett as "Scabtown").

The fort was abandoned at the end of the Indi-

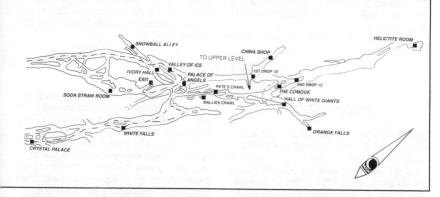

SNOWBALL ALLEY

CHINA SHOP

HELICTITE ROOM

TO UPPER LEVEL

VALLEY OF ICE

IVORY HALL

PALACE OF ANGELS

EXIT

1ST DROP 10'

2ND DROP 12'

PETE'S CRAWL

THE COMODE

SODA STRAW ROOM

HALL OF WHITE GIANTS

WALLIES CRAWL

WHITE FALLS

ORANGE FALLS

CRYSTAL PALACE

an Wars in 1883 and civilians took over the buildings. Because the fort structures have been in continuous use since the 1850s, they are in better condition than most. Fourteen buildings of the original 40 have been restored, including the officers' quarters, barracks, hospital, school, bakery, and post headquarters. Seven other buildings are in ruins, and the rest are gone. The hospital ward serves as a visitor center and contains interpretive exhibits that explain the natural and military history of the area. A nature trail leads to the old fort kiln and the "Government Springs."

To approach the fort from San Angelo, take US 277 43 miles south to US 190, then east 30 miles to FM 864, then southwest about six miles on FM 864 to the small town of Fort McKavett (pop. 105, many of them retirees who take advantage of the excellent San Saba fishing).

The Caverns Of Sonora

This cave is among many in the Lower Cretaceous Edwards Limestone found throughout the Edwards Plateau region, but nothing compares with the speleological beauty found here. The cave was in fact kept secret for several years after its discovery in 1955 by Dallas spelunkers who feared the cave would be overrun. The founder of the American Speleological Society has said the Sonora caverns are "the most indescribably beautiful caverns in the world. Their beauty can't possibly be exaggerated—even by Texans."

The cave is one of the state's longest, with nearly eight miles (an estimate, since mapping isn't yet complete) of passages through seven levels. The lower levels are the most striking, since they're still actively producing cave formations; these formations run the gamut of all known types, including some found nowhere else. Some are luminous and phosphorescent, some are crystalline and transparent, and all have shape-inspired names like "The Mummy," "The Passing Quarterback," and "The Ice Cream Cone." Some passages contain solid flowstone that covers the walls, floor, and ceiling, a rarity. Long "soda straws" or tubular stalactites up to six feet long but only a quarter inch in diameter are common in some passages. In the "Christmas Tree Room" are stalagmite formations known as coral trees. One of the most amazing rooms is full of helictites, bursting star-like formations formed by a water flow that's so slow that gravity doesn't affect the random shape as the crystals emanate outward in all directions. Looking around, it's hard not to imagine that you're standing in a world made of rock candy.

Tours through the cave are managed by a private enterprise, which means you have to put up with a somewhat tacky entrance and souvenir shop on the way in. The tour takes visitors through a mile and a half of the cave, a 1 1/2 to two-hour walk. The temperature in the cave is a constant 70° F with a 98% relative humidity, so even in the winter it can be a bit clammy. The lowest point on the walk is 150 feet and the highest is 2,230 feet, so the walk involves some elevation change. Tours are led from the souvenir shop seven days a week about every half hour, 8-6

May through September, 9-5 the rest of the year. Admission is $6.50 per adult, $5 children 6-11, under six free.

Outside the cave are picnic and camping areas. Overnight fees for tent campers is $5; for RVs it's $8. For more information contact Caverns of Sonora (tel. 915-387-2880), Box 213, Sonora, TX 76950.

DEL RIO

INTRODUCTION

Texans will argue over whether Del Rio is in West Texas or South Texas. The truth is it's a little of both. The Pecos River is less than an hour's drive west of town; terrain-wise, the Edwards Plateau meets the eastern edge of the Chihuahuan Desert here; it's at the same latitude as San Antonio (South Central Texas) yet west of San Angelo (usually considered West Texas). One thing's for sure, it's a long way from anywhere else—the nearest towns of any size are San Angelo (150 miles), Laredo (180 miles), and San Antonio (153 miles).

For many visitors to Texas, it's just a stopover on US 90 between San Antonio and Big Bend. Savvy Texans, however, know that Acuña, Lake Amistad National Recreation Area, and Seminole Canyon make Del Rio a worthwhile destination in its own right (with nearby Brackettville and Langtry as worthy side trips, too). "Winter Texans" have also discovered the Del Rio area, and more and more are coming here to avoid the winter crowds in Harlingen-Brownsville and McAllen.

Climate

July and August are the hottest months, with average high temperatures in the mid-90s and overnight lows in the 70s. Coolest months are December and January, when average lows are around 40° F. Average annual precipitation for the area is 23 inches, with spring and late summer months receiving the most rain.

History

Del Rio was originally settled by Spanish missionaries who arrived on St. Philip's Day, 1635, and named their mission San Felipe del Rio. But archaeological evidence suggests that the area around Del Rio, in particular the canyons of the Rio Grande and Pecos River, have been inhab-

ited for at least 12,000 years. Indian pictographs that remain on canyon walls are at least 4,000 years old (see "Seminole Canyon State Park" below for more details).

The Indians who resided in the area when the Spanish arrived were probably Coahuiltecans; whoever they were, they didn't submit to missionization and the San Felipe mission was short-lived. The Coahuiltecans mysteriously disappeared sometime during the 18th century and the area was abandoned until the 1850s when Fort Clark was established in nearby Brackettville to protect the San Antonio-El Paso Trail. As the area became "pacified," Anglo-American speculators became interested in the land around San Felipe Springs, which then, as now, pumped around 90 million gallons of water a day out of the rocky ground. The springs were an important water stop for stagecoaches on the San Antonio-San Diego route (which connected with the Chihuahua Trail as well) and for the U.S. Camel Corps during their Big Bend surveys. In 1869, five men formed an irrigation company, sold shares, and established farming homesteads. By the mid 1870s, San Felipe del Rio was still nothing more than a collection of adobe huts with thatched roofs; building materials were difficult to bring in since the town was in the middle of a burgeoning haven for Comanches and Mexican bandits.

A Fort Clark cavalry outpost called Camp del Rio was established nearby in 1876 and by the mid-1880s was abandoned as the Indian Wars came to a close. But what contributed most to the town's development was the meeting of the Southern Pacific and the Galveston, Harrisburg, and San Antonio railroads in 1883 at a nearby junction. After the commemorative silver spike was driven into the rails, Del Rio became connected to the outside world and began prospering almost immediately as irrigated farming expanded. That same year the post office shortened the town name to Del Rio (so as not to confuse it with another Texas town, San Felipe de Austin).

DEL RIO-
CIUDAD ACUÑA

TO
LAKE
AMISTAD

NATIONAL PARKS
SERVICE OFFICE

377
277
90

VAL VERDE COUNTY FAIRGROUNDS/
VAL VERDE DOWNS RACETRACK

DEL RIO
INTERNATIONAL
AIRPORT

17TH ST.
14TH ST.
9TH ST.
3RD ST.

BEDELL AVE.

N. MAIN ST.
AVE. O
AVE. H
AVE. F

SAN FELIPE
SPRINGS

SAN FELIPE
SPRINGS RD.

SAN FELIPE CREEK

TO
SAN
ANTONIO

90

GARFIELD

E. RODRIQUEZ

CIENEGAS RD.

DEL RIO

GIBBS
OGDEN

S MAIN ST.
BROADWAY ST.

FIREHOUSE
(DEL RIO COUNCIL
FOR THE ARTS)

PECAN

CANTU

BROWN
PLAZA

RODRIQUEZ

MARGARITE AVE.

BROADBENT AVE.

277

FARLEY LN.

NICHOLSON

GRINER

WHITEHEAD
MUSEUM

HUDSON DR.

TO
EAGLE
PASS

VAL VERDE
WINERY

239
277

QUALIA DR.

BRINKLEY MANSION

TO AMISTAD DAM

LOOP RD.

CARRETERA
PRESA AMISTAD

HIDALGO
MADERO
GALEANA
VICTORIA

MATAMOROS

MORELOS

BLVD. GUERRERO

CIUDAD ACUÑA

MEXICO

TEXAS

RIO GRANDE

MOON

0   1 mi

0   1 km

As Del Rio is on the edge of the Edwards Plateau—an environment perfect for cloven-hoofed livestock—sheep and goat ranches moved in and the town has become a major contender for the national "wool and mohair capital" title along with San Angelo farther north. Another boon to Del Rio development was the building of the Amistad International Dam in the 1960s, which created one of the largest manmade lakes in the U.S. (by impounding the Rio Grande, Pecos River, and Devils River), with nearly a thousand miles of shoreline. This not only added to the availability of water for irrigation, hydroelectric, and other utilitarian purposes, it made Del Rio and Acuña recreational centers on both sides of the border. The latest development has been the establishment of more than 30 *maquiladoras* or "twin plants," American-owned factories located in or near Acuña on the Mexican side, which has helped to expand Del Rio's population to its current 35,000 (Acuña has about three times as many people).

Another claim to fame for Del Rio-Acuña is that two famous radio figures broadcast their shows from a "pirate" radio station on the Mexican side, XER. The first was Dr. John R. Brinkley, the infamous goat gland surgeon of the '30s; the second was rock-'n'-roll DJ Wolfman Jack in the late '50s and early '60s. The facility was set up so that announcers could operate out of a Del Rio studio while the 500,000-watt transmitter (with a signal that reached all the way to Canada) was actually located in Acuña, thus circumventing FCC licensing. Mexican radio still rules the airwaves in this part of Texas.

SIGHTS

Historic Buildings

Del Rio has an unusually high percentage of buildings still standing from the late 1800s, some built by Italian stonemasons. The Gothic-style **Sacred Heart Church,** at 310 Mill St. downtown, was built in 1892. Nearby at 400 Pecan St. is the **Val Verde County Courthouse,** a huge Victorian built in 1887 of native limestone. At 1901 S. Main is the **Chris Qualia Home,** an 1898 Victorian with gingerbread and cupolas.

South of Canal St. is a residential area lined with historic old homes, including the **Second Taini Home** at 1100 S. Main, which Taini built for

his family in 1904. The **Taylor-Rivers House** at 100 Hudson Dr. was built in 1870 of adobe and is the oldest existing house in Del Rio.

The **Brinkley Mansion** on Qualia Dr., past the Val Verde Winery, is not so old (built in 1929) but is an impressive monument to probably the biggest medical fraud ever perpetrated in North America. "Dr." Brinkley (none of his claimed medical degrees were ever recognized by the AMA) built an empire on the "Brinkley operation," goat gland transplants for men that were supposed to preserve or restore virility (Woodrow Wilson supposedly asked to have one performed in secret). In the '30s, the city allowed Brinkley to establish a clinic in the Hotel Roswell downtown. Del Rio civic leaders still won't admit they harbored a fraud and a fugitive (fleeing indictments in Kansas and California), because they're still trying to save face and because they're grateful for his local philanthropy, which included donations to hospitals and schools. And of course, where would Wolfman Jack (and rock 'n' roll) be if Brinkley hadn't established the most powerful radio station on the continent?

San Felipe District

Across the Old San Felipe Canal to the south is the traditionally Mexican district of San Felipe; drive through here and you may think you've crossed the border. This is also one of the oldest parts of town, centered **Brown Plaza,** at Cantu and Cisneros, which was a favorite gathering place for Mexican residents at the turn of the century. Nowadays it's been co-opted by the community as a whole for local celebrations of all types.

Val Verde Winery

Established in 1883 by Italian immigrant Frank Qualia, Val Verde is the oldest winery in Texas and is still run by the Qualia family. During Prohibition it was one of the only licensed wineries in the country. The 18-inch-thick adobe walls provide a cave-like atmosphere for the aging process (done in French white-oak barrels); total output is around 7,000 gallons a year. The first vinifera the Qualias planted, a "Lenoir" variety from Madeira (called Jacquez in Spain), is still the mainstay of the winery's production. The Lenoir is a smooth, dry table red, similar to other Spanish varietals. Val Verde also produces a Cabernet Sauvignon (doesn't quite compare with the Cabernets from Texas's Llano Estacado region or from northern California), a dry and a semisweet Herbemont (light and nutty), a Johannisberg Riesling (suffers by comparison with the Lubbock wines), a Rio Grande Blush (okay), and an award-winning Tawny Port (good). Wine prices are quite reasonable. The winery offers free tours and winetasting Mon.-Sat. 9-5 at 100 Qualia Dr. (tel. 512-775-9714).

Whitehead Memorial Museum

The Whiteheads are a local ranching family that bought the old Perry Store (built in the 1870s) to preserve it from being demolished in the early '60s. They turned it into a museum that now encompasses several buildings on the same lot, including an Indian chapel, a log cabin, a barn, the Hal Patton Labor Office, and yet another replica of Judge Roy Bean's Jersey Lilly Saloon (which makes three—one each in Pecos and Del Rio, plus the original in Langtry). The judge himself and his son Sam are buried on the museum grounds. Each of the museum buildings contains exhibits related to area history; probably the most interesting is the exhibit on the Black Seminoles in the Patton building, along with the Indian religious art in the chapel. At 1308 S. Main St., tel. (512) 774-7568. Open Tues.-Sat. 9-11:30 and 1-4:30; admission $2 adults, 50 cents children.

The Firehouse

This 1932 building at 120 E. Garfield was originally a combination city hall, jail, and firehouse. Today it's headquarters for the Del Rio Council for the Arts (tel. 512-775-0888), which provides gallery space for regional artists and offers classes in fine arts, crafts, Spanish, dance, and music. The gallery features rotating exhibits including a Western art show in May associated with the Super Bull bull-riding competition (see "Events" below).

Ciudad Acuña

Across the Rio Grande from Del Rio via Spur 277 (Garfield/Las Vacas) is one of the Texas-Mexico border's least spoiled and cleanest towns. Acuña (Ciudad means "City") is just large enough (120,000) to be of varied interest to the casual visitor, yet small enough (and remote enough) to have escaped the Nuevo Laredo-Juarez "fleece-the-gringo" syndrome for the most part. It's named for Manuel Acuña, a revolutionary Mexican poet, and belongs to the Mexican state of

rancher in wool chaps, ca. 1890

Coahuila, which was itself once part of the larger Mexican state Coahuila y Texas. Perhaps because of this shared past, Acuña and Del Rio seem particularly compatible border sisters. The town's social center is shady Plaza Benjamin Canales (named after another revolutionary hero) just on the other side of the International Bridge; on warm evenings, the streets come alive with food vendors and evening strollers. On Sundays there are sometime band concerts at the plaza's gazebo. *Calandrias* or horse carriages take visitors around the old part of the city for around $5 an hour. The main tourist drag is Avenida Hidalgo, which is lined with craft and curio shops, saloons, and restaurants. Street touts don't hound gringos as in Juarez and sales pressure in the shops is low. Prices are also low: a liter bottle of Cuervo Especial tequila is only $4.25.

Unlike at some border towns, it's not as easy to walk across to Acuña (from city limit to city limit it's three miles), which is another reason the city isn't inundated with tourists. Instead, visitors can drive, catch public buses, or take taxis from downtown Del Rio. You shouldn't drive, though, unless you have Mexican insurance (see "Border Crossings," p. 66). There are parking lots on Las Vacas St. in Del Rio (closest point to the crossing) where you can park a car all day for $1. Buses pass regularly on the way into Acuña and cost 40 cents each way—get off at the plaza once you've crossed the bridge. A taxi from Del Rio (Las Vacas) is $7 one way; taxis coming the opposite way will ask for more, but you shouldn't pay over $8. Cab companies on the Del Rio side provide free parking if you hire one of their taxis.

Sanborn's (tel. 512-775-3252), near the bridge on Spur 239, can arrange Mexican auto insurance for longer journeys south of the border.

ACCOMMODATIONS

Hotels And Motels
The main hotel/motel strip in Del Rio is Avenue F (US 277 N/US 90 W). Here you'll find the inexpensive **Desert Hills** (tel. 512-775-3548) at No. 1300, with rooms for $20-27 (senior and long-term stay discounts available), the **Del Rio Motor Lodge** (tel. 775-2486) at No. 1300 for $20-25, and the **Motel 6** (tel. 774-2115) for $21 s, plus $6 for each additional adult. The moderately priced **Best Western Inn of Del Rio** (tel. 775-7511) is at No. 810 and has rooms for $43 s, $61 d; they also offer complimentary breakfasts and cocktail hour. The nicest rooms in town are at the **Ramada Inn** (tel. 775-1511), $50 s, $60 d.

There are a few hotels in Acuña that cater to gringos. One that belongs to the Del Rio Chamber of Commerce is **Los Alpes** (tel. 2-1221) on Blvd. Guerrero South. It's a bit away from the center of things, but the $28-36 room rates are good value. Out at Lake Amistad are several hotels and motels—see "Lake Amistad National Recreation Area" under "Vicinity of Del Rio" for details.

Camping
Yucca Trailer Village (tel. 512-775-6707) on US 90 W toward Lake Amistad has full hookups for $9.50 a night (weekly and monthly discounts available). **Fisherman's Headquarters** (tel. 774-

4172) is north of town where US 90 and US 277 split. Full hookup sites are $9.50 per night. Other campgrounds are available on the lake (see Lake Amistad National Recreation Area below).

FOOD

The Mexican presence in Del Rio is strong, so Tex-Mex restaurants far outnumber any other kind. One of the best is **Memo's** (tel. 512-775-8104) at 804 E. Losoya on the banks of San Felipe Creek. The same family has operated the restaurant since 1936, turning out dependable *chalupas,* fajitas, and enchiladas as well as steaks for moderate prices. A bonus is that one of the family members is "Blondie" Calderon, the pianist for C&W singer Ray Price's band. Whenever he's not on the road with Price, Blondie gets a band together for a jam session at Memo's to entertain diners.

For cheap, gutbucket Tex-Mex, you might try **Mi Casa** at 1912 Ave. F, which is inexpensive and open 24 hours; they have all the usual border specialties.

Of course, you could cross the river for Mexican food, with Mexico for atmosphere. An outstanding choice is **Asadero La Posta** at 350 Allende St. (left off Hidalgo eight blocks from the bridge) which specializes in fajitas, *queso con chile, queso fundido,* and *carne asada.* On weekends, the upstairs room occasionally hosts live *conjunto* music. La Posta is open daily for breakfast, lunch, and dinner. More well known is **Crosby's Restaurant & Bar** (tel. 2-2020) at 195 Hidalgo, which since the '30s has drawn a curious mix of Chihuahuan cowboys, Texas ranchers, and tourists—sort of the Acuña version of Nuevo Laredo's Cadillac Bar. House specialties include *cabrito,* Portuguese-style chicken, frogs' legs, roast quail, and the usual border dishes. Open daily 9 a.m.-midnight.

For American food, the favorite local spot is the **Cripple Creek Saloon** (tel. 512-775-0153) at US 90W just after it splits from US 277. The saloon specializes in mesquite-grilled steaks, swordfish, frogs' legs, prime rib, catfish, lobster, and shrimp; open Mon.-Sat. for dinner only.

EVENTS

May

George Paul Memorial Bull Riding Competition: Usually held the first Sunday in May, followed by a week of parades, art shows, and other PRCA rodeo events. Contestants in the event (formerly called Super Bull) are top-rated professional bull riders who compete here for the largest bull-riding purse in the world, around $60,000 in prize money and a 14-karat-gold belt buckle studded with rubies. At the Val Verde County Fairgrounds on N. Main Street.

Cinco de Mayo: Commemorates the Mexican defeat of a French naval invasion at Puebla on May 5 with music, dancing, and food at Brown Plaza in the San Felipe District.

September

Dies y Seis: Mexican independence celebration on Sept. 16, with fiestas in Del Rio and Acuña, including food, music, and dancing.

October

Fiesta Amistad: This is Del Rio's biggest annual event, held in cooperation with Ciudad Acuña to commemorate U.S.-Mexico relations. The festival has been held yearly since October 24, 1960, when U.S. President Dwight Eisenhower and Mexican President Adolfo Lopez Mateos agreed to build a dam across the Rio Grande for the benefit of both countries. The schedule of events lasts nine to 10 days and features Señorita Amistad and Miss Del Rio beauty pageants, an international parade from Del Rio to Acuña, a Battle of the Bands, foot and bike races, an arts and crafts show, an open house at nearby Laughlin Air Force Base, and an *abrazo* or friendly embrace between U.S. and Mexican dignitaries on the Amistad Dam.

INFORMATION

The Del Rio Chamber of Commerce (tel. 512-775-3551) at 1915 Ave. F distributes maps and brochures related to the Del Rio area. The area code for Del Rio is 512. To call Acuña telephone numbers from Del Rio, dial 011-52-877 plus the number.

VICINITY OF DEL RIO (LOWER PECOS)

LAKE AMISTAD NATIONAL RECREATION AREA

Lake Amistad *(amistad* means "friendship" in Spanish) came about after the governments of the U.S. and Mexico, through the International Boundary and Water Commission (IBWC), agreed to build the Amistad Dam across the Rio Grande (or the Rio Bravo as it's known in Mexico). Del Rio-Acuña was chosen as the best possible site since it's just below the confluence of the Rio Grande, the Pecos River, and Devils River—giving man control over three rivers at once. The primary functions of the dam are water conservation, flood control, hydroelectric power (about 161 million kwh per year on the U.S. side), and recreation (swimming, boating, camping, fishing, hunting, and scuba diving). The surface area of the reservoir varies between 65,000 and 89,000 acres and the shoreline is 800-1,000 miles (with over half on the U.S. side), which makes it one of the largest manmade lakes in the United States. The National Park Service administers nine sites along the American side of the lake, while Texas Parks and Wildlife manages those areas not under specific Park Service jurisdiction. As a national recreational site, it's probably the most undeveloped and noncommercial of any Park Service-supervised lake.

Boating

Sailors enjoy Amistad because it's large, uncrowded, and surrounded by side canyons; the three rivers that feed into the lake also offer opportunities for exploration. An added bonus is that some of the river canyons contain 4,000-year-old Indian pictographs that can only be seen by boat. Some of the most spectacular canyons are along Devils River, which also happens to pass through Indian Head Ranch, an exotic game preserve—sometimes the odd impala or wildebeest is visible along the cliffs from the river.

There are three marinas and eight boat launches on the American side. Boats can be rented from the **Lake Amistad Resort & Marina** (tel. 512-774-4157) at the Diablo East Marina, and from the **Creek Boat Rental** (tel. 774-3334) at Rough Canyon. The going rate for boat rentals is $25 an hour or $150 per day (plus gas) for a 16-foot deckboat (115 HP) or an 18-foot runabout (135 HP). A 16-foot bass boat (70 HP) can be rented for $15 an hour or $90 a day, and a 13-foot sailboat is $7 an hour or $35 a day. Water skis are also available for rent. Lake Amistad Resort rents houseboats for $1000 a week (36-foot) and $1195 (50-foot). Discounts on all rentals are available in the off-season (Oct.-May).

The other two marinas on the Del Rio side are the Park Service-administered Rough Canyon Marina to the north and the U.S. Air Force Marina near the dam. The USAF Marina is open only to the military and their families. A marina on the Mexican side is accessible by boat or by driving six miles across the dam into Mexico.

Fishing

Amistad is open to anglers year-round. The lake is stocked with walleye, smallmouth, striped bass, striped hybrid bass, white bass, Florida bass, six species of sunfish, two species of crappie, Rio Grande and African perch, freshwater drum, northern pike, buffalo, four species of gar, and five species of catfish. Anglers should keep an eye on the IBWC buoys that divide U.S. from Mexican waters; a Mexican fishing license is required to fish the Mexican side (but they're easily available from the U.S. marinas or bait shops in Del Rio).

Swimming

Shore swimming is permitted at all of the designated camping areas (see "Camping" below) and at the three designated swimming beaches at Governor's Landing, Rough Canyon, and Old 277 North. On the Mexican side you can swim just about anywhere but there's a designated Mexican swimming beach (with picnic ramadas) near the west end of the dam.

Hunting

Only certain shore areas (mostly to the east) are designated by Texas Parks and Wildlife for hunting. Hunting is allowed only in season and game animals (whitetail deer and javelina) may be hunted only with bow and arrow. Details on seasons and bag limits are available at the Diablo East and Rough Canyon ranger stations.

LAKE AMISTAD NATIONAL RECREATION AREA

LANGTRY
TO MARATHON
TEXAS
RIO GRANDE
S.P.R.R.
MEXICO
PECOS RIVER
ARROYO DE LA PARIDA
PECOS RIVER
SEMINOLE CANYON
★ = NAT'L PARK SERVICE-ADMINISTERED AREAS
ROUGH CANYON
TO OZONA
COMSTOCK
163
ARROYO DE LA ZORRA
ARROYO DEL CABALLO
COW CREEK CANYON
S.P.R.R.
CASTLE CANYON
LAKE AMISTAD
MEXICO MARINA
SPUR 406
DEVILS RIVER
AMISTAD DAM
MEXICAN CUSTOMS
ROUGH CANYON
USAF MARINA
GOVERNOR'S LANDING
ROUGH CANYON
MEXICO
DIABLO EAST
U.S. CUSTOMS
BLACK BRUSH POINT
TO SAN ANGELO
277
SAN PEDRO FLATS
OLD 277 NORTH
OLD 277 SOUTH
SAN PEDRO CANYON
AMISTAD-ACUNA RD.
NPS OFFICE
TEXAS
RIO GRANDE
0   5 mi
CIUDAD ACUNA
DEL RIO
0   5 km
TO EAGLE PASS
90
TO SAN ANTONIO
277
TO SAN ANGELO

© MOON PUBLICATIONS, INC.

Scuba Diving

Best underwater visibility is 25-30 feet, Nov.-April. Algae growth during the warmer months can cut visibility by five to 10 feet. The most popular dive site is at Diablo East, where a cove near the View Point Cliffs has been marked off for diving and swimming only. The depth exceeds 100 feet at the outer edge of the cove; a dive platform is anchored at 40 feet and there is a boat wreck for divers to explore. Other good spots include Castle Canyon, the US 90 bridge, Indian Springs (6½ miles up the Devils River via Rough Canyon), and the cliffs area in Cow Creek Canyon. Spearfishing is permitted (a valid fishing license is required), but only for "rough" fish, including gar, drum, buffalo, carp, and African perch. Divers must register at park headquarters before setting off on a dive.

Camping

Primitive drive-in campsites are available at Governor's Landing (17 sites), San Pedro Flats (12 sites), Old 277 North (8 sites), Old 277 South (four sites), and Spur 406 (12 sites). All designated camping areas provide chemical toilets and cooking grills but no drinking water or showers. Camping is also permitted anywhere along the shore below contour 1,144.3 feet except next to marinas and in posted noncamping areas. There

are no camping fees, but campers are limited to 14 days in a calendar year.

Near the Diablo East Marina are three commercial campgrounds, **American Campground** (tel. 512-755-6484), **Amistad Park** (tel. 775-6491), and **Holiday Trav-L Park** (tel. 775-7784). Site fees at each run $9-12 depending on hookups used (full hookups available at all three). Near the Rough Canyon Marina is the **Rough Canyon Trailer Park/Campground** (tel. 775-6707), where sites are $9 a night. All commercial campgrounds at the lake offer discounts for weekly and monthly stays.

Motels

The **Amistad Lodge** (tel. 512-775-8591) overlooks the lake off US 90 W between Black Brush Point and Diablo East and has rooms for $27 and up. The nearby **Angler's Lodge** (tel. 775-1586) has rooms starting at $25. Both are clean, well-maintained inns. Farther down US 90W toward the dam is the **Lakeview Inn** (tel. 775-9521), which is closer to the marina but farther from Del Rio; room rates are $30 and up. Over at Rough Canyon off US 277 is the more expensive **Laguna Diablo Resort** (tel. 774-2422), where rooms start at $58.50. There are also plenty of motel accommodations in Del Rio itself (see "Accommodations" under "Del Rio" above).

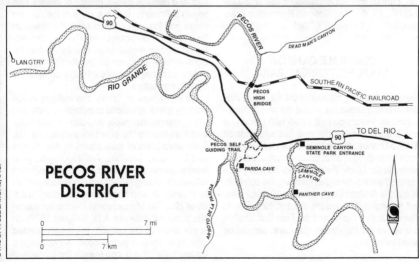

PECOS RIVER
DISTRICT

Seminole Canyon

Information

Park headquarters is at the US 90/277 split, where you can pick up a map of the lake as well as handouts on fishing, boating, hunting, and park-use regulations. At the mouth of the Pecos River, 44 miles west of park headquarters off US 90, is a quarter-mile, self-guiding nature trail that exhibits native regional plants. The Big Bend Natural History Association offers publications at the trailhead. For further information on Lake Amistad, contact the Superintendent (tel. 512-775-7491), Lake Amistad National Recreation Area, Box 420367, Del Rio, TX 78842.

SEMINOLE CANYON STATE HISTORICAL PARK

Seminole Canyon, named for the Seminole Indians who frequented the area at the time of Anglo-American expansion in the mid-19th century, is one of the larger river canyons that runs north off the Rio Grande. At least 200 Indian rock-art sites have been discovered in these canyons and elsewhere in the Lower Pecos region. As many as a hundred were submerged following the construction of the Amistad Dam, including 10 major sites, but fortunately three of the most striking, Parida Cave, Panther Cave, and the Fate Bell Shelter, are above the high-water mark and can still be seen today.

History

The first North American Indians, big-game hunters who followed herds of camel, mammoth, and bison, began living along the Rio Grande and in the Pecos and Devils river valleys 10,000-12,000 years ago. By around 8,000 years ago, they had been replaced by, or perhaps evolved into, groups of peaceful foragers who lived on the plants and small animals of the intersecting desert and chaparral terrains. By 4,000 years ago, and perhaps earlier, groups of Indians had begun painting on the rock walls of the canyon caves, and they continued to add to the collection for another 2,800 years or so. The resulting pictographs cover a wide range of subjects and designs, most of which can be identified with regional phenomena, though some are completely open to conjecture.

As elsewhere in Texas, the Indians made paint by grinding various minerals—ocher, iron oxide, manganese oxide, and clay—into powder and then mixing the powders with animal fat. They used parts of local plants or their hands and fingers for brushes. Anthropologists who have analyzed the paintings can discern different art periods, distinguished by a move from realism to abstraction, and from one set of colors to another (the Red Monochrome Period, for example, occurred between A.D. 600 and 1000). In some areas of the canyon, the artists painted layer upon layer of pictographs, without regard for "posterity"; this is one reason the function of the paintings is thought to be ceremonial. In the early historic period (beginning in the 16th century), it's known that Coahuiltecans were living in the canyons, but whether they were descended from the earlier canyon-dwellers hasn't been ascertained. By the time the Anglo-Americans had established Fort Clark in nearby Brackettville in the 1850s, only Comanches frequented the area (the Seminoles arrived later at the invitation of the Mexican government—see "Brackettville" below).

Visiting The Park

Seminole Canyon is 45 miles west of Del Rio. The park covers 2,173 acres in and around the canyon and protects a combination of flora and fauna that represents a meeting of Tamaulipan Thorn Scrub, Edwards Plateau, and Chihuahuan Desert terrains. Two trails have been established for exploring the area and these lead to the canyon's two main pictograph sites.

The short trail to **Fate Bell Shelter** can only be taken in the company of a park ranger. Fate Bell is a major Indian site, with a long series of painted cave shelters beneath a semicircular canyon ledge. The cave bottom has a 13-foot layer of debris accumulated over 6,000 years of continuous habitation, including intact thatched mats, sandals, and stone tools. Several levels of pictographs have been covered by this layering. The main rock-art period visible here is the Pecos River Style, marked by stick-like figures carrying *atlatls* (spear throwers) and pouches made from prickly pear cactus. Guided tours along this trail are led Wed.-Sun. at 10 a.m. and 3 p.m. year-round.

The other trail is a six-mile (roundtrip) self-guiding path that leads down to a Rio Grande overlook opposite Panther Cave. This is a worthwhile hike for enjoying the Lower Pecos environment, but to get a good look at the Panther Cave pictographs, you really need to go by boat via the Rio Grande (see "Boat Tours" below).

The visitor center is open daily 8-5 and contains excellent interpretive exhibits that depict daily life in the Archaic Indian period, including a life-size diorama that demonstrates hunting and foraging techniques. The staff can also answer questions about the pictograph sites and about area activities.

The park entry fee is $3 per vehicle or $1 for pedestrians and cyclists.

Camping

The park camping area has 31 drive-in sites, $6 a night with water and $9 a night with w/e. Restrooms have flush toilets and hot showers.

Boat Tours

By boat, visitors can explore the Pecos-Rio Grande River area in the vicinity of Seminole Canyon and see pictograph sites that aren't accessible on foot. Chief among these are Parida Cave and Panther Cave. **Parida Cave** is a few miles north of Seminole Canyon just below the mouth of the Pecos River. In 1987, the Park Service constructed a boat dock and rock-trail system with interpretive signs so that the general public could easily visit the cave by boat. Like the Fate Bell Shelter in Seminole Canyon, Parida was inhabited continuously for thousands of years, starting around 3000 B.C. and ending about 500 years ago. Hundreds of pictographs and a burnt rock midden have been left behind. When the Southern Pacific Railroad came through in 1883, Parida became the Painted

Fate Bell Rock Shelter

Jersey Lilly Saloon,
Langtry

Caves Station, where passengers rested while the train was being serviced. The remains of the station are now 50 feet below the surface of Lake Amistad.

Panther Cave is near the mouth of Seminole Canyon and is the model by which all other Pecos River pictographs are judged in terms of period, style, and color. The Sistine Chapel of painted caves, the shelter has pictographs covering the walls and part of the ceiling 12 feet above the floor. The cave got its name from a panther painting that's over 15 feet long. Because the cave is so popular, a chain link fence has been erected across the shelter to prevent vandalism, but there are camera portholes built into the fence. As at Parida, a Park Service dock allows visitors to approach by boat.

Another popular sightseeing stop for boaters is the **Pecos High Bridge**, about five miles up the Pecos River from the Rio Grande junction. The construction of the original span in 1882 was a significant event in the completion of the country's second transcontinental rail line and required a crew of 8,000 (who cut two 1500-foot tunnels through solid rock on either side of the river). The second version in 1891 was the highest bridge in the world when built (321 feet high—still the highest bridge in Texas), and its completion shortened the rail route by 13 miles. This bridge was replaced by another of about the same height in 1944, which is still used by transcontinental trains. The 1891 bridge was dissasembled and sold to

Venezuela and is reportedly still in use there.

If you don't have your own boat, you can rent one at Lake Amistad (see "Boating" under "Lake Amistad National Recreation Area" above) or join a guided boat tour. Only two experienced tour operators are licensed to lead tours in the Pecos-Rio Grande-Devils River area. Manuel and Inez Hardwick of **High Bridge Adventures** (Box 816 Comstock, TX 78837, tel. 915-292-4495) lead boat tours from the Pecos River Boat Ramp. Their three-hour tours visit Parida and Panther caves, several lesser-known pictograph sites, and the Pecos High Bridge for $20 per person. **American Watersports** (tel. 775-6484 or 800-LAKE-FUN), at Lake Amistad's Diablo East Marina, offers two different river/pictograph tours. One takes in the Pecos River area, the other lesser known Devil's River; either tour costs $45 per hour for up to six persons.

Jim Zintgraff, a professional photographer who has been documenting the Lower Pecos pictographs for over 36 years, leads boat tours from the Diablo East Marina on Lake Amistad. Tours all the way to the Pecos cost as much as $45 a person and take the better part of a day. Jim can be contacted by calling (512) 525-9907 in San Antonio.

Information

For more information, contact the Superintendent (tel. 915-292-4464), Seminole Canyon State Historical Park, Box 820, Comstock, TX, 78837.

LANGTRY

Langtry was established in the 1880s when the Southern Pacific and the Galveston, Harrisburg, and San Antonio railroads were joined at nearby Dead Man's Gulch. At the time, the only settlement in the area was a tent city named Vinegaroon with a reputation for extreme lawlessness. The railroad and the Texas Rangers commissioned Vinegaroon store owner Roy Bean to serve as justice of the peace at a new town site next to the rail line. Judge Roy Bean christened the town Langtry, after his idol Lillie Langtry, a famous English actress of the period, and opened a saloon called the Jersey Lily (her international title, which Bean misspelled as "Lilly") that also served as his courtroom. The rest, as they say, is history. With a volume of the 1879 Revised Statutes of Texas and a six-shooter, the judge declared himself the "law west of the Pecos," often fining defendants by ordering a round of drinks for the house. In 1896, Bean defied Texas and Mexico law by staging the Maher-Fitzsimmons championship prizefight on a sandbar in the middle of the Rio Grande (at the time, professional boxing was illegal on both sides of the river). Bean died in 1904. In 1972, director John Huston filmed Bean's story in *The Life and Times of Judge Roy Bean,* starring Paul Newman.

Judge Roy Bean Visitor Center
The visitor center itself is one of the State Highway Dept.'s 12 tourist bureaus and distributes information on travel throughout the state. Behind the center is the restored Jersey Lilly saloon, which is open to touring (free). Next to the center is a nature trail through a well-planned Chihuahuan Desert garden in which the plants are labeled with their scientific names and the medicinal and utilitarian uses of each.

BRACKETTVILLE

Brackettville (pop. 1,844), 32 miles east of Del Rio on US 90, grew up around Fort Clark, a frontier fort that opened in the 1850s and didn't close until 1946. It's the county seat for Kinney County, which is larger than the state of Rhode Island but has only one other town (Spofford, pop. 77, 10

miles south of Brackettville). It's mostly a ranching (cattle, sheep, goats) and farming community that is also a popular hunting area for deer, javelina, wild turkey, quail, and dove. Brackettville has two claims to fame: Fort Clark (home of the renowned Black Seminole Scouts) and Alamo Village.

Seminole Indian Scout Cemetery
This unassuming cemetery, about five miles south of Brackettville on FM 3348, is the only monument to a remarkable group of people with a remarkable history. Buried here along with some of their descendants are around a hundred Black Seminoles who served as Army scouts at nearby Ft. Clark. Their history goes back to the early 1800s when a group of slaves ran away from Georgia and South Carolina to Florida, where they became sharecroppers for Seminole Indians. In Florida, the blacks and the Seminoles intermarried and fought the U.S. Army together but kept separate camps. In the 1840s several bands of black and Seminole warriors were captured by the army and sent to a Cherokee reservation in Oklahoma. From here they escaped across Texas to northern Mexico, where they were employed by the Mexican government to keep the Apaches and Comanches at bay, thus earning a reputation as fearless Indian fighters. In exchange for their services, Mexico gave them land at Naciamente (below Piedras Negras).

Throughout the 1850s and 1860s, the mixed band of blacks and Seminoles kept to themselves and began to merge toward a single ethnicity that featured a mixture of Indian and African dialects (it is thought that most of the blacks originated from North Africa's Barbary Coast). As the Civil War came to a close, the U.S. Army approached the Black Seminoles for help in ridding the Fort Clark area of Comanches. Lieutenant John "Thunderbolt" Bullis led the Seminole-Negro Indian Scouts (as they were officially called) in 26 successful Indian campaigns between 1871 and 1881, during which three Seminole scouts earned Medals of Honor. A fourth scout was awarded the Medal of Honor during a campaign with MacKenzie's Raiders. All four of these scouts have grave markers in the cemetery.

The Seminole Indian Scouts were disbanded in 1914. Around 50 of their descendants live in Brackettville and another hundred or so in Naciamente, Mexico. Others live in Del Rio, Fort

Davis, San Antonio, and farther afield. The last scout to be buried in the cemetery was Curly Jefferson, who died in the 1950s. Black Seminoles living in Brackettville maintain the cemetery and occasionally hold barbecues to raise funds for grounds improvement.

Fort Clark Springs

Fort Clark is the only frontier fort in Texas to have been turned into a resort, complete with golf course, swimming pool, motel, bar, and RV park. Some of the original buildings have been restored (the 1872 barracks is now the motel), and you can tour the grounds during the day. It's on the east edge of town off US 90.

Alamo Village

This replica of the 19th-century Alamo Mission is the largest movie set ever built outside Hollywood. It took 5,000 men two years (1957-59) to build, using the original Spanish plans and adobe bricks made on-site by adobemakers from Mex-

ico—all to be used for the John Wayne epic film *The Alamo*. After the film was completed, the set was expanded to include an Old West town that has been used by production companies in making nearly 40 feature films (including the recent *Lonesome Dove)* and hundreds of TV shows and commercials. One end of town is said to represent San Antonio and the other Fort Worth in the 1880s.

Every Labor Day the Cowboy Horse Races are held here in which riders race through the town for distances of 200, 250, 300, 350, and 440 yards. The final race is a tribute to the original quarter-horse races, which were named after the quarter mile (440 yards) that the main streets of most Old West towns extended.

The complex is located on the Shahan HV Ranch, six miles north of Brackettville on RR 674. It's open to visitors daily 9-5, year-round (except Dec. 21-26). During the summer months there is live entertainment, including music and simulated gun duels. Admission is $5, children under six free.

BOB RACE

NORTH CENTRAL TEXAS

DALLAS

INTRODUCTION

Dallas tries to be all things to all people: Manhattan of the Southwest, cowboy capital, temple of consumerism, arts center, church center, and Sun Belt suburbia. To a certain degree, the city succeeds: it ranks third in the U.S. as headquarters for Fortune 500 companies; it's the only city in Texas with a weekly rodeo (actually in nearby Mesquite); it has more shopping centers and more retail space per capita than any other U.S. city; 60 downtown acres have been set aside as an arts district; it harbors the two largest Methodist and Baptist churches in the world; and it's encircled by planned suburban communities.

Dallas's one million residents are secure in feeling superior to other Texas cities (calling Dallas "the Cadillac of Texas towns") yet insecure about their status in relation to other U.S. metropolitan centers. They've gone from the city that shot J.F.K. to the city that shot J.R. (J.R. Ewing, the sleazy billionaire on TV's "Dallas"); the convention and vis-

itors bureau has even used the slogan "If you like the show, you'll love the city"), which probably makes average Dallasites feel like their city's not taken seriously. It's virtually impossible to arrive in Dallas for the first time without a bundle of preconceived images; in spite of this tendency (or perhaps because of it), most visitors seem to be surprised by how much they like Dallas. It's a city that invites parody, yet no one who spends any time there can deny that it's an extremely vibrant place.

Land

Of course, you can't achieve the "bright lights, big city" effect without cutting down a few trees and leveling a few hills. The terrain around Dallas used to be a series of wooded prairies collectively called the Cross Timbers. As the city grew from "Dallas" to "Greater Dallas" to the "Metroplex" (a linking of Dallas, Arlington, Fort Worth, and several smaller towns by spaghetti freeways), virtually all characteristics that distinguished the Cross Timbers from the Prairies were erased or covered over. Which is not to say there aren't plenty of

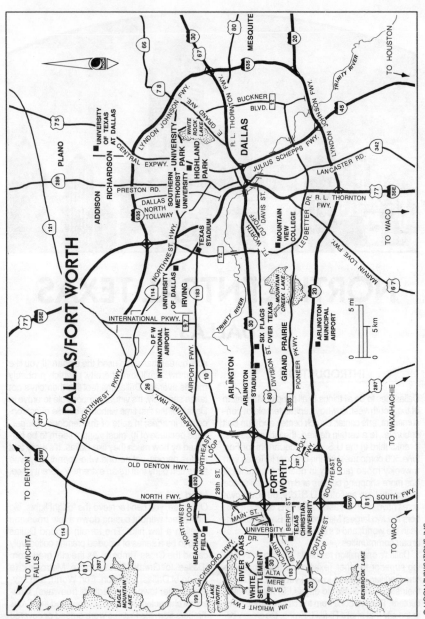

© MOON PUBLICATIONS, INC.

greenbelts in and around Dallas—but these are manmade oases.

Climate
Dallas weather is fairly moderate most of the year, thanks to its position between the chilly High Plains to the west and the muggy lowlands to the east. Average humidity is 50-60% year-round. Average temperatures range from 36-56° F in January to 74-95° F in July. Average annual rainfall is 39 inches, with April, May, and September the wettest months (three to four inches per month).

History
Dallas started as one log cabin in 1840, when John Neely Bryan came from Tennessee and established a small trading post on the Trinity River. Other settlers joined him, including his Arkansas neighbor Joe Dallas, for whom Bryan named the town. In 1855, around 350 French colonists from La Réunion moved to Dallas following the dissolution of their Texas colony, thus expanding the settlement. As with many Western towns, it was the coming of the railroads that really put Dallas on the map. Two rail lines came through: the Houston and Texas Central in 1872 and the Texas and Pacific in 1873.

Although a certain amount of ranching and farming was established in the Dallas area, the city stayed close to its trading-post roots—instead of riding herd or planting cotton, Dallas interests preferred buying and selling Texas assets. When oil was discovered elsewhere in the state, this is where the oilmen kept their money. After World War II, Dallas became a banking and insurance headquarters as other industries (high tech, communications, aviation, medicine, conventions, film, and fashion, to name a few) joined oil, livestock, and agriculture in boosting the economy. Since the city financiers were fairly diversified, the oil recession of the '80s affected Dallas little.

Costs
For its comparative size, Dallas enjoys a reasonable cost of living. Nonetheless, it's Texas's most expensive city, especially if you're staying or eating downtown. To save money, you might consider choosing a place to stay east or west of the city (there's not much available to the south, and north Dallas is just as expensive as central Dallas). Fresh fruits and vegetables are sold daily from dawn to dusk at the Farmer's Market off Pearl Expressway.

SIGHTS

Downtown Architecture
Of the many buildings that make up Dallas' Manhattan-like skyline, three distinguish it from other urban profiles. The structure that looks like a shiny sphere at the end of a 50-story shaft is the **Reunion Tower,** which is linked to the Hyatt Regency Hotel, the Union railway station, and the Reunion Arena (home to the Dallas Mavericks basketball team). The view from the tower is probably the best city view accessible to the public, especially at night. An elevator ride to the observation deck costs $2 adults, $1 for children under 12 and senior citizens. Or you can ride an elevator to the Top of the Dome Club bar, two floors higher than the observation deck, for free.

The **Renaissance Tower** is the 56-story glass-and-steel building that's illuminated at night

Reunion Tower, Dallas

DOWNTOWN DALLAS

© MOON PUBLICATIONS, INC.

with elongated double Xs. It's shown around the world on reruns of the TV show "Dallas" as J.R. Ewing's offices, but it actually belongs to Prudential Insurance. Another Dallas landmark is the red neon Pegasus flying over the much shorter **Mobil Building.** The corporate logo of the Magnolia Petroleum Co., it was originally erected in honor of the 1945 American Petroleum Institute, the first major convention held in the city (Dallas is now the number-two convention city in the

U.S.). The tallest high-rise in Dallas is the 72-story Nations Bank tower, which is outlined by two miles of green argon tubing at night.

Dallas Arts District

This ambitious project involves 60 acres of prime downtown real estate that are being developed by a mixture of private (Arts District Management Association) and public (Arts District Foundation, Arts District Friends) investment. The district is bounded on the north by Woodall Rogers Freeway, on the west by St. Paul, on the east by Routh, and on the south by Ross. Existing facilities include the Dallas Arts Magnet High School, the Dallas Museum of Art (see "Museums" below), the Dallas Theater Center, the Meyerson Symphony Center, and the Trammel Crow Center. The Trammell Crow Center is a multi-use building that often houses traveling folk-art exhibits from the Smithsonian and other American museums. It also features a sculpture garden that displays 22 French bronzes, including works by Rodin. Several historic buildings have been preserved within the district: the Greek Revival-style Belo Mansion, St. Paul United Methodist Church, and Catedral Santuario de Guadalupe.

Museums

The **Dallas Museum of Art** (tel. 214-922-1200) is the centerpiece of the Arts District. A modern, state-of-the-art facility, it houses an average of 10,000 items ranging from prehistoric art to contemporary painting and sculpture. Permanent gallery exhibits include pre-Columbian, African, 19th-century and early modern European, and 18th-century to post-WW II American collections. A Decorative Arts Wing features a re-created Mediterranean villa that houses the Hoblitzelle Collection of silver and the Wendy and Emery Reves Collection of European furniture, impressionist paintings, and Chinese porcelain. The museum is at 1717 N. Harwood. Free museum tours are given Tues.-Fri. at 11 a.m., Sun. at 2 p.m., starting at the Orientation Theater Entrance. General museum hours are Tues., Wed., Fri., and Sat. 10-5, Thurs. 10-9; Sun. and holidays 12-5. Admission to most of the galleries is free; there's a $3 admission to the Reves Collection, and special temporary exhibits may also charge.

The **Age of Steam Railroad Museum** (tel. 214-428-0101) at the Fair Park (Washington and Perry) is a must for railroad buffs. Here you'll find the world's largest steam locomotive, a 1903 depot, a 1930s passenger train (complete with dining car, sleepers, and several cabooses), and an authentic whistle tree. Open Thurs.-Fri. 9-1, Sat.-Sun. 11-5. Admission is $2 adults, $1 ages 16 and under.

Even non-Christians might be interested in the **Biblical Arts Center,** (tel. 214-691-4661) a non-denominational museum devoted to world art that evokes the early biblical era. The main work on display is the "Miracle at Pentecost" mural, which measures 124 feet by 20 feet; it took Dallas artists Torger Thompson and Alvin Barnes three years to paint it. Every half-hour, when the museum is open, the mural is the focus of a sound-and-light presentation. Two other galleries within the center house traveling exhibits and occasional performing arts. The center is at 7500 Park Ln. at Boedeker, six miles north of downtown Dallas off the North Central Expressway (US 75). Open Tues.-Sat. 10-5, Sun. 1-5. Admission to most exhibits is free, but the sound-and-light show costs $3.75 adults, $3 seniors, $2 children 6-12.

The **Museum of African-American Culture** (tel.214-565-9026) has moved from Bishop College to the WRR Building at Fair Park (1515 First Ave.). It features collections of African and African-American art and artifacts from pre-slavery Africa through modern times. Admission varies according to the exhibit.

Southern Methodist University (SMU) is the site for the **Meadows Museum of Art** (tel. 214-692-2516), a portion of a $35 million endowment made by oil tycoon Alger Meadows. The museum specializes in Spanish and Portuguese art, and has a permanent collection of works by Spanish masters, including Goya, Picasso, Murillo, Valázquez, and Miró. In the Owens Fine Art Center, SMU campus (at Bishop and Binkley). Open Mon.-Sat. 10-5, Sun. 1-5; admission free.

The **Sixth Floor** (tel. 214-653-6666) calls itself "a permanent educational exhibition examining the life, death, and legacy of John F. Kennedy within the context of American history." Formerly part of the Texas School Book Depository, this is the floor from which Lee Harvey Oswald allegedly shot JFK as he drove through Dealey Plaza on Nov. 22, 1963. The window area that Oswald used as a vantage point is protected behind a glass wall, and has been restored to the way it was on the day of the assassination. Other exhibits evoke American life in the Kennedy era. The building now contains offices of the Dallas County government and is located at 411 Elm Street. The Kennedy exhibit is open daily 10-6. Admission is $4 adult, $3 senior, $2 student with ID; an audio tour is available for $2.

*"Old Red," County
Courthouse, Dallas*

Dallas County Historical Plaza

This area, bounded by Elm, Market, Commerce, and Houston, is actually divided in two: Founder's Plaza, with a reconstruction of John Neely Bryan's original log cabin (see "History" above), and Kennedy Memorial Plaza, which contains a bizarre structure of concrete walls surrounding a small monument that's dedicated to Kennedy. Although Kennedy's limousine passed by here that fateful day in 1963, he was actually shot east of Houston St., in Dealey Plaza. On the east edge of Kennedy Memorial Plaza stands "Old Red," the huge Romanesque-style Dallas County Courthouse, built in 1891 of dark-red Pecos sandstone.

Old City Park

This recreated early Dallas village features 37 restored North Central Texas structures from 1840-1910, including the antebellum Millermore home, a general store, bank, post office, train depot, dentist's office, school, church, smokehouse, barbershop, Indian teepee, and various small houses and cabins. The 13-acre grounds have picnic areas and trails. The entrance is at 1717 Gano, just south of downtown at I-30 and Harwood. Open Tues.- Sat. 10-4, Sun. 1:30-4:30 p.m.

Dallas Arboretum And Botanical Gardens

The scenic 66-acre grounds of the former De-Golyer and Camp estates on White Rock Lake are the setting for this series of floral, herbal, and vegetable gardens. Best time of year for a visit is spring, when everything's blooming. The Spanish colonial-style DeGolyer mansion has been turned into a museum that contains 17th to 18th-century European art and furnishings. Open daily 10-6. Admission is free Fri. 3-6 p.m.; other times it's $6 adults, $5 seniors, $3 children 6-12.

Dallas Zoo

This zoo features over 1,600 animals in 20 environments, including a tropical rainforest. A train circles the zoo every 15 minutes. A schedule of feedings is available. In the summer, there's a children's petting zoo with goats, sheep, and rabbits. In Marsalis Park, 621 E. Clarendon Drive. Open daily 9-5; admission $5 adults, $1 children 6-12 and seniors.

Fair Park

Besides being the site of the enormous Texas state fair every October, Fair Park contains several science-oriented exhibitions year-round. The **Dallas Aquarium** (tel. 214-670-8441) is the nation's largest inland aquarium, with over 300 species of marine, tropical, and freshwater fish. It's open daily 10-4:30 and costs $1 for adults, 50 cents for children. The **Museum of Natural History** (tel. 670-8459) houses permanent exhibits on the plants and animals of Texas and the Southwest, including 50 dioramas and a fossil hall. The museum's Earth Science Hall contains a 32-foot reconstructed mosasaur, one of the world's largest prehistoric sea serpents, as well as a 15-foot mammoth from nearby Trinity River. Open Mon.-Sat. 9-5, Sun. noon-5; admission free. The **Science Place I** (tel. 214-428-5555) hosts traveling science exhibits (recently including rare documents from Einstein's experiments, robot dinosaurs, and an exhibit on Egyptian mummification techniques) and is open daily 9:30-5:30; admission is $5.50 adults, $2.50 children 7-16 and seniors. The **Science Place II** (tel. 428-8352) contains a planetarium plus hands-on exhibits like The Shadow Room, where bursts of light transpose visitors' silhouettes onto phosphorescent walls. Open Tues.-Sat. 9:30-5:30, Sun. noon-5:30; $2 adults, 50 cents children 7-16.

Union Station
This huge, beaux arts-style railway depot was built in 1914, but it decayed along with the importance of railway passenger travel over the next 60 years. In 1974 it was restored to its former glory and now contains the Dallas Visitors Center, restaurants, shops, and a small Amtrak depot (Amtrak still stops here). At 400 S. Houston, across from the Hyatt Regency; open 24 hours a day.

Dallas Farmer's Market
In the early 1900s, farmers came daily to Pearl and Cadiz streets to sell fresh produce to wholesale distributors. Traffic jams increased and city residents complained, but instead of barring the produce markets, the city built a farmer's market shed in the late '30s, just south of downtown. They added three more sheds in 1946, 1954, and 1982 (a fifth is planned for the '90s), so that it's now among the largest urban farmer's markets in the country. Over a thousand farmers sell fresh fruits and vegetables at the market daily; floral vendors participate March to December as well. The market sheds are on either side of the Pearl Expwy. between Harwood St. and the North Central Fwy. (US 75). Open daily, sunrise to sunset.

Adolphus Hotel
When it was built in 1912 by beer magnate Adolphus Busch, the Adolphus Hotel was said to be the most beautiful building west of Venice, Italy. Following its restoration and reopening in 1981, it's probably more impressive than it was then—21 stories of ornate brick and granite in the French Renaissance style on the outside, all marble and wood paneling on the inside. Common rooms are furnished with antiques and objets d'art like the 1805 Doré crystal chandelier and huge 1661 Brussels tapestries hanging in the lobby. The hotel's restaurants are just as posh; the French Room features a 59-color carpet that was custom-designed in Hong Kong and Italian hand-blown glass chandeliers. Many historic hotel restoration projects subdivide guest rooms to increase occupancy, but at the Adolphus they combined 800 rooms to make 439 larger rooms. All rooms are decorated with Chippendale- and Queen Anne-style furniture and Williamsburg paneling. At 1321 Commerce St. downtown. See "Dallas Hotels And Motels" chart for rates.

Southfork Ranch
The TV home of J.R., Sue Ellen, Bobby, and Miss Ellie was once a real ranch owned by another J.R., but only the exterior was used in the TV show. It's now a "Dallas" museum that features memorabilia from the cast and show, including the gun that shot J.R. and an 18-story oil rig. To get here, take I-75 north to Parker Rd., then go east six miles and make a right at FM 2551, then left at the Southfork sign. Admission (which includes a guided tour) is $7.95 adults, $5.95 children 6-12. Parking costs an additional $2 per vehicle. Call (214) 442-6536 for more information.

ACCOMMODATIONS

See the "Dallas Hotels and Motels" chart for hotel/motel accommodation.

Campgrounds
KOA Kampgrounds has two locations near Dallas: in Denton, 30 miles northwest off I-35 E (Corinth Exit 460), where tent/camper sites are $14, full hookups $16, and cabins $22.50; and at Caddo Mills, 36 miles northeast on I-30 E, exit FM 36 N, where tent/camper sites are $14, full hookups $16, cabins $24. Both have pools. Closer to the city is the **Dallas Hi-Ho Campground,** which is 18 miles south off I-35 E at Bear Creek Rd. (exit 412); full hookups are $14.50. There are also several RV parks near Fort Worth (see "Accommodations," p. 221).

DALLAS HOTELS AND MOTELS

Add 13% hotel tax to all rates. Area code: 214

NAME	ADDRESS	PHONE	RATES	FEATURES
DOWNTOWN				
The Adolphus	1321 Commerce	742-8200	$190-260	historic, refrigerators, wknd. discounts
Aristocrat Clarion Hotel Of Dallas	1933 Main	741-7700	$65-150	historic, refrigerators, wknd. discounts
Dallas Park Plaza Hotel	1914 Commerce	747-7000	$81-109	wknd. and senior discounts
Fairmont Hotel	1717 N. Akard St.	720-2020	$125-240	Arts District location, heated pool
Hotel Crescent Court	400 Crescent Ct.	871-3200	$205-285	near McKinney Ave. entertainment district, heated pool, spa
Hotel St. Germain	2516 Maple Ave.	871-2516	$225-450	historic, near McKinney Ave., Jacuzzi, fireplaces
Holiday Inn Downtown	1015 Elm	748-9951	$76-94	pool
Hyatt Regency	300 Reunion	651-1234	$150-190	pool, tennis courts
Ramada Inn	1011 S. Akard	421-1083	$45-55	near Convention Center, heated pool, airport shuttle
Southland Center Hotel	400 N. Olive	922-8000	$79-180	art gallery
DALLAS–FORT WORTH AIRPORT				
Airport Marriott	8440 Freeport Pkwy.	929-8800	$75-145	pool, airport shuttle, coin laundry, wknd. discounts
Embassy Suites	4650 W. Airport Fwy.	790-0093	$124	heated pool, airport shuttle, coin laundry, wknd. discounts
Exel Inn (Airport)	825 Esters	929-0066	$33-40	pool, airport shuttle
Harvey Hotel (Airport)	4545 John Carpenter Fwy.	929-4500	$95-130	heated pool, airport shuttle, wknd. discounts
La Quinta Motor Inn	4105 W. Airport Fwy.	252-6546	$47-61	pool, airport shuttle
Red Roof (Airport)	8150 Esters	929-0020	$31-40	—
Sheraton Grand Hotel	Esters	929-8400	$105-140	heated pool, airport shuttle, wknd. discounts
NORTH DALLAS (OFF LBJ FREEWAY)				
Comfort Inn	3536 W. Kingsley	340-3501	$44-48	heated pool

DALLAS HOTELS AND MOTELS

Add 13% hotel tax to all rates. Area code: 214

NAME	ADDRESS	PHONE	RATES	FEATURES
NORTH DALLAS (OFF LBJ FREEWAY) (continued)				
Courtyard by Marriott	2930 Forest	620-8000	$69-85	pool, wknd. discounts
Dallas Parkway Hilton	4801 LBJ Fwy.	661-3600	$85-125	heated pool, wknd. discounts
Econo Lodge	9356 LBJ Fwy.	690-1220	$42-48	pool, coin laundry, senior discounts
Grand Kempinski	15201 Dallas Parkway	386-6000	$125-200	indoor/outdoor pool, health club, wknd. discounts
Motel 6	2753 Forest Lane	620-2828	$23 +$6 ea. add.	pool
The Westin Hotel Galleria	13340 Dallas Parkway	934-9494	$160-180	pool, refrigerators, jogging track, linked to Galleria
NORTHWEST (INCLUDING MARKET CENTER)				
Best Western Market Center	2023 Market Ctr.	741-9000	$55-75	pool, comp. eve. beverage
The Clarion Hotel	1241 W. Mockingbird	630-7000	$77-97	pool, coin laundry
Days Inn Texas Stadium	2200 E. Airport Fwy.	438-6666	$42-58	pool, coin laundry
Embassy Suites Market Center	2727 Stemmons Fwy.	630-5332	$139-149	heated pool, coin laundry, comp. eve. beverage
Holiday Inn Market Center	1955 Market Center	747-9551	$58-68	pool, airport shuttle
Le Baron Hotel	1055 Regal Row	634-8550	$70-85	pool, tennis courts, airport shuttle
Ramada Hotel	3232 W. Mockingbird	357-5601	$57-66	near Love Field, pool, airport shuttle
Red Roof MC	1550 Empire Central	638-5151	$31-40	—
Travelodge MC	4500 Harry Hines	522-6650	$54-76	seasonal and senior discounts
EAST				
Days Inn Dallas	6222 Belt Line	226-7621	$32-37	pool
La Quinta Motor Inn East	8303 E. Thorton Fwy.	324-3731	$44-58	pool
Motel 6–Mesquite	3629 US 80	613-1662	$21 + $6 ea. add.	—
Motel 6	3629 I-30 and Belt Line	226-7140	$23 +$6 ea. add.	pool
Red Roof Inn Dallas East	8108 E. Thorton Fwy.	388-8741	$40-48	—

*Southfork Ranch,
Dallas*

DALLAS CONVENTION & VISITORS BUREAU

Bed And Breakfasts

Bed & Breakfast Texas Style (tel. 214-298-8586) is the largest B&B registry in the state, covering not only Dallas but most of north and northeast Texas. To book a B&B in Dallas, Fort Worth, Arlington, Waco, or Waxahachie, contact director Ruth Wilson, 4224 W. Red Bird Ln., Dallas, TX 75237.

FOOD

As you would expect for a city of its size, Dallas has food for virtually every taste and budget. It's definitely the state's gourmet capital, even if many of the big-name places are corporate-owned. Meal prices tend to be on the high side if there's anything Southwestern on the menu.

American/Southwestern

$$ **Baby Routh:** An offshoot of the highly acclaimed and more expensive Routh Street Café. Like its progenitor, this one features elevated Southwestern cuisine. At 2708 Routh downtown (tel. 214-871-2345); open Mon.-Sat. for lunch and dinner, Sun. for brunch and dinner.

$$$ **Dakota's:** More nouveau Southwestern, with the emphasis on mesquite-grilled items served amidst a marble-floored, wood-paneled atmosphere. Great key lime pie. At 600 N. Akard downtown (tel. 740-4001); open Mon.-Fri. for lunch and dinner, Sat.-Sun. dinner only.

$$ **Deep Ellum Café:** Serves a creative variety of Texas-American dishes, from Southwestern to Tex-Mex to Cajun to down-home. Very chic Deep Ellum location at 2706 Elm (tel. 741-9012); open Mon.-Fri. for lunch and dinner, Sat.-Sun. brunch and dinner.

$ **8.0:** Ultra-chic, eclectic, health-oriented menu featuring such memorable dishes as "Ecraser dans la Rue (the Roadkill Platter)." Popular *après-soir* hangout—the CD jukebox has over 1,500 selections. At 2800 Routh (tel. 979-0880); open Mon.-Tues. 11 a.m.-1 a.m., Wed.-Sat. 11 a.m.-2 a.m., Sun. 10 a.m.-midnight.

$$$+ **The Mansion on Turtle Creek:** This is where Dallas's rich and famous eat to be seen. The menu is always changing but is, as usual in Dallas, first-class Southwestern. At 2821 Turtle Creek (tel. 526-2121); open daily for lunch and dinner.

$$$+ **Routh Street Café:** One of the nation's seminal nouveau Southwestern kitchens, operated by famous Texan chef Stephan Pyles. Jalapeño sorbet, anyone? The five-course, prix-fixe menu changes nightly. At 3005 Routh St. downtown (tel. 871-7161); open Tues.-Sat. for dinner.

$$ to $$$ **Sam's Café:** This is another branch of Mariel Hemingway's New York eatery, featuring a nouveau Southwestern menu with Thai influences. Popular with the young, upscale, and single. At 100 Crescent Court in the McKinney district (tel. 855-2233); open Mon.-Fri. for breakfast, lunch, and dinner, Sat.-Sun. dinner only.

Barbecue

$ Gene's Stone Pit Barbecue: This Deep Ellum smokehouse has been serving mighty good barbecue for over 40 years. On Friday nights there's occasionally live blues. At 3002 Canton (tel. 214-939-9419); open Mon.-Sat. for lunch and dinner.

$ Sonny Bryan's Smokehouse: Most Dallasites say Sonny's has the best barbecue in town (it's so popular the meat often sells out by 2 p.m.). Its quirky interior features chintzy Americana like car-hood tables and school-desk chairs. At 2202 Inwood (tel. 357-7120); open Mon.-Fri. 10 a.m.-5 p.m. (or until they run out of barbecue), Sat. 11 a.m.-3 p.m. (ditto).

Burgers

$ Andrew's: Features *haute* hamburgers and side orders like blue cheese burgers and cheese-stuffed jalapeños. At 3301 McKinney (tel. 220-0566); open daily for lunch and dinner.

$ to $$ Hard Rock Café: Corporate rock 'n' roll America (same chain as in New York, London, Tokyo, etc.) with burgers, pig sandwiches, fajitas, and rock memorabilia. At 2601 McKinney (tel. 855-0007); open daily 11 a.m.-2 a.m.

$ Joe Willy's Market & Grill: Features big, do-it-yourself burgers with homemade fries and onion rings. At 7033 Greenville (tel. 691-8930); open daily for lunch and dinner.

$ Prince of Hamburgers: A locally famous, pre-McDonald's drive-in (with curb service) that's been serving burgers, fries, and shakes since 1927. At 5200 Lemmon Ave. in the Oak Lawn district (tel. 526-9081); open daily for lunch and dinner.

Cajun/Creole

$$ Café Margaux: Serves a mixture of Cajun and Creole dishes, with the accent on the latter. Good oysters Bienville and sautéed veal in Creole sauce. At 3710 Rawlins in Oak Lawn (tel. 520-1985); open Mon.-Fri. for lunch and dinner, Sat.-Sun. dinner only.

$ Crescent City Café: Great variety of inexpensive New Orleans dishes (po' boys, muffalettas, red beans and rice, etoufée—even café au lait and beignets) in the Deep Ellum district, right around the corner from Tommy's (see "Entertainment" below). At 2730 Commerce (tel. 745-1900); open Mon.-Sat. for lunch and dinner (till 1 a.m. Fri. and Sat.).

$$ Pappadeaux Seafood Kitchen: A boisterous branch of Houston's highly reputed Greek-owned Cajun seafood restaurant. All seafood is fresh and expertly prepared; house specialities include oysters Pappadeaux, boudin, and bread pudding. At 3520 Oak Lawn (tel. 521-4700); open daily for lunch and dinner.

Down-home

$ Bubba's: Serves all the classics: fried chicken, catfish, biscuits and cream gravy, and chicken-fried steak. At 6617 Hillcrest (tel. 214-373-6527); open daily 6:30 a.m.-10 p.m.

$ Celebration: Down-home cooking that's actually served in a converted home. Adds middle-America fare like pot roast and meatloaf to the usual southern-style menu. At 4503 W. Lovers Ln. (tel. 358-0612); open daily for lunch and dinner.

European

$$ L'Ancestral: Family-owned, bistro-style restaurant that serves country French cuisine. At 4514 Travis (tel. 528-1081); open Mon.-Sat. for lunch and dinner, Sun. dinner only.

$$ Le Boul'Mich Bistro: Specializes in French-style seafood. At 2704 Worthington (tel. 220-2115); open Mon.-Sat. for lunch and dinner.

$$ La Tosca: A trendy Highland Park restaurant that specializes in northern Italian cuisine. At 7713 Inwood (tel. 352-8373); open Tues.-Sun. dinner only.

$ to $$ Momo's Italian Specialties: Has probably the most authentic Italian food in town, also the best calzones and pizza. At 9191 Forest Ln. (tel. 234-6800); open Mon.-Fri. for lunch and dinner, Sat.-Sun. dinner only.

Indian

All of the Indian restaurants in Dallas serve a similar, North Indian, tandoor-based cuisine (South Indian restaurants apparently haven't made it this far south yet). Good bets are:

$ India Palace: At 13360 Preston (tel. 214-392-0190); open daily for lunch and dinner.

$ Kebab-N-Kurry: Good lunch buffet on weekdays. At 401 N. Central, Ste. 300 (tel. 231-5556); open Mon.-Fri. for lunch and dinner, Sat.-Sun. dinner only.

$ Taj Mahal: At 9100 N. Central (tel. 692-0535); open Mon.-Fri. for lunch and dinner, Sat.-Sun. dinner only.

Mexican

$ Taco Cabaña: Best Mexican take-out in the city. At 3923 Lemmon (tel. 522-3770); open daily for breakfast, lunch, and dinner.

$ Casa Rosa: Among the most popular of the city's Mexican restaurants, with trendy specialities like blue corn enchiladas along with fajitas and other Texas standbys. At Inwood Rd. at Lovers Lane (tel. 350-5227); open daily for lunch and dinner.

$ La Suprema Tortilleria: Specializes in no-lard, organic-grain tortillas and all-natural meats (cottage cheese enchiladas and oat bran tortillas may be going a bit far, though). At 7630 Military Pkwy., in Urbandale (tel. 388-1244); open Mon.-Thurs. 10 a.m.-9:30 p.m., Fri.-Sun. 8 a.m.-10:30 p.m.

$ to $$ Mario's Chiquita: Tasty, upscale Tex-Mex menu that includes *ceviche, tacos al carbon,* and *carne asada.* At 4514 Travis, Ste. 105 (tel. 521-0721); open daily for lunch and dinner.

$ Martinez Café: Solid, inexpensive Tex-Mex. At 3011 Routh (tel. 964-7898); open Mon.-Fri. for lunch and dinner, Sat. dinner only.

$ Mia's: A family-run place with the best chiles rellenos in town—expect long lines during peak dining hours. This is where the Dallas Cowboys like to fatten up. At 4322 Lemmon (tel. 526-1020); open Mon.-Sat. for lunch and dinner.

Oriental

$ First Chinese B-B-Q: In spite of the name, this restaurant caters to a primarily Chinese clientele. Good Chinese-style barbecued pork ribs, marinated chicken. At 111 S. Greenville, Richardson (tel. 680-8216); open daily for lunch and dinner.

$ to $$ Han-Chu: Excellent northern Chinese menu (same owner as the Taiwan). At 9100 N. Central (tel. 214-691-0900); open daily for lunch and dinner.

$ to $$ New Big Wong: A primarily Cantonese place with lots of fresh seafood selections. Another favorite late-night spot. At 2121 Greenville (tel. 821-4198); open daily for lunch and dinner till 3 a.m.

$ to $$ Taiwan Restaurant: Probably the best Chinese restaurant in Dallas, featuring a range of regional cuisines. At 4890 Belt Line (tel. 387-2333); open daily for lunch and dinner.

$ Tong's House: Good Szechwan and Cantonese menu, very reasonable prices. At 1910 Promenade Center, Richardson (tel. 231-8858); open Tues.-Sun. for lunch and dinner.

$$ to $$$ Uncle Tai's Hunan Yuan: A branch of the famous Hunan restaurant of the same name in New York; the menu includes unusual dishes like venison in chile sauce. Elegant atmosphere. In the Galleria, north Dallas (tel. 934-9998); open daily for lunch and dinner.

$ Thai Lanna: All the usual noodle and curry dishes. At 4315 Bryan St. (tel. 827-6478); open daily for lunch and dinner.

Seafood

$$ Bay Street Restaurant: Mesquite-broiled seafood is the specialty here. At 5348 Belt Line (tel. 214-964-8843); open daily for lunch and dinner.

$ Dinger's Catfish Café: Excellent mesquite-smoked catfish in lime sauce and seafood salad; funky atmosphere, reasonable prices. At 8989 Forest (tel. 235-3251); open Mon.-Sat. for lunch and dinner.

$ to $$ S&D Oyster Company: The reliable kitchen specializes in fresh Gulf seafood, raw, boiled, or fried. At 2701 McKinney (tel. 880-0111); open Mon.-Sat. for lunch and dinner.

Steak

$$ to $$$ The Butcher Shop: A grill-it-yourself steak place (add $2 and they'll cook it for you). At 808 Munger at Lamar (tel. 214-720-1032); open daily for dinner only.

$$$ Del Frisco's Double Eagle Steak House: Often cited as the city's best steakhouse; cuts are huge. Seafood selections are also available. At 4300 Lemmon (tel. 526-9811); open Mon.-Sat. dinner only.

$$$+ Morton's of Chicago: A branch of Chicago's famous surf 'n' turf place. In the basement of a restored West End building at 501 Elm (tel. 741-2277); open Mon.-Sat. for dinner.

$$-$$$ Ruth's Chris Steak House: Famous nationwide for custom-aged, handcut, USDA prime beef; seafood is also available. At 5922 Cedar Springs Rd. (tel. 902-8080); open daily for dinner only.

ENTERTAINMENT

Clubs And Bars

Dallas is a good town for club- and pub-crawling, with something for every predilection. As elsewhere, names come and go with astonishing reg-

Famous blues musician Mance Lipscomb created his style from watching Blind Lemon Jefferson play in Deep Ellum, Dallas.

ularity, so it's best to read the local papers for what's happening. The *Dallas Morning News's* "Guide" section (published every Friday) is an excellent source of information since clubs are listed by category ("Country," "Blues," "New Music/Underground," "Polka," etc.). Another good source (though not as meticulously organized) is the *Dallas Observer,* which is published every Thursday and emphasizes local music, art, and film criticism. Most clubs close at 2 a.m.

Several Dallas clubs specialize in satisfying "polka-holics," including the hot **Czech Club** (tel. 214-381-9072) at 4930 Military Pkwy., Sat. nights only. Other roots/ethnic dancing places are the Afro-Caribbean **Exodus** (tel. 748-7871, 210 N. Crowdus, Wed.-Sun.) and two Tejano/*conjunto* places, **Grand Central Station** (tel. 922-8122, 703 McKinney, Wed.-Sun.) and the **Longhorn** (tel. 428-3128, 216 Corinth at Industrial, Fri.-Sat.).

One of the most popular urban cowboy-type dance halls in Dallas is the **Country Connection** (tel. 869-9923, 2051 W. Northwest Hwy.), which is generally open Tues.-Sunday. **Palms Dance-land** (tel. 388-1922, 4906 Military Pkwy.) used to be a daytime dance hall where housewives and truckers got together; in its latest incarnation, it's open Mon.-Sat. nights. The Palms gives lessons in two-step, schottische, and other country dances on Monday evenings. The **Top Rail** (tel. 556-9099, 2110 W. Northwest Hwy.) has live country nightly, and gives lessons on Sunday evenings.

Deep Ellum is the district for new rock and experimental music. Some of the clubs here aren't even labeled with signs, people just cruise the area and gather in Soho-style warehouses for a night of light and sound pulsations. The **Asterisk** (tel. 214-748-7073, 2556 Elm) presents an eclectic mix of bands Tues.-Sun., including funk, world beat, and jazz. The **Club Dada** (tel. 744-3232, 2720 Elm St.) features a similar mix. **Club Clearview** (tel. 939-0006, 2806 Elm) presents a harder-edged sound ranging from roots rock to punk funk. At **The Video Bar** (tel. 939-9113, 2610 Elm), patrons dance to the latest rock videos, including quite a few that never make it on MTV.

One of the hottest dance spots in town is the **Pinnacle** (tel. 214-744-3533; 2708 Main), which plays progressive dance music in the main room, jazz and reggae in the back. At the other end of the dance spectrum is **Dallas Alley** (tel. 988-WEST) in the West End district, where a complex of five dance clubs is frequented mostly by tourists and conventioneers.

Jazz fans will find several Dallas havens, including the **Collateral Club** (tel. 214-241-1969, 11407 Emerald, live music on weekends), **D' Jazz Club** (tel. 361-4338, Caruth Plaza Shopping Center, Park at Central, live music nightly), **Dream Café** (tel. 954-0486, 2800 Routh, live music on weekends), and **Strictly Tabu** (tel. 528-5200, 4111 Lomo Alto, nightly).

For blues, try **Blues Alley** (tel. 421-9867, 2715 Meadow, South Dallas, open Thurs.-Sun.), **Blue**

Texas Stadium, Dallas

DALLAS CONVENTION & VISITORS BUREAU

Cat Blues (tel. 744-CATS, 2617 Commerce, Wed.-Sun.), **RJ's Sho-Nuff** (tel. 528-5230, 3910 Maple, Mon.-Sat.), or **Schooner's** (tel. 821-1934, 1212 Skillman, Wed.-Sun.) For the latest blues happenings, you can also call the Dallas Blues Society's recorded hotline at 521-BLUE.

Amusement Parks
Six Flags Over Texas is a monster attraction located in Arlington—see "Fort Worth," p. 226 for details.

SPORTS AND RECREATION

Rodeo
Every Friday and Saturday night from the first week in April through the last week in September, the **Mesquite Championship Rodeo** is held in Mesquite Arena, about 15 minutes southeast of Dallas. This professional event has been a tradition since 1958; nowadays a "skybox" at the covered arena leases for $6500-9052 a season and the rodeo is broadcast weekly on the Nashville Network. The show is very well executed—if you've never been to a rodeo this is a good one to start with, since the excitement level here rivals that of a professional football game. The two-hour rodeo starts at 8 p.m., but gates open at 6:30. The Bull's-Eye Bar-B-Q Pavilion serves barbecue plates for $7.50 adult portion, $4.25 children's.

The rodeo arena is off LBJ Fwy. (South) at the Military Pkwy. exit. Grandstand seating is $7

adults, $3 children 12 and under; reserved boxes are $12. For information and reservations, call 222-BULL.

Baseball
The **Texas Rangers** American League team plays ball in Arlington Stadium near Fort Worth from mid-April to early October. For ticket information, call (817) 273-5100.

Basketball
The **Dallas Mavericks** is a young basketball team (less than 10 years old), but already they're getting into the play-offs every year. They play at Reunion Arena in the Reunion district between November and April. Call (214) 658-7068 for ticket information.

Football
Under the leadership of coach Jimmy Johnson and quarterback Troy Aikman, the **Dallas Cowboys** seem to be coming out of their multi-year slump. They play from late August through mid-December (and later if they make it to the playoffs) at Texas Stadium off E. Airport Freeway. Call (214) 579-5000 for ticket information.

Polo
The **Willow Bend Polo and Hunt Club** is headquartered in Plano, north of Dallas. The season is May-June and Sept.-November. Many of the matches pit international teams against the Texans. For information, call (214) 248-6298.

Nature Trails
The **Mountain View College Nature Trail** winds through 40 acres of the northern section of this campus, which is off W. Illinois Ave. southwest of Dallas near Grand Prairie. Open daily; free admission. In southwest Dallas is the **Dallas Nature Center,** a preserve of wooded hills and rolling prairies that is a living example of how the whole area once appeared. It's at 7575 Wheatland (tel. 296-1955); admission is $1 adults, 50 cents children, and it's open daily, 9-5. The **L.B. Houston Nature Trail** is part of L.B. Houston Park, a large nature preserve maintained by Dallas Parks and Recreation. It's just north of the University of Dallas on the west edge of the city limits. Open daily; free admission.

Wet 'n' Wild
This water park is northeast of Dallas in the satellite city of Garland. It features the usual water fun: a Surf Lagoon wave pool, Hydramaniac and Blue Niagra water rides, plus swimming pools and food concessions. At the intersection of LBJ Fwy. and Northwest Highway. Open daily May through Labor Day 10-9, weekends the rest of the year 10-6. Admission is $14 adults, $12 children 3-12. Call (214) 840-0600 for additional information.

EVENTS

January
Cotton Bowl: A nationally televised, college postseason football game, preceded by a New Year's Day parade through town. The half-time show sometimes features the famous Kilgore Texas Rangerettes.

March-April
Greater Southwest Guitar Show: Once a year (usually the last weekend in March or April), some 8,000 musicians, dealers, and guitar collectors from around the globe attend the world's largest guitar show to wheel and deal on new and vintage instruments. Occasionally there are impromptu "superstar" jam sessions. At the Dallas Convention Center (tel. 214-243-4201), 650 S. Griffin.

Prairie Dog Chili Cookoff and Pickled Quail Egg-Eating World Championship: The oldest and largest chili cook-off in the Metroplex area. There aren't any prairie dogs in the chili, but the pickled quail eggs are for real. At Traders Village, 2602 Mayfield Rd., Grand Prairie. Usually the first weekend in April.

May
Cinco de Mayo: A Mexican holiday celebrated with zest at Traders Village, 2602 Mayfield Rd., Grand Prairie, with music, dancing, and food.

June
Juneteenth: June 19 is the anniversary of the emancipation announcement at Galveston, Texas, at the close of the Civil War. Several events take place in Dallas, highlighted by the Benson & Hedges Blues Festival, a week of blues performances at various venues throughout the city.

July
Shakespeare Festival of Dallas: Takes place at the Fair Park Bandshell at 1st and Parry, Tues.-Sun. throughout the month. Two plays are presented, beginning at 8:15 p.m. Admission is free, but if you don't get there by 6 p.m., you probably won't get a seat. Concessions sell food, beer, and wine for picnics.

Fourth of July: Fireworks show at Fair Park.

September
National Championship Pow-Wow: Indian tribes from all over the U.S. come to Trader's Village (Grand Prairie) the first weekend after Labor Day to celebrate Amerindian culture. Activities include an Indian dance competition with 11 different categories, archery contests, an arts and crafts show, and Indian food concessions. Sponsored by the Dallas-Fort Worth Intertribal Association (tel. 214-647-2331).

October
Texas State Fair: This combination livestock show, fireworks display, country music festival, rodeo, and fashion show is over a hundred years running and is the largest state fair in the country. Held mid- to late October; average attendance is around three million. At the Fair Park, where it's always been.

December
Candlelight Tour: The grounds and historic structures of the Old City Park are decorated for Christmas, and during the first week of the month,

Dallas residents gather for caroling, storytelling, square dancing, and a candlelight promenade.

SHOPPING

Dallas boasts 630 shopping centers, more per capita than anywhere else in the United States. Most are just like shopping centers anywhere else, rows of chain stores or trendy boutiques. Also, if you're looking for bargains, this isn't the place (try Fort Worth, or better yet, El Paso). That said, there are a few shopping places worth visiting as attractions in themselves.

The **Galleria** (Dallas Pkwy. at LBJ Fwy., north Dallas) is a "supermall" with an attached Westin Hotel, four-star restaurants, a five-theater cinema, a year-round ice rink, and 195 stores, including Tiffany & Co., Gucci, Louis Vuitton, Saks Fifth Ave., the American Museum of Historical Documents (they're for sale), FAO Schwarz, and many other ritzy names. **Highland Park Village** (Preston and Mockingbird, central Dallas) claims to be

The Galleria, Dallas

the first shopping center in Texas (est. 1931). It's situated on the line between two fashionable neighborhoods, Highland Park and University Park. The parking lot is full of German cars; stores in this Rodeo Drive wannabe include Polo-Ralph Lauren, Chanel of Paris, and Guy Laroche.

Back on earth, there's **Olla Podrida,** with over 60 arts, crafts, and antique specialty shops. At 12215 Coit Rd., south of the LBJ Fwy. in north Dallas. For bargains, try **Trader's Village,** a 106-acre flea market that attracts an average of 1,600 vendors every weekend (Sat.-Sun., 8 a.m. to dusk). It's at 2602 Mayfield Rd. in Grand Prairie, west of Dallas off State 360; there's no admission charge, but parking costs $2.

The **West End MarketPlace** in the historic West End district features around 100 retail shops intermixed with restaurants. Then across town at Main and Ervay, there's the original **Neiman-Marcus,** the department store that started the American craze for expensive gifts. One of their recent catalogs offered pairs of Shar-Pei puppies ($4000) and Private Reserve Barbecue Sauce ($14). (When Stanley Marcus sent out his first mail-order catalog in 1959, he advertised a Black Angus steer, delivered alive or in steaks.)

DALLAS INFORMATION

Tourist Offices
The **Dallas Visitors Center** on the first floor of Union Station (across from the Hyatt Regency) carries a large selection of maps and brochures about Dallas and North Central Texas. It's open daily 9-5. Another branch of the visitor center is located on the first floor of the West End Market-Place. The **Dallas Convention and Visitors Bureau** (tel. 214-746-6677) is headquartered in Renaissance Towers on Elm St. in the offices of the chamber of commerce. They're open Mon.-Thurs. 7:30-7, Fri. 7:30-5, Sat. 9-12. For up-to-the-minute information on Dallas happenings, call the Bureau's 24-hour Special Events Hotline at (214) 746-6679.

Publications
The *Dallas Observer* is a free weekly newspaper with plenty of information on local events, arts, music, cinema, and restaurants. It's distributed mostly in restaurants and clubs, and in some

1. Cadillac Ranch, Amarillo; **2.** boots, Cadillac Jack Boot Co., Austin (photos by Joe Cummings)

1. longhorn steer; **2.** End of the line in the beef industry;
3. Y.O. Ranch entrance, Mountain Home (photos by Joe Cummings)

shops. *D Magazine* is a monthly that focuses on a mix of local politics, civic happenings, fashions, and personalities. *D* is available at local newsstands.

Maps

The AAA Dallas map is quite good and is available free to AAA members from their offices at 4425 N. Central Expwy. (tel. 214-526-7911) and 12300 Inwood Rd., Ste. 110 (tel. 661-3300). Both offices are open Mon.-Fri. 8:30-5, Sat. 9-1. Serious map-users will want to obtain the Mapsco Dallas set of maps ($21.50), which are revised annually (Mapsco, Inc., 5308 Maple Ave., Dallas, TX 75235, tel. 521-2131).

Telephone

The area code for Dallas is 214.

TELEPHONE AND EMERGENCY INFORMATION

Emergency (police, fire, medical)	911
Telephone Directory Assistance	411
Weather Service	787-1700
Amtrak	(800) 872-7245
DART	979-1111
Road Conditions	320-6100
Time/Temperature	844-4444

DALLAS TRANSPORT

City Buses

Dallas Area Rapid Transit (DART) has bus routes through town as well as to DFW International Airport and Love Field. One very useful service is the three "Hop A Bus" high-frequency routes (look for the buses painted like rabbits, kangaroos, and frogs) that circulate downtown through the Arts District, Deep Ellum, the Core, West End, and Reunion areas. These cost 35 cents one way with unlimited transfers on any one route (in one direction). Depending on the route, the Hop A Bus runs every five to 12 minutes from 6:30 a.m. till 6:30

p.m. A Hop A Bus route map is available at the Dallas Visitors Center, or you can call (214) 979-1111 for schedule information.

Taxis

Two taxi services in Dallas include **Lone Star Cab** (tel. 214-821-6310) and **Sterling** (tel. 421-9400).

Airports

Dallas-Fort Worth International Airport is the world's third-busiest airport and the largest U.S. airport. Over 20 airlines offer daily service to 150 U.S. and 23 international destinations. The airport is 18 miles northeast of Dallas (same distance from Fort Worth); allow 30 to 45 minutes' driving time from the downtown area ($20-25 by taxi, $8-10 by airport shuttle). DFW is practically a self-contained city, enhanced by the attached Hyatt Regency DFW (Terminal 3). The Hyatt's health club, golf course, tennis, and racquetball courts are open to airport travelers, as is the 24-hour Business Communication Center (for faxes, copying, etc.). The DFW Airport Assistance Center (Terminal 2W, Gate 4) is also open 24 hours. The best restaurant choice is the **Texas Café** (Terminal 2W, Gate 2).

Love Field is a commuter airport seven miles northwest of town (taxi $12-15, shuttle $8-10, city bus to the Arts District 25 cents). The main user of Love Field is Southwest Airlines.

Super Shuttle offers van service to both airports and Dallas. The airport terminals have designated waiting zones; from Dallas, you must call for a reservation (tel. 817-329-2000).

Tours

D-Tours (tel. 214-241-7729) offers custom, escorted sightseeing of Dallas and vicinity to individuals and groups (bilingual and multilingual guides available on request). **Silver Cloud Tours** (tel. 521-1664) has several prearranged itineraries covering the city's main attractions that range from $15 for a two-hour tour to $40 all day. **Dallas Gray Line Tours** (tel. 824-2424) leads similar tours at similar rates.

FORT WORTH

INTRODUCTION

"Cowtown, U.S.A." is Dallas's smaller brother in the Metroplex's double heart. It's been said that while Dallas is yuppie, Fort Worth is just "yup" (cowboyese for "yes"), but in several respects the city is more sophisticated than Dallas will ever be. Despite the fact that its population (440,000) is less than half that of the Big D's, its art museums are as good or better than anything found in Dallas, it has a modern music/theater/dance center that's a world treasure, and its liquor laws are much more liberal (a recent survey found one tavern for every 26 people compared with one per 3,500 in Dallas). City planning is, for the most part, exemplary; the park network is second in total acreage only to Chicago. In 1989, *Newsweek* magazine named Fort Worth in its "America's Best Places to Live and Work" top 10.

But the city really shouldn't be compared to Dallas. Since the early 1900s, it's been the pet project of a succession of local millionaires, from publisher Amon Carter to the financier Bass brothers, who have taken it upon themselves personally to make Fort Worth a livable city (examples: a Bass private security force patrols the downtown area; the city subway is owned by the Tandy Corporation). If you ask city residents how they feel about this patronization, most say they prefer a well-run monarchy to a potholed democracy. One thing's for certain: there's not another town anything like it in the United States.

Climate
Fort Worth's weather is virtually the same as Dallas's, ranging from 36-56° F in January to 74-95° F in July. The most frequent precipitation occurs April-May and September.

History
Fort Worth got its start when the U.S. Army's Company F, Second Dragoons, established Camp Worth (named for Major General W.J. Worth, a hero of the War of 1812 and the just-finished War with Mexico) on a bluff overlooking the Trinity River. In the 1850s, a settlement grew up around the camp and it was upgraded to Fort Worth. Following the Civil War, the great Texas cattle drives flourished and it's estimated that between 1866 and the mid-1880s around 10 million head of Texas cattle were driven north along the Chisholm, Dodge City, and Loving-Goodnight trails. The Chisholm Trail (named for Texas cattleman Jesse Chisholm), ran right through Fort Worth, which soon became known as "Cowtown." This was the last major outpost along the trail before it continued to Abilene, Kansas, so cattle drovers always stopped here for supplies and last-minute revelry; on the way back from delivering beeves, it was the first stop where they could spend their newly earned money. Hence, the town quickly grew into an assemblage of saloons, casinos, and brothels. The wildest part of town was Hell's Half Acre (where the Convention Center and Water Gardens are now situated), which was also a favorite hiding place for George Parker and Harry Longbaugh, better known as Butch Cassidy and the Sundance Kid.

When the railroad came to town in 1876, Fort Worth was transformed from a place where cattle drives started to where they ended and livestock continued northward by rail. By the turn of the century, Armour and Swift had established meat-packing plants at the Fort Worth Stockyards so that fewer live cattle had to be transported. By the mid-20th century, trucking had entered the picture, which meant that meat and livestock could be moved northward more quickly and in smaller units. This resulted in the gradual decline of the stockyards, since the need for thousands of pens, feed lots, water facilities, yard-hand personnel, and other services was greatly reduced.

In the post-WW II era, Fort Worth's fortune waxed and waned with livestock and agriculture, but in recent years the city has been aggressive in attracting high-tech interests to the area, including defense and aerospace contractors. The Tandy Corporation, owner of the nationwide Radio Shack chain, is a major local employer, as are American Airlines, General Dynamics, and Bell Helicopter. The city is also home to one of the major U.S. currency plants outside of Washington, D.C.

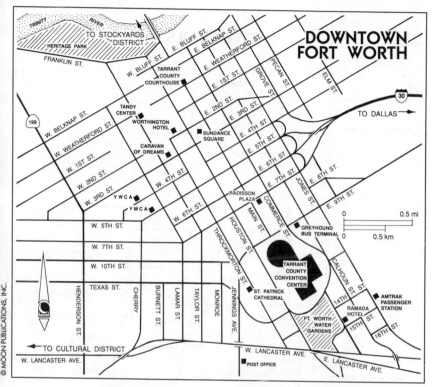

DOWNTOWN FORT WORTH

SIGHTS

Fort Worth Stockyards
National Historic District

In the early part of the century, the Fort Worth stockyards were the largest in the world. Their size and importance declined with the advent of the trucking industry, but in 1976 the U.S. Department of the Interior added the entire district to the National Register of Historic Places, thereby saving the area from further modification. The yards still play a very active role in the Texas livestock industry and are host to 42 livestock commission companies who participate in weekly auctions. Around 50 restaurants, saloons, dance halls, art galleries, and western-wear shops in the district add to the daily and nightly activity.

The center of the Stockyards is the **Livestock Exchange** at 131 E. Exchange Ave., an immense mission-style structure that was built in 1902. In addition to livestock commission offices, the complex houses the offices of a number of Fort Worth attorneys and architects, the North Fort Worth Historical Society, and art galleries. Behind the exchange are the stock holding pens and the auction arena. Weekly cattle auctions are held Mon. at 10 a.m.; hog auctions are Mon.-Tues. at 9 a.m., and special auctions are held the last Thurs. of every month. Next door is the **Cowtown Coliseum,** which was built in 1907-08 to house the annual Southwestern Exposition and Stock Show and was the site of the first indoor rodeo in 1918. (See "Sports and Recreation" for more information on the weekly Fort Worth Championship Rodeo.)

The Fort Worth Visitor Information Center is in a small building opposite the Livestock Exchange

CATTLE TRAILS

MONTANA TERRITORY

FORT BUFORD

MILES CITY

YELLOWSTONE RIVER

POWDER RIVER

DAKOTA TERRITORY

MISSOURI RIVER

MINNESOTA

WYOMING TERRITORY

FORT LARAMIE

IOWA

CHEYENNE

GALLALA

NEBRASKA

PLATTE RIVER

MISSISSIPPI RIVER

COLORADO

DENVER

KANSAS RIVER

ELLSWORTH

KANSAS CITY

ABILENE

BEDALIA

ST. LOUIS

PUEBLO

DODGE CITY

WICHITA

KANSAS

MISSOURI

NEW MEXICO TERRITORY

INDIAN TERRITORY

ARKANSAS RIVER

RED RIVER

ARKANSAS

TEXAS

RED RIVER STATION

RIO GRANDE

ABILENE

FORT WORTH

DALLAS

LOUISIANA

SAN ANTONIO

HOUSTON

VICTORIA

GULF OF MEXICO

CORPUS CHRISTI

BROWNSVILLE

	WESTERN TRAIL	
	CHISHOLM TRAIL	
	SHAWNEE TRAIL	
	GOODNIGHT - LOVING TRAIL	

0   200mi

0   200km

© MOON PUBLICATIONS, INC.

Building. Across the street from the Coliseum are mule barns built in 1911, which are now used to house hogs, goats, and sheep on auction days. On the next block east from the Coliseum is the **Stockyards Hotel** (Thannisch Building), which was constructed in 1906-07 and was restored in 1984. Bonnie and Clyde once stayed here, and now the "Bonnie and Clyde Room" is one of several Texas theme rooms offered to guests. On the first floor of the hotel is **Booger Red's Saloon & Restaurant** and the **Stockyards Drugstore;** both have been in continuous operation since 1913. Other buildings along N. Main and Exchange vary in age, with most dating from 1910-22.

The Stockyards really come alive during Pioneer Days in September, during the Chisholm Trail Roundup in June, and most of all during the Southwestern Exposition Stock Show and Rodeo (see "Events" for more information) in January. On Sunday mornings you can visit the interdenominational **Cowboy Church** in a dirt corral behind the auction arena. Practically everybody who attends (mostly rodeo cowboys, livestock traders, and ranchers) will be wearing Resistols and Wranglers, including the pastor.

The Stockyards District is approximately 2.5 miles north of downtown Fort Worth via N. Main (turn right on E. Exchange to reach the coliseum, livestock exchange, and visitor center).

A guided walking tour of the Stockyards can be arranged through the visitors center on E. Exchange Avenue.

Fort Worth Cultural District

If you're keeping score, note that Fort Worth has four museums in its arts district while Dallas has only one. None of the museums described below charges admission except for occasional special exhibits. Foremost is the **Kimbell Art Museum** at the intersection of Arch Adams St. and Camp Bowie Boulevard. Fort Worth industrialist Kay Kimbell left his art collection and his entire fortune to the Kimbell Art Foundation, which opened the museum in 1972. The building was designed by architect Louis Kahn and is an optimal combination of vaulted ceilings and natural light sources. The permanent collection includes works by Picasso, Tinteretto, Murillo, Van Dyck, El Greco, Rembrandt, Monet, Cézanne, and other big names, as well as collections of Greek, pre-Columbian, Asian, and African art. This museum is said to have the second-highest acquisition budget in the U.S., and since it's a fairly young institution, new acquisitions are still accumulating (a recent purchase was Caravaggio's $15 million "The Cardsharps"). The Kimbell also regularly hosts traveling exhibits, art seminars, lectures, films, and musical performances. Open Tues.-Sat. 10-5, Sun. noon-5; admission is free. Call (817) 332-8451 for information.

The **Amon Carter Museum** is off Camp Bowie Blvd. between Lancaster and Montgomery. Amon Carter, the founder of the *Fort Worth Star-Telegram,* left his collection of Western art by Frederic Remington and Charles Russell, as well as a considerable sum of money to the city for the establishment of a museum devoted to American art and photography. Other artists whose works are on display include Georgia O'Keeffe, Winslow Homer, Laura Gilpin, Ansel Adams, Grant Wood, Martin Johnson Heade, and William Michael Harnett. Open Tues.-Sat. 10-5 and Sun. noon-5. Admission is free.

The **Modern Art Museum of Fort Worth** is across Lancaster St. from the Amon Carter. This was the city's first museum, originally occupying the second floor of the Carnegie Library downtown starting in 1901. The new location houses the best collection of modern art in the Southwest, including works by Picasso, David Hockney, Mark Rothko, Frank Stella, Andy Warhol, and Jackson Pollock. Open Tues.-Sat. 10-5, Sun. 1-5. Free admission.

At Montgomery and Crestline is the **Museum of Science and History,** which includes the **Noble Planetarium** and the **Omni Theater.** At the Omni, a six-foot, one-ton film projector projects 70-mm images on a tilted dome screen that's 80 feet in diameter. Together with a 72-speaker, six-track sound system, the theater's science presentations are guaranteed to keep you awake. Hours are Mon.-Thurs. 9-5, Fri.-Sat. 9-8:30, and Sun. 12-5. The museum exhibits are free, but Omni shows cost $5.50 adults, $3.50 seniors and children under 12. Planetarium admission is $3. Call (817) 732-1631 for program information.

Other Museums

The **Cattleman's Museum** (tel. 817-332-7064) at 1301 W. 7th (first floor of the Texas and Southwestern Cattle Raisers Foundation) is a small collection of exhibits that chronicle the development of the ranching and cattle industry. Open Mon.-Fri. 8:30-4:30; free admission.

Seven restored Texas log cabins make up the **Log Cabin Village** (tel. 926-5881) off University Dr. (2100 Log Cabin Village Ln.) near Texas Christian University. Each was once owned by a different Tarrant County pioneer family; one belonged to the uncle of Cynthia Ann Parker, a young girl who became famous when she was kidnapped by Comanches. Years after her capture, she was rescued but couldn't reaccustom herself to Anglo culture; she eventually married Chief Nocona and gave birth to Quanah Parker, the last Comanche war chief. During tours of the cabins, there are demonstrations of candle-dipping, weaving, spinning, quilting, and flour-milling. Open Mon.-Fri. 8:30-4:30, Sat. 11-4:30, and Sun. 1-4:30. Admission is $1 adult, 50 cents for children under 12.

Sundance Square

Named for the Sundance Kid, who used to hole up in Fort Worth between bank robberies, this downtown district preserves some of the city's turn-of-the-century architecture. It covers four historic city blocks, separated by red-brick streets. At the north end of the square is the massive Tarrant County Courthouse, which was built of pink granite and marble in the Renaissance Revival style around 1895. Half the structure now houses the Worthington Hotel, the other half City Center offices.

The oldest building in the square is the **Knights of Pythias Hall** at 317 Main. On the National Register of Historic Places, the turreted building was erected in 1881 as the world's first Pythian Temple by Justus H. Rathbone, the fraternal order's founder. Haltom's Jewelers on the bottom floor has been in business since 1893. The top floor is now home to Casa Mañana On the Square, with year-round live-theater performances. The **Plaza Hotel,** at 301 Main, was built in 1908 and was one of the town's last working brothels before it was restored in 1982 as an office building with urbane Prego Pasta House Restaurant on the bottom floor.

The unnamed building at 309 Main was erected in 1895 and now houses the **Sid Richardson Collection of Western Art,** an assortment of 52 paintings by Frederic Remington and Charles Russell. Other buildings of historic interest include the Weber Building (1880-1915) at 302 Main, the Conn Building (1906) at 310 Main, the Jetts Building (1907) at 400 Main (with Richard Haas's trompe l'oeil mural "The Chisholm Trail"), the City National Bank Building (1886), and Fire Station No. 1 (1907), which houses an interpretive exhibit that recounts Fort Worth history.

Caravan Of Dreams

The hard-to-classify Caravan of Dreams experiment could be placed under several different headings, but as much as anything else belongs alongside museums and historic buildings as one of Fort Worth's unique attractions. Backed by billionaire "ecopreneur" Ed Bass, the Caravan's location at the east edge of Sundance Square supports a live theater, a multitrack and MIDI record-

theater mural,
"Caravan of Dreams,"
Fort Worth

ing studio, a rooftop desert garden, a multicultural mural group, and a nightclub/restaurant. It's one of various Bass ventures found throughout the world, including Synergetic Press and Biosphere II in Arizona, and the October Galleries in London and Kathmandu. (For an excellent account of Ed Bass's multiple interests, read "The Long, Strange Trip of Ed Bass" in the June 1986 *Texas Monthly.)* Jazz musicians often claim that the Caravan is at the top of their list of places to play in the world; seminal alto saxophonist/composer Ornette Coleman has recorded several albums on the Caravan's label. The center's Theater of All Possibilities presents everything from Greek tragedies to Asian classical drama to experimental theater.

The landmark geodesic dome on the roof contains a controlled biosphere for some 300 varieties of cacti and succulents, including rare species like the Malagasy thorn forest's *Didierea trolii*. Inside the building are several murals created by Caravan artists Zara Kriegstein, Flash Allen, Corinna MacNeice, and Felipe Cabeza de Vaca. Two Jazz Murals cover a total of 720 square feet and recount the history and development of jazz from the arrival of African slave ships to its ascension as a world art. A gift shop in the lobby sells records, CDs, books, and Caravan souvenirs. It's at 312 Houston (tel. 817-877-3000) and is open to the public Mon.-Fri. from 11 a.m., Sat.-Sun. at 4 pm. See "Entertainment" below for more music information.

Fort Worth Water Gardens

Architect Philip Johnson designed this descending series of terraces and water sculptures that were built in 1974. The park covers four city blocks in an area that was called "Hell's Half Acre" during the Wild West era. Now it's a quiet place to get away from the downtown summer heat. The final scenes of the 1976 film *Logan's Run* were filmed here. Between Houston and Commerce streets near the Convention Center.

Fort Worth Zoo

Once again, Fort Worth outdoes Dallas. Established in 1909, this 35-acre zoo holds nearly 5,000 animals, including the largest collection of reptiles in the country. The James R. Record Aquarium features an extensive selection of fresh- and saltwater fishes, and the elephant grounds is one of the most successful in the U.S. for Asian elephant breeding. The new World of Primates exhibit allows visitors to observe endangered lowland gorillas in an indoor, climate-controlled tropical rainforest. Near TCU at 2727 Zoological Park Dr. (off University Dr.); open daily 9-5. Admission is $5 adults, $2.50 seniors over 65 and children 4-12. Call (817) 871-7050 for more information.

ACCOMMODATIONS

See the chart on p. 222 for hotel and motel information.

Campgrounds And RV Parks

The U.S. Army Corps of Engineers administers eight public campgrounds on Benbrook Lake, six miles southwest of town off Loop 820 at US 377. Seven have drive-in sites with w/e only for $4-9 a night: **Holiday Park, Bear Creek Park, Shady Rest Park, Mustang Point Park, Rocky Creek Park,** and **Westcreek Park.** Mustang Point Park is closed Oct. 1 to March 31. One campground, **Mustang Creek Park,** is a no-fee, three-acre primitive site without water. All campsites have a 14-day limit; call (817) 292-2400 for more information.

Cowtown RV Park (tel. 817-441-RVRV) is in Aledo off I-20 W (between the Farmer Rd. and Willow Park Rd. exits) about 20 minutes' drive west from Fort Worth. Facilities include a convenience store, pool, bicycle rental, laundry room, and full hookups for $15 a night.

FOOD

As you would expect from a livestock and meat-packing center, in Cowtown restaurants the emphasis is on meat, from burgers to barbecue. Chili is also a local favorite, with many area restaurants serving bowls o' red during the winter.

American

$ to $$ **Booger Red's Restaurant & Saloon:** In business since 1907; the bar has saddles for stools. The varied menu includes chicken-fried steak, veal, duck, calf fries, seafood, burgers, barbecue, omelets, and sandwiches. In the Stockyards Hotel, Stockyards district (tel. 625-6427); open daily for breakfast, lunch, and dinner.

$ to $$ **Hubba Hubba's Great American Diner:** '50s decor with burgers, steaks, chicken, seafood, some Tex-Mex, and biscuits and gravy for breakfast. At 8320 State 80 W (tel. 560-2930); open daily for lunch and dinner (bar open till midnight).

$ to $$ **Vance Godbey's:** A local institution that serves roast beef, ham, barbecue, chicken (fried, barbecued, or roasted), and other American dishes cafeteria-style. All-you-can-eat deals are $6.95 weekdays, $7.95 weekends. At 8601 Jacksboro

FORT WORTH HOTELS AND MOTELS

Add 13% hotel tax to all rates. Area code: 817

NAME	ADDRESS	PHONE	RATES	FEATURES
DOWNTOWN				
The Chisholm	600 Commerce	332-6900	$51-55	coin laundry, weekly and monthly rates
Park Central Hotel	100 Houston	336-2011	$45-51	pool, monthly rates
Radisson Plaza	815 Main	870-1000	$79-143	heated pool, sauna
Ramada Hotel	1701 Commerce	335-7000	$62-84	coin laundry
The Worthington	200 Main	870-1000	$89-144	historic, heated pool, sauna, tennis courts
WEST				
Best Western W. Branch Inn	7301 W. Fwy.	244-7444	$38-56	laundry, senior discount, refrig. on request
Caravan Motor Hotel	2601 Jacksboro Hwy.	626-1951	$28-33	pool
Days Inn West	I-30 at Las Vegas Trail	246-4961	$34-42	senior discount
Green Oaks Inn	6901 W. Fwy.	738-7311	$68-98	pool, tennis courts
La Quinta Motor Inn Fort Worth	7888 I-30 (Cherry Rd. exit)	485-2750	$42-52	kitchenettes, monthly rates, comp. eve. beverage
Motel 6	I-30 at Las Vegas Trail	244-9740	$22.95 + $6 ea. add.	pool
Ramada Inn	1401 S. University	336-9311	$45-65	pool, coin laundry
NORTH–NORTHEAST (NEAR MEACHAM FIELD)				
Downtown Motor Inn	600 N. Henderson	332-6197	$27-36	coin laundry
Holiday Inn Conf. Cntr.	2540 Meacham	625-9911	$69-75	heated pool, sauna, tennis courts
La Quinta Inn	7920 Bedford-Euless	485-2750	$42-52	pool, airport shuttle
Ramada Inn	Jct. Loop 820 and State 10	284-9461	$38-60	pool, airport shuttle, senior disc., comp. eve. beverage
Sandpiper Inn	4000 N. Main	625-5531	$40-50	heated pool, coin laundry, weekly rates
Stockyards Hotel	109 E. Exchange St.	625-6427	$65-105	historical district

Hwy. (tel. 237-2218); open Wed.-Sat. for dinner, Sun. for lunch and dinner.

Barbecue

$ Angelo's Barbecue: This local legend serves the standard Texas barbecue fare, plus ham and braunschweiger. At 2533 White Settlement Rd. (tel. 332-0357); open Mon.-Sat. for lunch and dinner.

$ Jim Riscky Grocery: The 18-spice "Riscky dust" that Jim puts in his barbecue has a cult following. Although he has several locations throughout Fort Worth now, this grocery (tel. 624-8662) is where it all started. At 2314 Azle Ave. (FM 1220), south of Ephriham Ave. (State 183), east of the Stockyards district; open Mon.-Sat. for breakfast, lunch, and dinner.

Burgers

$ B.J. Keefer's: A build-your-own burger place where they grind the beef on the premises (they also make their own hamburger buns). At 909 W. Magnolia (tel. 817-921-0889); open Mon.-Sat. for lunch and dinner.

$ Charles Kincaid Grocery & Market: Selected by 400 food critics around the country as serving the best burgers in America. Besides burgers, Kincaid's offers chicken and dumplings, plate lunches with fresh vegetables, and chicken-fried steak. At 4901 Camp Bowie Blvd. (tel. 732-2881); open Mon.-Sat. for lunch and dinner.

Down-home

$ Ashley's Country Restaurant: Features chicken-fried steak, liver and onions, steak, chicken, and catfish. Breakfast buffet on weekends, all-you-can-eat deals during the week. At 6809 McCart (tel. 817-346-8643); open daily 6 a.m.-10 p.m.

$ Celebration: A branch of the Dallas restaurant that serves the usual down-home dishes plus pot roast and broiled fish. At 4600 Dexter (at Camp Bowie and Hulen, tel. 731-6272); open daily for lunch and dinner.

European

$$ Bella Italia: Innovative northern Italian cuisine, featuring fresh seafood, quail, veal with shrimp, and calamari with walnuts and pink peppercorns. At 2913 Walton (tel. 817-294-7979); open Tues.-Sat. for dinner only.

$$ Edelweiss: A Bavarian-style bierhalle with all the German standards, including schnitzel,

sauerkraut, sauerbraten, and Black Forest cake, as well as marinated herring and Shashlik Caucasian ("steak on a stick"). Live German music and dancing nightly. At 3801A Southwest Blvd. off Loop 820 (tel. 738-5934); open Tues.-Sat. dinner only.

$$$ Saint Emilion: Country French cuisine served in a country atmosphere. À la carte menu and two prix-fixe menus ($16-22), daily lunch buffet. At 3617 W. 7th (tel. 817-737-2781); open Tues.-Fri. for lunch and dinner, Mon. and Sat. dinner only.

Indian

$ to $$ Maharaja: Northern Indian tandoor and curry dishes. All-you-can-eat buffet weekdays. At 6308 Hulen Bend Blvd. (tel. 817-294-4249); open Mon.-Fri. for lunch and dinner, Sat.-Sun. dinner only.

Lebanese

$ to $$ Hedary's Lebanese Restaurant: Good selection of shish kebabs, *sfiha* or "Lebanese pizza," baked chicken, and broiled lamb, all prepared with fresh ingredients. At 3308 Fairfield Ave. (tel. 731-7961); open Tues.-Fri. for lunch and dinner, Sat.-Sun. dinner only.

Mexican

$ Joe T. Garcia's Mexican Bakery: The place to get away from the gringo lunch crowds at Joe T's larger branch (see below). Great Mexican breakfasts *(chilaquiles, migas,* huevos rancheros). Too bad the dining room isn't open at night; the bakery sells Mexican pastries until 8 p.m., however. At 2140 N. Main St. (tel. 626-5770); kitchen open daily 7 a.m.-3:30 p.m.

$ to $$ Joe T. Garcia's Mexican Dishes: In business since 1935, Joe T's is often named as one of the best Tex-Mex restaurants in the state. It's a huge, plaza-style place (part of the building looks like it's about to fall over), and there are no menus; the choice is the regular dinner (or lunch), which consists of nachos, two tacos, two enchiladas, rice, beans, guacamole, tostaditos, and salsa, or fajitas (chicken or beef) with beans, tortillas, *pico de gallo,* and guacamole. At lunch they usually offer tamales, chiles rellenos, *flautas,* and steak ranchero as well. At 2201 N. Commerce (tel. 626-4356 or 429-5166), around the corner from Joe T. Garcia's Mexican Bakery; open daily for lunch and dinner.

$ **Taco Cabaña:** A classic, all-night Tex-Mex drive-in (and outdoor patio) with great fajitas and *frijoles borrachos,* "drunken beans" (beer and margaritas, too). At 6600 Camp Bowie Blvd.; open 24 hours.

Oriental

$ to $$ **Autumn Moon:** Features Hunan and Szechwan dishes; lunch buffet daily. At 5516 Brentwood Stair Rd. (tel. 817-496-6633); open daily for lunch and dinner.

$ **Bangkok In Dream:** Serves traditional Thai dishes like *yam* (spicy meat salads), *moo satay* (marinated pork kebabs), and *po taek* ("broken fish trap"), a hot and tangy seafood soup. At 3436 Williams Rd. (tel. 244-9277); open Mon.-Sat for lunch and dinner, Sun. lunch only.

$ to $$ **China Jade Restaurant:** Extensive menu featuring several regional cuisines. At 5274 Hulen St. (tel. 292-1611); open daily for lunch and dinner.

$ **Fort Worth Dong Khanh:** An inexpensive, lunchtime only place with Cantonese and Szechwan dishes, including clams in black bean sauce. At 3310 E. Lancaster (tel. 536-1002); open daily 11 a.m.-3 p.m.

Seafood

$ to $$ **Catfish & Co.:** Specializes in fresh, farm-raised catfish (all-you-can-eat for $10) and oysters on the half shell. At 4004 White Settlement Rd., (tel. 817-738-8833); open Mon.-Sat. for lunch and dinner, Sun. lunch only.

$ to $$ **J&J Oyster Bar:** New Orleans-style seafood, featuring oysters (raw, fried, barbecued), catfish, crawfish (in season), and gumbo. At 929 University Dr. (tel. 335-2756); open Mon.-Sat. for lunch and dinner, Sun. dinner only.

Steaks

$$ to $$$ **Cattleman's Steak House:** A rustic, Stockyards institution (est. 1947) with a wide variety of charbroiled steaks, as well as barbecue, chicken, and seafood. At 2458 N. Main St. (tel. 817-624-3945); open Mon.-Fri. for lunch and dinner, Sat.-Sun. dinner only.

$ to $$ **Mac's House:** Highly acclaimed, moderately priced steak served in a semi-elegant atmosphere. At 2400 Park Hill Ave. (tel. 921-4682); open Mon.-Fri. for lunch and dinner, Sat.-Sun. dinner only.

$ **Star Café:** An 80-year-old Stockyard café with the least expensive steaks in town, offered two ways: grilled in lemon butter or chicken-fried. The chili here is also a big draw. At 111 W. Exchange Ave. (tel. 624-8701); open Mon.-Sat. for lunch and dinner.

ENTERTAINMENT

Caravan Of Dreams Performing Arts Center
The Caravan's well-designed nightclub features live music (mostly national and international jazz, fusion, folk, and new music artists or ensembles) Wed.-Sun. nights, with most shows starting at 8 p.m. The equally well-designed theater hosts dance and drama performances from a wide variety of traditions throughout the year. Most events have cover charges (a membership is available that allows free or half-price entry to all Caravan nightclub performances). The **Rooftop Grotto Bar** is open nightly from 4 p.m. till 1:30 a.m. The center is on Sundance Square at 312 Houston St.; for more information call (817) 429-4000 or 877-3000.

Stockyards District
At least a dozen saloons and dance halls grace the Stockyards district, some of them dating from the turn of the century. All are within walking distance of each other, along East and West Exchange or along N. Main. One of the newer ones is **Billy Bob's Texas** (tel. 817-624-7117) at 2520 Rodeo Plaza. Billed as "the world's largest honkytonk," it's got to be seen to be believed—100,000 square feet with 42 bar stations, a restaurant, and a bull ring for live bullriding (Fri. and Sat. only). Live music on weekends at Billy Bob's tends toward urban-cowboy country crossover, featuring big-name acts like Joe Ely, Jerry Jeff Walker, and Highway 101. Very commercial. It's open Mon.-Tues. 10-5, Wed-Sat. 10 a.m.-2 a.m., Sun. noon-7.

At the other end of the Stockyards spectrum is the **White Elephant Saloon** (tel. 817-624-1887), which has been around since 1887 and features traditional C&W and country swing nightly (cover charge only on weekends). It's at 106 E. Exchange and is open Mon.-Sat. till 2 a.m., Sun. till midnight. *Esquire* magazine has listed the White Elephant in its "100 Best Bars in America." The saloon has been expanded to include **Upstairs** at the White Elephant, a cabaret theater, and the White Elephant Beer Garden (next door), which is open for country dancing April-October.

Folk, Rock, Blues, And R&B
The Hare 'N' Hound (4400 White Settlement Rd., tel. 731-4139) and the Pig and Whistle (5731 Locke Ave., tel. 731-4938) showcase live folk and pub rock nightly. West Side Stories (3900 State 377 S, tel. 560-7632) offers a mixed bag, from roots to modern rock and comedy acts.

Fort Worth has one club that regularly features blues and R&B, J&J Blues Bar (937 Woodward, tel. 870-2337). They book live bands Wed.-Saturday.

EVENTS

January
Southwestern Exposition and Livestock Show: One of the largest of its kind in Texas. The highlight of the two-week series of events is the all-Western parade (no motor vehicles allowed) that starts at the corner of W. Weatherford and Houston, then proceeds south on Houston to 9th, east to Main and north again to the Tarrant County Courthouse. As many as 2,000 horses participate in the parade. There are rodeos nightly as well as rodeo matinees on weekends. Usually held the last week of January and first week of February, with most events taking place at the Will Rogers Memorial Coliseum on W. Lancaster.

February
The Last Great Gunfight: In 1887, Luke Short, the owner of the White Elephant Saloon, outdrew ex-Fort Worth Marshall Jim "Longhair" Courtright in front of the saloon. This was supposedly the last gunfight of significance in the town, and every year the duel is reenacted in mock gunfights on Exchange Ave., in front of the White Elephant. Usually the first weekend in February.

April
Main Street Ft. Worth Arts Festival: A street festival held on Main St. between the Convention Center and the County Courthouse (Sundance Square). Features arts and crafts shows, food vendors, and outdoor concerts. Usually the second weekend of the month.

May-June
Every four years, the prestigious Van Cliburn International Piano Competition is held over a two-week period in Fort Worth (preliminaries at Landreth Auditorium, TCU; finals at the Tarrant County Convention Center Theater). Van Cliburn is a Fort Worth native who won the Tchaikovsky International Piano Competition in Moscow in 1958. The Van Cliburn competition is now among the top three such contests in the world. The next competitions are scheduled for 1993 and 1997. Contact the Fort Worth Convention and Visitors Bureau (tel. 817-336-8791) for more information.

June
Chisholm Trail Roundup: A three-day event usually held the second weekend in June, featuring barbecue and chili cook-offs, chuckwagon races, mock gunfights, street dances, armadillo races, livestock shows, an Indian dance competition, a Western writers workshop, mariachi competitions, C&W concerts, and the Chisholm Trail Ride. A high point of the weekend is the Texas Old Time Fiddlers Contest, which attracts the cream of the Texas fiddle tradition. All events except the trail ride are held within the Stockyards District—at the Cowtown Coliseum, the Mule Barns, or on Exchange Avenue.

Juneteenth Heritage And Jazz Festival: A three-day jazz, blues, and gospel music festival held around June 19th at the Convention Center (Friday evening) and Rolling Hills Parks (Sat. and Sun. daytime). The most recent festival featured Stanley Turrentine, David "Fathead" Newman, Gil-Scott Heron, Wynton Marsalis, and other name artists. Food vendors serve Cajun catfish, barbecued goat ribs, fried chicken, and a variety of other dishes. Tickets are usually $7-12.

September
Pioneer Days: A three-day celebration during the third weekend in September that pays tribute to early Fort Worth settlers. Events include a fajitas cook-off, music and dancing, and the annual Police Rodeo. At the Stockyards.

November-December
National Cutting Horse World Futurity: Sponsored by the National Cutting Horse Association, this event is a trial for three-year-old cutters (horses used to separate herds of cattle). The action is

simple: a cowboy and his horse cut a calf from the herd, and then the rider loosens the reins to allow the horse to keep the calf from rejoining the other cows. The most skilled horses win as much as $2 million for their owners. Held at Will Rogers Memorial Coliseum.

SPORTS AND RECREATION

Fort Worth Championship Rodeo
The Stockyards' Cowtown Coliseum was the site of the first indoor rodeo in 1917. The tradition continues every Saturday night between the first Saturday in April and third Saturday in September with a series of PRCA-sponsored contests. Rodeo events begin at 8 p.m. and last about two hours. Special amateur competitions are occasionally held during the season, such as the Texas High School Rodeo Finals in early June and the Chisholm Trail Roundup Rodeo in mid June. Regular admission is $5 adults, $3 seniors, $2 children 12 and under. Call (817) 626-2228 for information.

Texas Rangers
Both Dallas and Fort Worth lay claim to this professional baseball team, but the truth is they're based in Arlington (but Arlington's closer to Fort Worth). Home games are played in season at Arlington Stadium, about 15 miles east of downtown Fort Worth at 1700 Copeland Road. Call (817) 273-5100 for schedule and ticket information.

Trinity Meadows
First opened in May '91, this parimutuel racetrack nine miles west of town off I-20 (exit 418) holds horse races Wed.-Sun. throughout the year except January and February. General admission is $5 including parking and program. Post times vary; call (817) 441-9240 for information.

Parks And Gardens
The Fort Worth Botanic Gardens covers 114 acres and contains thousands of varieties of flowers, plants, and trees. Of note are the Rose Garden, with over 3,500 rosebushes, and the Fragrance Garden, designed for the blind. The gardens are at 3220 Botanic Garden Dr. off University Dr. west of downtown. Open daily from 8 a.m. till dusk; free admission. The gardens also con-

tain a Conservatory for tropical flora; hours are Mon.-Fri. 10-9, Sat. 10-4, Sun. 1-4. Admission is $1 adults, 50 cents children 4-12.

Adjacent to the Botanic Gardens is the Fort Worth Japanese Garden, a 7.5-acre compound of shrubs, rocks, and water arranged in the traditional Japanese style. Open Tues.-Sun. 10-5; admission $1 adults on weekdays, $1.50 on weekends, 50 cents children 4-12.

Fort Worth Nature Center And Refuge
A 3,400-acre preserve and National Natural Landmark between Lake Worth and Eagle Mountain Lake with a variety of recreational possibilities: hiking trails (including a boardwalk over a living marsh), equestrian trails, birdwatching, wildlife viewing, and picnicking. Buffalo and white-tailed deer wander the area, and there's a prairie dog town. Northwest of downtown off Jacksboro Hwy. (State 199) about seven miles. Open Mon.-Fri. 8-5, Sat.-Sun. 9-5; free admission.

Benbrook Lake
This 3,770-acre lake, administered by the U.S. Army Corps of Engineers, is a favorite local spot for swimming, fishing, boating, picnicking, trail riding, hiking, and camping. Recreation areas around the lake offer varying facilities, e.g., campsites, picnic areas, trails, boat ramps, and fishing piers. A stable at Dutch Brand Park rents horses for trail riding. Admission to the various parks is free. See "Accommodations" for camping information. The lake is about 12 miles southwest of downtown Fort Worth off US 377. For further information, contact the manager (tel. 817-292-2400), Benbrook Lake, P.O. Box 26619, Fort Worth, TX 76126.

Amusement Parks
Every kid in Texas has to make a pilgrimage to Six Flags Over Texas at least once in his or her life. The latest heart-stopping ride addition is the Flashback, in which cars drop forward from a 125-foot tower through three loops, then backward to the starting point. Other stars of the show include the Shockwave, Cliffhanger, and Splashwater Falls (a boat ride over a five-story falls).

Six Flags is in Arlington, about 15 miles from downtown Fort Worth off I-30 (next to Arlington Stadium). Open March 4 to Nov. 12 from 10 a.m. (closing time varies from week to week). Admission fees are $23 adults, $17 seniors and children under 48 inches tall. Call (817) 640-8900 for information.

Across from Six Flags in Arlington is **Wet 'n' Wild** (tel. 265-3013), an amusement park devoted to water recreation, including a wave pool, waterslides (the Kamikaze has a 300-foot drop), and Lazy River, an artificial river for rafting. Open daily May through Labor Day, weekends the rest of the year. Admission is $13 adults, $11 children 3-12.

SHOPPING

Western Wear
Williams Western Tailors (tel. 817-625-2401) design, cut, and sew Western-style shirts for Texas celebrities, including country music stars, prorodeo cowboys, and the cast of "Dallas." They also tailor Western suits and just about anything else made of cloth. Figure around $50 for a basic shirt. At 1104 N.W. 28th, northwest of the Stockyards. For ready-mades, try **Luskey's Western**

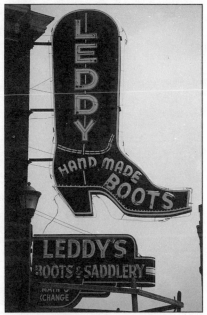

Leddy's Boots, Fort Worth

Wear (tel. 817-335-5833) at 101 Houston St., which has been serving Fort Worth cowboys and cowgirls since 1919.

Boots And Saddles
Two shops in the Stockyards district make custom boots. **M.L. Leddy's Boots and Saddlery** (tel. 817-624-3149) is at 2455 N. Main. Boots here start at around $400, saddles from $1400. They also sell used saddles, tack, and Western wear. **Ryon's Saddle and Ranch** (tel. 625-2391) is just up the street at No. 2601. Boots cost about the same as at Leddy's, saddles a bit less.

The **Justin Boot Co. Factory Outlet** (tel. 654-3101) at W. Vickery Blvd. and Lipscomb sells ready-made boots that are factory seconds or overstocks at 40-50% below retail.

Antiques
Antique Avenue (tel. 817-877-3997) brings around 50 antique dealers under the roof of the old King Candy Factory. At 813 E. 9th St.; open daily. **Central Antiques** (tel. 332-5981) has two floors of antiques and collectibles. In back is a barn where estate auctions are occasionally held. At 401 S. Freeway (I-35 W).

FORT WORTH INFORMATION

Tourist Offices
The **Fort Worth Visitor Information Center** (tel. 817-624-4741) is opposite the Livestock Exchange in the Stockyards district. Downtown in Sundance Square is the **Fort Worth Convention and Visitors Bureau** (tel. 336-8791).

Both offices distribute useful brochures on local attractions (including a map of the Cultural District), dining, and accommodations.

Publications
On Friday, the *Fort Worth Star-Telegram* publishes "Star Time," a detailed datebook that contains information on dining and entertainment in the area. The chamber of commerce publishes the monthly *Fort Worth* magazine, which focuses on local business news.

Maps
The chamber of commerce distributes a free, detailed street map of Fort Worth at the Stockyards

visitor center. Somewhat better is the AAA map, which can be obtained at the Fort Worth AAA office (tel. 817-335-4871), 28 W. 7th St.; it's open Mon.-Fri. 8:30-5, Sat. 9-1.

Telephone

The area code for Fort Worth is 817.

FORT WORTH TRANSPORT

Downtown

Fort Worth has made it easy for visitors to get around downtown without a car or even bus fare. The Fort Worth Transit Authority bus system (the "T") is free downtown along Throckmorton (northward) and Houston (southward). There's also a free subway from the Tandy Center at the north end of Throckmorton out to the free Trinity Riverside parking lot, so out-of-towners can park outside the downtown area and take free public transport. Elsewhere in Fort Worth, the "T" costs 75 cents. For schedule information, call (817) 870-6200. **Yellow Checker Cab** can be reached at tel. 534-5555.

TELEPHONE AND EMERGENCY INFORMATION

Emergency (police, fire, medical)	911
Telephone Directory Assistance	411
Weather Service	336-4416
Amtrak	(800) 872-7245
Texas State Highway Patrol	359-4751
Road Conditions	358-6300

Dallas-Fort Worth Airport

DFW is equidistant between Fort Worth and Dallas. **Super Shuttle** (tel. 817-329-2000) provides pick-up van service between the airport and town. For more details, see "Dallas Transport," p. 215.

Tours

Gray Line (tel. 817-429-7563) does a standard tour of the Stockyards, cultural district, and downtown for $15 per person.

VICINITY OF DALLAS-FORT WORTH

WAXAHACHIE

The rich blackland prairies of Waxahachie (an Indian name meaning "Buffalo Creek") attracted farmers beginning in the early 19th century. One of the oldest towns in North Central Texas, it was incorporated as the Ellis County seat in 1850 and by 1900 was a prosperous cotton center. The early cotton kings built lots of Victorian homes, earning Waxahachie the nickname "Gingerbread City." Filmmakers have found the town to be the perfect backdrop for Texan Americana—*Bonnie and Clyde, Tender Mercies, Places in the Heart,* and *Trip to Bountiful* were all filmed here.

Long dependent on farming and ranching, this city of 15,000 recently beat 80 other prospective sites for the location of the federal government's new superconducting supercollider.

Historic Buildings

Over 225 properties in town are listed on the National Register of Historic Places. Street signs indicate the way to the major sites. The chamber of commerce distributes "Historic Waxahachie Downtown Walking Tour" and "Driving Tour" brochures, available at the chamber (102 YMCA Dr., off US 277, tel. 214-937-2390), at the Ellis County Historical Museum, or at the Mahoney-Thompson House. Some of the historic downtown houses now contain antique and craft shops, like **Country Cottage** at 113 N. College.

The 1896 **Ellis County Courthouse** at Main and College is the most spectacular courthouse in Texas (and Texas has a lot of spectacular courthouses). Its elaborate arches, balconies, turrets, carved faces, and clock tower make it look more like a medieval castle than a government building. Like many of the larger turn-of-the-century courthouses in the state, it was designed by architect J. Reily Gordon and built of granite and sandstone by Italian stonemasons. The building is open to the public Mon.-Fri. 8-5; free admission.

The **Mahoney-Thompson House** at 604 W. Main was built in the Greek Revival style in 1904 and now belongs to the Ellis County Historical Museum. It has been redecorated in period furnishings and is open for tours Sat. 10-5, Sun. 1- 5, or by appointment. A $2 donation is requested for admission.

The **Ellis County Historical Museum** is housed in a restored 1889 Masonic Temple built in the Romanesque Revival style. Exhibits feature artifacts from Waxahachie's late 1800s heyday, including a rare fan collection. It's open Tues.-Sat. 10-5, Sun. 1-5. Admission is free.

Gingerbread Trail

During the first weekend of June every year, several privately owned Victorians, the county museum, the Mahoney-Thompson House, and the courthouse are open to the public for touring. Other activities include a street dance, performances on the square and at Getzendaner Park, and an arts and crafts show. Tickets are $10 adults, $4 children (ticket gazebos are set up at all town entry points). There is a 20% discount for advance-ticket purchases (call 214-937-2390 for information).

Scarborough Faire

A recreation of an English Renaissance-period country fair, with jugglers, jesters, wizards, jousting, music, food, arts and crafts. The event takes place over seven weekends in April and May at a site on FM 66, two miles west of I-35 E. For information call (214) 937-6130.

Radio

If you've got an AM radio and are within range, tune in KBEC 1390 AM on Sunday, 2-6 p.m., for the "Ranch Road 13 with Ranger Rita" program. Statewide-acclaimed Ranger Rita devotes her show to up-and-coming Texas singer-songwriters like Robert Earl Keen, Jr. and James McMurtry.

Getting There

Waxahachie is 35 miles south of downtown Dallas off I-35 E.

HAGERMAN NATIONAL WILDLIFE REFUGE

This 11,230-acre preserve straddles the Big Mineral arm of Lake Texoma on the Texas-Oklahoma border, around 60 miles north of Dallas via US 75.

Wildlife

About 3,000 acres of the refuge are marsh and wetlands, the rest uplands and farmlands (cultivated for waterfowl feed—milo, corn, and green wheat). Hagerman is home to a variety of native mammals, including **white-tailed deer, bobcat, beaver,** and **raccoon.** But the most honored residents are the thousands of waterfowl that spend portions of fall, winter, and spring on the wetlands and marshes. Around 10,000-15,000 **Canada geese** winter at Hagerman, along with **white-front** and **snow geese.** Duck varieties include **mallards, pintail, green-winged teal, blue-winged teal, shovelers, redheads, canvas-backs, scaup,** and **ringbacks.** Other birds who reside at the refuge include **bobwhite quail, mourning doves,** and various other songbirds.

Visitor Activities

Sightseeing: A four-mile auto tour route winds through the refuge; maps are available at the refuge headquarters. Several nature trails and field roads are open to hiking and are equipped with footbridges and photography blinds. Fall and winter are the best times of year for birdwatching; if you visit during the summer, bring insect repellent.

Fishing and hunting: Daytime shoreline fishing is permitted year-round. Boats are allowed on the lake April 1-Sept. 30 only and there are three boat ramps available. Hunting is permitted during announced "special hunts"—contact the refuge staff for the latest information.

Camping: Not permitted in the refuge, but there are Corps of Engineers-administered campgrounds north of the refuge boundary along Lake Texoma shores. Primitive, no-fee camping is permitted at 125-acre **Paradise Cove Camp** (FM 120 off US 69/75), where facilities include pit toilets, grills, and a boat ramp. Before camping at Paradise Cove, you must obtain a permit from the project office on Park Road 2 (off US 69/75). Dozens of other campgrounds on Lake Texoma are available for drive-in campers for fees of $5-11 a night.

Information

Contact the Refuge Manager (tel. 214-786-2826), Hagerman National Wildlife Refuge, Route 3, Box 123, Sherman TX 75090.

WACO

History

Waco (pronounce WAY-co) was named for the Waco Indian tribe that once lived in the area along the Brazos River. The town grew up around a ferry service that carried westward immigrants across the river in the mid-19th century. In 1870, the ambitious townspeople substituted a toll bridge (at the time the longest suspension bridge in the U.S.) for the ferry. When the railroad arrived in 1872, the town became an important transportation crossroads. As at Waxahachie to the north, cotton was (and still is) an important part of the local economy, but Waco took further advantage of its geographic position to become an intermediate trading center between San Antonio and Dallas. In 1886 Baylor University, the largest Baptist university in the world, was moved here from Independence.

The Waco business community continued to diversify in the 20th century and managed to attract dozens of manufacturing interests. Two soft drinks were born here—Dr. Pepper (formulated at the Old Corner Drug Store in 1885 and named after the father of the inventor's girlfriend) and the all-time Texas favorite, Big Red. Today Waco's a half-college, half-industrial town of around 100,000. Celebrity claims to fame: local band Hank Thompson and the Brazos Valley Boys put Waco on the map with their hit "Six Pack to Go," and comedian Steve Martin was born here.

Texas Ranger Hall Of Fame And Museum

The Rangers are an integral part of Texas frontier legend. They began as privately hired "rangering companies" that provided security for land *empresarios* along the Indian frontier in West Texas (Stephen F. Austin hired the first 10 Texas Rangers in 1823). They played a significant role in the Texan Revolution against Mexico, and eventually developed into a state paramilitary force that fought Indians and patrolled the Mexican border with virtually no supervision. It was said that a Ranger could "ride like a Mexican, trail like an Indian, shoot like a Tennessean, and fight like the devil." But not all their activities were heroic, and in 1935 the state government reigned them in under the jurisdiction of the Dept. of Public Safety as a special investigative unit (there are only about 100 active Rangers in the state presently). But Texans prefer to remember them fondly as an elite and noble police force. An oft-told story describes the Ranger who steps down from a train in a riot-torn town and is asked, "You mean they sent only one Ranger?" to which he stoically replies, "You only got one riot, don't you?"

The museum and hall of fame are part of a 35-acre park that has been built around a replica of the Texas Rangers' Fort Fisher. This temporary Ranger outpost was originally established in 1837 and is now the active headquarters of Ranger Company F. The museum features a number of exhibits chronicling the history of the Rangers, including dioramas, audio-visual presentations, paintings, memorabilia, a library, and impressive gun collections (the Colt display traces the development of the pistol that won the west). The Hall of Fame honors 23 Rangers who were considered exemplary figures.

Fort Fisher Park is off I-35 at University Parks Dr. (exit 335B). Open daily 9-6 from June 1 to Aug. 31, 9-5 the rest of the year. Admission is $2.50 adults, $1.50 children 5-12. For additional information, contact the Texas Ranger Hall of Fame (tel. 817-754-1433), Box 2570, Waco, TX 76702.

Baylor University

Founded in 1845 (and moved here from Independence in 1886), this is the state's oldest institution of higher learning and the largest Baptist-sponsored university in the world (11,000 students). The 425-acre campus is worth visiting for a look at the **Armstrong-Browning Library** (tel. 817-755-3566), which contains the most extensive collection of Robert and Elizabeth Barrett Browning material in the world. The library contains all of the poets' first editions, thousands of their letters and manuscripts, and just about everything ever written about the Brownings in the English language. The building itself was constructed in the 18th-century Italian Renaissance style and features 54 stained-glass windows, each depicting a different Browning poem. Ten of their poems are also illustrated on the bronze-paneled entrance doors. The library is open to the public Mon.-Fri. 9-12 and 2-4, Sat. 9-12. Free admission.

Also on campus is the **Strecker Museum** (Sid Richardson Science Building, tel. 817-755-1110), which contains natural history exhibits in the fields of geology, biology, Indian lore, anthropology, and archaeology. Outside the hall is a reconstructed town that is supposed to represent life along Texas waterways in the 19th century. Open Mon.-Fri. 9-4, Sat. 10-1, Sun. 2-5. Free admission.

Baylor's main entrance is near Fort Fisher Park off University Parks Dr. (I-35 exit 335B).

Lake Waco

This 7,260-acre lake is the largest in Texas inside city limits. Facilities for swimming (long sand beaches), boating, fishing, water-skiing, and picnicking are available at seven parks along 60 miles of shoreline. As at many dam-built lakes, the recreation areas are administered by the Corps of Engineers (tel. 817-756-5359). The easiest access to the lake is via State 6 W from I-35 South.

Accommodations

Cheapest single rooms in town are at the **Motel 6** (tel. 817-799-4957), 1509 Hogan Ln. (Behrens Circle exit off I-35): $19 a night plus $6 for each additional person. For two to more, the nearby **Viking Inn** (tel. 799-2414), 1300 New Dallas Hwy., is a better deal—$20 s, $23 d—and the Viking has efficiencies on request. The popular **Best Western Old Main Lodge** (tel. 753-0316) at 215 Dutton (I-35 exit 335A) has rooms for $47 s, $53 d and complimentary continental breakfast. The **Riverplace Inn** (tel. 752-8222) at 101 I-35 N (exit 335C) is on the Brazos River; some rooms overlook the water. Rates are $34-54 and continental breakfasts here are also on the house. Top drawer is the **Waco Hilton** (tel. 754-8484), 113 S. University Parks Dr., where rooms are $75-85.

Food

The famous **Elite Café** ("Where the Elite Meet to Eat") serves classic Texas diner food, including their house specialty, chicken-fried steak. It's at 2132 S. Valley Mills at I-35 (tel. 817-754-4941) and is open daily for breakfast, lunch, and dinner.

Nick's (tel. 817-772-7790), 4508 W. Waco Dr., is a Greek-American restaurant that's been serving dependable *souvlaki* and *dolmathes* to wacky Waco for three generations. Besides Greek dishes, they also serve steak and seafood; open Mon.-Fri. for lunch and dinner, Sat. dinner only.

For real Tex-Mex, try **El Conquistador** (tel. 817-772-9751) at University Parks Dr. and

LaSalle. House specialties include *tacos al carbon* and *carne guisada*.

The traditional Baylor student hangout for the last 50 years has been **George's** (tel. 817-753-9507) at 1525 Circle Rd. ("The Circle"). Chicken-fried steak is a favorite here, along with the "Big O," a huge, frosted globe of beer; they're open Mon.-Sat. 7 a.m.-11 p.m. You'll also find all the usual fast-food joints along I-35 near Baylor University.

Camping

Fort Fisher Park (tel. 817-753-4931) has a campground along the Brazos River with facilities for both tent ($8) and RV camping ($13), as well as screened shelters ($19). At Lake Waco, there are six camping areas: **Airport Park, Speegleville Park I,** and **Speegleville Park III** have basic drive-in sites for $6-8 a night, or with w/e for $10 a night, plus hot showers on site; **Speegleville Park II** is a 575-acre primitive camping area with dump station, pit toilets, and grills for $6; **Midway Park** and **Flat Rock** both have primitive, free camping areas with pit toilets and a nearby snack bar.

Getting There

Waco is off I-35, around 90 miles south of Dallas-Fort Worth and 100 miles north of Austin.

FOSSIL RIM WILDLIFE CENTER

This unique enterprise dedicates 3,000 acres of North Central Texas grasslands to the protection and breeding of exotic and endangered species from around the planet. The only privately owned wildlife park in the nation accredited by the American Association of Zoological Parks and Aquariums, the center is also a participant in the association's Species Survival Plan (SSP). The program's objective is to breed severely threatened animal species and reintroduce them to their natural habitats.

In numerical terms, the emphasis at Fossil Rim is on African species, including white rhinoceros, scimitar-horned oryx (currently extinct in its native North Africa), reticulated giraffes, cheetah, dama gazelles, Grevy's zebra, and addax.

Visitors may observe some of the nearly 1,000 animals protected by the facility by taking the 9.5-mile drive-through tour. Facilities along the drive include an education center, petting pasture, restaurant, self-guiding nature trail, nature store, playground, and picnic areas. The drive-through is open daily (except Thanksgiving and Christmas) from 9 a.m. until two hours before sunset. Admission is $9.95 adults, $8.95 seniors, $6.95 children 4-11.

The staff also leads 1½-hour horseback rides for $20 per person from the center's Overlook Stables. Overnight camping, including the trail ride, meals, and all camp necessities, cost $100. Visitors with a keen interest in the work of the center may want to take the "behind-the-scenes" tour ($35), which includes a visit to the white rhino breeding facility and the Intensive Management Area, where captive breeding of such rarities as the Mexican wolf, red wolf, margay, coati, and Attwater's prairie chicken is taking place.

The Fossil Rim Wildlife Center is located three miles southwest of Glen Rose off US 67. Glen Rose is 70 miles northwest of Waco, 58 miles southwest of Fort Worth, and 75 miles southwest of Dallas. For more information on Fossil Rim activities, call (817) 897-2960.

Foothills Safari Camp

Another way to experience Fossil Rim is by signing on for a three- to five-day stay at the safari camp. During the day, participants are guided on jeep and horseback animal-watching tours, nature hikes, and fossil hunts. Evenings feature gourmet meals served by the camp chef, after which guests may gather around a bonfire or gaze at the stars through the camp's telescope. Guests stay in safari-style tents (air-conditioned in summer, heated in winter) with private baths.

Rates are $375 ($450 March-May and late Sept.-Nov.) per person for a two-night/three-day safari and $562.50 ($675 March-May and late Sept.-Nov.) for three nights/four days; children 2-6 accompanying their parents are charged $300/375 and $450/562.50 respectively (children two and under are free). Included in the price are accommodations, all meals, activities, lectures, and guided tours. For further information, call (817) 897-3398 or (800) 245-0771.

BOB RACE

SOUTH CENTRAL TEXAS

Many people find this the most culturally interesting region of Texas. Historically, South Central Texas was the area of choice for land *empresarios* (who obtained land grants from Spain and later Mexico for their private colonies) because of the abundance of water and the relatively mild climate. Many of the towns that dot the area were started in the early 19th century by European immigrants—Czechs, Poles, Germans, French, and Belgians—and most of these show discernible traces of their origins. While other parts of Texas were settled by frontiersmen looking for cheap land, the *empresario* colonists were often fleeing some degree of political or economic oppression; hence, their descendants have tended to sympathize with social causes. During the Civil War,

South Central Texas claimed the largest stronghold of Union supporters in the state. Today, Austin and San Antonio are the state's most politically progressive cities, largely because of this early immigrant heritage.

The unique topography of South Central Texas is determined by the falling away of the Edwards Plateau as it meets the coastal plains of South Texas. This drop, the Balcones Escarpment, extends all the way from San Antonio to just below Dallas, but is most conspicuous in the Hill Country and the Llano Uplift west of Austin and San Antonio. The hilly terrain and the springs, creeks, rivers, and 150-mile chain of Highland Lakes attract visitors from all over the state and beyond.

AUSTIN

Austin is a combination state capital, university town, and high-tech center. You'd think this might result in a big, busy city, but it doesn't; within the city limits there are less than 500,000 people (of

course, this might seem huge if you're coming from a burg of, say, 50,000). Austin residents are proud of their city's reputation for having both small-town atmosphere and urban sophistication.

CLIMATE

Austin has mild winters with occasional cold snaps. Summers are hot and humid (though not as humid as South Texas or the Gulf coast), averaging 64% relative humidity in July. The average annual precipitation for the area is 31 inches, with most rain falling in May (average 4.19 inches) and September (average 3.60 inches).

SELECTED MONTHLY AVERAGE MAXIMUM/MINIMUM TEMPERATURES

Month	Max. (°F)	Min. (°F)
Jan.	60	41
March	71	49
May	85	65
July	95	75
Sept.	90	69
Nov.	70	48

HISTORY

Spanish priests from San Antonio established a short-lived mission at Barton Springs in 1730, but apparently the local Tickanwatic Indians didn't take to missionizing—the priests gave up after a year. In 1838 trader Jake Harrell set up camp at a spot that later became the center of downtown Austin; he was soon joined by a sprinkling of other settlers, who built log cabins and a stockade. They called the settlement Waterloo. Republic of Texas Vice President M.B. Lamar was apparently an acquaintance of Harrell's, since he joined him for a buffalo shoot in Waterloo that same year. When Lamar succeeded Sam Houston as president, he decided to establish the state capital at Waterloo. The capital buildings began construction in 1839. Perhaps because of the unfortunate associations of the name "Waterloo" (Lamar's middle name was Bonaparte), the capital was soon named Austin, after land *empresario* Stephen F. Austin.

By 1860 Austin had a population of around 3,500. City residents, along with those of surrounding Travis County, voted against secession from the Union in 1861. The Civil War had little effect on the state capital, except for the year the Confederacy fell (1865), when a unit of renegade Texas Confederates raided the State Treasury for gold and silver coins. The University of Texas was opened in 1883, thus establishing Austin as a town of scholars and bureaucrats.

Austin remained a college and government town until the Tracor electronics company arrived in the 1960s. They were eventually followed by Motorola, IBM, and Texas Instruments. The latest industry to take root in Austin has been the music industry. Within the last 20 years, Austin has become the pop-music world's Third Coast, joining Nashville, New York, and Los Angeles as a performance and recording center.

SIGHTS

Congress Avenue And East Sixth Street

These streets have been the center of Austin's downtown life since the mid-1800s. Congress Ave. was the main north-south artery, leading to the magnificent State Capitol, while E. Pecan St. (which became E. 6th) led east to Houston. The original buildings along the two streets are dated between 1854 and 1909, with most built in the 1870s and 1880s. They feature a combination of Victorian and Renaissance Revival styles, in brick and native stones (limestone and pink granite). The Austin tourist office distributes the excellent *Austin Historic Walking Tour* pamphlet, which guides visitors along a nine-block section of 6th St. and a 10-block section of Congress with descriptions of historic buildings along the way. Office staff also lead guided walking tours of downtown Austin Thurs.-Sat. at 9 a.m. and Sun. at 2 p.m. The tourist office also offers an audio-cassette tour of the same routes called *Walk of the Town* that sells for $5 or rents for $2.

Sixth St. itself has been designated a National Historic District. As Pecan St., it was the town center in the 1870s and early 1880s (it was changed to E. 6th in 1884); most of the two- and three-story buildings are former mercantile houses of Victorian design. But its respectability has been somewhat suspect ever since the 1888 completion of the State Capitol shifted the downtown emphasis to Congress Avenue. Short-story writer O. Henry, who lived in Austin during the 1890s as editor of *Rolling Stone* (the original), wrote that E. 6th St. was "bold, bad, and hard to

AUSTIN

COLORADO RIVER

BEE CAVES RD.

BARTON SPRINGS RD.

ZILKER PARK

FREDERICKSBURG RD.

UNIVERSITY OF TEXAS

MEDICAL PKWY.

SHOAL CR. RD.

BURNET RD.

LAMAR BLVD.

KOENIG LN.

45th ST.

34th ST. 38th ST.

31st ST.

RED RIVER ST.

ROBT. MUELLER AIRPORT

MANOR RD.

MARTIN LUTHER KING JR. BLVD.

E. 12th ST.

ROSEWOOD AVE.

OAK SPRINGS DR.

7th ST.

1st ST.

CONVENTION CENTER

TOWN LAKE

PLEASANT VALLEY RD.

SPRINGDALE RD.

AIRPORT BLVD.

LAMAR BLVD.

OLTORF ST.

S. 1st ST.

S. CONGRESS AVE.

STASSNEY LN.

BURLESON RD.

E. RIVERSIDE DR.

WILLIAM CANNON DR. WEST

MOON

1.5mi

1.5km

EAST WILLIAM CANNON DR.

McKINNEY FALLS STATE PARK

SCENIC LOOP

BERGSTROM AIR FORCE BASE

GUADALUPE ST.

SAN JACINTO BLVD.

© MOON PUBLICATIONS, INC.

curry." By the 1960s, it had become something of a skid row.

A neighborhood renaissance began in the late '60s, as local entrepreneurs started restoring historic 6th St. structures. As the Austin music scene burgeoned in the '70s, 6th St. developed into a popular live-music venue. By 1980 it was a nightly street party, but when the Texas Legislature raised the drinking age from 18 to 21, things calmed down a bit. An older crowd began patronizing the district and 6th St. grew up to a certain degree. It's still Austin's primary entertainment district, dotted with live-music clubs and restaurants ("Austin's Bourbon St.," as journalists are wont to say—only it's a lot less touristy than New Orleans's Bourbon St.). During the last weekend in September there's an Old Pecan Street Festival.

State Capitol

This is the largest state capitol building in the country—Texas size. It's seven feet taller than the U.S. Capitol in Washington, D.C. At the time of its

CENTRAL AUSTIN

UNIVERSITY OF TEXAS

ERWIN SPECIAL EVENTS CENTER

35
290
81

W. 15th ST.　E. 15th ST.

RED RIVER ST.

SHOAL CK. BLVD.

STATE CAPITOL

W. 12th ST.　E. 12th ST.

W. 11th ST.　E. 11th ST.

STATE HIGHWAY BUILDING　AUSTIN MARRIOTT

W. 10th ST.　E. 10th ST.

POST OFFICE

W. 9th ST.　E. 9th ST.

GUADALUPE ST.
LAVACA ST.
COLORADO ST.
CONGRESS AVE.
BRAZOS ST.
TRINITY ST.
NECHES ST.

RADISSON PLAZA HOTEL

W. 8th ST.　E. 8th ST.

W. 7th ST.　E. 7th ST.

WEST AVE.

DRISKILL HOTEL

W. 6th ST.　E. 6th ST.

SAN JACINTO BLVD.

343

W. 5th ST　E. 5th ST.

O. HENRY MUSEUM

LAMAR BLVD.

343

EAST ST.

AMTRAK STATION

CONVENTION CENTER

W. 1st ST.　E. 1st ST.

CREST HOTEL　FOUR SEASONS HOTEL

Colorado River

HYATT REGENCY

S. 1st ST.

RIVER ST.

CHAMBER OF COMMERCE

W. RIVERSIDE DR.

VISITOR INFORMATION CENTER

PALMER AUDITORIUM

BOULDIN AVE.

BARTON SPRINGS RD.

TOWN LAKE

E. RIVERSIDE DR.

343

0　0.25mi
0　0.25km

© MOON PUBLICATIONS, INC.

completion in 1888, it was said to be the seventh-largest building in the world, with 8.5 acres of floor space on three acres of land. Like many of the grander government buildings built in Texas in the late 1800s, it was designed in the Renaissance Revival or neoclassic style (although this is one of the more sober-looking interpretations of that style in the state—county courthouse fans may be disappointed). It took 15,000 railroad cars of pink granite, quarried at Marble Falls, to complete the cruciform exterior. The cornerstone alone weighs eight tons. No expense was spared for the interior, either, which contains seven miles of oak, pine, cherry, cedar, ash, walnut, and mahogany wainscoting. The roof is covered with 85,000 square feet of copper. The 500 doors and 900 windows are framed in oak, pine, and cherry.

The impressive rotunda interior displays the usual paintings of Texas statespersons and historic documents, including the Texas Declaration of Independence and Ordinance of Secession. Free tours of the Capitol are given daily between 8:30 a.m. and 4:30 p.m., starting at the Tourist Information Center (in the south foyer). The entrance foyer and rotunda are open 24 hours, however, so you could come by anytime for a self-guided tour.

Museums

The **Laguna Gloria Art Museum** is housed in a 1915 Spanish-style villa (built as a "winter retreat" by the founder and publisher of the *Austin American*) on 28 acres overlooking Lake Austin. The galleries host traveling exhibits of 20th-century American painting and photography, about half of which tends to be by local/regional artists, half by nationally and internationally known names. In addition, the museum offers film, lecture, and music series as well as art classes. Perhaps the best part of the museum is the palm- and pecan-shaded grounds—a natural relief from Austin's summer heat. It's at the end of W. 35th St. (tel. 512-458-8191); open Tues.-Sat. 10-5 (Thurs. till 9 p.m.), Sun. 1-5. Admission is $2 adults, $1 seniors and students, children under 16 free.

German sculptress Elisabet Ney built a home and studio in Austin in 1892. After she died in 1907 it was turned into the **Elisabet Ney Museum,** thus preserving one of only four intact 19th-century sculptor's studios in the country (now a designated National Historic Site). Ney's sculptures and the

Texas State Capitol, Austin

tools of her trade are on display, and the building itself is an artful design of stonemasonry with cast-iron fittings and wood flooring. A spiral staircase leads to a loft where there are several interpretive exhibits on Ney's life and work. The museum also offers art classes. At 304 E. 44th Ave. (at Ave. H) in the historic Hyde Park district. Open Wed.-Sat. 10-5, Sun. noon-5; free admission.

O. Henry Museum

Another artist who lived in Austin in the late 19th century was American writer William Sydney Porter, better known by his pen name "O. Henry." While living in Austin (1885-95), Porter worked as a bank clerk and was editor and publisher of an Austin weekly called *Rolling Stone.* A small collection of Porter memorabilia, along with original and period furnishings, is kept in his Victorian cottage at 409 E. 5th St. (at Neches St.). In May the museum sponsors an annual O. Henry Pun-Off. Open Wed.-Sun., noon-5; free admission.

Other museums of note in Austin are on the UT campus (see "University of Texas at Austin").

Austin's historic
Driskill Hotel

Driskill Hotel

Cattleman Jesse Lincoln Driskill built this striking, Richardson Romanesque-style hotel on Pecan St. (now E. 6th) in 1886. A bust of Driskill sits atop the south facade facing E. 6th St., and busts of his sons A.W. and J.W. decorate the other entrances. While the state Legislature was waiting for the capitol to be completed (1888), Driskill let them use the hotel for meetings and official sessions. Governor Sul Ross established an Austin tradition by holding the first gubernatorial inaugural ball here in 1887. Lyndon B. Johnson used the hotel as headquarters for his first Senate campaign, as well as in his successful bid for the presidency in 1964. The hotel now has its own curator who looks after the governors' memorabilia on display on the first-floor hallway between the lobby and the Lobby Bar.

The hotel has had several different owners since Driskill died in 1890. The most recent management completed a full restoration in 1989, elevating the facilities to first-class standards while preserving the historical (among the 15 terraced suites are the Governor's Suite and the LBJ Suite). See "Austin Hotels And Motels" chart for room rates.

University Of Texas At Austin

Since its inception in 1883, UT has grown to encompass a 357-acre campus with an enrollment of 50,000 (over 10% of Austin's population). Academic headquarters for the entire UT system (14 insti-

tutions statewide), three of its graduate programs have been ranked in the U.S. top five (botany, linguistics, and Spanish) and five more (Germanic languages, civil engineering, classics, zoology, and computer science) among the top 10. The Austin campus also has the sixth-largest university library in the country, with nearly six million volumes.

It takes money to achieve these kinds of rankings, and UT has one of the largest public endowments of any educational institution in the world. The state Legislature gave the university two million acres of West Texas desert during the latter half of the 19th century, which might not have amounted to much except that oil was discovered on the land in 1921. Royalties from drilling rights led to the establishment of the Permanent University Fund, and it's been fat city ever since. (Now that oil prices are slumping, the fund may turn out to be not so permanent.)

Austin's best museums are located on the UT campus. The **Harry Ransom Humanities Research Center** (512-471-9111), housed in the Harry Ransom Center and the Academic Center, is comprised of the Leeds Gallery (rare books and manuscripts), the Photography Collection (over five million prints and negatives, including the world's first photograph, and 3,000 pieces of antique photographic equipment), the Iconography Collection (iconographic artwork spanning four centuries), and several other smaller humanities-oriented collections. One of the five existing Gutenberg Bibles (the first books to be printed in

Europe using movable type) is on display on the first floor of the Ransom Center. Both buildings are located at the west edge of campus, at W. 21st and Guadalupe. Hours are Mon.-Fri. 9-5; free admission.

The **Archer M. Huntington Art Gallery** (tel. 471-7324) is housed in two halls, the Ransom Center and the Art Building. The permanent exhibits include collections of 19th- and 20th-century North American and contemporary Latin American art, Greco-Roman art, and 2,000 other works of various provenance. Traveling exhibits are also on display. The Art Building is at E. 23rd and San Jacinto. Hours for both halls are Mon.-Fri. 9-5, Sun. 1-5; free admission.

The **Texas Memorial Museum** (tel. 471-1604) is a collection of research exhibits in the sciences, including the fields of geology, paleontology, anthropology, archaeology, and natural history. At 2400 Trinity; open Mon.-Fri. 9-5, Sat.-Sun. 1-5. Free admission.

The first presidential museum built on a university campus, the **Lyndon Baines Johnson Library and Museum** displays LBJ memorabilia, four stories of presidential manuscripts, and a replica of the Oval Office during LBJ's administration. There is also a general exhibit of presidential campaign memorabilia that covers the George Washington era to the present. The "First Lady Theater" presents a short film on the life and work of Lady Bird Johnson. At 2313 Red River; open daily 9-5. Free admission.

The **Frank C. Erwin Jr. Special Events Center** at 1701 Reed River is an 18,000-seat arena that hosts everything from UT basketball games to big-name rock concerts. The center's monthly *Applause* magazine contains details on upcoming events; call (512) 477-6060 for ticket information.

The general information number for the university is (512) 471-3434.

French Legation

France was the first country to recognize Republic of Texas sovereignty, and in 1840 they sent French chargé d'affaires Alphonse Dubois de Saligny to Austin to set up a foreign-service outpost. In 1841 Dubois had a Louisiana Bayou-style house built of Bastrop pine that surpassed in elegance all other houses in town besides the president's. All the window glass and furniture was imported from France, all the hardware (brass hinges, locks, keys) from England. Dubois left town before he'd completed a year's residence (because of a dispute with a local hotelier over unpaid bills), and the house passed into the hands of a bishop and later a doctor. The state purchased the house in 1948 and allowed the Daughters of the Republic of Texas to restore it for public viewing. It now stands as probably the best example of French colonial style in the U.S. outside Louisiana; the free-standing kitchen is said to be the only fully restored early French kitchen in the country. At 8th and San Marcos (tel. 512-472-8180); open Tues.-Sun. 1-5. Admission $2 adults, $1 ages 10-18, 50 cents ages 5-9.

AUSTIN ACCOMMODATIONS

Hotels And Motels

See "Austin Hotels and Motels" chart.

Bed And Breakfast Inns

La Prelle Place (tel. 512-441-2204) is a 1912 American four-square with four large rooms furnished with antiques. Rates are a reasonable $49-79 a night, including continental breakfast. At 2204 Lindell Ave. off S. Congress at Live Oak.

Ziller House (tel. 512-462-0100, fax 462-3922) at 800 Edgecliff Terrace is near the downtown area and has a view of Town Lake. Tastefully decorated rooms with private bath cost a reasonable $40 s, $45 d including a fix-it-yourself breakfast.

Seven blocks west of the University of Texas in a 1936-vintage house, **The Wildflower Inn** (tel. 512-477-9639), 1200 W. 22½ St., offers country-furnished rooms for $59-69 a night including continental breakfast.

Bed & Breakfast Texas Style (tel. 214-298-5433, 4224 W. Red Bird Ln., Dallas, TX 75237) can handle reservations for the above B&Bs or suggest others in the Austin area.

AYH Hostel

The recently opened **Austin International AYH Hostel** (tel. 512-444-2294) is housed in the renovated Old Rowing Club Boathouse on Town Lake, 2200 S. Lakeshore Blvd. (take Capital Metro bus #8 from downtown to Pleasant Valley and S. Lakeshore). The hostel has a fully equipped self-service kitchen and a large com-

AUSTIN HOTELS AND MOTELS

Add 13% hotel tax to all rates. Area code: 512

NAME	ADDRESS	PHONE	RATES	FEATURES
NORTH (INCLUDING AIRPORT)				
Austin Hilton	6000 Middle Fiskville Rd. (off I-35)	451-5757	$84	pool, airport shuttle
Austin Motor Inn	11400 I-35 North	835-0333	$22-24	pool
Best Western Chariot Inn	7300 I-35 North	452-9371	$30-42	pool, airport shuttle
Budget Host Inn of Austin	820 E. Anderson (off I-35 N at US 183)	835-4311	$29-39	—
Days Inn	8210 I-35 North	835-2200	$41-45	pool, airport shuttle
Heritage Inn	9121 I-35 North	836-0079	$27-35	pool, airport shuttle
Holiday Inn-Airport	6911 I-35 North	459-4251	$53-61	pool, coin laundry, airport shuttle
Holiday Inn Northwest Plaza	8901 Business Park (US 183 and Loop 1)	343-0888	$75-80	heated pool, airport shuttle, weekly rates
La Quinta Motor Inn-North	5812 I-35 North	452-9401	$53-59	pool, airport shuttle
Motel 6-North	9420 I-35 North	339-6161	$22.95 + $6 ea. add.	pool
Red Lion Hotel	6121 I-35 North	328-5466	$61-109	pool, sauna, coin laundry, airport shuttle, wknd. disc.
Rodeway Inn Airport	5526 I-35 North	451-7001	$38-48	pool, airport shuttle
CENTRAL				
Austin Marriott at the Capitol	701 E. 11th	478-1111	$89-139	heated pool, saunas airport trans., wknd. discount
Best Western Quarters at the Capitol	300 E. 11th	476-7151	$48-54	pool, airport shuttle
Budget Inn Capitol	1201 I-35 North	472-8331	$30-40	pool, weekly rates
Crest Hotel	111 E.1st and Congress	478-9611	$85-108	pool, airport shuttle
Driskill Hotel	604 Brazos at E. 6th	474-5911	$119-139	historic, valet parking, airport shuttle
Embassy Suites Downtown	300 S. Congress	469-9000	$119-129	heated pool, sauna, airport shuttle, wknd. discount, comp. eve. beverage
Four Seasons Hotel Austin	98 San Jacinto, on Town Lake	478-4500	$135-175	heated pool, saunas, health club, airport shuttle

AUSTIN HOTELS AND MOTELS

Add 13% hotel tax to all rates. Area code: 512

NAME	ADDRESS	PHONE	RATES	FEATURES
CENTRAL (continued)				
Guest Quarters Suite Hotel Austin	303 W. 15th	478-7000	$130-150	1-2 bed. apts w/ kitchens, pool, coin laundry, airport shuttle, wknd. discount.
Hyatt Regency Austin	208 Barton Springs	477-1234	$109-150	some rooms overlook river, heated pool, airport shuttle, wknd. discount
Kensington Motor Lodge	3300 Manor (west off I-35)	478-5959	$18-32	kitchens in all units, weekly rates
Motel 6 Central	5330 N. Interregional Hwy. (I-35 exit 238A)	467-9111	$28.95 + $6 ea. add.	pool
Stouffer Austin Hotel	9721 Arboretum	343-2626	$119-154	heated pool, sauna, valet parking, airport shuttle
SOUTH				
Best Western Seville Plaza	4323 I-35 South	447-5511	$40-45	pool, coin laundry weekly rates
Capitol Motor Inn	2525 I-35 South	441-0143	$27-35	pool, weekly rates
Best Western South	3909 I-35 South	444-0531	$39-54	pool, coin laundry, airport shuttle
Exel Inn of Austin	2711 I-35 South (exit 231)	462-9201	$28-37	pool
La Quinta Motor Inn	Ben White 4200 I-35 S	443-1774	$52-64	pool
Motel 6 South	2707 S. Interregional Hwy. (I-35 exit 231/232A)	444-5882	$23.95 + $6 ea. add.	pool
Ramada Inn South	1212 W. Ben White (off US 290)	447-0151	$52-60	pool

mon room that overlooks Town Lake. Dormitory beds are $10 a night for AYH members ($3 additional for a temporary membership card). There's also a couples room with a king-size waterbed (same per-person rate).

Austin Area Campgrounds And RV Parks

Austin has an abundance of campgrounds and RV parks. The **Austin KOA** (tel. 512-444-6322) is the most expensive in the state at $16 for a tentsite, $17 RV site with no hookups, $21 full hookup (weekly and monthly discounts are available). Cabins are $24. It's got a pool (as do the other 24 Texas KOAs) and a lounge with fireplace, but otherwise isn't worth more than any other KOA. South of Austin off I-35 at the Wm. Cannon Dr. exit (exit 228).

At nearby **McKinney Falls State Park** (tel. 243-1643) off US 183 S (southeast edge of town), drive-in sites with water are $6, with w/e $9; screened shelters are $18. Dump stations are

HIGHLAND LAKES CAMPING

Campgrounds listed with phone numbers 472-7483 or 473-4083 (area code 512) are Lower Colorado River/Travis County facilities; stays are limited to 14 days in a 30-day period.

CAMPGROUND/ RV PARK	LOCATION	DAILY RATES	PHONE	FACILITIES
LAKE TRAVIS				
Arkansas Bend	near Lago Vista off Lohman's Ford	free	472-7483	tentsites, boat ramp
At the Pace	FM 2322 near Pace Bend Park	$5-7	264-1395	w/e, full hkups, senior discount
Cypress Creek	FM 2769 and Old Anderson Mill	free	472-7483	tentsites, boat ramp
Hudson Bend Camper Resort	Hudson Bend near Mansfield Dam	$12-15	266-1562	full hookups
Mansfield Dam Park	FM 620 at Mansfield Dam	free	472-7483	tentsites
Pace Bend Park	FM 2322, 4.6 mi. east of US 71	$2	472-7483	tentsites, full hkups, boat ramp
Sandy Creek Park	Lime Creek near FM 1431	free	472-7483	primitive
Windy Point/ Bob Wentz Park	off Comanche Trail, near Mansfield Dam	free	472-7483	tentsites, boat ramp
LAKE MARBLE FALLS				
Falls Creek Trailer Park	S. Marble Falls	$12	693-2674	full hookups
Kampers Korner	S. Marble Falls	$12	693-2291	full hookups
River View RV Park	S. Marble Falls	$15	693-3910	full hookups
LAKE LBJ			(area code 915)	
Kingsland Lodge	Kingsland	$15, $50-60	388-4830	full hookups, cabins, boat slips
LA-Z-L RV Park	Kingsland	$14	388-3473	full hookups, boat ramp, fish dock
Longhorn Resort	Kingsland	$8-12 RV, $42-70 cabins	388-4343	full hookups, cabins, marina
Plainsmen Lodge	Kingsland	$10; $50-60	388-4344	full hookups, cabins, boat dock
Rio Vista Resort	Kingsland	$8, $11	388-6331	tentsites, full hookups, boat/fishing docks, laundry, boat slips

HIGHLAND LAKES CAMPING

Campgrounds listed with phone numbers 472-7483 or 473-4083 (area code 512) are Lower Colorado River/Travis County facilities; stays are limited to 14 days in a 30-day period.

CAMPGROUND/ RV PARK	LOCATION	DAILY RATES	PHONE	FACILITIES
INKS LAKE				
Inks Lake State Park	Park Rd. 4 off US 29	$6, $9, $12	793-2223	boat ramp, tentsites, w/screen shelter
Rock-A-Way Park		$14	793-2314	tentsites, w/boat ramp, fishing dock
Shady Oaks	near Inks Dam	$8 tent, $14 RV	793-2718	tentsites
LAKE BUCHANAN				
Black Rock Park	FM 261, 4 mi. north of US 20	free	473-4083	primitive, boat ramp
Cedar Lodge	US 261	$13.50 RV, $45 cabins	793-2820	full hookups, cottages
Colorado Bend State Park	RR 501	$5	—	primitive
The Edgewater	US 261	$11, $47	793-6861	full hookups, cabins
Roy's Lakeside	US 261	$7, $10, $24	793-2393	tentsites, full hookups, cabins, boat rentals
Shaw Island	4.2 mi. off US 261	free	473-4083	primitive
Silver Creek RV Park	RR 2341	$12	756-2381	full hookups
Waterfront	US 261	$12	793-2819	full hookups, boat ramp

available. Also off US 183 S (at US 71 near Bergstrom AFB) is the **Royal Palm Mobile Home and RV Community** (tel. 385-2211), which is oriented toward long-term residents but will take RVs for $15 a night.

The **Shady Grove RV Park** (tel. 499-8432) is within the city limits and very close to downtown Austin at 1600 Barton Springs Rd., near Zilker Park. Rates are $13 per site. Nearby at 1518 Barton Springs is the similar **Pecan Grove RV Park** (tel. 472-1067), where RV sites are $14.

Northwest of town at **Emma Long Metropolitan Park** (tel. 346-1831), tentsites are $5, drive-in sites w/e are $10 (plus a one-time $5 entry fee Fri.-Sun.).

The following Highland Lakes have campgrounds on their shores: Lake Travis, Lake Marble Falls, Lake LBJ, Inks Lake, Lake Buchanan, and Lake Bastrop. See "Highland Lakes Camping" chart for details.

FOOD

There are probably more restaurants per capita in Austin than in any other Texas town. Quantity doesn't mean quality, though, and this is especially the case in a college town (students will eat anything). Safe bets:

American
$$ **City Grill:** Specializes in mesquite-grilled beef and seafood, including fresh tuna, redfish, and swordfish, served in a renovated warehouse. At 401 Sabine (tel. 512-479-0817); open daily, dinner only.

$ to $$ Good Eats Café: A fairly successful attempt at updating the classic Texas café, adding seafood to a meatloaf and barbecue menu. Country breakfasts. At 1530 Barton Springs Rd. (tel. 476-8141); open daily for breakfast, lunch, and dinner.

$$$ Hudson's On The Bend: Hunting-lodge decor with a variety of local cuisines, including Southwest and German, with an emphasis on fresh, pecan-smoked game. On Mimi Sheraton's list of top-50 restaurants in the United States. At 3509 FM 620 (tel. 266-1369); open Tues.-Sun. for dinner only.

$$$ Jeffrey's: A nouvelle cuisine that borders on French. Long lines, good food. At 1204 W. Lynn (tel. 477-5584); open Mon.-Sat. dinner only.

$ Magnolia Café: Good pancake breakfasts, vegetarian dishes. At 1920 S. Congress (tel. 478-8645); open daily for breakfast, lunch, dinner.

$ Scandals: Great deals for grazers: all-you-can-eat soup and salad bar Mon.-Fri. 11 a.m.-2 p.m., happy hour with free hors d'oeuvres 5-7. In the Driskill Hotel, 6th and Brazos (tel. 473-5911).

$ Scholz Garten: A beer garden founded by August Scholz in 1862, with the Saengerrunde Hall next door. Serves an American hybrid of German, Texan, Italian, and Cajun dishes. An Austin institution. At 17th and San Jacinto (tel. 477-4171); open Mon.-Sat. for lunch, dinner.

$ to $$ Threadgill's: Diner-style down-home featuring chicken-fried steak, black-eyed peas, okra, and the best pecan pie in Austin. Janis Joplin got her start here, but nowadays live music is intermittent (try Wednesday night). At 6416 N. Lamar (tel. 451-4550); open daily for breakfast, lunch, dinner.

Barbecue

$ to $$ County Line On The Hill: Great Hill Country view and great, lean barbecue, including smoked turkey and duck, blue-plate specials. At 6500 Bee Caves Rd. (tel. 512-327-1742); open daily for dinner only.

$ to $$ Green Mesquite Barbecue: Another Austin classic; standard barbecue plus smoked turkey and homemade peach cobbler. At 1400 Barton Springs Rd. (tel. 479-0485); open daily for lunch, dinner.

$ to $$ County Line On The Lake: Same as County Line On The Hill except at 6204 FM 2222, on Lake Austin.

$ Ruby's BBQ: Updated, "clean" barbecue, with USDA-certified, hormone-free beef. Black

beans instead of the same old pintos, and a choice of creamy or vinaigrette slaw. Great chicken. Convenient location next to Antone's, 512 W. 29th at Guadalupe (tel. 477-1651).

Belgian

$$ L'Estro Armonico: The menu changes daily and features dishes strong on Belgian sauces—fish in *soubise* (puree of onions and rice) or potatoes in béchamel, for example. Good value considering all the work that goes into the cuisine. At 3520 Bee Cave Rd. (tel. 512-328-0580); open Tues.-Sun. for dinner only.

Chili

$ Texas Chili Parlor: The only place in town that specializes in chili, and in every possible permutation—in bowls, in chili pie, on hot dogs, in flour tortillas, to name a few. You choose the degree of hotness—X, XX, or XXX. At 1409 Lavaca (tel. 472-2828); open daily for lunch and dinner till 2 a.m.

German

$$ Gunther's Restaurant: Authentic Bavarian cuisine, including *schweinshaxe* (pork joint) and *jaegerschnitzel* (veal cutlet in mushroom and wine sauce); Spaten beer on tap, served in the half-liter as in Germany. At 11606 I-35 N (tel. 512-834-0474); open Tues.-Sun. for dinner only.

Health

$ to $$ Mother's Café and Garden: Austin's best vegetarian food, including health-conscious Tex-Mex. At 4215 Duval (tel. 512-451-3994); open Mon.-Sat. for lunch, dinner, Sunday for brunch.

$ High Time Tea Bar & Brain Gym: Austin's only no-booze, no-smoke bar serves a few snacks and nutrient-rich drinks. At 314 S. Congress; open 1 p.m.-2 a.m. daily.

$ Mr. Natural: A bakery and juice bar with light buffets and takeout, all vegetarian. At 1901 E. 1st St. (tel. 477-5228); open Mon.-Fri. 8-6, Sat. 10-6.

Italian

$$$ Basil's: Innovative Italian kitchen that uses only fresh herbs and homemade pasta, with an emphasis on seafood; make reservations to avoid the line. At 10th and Lamar (tel. 512-477-5576); open daily for dinner only.

$ to $$ **Brick Oven Restaurant:** Chicken, lasagna, stromboli, pizza (Austin's best)—all baked in an 1890 wood-fired brick oven. At 1209 Red River (tel. 477-7006); open Mon.-Sat. lunch and dinner, Sun. dinner only. Second location at 10710 Research Blvd. (tel. 345-6181); same hours.

Mexican

Austin is very strong in Tex-Mex, rivaling its more Hispanic neighbor to the south, San Antonio.

$ to $$ **Chuy's:** Popular place with trendy dishes like blue corn tortilla enchiladas as well as traditional chiles rellenos. Good margaritas and amusing Mexican kitsch decor, including Elvis shrine and Hubcap Room. At 1728 Barton Springs Rd. (tel. 512-474-4452); open daily for lunch, dinner.

$ **Cisco's:** Longhorn (UT team) fans fill the place up on weekends for breakfasts of *migas* or *huevos rancheros* (the kind they made before Tex-Mex became trendy—thick sauces). LBJ used to eat here. At 1511 E. 6th (tel. 478-2420); open daily for breakfast and lunch.

$ to $$ **Fonda San Miguel:** A contender for best Mexican in Austin; specializes in dishes from Yucatan, Veracruz, and Oaxaca. Heart-stopping Sunday buffet. At 2330 W. North Loop (tel. 459-4121); open daily for lunch, dinner.

$ to $$ **La Zona Rosa:** In a town of great Mexican restaurants, this trendy place wouldn't rate except for the chili (which, of course, isn't really Mexican). The owner, Gordon Fowler, is the son of the late Wick Fowler of "Two-Alarm Chili" fame. At 612 W. 4th St. (tel. 482-0662); open daily for lunch, dinner till late.

$ **Las Manitas Avenue Café:** Best Mexican breakfasts in town, including *migas especiales con hongos* (eggs scrambled with corn tortilla strips and mushrooms), served with black beans. Different lunch specials every day, from *caldo azteca* to *tamal vegetariano;* Saturdays feature menudo and *barbacoa.* Walk through the kitchen to get to the patio out back. *Conjunto* music on occasional Friday evenings in the summer (see "Entertainment" below). At 211 Congress (tel. 472-9357); open Mon.-Fri. 7-4, Sat.-Sun. 7-2:30.

$ to $$ **Mexico Tipico:** Another café-style place with great breakfasts, serving *migas* with fried potatoes, just like on the border, plus great *licuados* (Mexican fresh-fruit smoothies). At 1707 E. 6th (tel. 472-3222); open daily for breakfast, lunch, dinner.

$ **Pinch-A-Pollo:** Specializing in marinated grilled chicken and interior cooking, including Yucatecan specialties like *chiles habañeros.* Good *sopa de tortillas.* At 7915 Burnet Rd. (tel. 452-3088); open daily for lunch and dinner.

$ **Seis Salsas:** "Six Salsas" is what you'll find on the table *(tomatillo, chile arbol, serrano, chipotle, pico de gallo,* and *ranchera).* Fresh handmade tortillas and consistent, traditional Tex-Mex, including *carne guisada* and killer breakfast tacos. At 2004 1st St. (tel. 445-5050); open daily for breakfast, lunch, dinner.

Oriental

$$ **Azuma:** Traditional Japanese cuisine, including sushi and *teishokus* (set dinners). Sushi happy hour 5:30-7 and after 8. At 11906 Research Blvd. (tel. 512-258-3780); open Mon.-Sat. for lunch and dinner.

$$ **Beijing Imperium:** Semiformal restaurant specializing in Hunan and Szechwan cuisine. At 10000 Research Blvd. in the Arboretum Center (tel. 343-2944); open daily for lunch and dinner.

$$ **China Palace:** Huge, popular place with a long menu that features everything from *dim sum* to hotpots. At 6605 Airport (tel. 451-7104); open daily for lunch and dinner.

$ **Chou Down Stir-Fry Bar:** This innovative downtown restaurant features Mongolian barbecue-style buffet service. You heap your plate with various meats and/or vegetables plus a choice of six different sauces from the "stir-fry bar" then hand it to the cooks to be quickly seared over a helmet-shaped grill. Won-ton chips served with a sweet-hot sauce are on the house, along with chocolate-dipped fortune cookies. At 117 San Jacinto Blvd. (tel. 476-3938); open daily for lunch and dinner.

$$ **Kyoto:** Standard Japanese fare, sushi bar. At 315 Congress (tel. 482-9010); open Mon.-Fri. for lunch and dinner, Sat. dinner only.

$ to $$ **Satay:** Features food from countries on the South China Sea (Thailand, Malaysia, Indonesia, etc.), including the restaurant's namesake—small, marinated meat kebabs served with peanut sauce. Vegetarian dishes available. All-you-can-eat Sunday buffet. At 3202 W. Anderson Ln., Shoal Creek Plaza (tel. 467-6731); open Mon.-Sat. for lunch and dinner, Sun. noon-3.

$$ **Thai Kitchen:** Standard Thai; above-standard service. At 830 E. Wm. Cannon (tel. 445-4844); open Mon.-Sat. for lunch and dinner.

Seafood

$ to $$ **Maceo's Seafood Co.:** Basic surf-and-turf menu, with an all-you-can-eat catfish special for lunch Friday. At 3-4 W. 4th St. (tel. 512-477-0970); open Mon.-Fri. for lunch and dinner, Sat. dinner only.

$$ **Pearl's Oyster Bar:** Features a mostly Cajun-Creole menu, including blackened redfish, and fresh Gulf oysters. At 9033 Research Blvd. (tel. 339-7444); open daily for lunch and dinner.

$$ **South Point Seafood:** Fresh fish prepared in several ways—fried, steamed, baked, or grilled—and served with baskets of hush puppies. Next door to a fish market. At 2330 S. Lamar (tel. 442-6077); open Mon.-Fri. for lunch and dinner, Sat.-Sun. dinner only.

Steak

$ to $$ **Dan McKlusky's:** Considered by many to have the best steaks in town; the waiters bring the raw meat to your table for inspection before grilling it. Chicken and seafood also available. At 419 E. 6th (tel. 512-472-8924); open Mon.-Fri. for lunch and dinner, Sat.-Sun. dinner only. Second location at 1000 Research, Arboretum Center (tel. 346-0780); same hours.

$$ **Night Hawk:** An Austin institution for over 50 years, and a favorite Longhorn hangout. Menu extends beyond steaks (a rival for McKlusky's) to catfish and oysters. Children's menu available. Two locations—the "Frisco Shop" at 5819 Burnet Rd. (tel. 459-6279), which is open daily for breakfast, lunch, and dinner; and "The Steakhouse" at 6007 N. I-35 at US 290 (tel. 452-0296), open daily for lunch and dinner.

$$ to $$$ **Ruth's Chris Steakhouse:** Another Austin contender for the steak title. Serves only U.S. prime (chicken and seafood available). At 3010 Guadalupe (tel. 477-7884); open daily for dinner only.

ENTERTAINMENT

Austinians are fond of mentioning the fact (over and over) that Austin has more musicians and more music venues per capita than any place else in the country. It's true, and what's more, there's an incredible variety of bands, definitely a wider spectrum than in most Texas cities. That's the good news, especially for residents trying to keep up with the national/international music scene. The bad news, for out-of-staters in search of unique, regional styles, is that Austin tries too hard to be trendy and ends up with bands that could be from anywhere else—the same modern rock, the same heavy metal, the same punk, and the same urban country—with less of what American-music lovers make pilgrimages to Texas for: blues, swamp music, Tex-Mex, and pre-Nashville country (there are exceptions, of course, most notably at Antone's). For Texas roots music, you're sometimes better off in San Antonio or Houston. That said, if you just want to party (and forget the ethnomusicology), you're in the right place. Welcome to Party City, Texas.

Live Music

If you're serious about hearing live music in Austin, you've got to have the right publications in hand. Amateurs can get by with the latest issue of the *Austin Chronicle* weekly, distributed free from street-corner stands downtown and in many restaurants and bars. The *Chronicle* lists all the acts for the week at the major venues and many of the minor ones. The *Chronicle*'s "Onward" section, issued on Thursday, also outlines current musical happenings. Pros (talent scouts, record company A&R staff, real music addicts) should seek out the *Chronicle*'s annual *Austin Music Industry Guide,* which lists 77 live music venues (not bad for a city of less than half a million), as well as 47 record labels. The guide is published once yearly in May or June; to obtain a back issue ($3), call or stop by the *Chronicle*'s office at 4000 I-35 (at 40th St. off I-35), tel. (512) 473-8995; the mailing address is P.O. Box 49066, Austin, TX 78765.

Most live music clubs are in the E. 6th area; a few are concentrated along "the Drag," which is the section of Guadalupe (Austinians say "GWAD-a-loop") next to the UT campus. Here are a few of the best:

Antone's: (tel. 512-474-5314) 2915 Guadalupe calls itself "Austin's Home of the Blues" but it's more like the Texas roots music headquarters for the entire state (and one of the few places in Austin that books zydeco acts). The Fabulous Thunderbirds, the late Stevie Ray Vaughan, and other national names got a leg up here. Live music Mon.-Saturday.

Austin Outhouse: (tel. 451-2266) 3510

1. MacDonald Observatory, Fort Davis; 2. cactus garden, Caravan of Dreams, Fort Worth; 3. Sabal Palm Grove Sanctuary, Brownsville; (photos by Joe Cummings)

1. Dallas skyline (Dallas Convention & Visitors Bureau); **2.** Cowboy Artists of America Museum (Joe Cummings); **3.** Fiesta Noche del Rio, San Antonio (San Antonio Convention & Visitors Bureau); **4.** Houston by night (Tracey Maurer); **5.** Zydeco Creole Dust Fest, Beaumont (Joe Cummings)

Guadalupe. Blues, folk, country, some rock, every night. Honky-tonk atmosphere.

Back Room: (tel. 441-4677) 2015 E. Riverside. Hard rock, metal, some touring acts. Live music Mon.-Saturday.

Broken Spoke: (tel. 442-6189) 3101 S. Lamar. Classic country dance hall, with café in front. Mostly traditional C&W and country swing—look for Alvin Crow and the Pleasant Valley Boys. Live music Wed.-Saturday.

Chez Fred: (tel. 477-7777) 9070 Research Boulevard. Only a real music town could support live jazz nightly (mostly local acts, nothing too lively).

Club Palmeras: (tel. 473-0798) 217 Congress. Latin and Caribbean music. Live music Mon.-Saturday.

Continental Club: (tel. 441-2444) 1315 S. Congress. Roots rock, blues, and zydeco, some touring acts. Live music Mon.-Saturday.

Green Mesquite: (tel. 479-0485) 1400 Barton Springs. Mix of rock, country, blues, jazz. In the summer, they have outdoor performances in the beer garden. Live music every night.

Headliner's East: (tel. 478-3488) 406 E. 6th. Mostly C&W, some rockabilly, nightly.

Hole In The Wall: (tel. 472-5599) 2538 Guadalupe. Classic Austin digs with mostly roots rock, some country and folk. Live music every night.

Jamaica Racquet Club: E. 6th and Red River. R&B and Caribbean, Wed.-Saturday.

Jelly Club: (tel. 472-2002) 306 E. 6th. New and established local acts nightly.

Joe's Generic Bar: (tel. 480-0171) 315 E. 6th St. Blues and R&B nightly.

Las Manitas/La Peña: (tel. 477-6007) On several Friday evenings during the summer (6-8 p.m.), Las Manitas Avenue Café hosts "Ramon's Ice House," *conjunto* and Latin American music performances in support of La Peña, a nonprofit Latino arts organization. Politically correct fun.

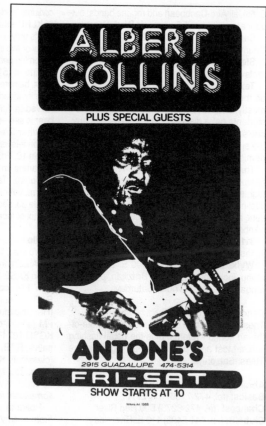

La Zona Rosa: (tel. 482-0662) 612 W. 4th St. A warehouse-like area in back of the restaurant hosts rock, *conjunto,* and R&B Thurs.-Sunday.

Liberty Lunch: (tel. 477-0461) A reincarnation of Armadillo World Headquarters, this semi-outdoor venue books the best of roots, reggae, and world beat, Thurs.-Saturday.

Lumberyard: (tel. 255-9622) 16511 Bratton. Large venue emphasizing local and touring progressive country acts. Live music Mon.-Saturday.

Maggie Mae's: (tel. 478-8541) 323 E. 6th. Three stages: downstairs, upstairs, and in back ("old side"). Mostly pop and funk, occasional acoustic acts. Live music Mon.-Saturday.

Mercado Caribé: (tel. 469-9003) 508 Trinity. Off

E. 6th, all Afro-Caribbean and reggae bands; outdoor area with sand. Live music Wed.-Saturday.

Saxon Pub: (tel. 448-2552) 1320 S. Lamar. Country and Texas singer-songwriters, nightly.

Steamboat: (tel. 478-2912) 403 E. 6th. Local roots and alternative rock, Mon.-Saturday.

Texas Tavern: (tel. 471-9231) Texas Union, on the UT campus. Pop, rock, and funk acts, mostly local favorites, some touring acts. UT students get a discount on the cover, but anyone's welcome. Live music Fri. and Sat. during the summer, plus other nights during the academic year.

Threadgill's: (tel. 451-5440) 6416 N. Lamar. Features acoustic folk or country acts one or two nights a week—usually someone good. Janis Joplin used to sing here when she was a UT student, as attested by a plaque mounted next to the jukebox.

311 Club: (tel. 477-1630) 311 6th St. Local and Texas acts—mostly roots rock—nightly.

Wylie's: (tel. 472-3712) 400 E. 6th. Varied menu, including roots rock, Brazilian, pop, and reggae. Live music Thurs.-Saturday.

Dance Clubs (Discos)
These clubs feature canned music and state-of-the-art sound systems, plus the usual flashing lights. Most are open Mon.-Sat. nights, some Thurs.-Sat. only.

Abratto's : (tel. 477-1641) 318 E. 5th
Basics: (tel. 472-7136) 611 E. 7th
Chances: (tel. 472-8273) 900 Red River
Club XS: (tel. 441-5498) 110 E. Riverside
Dallas: (tel. 452-2801) 7115 Burnet
Heartbreak: (tel. 478-5400) W. 6th St.
Infinity: (tel. 472-2711) 600 E. 6th
Lizard Lounge: (tel. 476-6463) 404 Colorado
Mirage: (tel. 474-7531) 222 E. 6th
New West: (tel. 467-6134) 7934 Great Northern Blvd.
Phaces: (tel. 472-8008) 709 E. 6th
Sanitarium: (tel. 477-6626) 705 Red River
Sneakers: (tel. 832-5922) 9515 N. Lamar

Television Shows
"Austin City Limits" premiered in 1975 and has been broadcast by over 280 public TV stations since. Featured bands cover the American folk music spectrum: country, bluegrass, folk, zydeco,

conjunto, and western swing. The shows are taped at KLRU studios on the UT campus, weekday nights only. Tickets are free but must be picked up a day or two in advance at KLRU. To find out about upcoming performances, call the Austin City Limits Hotline at (512) 471-4811. Once you've got the ticket, be sure to arrive at the studios at least a half-hour in advance, since seating is first-come, first-served (a ticket doesn't guarantee a seat). Free beer is served before the performance.

Other live music programs to watch for on Austin television include "Live from Austin, Tejas" (cable 10, Fri., 8 p.m., local Latino performances), "Estamos en Tejas" (cable 10, Wed., 12:30 p.m., conjunto), "Texas Music Show" (cable 10, Wed., 8 p.m., various Texas acts), and "Lost in Austin" (cable 33, second Fri. of the month, 7 p.m., eclectic mix of local acts).

Radio
There are 24 AM and FM radio stations based in the Austin area. Some of the more listenable include KASE 101 FM (progressive country), KAZI 88.7 FM (community radio that emphasizes R&B, gospel, blues, and jazz), KELG 1440 AM (Hispanic music, including local artists), KLBJ 94 FM (album-oriented rock, some local music), KGSR 107 FM (eclectic mix of folk, blues, alternative, R&B, and Austin artists), KMFA 89.5 FM (classical), KTXZ 1560 AM (bilingual programming, Tex-Mex), KUT 90.5 FM (UT station, eclectic), KVET 1300 AM (traditional country, some local music).

Polka fans should tune in KTAE 1260 AM (from nearby Taylor) to hear "Polka Time," Mon.-Sat. 11-noon, Sun. 1-2. Features traditional Bohemian polkas with one 15-minute break for classified ads.

Comedy Clubs
Esther's Follies: (tel. 512-320-0553) 501 E. 6th. A 14-year running musical comedy revue. Features a series of evolving ensemble skits, sometimes involving the participation of a local or touring stand-up comic. Thurs.-Saturday.

The Laff Stop: (tel. 512-467-2333) 8120 Research Boulevard. Local and touring stand-up acts Tues.-Saturday.

The Velveeta Room: (tel. 512-320-0553) 317 E. 6th. Thursday is open-mike night, Fri. and Sat. feature local and touring stand-up comedy.

EVENTS

March
South By Southwest Music and Media Conference ("SXSW"): Put on for the benefit of music writers and record company people, who converge on Austin in droves for this event, but the whole town profits from a week of general craziness and free concerts. Bands play their best, hoping they'll be picked up by a national label.

March-April
Austin-Travis County Livestock Show And Rodeo: Ten days in late March or April devoted to livestock exhibits, auctions, live C&W music, a barbecue cook-off, and the rodeo. At the Texas Exposition and Heritage Center, 7311 Decker Ln. (tel. 512-928-3710).

Highland Lakes Bluebonnet Trail: The "trail" is an auto route from Austin through Marble Falls, Burnet, Llano, and Kingsland, where hordes of Texas bluebonnets are in peak bloom this time of year. On weekends, each of these towns hosts small arts and crafts fairs and other events. Best place in the state for bluebonnet viewing.

May
Cinco De Mayo: The 5th of May is a celebration of Mexican culture that commemorates the defeat of the French navy at Puebla, Mexico, on that day in 1862. Activities include music, dance, arts and crafts exhibits, and a menudo cook-off. At Fiesta Gardens, 2101 Bergman.

Fiesta Laguna Gloria: An event held as a fund-raiser for the Laguna Gloria Art Museum, usually the third weekend in May. Features food vendors, jugglers and mimes, mariachis, art shows, and an art auction. At the museum, 3809 W. 35th (tel. 458-8191).

June
Green Mesquite Rhythm & Blues Festival: First weekend in June at Green Mesquite Barbecue (tel. 479-0485). A strictly local festival featuring home-grown blues acts.

Clarksville/West End Jazz Festival: A new festival dedicated to the celebration of Austin's West End, a predominantly black neighborhood. Features local jazz, Brazilian, and African talent. On W. 6th St. and other West End venues.

July/August
Austin Aquafest: A series of events held over the last weekend in July and the first two weekends in August to distract residents from the heat. Events include a water-skiing exhibition, music and dance festivals, a softball classic, fishing tournaments, and a nighttime water parade at Town Lake's Auditorium Shores.

November
Dia De Los Muertos: The Mexican Day of the Dead is celebrated on the first two days of November with a downtown skeleton parade and various Latino art exhibits.

RECREATION

Ballooning
Somehow hot-air ballooning has taken hold in Austin. Most trips take in aerial views of the city, Hill Country, and/or the Highland Lakes followed by post-flight refreshments (dawn flights are the most popular). Rates start at around $130 for an hour's flight. The following companies feature federally licensed pilots and federally inspected equipment: **Austin Aeronauts** (tel. 512-440-1492), **Balloonport of Austin** (tel. 835-6058), and **Hendrix Ballooning** (tel. 288-0403). Hendrix Ballooning also offers pilot training and ballooning equipment for purchase.

UT Outdoor Program
UT Recreational Sports (Gregory Gym, UT campus, tel. 512-471-1093) has an excellent Sept.-May roster of guided outdoor trips throughout the state that are open to the public. Prices are low (and even lower for UT students). Programs vary in length from a day ("Rafting the Guadalupe") to 10 days ("Canoeing the Rio Grande"). Other programs include "Snorkel the San Marcos," "Backpack Big Bend," "Hike Seminole Canyon State Park," "Rockclimb Clinic at Lake Travis," and "Kayak the Salt River."

Parks
Town Lake Park is really a series of small parks that run along a section of the Colorado River between Tom Miller Dam to the west and Longhorn Dam to the east. An 8.5-mile walking-jogging-biking trail runs through the parks and there are sev-

eral picnic areas. Fishing and boating (no motors) are allowed, but swimming is prohibited. These parks are along the south edge of town; when Austin residents refer to "the river," they mean Town Lake (which is, of course, an impounded section of the Colorado River).

Zilker Park is the site of Barton Springs, a 1,000- by 125-foot natural swimming pool that's extremely popular during the hot summer months. The clean, limestone-filtered water stays a constant 69° F. Other facilities scattered throughout the 400-acre park include ballfields, picnic areas, playgrounds, and boat ramps along Town Lake. Off Barton Springs Rd. to the southwest of the city center.

Emma Long Metro Park, the oldest park in town, is usually called just City Park. The park has about three miles of Lake Austin shoreline with cliffs, beaches, and boat ramps. Boats and canoes can be rented on-site.

McKinney Falls State Park

The park is named for Thomas F. McKinney, one of Stephen Austin's original colonists, who settled next to Onion Creek in the 1850s and bred racehorses. The ruins of his stables and homestead can be seen in the park. The creek is the park's centerpiece, winding 1.7 miles with scenic pools and two waterfalls. Flora along the creek includes bald cypress, Texas oak, pecan, elm, sycamore, and other water-loving trees, while the uplands of the 640-acre park are characterized by mesquite, cedar, live oak, cacti, and various grasses. The Smith Rockshelter Trail is an interpretive trail with labeled flora. Fauna that may be spotted in the park include white-tailed deer, raccoons, armadillos, wild turkey, and various songbirds. The park contains several picnic sites, playgrounds, and a hike/bike trail, as well as 84 campsites. (See "Austin Area Campgrounds and RV Parks," for camping details.) The park can be reached via US 183 south to FM 812 (scenic loop) west, seven miles southeast of the city center. For more information, contact the Superintendent (tel. 512-243-1643), McKinney Falls State Park, 7102 Scenic Loop Rd., Austin, TX 78744.

Horse Racing

Pari-mutuel betting has become a reality in Texas. **Manor Downs** (US 290 and Manor, tel. 272-5581) hosts races monthly except in December.

Bat Watching

Bat Conservation International says that Austin has the largest urban bat population in the world. Between April and October bat-lovers gather on the Congress Ave. bridge over the Colorado River (Town Lake) at sunset to watch up to 750,000 Mexican free-tail bats come out in search of their evening bug meal. It's estimated that they eat as much as 20,000 pounds of bugs a night.

SHOPPING

Austin isn't a big shopping mecca like Dallas, Houston, San Antonio, or the border towns—just the usual assortment of shopping malls and unimpressive antique-junk stores. A few places are worth mentioning, however.

Markets

The **Austin Country Fleaworld** at 9500 US 290 E spreads across 130 acres; 360 covered stalls offer everything from antiques to fresh produce. The **People's Renaissance Market** at W. 23rd and Guadalupe is a throwback to the '60s when arts and crafts street vendors set up along the Drag; now they're confined to one block, but the merchandise is still occasionally innovative. At the **Travis County Farmers Market,** 6701 Burnet Rd., you'll find trucked-in produce at great prices (open April-October, Sat. only).

Unique

Unique shops in town include the **Eclectic Ethnographic Gallery** (tel. 512-477-1863) at W. 12th and Lamar, which offers a collection of ethnic arts, crafts, jewelry, and clothing from all over the Third World.

Out of Africa focuses on African crafts and has locations at 2901 S. Capital of Texas Hwy. (tel. 480-8149) and 606 Blanco (tel. 480-8149). **Tesoros Trading Co.,** 2095 Congress Ave. (next door to Las Manitas Restaurant) sells Latin American folk art.

Electric Ladyland (tel. 444-2002) at 1306 S. Congress carries vintage American clothing (men's and women's) as well as Halloween costumes. Bob Dylan has made purchases here.

Boots

Cadillac Jack Boot Co. (tel. 512-452-4428) at 6623 N. Lamar sells reconditioned cowboy boots from before the decline of handmade boots (pre-1970s), plus other vintage western wear. Reconditioned boots start at around $90 a pair. Owner Jimmy James keeps a row of colorful boots behind the counter that are part of his private collection—they're not for sale but you can look for free.

If you've come to Austin to seek bootmaker Charlie Dunn of Jerry Jeff Walker song fame, you're too late—he retired a few years ago and moved to Raymondville. Lee Miller of **Texas Traditions** (2222 College, tel. 443-4447) has taken over where Charlie left off and is considered one of the best bootmakers in the state. **Capitol Saddlery** (1614 Lavaca, tel. 478-9309) is where Dunn started out, and they still make custom boots as well as other leather cowboy gear. **Texas Custom Boots's** Noel Escobar, Jr. also comes highly recommended as a local bootmaker. Noel's shop (tel. 327-7969) is in nearby Oak Hill (southeast edge of Austin) at 3654 Bee Caves Road. At any of these custom shops, a pair of boots will cost a minimum of $500-600.

INFORMATION

Tourist Offices
The **Austin Convention and Visitors Bureau** (tel. 512-474-5171) has its main office at 900 Congress Ave., Suite 300. Their visitor information center (tel. 478-0098 or 800-888-8AUS) is at 300 Bouldin Avenue. Both offices are open Mon.-Fri. 8:30-5. The **State Dept. of Highways** maintains a visitor center in the State Capitol at 11th and Congress. The staff distributes travel information on Austin as well as the rest of Texas; best of all, it's open daily 8-5.

Yet another source of tourist information is the hospitality desk at the **Old Bakery and Emporium** (tel. 512-477-5961) at 1006 Congress. They have the usual selection of maps and brochures as well as specific information for senior citizen services and activities; open Mon.-Fri. 9-4. For info on UT, visit the **University of Texas Visitors Center** (tel. 471-1420) at UT's Little Campus (Martin Luther King and I-35); open Mon.-Fri. 8-4:30.

Publications
The weekly *Austin Chronicle* (published every Fri.) is distributed free throughout the city and contains up-to-date information on Austin hap-

penings, including recreation, dining, music, and local politics. For local business news (and occasional general-interest features), check the chamber of commerce's monthly *Austin,* which maintains an up-to-date calendar of events and list of restaurants. Austin's one daily paper is the *Austin American-Statesman.*

Maps
At least five maps of Austin are available. The Austin CVB's giveaway map is sketchy but useful for general orientation. The Old San Francisco Steak House's cute and colorful map (also distributed by the CVB) helps pinpoint landmark attractions in and around town, but its distorted scale undermines its usefulness as a streetfinder. Rand McNally's (not enough color contrast, hard to read) and Continental Map's (too densely colored, hard to read) lose out to the accurate and easy-to-read AAA map. AAA's Austin office (tel. 512-444-4757) is at 321 W. Ben White Blvd., Suite 205; open Mon.-Fri. 8:30-5, Sat. 9-1.

Telephone
The area code for Austin and the surrounding area is 512 (915 for Kingsland).

TRANSPORT

Taxis
Two established cab companies offer 24-hour taxi service: American Cab (tel. 512-452-9999) and Yellow Cab (tel. 472-1111).

City Buses
Austin is blessed with one of the better city bus systems in the state, Capital Metro. There are over 50 neighborhood routes, seven express and feeder routes, and two special downtown routes

---

TELEPHONE AND EMERGENCY INFORMATION

Emergency (police, fire, medical)	911
Crisis Intervention Hotline	472-4357
National Weather Service	476-1700
Telephone Directory Assistance	1-411
University of Texas Information	471-3434

nicknamed 'Dillos (Armadillo Express). The Congress/Capitol 'Dillo runs from the Park & Ride lot at the City Coliseum and Palmer Auditorium (south of Town Lake) and Martin Luther King, Jr. Blvd., via Congress Ave., Lavaca St., and San Jacinto St.; the bus operates 6:30 a.m.-7:15 p.m. weekdays, 11 a.m.- 7 p.m. Saturday. The ACC/Lavaca 'Dillo also starts at the Park & Ride lot and runs north-south along Guadalupe and Lavaca all the way to 21st St.; hours of operation are 6:45 a.m.-10:15 p.m. weekdays. Parking at the Park & Ride lot and at the State Parking Garages along San Jacinto and Trinity is free.

Even if you're driving an auto, riding the Capital Metro can save *mucho dinero* on parking fees during the day. Capital Metro fares are 50 cents for adults, 25 cents for students with ID, and free for seniors. 'Dillo fares are only 25 cents for adults, free for seniors and students. The Capitol Metro

office at 2910 5th St. has Capital Metro schedules and route maps, or you can call Capital Metro at (512) 474-1200 for information.

Tours
Gray Line (tel. 512-345-6789) offers a three-hour city tour for $16 that visits the State Capitol, LBJ Library, Governor's Mansion, UT, Barton Springs, Town Lake, E. 6th St., the O. Henry Museum, and historic buildings.

Robert Mueller Municipal Airport
Austin's small airport is only three miles from the city center. A handful of airlines provides daily service to 20 cities, mostly in Texas. Taxis between the airport and downtown charge around $7 a trip. Capitol Metro bus 20 goes to the airport from downtown Austin for 50 cents.

VICINITY OF AUSTIN

HIGHLAND LAKES

After a series of catastrophic floods, Austin persuaded the state to dam the Colorado River in several places northwest of the city over a 23-year period. (This Colorado River, incidentally, is not the one in Colorado; this one starts and ends in Texas.) The impoundment system is administered by the Lower Colorado River Authority (LCRA). Ecologists lament the fact that it destroyed the surrounding flood-plain ecosystem, but most Austinians love the fact that they now have a weekend playground of seven artificial lakes; from north to south they are Buchanan, Inks, LBJ, Marble Falls, Travis, Austin, and Town. Of these seven, only Buchanan, LBJ, and Travis are of any significant size (Lake Austin and Town Lake are within or adjacent to the city).

The LCRA, in conjunction with Travis County, operates a number of free or very inexpensive lakeshore campgrounds in the lake country; see the "Highland Lakes Camping" chart (pp. 240-241) for details.

The "capital" of the Highland Lakes area is **Burnet** (pronounced BURN-it), 62 miles northwest of Austin. Although the Highland Lakes Tourist Association has its mailing address in

Austin (P.O. Box 1967, Austin, TX 78767), you can get the same information from the Burnet Chamber of Commerce (tel. 512-756-4297), 705 Buchanan Dr., about a mile west of US 281. One of the best times to visit the lake country is in April when the bluebonnets are in bloom. Burnet holds a **Bluebonnet Festival** the second weekend in April in the town square, featuring a parade, arts and crafts fair, foot races, and a street dance.

Lake Buchanan
This 23,060-acre body of water is the largest in the Highland Lakes system and is formed by Buchanan Dam (built in 1937, the first in the series). A number of public and private facilities along its shores support fishing, boating, swimming, and other water recreation. One of the highlights of Lake Buchanan activities is the **Vanishing Texas River Cruise**, which takes visitors in search of bald eagles. The American bald eagle is extremely rare these days, but a population of 18-30 (including both varieties, the northern and the southern) spends winters at the lake. The cruises run daily between mid-November and late March at 8 and 11 a.m. Peak eagle-watching times are January and February. During the 2 1/2-hour trip, other birds including great blue herons, egrets, terns, cormorants, and pelicans are commonly sighted.

Rugged cliffs surround the lake, and the cruise passes 50-foot Fall Creek Falls. The boat leaves from the northeast shore off FM 2341, and has a heated cabin and food galley serving coffee and hot chocolate. Rates are $12.95 adults, $11.95 seniors and military, $8.95 children 6-12. Contact Vanishing Texas River Cruise for reservations (required): P.O. Box 901, Burnet, TX 78611 (tel. 512-756-6986).

The lake is surrounded by a variety of private and public campgrounds and lodges. The quickest way to the lake from Austin is via I-35 N to Georgetown, then west on State 29 (about 75 miles total). A more scenic route is US 290 west to State 71, then west to US 281, north to State 29 at Burnet (about two miles farther).

Longhorn Cavern State Park

This is the only cave in Texas administered by the park system (but only remotely, since a local concession handles day-to-day operations). A long limestone cave formed by ancient underground streams, Longhorn was once used by early Indian tribes as temporary shelter, as evidenced by bones and arrow tips found on the cavern floor. During the Civil War, Confederate troops manufactured gunpowder here. In the early 1900s, Burnet and Llano County residents used the cave as a social center for dancing and dining during the hot summer months (the interior temperature is a constant 64° F). Various chambers in the cave are named for their shapes or for the predominant cave formations contained therein: Frozen Waterfall, Crystal City, Hall of Gems, Queen's Throne, Viking's Prow, among others.

Facilities in the 634-acre park include picnic areas, a snack bar, hiking and nature trails, and a gift shop. Cavern tours last about an hour and a half for a 1.25-mile roundtrip walk. During the summer (Memorial Day through Labor Day) tours are given hourly 10-6, seven days a week; the rest of the year 10-5. The cave is off US 281 between Burnet and Marble Falls (12 miles southwest of Burnet), not far from Lake LBJ. Admission is $6 adults, $4 children 5-12. For further information contact Longhorn Cavern State Park, Route 2, Box 23, Burnet, TX 78611 (tel. 512-756-6976).

Lake LBJ
This is a medium-sized lake of 6,375 surface acres formed by the Alvin Wirtz Dam. The fishing is good here because of the many caves and coves among the limestone cliffs. It's also popular among water-skiing enthusiasts because it's protected from high winds. There are several resorts and private campgrounds around LBJ, but no free public campgrounds.

Lake Travis
Travis is the second-largest Highland Lake, with an average surface area of 18,900 acres. It's impounded by Mansfield Dam, built in 1941. Because it's large and relatively close to Austin, Travis gets heavy use from boaters, anglers, waterskiiers, and scuba divers. Besides an assortment of private facilities, there are five public parks on her shores with free or nearly free ($2) camping.

Wineries
Two highly regarded wineries in the Highland Lakes area are open to the public for tastings and tours. **Slaughter Leftwich** (tel. 512-266-3331), at 4209 Eck Ln. (off FM 620 near the south shore of Lake Travis) is the originator of the Texas Chardonnay varietal, which earned a double gold medal at the 1984 San Francisco Fair and since 1986 has been the most awarded Chardonnay in the state. The winery's Austin Blush, Sauvignon

Blanc, and Cabernet Sauvignon have also been acclaimed at wine competitions. Slaughter Leftwich is open to the public 1-5 daily for tastings and sales; tours of the winery are included on weekends.

Fall Creek Vineyards (tel. 915-379-5361) can be found off FM 2241 near the northwestern shore of Lake Buchanan. Many wine critics say Fall Creek makes the state's finest wines. The winery's 65 acres of vinifera produce award-winning Sauvignon Blanc, Emerald Riesling, Chardonnay, Cabernet Sauvignon, Carnelian, and Zinfandel. Open for tastings and sales Mon., Wed., and Fri. 11-2 or for tours and tastings each Sat. noon-5. For reservations contact the Fall Creek Vineyards office at 1111 Guadalupe St. (tel. 512-476-4477) in Austin.

GEORGETOWN

Originally a stop for cattle drovers along the Chisholm Trail, then a railhead for the shipping of local cotton, Georgetown languished for decades after cotton prices bottomed out during the Depression. A 1982-83 restoration of its quaint Victorian square turned the town of 15,000 into one of Austin's favorite weekend playgrounds. A growing number of people who work in Austin choose to commute from Georgetown, which is 26 miles north of the state capital via I-35.

The late-18th-century buildings that line the square contain restaurants, art galleries, antique shops, and other tourist-oriented ventures. In addition to the town square, Georgetown boasts two residential districts on the National Historic Register. Stop by the **History and Visitors Information Center** at 101 W. 7th St. for pamphlets that outline suggested walking or driving tours through historic districts. For further information, contact the Georgetown Convention and Visitors Bureau (tel. 512-869-3545, P.O. Box 409, Georgetown, TX 78627).

Nearby **Lake Georgetown**, maintained by the U.S. Corps of Engineers, offers three shoreline recreational sites with boat ramps, picnic areas, and rest room/shower facilities: Cedar Breaks Park, Russell Park, and Jim Hogg Park.

Accommodations
The following hotels have rooms in the $45-55

range: **Comfort Inn** (tel. 512-863-7504, 1005 Leander Rd.), **Georgetown Inn** (tel. 863-5572, I-35 North), **Ramada Inn** (tel. 869-2541, 333 I-35 North). **Bed & Breakfast Texas Style** (tel. 214-298-8586) can arrange stays at local Victorian B&Bs for $40-70 including breakfast.

SAN MARCOS

San Marcos is on the far eastern edge of the Hill Country, 26 miles south of Austin via I-35. The town (pop. 28,000) takes its name from the San Marcos River, which was named by 18th-century Spanish explorers who "discovered" it on St. Mark's Day. The Spaniards attempted to missionize the area several times without success. It was finally settled by Anglo-Americans in the 1840s.

But long before any Europeans had laid eyes on the San Marcos River, it was an important source of water for Indian tribes. The river's constant temperature (about 71° F) and crystal clarity sustains two globally rare fish species, as well as the world's only known occurrences of Texas wild rice *(Zizania texana)*. Evidence found in the bottom of Aquarena Springs, source of the San Marcos, shows that Indians inhabited the area 12,000 years ago—this may, in fact, be one of the oldest Indian sites in North America, along with the Lower Pecos River Valley. The Texas Nature Conservancy has recently undertaken a San Marcos River project to try and protect the riparian system from further encroachment by city and county development.

Aquarena Springs

The headwaters of the San Marcos River is the site of a water-oriented amusement park. One highlight of the park is the glass-bottom boat ride, which guides visitors over aquatic plant varieties and schools of fish as well as bubbling spring sources. You may also see a crew of underwater archaeologists from SMU scavenging for Indian relics. Another attraction is the Submarine Theatre, which is lowered under the water (only about six feet) for a 30-minute aquatic show that features Ralph the Swimming Pig (yes, the one and only) and his human cohorts. The Sky Spiral lifts a revolving dome 250 feet above the park for a panoramic view of San Marcos and the surrounding hills, while the Swiss Sky Ride crosses over

the springs to the Hanging Gardens. Also on the grounds is the remains of a 1753 Spanish mission and a replica frontier village.

Aquarena Springs (tel. 512-396-8900) is just off I-35 (exit 206) and is open daily 10-6 and the remaining months till 5. Admission is $14.95 adults, $12.95 seniors, $11.95 children 4-15.

Wonder World

This large cave was formed by a prehistoric earthquake along the Balcones Escarpment, rather than by the erosive processes common in most limestone caves. The 45-minute cave tour exits the cave via an elevator ride to the top of a 146-foot observation tower; from the tower visitors can clearly see the Escarpment where the Edwards Plateau ends and the coastal plains start. Other attractions include an anti-gravity house and a train ride through a wildlife park. You can purchase separate tickets for each attraction, or buy an all-inclusive ticket for $10.50 adults, $8.50 seniors and children 4-11. Open Memorial Day to Labor Day 8-8, the rest of the year 9-6. Call (512) 392-3760 for further information.

Canoeing And Tubing The San Marcos

The San Marcos River is popular among canoeists and kayakers. Equipment can be rented from **Spencer Canoes** (tel. 512-357-6113) at 360 S. LBJ Dr. and **T.G. Canoes** (tel. 353-3846), on State 80.

The local **Lions Club** (tel. 512-392-8255) also rents large inner tubes for floating the river between May and September. Rates are a reasonable $3 a day (plus $7 deposit, and $1.25 for shuttle service if needed). At City Park, Bugg Ln. and Aquarena Springs Drive.

Events

In early June San Marcos is the starting point for the **Texas Water Safari**, a grueling marathon canoe ride along 260 miles of the San Marcos and Guadalupe rivers to the Gulf of Mexico. Billed as "the world's toughest boat race," crews must paddle and portage nonstop through rough water, log jams, dams, and other hazards to arrive in Seadrift on the coast within a 100-hour time limit. For information on the race, call (512) 357-6113.

The **Republic of Texas Chilympiad** is the world's largest CASI-sanctioned chili cook-off (don't laugh, they're held as far away as Singapore). It usually convenes the third weekend in September (three days) and attracts as many as 500 teams from around the world. Spectators are invited to taste, though it always pays to ask what's in the pot first (rattlesnake is a popular ingredient). Other activities include music performances, nightly dances, and an arts and crafts show. At the Hays County Civic Center (I-35 exit 201).

Accommodations And Food

Motel 6 (tel. 512-396-8705) has single rooms for $22.95 plus the usual $6 per additional person; at 1321 I-35 N (exit 206). Next least expensive is the **University Inn** (tel. 396-6060) at 1507 I-35 N (exit 206); rooms here are $50 s, $60 d June-Sept., $5 less the rest of the year. **Aquarena Springs Inn** (tel. 396-8901) is on the grounds of the Aquarena Springs amusement park; rooms are $55 s or d with one bed, $70 with two beds. The **Holiday Inn** is at the junction of I-35 and Loop 82; $52 s, $54 d. 24. **Motel 6** (tel. 396-8705), off I-35 at exit 206, has

the least expensive rooms in the area for $22.95 s plus $6 for each additional person.

The **Crystal River Inn** (tel. 396-3739) is a bed and breakfast housed in a restored 1883 Greek Revival-style home in San Marcos's historic downtown (326 W. Hopkins). Rooms are $60-90 a night, including a full breakfast. On weekends they're open to the public for brunch.

San Marcos has all the usual fast-food joints along I-35, mostly clustered around exit 205. For a little atmosphere, try the **Katy Station Restaurant** (tel. 396-5010) at 400 Cheatham, off Allen Parkway. The building is a former "Katy" (Missouri, Kansas, and Texas) railroad depot, built in 1890. They serve a variety of steak, chicken, and seafood. Open Mon.-Sat. for lunch and dinner. **Pepper's At The Falls** (tel. 396-5255) is a popular family restaurant serving American food at 100 Sessom Dr. (I-35 exit 206) on the river. Open daily for lunch and dinner.

HILL COUNTRY

Practically every person living in South Central Texas suggests different borders for the Hill Country. The Texas Hill Country Association, an organization of businesses in 23 South Central Texas counties, would have you believe that towns as distant as Uvalde, San Antonio, San Marcos, and Austin all belong to it (no way). The Highland Lakes area (covered under "Vicinity of Austin") is often included since it's hilly. But for purposes of this book, we're considering only the hills formed where the southeastern edge of the Edwards Plateau meets the Balcones Escarpment—not the geologically separate rise formed by the Llano Uplift around Austin—which predominantly includes the counties of Real, Bandera, Gillespie, Kerr, Kendall, Comal, northern Uvalde, northern Medina, and northwestern Bexar.

The reason everyone's trying to get in under the Hill Country banner is because it's a significant tourist draw for this part of the state, especially for elevation-starved South and East Texans. And these aren't alpine heights either; 1,400-1,700 feet is the high norm. In the heat of a South Texas summer, however, the Hill Country breezes and relatively low humidity can make it feel like Eden rediscovered. Beyond the mild climate,

there's also a seductive Hill Country culture of sorts, a combination of small town quaintness and Texas self-sufficiency. It's been called the state's "heartland," like England's Lake District, France's Provence, or Germany's Black Forest. Most of the towns date to the mid-1800s and were settled by Europeans of German, Polish, and Czech descent. Historic buildings are constructed of cream-colored, locally quarried tufa limestone. Many people find the scenery beautiful, but one really has to seek out the beauty, since much of the Hill Country is like South Texas—lots of cacti, mesquite, and caliche— with added hills. Hint: the most scenic areas are along the Hill Country rivers, most notably the Frio, Sabinal, Guadalupe, Medina, and Pedernales. Many a Texan's dream is to retire with a little rancho along one of these rivers.

San Antonio is a popular jumping-off point for Hill Country road tours, whether by car or bicycle (public transport is virtually nonexistent in these parts). Hill Country aficionados often make a loop via State 16 northwest to Bandera and Kerrville, then west on FM 337 (the most scenic) or State 39 (so they don't have to backtrack to Medina) to the Frio Canyon area (Leakey, Rio Frio, and Concan), then back to San Antonio via US 90 (taking in non-Hill Country towns Uvalde and Castroville along the way). This general route offers a good sampling of the area's best without running into hordes of tourists; the approximately 200 road miles could take anywhere from two days to a week, depending on how long you stop over along the way. Recommended side trips off the loop include the pleasantly named Comfort (near Kerrville) and Utopia (near Frio Canyon). But there are lots of other "itty-bitty" towns (and bigger towns like Fredericksburg) off this circuit worth visiting as well.

All phone numbers in this section are in the 512 area code unless otherwise noted.

BANDERA

The first settlers in the Bandera area were wood cutters who came in the 1840s to make shingles from the bald cypress that grows along the Medina River. They were followed by a Mormon contingent and later by Polish immigrants; the Polish built the town that became modern Bandera.

The U.S. Army also contributed to the development of Bandera (and Kerrville farther north) by establishing nearby **Camp Verde.** Troops stationed at Camp Verde called it "Little Egypt" since it was the headquarters for the short-lived U.S. Army Camel Corps, a unit that played a significant role in the exploration of Far West Texas's Big Bend region.

Billing itself as the "Cowboy Capital of the World," Bandera today (pop. 1,000) is more of a weekend-cowboy destination than a true ranch town ("Dude Ranch Capital" would be more descriptive). The town claims more rodeo champions than any Texas town of comparable size. Local legends Toots Mansfield, Scooter Fries, Clay Billings, and others are commemorated by a plaque in front of the 1890 Renaissance Revival-style courthouse (constructed of locally quarried limestone) on Main Street. Other buildings in the Main St. area are typical 1880s ranch-style clapboard or stucco, some with intact boardwalks out front.

Main St. businesses include a honky-tonk, several restaurants, and a couple of western-wear stores. Horse-and-buggy tours are available on weekends, when the town fills up with racetrack enthusiasts and visitors from San Antonio.

Frontier Times Museum

This is the kind of museum you find only in small-town America. It's basically a collection of everything the townsfolk have thought was memorable since the museum was established in 1927. The 40,000 objects on display include an impossibly eclectic range of old photos, artwork, bells from around the world, plates, and unique items like a two-headed goat, a shrunken head from South America, a baby incubator, and a camel-hair pillow from Camp Verde. At 506 13th St.; open Mon.-Sat. 10-4:30, Sun. 1-4:30. Admission is $1.50 for adults, 25 cents for children 6-18.

Historic Sites

Polish immigrants built **Saint Stanislaus Catholic Church,** at 7th and Cypress, of tufa limestone in 1876 (it's the second-oldest Polish church in Texas after the one in Panna Maria). Behind the church is the **St. Joseph's Convent-Parish Museum,** built in 1874. The nearby **Catholic Cemetery** on Cypress (between 7th and 8th) was established by the first 16 Polish families who arrived in 1855. Many of the headstones date to the mid-19th century and are inscribed in Polish. The limestone **Old Bandera Courthouse and Jail** on 12th and Cypress were constructed in 1868 and 1881 respectively.

Camp Verde

Camp Verde's camel corps imported the beasts, along with camel handlers (one famous handler, Hadji Ali, was nicknamed "Hi Jolly" by his Army employers), from North Africa by boat via the now-defunct port of Indianola, Texas. The camels made very successful pack animals for the Army's Trans-Pecos explorations. They didn't consume as much water as horses or mules (though this characteristic has been highly exaggerated in camel mythology), they were more sure-footed in rough terrain, and Indians wouldn't steal them (Indians were said to fear the odd-looking creatures). The outbreak of the Civil War ended the camel experiment—when Confederate troops took over Camp Verde they set some of the 80 animals loose and killed others. There are no physical remains of Camp Verde, just a historical marker narrating a short history of the post at the former site of the camel pens. But you could stop at the **Old Camp Verde General Store and Post Office** on State 173, 11 miles north of Bandera, which sells food, souvenirs, and Texana. The store has been in continuous operation since 1857. Across the road is a picnic area.

Dude Ranches

There are eight dude ranches in the Bandera vicinity, all oriented toward family vacations for urbanites seeking a "ranch experience." Lodging is generally in rustic cabins and meals are "ranch-style." Common Bandera dude ranch activities include trail rides, hay rides, outdoor barbecues, and Medina River recreation. Guests are not obliged to participate in any group activities and can choose instead to make use of the facilities on their own. Kids love these places, so there are always lots of kids around; a guest ranch that might be more suitable for adults traveling without children is the Y.O. Ranch (see "Kerrville"), although couples without children are welcome at those listed below as well.

The most renowned of the Bandera bunch is the **Mayan Ranch,** which is off Pecan St. about 1.5 miles west of Bandera's Main Street. The Mayan's 326 wooded acres abut the Medina River, so the scenery is especially pleasant. Rates include lodging, all meals (with the "cowboy breakfast" option—served on an early morning trail ride), swimming and tubing on the Medina River, horseback riding (two different trail rides per day), hiking, tennis, country dance lessons, and various other activities that the Hicks family dreams up on the spot. Rates are $85-90 a day for adults, $50 per

day for teens, and $40 daily for children. Rates are $5-10 per day less for weekly stays. For reservations, call or write Don and Judy Hicks (tel. 512-796-3312), Box 577, Bandera, TX 78003.

The **Dixie Dude Ranch** has been a working ranch since 1901 and offers perhaps the most authentic ranch experience. The 711-acre spread has plenty of room for experienced equestrians but they also lead trail rides for the less experienced. Rates are $65-85 per adult, $25-55 per child under 16 per night (depending on the cabin and season), and include horseback riding, hayrides, swimming, bonfires, cookouts, and live entertainment (owner Clay Conoly plays fiddle). The ranch is also open to day use only for $10-30 depending on the activities chosen. The Dixie is nine miles southwest of Bandera on FM 1077. Contact Billie Crowell (tel. 512-796-7771, 800-375-9255), Box 548, Bandera, TX 78003.

Just a bit farther on FM 1077 is the **Silver Spur Dude Ranch** (tel. 512-796-7170, P.O. Box 1657, Bandera, TX 78003), a 275-acre, family-owned guest ranch built in 1980 on dry, hilly rangeland. Accommodations are in modern cabins with color TV. All the usual activities (including a large swimming pool), $78 for adults, $30-58 for children (depending on age) a night, $20 for day use only.

Other Bandera guest ranches include: **Flying L Guest Ranch** (tel. 512-796-3001, 800-292-5134, HCR 1, Box 32, Bandera, TX 78003), **LH7 Ranch Resort** (tel. 512-796-4314, P.O. Box 1474, Bandera, TX 78003), **Lost Valley Resort**

Cowboys come in all sizes.

Ranch (tel. 512-796-3117, P.O. Box 1509, Bandera, TX 78003), **Peaceful Valley Ranch** (tel. 512-796-3681, Rt. 3, Box 900, Bandera, TX 78003), and **Twin Elm Guest Ranch** (tel. 512-796-3628, P.O. Box 117, Bandera, TX 78003).

Motels
The **Econo Lodge** (tel. 512-796-3093) at 1900 State 16 South has rooms for $49-58 (senior discounts available) and a pool. The **River Front Motel** (tel. 796-3690), facing the Medina River at 1004 Maple, has individual cottages for $40-45 a night. The **Frontier Hotel** (tel. 796-4100) on State 16 and Cherry St. in town costs $35 s a night.

Three miles north of town on State 173 is the small **Horseshoe Inn** (tel. 512-796-3105, 800-352-3810), where simply furnished but charming rooms with private bath are $35 d during the week, $45 d on weekends. Rates include a full breakfast and the use of tubes for floating on the nearby Medina River. **Bandera Creek Bed & Breakfast** (tel. 512-796-3517), southeast of town on State 16 near Bandera Downs, has two rooms with shared bath for $65 including continental breakfast.

Campgrounds And RV Parks
Each of the RV parks in and around Bandera charges a moderate $10 a night for full-hookup sites, even less for long-term stays. **Koehler Park** (tel. 512-796-8153) is at 1503 Main St. in Bandera. **Old Mill Trace RV Park** (tel. 512-796-4595) is two blocks off Main on the Medina River. **Skyline Ranch RV Park** (tel. 796-4958) is a mile west of town on State 16 and features a lounge and pavilion. The family-oriented **Yogi Bear's Jellystone Park** (tel. 796-3751) is on the river near the River Front Motel. In addition to full hookups, the park has a swimming pool and facilities for canoeing and tubing. **The Farm** (tel. 589-2276) is 7.5 miles northwest of Bandera off FM 2828 on the river and has tent camping for $7 a night in addition to RV sites. No-fee primitive camping is permitted at the **Hill Country State Natural Area** (see below).

Food
Locals enjoy the **O.S.T. Restaurant** (tel. 512-796-3836) at 305 Main, which serves time-warp Tex-Mex (like enchiladas served with a thick tomato sauce and chili) and down-home fare like home-

made soups, chicken-fried steaks and biscuits. The acronym stands for Old Spanish Trail, which used to pass through Bandera. They also serve Mexican or American breakfasts at any hour—a real plus. Open daily for breakfast, lunch, and dinner. **Harvey's Old Bank Steakhouse** at 309 Main offers steak and other Texas dishes. A pleasant outdoor eating area is open in good weather. Open daily for lunch and dinner.

Rustic **Busbees Bar-B-Q** at 319 Main has barbecued beef, sausage, chicken, and ribs Wed.-Sun. 10:30 a.m.-8 p.m. or until sold out. Tiny **El Jacalito** at 304 11th (one block west of Main) turns out respectable Tex-Mex.

North of Bandera on State 16 is **Thuy's** (tel. 796-8496), a stranded Vietnamese restaurant that's open Tues.-Sat. for dinner only. Nearby is the best local Mexican place, **Un Taco Mas, Etc.** (tel. 796-7257), which serves enchiladas, tacos, chalupas, menudo, and breakfast tacos daily, 9 a.m.-2 a.m.

One place most tourists don't know about is the incomparable **Pipe Creek Junction Café** (tel. 512-535-4742), which is about 12 miles east of Bandera at the junction of State 16 and FM 1283. It looks like a country store from the outside but the eye-popping menu inside has farm-raised catfish (all-you-can-eat Wed., Fri.), frog legs, rabbit, catfish-fried chicken livers, grilled teriyaki chicken, and homemade breads, plus daily specials written on a chalkboard. They also serve breakfast tacos and incredible buttermilk pie. Open Tues.-Sun. 6 a.m. to 11 p.m.

Dance Halls
Can't have a cowboy capital without a couple of honky-tonks. The **Cabaret Dance Hall** (tel. 796-3095), at 801 Main, has been a big draw for over 50 years. Texas names like Johnny Bush and the Bandeleros and Hank Thompson play on weekends, and Billy Joe Shaver and Willie Nelson recently filmed a performance here. Open Fri.-Sun. till 2 a.m. A bit funkier is **Arkey Blue's Silver Dollar** (tel. 796-8826) at 308 Main, where Arkey Blue and the Blue Cowboys motivate boot heels on a sawdust dance floor Fri. and Sat. nights.

Bandera Downs
At this recently opened racetrack, horses run daily Thurs.-Sun. from late February to late November.

General admission is $3 including parking; other seating options include Grandstand ($5), Turf Club ($7) and air-conditioned Jockey Club ($10-12). For further information or ticket reservations, call (512) 796-7781 or (800) 572-2332.

Hill Country State Natural Area

This 4,753-acre park, 10.5 miles southwest of Bandera via FM 681 and FM 1077, is a chunk of the Hill Country preserved in its natural, undeveloped state. The terrain varies from the Bandera Creek bottom to the tops of rocky hills. The former Merrick Ranch on the site is being allowed to revert to its natural state.

There are equestrian and hiking trails but the state Parks and Wildlife Dept. has no plans to expand the facilities. Free camping is allowed except Tues. and Wed. when the park is closed. Water is available at park headquarters; no ground fires are permitted (bring a campstove). For further information, contact the Manager (tel. 512-796-4413), HCSNA, Rte. 1, Box 601, Bandera, TX 78003.

Medina Lake

The floor of 5,575-acre Medina Lake was once the site of Mountain Valley, an early Mormon colony that was destroyed by a 1900 flood. Before it was dammed, the Medina River valley was probably the most beautiful in the Hill Country. The wooded bluffs that ringed the dramatic valley, now filled with water, still lend an added beauty to the lake. Unlike many Texas dams that are state or federally funded, the Medina Dam was built (in 1912) by private interests. The dam and the entire lakeshore are still privately owned, though there are public facilities at a few commercial campgrounds and marinas. Many San Antonio families have weekend homes here. The lake is suitable and very popular for boating, water-skiing, swimming, and fishing.

Medina Lake is 22 miles from Bandera, via State 16 east to Pipe Creek, then FM 1283 south to Park 37. Two small, unincorporated communities, Mico and Lake Hills (sometimes spelled Lakehills), offer minimal grocery and gas facilities. There are four RV parks in Lake Hills, all with sites for $10 a night (long-term discounts are available). **Goat Hill Camp** (tel. 512-751-2072) is on the lakeshore at the end of 19th St. (Goat Hill Rd.), off Park 37; full hookups are available. **Bob's Cove** (tel. 751-9923) is at a cove off a dirt road that starts where Park 37 ends; $8 w/e only, tents allowed. **Lakehills Mobile Home & RV Park** (tel. 751-3030) is off Park 37 next to the EMS barn; full hookups. The **Hitching Post** (tel. 751-3222) is on Park 37 a mile west of FM 1283; full hookups. **Cedar Point Landing** (tel. 751-3115) on Medina Dam Rd. (just off FM 1283) has a boat ramp open to the paying public.

KERRVILLE

This town of 17,000 has grown beyond its quaint Hill Country roots into an arts center of sorts. The town itself is not much of an attraction except at the end of May when the Kerrville Folk Festival and Texas State Arts and Crafts Fair take place and during September's Jimmie Rodgers Jubilee. The surrounding area is dotted with youth camps and ranches.

Cowboy Artists Of America Museum

The Cowboy Artists of America is an organization (founded in 1965) of around 25 active artists, plus eight emeritus members, from the school of Western American Realism. The museum features rotating exhibits by member artists and occasionally by nonmembers. The facility, built in 1985, is quite large and includes a research library, auditorium and museum store. An artist in residence sometimes paints or sculpts in public view in a studio off one of the galleries. The museum also regularly sponsors workshops for aspiring Western artists. The works themselves are always a bit of history (meticulously researched down to the last spur and Indian feather) mixed with romanticism. Member Bill Owens has said it's important "to show the public who the true cowboy is, and what he does. In some ways, he doesn't fit into a mold, but there are some things about him that are very characteristic. There is a code, an unspoken etiquette, that the cowboy has that separates him from other people." Even if you don't buy that statement, you'll probably enjoy the exhibits for the sheer technique involved—these guys are good.

The museum (tel. 512-896-2553) is at 1550 Bandera Hwy. (State 173) east off State 16; open Tues.-Sat. 9-5, Sun. 1-5. (June through August it's also open on Mondays, 9-5.) Admission is $2.50 adults, $2 seniors, $1 12 and under.

Cowboy Artists of America Museum, Kerrville

Hill Country Museum

This turreted, limestone mansion was originally the home of cattle baron and ex-Texas Ranger Charles Schreiner (see "Y.O. Ranch" below). Then for a while it was a Masonic temple. It now contains exhibits interpreting the history of the Schreiner family and Kerr County. The house itself is the most interesting exhibit, with a parquet floor made of 10 kinds of wood and other flourishes. At 216 E. Garrett; open Tues.-Sat. 9:30-noon and 1:30-4:30 p.m. Admission is $2.50 adults, $1 children 6-12.

Y.O. Ranch

Texas Ranger Captain Charles Schreiner (a native of Alsace-Lorraine) founded this ranch in 1880 after he'd made his fortune by driving 300,000 head of longhorn cattle to Dodge City, Kansas. Schreiner bought the Y.O. brand from another rancher (it stood for Young-Olsten at the time). Over the years, the ranch has shrunk from 550,000 to 40,000 acres, still quite a spread. Charles Schreiner III ("Charlie III") brought the longhorn breed back from near extinction in the 1950s and the Y.O. now has the largest quality registered herd in the country. Charlie III has also been breeding "exotic" game on the ranch for the last 30 years, one of the first to do so in Texas.

Some of the species bred on the ranch are endangered in their native countries; the blackbuck antelope had been completely wiped out in Pakistan before they began importing from the Y.O. in recent years. Other cloven-hoofed creatures who inhabit the ranch include axis and sika deer, mouflon, red, and aoudad sheep, addax, Persian ibex, barasingha, oryx, and eland. They also breed emu, ostrich, rhea, giraffe, and zebra—a virtual zoo collection of African and Australasian animals. The game species are hunted when the herds get too big (the ranch claims that only 5% are taken by strictly regulated hunting, less than the percentage that would die of natural attrition in the wild).

But most of the visitors to the Y.O. are non-hunters who come for the ranch tour or to spend a day or two in the antique-furnished, century-old guest cottages (listed on the National Register of Historic Places). A half-day tour takes visitors through the wildlife areas and includes a large ranch-style lunch in the cowboy mess. The cost is $23 adults, $12 children 6-12. Overnight stays cost around $75-85 for double accommodations, depending on the cottage, including three meals a day. Facilities include horse stables, swimming pool, guest lodge (with liquor, wine, and beer), tennis court, and a hot tub.

On Memorial Day weekend in late May the ranch hosts the three-day **Y.O. Ranch Longhorn Cattle Drive** across the ranch. Besides herding longhorn, activities include campfire entertainment and chuckwagon cook-outs. The cost is $175 per person if you bring your own horse, additional fees if you have to rent one.

For more information, contact the Y.O. Ranch (tel. 512-640-3222), Mountain Home, TX 78058. To get to the ranch, take I-10 west from Kerrville to Mountain Home (18 miles), then State 41 south another 14 miles till you see the Y.O. sign.

Accommodations

The **Inn of the Hills River Resort** (tel. 512-895-5000), 1001 Junction Hwy. (State 27), has basic rooms for $48 s, $60 d, plus more expensive rooms with a river view. The **Sands Motel** (tel. 896-5000) on State 27 and the **Save Inn Motel**

(tel. 896-8200) on State 16 each have rooms for $25-40. Also on State 16 is the **Sunday House Motor Inn** (tel. 896-1313), which features rooms for $56-66 s, $58-88 d.

The **Y.O. Ranch Hilton** (tel. 512-257-4440), is Kerrville's poshest digs and has a hunting lodge atmosphere. September through March rooms are $55-65 s, $65-75 d. The rest of the year, add $10 to all rates.

RV Parks And Camping

Kerrville KOA (tel. 512-895-1665) on FM 1338 a half mile south of I-10 (exit 501) has full hookups for $10.50-12 per couple per night. **AmeriCamp Leisure Resort** (tel. 896-6052) is a half mile west of the State 16 and I-10 junction on Benson Rd. and costs $8 for tentsites, $13 for full hookups. **The Woods of Texas** (tel. 257-6110), three miles north of I-10 on State 16, is surrounded by 45 wooded acres and has full hookups for $10-13 a night.

Tent and RV camping is also permitted at Kerrville-Schreiner State Park (see below).

Food

Beyond the fast-food chains crowding the State 27 and 16 junction, there isn't a huge selection of places to eat. **Annemarie's** (tel. 512-257-8282) at 2124 Sidney Baker (State 16) offers various schnitzels and sausage platters, as well as American standbys like steak and fried chicken. Open daily for breakfast, lunch, and dinner. More downhome cooking is available at **Joe's Jefferson Street Cafe** (tel. 257-2929), housed in a 100-year-old building at 1001 Jefferson Street. The menu includes homemade breads and pastries, chicken-fried steak, seafood, and steaks. **Bill's Barbecue** (tel. 895-5733) at 1909 Junction Hwy., (State 27), serves brisket, links, ribs, chicken, and, on occasion, *cabrito*. Open Tues.-Sat. 11-3 (or until the meat runs out). East a few blocks on Junction Hwy. is the **Acapulco Restaurant** (tel. 895-2232), which, despite its name, serves border food like *carne guisada, tacos al carbon,* and *chalupas*. Open daily for lunch and dinner.

Events

May-June: The **Kerrville Folk Festival** is an 18-day event (live music every day and night) from late May to early June that's been held annually for 20 years. "Folk" in this case means just about any original music performed at below 120 decibels. A more appropriate name might be "Kerrville Songwriting Festival" since it not only showcases the best Texas songwriting talent but offers songwriting workshops. The 1989 lineup included Lyle Lovett, Michelle Shocked, Nanci Griffith, Shawn Phillips, Gary P. Nunn, Carolyn Hester, Peter Yarrow, Robert Earl Keen, Jr., and many more. The festival is held at Quiet Valley Ranch, nine miles south of Kerrville on State 16. Advance single-day tickets cost $8 weekdays, $10 Sat.-Sun. (add $2 if bought at the door) and multiple-day tickets range from $24 for three days to $125 for all 18 days. Camping is free for multiple-day ticket holders, $3 a day for others.

The **Texas State Arts and Crafts Fair** runs concurrently with the Folk Festival, usually for four days over the Memorial Day weekend in late May. The number of exhibitors at this fair is limited to 250 and they're carefully selected for quality. In addition to the exhibits, there are also performances of music and cowboy poetry. The fair is held on the Schreiner College campus. Tickets are $6 a day adults, $3.50 children 6-12. Two-day and four-day passes are $10/6 and $16/7 respectively. For more information, contact TACF, Box 1527, Kerrville, TX 78209.

As if there weren't enough events in May already, the Y.O. Ranch hosts a three-day longhorn commemorative cattle drive. See "Y.O. Ranch" for details.

September: Jimmie Rodgers, the "Blue Yodeler," was born in Mississippi in 1897, contracted tuberculosis in 1924 while working on southern railroads, and was forced to take up another line of work. He began performing, became a recording star in 1927, and moved to Kerrville in 1929 in hopes that the clear air and mild climate would mitigate the TB. A white singer who learned to sing the blues from black railway workers, he forged his own style of country blues by adding a yodeling technique to the melodic lines. He continued to perform in Texas and had his own radio show in San Antonio, but he died in a New York hotel room in 1933 after attending a recording session. In his memory, Kerrville holds a **Jimmie Rodgers Jubilee** during the third weekend in September. Blue yodelers from around the region meet at the jubilee for performance competitions, which are held at **Schreiner College**. Rodgers sang a lot of hobo songs, so on Saturday there's a hobo stew cook-off. For information on upcoming jubilees, contact the Kerrville Chamber of Commerce (tel. 512-896-1155), 1200 Sidney Baker (State 16), Kerrville, TX 78209.

Kerrville-Schreiner State Park

This 517-acre facility begins 2.5 miles south of town on State 173 and runs along the Guadalupe River. There are facilities for swimming, boating, fishing, picnicking, and camping, as well as hiking trails with scenic views. Tent/camper sites with water only are $6 a night on weekends, $4 on weekdays; RV/camper sites with w/e are $9/11, and RV sites with full hookups are $10/12. There are also 23 screened shelters for $15/16 a night. Contact the Superintendent (tel. 512-257-5392), Kerrville-Schreiner State Park, 2385 Bandera Hwy., Kerrville, TX 78208.

COMFORT

German immigrants founded Comfort (named because it was the first "comfortable" spot they came to after a hard journey from New Braunfels) in 1854. Like many European immigrants, they had fled political and religious persecution in the Old World, but unlike other German groups who came to Texas, the Comfort settlers weren't particularly religious (not a single church was built in Comfort for 40 years after its founding). They also held strong pro-Union and antislavery views, a stance that brought them Confederate persecution.

Today, Comfort remains a small, unincorporated town of around 1,500. Ten blocks of pre-1900 buildings in the downtown area have been listed on the National Register of Historic Places. Most are in the characteristic Central Texas style—creamy limestone cubes. A few are wooden Victorians. The chamber of commerce office (tel. 995-3131) at 7th and High distributes a free *Tour Through Comfort History* booklet that details the location and history of structures within the Comfort Historic District.

If you're traveling the San Antonio-Kerrville-Frio Canyon loop, you'll have to make an 18-mile detour east on State 27 from Kerrville to find the little town of Comfort.

Truer Der Union Monument

A simple obelisk on High St. between 3rd and 4th,

erected in 1865, commemorates 68 local Union sympathizers who were assaulted by Confederate troops during the Civil War. Persecuted for refusing to sign a Confederate oath of allegiance, these men, mostly Germans, attempted to flee to Mexico in 1862. While camped on the Nueces River near Brackettville, only about 35 miles from the Rio Grande, a Confederate cavalry unit caught up with them. Nineteen were killed in the ensuing battle, 15 were captured and later executed, and the remainder made it to Mexico or back to the Comfort vicinity. Comfort residents later gathered the remains of the slain (who were left unburied) and interred them in a community grave beneath the 1865 "True to the Union" marker.

Ingenhuett Store

Built in 1867, this is one of the oldest continuously operating general stores in the state, run by the same German-American family for four generations. They carry everything from work clothes to parts for a 1920 Lavelle cream separator, fresh meat, and single bolts or nails. At 830 High Street.

Antiques

Several antique shops line High St. and 7th St. off High. One of the better selections is at **Comfort Common,** 818 High, which is on the bottom floor of the restored 1880 Faust Hotel (now a bed and breakfast). Perfect for the toy town of Comfort is the **Little People Car Co.** (tel. 512-995-2905) on High near 6th Street. Housed in a former blacksmith shop, this father-and-son enterprise rebuilds antique pedal cars, the kind that were a popular children's toy in the '20s and '30s. They also make all-new pedal cars based on the same specifications of the classic models. They're the only company in the country that still manufactures and restores the little cars, most of which are bought by collectors. An average car costs $300-400, highly collectible restored models (e.g., a 1928 Cadillac) much higher.

Accommodations And Food

The **bed and breakfast** above the Comfort Common (tel. 512-995-3030) has three suites that are around $43-53 a night for two persons, including coupons for breakfast at nearby **Christine's** restaurant. Additional guests are charged $12 a night, and there's a discount for stays of two or more consecutive nights. The Comfort Common staff can also arrange B&B stays in local homes for $25-40 a night.

Christine's serves tasty omelets and apple crêpes. The new beer garden attached features German and Tex-Mex dishes (including combinations thereof), as well as German and French pastries. Open Tues.-Sat. for breakfast and dinner. Also good is the **Old Post Office Café,** a lunch spot next door to Comfort Common. The owner, a food columnist for the *San Antonio Express-News,* has compiled a short but imaginative menu (along with daily specials) that includes items like chicken-and-new-potato salad in Dijon dressing and apple-raisin-sour cream pie. Open Thurs.-Sat. 11-4, Sun. 11:30-4.

FREDERICKSBURG

The Society for the Protection of German Immigrants in Texas founded their second colony here in 1846, a year after the founding of New Braunfels. Baron Ottfried Hans von Meusebach (who dropped his title and changed his name to John O. Meusebach the day he sailed for Texas) led 120 Germans to this spot in the middle of Comanche territory and named it for Prince Frederick of Prussia. Meusebach was able to negotiate a treaty that allowed the colonists to stay (this treaty earned the distinction of being the only agreement between Indians and whites in Texas never to be violated by either side). And like many South Central Texas colonies, the citizens of Fredericksburg and surrounding Gillespie County voted overwhelmingly against Texas secession from the Union prior to the Civil War.

Many of the descendants of the first settlers still live in Fredericksburg. Some of the older generation speak German as a first language (one town church still holds services in German), and as in New Braunfels there are occasional German festivals. The downtown architecture hasn't changed much since the turn of the century, and it shows its German heritage in mansard roofs, *fachwerk* (half-wooden) walls, and lacy storefronts. On weekends, Main St. is filled with daytrippers from Austin and San Antonio (it's more or less equidistant between the two), so if you want to avoid the crowds, it's best to visit Fredericksburg on a weekday (certain attractions are closed on weekdays, however).

Museums
The **Vereins Kirche Museum** (tel. 512-997-3832) is off W. Main in the old town square, opposite the County Courthouse. Vereins Kirche, German for "People's Church," was the first public building erected in the new colony. The current structure is a 1936 replica that was built for the Texas Centennial. It now houses the Gillespie County Archives as well as a small historical collection of photos, documents, and other local artifacts. Open Mon.-Fri. 10-4; admission is 50 cents per person over 12.

The **Pioneer Museum Complex** (tel. 512-887-9394), 309 W. Main, is a collection of 19th-century structures with period furnishings, including the 1849 Kammlah House, the 1870s Fassel House, the 1855 First Methodist Church, a barn, smokehouse, log cabin, and a "Sunday house." Farmers built one-room Sunday houses with sleeping lofts in town so that when they came in on Sundays for church and shopping, they'd have a place to stay. Open May 1-Labor Day, Mon.-Sat. 10-5, Sun. 1-5; the rest of the year, Sat. 10-5, Sun. 1-5.

World War II buffs may want to visit **Admiral Nimitz State Historical Park and Museum of the Pacific War** (tel. 997-4379) at 340 E. Main. Nimitz was born in Fredericksburg of German parents in 1885. His grandfather built the Steamboat Hotel which now houses the museum in the 1850s. Exhibits chronicle events in the war's Pacific theater as well as the life and naval career of the admiral. Behind the former hotel is the Garden of Peace, a gift from the Japanese government, which contains replicas of Admiral Togo's office and teahouse. Two blocks east is the History Walk of the Pacific, a four-acre outdoor exhibit of war machinery used in Pacific battles. Open daily 8-5; admission $3 adults, $1.50 children 6-12, free for seniors and children under six.

Accommodations
Bed And Breakfast: Fredericksburg claims to have been the first town in Texas to establish B&B-type lodging. **Bed And Breakfast Of Fredericksburg** (tel. 512-997-4712, 307 W. Main, Fredericksburg, TX 78624) now has a list of nearly 20 private homes that take guests at rates from $30 to $100 a night. Three will take bookings directly: **Country Cottage Inn** (tel. 997-8549), across from the Nimitz Park on Main St., is housed in the town's first two-story stone resi-

dence (1850). **Baron's Creek Inn** (tel. 997-9398, 110 E. Creek, Fredericksburg, TX 78624)) is a 1911 German house with a grape arbor and windmill.

Nine miles northeast of town off FM 1631 is the quiet, secluded **Landhaus** (tel. 997-4916, 997-9624), an 1887-vintage B&B on 50 acres of land.

Motels: The **Dietzel Motel** (tel. 512-997-3330) is on US 290 at US 87, a mile west of the town center. Adequate rooms are $30 s, $35 d. South of Main St. at 908 S. Adams (State 16) is the **Comfort Inn** (tel. 997-9811), which has rooms for $49 s, $54 d. At 501 E. Main is the **Best Western Sunday House Inn** (tel. 997-4333), the biggest place in town with rooms for $48 s, $58 d. All three motels have swimming pools.

Hostel: The AYH-sponsored **Hill Country Home Hostel** (tel. 512-644-2419, Peach and Loring streets) is in Stonewall, 16 miles east of Fredericksburg on US 290. Member rates are $7.25 a night. There are only eight beds, so be sure to make reservations well in advance.

Camping

At **Lady Bird Johnson Municipal Park** (tel. 512-997-4202, three miles southwest on State 16) on the Pedernales River (pronounced Purd-NAL-lez), tent/camper sites with w/e are $5 a night and full hookups are $10. Facilities include boat ramp, bathhouses, fishing, tennis courts, and a nine-hole golf course. Six miles east of town on US 290 is **Madison's Hill Country KOA** (tel. 997-4796), where tentsites are $10, full hookups $13.75. A swimming pool is open in the summer.

Food

Many of the restaurants in Fredericksburg are owned and operated by German-Americans. **Friedhelm's Bavarian Inn** (tel. 512-997-7024), at 905 Main, serves authentic Bavarian-style cuisine (the *jagerschnitzel,* potato dumplings, and imported sauerkraut are tops). Open Tues.-Sun. for lunch and dinner. The **Altdorf Biergarten And Restaurant** (tel. 997-7774), in an 1860 tufa limestone building at No. 301, has German as well as steaks and Tex-Mex. Open Mon.-Sat. for lunch and dinner, Sun. lunch only. An 1850s wagon house at No. 312, **Oma Koock's** (tel. 997-8107), features yet more German food, plus other continental dishes, steak, and seafood.

Dietz Bakery at 218 Main is the oldest bakery in town (established in 1876 at 312 Main, now a bank). Everything in the shop is made fresh daily, including country-style breads and pastries. Across the street at No. 141 is the **Fredericksburg Bakery,** which has been in operation since 1923 (the building was erected in 1889). More delicious breads and pastries, plus ice cream. At either of these bakeries, the best bread selection is early in the morning after they open (8 a.m.); by afternoon, there may not be much left. **Fredericksburg Fudge** at 128 E. Main sells a couple dozen varieties of chocolate concoctions, some from traditional German recipes, some local creations.

Sausage fans should tour **Opa's Smoked Meats** at 410 S. Washington, a third-generation smokehouse with fresh and dried sausages, ham, turkey, bacon, pork and beef jerky, and other smoked meats (open Mon.-Sat.). **Sunday House** at No. 122 is another smokehouse, this one known for its smoked turkey—whole birds, turkey sausage, legs, thighs, wings, and breasts.

Another local favorite is **Rabke's Table Ready Meats** (tel. 512-685-3266), a market and deer-processing facility 13 miles north of town via State 16 (then right at the Eckert Rd. turnoff and four miles along a signed, narrow road). Rabke's offers all the smoked standards including whole smoked turkeys, plus tamales, venison, beef-and-pork sausage, venison of all kinds, and for the health-minded, turkey jerky—a tender, spicy alternative to beef jerky. Open Mon.-Fri. 8 a.m.-5 p.m., Sat. 8 a.m.-noon and 1:30-5 p.m., Sun. 1:30-5 p.m.

Events

April: The **Easter Fires Pageant** is held the night before Easter Sunday at Gillespie Fairgrounds. A 600-plus cast recreates the history of Fredericksburg's founding and the signing of the peace treaty with the Comanches. During the mid-1800s, parents told their children that the Indian fires burning in the hills were set by the Easter Bunny for boiling Easter eggs. Call the Fredericksburg Chamber of Commerce (tel. 512-997-6523) for information.

June: During the summer, Fredericksburg is awash in peaches, since three quarters of the peaches sold in Texas are grown here. Local restaurants often feature peach cobbler and fresh peach ice cream. On the third weekend of June, the nearby town of Stonewall (16 miles east on US 290) holds the **Stonewall Peach Jamboree** in the Stonewall Rodeo Arena. Events include a rodeo, parade, fiddler's contest, peach pie-baking contest, country dancing on Friday and Saturday nights, and a chicken-flying contest—a Stonewall chicken holds the world's record in chicken flight: 236 feet.

August: The century-old **Gillespie County Fair** is held at the County Fairgrounds, three miles south of town on State 16. All the usual county fair activities, including livestock and agricultural exhibits, arts and crafts, a carnival, music, and horse races. Usually the fourth weekend in August.

October: The biggest event of the year in this German-Texan town is of course **Oktoberfest.** Activities are centered on the old town square, with German music and dancing, sausage-eating, and lots of beer-drinking. Everyone dresses in variations of traditional German clothing. First weekend in October.

December: At the annual **Kristkindl Market,** open the second weekend of December, the Fredericksburg Shopkeepers Guild offers a special array of locally made Christmas gifts. The Guild also sponsors wandering minstrels and carolers, so the town takes on an especially festive air this weekend. Call (512) 997-8515 for details.

VICINITY OF FREDERICKSBURG

Wineries

Two wineries near Fredericksburg are open to the public. **Bell Mountain/Oberhellmann Vineyards** (tel. 512-685-3297), 15 miles north of town on State 16, makes the best wine in the area; tours and tastings are held every Saturday 10-4 in the Bavarian-style winemaker's house. **Pedernales Vineyards** (tel. 512-997-8326), also off State 16, is open for tours and tasting Mon.-Fri. 9-5, Sat. 9-4 .

Enchanted Rock State Natural Area

Enchanted Rock is a massive, pink granite dome. In geologic terms, it's a batholith, the second largest in the country (70 acres across, 325 feet from its exposed bottom—a much larger portion remains underground) after Stone Mountain in Georgia. As part of the Llano Uplift formed in the Precambrian Era, it's also one of the oldest exposed rock surfaces in the state.

The Enchantment Of The Rock: Amerindian sites at Enchanted Rock show evidence of human habitation (Pre-Archaic and Archaic Indians) 8,000 years ago. Indians from Late Prehistoric and early Historic eras also inhabited the area and evidence shows that Enchanted Rock was sacred to the latter. Legend has it that the Comanches held human sacrifices upon boulders at the base of the rock. An 1883 *New York Mirror* reported that Comanches performed annual ceremonies known as *paynim* here, but failed to describe the ritual. Most anthropologists agree that the Indians held the rock in fearful veneration and believed it to be haunted. At night, the rock fills the air with spooky creaks and groans, probably from the contraction of the granite as it cools. Under a full moon, the surface sparkles and glistens—partly from minute reflections in the granite itself, partly from small *huecos* or rock hollows where water collects. Today, New Agers occasionally gather at Enchanted Rock on full-moon nights, believing it to be a source of spiritual power.

The park is listed as an "archaeological district" on the National Register of Historic Places.

Flora and Fauna: Around the base of the dome run two creeks, Sandy and Walnut Spring. Some of the park's vegetation is typical of the Edwards Plateau—live oak, mesquite, Texas persimmon, Mexican buckeye, prickly pear, and various grasses. Other species that aren't usually found in the Hill Country grow well here, such as blackjack oak, hickory, and post oak. The native animals are more typically Hill Country—jack rabbits, wild turkey, armadillos, and white-tailed deer.

Facilities: A four-mile loop trail winds through the four major rock outcroppings in the 1,643-acre park, and one moderately difficult trail leads to the dome's crest (nice view). Rock climbing and rappelling are permitted and Enchanted Rock is one of the country's great challenges.

Walk-in tentsites with water are available for $6 a night on weekdays, $8 on weekends, and flush toilets and showers are available. Primitive sites without water are $4/6. No RVs. The park entry fee is $3 per vehicle, $1 for pedestrians or cyclists. For further information or campsite reservations, contact the Superintendent (tel. 512-247-3903), Enchanted Rock State Natural Area, Rte. 4, Box 170, Fredericksburg, TX 78624.

Getting There: Enchanted Rock is 18 miles north of Fredericksburg on RR 965.

Luckenbach

In the song that made this little town famous, Waylon Jennings and Willie Nelson sang "... in Luckenbach, Texas, ain't nobody feelin' no pain." With a population optimistically set at 25, there's hardly anyone here to feel anything. Before Waylon and Willie's song put Luckenbach on the map in the '70s (bringing country music pilgrims from all over who wanted to say they'd been here), it was just a place that Austinians knew about. The **Luckenbach Dance Hall** (a ramshackle 1880 building that also serves as the town's post office and general store) occasionally holds a Saturday night dance, and on the first Saturday of October there's a ladies-only chili cook-off.

The late owner of the dance hall-general store-post office was humorist Hondo Crouch, who was really the main draw in town. There's a bust of Hondo in front of the store. A small bar in back of the store/post office sells beer; regulars come here to play dominoes. When the weather s decent, there are usually a couple of guitar-pickers out back playing music and sipping longnecks under the shady oaks. A few steps away are a woodworking studio and, on weekends, Big Daddy's Bar-B-Q.

Getting There: It's easy to drive right past Luckenbach without knowing it, since souvenir-seekers perpetually steal the city limits signs on either side of town. From Fredericksburg, go east on US 290 (toward Austin) about six miles to FM 1376, then south another 4.5 miles to Luckenbach. Take the second left posted "Luckenbach Road." Coming from the north along FM 1376, take the first signposted right.

FRIO CANYON

Frio Canyon is a beautiful stretch of river valley and small canyons along the Frio River between Leakey to the north and Concan to the south. The river runs clear and cold year-round (*frio* is Spanish for "cold") and is lined with cypress, pecan, live oak, cedar, walnut, wild cherry, piñon, and mountain laurel. Some areas also have bigtooth maple and sycamore, which are a major tourist attraction in the late fall as the leaves turn color. State 83 parallels the river and you'll find a dozen or more camps and lodges between the highway and the river, which is popular for fishing and tubing. About 15 miles east of the Frio is the equally

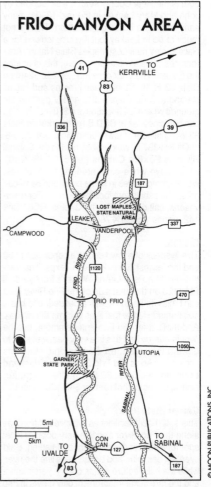

beautiful Sabinal River, which runs along the same north-south axis. The drive between the two rivers on FM 337 (and on the same road farther west to a third river, the Nueces) is one of the most scenic in the state, as it winds gently through high limestone cliffs and spare forests of piñon, madrone, and oak.

Leakey

Pronounced LAY-key, this small community (pop.

500) is the Real County seat. It was founded by John and Mary Leakey in the mid-1800s; many early limestone buildings still stand. There's not much to do in Leakey, but if you're looking for a place to stay near Lost Maples State Natural Area (besides the state campgrounds), this is among the closest. The **Welcome Inn** (tel. 232-5246) on State 83 at 7th St. has motel rooms and cabins starting at $30. There's also an RV park on the grounds where full hookups are $10 a night. You can buy groceries at **D&D Supermarket** on State 83 in the middle of town; open Mon.-Sat. 7:30-6.

Off FM 337 in Vanderpool, next to the Sabinal River, is **Foxfire Cabins** (tel. 512-966-2200), which have white-pine interiors, full kitchens, woodburning stoves in some units, and barbecue grills. The cabins rent for $49-69 a day. For reservations, call or write Foxfire Cabins, HC01 Box 142, Vanderpool, TX 78885.

Rio Frio

This flyspeck of a town sports a population of 50 and the largest live oak tree in Texas. The centuries-old tree is in LeAnn Walker's front yard off FM 1120 on the east side of the Frio River (you can't miss it). LeAnn keeps a pet deer and has a dog named Hunter that likes to climb the big oak. And that's it for Rio Frio entertainment; but the river is nearby and this is a very peaceful spot to unwind that even few San Antonio residents know of. LeAnn's **Rio Frio Bed & Breakfast and Lodging** (tel. 512-232-6633) offers eight furnished cottages that rent for $45-120 a night.

Garner State Park

This 1,420-acre facility has 1.5 miles of frontage along the Frio River and is a very popular local spot for swimming, canoeing, and fishing. Bald cypress, oak, elm, and pecan trees line the river, while the hills feature cedar, cherry, persimmon, and the rare Texas madrone (it only grows in Frio Canyon, Big Bend, and the Guadalupe Mountains). There are a few short hiking trails, plus a miniature golf course, paddleboat rentals, and a dance terrace. The dance terrace is the social center for Frio Canyon summers, since it has a free jukebox stocked with Johnny Cash, George Strait, and Jimmie Rodgers records. In May, there's a "dance reunion" with live music. Summers can get crowded, especially on weekends.

Facilities: Garner offers every type of overnight facility in the state park system except for a hotel: campsites with water only ($7 weekdays, $9 weekends), with w/e ($10/12), with full hookups ($11/14), screened shelters ($15/18), and cabins ($35 for two persons, plus $5 each additional adult, $2 each additional child 6-12). For a summer cabin, reserve early (up to 90 days in advance).

For further information or reservations, contact the Superintendent (tel. 512-232-6132), Garner State Park, Concan, TX 78838.

Getting There: The park is a mile south of the US 83 and FM 1050 junction, nine miles south of Leakey.

Concan

Outside of the Lost Maples and Garner state parks, this is the prettiest part of Frio Canyon. River vistas in the Concan area are particularly stunning, with the crystal-clear Frio River winding around smooth-topped boulders banked by tall stands of pecan and oak. As with Garner State Park, summer is the local season and lodging may be booked out on weekends then.

Nobody knows for sure how the town got its name but everyone likes to speculate. At one time it was spelled Con Can, but an 1885 postmaster changed it to one word. "Concan" or "Con Can" may have been a Mexican game of chance played by Mexicans in tent camps on the banks of the Frio—that's the story that gets reported the most (but no one today knows anything about the game).

Accommodations: Among the better places off US 83 in Concan (there are several to choose from) is **Yeargan's River Bend Camp** (tel. 512-232-6616). It's open year-round (not all Frio Canyon lodges are) and offers several different kinds of overnight facilities with rates that depend on the number of persons and time of year. Motel rooms with kitchenettes range from $30 (one to four persons, Jan. 1-March 1) to $71 (10 persons, May 1-Oct. 1). Cottages range from $30 (one to four persons, Jan. 1-March 1) to $50 (six persons, May 1-Oct. 1). Camping rates vary from $9 for tents or RVs in the "bargain season" (Jan. 1-March 1) to $14 for a screened shelter in the "regular season" (May 1-Oct. 1). Camping rates are fairly reasonable for small groups, since one fee admits two vehicles and up to eight persons. Rates in the "low season" (March 1-May 1 and Oct. 1-Jan. 1, excluding holidays) are in between the regular and bargain seasons.

Frio River, Concan

A longtime Texas favorite among the Concan places is **Neal's Lodges** (tel. 512-232-6118), which was established in 1926. Neal's features 60 cabins, nine RV hookups, and tentsites on the river, plus a grocery store, restaurant, and laundromat. The cabins are $38-150 a day per four persons, depending on the cabin; all but four have kitchenettes. All have either "refrigerated air" (air conditioning) or evaporative coolers. Rates are 30-40% lower in the winter. RV hookups are $16.50 a night for one to four persons, plus $3 for each additional person. There are 25-30 campsites on the river (depending on tent size!); rates are $14.50 per vehicle with up to four persons, $3 each additional person. No reservations are taken for campsites.

Neal's rents inner tubes for river floating ($3 a day, $2 for shuttle service up the river), and also leads horseback trail rides for $10 a person and sunset hayrides for $3 a person. For further information or cabin reservations, contact Neal's Lodges, Box 165, Concan, TX 78838.

Getting There: Concan is 17 miles south of Leakey on US 83.

UTOPIA

As you enter town on US 83 a sign reads "Welcome to Utopia—Let's Keep It Nice." You might think the town was named for the mild climate, clean air, and clean water (it's on the banks of the Sabinal River and is the location of the Utopia Spring Water plant), but it could have been named by frontier circuit preachers who found it a heavenly place to hold camp meetings and save souls. Utopia has a population of only 360 but there are seven churches in town. It recently gained temporary national recognition after a famous hamburger chain filmed one of its television commercials here.

Specialty Shops
Huajillo honey is a local specialty and there's no better place to buy a jar than the **Utopia Honey House** on FM 187, which is the main drag running through town. The Honey House is also the official dispenser of tourist information for Utopia and vicinity. **Utopia Organic Gardening** on the same road sells fruits and vegetables grown without the use of chemical pesticides or fertilizers (how Utopian!).

Accommodations
Two miles south of town on FM 187 is the turnoff for **Utopia On The River** (tel. 512-966-2444), a large inn built of native stone and cedar. Each of the 12 rooms has a microwave and refrigerator. In back of the inn are a sauna, small pool, and jacuzzi, plus a 2.5-mile trail along the Sabinal. A large cypress near the river is an estimated 750-800 years old. The proprietors allow deer and turkey hunting on the 650-acre property (guests only). Room rates are $59 s, $69 d including a full country breakfast of pancakes, sausage, eggs, bacon, and hashbrowns.

The **Bluebird Bed & Breakfast Inn** (tel. 512-966-3525 or 966-2320), 10 miles west of Utopia on FM 1050, has stone and wood cabins for $65 a night, including a full breakfast.

Off FM 187, the family-owned **Good Shepherd Campground** (tel. 966-2325 or 966-2402, Box 457, Utopia, TX 78884) offers RV sites with full hookups ($15), and apartments ($35). All rates are discounted for stays of two or more nights.

Food

There are a couple of restaurants in the center of town on FM 187. The **Lost Maples Inn** serves sandwiches and Tex-Mex; the **Paradise Café** has barbecue.

Recreation

Inner tubes for floating the Sabinal can be rented at the Good Shepherd Campground (see "Accommodations" above) for $2 a day. They also rent canoes for $4 an hour or $10 a day (10% off if you rent two canoes, 20% off for four canoes).

Another place that rents tubes is **Conrad's Trading Post** at 544 Main (FM 187). About three miles north of Utopia off FM 187 to the east is **Wagon Wheel Riding Stable** (tel. 512-966-3678), which rents out horses for $10 an hour.

Getting There

Utopia is at the junction of FM 187 and FM 1050. From Leakey, it's 24 miles via US 83 south and FM 1050 east. You could also come here directly from Bandera by following FM 470 west (off State 16) through Tarpley for 29 miles till it terminates at FM 187; then south on FM 197 two miles to Utopia.

LOST MAPLES STATE NATURAL AREA

The hundreds of "lost maples" here are leftovers from an earlier geologic era (the Pleistocene Ice Age) when the region was wetter and cooler. High canyon walls along the Sabinal River continue to protect the park's flora from dry winds and high summer temperatures. Other trees in the canyon bottoms include sycamore, various oaks, pecan, hackberry, and walnut. Even more rare than the bigtooth maples are American smoke tree, Canada moonseed, and witch hazel, all of which are hundreds of miles from their native habitats. On the densely wooded upper slopes

you'll find lacey, Texas, and live oak, Texas ash, and Ashe juniper. Still higher are upland plateaus with mostly live oak and Texas madrone.

Notable birdlife includes canyon wrens, golden-cheeked warblers, black-capped vireos, the green kingfisher, and in the winter, golden and bald eagles. The 2,208-acre park is also home to three unique amphibians—the rare barking frog, the Texas salamander, and the Texas cliff frog. Animals living in the park include white-tailed deer, armadillo, gray fox, Russian boar, javelina, bobcat, opossum, raccoon, and mountain lion.

Fall Color Changes: The maples usually hit their peak colors (brilliant red, yellow, and orange) sometime during the last two weeks of October and the first two weeks of November. During this four-week period, it gets quite crowded Sat. and Sunday; if you can, visit the park during the week instead. The timing and brilliance of the color depends on environmental factors such as rainfall and temperature over the previous months. The park maintains a "Maple Hotline" (800-792-1112, in Texas only) after Oct. 1 that offers a recorded color forecast to help color-crazy visitors time their visits.

Trails: The park has 10.5 miles of hiking trails. Contour maps are available free from the park headquarters (elevations are between 1,500 and 2,400 feet). The most popular hike is the easy Maple Trail (half a mile roundtrip), which starts at the designated picnic area and leads along the Sabinal River through stands of maple, pecan, sycamore, and walnut. If you cross the river (there are stones and shallow places), you can connect with the 4.2-mile (one way) **East Trail**. This trail proceeds north along the river, then crosses west to Primitive Camping Area A at mile 1.5, then down along a steep ridge to an overlook, and along Can Creek back to the overflow parking lot near the visitor center. The **West Trail,** a large, 3.4-mile half loop between the top of Can Creek and one of the park residences, passes through steep Mystic Canyon. There are three primitive camping areas along this trail, and two more on a 1.8-mile side loop northwest of the trail.

Facilities: The visitor center features interpretive exhibits on local natural and cultural history and is open daily 8:30-5. The main campground has drive-in sites with water only, $6 a night on weekdays, $8 on weekends. There are also eight primitive camping areas throughout the park near hiking trails; these are $4/6 a night. As at all state parks, there's a $3 entry fee per vehicle, $1 for pedestrians or cyclists. For further information, contact the Superintendent (tel. 512-966-3413), Lost Maples State Natural Area, HC01, Box 156, Vanderpool, TX 78885.

Getting There: The park entrance is about four miles north of Vanderpool off FM 187. Vanderpool is 17 miles east of Leakey on FM 337.

SAN ANTONIO

INTRODUCTION

San Antonio is every Texan's favorite town. It's also quite popular with out-of-state tourists, over a third of whom make it to Alamo City during their Texas travels (more than any other place in the state). Year in and year out San Antonio tops the list in tourist surveys of best places to visit in Texas, along with four of the state's top-10 attractions—the Alamo, the River Walk, the San Antonio missions, and Sea World.

If you're the type of traveler who usually avoids hordes of tourists, rest assured that this city of nearly a million (10th-largest city in the U.S.) absorbs them rather well. With the relaxed attitude of the locals, it's not always easy to tell who's on vacation and who's not.

What makes San Antonio so popular? To be sure, the Alamo is an American pilgrimage point, like the Grand Canyon and the Empire State Building. But most folks find the Alamo a rather puny monument when sized up against their imagination—you'd think word would get around. It's more likely the strong historical and cultural appeal, which led Will Rogers to call San Antonio "one of four unique cities in America" (Boston, New Orleans, and San Francisco were the other three). First and foremost, it's a "Texican" town, a bicultural blend of Old World and New World and the largest city in the U.S. with a Hispanic majority. It's also one of the state's most progressive cities. Things are relaxed; while even in laid-back Fort Worth just about every man walking around downtown on a midweek afternoon is wearing a tie, in San Antonio you're more likely to see *guayaberas,* short-sleeved, open-at-the-neck shirts worn in tropical capitals from Mexico City to Manila. Long lunch breaks are common, a custom dating to the pre-air-conditioning era when summer temperatures and humidity mandated a two-hour siesta.

The city's cultural keynote is not the stereotypical *mañana* attitude sometimes associated with Mexico, but rather a social ethic in which people are encouraged to live and work with a festive outlook. It's hard not to be festive in a city that holds fiestas or celebrations of some sort every month of the year. Even going to church can be an occasion for exuberance, if you happen to be attending Mission San José's mariachi mass on Sunday. It's a city that looks as festive as it acts: flower gardens are everywhere, from the barrios of the West Side to the mansions of Alamo Heights. Most of the buildings downtown were built before 1930, many before 1900, which adds to the overall visual romanticism.

A recent testimony to the city's allure came from the U.S. Conference of Mayors, who, in 1988, named San Antonio the most livable city in America with a population over 100,000. City leaders are building on favorable press like this by attempting to make the city even more attractive to visitors. In 1989, resident voters gave the city permission to build the $160 million Alamodome (financed by a new half-cent VIA Metropolitan Transit tax) near the current convention center and arena. The 65,000-seat facility is expected to attract major conventions (San Antonio is already one of the nation's top convention towns), sports events, and performances after its projected completion date of February 1993.

Land

San Antone (some locals hate the term "San Antone," but like the nickname "Frisco" for San Francisco, its use predates the lives of current residents—lots of Texans pronounce it "San 'Tone") is uniquely positioned between the Edwards Plateau to the north and the brush country of the Coastal Plains to the south. Hence, it's a mixture of hilly and flat (mostly the latter). The San Antonio River bisects the city along a north-south axis, with a 2.5-mile horseshoe-shaped section that runs through six downtown blocks (developed as the Paseo del Rio or River Walk). Other notable waterways include San Pedro and Salado creeks, both of which feed into the river.

Climate
With an average relative humidity of 66% (as high as 87% on July mornings) and an average temperature of 60° F, the city borders on subtropical. Optimum months weatherwise are October-Novermber and March through early June. June through Sept. are hot and muggy, and December-January can be on the cool side (with maybe a week's worth of intermittent freezing weather). Average annual precipitation is 29 inches, with the most frequent rains in May, June, and Sept. (over three inches, on average, in each of these months). Overall, the city has clear skies 60% of the time (from 48% in January to 75% in July).

History
The Founding Of The Alamo: Dominga Teran de los Rios, governor of the Spanish colonial province of Texas, arrived at what's now south San Antonio in 1691 and encountered a hospitable group of Coahuiltecan Indians. They were living on the banks of a river they called "drunken old man going home at night" (named for its curves). The date happened to be Saint Anthony's Day, so the governor named the spot San Antonio. Word spread that the Coahuiltecans at San Antonio were "friendly" (easily dominated), and in 1718 a Franciscan priest established a mission called San Antonio de Valero (Valero was the viceroy of Mexico at the time). A military contingent founded a presidio at San Antonio that same year and by 1731 there was a civilian settlement called Villa de Bexar. In order to boost the non-Indian population at Villa de Bexar, Spain allowed 55 colonists to im-

SELECTED MONTHLY AVERAGE MAXIMUM/MINIMUM TEMPERATURES		
Month	**Max. (°F)**	**Min. (°F)**
Jan.	62	42
March	72	50
May	85	65
July	94	74
Sept.	89	69
Nov.	70	49

migrate here from North Africa's Canary Islands (whose modern-day descendants still proudly declare their roots). Four other missions were established in the intervening years—San José, Concepción, San Juan, and Espada.

By 1794, the heathen-converting function of the missions had become less important to the Spaniards as San Antonio grew and was made the capital of Spanish Texas. They were gradually secularized, beginning with San Antonio de Valero. By 1801, Misión San Antonio had been turned into a garrison for a cavalry unit from Alamo de Parras in northern Mexico. The shortened name for the place was Alamo ("cottonwood" in Spanish), which eventually became applied to the garrison as well.

Revolution And Resettlement: Following the Mexican Revolution of 1821, San Antonio became part of the Republic of Mexico. That same year, Stephen F. Austin came to the war-torn town and negotiated a land grant from Mexico which allowed him to bring 300 Anglo-American colonists into Texas. By 1836, San Antonio had an Anglo population of 3,500. When General An-

Nacho Guarache   BY LEO GARZA

SAN ANTONIO

© MOON PUBLICATIONS, INC.

tonio López de Santa Anna seized the Mexican presidency and abolished the 1824 Mexican constitution, many Texans (both Anglos and Hispanics) refused to recognize his dictatorship. This led to the famous Battle of the Alamo in March 1836 in which every Texan defender was killed. In the midst of the Alamo siege, Texas leaders declared independence from Mexico, which they later won at the Battle of San Jacinto.

Immediately following the Alamo siege, the city was more or less abandoned by non-Hispanics until German settlers began arriving in the 1840s. They established the historic King William district (named for King Wilhelm of Prussia) and erected trilingual street signs in German, English, and

Spanish. After the Republic of Texas was annexed to the U.S. in 1845, other groups began moving to San Antonio; the population had grown from 800 to 8,000 by 1860. The Civil War stifled growth again, but in the 1870s the city developed into a ranching center as it became the starting point for the Chisholm Trail cattle drives to Kansas. The railroad arrived in 1877 and within 10 years the city had telephones and electricity.

Economy
San Antonio's military heritage began with the arrival of Spanish conquistadors in 1718 and continued with the occupation of the missions by various Spanish, Mexican, and Texan army units.

DOWNTOWN SAN ANTONIO

© MOON PUBLICATIONS, INC.

Because it was the crossroads of important north-south (Chisholm Trail) and east-west (San Antonio-El Paso-Chihuahua Trail) trade routes, it was naturally viewed as a strategic area. Fort Sam Houston was founded in 1876 and is still in business. In 1898, Teddy Roosevelt recruited his Rough Riders (for the war with Spain in Cuba) in San Antonio saloons and outfitted them at Fort Sam. The U.S. Army post was joined by four Air force bases: Brooks and Kelly in 1917, Randolph in 1930, and Lackland in 1941. Needless to say, these five bases comprise one of the linchpins of San Antonio's economy, bringing in billions in federal funds and creating thousands of jobs.

Another linchpin is tourism, since San Antonio is the number-one tourist destination in the num-ber-three state (after New York and California). The fact that the city wants to preserve its share of tourism explains why it's so anxious to create projects like Sea World and the Alamodome. Education is also important, another legacy of the Spanish missions. St. Mary's University (1852), Trinity University (1869), Incarnate Word College (1881), and Our Lady of the Lake College (1911) established the city as an educational center, followed by the University of Texas at San Antonio and eight other institutions of higher learning, including a branch of the University of Mexico, two medical research centers, a theology school, and the largest junior college in the state, San Antonio College. A variety of regional manufacturing interests round out the picture, such as Pace hot sauces (who buy their chiles directly from the *chileros* of Mexico's Jalapa—as in jalapeño), and two Texas beers, Pearl and Lone Star.

Even more so than in the 19th century, the city is a major transportation crossroads. The Chisholm Trail has become I-35, joining Laredo with Kansas City and extending all the way to Duluth, Minnesota, on the banks of Lake Superior. The San Antonio-El Paso Trail has been buried by I-10, which now connects the Atlantic (Jacksonville) and the Pacific (Los Angeles). One of the biggest interstate loops in the country, Loop 410, keeps tractor trailers from plowing through downtown San Antone. Five other U.S. highways converge on the city as well, which makes for some interesting traffic configurations.

SIGHTS

San Antonio Missions National Historical Park

San Antonio is the only city in the U.S. with five Spanish missions within its city limits. All were built along the San Antonio River, establishing a pattern around which the modern city eventually developed. The Alamo (originally Misión San Antonio de Valero) was the first (est. 1718), but is a separate state historic site (see "The Alamo State Historic Site" below). The other four were established as missions between 1720 and 1731, although the stone chapels that stand today were begun in the 1740s and 1750s. Three of the missions, San Juan, Espada, and Concepción, were moved from earlier sites in East Texas because of French and Indian pressures (in East Texas, they attempted to missionize Caddo Indians, who eventually revolted; in San Antonio it was the more docile Coahuiltecans). The fourth, San José, is considered the "queen of the missions" because of its historic success and because it's the most impressive architecturally. All four of the mission chapels are active Roman Catholic parishes which serve the surrounding communities. They're administered cooperatively by the National Park Service, the state of Texas, and the local Catholic archdiocese.

Each of the four missions can be visited along a 5.5-mile Mission Trail that runs south of I-10 from the downtown area. If you start from the Alamo, add another 2.5 miles (follow Alamo St. to S. St. Mary's, which eventually becomes Mission Parkway). All four missions are worth visiting, but

if you're pressed for time, San José is the most extensively restored and the most ornate. The historical park also includes a Spanish dam and aqueduct near the San Juan and Espada missions. These 250-year-old waterworks are still a functioning part of the local irrigation system.

The park facilities are open to the public daily 8-5 Central Standard Time and 9-6 Central Daylight Saving Time. Admission is free, but donations are gratefully accepted in the chapels.

Worship services are held on Sunday mornings and on religious holidays, so these times may not be the best for visits unless you would like to attend a service. For further information, contact the Superintendent (tel. 210-229-5701), San Antonio Missions National Historical Park, 2202 Roosevelt Ave., San Antonio, TX 78210.

Mission Concepción: Established as Misión Nuestra Señora de la Purisima Concepción de Acura in 1731, this is the oldest unrestored stone Catholic church in the country. One reason it's so well preserved is that it was built on bedrock, so the earth's movements have had little effect on building decay. The chapel design includes the typical twin bell towers and cupola, with simple, carved-stone embellishments around the doorway. Some of the original interior frescoes remain. In the front of the chapel is an original *noria* (well). By 1772, the church, *convento* (convent), *labores* (farmlands), and ranch at Mission Concepción were self-sufficient. Between 1794 and 1824, the mission underwent secularization but in 1855 the Catholic Church regained the mission. On the first Sunday in August the mission holds a **parish festival** featuring Latino music, food vendors, and other festivities. The mission is at 807 Mission Rd. at Felisa (tel. 210-532-3158).

Mission San José: Founded in 1720 (two years after the Alamo) by Fray Antonio Margil de Jesus as Misión San José y San Miguel de Aguayo, this important Texas mission settlement was moved along the San Antonio River several times before settling at its present site in 1740. The chapel/sacristy was designed and built between 1768 and 1782 in the Churrigueresque, late Spanish Renaissance style and is considered one of the finest examples of Spanish mission architecture in the United States. When Spain sent Fray Juan Augustín Morfi on a tour of frontier missions in 1777, he reported: "[San José] is in truth the first mission in America, not in point of time, but in point of beauty, plan, and strength, so that there is not a presidio along the entire frontier line that can compare with it."

Today, it is the most well restored of the San Antonio missions and serves as headquarters for the entire historical park. The surrounding compound has been restored so that visitors may view the Indian quarters, granary, mill, kilns, *convento*, and Spanish residence. An *horno*—a small dome-shaped oven made of tufa limestone— stands in the courtyard. The mission-dwellers burned wood inside until the oven was hot, then the coals were raked out, food inserted, and the *horno* sealed until the food was cooked.

The chapel's asymmetrical front features a bell tower on one side and a flat-topped, ventilated facade on the other. In the middle of the lengthy roof behind is a large dome which makes that section of the church taller than the building's entire length. The lavishly sculptured entryway is said to have been carved by descendants of the original artisans at Spain's Alcazar. On the south side of the building (the sacristy) is "Rosa's Window," bordered by stone scrolls and foliage that has made it a San Antonio mission highlight. At least two sto-

Mission San José

ries offer an explanation for the window's name: that the sculptor worked on it for five years while mourning the death of his wife Rosa, or that it was somehow associated with St. Rose's Day.

The Park Service has established several interpretive exhibits in parts of the Indian quarters near the main entrance to the complex, including a six-minute audio-visual presentation on the mission's history. At noon on Sundays, there is mariachi mass at the church. Annual events at Mission San José include El Dia de las Misiónes on August 6, which commemorates the founding of the mission and kicks off the Semana de las Misiónes, a week-long celebration at all five of San Antonio's missions. At 2200 Roosevelt Ave. and Mission Rd. (tel. 210-229-4770).

Mission San Juan: This outpost is thought to have been established at or near the spot that was first claimed as San Antonio by the Spanish in 1691. Originally called Misión San Juan Capistrano (est. 1731), it was smaller than either Concepción or San José. For the first few years it consisted only of a friary and granary. In 1756, a small church was built, which has since been reduced to its foundation; a larger church was started on adjacent grounds in the 1760s (these ruins are also still visible), but was never completed before secularization began in 1792. The current church is actually a former granary that was transformed by the addition of Moorish arches in the early 1900s, when the Catholic diocese regained the parish. Inside and out, the building is quite simple; altars inside display rare Christ and Virgin figures of cornstalk pith.

The *convento* has been made into a small museum with good exhibits on mission archaeology and the Coahuiltecan Indians. Much of San Juan's charm is that it's in a quiet, relatively rural area. A daily mass is performed at 7 p.m. San Juan holds its **parish festival** on the last Sunday in May (Memorial Day weekend), beginning with an outdoor mass. At 9101 Graf Rd. (tel. 210-532-5840).

Mission Espada: The most remote of the five missions, Misión San Francisco de la Espada is still encircled by *labores* (farmlands) owned by descendants of the original mission community. Like San Juan and Concepción, the Espada missionaries had moved from an earlier site in East Texas, in this case the oldest of the three, San Francisco de los Tejas (est. 1690). The original adobe church no longer stands. A larger limestone church was begun in 1756 but was never finished, though the

Mission San Juan

sacristy for this larger structure was completed and became part of the current church in the late 1800s. Double-tiered Moorish arches support three bells over the church's simple stone facade.

The interior is well cared for, and the St. Francis figure at the front is thought to date from the 1780 completion of the original sacristy.

Next to the chapel is a *noria* similar to the one at Mission Concepción. The restored *convento* is closed to the public since it's now the church rectory. The Park Service information center is at the southeast corner of the compound in rooms adjoining the only remaining bastion. Various other walls and ruins encircle the courtyard. Espada's **parish festival** is held in late September or early October. At 10040 Espada Rd. (tel. 210-627-2021).

Espada Aqueduct: Between 1719 and 1740, the Spanish constructed a sophisticated *acequia* system for irrigating cultivated lands around San Antonio. Much of the system is still in use to the south of the city and there are even a few *acequias* or canals remaining in downtown San Antonio. Of the several engineering feats the missionaries accomplished, perhaps the most impressive is the aqueduct they built over Piedras Creek, about a mile and a half northwest of Mission Espada. This arched stone structure has been carrying water over the creek to Espada fields by force of gravity for two and a half centuries, making it the oldest Spanish water system in the country. In 1965 it was declared a national historic landmark and the small **Aqueduct Park,** now a favorite local picnic spot, was laid out next to it.

The Alamo State Historic Site

This big chunk of limestone in the middle of downtown San Antonio has become a national icon,

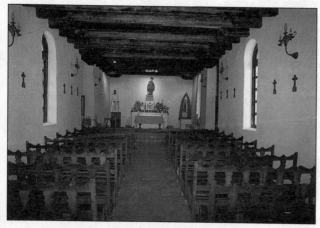

interior of Mission Espada, San Antonio

THE ALAMO

ACEQUIA

MUSEUM AND SOUVENIRS

SHRINE

CALVARY COURTYARD

TO LIBRARY

CONVENT GARDEN

WISHING WELL

ENTRANCE

LONG BARRACK MUSEUM

NOT TO SCALE

© MOON PUBLICATIONS, INC.

symbolic of America's one-time frontier spirit and a willingness to die for independence. How many died here in the Battle of the Alamo is still a matter of debate but the figure on the defenders' side was probably 187 or 188 (including 10 Hispanics), who fought a Mexican force of 5,000, around 1,600 of whom were also slain in the heated battle. Alamo lore is still a sacred subject among a very small group of Texans who haven't yet figured out that Texas is no longer a republic. One fellow has even fueled the fire by publishing the provocatively titled *Forget The Alamo!* which, despite its title, is a perfect example of the subculture.

History: What tends to get lost, even among the site's historical exhibits, is the history of the Alamo as Misión San Antonio de Valero, its original name. Had it not been for the founding of this mission in 1718, the city of San Antonio wouldn't exist. The Spaniards established San Antonio as a halfway point between northern Mexico and their short-lived East Texas missions (the route they

plied became known as El Camino Real, "the Royal Road," which Anglo settlers later called the Old San Antonio Road). The mission started out on the San Antonio River's west bank, at its junction with San Pedro Creek, but was moved upriver to its current site in the 1720s. The chapel made famous by countless postcards was erected in 1744. By the mid-1700s, it was a thriving mission community with *acequia*-irrigated farmlands, a cattle ranch, granary, chapel, and *convento,* as well as blacksmith, carpenter, and textile shops. As the Texas missions began declining in the late 18th century because of problems with migrating Apaches, the Catholic Church secularized Mission San Antonio and distributed the farmlands among the mission Indians. The church then leased the abandoned mission grounds and buildings to a Spanish cavalry unit from northern Mexico's Alamo de Parras in the early 1800s, and the compound gained the nickname "El Alamo."

The famous Alamo fight (p. 273) took place in 1836, after which the Alamo was again abandoned. Beginning in 1845, a succession of other tenants leased the buildings from the Catholic Church, including the U.S. Army (and the Confederate army during the Civil War) and a couple of mercantile interests who used the chapel as a warehouse. The state bought the chapel from the Catholic Church in 1883. In 1903 the Daughters of the Republic of Texas (DRT) bought the "long barracks" (originally a *convento)* and the state turned over the remainder of the property to the DRT shortly thereafter.

Exhibits And Facilities: The heavily restored chapel and long barracks are the only buildings remaining from the original mission compound. The Museum-Souvenir Shop, the DRT Research Library, the walls, and other limestone structures on the grounds are 20th-century additions that have been carefully designed to blend with the original architecture. The grounds are well kept and flower-filled in the spring; behind the chapel you can see the original San Antonio *acequia.*

The modest displays in the chapel itself are mostly oriented around the 1836 battle, including a miniature three-dimensional model of the compound as it looked at that time. The information desk at the front distributes self-guiding tour pamphlets, or you can take one of the free 30-minute tours that leave periodically. In his last visit, the author was glad to see that the DRT had removed the large, tacky painting from the north interior wall which had featured Davy Crockett swinging his flintlock at a mob of Mexican soldiers—the figure's face was unmistakably John Wayne's!

Tourist traffic through the chapel is channeled so that you end up leaving by a rear door to the left, where a path leads directly to the Museum-Souvenir Shop. Unfortunately, this means that many visitors miss the Long Barracks Museum which is well to the left of the exit, against the front wall of the compound. In this latter museum are two automated slide shows, one on the battle, one on the mission's overall history. The remainder of the exhibits are again battle-oriented. In the Museum-Souvenir Shop are exhibits of Sam Houston memorabilia, an early gun collection, and piles of Alamo souvenirs, from imitation coonskin caps to "Remember the Alamo" bumper stickers. And of course a dozen or more versions of Alamo postcards.

Visitors sometimes have trouble finding the Alamo among all the taller buildings which surround it; it's on Alamo St. between E. Houston and E. Crockett, on Alamo Plaza. Admission to the complex is free. Hours are Mon.-Sat. 9-5:30, Sun. 10-5:30. Go just after it opens or just before it closes to avoid the crowds. Sundays are usually less crowded, since fewer conventions are in town that day. For further information, call (210) 225-1391.

SAMA Museums

The **San Antonio Museum Association** operates two museums; paying the admission fee ($4 adults, $2 seniors, $1.75 children 6-12) to either one of them grants the purchaser a 50% discount admission to the other. The hours for each are the same: Mon.-Sat. 10-5 (till 6 June-August), Sun. noon-5. On Tuesdays they're open till 9 and admission is free 3-9.

The Association's **San Antonio Museum of Art** (tel. 210-829-7262) is housed in a former Anheuser Busch brewery at 200 W. Jones, off Broadway, and has only been open since 1983. There are nine galleries total in the tastefully renovated building, four in each of two towers plus one in the hall that connects them. The museum is strong in Latin American art as well as folk art from a variety of cultures. Permanent collections include the excellent pre-Columbian and Spanish Colonial exhibit, which features sculpture and ceramics from the Colima, Nayarit, Jalisco, Olmec, and Mayan cultures. The equally splendid Mexican Folk Art gallery contains 2,500 pieces from the Nelson Rockefeller Collection as well as 2,000-2,500 other pieces collected by SAMA.

Another gallery displays ancient Greco-Roman art, including rare Greek urns and sculpture from the 3rd-5th centuries B.C. The Asian art gallery has a fairly standard collection of ceramics, sculpture, jewelry, and painting, as do the historical American and European galleries. Remaining galleries contain rotating displays of contemporary American art and other traveling exhibits. The museum also hosts various lecture series; SAMA's Friends of Folk Art organization, for example, presents lectures on topics such as "Tradition and Symbolism of Indian Textiles in Guatemala," "Caribbean Folk Art and Festivals," and "Indigenous Arts of Rural India."

The **Witte Museum** (tel. 210-978-8100) in Brackenridge Park (off Broadway) has long been popular among children because some of the exhibits invite visitor participation, with an emphasis on science and natural history. An exhibit called "Texas Wild: Ecology Illustrated" explores the state's ecological diversity. Another exhibit is devoted to dinosaurs that once roamed the Texas plains, while a third chronicles the daily life of the Southwest's Archaic Indians of 8,000 years ago.

Other Museums

The **Marion Koogler McNay Art Museum** (tel. 210-824-5368) is at 6000 N. New Braunfels in the upscale northeast section of the city. A blend of Mediterranean and Southwest architectural styles, the building, courtyard, and gardens of the McNay make up one of the most pleasant art facilities in the Southwest, with 10 galleries and 10,200 square feet of support space in all. Formerly the residence of oil heir Marion McNay, it opened as an art museum in 1954 and houses a variety of collections. The Oppenheimer Collection includes medieval and Gothic wood and stone sculptures, stained glass, tapestries, and panel paintings. In other collections, the emphasis is on modern European and American paintings of the late 19th and early 20th centuries, with works by Monet, Gauguin, Van Gogh, Klee, Degas, Pissarro, Matisse, Renoir, Cezanne, O'Keeffe, and Picasso, as well as the graphic art of Toulouse-Lautrec, Goya, Jasper Johns, Willem de Kooning, and Robert Rauschenberg. The Tobin Collection of Theater Arts displays rare books and sketches on theater architecture, set and costume designs, and stage models.

The McNay also offers a year-round calendar of activities, including receptions, teas, musical performances, lectures, and art classes (as part of the museum's San Antonio Art Institute). Open Tues.-Sat. 9-5, Sun. 2-5; admission is free (donations accepted).

The University of Texas sponsors the **Institute of Texan Cultures** (tel. 210-226-7651) at 801 S. Bowie in HemisFair Park. The Institute is a center for the study of some 25 different cultural groups who have contributed to Texan history. Besides the research facilities, there are several galleries with revolving exhibits, so it's worth revisiting if you've been here before. The "Faces and Places of Texas" film presentation in the Dome Theater offers a good multicultural overview. Occasional special presentations by visiting experts on Texas culture include slide shows and lectures. A gift shop features a wide selection of books on Texana as well as folk crafts. The galleries and gift shop are open Tues.-Sun. 9-5; free admission (parking is $1 a day).

The **Mexican Cultural Institute (Instituto Cultural Mexicano)** (tel. 210-227-0123), also at Hemisfair Plaza, is sponsored by the University of Mexico (see "Universities" below) and is devoted to Mexican history and culture. The galleries host traveling art exhibits, films, lectures, workshops, and concerts. Gallery hours are Mon.-Fri. 9-5:30, Sat.-Sun. noon-6. Free admission.

One of the largest Hispanic art institutes in the country, the **Guadalupe Cultural Arts Center** (tel. 210-271-3151) at 1300 Guadalupe (northwest of downtown), focuses on Chicano art. Besides changing visual art exhibits, the center offers art classes, films, and music and dance performances. One of the highlights of the yearly calendar is the Tejano Conjunto Festival (see "San Antonio Events" below).

The **Hertzberg Circus Collection** (tel. 210-299-7810), 210 W. Market, is a unique museum devoted to the circus world. The centerpiece of the exhibit is a miniature model of a traditional three-ring circus, complete with big top, side show, animal stables, and dining tents. There are over 20,000 other pieces of circus memorabilia on display, including circus posters and literature, costumes, and various props. Open Mon.-Sat. 9-5. Admission is $1 for adults, 50 cents for children.

Paseo Del Rio (River Walk)

One of the biggest tourist attractions in San Antonio, the River Walk is a set of cobblestone and flagstone paths that extend for about 2.5 miles along the San Antonio River from the Municipal Auditorium on the north end to the King William district at the south. The river itself is below street level, so one descends stone stairways at various intersections to arrive on the paths. Scenic arched bridges cross over the river at intervals. The paths, bridges, and stairways were built by WPA crews between 1935 and 1941 and were meant to be used as an urban park but the area remained neglected; during the 1968 HemisFair, the city allowed commercial development and it's now the center of downtown life. The city maintains a selection of lush flora along the river, including 75 species of trees (predominantly the native bald cypress, pond cypress, and crepe myrtle), subtropical plants, and flowers.

LA MANSIÓN DEL RÍO HOTEL

*Paseo del Rio
(River Walk)*

A variety of indoor/outdoor restaurants, cafes, bars, hotels, boutiques, and the recently added Rivercenter shopping mall now line the River Walk. Barges (for groups) and river taxis (for individuals) carry visitors up and down the river—there are even nighttime dinner cruises on the flat-bottomed boats. Where the river curves by La Villita, the Arneson River Theater features live theatrical and music performances during the warmer months. The River Walk is also an important focus for many of the city's festivals.

La Villita National Historic District

"The Little Town" developed as a Spanish squatters' settlement along the east bank of the San Antonio River, next to the original Mission San Antonio de Valero, in the mid- to late 18th century. In the mid-19th century, Anglo and European immigrants began arriving, La Villita's adobe huts were replaced by sturdier limestone buildings, and the district became the town center. In the early 20th century, it declined into a virtual slum until artists and other "bohemian" elements moved in during the '40s and '50s and renovated the old structures. As often happens when artists take up residence in a low-rent area and make improvements, the city decided it would make a good tourist attraction; after a major renovation in the early '80s, it's now a showcase for middle-of-the-road artists and craftspersons. Many of the

crafts now hail from Mexico and Central America, including pottery, weavings, jewelry, and clothing.

Among the small district's historic attractions are the 19th-century "Little Church," a frequently chosen site for wedding ceremonies, and the Arneson River Theater (see "Paseo del Rio"). Several festivals hold all or part of their customary events at La Villita.

Market Square

West of the downtown area at Commerce and San Saba, just off I-35, this restored market plaza is surrounded by buildings that date from as early as 1840. A farmer's market, Mexican restaurants, and a large Mexican-style market building (the largest outside Mexico) have made this another important tourist attraction (see "Shopping" below). The **Centro de Artes del Mercado,** housed in a renovated 1922 building on the square, is a recently established arts center that offers art exhibits as well as music and dance performances; it also serves as a meeting place for civic and social functions. The city plans to use the Centro to house permanent art and historical exhibits in the future.

Overlooking Market Square is a statue of St. Cecilia, the patron saint of musicians, and there's always live Mexican music somewhere in the square. During the summer, music and dance performances are usually presented around noon in the center of the square (Mariachi Plaza). Mi Tierra

Café and Bakery usually features a few *trovadores* (singing guitarists) strolling around the restaurant, and twice a year (August and November) the square is the site of a Trovadores Festival that draws wandering Mexican guitarists from near and far.

King William Historic District
German settlers established this 25-block district on the east bank of the river (now south of downtown) in the late 1800s and named it after Prussia's King Wilhelm I. At the time it was the most elegant neighborhood in San Antonio. Over the years it decayed, but many of the distinctive Victorian houses built between the 1850s and 1920s are now being restored to their former glory. King William St. itself has the most striking set of homes—the media often describe it as the most beautiful residential street in the state.

The highly active San Antonio Conservation Society (tel. 210-224-6163) has its headquarters at 107 King William; they distribute a free brochure map that describes a walking tour of the district. The society bought and renovated one house that is now open to the public: the **Steves Home** (tel. 225-5924) at 509 King William. The restoration includes period furnishings and a period kitchen. Open daily 10-5; admission is $2 adults, free for children under 12.

San Antonio Zoo
This widely acclaimed zoo (tel. 210-734-7183) is nicely situated among the rock cliffs of an old limestone quarry in Brackenridge Park, off Broadway and Hildebrand (north of downtown). The zoo was established in 1929 and some of the exhibits, like the Barless Bear Pits, have served well ever since; other sections have been upgraded and expanded. All in all, there are now over 3,600 animals from over 670 species on 50 acres of well-kept grounds. The setting and weather must agree with the animals here, since the zoo has a national reputation (among the top 10) for captive breeding; it was the first to hatch a flamingo and the first to deliver a white rhino. The impressive bird collection exhibits everything from penguins to an endangered whooping crane (this is the only zoo in the U.S. with a whooper) and the African antelope collection here is one of the most extensive in the world. The cat exhibit includes the rare jaguarundi, a feline species native to South Texas, Mexico, and Central America. The monkey and ape collection is also outstanding. The Children's Zoo fea-

tures a boat ride past an Everglades exhibit, a petting zoo, and an educational Rain Forest exhibit. Camera loans are available at the zoo entrance. Open daily 9:30-5, summer till 6:30. Admission is $5 adults, $3 children 3-11.

Southwest Craft Center (Ursuline Academy)
This complex of mid-19th-century buildings at 300 Augusta at Navarro once housed the first girls school in San Antonio, the Ursuline Academy (which has since moved to a different location). Founded by Catholic nuns, the Gothic-style convent, courtyards, and school buildings are now owned by the **Southwest Craft Center** (tel. 210-224-1848), which offers a variety of arts and crafts classes (woodworking, pottery, weaving), workshops, exhibits (two galleries—one for visiting artists, one for staff and students), and the Copper Kitchen restaurant (open Mon.-Fri. for lunch). There are usually a few artists or craftspersons working on the premises; crafts are for sale as well. Open Mon.-Sat. 10-4; free admission.

Spanish Governor's Palace
This building (tel. 210-224-0601) was built in 1749 as a residence for the Spanish governor of Texas province and is one of the most evocative of all colonial structures left standing in San Antonio. The San Antonio Conservation Society has lovingly restored the building and fitted it with period furnishings. The fountain and foliage in the garden patio, at the back of the house, make a welcome oasis from summer heat. Open Mon.-Sat. 9-5, Sun. 10-5; admission is $1 adults, 50 cents children 7-13.

Breweries
Neither of San Antonio's two breweries, Lone Star and Pearl, gives tours anymore, but each has a visitors center where you may buy items emblazoned with beer logos. Lone Star Brewery also features the **Buckhorn Hall of Horns, Fins, and Feathers** (tel. 210-270-9467) at 600 Lone Star Blvd. downtown. The original Buckhorn Bar was an elegant saloon built in 1881 that was distinguished by its collections of animal horns and antlers. This collection was expanded and later moved to the Hall of Horns, which now displays over 3,500 specimens of horned game animal trophies from all over the globe. The Hall of Fins and Hall of Feathers contain, what else, fish and bird trophies. Buckhorn Hall is supposedly the second-most-visited attraction in the city after the Alamo.

Open daily 9:30-5; admission is $3.50 adults, $3 seniors, $1.50 children 6-12. Complimentary beer is served in the replica Buckhorn Bar.

The **Pearl Brewery** (tel. 210-226-0231) is north of downtown at 312 Pearl Pkwy. and Ave. A—you can't miss the towering yellow Victorian. Pearl was founded by a German brewmaster in 1886.

Sea World Of Texas

This is the largest of the four Sea Worlds in the U.S. (the other three are in San Diego, Orlando, and Aurora, Ohio) and is quickly becoming one of San Antonio's top tourist spots. The 250-acre park (tel. 210-523-3611) is 16 miles northwest of the city center off State 151, between Loop 1604 and Loop 410 W. The central attraction is Shamu Stadium, the largest facility for the presentation of marine animals in the world (4,500 seats, seven million gallons). Killer whales Shamu, Namu, Kandu, and the 1988-born Baby Shamu thrill audiences here with their aquabatic skills, while the smaller New Friends Stadium presents four other species of dolphins and whales.

Other venues feature trick water-skiing, a penguin exhibit (in a simulated Antarctic environment, complete with snow), a 450,000-gallon shark tank, and a 300,000-gallon Indo-Pacific reef aquarium. The 12-acre Cypress Gardens has paths that wind through a display of native Texas flora; *doncellas,* young women in traditional Spanish gowns, are stationed amid the gardens to answer questions and pose for pictures. The usual assortment of restaurants, ice-cream parlors, and gift shops (with Shamu caps and T-shirts) are on hand, plus a four-acre playground with a nautical theme and a carnival midway. In 1991 the park added Texas Splashdown, a six-minute flume ride, and Rio Loco, a simulation of Central Texas river tubing—perfect for cooling off during summer visits. Open daily 9-7 (extended hours in the summer). Admission is $24.61 adults, $17 children 3-11; group discounts and season passes are available.

Sea World has a downtown information center across from the Alamo that offers a free film preview of the park, a miniature 3-D model of the layout, and information on express buses to the park.

Fiesta Texas

Opened in 1992, this new theme park joins Sea World as one of the San Antonio area's top attractions. The 200-acre facility, partially surrounded by the 100-foot cliffs of a former limestone quarry, contains four Texas theme areas, each of which offers an array of musical entertainment, rides, and food. **Los Festivales** represents the state's Hispanic heritage and features two performance venues, the 2,000-seat, air-conditioned Zaragoza Theater (with Mexican folkloric performances and the "Heart of Texas" historic show) and the 746-seat, open-air Teatro Fiesta (*conjunto* and Tejano music). A large restaurant and a couple of cafes in this section serve Mexican and Tex-Mex foods.

A Western theme dominates **Crackaxle Canyon**, which is constructed to resemble a 1920s Texas boom town and features 4,000-seat Lonestar Lil's (hosting a choreographed music-

The Rattler, Fiesta Park

dance production based on the West Texas oil-boom era) and the 1,500-seat Sundance Theater (country music and comedy performances). This section of the park also contains what is likely to become Fiesta Texas's biggest draw, The Rattler—the world's tallest (180 ft., six inches), fastest (73 mph top speed), and steepest (61.4-degree angle on the first drop) wooden roller coaster. This coaster winds over and *through* the natural limestone canyon surrounding the park; take my word for it, this is one terrifying coaster ride! Crackaxle Canyon also features the Gully Washer, a simulated whitewater rapids tube-ride, and the Ol' Waterin' Hole, a complex of other water rides, slides, and pools. Old Blues Bar-B-Que offers West Texas-style barbecue ribs, chicken, brisket, steaks, and sausage along with the usual accompaniments.

The theme of the Rockville section of the park is 1950s-era small-town Texas. So far the park's favorite musical show seems to be the 45-minute Broadway-style musical performed in the realistic, 1,000-seat Rockville High School auditorium. Called "Rockin' at Rockville High," the performance weaves a humorous story line around a collection of top-10 '50s teen anthems. Rockabilly and '50-'60s oldies bands play at a smaller open-air theater next door. Rides in Rockville include the Power Surge, in which a large boat plunges down a 100-foot waterfall to a tremendous splashdown at the bottom, and the Motorama, a track with scaled-down, electric-powered models of classic '50s American cars, complete with car radios playing vintage rock 'n' roll.

The fourth theme section is the German-inspired **Spassburg** ("Fun Town"), centered around the 1,000-seat Sangerfest Halle. This combination beer garden, theater, and restaurant presents a menu of German specialties along with live tuba, accordion, and German choir ensembles. The rides at Spassburg are tamer than those in the rest of the park and include an early 1900s-style German carousel, a Bavarian swing ride, and various other mild thrills mostly oriented toward children.

Fiesta Texas opens at 10 a.m. and closes after sunset following a spectacular laser and fireworks show. Admission prices (not including 8.25% sales tax) is $22.95 for adults, $15.95 for children 4-11; two-day passes are available for $34.95 adults, $ 24.95 children 4-11. USAA members are offered a $5 discount on admission rates at a special ticket window near the entrance.

Universities

San Antonio boasts nine colleges and universities (10 if you count the Health Science Center separately). The **University of Texas at San Antonio** (tel. 210-691-4011) has an enrollment of 13,000 in Bachelor's and Master's degree programs (liberal arts, fine arts, and engineering) on a 600-acre campus northwest of town (Loop 1604). The UT Health Science Center (tel. 567-7000), nearby at 7703 Floyd Curl, enrolls around 2,300 students in medical, dental, nursing, biomedical sciences, and allied health sciences.

Trinity University (tel. 210-736-7011), on Stadium and Hildebrand near Brackenridge Park, was founded by the Presbyterian Church in 1869 (though San Antonio was not the original location). It is one of the most attractively situated of the city's universities, since it's on a hill that overlooks San Antonio. It's small (3,000 students) and expensive, with a fair academic reputation (education and communications are among its strongest departments). The tennis team has won several national championships.

San Antonio boasts two Catholic universities. **St. Mary's University** (tel. 210-436-3011) at Camino Santa Maria and Cincinnati is the city's oldest, founded by the Society of Mary (a French order) in 1853. The school has an enrollment of about 3,200 and is most known for its law and business programs. Dwight Eisenhower was a football coach here in 1916. The other Catholic university is **Our Lady of the Lake University** (tel. 434-6711) at 411 S.W. 24th at Commerce. Founded in 1911, OLLU emphasizes programs for lower-income students and Hispanics. Enrollment is around 1,700. The Sacred Heart Chapel on campus, built in 1896, is a splendid structure of carved wood, marble, gold leaf, and stained glass.

The largest institute of higher education in the city is **San Antonio College** (tel. 210-734-7311), which also happens to be the largest two-year college in Texas (enrollment of 22,000). Its urban campus, at San Pedro and Dewey just north of downtown, was established in 1925. The college **planetarium** (tel. 733-2910) offers free shows on Sundays at 5, 6:30, and 8. Also on campus is the **Koehler Cultural Center,** a Victorian built by Pearl brewmaster Otto Koehler that now features art and cultural exhibits (jointly administered by the San Antonio Art League).

The **Autonomous National University of Mexico** (Universidad Nacional Autonoma de

Mexico), tel. (210) 222-8626, has a small branch at 600 HemisFair Park. It serves mainly as a Mexican cultural center (no degree programs here); courses offered include Spanish (four levels) as well as Latin American art, history, and anthropology. The Spanish courses are offered on a regular semester basis or as summer intensives, and all instructors are from Mexico.

SAN ANTONIO ACCOMMODATIONS

Hotels And Motels
The city has a range of places to stay to fit any budget. Most are clustered in four areas: downtown, off N.E. Loop 410, near the airport (north), and off N.W. Loop 410. There are also a few places west of the city near Sea World and Lackland AFB. Downtown hotels are the most expensive, but are within walking distance of the River Walk, the Alamo, La Villita, Market Square, and other attractions.

Historic Hotels: San Antonio has more historic hotels still in business than any other city in Texas. The oldest is the **Menger Hotel,** built by brewer W.A. Menger in 1859; at the time, it was said to be one of the finest hostelries west of the Mississippi. The original limestone and ironwork edifice still stands next to the Alamo and offers period rooms as well as newer rooms in the "motor hotel" addition. The old Rotunda lobby is worth a visit even if you're not staying here. Likewise for the Menger Bar (sometimes called the Roosevelt Bar), which was originally built as a replica of a pub in London's House of Lords. Teddy Roosevelt is supposed to have recruited some portion of his Rough Riders at this bar for the Spanish-American War.

The **St. Anthony** at 300 E. Travis was erected in 1909 and certainly gave the Menger a run for its money as one of the best hotels of its time in the Southwest. Now owned by Hong Kong's Park Lane Hotels International, it has been completely restored and remains a favorite among hotel patrons who wouldn't dream of staying at a chain hotel (no two rooms are alike). Another 1909 hotel that was recently renovated is the **Gunter Hotel** at 205 E. Houston. The Sheraton group is the current owner and they've made the Gunter one of the city's top-drawer places to stay, with lots of wood and brass in the public areas.

Yet a third place built in 1909 is the **Crockett Hotel** at Bonham and Crockett. Similar on the outside to other buildings made of native stone, the inside is decorated in a tasteful, modern Southwest style rather than in period style.

In 1910, rooms at the **Fairmount Hotel** were 75 cents a night. In 1985, investors moved the building from its original location on E. Commerce (the Rivercenter Mall took its place) to S. Alamo; now rooms are nearly 200 times the original tariff. It's listed in the Guinness Book of World Records under "world's largest building move"—it took six days to move the Italianate Victorian structure six blocks, using 38 specially designed hydraulic dollies. Another venerated San Antonio hotel is **La Mansión del Rio**, housed in a multi-story, mission-style edifice on the river (with a street entrance on College between Navarro and St. Mary's). The core building was originally constructed in 1852 as a Catholic boys school, which later became St. Mary's College and then St. Mary's University of Law. Since 1967, when it was transformed into a hotel, it has had the same owner—unusual in the fast-paced world of hotel deals in which Sheraton, Radisson, and Hyatt swap luxury properties with regularity. Because of its location on a quiet, out-of-the-way corner of the River Walk, La Mansión is a favorite among visiting entertainers and dignitaries (recent guests have included Mexican President Carlos Salinas and composer/performer David Byrne).

For addresses, phone numbers, and room rates, see the "San Antonio Hotels And Motels" chart.

Bed And Breakfast Inns
At last count, the city had around 20 B&Bs, all of which can be booked through **Bed & Breakfast Hosts of San Antonio** (tel. 210-824-8036), 166 Rockhill, San Antonio, TX 78209. Rates vary from $40 to $114 a night. One that will take reservations directly is **Terrell Castle Bed & Breakfast** (tel. 271-9145) at 950 E. Grayson. This 1880s Richardson Revival-style mansion has 26 rooms at $75-85 a night including a full breakfast. See also Bullis House Inn below.

AYH Hostel
The **Bullis House Inn/San Antonio International Hostel** (tel. 210-223-9426) is located opposite Fort Sam Houston at 621 Pierce Street. The historic, Greek Revival-style mansion was built in

SAN ANTONIO HOTELS AND MOTELS

Add 13% hotel tax to all rates. Area code: 210

NAME	ADDRESS	PHONE	RATES	FEATURES
DOWNTOWN				
Crockett Hotel	320 Bonham	225-6500	$75-125	historic, pool, weekly rates
Emily Morgan at Alamo Plaza	705 E. Houston	225-8486	$75-95	near Alamo, heated pool, saunas, refrig. on request
The Fairmount Hotel	401 S. Alamo	224-8800	$145-185	health club privileges, famous restaurant (Polo's)
Hilton Palacio del Rio	200 S. Alamo	222-1400	$145-207	on River Walk, some rooms w/river views, pool, refrig.
Holiday Inn Market Sq.	318 W. Durango	225-3211	$61-79	pool, coin laundry
Holiday Inn River Walk	217 N. St. Mary's	224-2500	$95-115	heated pool
Hyatt Regency	123 Losoya	222-1234	$130-160	River Walk, some rooms w/view, pool, wknd. discount
La Mansion del Rio	112 College	225-2581 or 800-531-7208	$110-185	River Walk, many rooms w/view, pool, refrig., wknd. disc.
La Quinta Motor Inn Convention Center	1001 E. Commerce	222-9181	$70-80	opposite HemisFair Park, pool
La Quinta Motor Inn Market Square	900 Dolorosa	271-0001	$64-80	pool
Marriott Rivercenter	101 Bowie	223-1000 or 800-228-9290	$140-160	heated pool, saunas
Marriott River Walk	711 E. River Walk	224-4555 or 800-228-9290	$130-170	many rooms w/view, heated pool, saunas
Menger Hotel	204 Alamo Plaza	223-4361 or 800-345-9285	$74-94	historic, next to the Alamo
Motel 6 Downtown	211 N. Pecos	225-1111	$31.95 + $6 ea. add.	near Market Square pool
Plaza San Antonio Hotel	555 S. Alamo	229-1000	$130-190	heated pool, saunas, tennis courts, wkly. rates
Rodeway Inn Laredo St.	1500 I-35 S (at Laredo)	271-3334	$35-51	pool, free shuttle to Market Square
Rodeway Inn Main	900 N. Main	223-2951	$48-62	pool
St. Anthony Hotel	300 E. Travis	227-4392 or 800-338-1338	$106-126	historic, heated pool
Sheraton Gunther Hotel	205 E. Houston	227-4392 or 800-222-4276	$89-129	historic, heated pool

SAN ANTONIO HOTELS AND MOTELS

Add 13% hotel tax to all rates. Area code: 210

NAME	ADDRESS	PHONE	RATES	FEATURES
DOWNTOWN (CONTINUED)				
Travelodge On The River	100 Villita	226-2271	$54-79	on River Walk, some rooms w/view, pool
Traveler's Hotel	220 N. Broadway	226-4381	$19-24	near Alamo and River Walk, weekly and monthly rates available
NORTHWEST				
Amerisuites	10950 Laureate (off US 281 N)	342-4800	$44-60	1-bdrm suites w/ kitchenettes, pool, coin laundry, airport shuttle
Holiday Inn Northwest	3233 N.W. Loop 410 (I-10 Junction)	377-3900 or 800-HOLIDAY	$59-84	pool, health club priv., coin laundry airport shuttle
La Quinta Motor Inn/ Vance Jackson	5922 N.W. Expwy. (Vance Jackson exit)	734-7931 or 800-531-5900	$52-62	pool, senior discount
La Quinta Motor Inn/ Wurzbach	9542 I-10 W (Wurzbach Exit)	690-8810	$42-52	pool, senior discount
Lexington Hotel Suites	4934 N.W. Loop 410 (exit 13B)	680-3351	$53-72	suites, pool, coin laundry, airport shuttle
Motel 6/Northwest	9400 Wurzbach	593-0013	$30.95 + $6 ea. add.	pool
Oak Hills Motor Inn	7401 Wurzbach	696-9900 or 800-468-3507	$54-60	opp. S. Texas Medical Center, pool, airport shuttle
Siesta Motel	4441 Fredericksburg	733-7154	$27-35	pool, weekly rates
Warren Inn	5050 Fredericksburg	342-1179	$29-38	pool, saunas, coin laundry, wkly. rates
Wyndham Hotel San Antonio	9821 Colonnade (off I-10 Wurzbach exit)	691-8888	$139-149	heated pool, sauna, airport shuttle
NORTHEAST				
Aloha Motel	1435 Austin Hwy.	828-0933	$26-35	pool, coin laundry, weekly and monthly rates, senior discount
Best Western Continental Inn	9735 I-35 N (exit 166/167A)	655-3510 or 800-528-1234	$36-52	pool, coin laundry
Days Inn Northeast	3433 I-35 N (Coliseum exit)	225-4521	$34-68	pool, weekly rates

SAN ANTONIO HOTELS AND MOTELS

Add 13% hotel tax to all rates. Area code: 210

NAME	ADDRESS	PHONE	RATES	FEATURES
NORTHEAST (continued)				
Holiday Inn/Northeast	3855 N. Pan American Expressway	226-4361 or 800-HOLIDAY	$54-64	pool, coin laundry, senior discount
Motel 6	9503 I-35 N (exit 167)	650-4419	$27 + $6 ea. add.	pool
Oak Motor Lodge	150 Humphreys (off Broadway and US 81)	826-6368	$30-42	pool, kitch. on request, (add $5) weekly rates
AIRPORT				
Best Western Town House Motel	942 N.E. Loop 410 (Broadway exit)	826-6311	$35-50	pool, airport shuttle
Courtyard by Marriott Airport	8615 Broadway	828-7200 or 800-321-2211	$72-82	pool, coin laundry, airport shuttle, senior discount
Drury Inn Airport	143 N.E. Loop 410 (airport exit)	366-4300 or 800-325-8300	$56-64	pool, airport shuttle, comp. eve. beverage
Embassy Suites Hotel/ Airport	10110 US 281 N (Jones Maltsberger exit)	525-9999 or 800-EMBASSY	$129-139	refrig., suites, heated pool, sauna, airport shuttle, monthly rates, comp. bev.
Sheraton Fiesta San Antonio	37 N. E. Loop 410 (McCullough exit)	366-2424 or 800-325-3535	$110-125	suites, pool, airport shuttle, sr. disc.
Hilton/Airport	611 N.W. Loop 410 (San Pedro exit)	340-6060 or 800-333-3333	$80-90	heated pool, saunas, health club privileges, airport shuttle
Holiday Inn/Airport	77 N.E. Loop 410 (airport exit)	349-9900 or 800-HOLIDAY	$85-95	pool, coin laundry, airport shuttle, sr. disc.
La Quinta Motor Inn/ Airport East	333 N.E. Loop 410 (airport exit)	828-0781 or 800-531-5900	$56-66	pool, airport shuttle senior discount
Ramada Hotel Airport	1111 N.E. Loop 410 (Naçogdoches exit)	828-9031 or 800-288-9031	$65-85	(seasonal) pool, health club privileges, airport shuttle
WEST/SOUTH				
Best Western Lackland Lodge	6815 State 90 W (1½ mi. E. of Loop 410)	675-9690	$34-47	pool
La Quinta Motor Inn/ Ingram Park	7134 N.W. Loop 410 (Culebra exit)	680-8883 or 800-531-5900	$56-66	pool, senior discount
La Quinta Motor Inn/ Lackland	6511 Military W	674-3200 or 800-531-5900	$49-59	heated pool

SAN ANTONIO HOTELS AND MOTELS

Add 13% hotel tax to all rates. Area code: 210

NAME	ADDRESS	PHONE	RATES	FEATURES
WEST/SOUTH (continued)				
La Quinta Motor Inn South	7202 S. Pan American Expwy.	922-2111	$51-61	pool
Motel 6	2185 S. W. Loop 410 (exit 7)	673-9020	$26 + $6 ea. add.	near Sea World and Fiesta Park, pool
Travelers Inn	6861 US 90 W at Military	675-4120 or 800-433-8300	$30-36	pool, senior discount

1906-09 for General John L. Bullis, a former Union army officer who came to Texas after the Civil War to serve in the Indian Wars (he led the famous Seminole Indian Scouts of Brackettville). The house is divided into two sections, a bed and breakfast inn and gender-segregated hostel dormitories. Rooms in the B&B section vary depending on room size, from $40 for a single with breakfast and shared bath to $59 for a large double with private bath and breakfast; $3 is subtracted from rates if guests elect not to have breakfast. Extra persons in a room are $10 with breakfast, $6 without.

Dorm beds are $13.50 for AYH members, $16.50 for nonmembers; weekly rates (members only) are $70 per person.

Bus nos. 15 and 22 run from nearby the Bullis House to downtown San Antonio (Houston St.).

To get here by car, take the New Braunfels/Fort Sam Houston exit off I-35 N, then take New Braunfels St. north to Grayson and make a left (west), then another left (south) on Pierce Street.

Campgrounds And RV Parks

The campground nearest to downtown San Antonio is the **Alamo KOA Kampground** (tel. 210-224-9296 or 800-833-KAMP), which is at 602 Gembler Rd. (three miles east on I-35, then a half mile south on Coliseum to Gembler, then follow the signs). The facility is next to a small lake and Salado Creek, so there's fishing and other water recreation, plus a heated pool and 18-hole golf course. Tent/camper sites are $12.75 a night; add $2 for w/e. Full hookups are $16.75 a night for two adults, plus $2 for each additional adult. Cabins are available for $21. Northeast of the airport

*Bullis House Inn/
San Antonio
International Hostel*

at Jones-Maltsberger and Buckhorn, the 856-acre **McAllister Park** (tel. 821-3000) has a tent-camping area that's $5 a night on weekdays, $10 on weekends.

Mission RV Jellystone Park (tel. 210-532-8310) is at 2617 Roosevelt Ave., three miles south of the city off Military Dr., then another mile or so on Roosevelt. RV sites are $16 a night for two, plus $2 per person for additional adults. Weekly and monthly rates are available.

Greentree Village North RV Park (tel. 210-655-3331) is about 12 miles north of the city off I-35 at the 12015 O'Conner Rd. (O'Conner Rd. exit). RV sites are $12.50 for two persons, plus $1 for each additional adult. Weekly and monthly rates are available. **Admiralty Park** (tel. 800-999-RSVA) is west of the city near Sea World at 1485 N. Ellison Dr. (Military Dr. exit off Loop 410). RV sites are $15 a night plus $2 for additional adults; weekly and monthly rates are available.

SAN ANTONIO FOOD

Ever since the chili queens served bowls of red on the streets of 19th-century San Antonio, the city has been regarded as something of a culinary adventureland. Unlike Dallas and Houston, restaurants here tend to be moderately priced, so gastronomic experiments needn't eat up your savings (more restaurants seem to be open on Sundays here, too). A lot of the better restaurants are north of the city center on and off Broadway. The River Walk establishments aren't known for culinary excellence since the steady flow of tourists and conventioneers assures a profit for any restaurateur who can get space there but in recent years the overall quality has improved. Local connoisseurs agree that The Bayous, Zuni Grill, and Rio Rio are among the best River Walk eateries.

Does San Antonio have the best Mexican food in Texas? Maybe—at the very least, it has the largest number and largest variety of Mexican and Tex-Mex places of any city in the state. A bit of trivia: Fritos were invented here in 1942.

American/Texan
$ **Alamo Cafe:** Among the most popular restaurants in San Antonio and recently ranked fifth statewide by *Texas Highways* readers, the two Alamo Cafes offer state-of-the-art Tex-Mex food (all tortillas made on the premises), chicken-fried steak, huge salads, creative desserts (especially good are coffee-flavored flan and lime margarita pie), and reasonable prices. At 9714 San Pedro (tel. 341-4526) and 10060 I-10W (tel. 691-8827). Both locations are open daily for lunch and dinner.

$$ **Biga:** Another original by San Antonio's premier chef, Bruce Auden (who earned his national reputation in the Fairmount Hotel's kitchens), this casual, moderately priced restaurant serves such creations as poblano bisque, sauteed soft-shell crab with cilantro lime on angel hair pasta, and oak-fired pizza topped with spicy chicken, basil, and fontina cheese. The menu changes daily but perennials include the onion rings served with habanero ketchup and Debra Auden's "rustic breads" (the restaurant's name comes from the sourdough starter used in many of the baked-on-the-premises breads and pastries). At 206 E. Locust, in an old house on the corner of Locust and McCullough St. (tel. 225-0722)—the former site of La Provence—at the edge of the Monte Vista Historical District; open Tues.-Fri. for lunch and dinner, Mon. and Sat. for dinner only.

In the back of the same building is the **Locu-Street Bakery** (tel. 225-0723), which is open Mon.-Sat. and sells muffins, scones, cookies, and other pastries (along with coffees, teas, and juice) from 7 a.m. till sellout and breads from 11 a.m. till sellout.

$$ **Cappy's:** A renovated lumber warehouse that serves everything from salad and seafood to burgers, including a few low-fat, low-cholesterol dishes. At 5011 Broadway (tel. 210-828-9669); open daily for lunch and dinner.

$ to $$ **Earl Abel's:** A classic, all-day, all-night (well, almost) American eatery with fried chicken, steak and fries, and other meat-and-potatoes fare. At Broadway and Hildebrand (tel. 822-3358); open 6:30 a.m. to 1 a.m. daily.

$$ **Liberty Bar:** An exceptionally good, moderately priced restaurant that's housed in an ancient, former general store/brothel. The rootsy, nouvelle-Americain menu changes regularly but specializes in mesquite-grilled meats, fresh-sautéed vegetables, homemade bread, and desserts. At 328 E. Josephine (tel. 227-1187); open daily for lunch and dinner, plus Sunday brunch.

$$ **Mama's:** A friendly restaurant with the most American menu in town—meatloaf to chocolate cake. At 9907 San Pedro (tel. 349-5662); open daily for lunch and dinner.

$$$+ Polo's Restaurant: Extremely chic restaurant in the historic Fairmount Hotel. Chefs come and go here, but the dishes are always avant-garde Texas, e.g., wok-charred lamb in peanut sauce, braised blackbuck antelope, *boudain*-stuffed quail, prawns in pineapple salsa, and my favorite dish title: fricassee of Texas rabbit with roast peppers and *nopalitos*. At 401 S. Alamo (tel. 225-4242); open daily for breakfast, lunch, and dinner.

$ Twin Sisters Bakery & Café: A popular Alamo Heights breakfast-and-lunch place with good omelets, soups, homemade breads, sandwiches, and baked desserts (cookies and muffins). Decent coffee, too. At 6322 N. New Braunfels (tel. 822-2265); open Mon.-Sat. for breakfast and lunch.

$$ Zuni Grill: Under the same ownership as Paesano's and Rio Rio, this daring Texan/Southwestern cafe turns out the most inventive dishes of any restaurant on the River Walk, e.g., pecan-crusted chicken with mixed greens and Texas goat cheese with spinach in chile vinaigrette. Also vegetarian enchiladas, duck nachos, and a variety of quesadillas and flautas. Next to La Paloma del Rio at 511 River Walk (tel. 227-0864); open daily for lunch and dinner.

Barbecue
$$ The County Line: Another link in the state's best barbecue chain. Features all the standards plus smoked duck, chicken, pork ribs, steaks, and fish. At 606 W. Afton Oaks Blvd. (tel. 210-496-0011); open daily for dinner.

$ Miller's Barbecue: Serves East Texas or "southern-style" barbecue cooked over oak in a rustic, pre-World War II atmosphere. Great prices. West central area, at 1020 Morales (no phone); open Mon.-Sat. for lunch or until the barbecue runs out.

$ Pig Stand: The city's oldest continually operating restaurant and a classic '50s-style take-out barbecue (including their famous "pig sandwich"). The management claims they were the first in the U.S. to feature curb service, too. At 1508 Broadway (tel. 222-2794); open 24 hours.

Cajun-Creole
$$ Huey's: Dependable Cajun and Creole fare, from blackened redfish to oysters Rockefeller, are served here in a casual, occasionally boisterous ambience. And it's right in the middle of the St. Mary's St. club district. At 2734 N. St. Mary's (tel. 736-6666); open Mon.-Sat. for lunch and dinner, Sun. dinner only.

$$$ La Louisiane: A San Antonio institution that serves classic French Creole dishes like red snapper Ponchartrain and chicken Marengo. At 2632 Broadway (tel. 225-7984); open Tues.-Sat. for lunch and dinner.

Chili
San Antonio's hometown dish is found on many menus, mostly in inexpensive diners and cafes. Among the better bowls of red are those served at the **Lone Star Café** at 237 Losoya, **Coney Island** at 225 N. St. Mary's and 300 Broadway, **Luther's Café** at 1325 N. Main, **Republic of Texas** at 429 E. Commerce (on the River Walk), and **Zweig's** at 126 Losoya.

French
$$$+ Chez Ardid: Classic French dishes like coquilles Saint-Jacques served in an elegant, early 1900s home. At 1919 San Pedro at Woodlawn (tel. 210-732-3203); open Mon.-Fri. for lunch and dinner, Sat. dinner only.

$$ to $$$ L'étoile: A rare find—top-drawer French cuisine at reasonable prices. Outdoor tables are available during warm weather. At 6106 Broadway (tel. 826-4551); open Mon.-Sat. for lunch and dinner, Sun. for dinner only.

German
$$ Edelweiss: The Swiss-German menu here leans heavily on veal and pork, including the reliable *Jagerschnitzel* and Zurich-style veal cutlets. The German beer and wine list, along with the friendly service, bring in the crowds. At 4400 Rittiman (tel. 829-5552).

$$ Karla's Restaurant & Gaststube: Standard Bavarian specialties and decor. At 5512 FM 78 (tel. 661-7617); open Tues.-Sun. for lunch and dinner.

$ to $$ Schilo's: A German-American-style deli with sausage, cold cuts, hot plates, sandwiches, sauerkraut, and homemade root beer; a downtown institution. At 424 E. Commerce (tel. 223-6692); Mon.-Sat. lunch and dinner.

$$ Vienna Weinstrube: German and Austrian cuisine served in an atmospheric, 120-year-old estate. At 1006 Holbrook (tel. 650-0097); open Mon.-Fri. for lunch only, Sat. for lunch and dinner.

Italian

$$ to $$$ La Buca: Upscale north Italian menu created by a big-name chef, strong on pasta and salads. At 7720 Jones-Maltsberger (tel. 210-826-2397); open Mon.-Fri. for lunch and dinner, Sat.-Sun. dinner only.

$$ to $$$ Nona's Homemade Pasta: Specializes in pizzas baked in a woodburning oven with unusual toppings (jalapeños and sausage, cream cheese and caviar, fresh fruit), as well as fresh, homemade pastas and *schiacciatine,* flat bread baked with olive oil, herbs, and cheese. During the week, a jazz ensemble performs for diners; on weekends there's belly dancing. Casual atmosphere at 2809 N. St. Mary's (tel. 736-9896); open Mon.-Thurs. 11-11, Fri. till midnight, Sat. 3-midnight.

$$ to $$$ Paesano's: The city's most popular Italian restaurant. The house specialty is seafood sautéed in a delicate wine, lemon, and garlic sauce (e.g., shrimp Paesano). At 1715 McCullough (tel. 226-9541); open Tues.-Fri., for lunch and dinner, Sat. dinner only.

Mexican

Listing all the *good* places in San Antonio would take up way too much space, so here are the simply *great:*

$ Big Ern's Taco Palace: This popular taco joint opposite La Mansión del Rio Hotel is famous for its chilaquiles and puffy chicken tacos. Half the fun is hearing Big Ern call out the orders in his operatic tenor. At 203 College (tel. 227-1830); open 7 a.m.-2 p.m. daily.

$$ El Jarro de Arturo: Reliable border food, including fajitas, chiles rellenos, flautas, and chicken *fundido.* At 13421 San Pedro at Bitters (tel. 494-5084); open daily for lunch and dinner.

$ El Mirador: Inexpensive Mexican and Tex-Mex with an especially good *almuerzo* (Mexican brunch) menu. Saturday morning the place is jammed with Mexican soup devotees. Specialties are *sopa Azteca* (spicy tomato broth with chicken, avocado, spinach, chiles, cheese, and tortilla strips), *caldo xochitl* (chicken broth with lime, vegetables, cilantro, and rice), and *sopa tarasco* (bean soup). Convenient downtown location at 722 St. Mary's (tel. 225-9444); open Mon.-Fri. for breakfast, lunch, and dinner, Sat. for breakfast and lunch.

$ to $$ La Calesa: A converted, tastefully decorated home that serves traditional Yucatecan specialties, including *cochinita pibil* (pit-cooked pork) and *pollo en escabeche* (marinated chicken). At 2103 Hildebrand (tel. 822-4475); open daily for lunch and dinner.

$$ La Fogata: Extremely popular indoor-outdoor restaurant with a northern Mexican menu. The main menu items are good, but it's in the appetizers and side dishes that the kitchen shines: *queso fundido* (melted cheese with chiles and chorizo), *ceballos al carbon* (grilled scallions), and *frijoles borrachos* ("drunken beans," whole pintos in a fragrant sauce). At 2724 Vance Jackson (tel. 341-9930); open Tues.-Sun. for breakfast, lunch, and dinner.

$ to $$ La Fonda: This San Antonio institution doesn't have the most daring Mexican kitchen in town, but the consistent quality and warm, friendly service has a loyal following. Extensive, traditional Tex-Mex menu. At 2415 N. Main (tel. 733-0621); open Mon.-Sat. for lunch and dinner.

$ to $$ Mi Tierra Café & Bakery: Right on Market Square, Mi Tierra gets a lot of tourists during the day. But slide in after midnight and it's a different crowd altogether. Classic border cuisine, with exemplary enchiladas and chiles rellenos. The *panadería* offers a large selection of Mexican baked goods. There are strolling guitarists during prime-time dining hours. At 218 Produce Row (tel. 225-1262); open 24 hours.

$$ Rio Rio Cantina: This casual bar/restaurant serves the most consistent Mexican food on the River Walk. The varied menu offers all the Tex-Mex standards—fajitas, chiles rellenos, enchiladas, etc.—plus regional dishes like *pollo en mole* and others, each prepared with the freshest ingredients. Great margaritas, too. At 421 E. Commerce St., with a River Walk entrance (tel. 226-8462); open daily for lunch and dinner.

$ to $$ Rosario's: According to the *New York Times,* this is the most authentic interior-style cuisine in San Antone (most San Antonio diners couldn't care less). Dishes from north central and Gulf coast Mexico predominate, including savory black bean soup, *camarones al mojo de ajo* (shrimp in garlic sauce), lobster tacos, crab enchiladas, and *rajas con queso blanco (chile poblano* strips in melted cheese). At 1014 S. Alamo (tel. 223-1806); open daily for lunch and dinner.

$ Taco Cabana: You can find take-out taco chains all over Texas, but San Antonio has the best. This one started as a small family-run joint at San Pedro and Hildebrand and has expanded to eight or more locations. Reliable fajitas, breakfast tacos (served anytime), *chalupas,* and enchiladas. Locations: all over the city; open 24 hours.

Natural Foods

$ **Adelante:** Features an inexpensive, health-oriented Tex-Mex menu (lard-free beans, natural meats). The veggie combo plate allows vegetarians entry into the Tex-Mex world. Opposite the Bookstop and very casual (they don't mind if you sit and read long after you finish eating). At 21 Brees, off Austin Hwy. (tel. 210-822-7681); open Mon.-Fri. 7:30-8:30, Sat. 8-5:30.

$ to $$ **Gini's Homecooking & Bakery:** Low-fat, low-cholesterol, and vegetarian American dishes, strong on homemade breads, soups, and salads. At 7214 Blanco at Loop 410 (tel. 342-2768); open daily for breakfast, lunch, and dinner.

Oriental

$$ to $$$ **Chinatown Café:** Features a nouveau Asia menu, mixing Hunan ("General Tao's Chicken") and Thai ("Tai Pepper Basil Shrimp") dishes. At Broadway and Nacogdoches (tel. 210-822-3522); open daily for lunch and dinner.

$ to $$ **Hung Fong:** The oldest Chinese restaurant in the city (est. 1939) and full of Chinatown kitsch, like the pair of neon flags on the ceiling (one U.S., one Taiwan). Mostly Cantonese dishes, large portions. At 3624 Broadway (tel. 822-9211); open daily for lunch and dinner.

$ to $$ **Dang's Thai:** Good standard Thai dishes, plus some northern-style Thai and Vietnamese. At 1146 Austin Hwy. (tel. 829-7345); open daily for lunch and dinner.

$$ to $$$ **Niki's Tokyo Inn:** Choice of Western and Japanese seating, plus a sushi bar. Best sushi in town. At 819 W. Hildebrand (tel. 736-5471); open Tues.-Sat. for dinner.

$ **Vietnam Restaurant:** A neighborhood favorite for the low prices and tasty lemon grass chicken, crab noodles, and crab rolls. At 3244 Broadway (tel. 822-7461); open daily for lunch and dinner.

Seafood

$$ to $$$ **The Bayous:** Cajun/Creole seafood, including gumbo, crawfish (in season), oysters, and shrimp. One of the more reliable River Walk restaurants, and they also arrange barge dining cruises. On the River Walk off N. Presa (tel. 223-

6403); open Mon.-Sat. for lunch and dinner, Sun. dinner only.

$$ **Landry's:** Another place with a Cajun/Creole emphasis. The menu offers an assortment of gumbos, and the snapper Pontchartrain gives La Louisiane a run for its money. At 600 E. Market (tel. 229-1010); open daily for lunch and dinner.

$$ **Water Street Oyster Bar:** Branch of the popular Corpus Christi eatery. Fresh seafood specials daily, plus a variety of oysters—raw, baked, steamed, or grilled. Oyster happy hour 5-7 daily. At 999 E. Busse, off Broadway (tel. 829-4853); open daily for lunch and dinner.

Steaks

$$ **The Barn Door:** Friendly, high-volume steak house with 10 cuts of prime beef, plus all the fixin's. At 8400 N. New Braunfels (tel. 210-824-0116); open Mon.-Fri. for lunch and dinner, Sat. dinner only.

$$ to $$$ **The Grey Moss Inn:** Grilled steaks (including pepper steak) served in a romantic, old stone house with outdoor patio. Seafood and chicken also served. About 12 miles northwest of the city on Scenic Loop Rd., between State 16 and I-10 (tel. 695-8301); open daily for dinner only.

$$$+ **Little Rhein Steakhouse:** This 1847 stone house on the River Walk is the oldest two-story structure in the city. The steaks are 100% USDA center-cut prime, the best and the most expensive San Antonio has to offer. Seafood available, also. At 231 S. Alamo (tel. 225-2111); open daily for dinner.

PIPE CREEK JUNCTION CAFE
BUTTERMILK PIE

3 eggs, beaten	2 cups sugar
1 Tsp. vanilla	$^1/_3$ cup flour
$^1/_2$ cup melted butter	$^3/_4$ cup buttermilk
or margarine	1 deep-dish pie shell

Mix all ingredients except buttermilk in a large bowl. Add buttermilk and stir well. Pour mixture into pie shell and bake in pre-heated 325° oven until "set"–about 1 hour and 15 minutes. Chill and serve.

SAN ANTONIO
ENTERTAINMENT

Live Music

San Antonio may have the most authentically regional music scene in Texas. Whether it's country, blues, swamp, *conjunto*, or German polkas, they've got it. To find out who's playing where, study the *San Antonio Express-News* "Weekender" section, published every Friday. The club listings are comprehensive and up-to-date, and the "Night Lights" column will help separate wheat from chaff. The *San Antonio Light* publishes a similar music column, that's also worth reading, in its weekend section (published on Thursdays) *Current* is a free biweekly that lists upcoming musical performances, but not as comprehensively as the Weekender. The free monthly *SA News* is somewhat better about music listings (including weekday as well as weekend performances), though it only lists the more well-known clubs.

The best part of town for music is the N. St. Mary's club strip, which is similar to Austin's E. 6th St. scene except that it's more funky and less touristy. Stretching between Josephine and Magnolia streets, near both San Antonio College and Trinity University, you'll find live music of several varieties most nights of the week. It's convenient to the downtown area and cover charges run a reasonable $2-5 (sometimes there's no cover during the week).

Below is a list of San Antonio's better live music venues. Most have bands Thurs.-Sun. nights only; on other nights of the week they may be open but you should call first to find out whether live music is happening.

Acapulco Sam's: (tel. 522-1707) 4903 N.W. Loop 410. Rock, world music.

Billy Blue's Barbecue & Icehouse: (tel. 225-7409) 330 E. Grayson St. Blues and R&B.

Billy Marbles: (tel. 227-9144) 409 E. Commerce St. Rock and R&B.

Blue Bonnet Palace: (tel. 651-6702) 16845 I-35 (north of Selma). Urban cowboy dance hall with live country music and indoor bull-riding.

Boardwalk Bistro: (tel. 824-0100) 4011 Broadway. Eclectic.

Cibolo Creek Country Club: (tel. 651-6652) 8640 Evans Road. Roots rock.

Country On The Rocks: (tel. 656-6463) 8024 Cross Creek. C&W and country rock.

Desperado: (tel. 680-7225) 6844 Ingram Road. *Tejano.*

El Fandango: (tel. 532-0377) 114 W. Carolina. *Conjunto.*

Eva's Cozy Spot: (tel. 732-4538) 2217 Blanco Road. *Conjunto*, some Tejano pop.

Farmer's Daughter: (tel. 333-7391) 542 N.W. White Road. Classic country dance hall.

Floore Country Store: (tel. 697-8827) Old Bandera Rd. (State 16), Helotes (two miles west of Loop 1604). A country classic since 1949; C&W, Texas singer/songwriters.

Hangin' Tree Saloon: (tel. 651-7391) 18425 2nd St., Bracken. Country.

Leon Springs Cafe: (tel. 698-3338) Boerne Stage Rd., Leon Springs (12 miles north of San Antonio off I-10). Major singer/songwriter venue; also blues, bluegrass. etc.

The Landing: (tel. 223-7266) Hyatt Regency, River Walk. Traditional jazz.

Lerma's: (tel. 732-0477) 1602 N. Zaragoza Ave. *Conjunto.*

Los Mesquites: (tel. 628-1259) 9901 N. Zarzamora Avenue. *Conjunto*

Monterey Jack's: (tel. 647-8055) 1620 Ingram Rd., and (tel. 496-8055) 2950 Thousand Oaks. Eclectic.

Riverbend Saloon: (tel. 229-9696) Hyatt Regency, River Walk. Country.

Rock Island: (tel. 641-6877) 8779 Wurzbach Road. Rock.

Sneakers: (tel. 653-9176) 11431 Perrin-Beitel Road. San Antonio's premier rock club, with local and touring acts.

Taco Land: (tel. 223-8406). Modern rock, alternative.

Texas South: (tel. 569-8700) State 97 (west of Pleasanton). Country, *conjunto.*

T Town: (tel. 340-8026) 7011 San Pedro. Tejano.

Tropical Drink Co.: (tel. 271-0396) 126 Losoya. Rock, R&B, Caribbean.

Tycoon Flats: (tel. 737-1929) 2926 N. St. Mary's Street. Rock, eclectic.

Wacky's Kantina: (tel. 732-7684) 2718 N. St. Mary's Street. Rock, alternative.

Yosemite Sam's: (tel. 558-488) 5999 De Zavala Road. Rock, blues, R&B.

Beethoven Mænerchor Halle und Garten, 422 Pereida St., presents monthly garden concerts of the Beethoven Mænerchor between Maifest (mid-May) and Oktoberfest (early October) every year. Besides German singing, there's also German food, beer, and wine. During festival times, the schedule includes lively German band performances as well.

The **Majestic Performing Arts Center** (tel. 210-226-2626), 212 E. Houston, is a magnificent restoration of the old Majestic Theatre, one of the few theaters in the country designed by celebrated architect John Eberson. It's now primarily a performance venue for the San Antonio Symphony, but other musical and theatrical performances are held here as well. It's worth attending an event here at least once just to view the breath-taking interior— the domed ceiling features a twilight sky, complete with twinkling stars, birds, and swirling clouds.

Bars

If you're just looking for a good bar and don't care about live music, try **The Esquire** (tel. 210-222-2521) at 115 E. Commerce (off the River Walk). Like any good Texas bar, they only serve beer in longnecks. In 1988, the bar celebrated its 50th anniversary with a contest in which patrons guessed how many longnecks could fit on the 76-foot-long wooden bar. Answer: 4,392. Another place with some history is the **Menger Bar** (tel. 223-4361) in the Menger Hotel, next door to the Alamo. Well over a hundred years old, the bar is reputed to have been a recruitment site for Teddy Roosevelt's Rough Riders.

Durty Nelly's Irish Pub, on the River Walk, is a big favorite with both locals and tourists. Guinness on tap, peanut shells on the floor, and piano players who urge the crowd to sing along (and hand out lyric sheets for this purpose) add to the charm.

Radio

For all its impressive cultural arts, San Antonio doesn't offer much in the way of good regional radio. Music pilgrims might try KONO-AM 860, which emphasizes music born in South and Southeast Texas, such as the Sir Douglas Quintet, Augie Meyers, Charlie and the Jives, or Rudy and the Reno Bops.

For country your best frequency is usually Y-100 (KCYY-100.3). For Tejano/*conjunto* sounds, tune in KXTN-FM 107.5 or KEDA-AM 1540. Another good bet is KSYM-FM 90.1, which plays an eclectic mix of jazz, folk, new music, Texas artists, and other music not usually heard on the radio.

Television

The weekly San Antonio cable-TV program "Bailando," sort of a Latin version of "American Bandstand" or "Club MTV," has satellite feeds to 520 Spanish-language TV stations throughout the U.S. and Mexico.

SAN ANTONIO EVENTS

January

Los Pastores: Various Catholic churches throughout the city put on Christmas plays that tell the story of sheperds in search of the infant Jesus. The most elaborate is held at Mission San José (tel. 210-224-6163) on the first or second weekend of the month.

February

San Antonio Stock Show And Rodeo: A 10-day event in mid-February with the usual rodeos, livestock judging, and carnival midway, plus auctions, Western art shows, parades, and country music concerts. At the Freeman Coliseum (tel. 210-225-5851), Houston St. and Coliseum Road.

Cine Festival: North America's largest Latino film festival, sponsored by the Guadalupe Cultural Arts Center (tel. 210-271-3151). Films are shown over a period of 10 days early in the month.

March

Texas-Irish Festival: A St. Patrick's Day celebration held at La Villita. The city dyes the river green for the occasion (the river is even renamed "the River Shannon" for the weekend) and there's lots of beer, food, and music. On Saturday, events include a 10-kilometer run at Brackenridge Park and a street parade downtown. On the weekend nearest March 17.

Spring Renaissance Fair: A medieval Europe-style event held at Market Square the weekend after the St. Patrick's Day celebration. Features costumes, entertainment, arts and crafts, and food vendors.

Paseo de Marzo: A Mexican spring fair, with Mexican food, music, and dance at Market Square, held the second or third weekend.

Carnaval del Rio: A Texas music festival that covers the regional spectrum, including blues, country, jazz, rock 'n' roll, salsa, zydeco, and *conjunto*. Sponsored by the Paseo del Rio Association (tel. 210-227-4262), the three-day event takes

Texas Folklife Festival

place five days before Ash Wednesday in various venues along the river.

April
Viva Botanica: Also called the Spring Flower Show, held the second weekend in April at the San Antonio Botanical Center (tel. 210-821-5115). Art show, food vendors, and lots of flowers.

Starving Artists Show: A large arts and crafts festival held along the River Walk and at La Villita. Part of the proceeds goes to the Little Church's program to feed the hungry. Some good bargains are usually available.

Fiesta San Antonio: This is the city's biggest annual festival, consisting of as many as 150 separate events over a 10-day period (Friday to Sunday, second and third weeks of the month). Parades, feasting, carnivals, *charreadas,* music, street dances, fireworks, and foot races are just a few of the festivities. Don't-miss events include the St. Mary's University oyster bake (first Saturday), A Day in Old Mexico Charreada (both Sundays at the San Antonio Charro Ranch—see "Sports And Recreation"), a march to the Alamo in commemoration of those who died there (Monday afternoon), the King's River Parade (river floats to celebrate the coronation of King Antonio), A Night in Old San Antonio (a huge, rollicking event at La Villita Tues.-Fri.), the Battle of Flowers Parade (downtown, Friday afternoon), the King William Fair (block party in the King William District Saturday afternoon), the Fiesta Night Parade (downtown, Saturday evening), and the Fiesta Finale

Street Dance (St. Luke's Catholic Church, 4603 Manitou, Sunday evening). For more information, call (210) 227-5191.

May
Cinco De Mayo: Two days of food, music, and dancing at Market Square to celebrate the Mexican defeat of the French at Puebla, Mexico, on May 5, 1862. Held the nearest weekend to May 5.

Tejano Conjunto Festival: A four-day music festival that features the best *conjunto* performers from Texas and northern Mexico. Held at various parks in the city, it's sponsored by the Guadalupe Cultural Arts Center (tel. 210-271-3151). In 1989, the center brought in a few Cajun and zydeco performers, which brought attendance up to nearly 40,000; as a result, there's talk that the name of the festival may be changed to the "San Antonio Accordion Festival" in the future so that Cajun/zydeco sounds can become a permanent feature.

Return of the Chili Queens: On Memorial Day weekend (last weekend of the month) at Market Square, this two-day event celebrates the 19th-century chili queen tradition with lots of chili and other local foods, plus continuous live entertainment. Sponsored by El Mercado Merchants Association (tel. 210-299-8600).

May-September
Fiesta Noche del Rio: Every Tuesday, Friday, and Saturday from Memorial Day weekend through Labor Day, the Alamo Kiwanis Club sponsors Latino music and dance performances

at the Arneson River Theater. The quality of the lineup varies from year to year, but is usually quite good and includes both folk and classical elements. Performances begin at 8:30 p.m. and admission is $7 adult, $3 children under 14. The proceeds go to various charities.

Beethoven Hall Concerts: From Maifest through Oktoberfest, Beethoven Hall (tel. 210-222-1521, 422 Pereida) hosts Friday night outdoor concerts of German music; German food and beer/wine are served.

June-August

Ballet Folklórico de San Antonio: This professional Latino ballet troupe (tel. 210-733-3708) has been performing at the Arneson River Theater every Sunday during the summer since 1974. The rest of the year they tour the country. Polished and very colorful entertainment. Admission is $7 adults, $1 for children 6-12.

June

San Antonio Festival: A two-week international arts festival patterned after Europe's Salzburg Festival, featuring everything from Tokyo's Grand Kabuki to Steve Reich to the Bolshoi Ballet. Ticket prices and venues vary. For information, call (210) 226-1573.

July

Fourth Of July: A five-day bash celebrated at several locations around the city, including La Villita, Market Square, Japanese Tea Gardens, Sea World, and Fort Sam Houston. The celebrations at La Villita and Market Square emphasize Tejano music, while at the Japanese Tea Gardens it's blues. There are evening fireworks displays at La Villita, Fort Sam Houston, Lackland AFB, and Sea World.

August

Texas Folklife Festival: A huge, four-day event that showcases some 30 different cultures with art and crafts shows, food, and entertainment at the Institute of Texan Cultures (tel. 226-7651). Usually the first weekend in August.

Semana de Las Misiónes: Mission Week starts with *El Día de Las Misiónes* on August 6 at Mission San José, than features celebrations at each of the city's five Spanish missions on the following five days.

September

Labor Day Festival: Three days of Mexican music and food at Market Square. Labor Day weekend.

Diez Y Seis: Mexican Independence Day, with public celebrations at Market Square and La Villita that include lots of food and music. Some of the battles for independence were actually fought in San Antonio, which at the time was part of Mexico. On the weekend nearest September 16.

Great Country River Festival: Three days of free country and western music along the River Walk and at Arneson River Theater, co-sponsored by radio station KKYX and the San Antonio River Association. Usually the last weekend of September.

October

Greek Funstival: A weekend celebration of Greek culture, held at La Villita and at St. Sophia Greek Orthodox Church (tel. 210-735-5051), 2504 St. Mary's. Food, music, and folk dancing. Usually the first or second weekend in October.

Missionfest: Also called Feria de las Americas, this event is held at the missions and at La Villita around Columbus Day. Sponsored by Los Compadres de San Antonio Missions Historical Park, activities include food concessions, music, and dancing in the spirit of Renaissance Spain, complete with the coronation of King Ferdinand and Queen Isabella. Proceeds from the concessions go toward further restoration of the San Antonio missions.

Oktoberfest: Sausage, beer, and German music at Beethoven Hall (tel. 210-222-1521, 422 Pereida). Spirited performances by the Mænechor and Damenchor, men's and women's singing societies.

December

Festival Guadalupano: Our Lady of Guadalupe Church (tel. 226-4604) at 1321 El Paso St. is an official regional shrine for the feast day of the Virgin of Guadalupe, December 12 (the anniversary of the New World's first miracle—the appearance of the Virgin before Indian peasant Juan Diego outside Mexico City in 1531). The festival is a 24-hour event that begins at midnight on the 12th and ends at midnight on the 13th, with over 20 local parishes participating. Many parishioners begin arriving around 3:30 a.m. for the *mañanitas* or morning serenades and by dawn celebrations are in full swing.

Ten special masses are held at intervals throughout the day; each mass features a different music and dance performance. Dancers wear satin robes emblazoned with the Virgin's image and imaginative headdresses. Between masses churchgoers help themselves to *champurrado* (hot chocolate), tacos, and *buñ* (sweet rolls). Visitors are welcome (best time to come is 7 p.m. when they hold the colorful Children's Mass, followed by performances by the Ballet Folklórico de San Antonio).

Christmas: From mid-December through early January, San Antonio lights up for Christmas. On the first and second weekends, trees are strung with lights and thousands of candles are lit along the River Walk for the **Fiesta de Las Luminarias.** During the following week, the **Fiesta Navideña** is held at El Mercado and features mariachi music, piñata-breaking, and traditional Mexican holiday food like *pan dulce* (sweet pastries). On the second weekend, Joseph and Mary's search for lodging on the eve before Jesus' birth is reenacted in **Las Posadas,** a procession of candle-bearing singers along the River Walk. After Christmas, Catholic churches hold **Los Pastores** (see "January") on various weekends through early February.

SHOPPING

Shopping Centers
San Antonio has the usual assortment of shopping malls, large and small, and like most American shopping centers, they're far from downtown (several are located along Loop 410, which encircles the city). But the jewel in the crown is the downtown **Rivercenter,** an attractively designed three-level mall at one end of the River Walk, next to the two Marriott hotels. The architects tried to make the mall the modern equivalent of a town square, and it almost succeeds. The three floors (river level, street level, and "fashion" level) feature some 125 shops and restaurants arranged in a "U" shape around a fountain plaza.

Mexican Goods
Much of the same crafts and souvenir items that you'd find in Mexico's tourist centers are also sold in San Antonio. Topping the list of places to shop

for such merchandise is **El Mercado** at Market Square (514 W. Commerce). It's basically a large warehouse divided into vendor stalls that carry everything from *huaraches* (Mexican leather sandals) to pottery and Mexican kitchen utensils. As in Mexico, bargaining is usually acceptable. Nearby **Nila's,** at 206 Produce Row, carries Mexican dresses for women and *guayabera* shirts for men. **Botica Guadalupaña** at 106 Produce Row, Market Square, is the oldest pharmacy in the city, and as the name suggests, they sell traditional Mexican herbal remedies. Also on Market Square is **La Villita Tortilleria** (905 Dolorosa), where you can get fresh tortillas and other Mexican groceries. The **Farmers Market** (612 W. Commerce) has fresh produce, including an extensive selection of Mexican chiles, plus a small assortment of arts and crafts.

Along Commerce St. between Market Square and the River Walk are several Mexican-owned shops selling Spanish-language books and records. **Kerr's Mexican Curios** at 428 E. Commerce, just above the River Walk, is jammed with Mexican souvenirs of the kind you'd find in Nuevo Laredo or Juarez. Down on the River Walk, **Mayan Tejidos de Guatemala** specializes in crafts from lower Mexico and Central America.

If you've been looking for a place that makes custom piñatas, look no further than **Sanchez Piñata Land** at 709 S. Alamo. Señor Sanchez will make a piñata in virtually any requested shape or size, and fill it with whatever you like. Or you can settle for a ready-made donkey (or other animal) stuffed with candy.

Dos Carolinas at 707 S. St. Mary's has handmade guayaberas (Yucatan-style shirts) in linen, silk, and lightweight wool, plus other Mexican classic and original Southwestern creations.

Antiques
Antique Conglomerate (tel. 210-494-7490) at 5525 Blanco, north of downtown, is a complex of around a dozen antique shops, the kind in which the word "antique" means almost anything used. More authentic, but more high priced, is **Chadwick's** (tel. 734-2798), which is also north of the city center at 2524 N. Main.

Bookstores
The city has a fair number of independent book-

stores, something most Texas cities lack. The greatest selection overall is at either of the **Bookstop** stores; best of all, they sell at a discount to the public (and at an even better discount if you buy a membership). The Alamo Heights location (tel. Brees) is the best—they have an excellent magazine selection and books covering every topic from computers to Texana. The **Book Worm** (tel. 210-342-4258), 4707 Blanco in northwest San Antonio, offers a mix of new and used books. The **Antiquarian Book Mart** (tel. 828-4885), 3127 Broadway, carries only used and rare books.

Western Gear

Sheplers (tel. 210-681-8230) at 6201 N.W. Loop 410 at Ingram bills itself as the largest western-wear store in the world, and it looks it. They carry all the standard boots, hats, jeans, and saddle tack, as well as piles of tacky pseudo-western junk, like ashtrays in the shape of a boot. Much more authentic is **Kallison's Farm and Ranch Store** (tel. 222-8411) at 1025 Nogalitos, which offers everything from fencing pliers to woodburning stoves. If you're making a tour of Texas's bootmakers, check out **Johnny Little's Boot Shop** (tel. 732-8137), where three generations of Littles have supplied San Antonians with custom boots for half a century. For custom saddles and other leather gear, trot over to **Lebman's Corral** (tel. 680-7117), at 6504 Bandera.

Paris Hatters (tel. 210-223-3453) at 119 Broadway carries a wide selection of hats, both western and eastern styles, plus name-brand Texas boots such as Justin, Tony Lama, and Nocona.

SPORTS AND RECREATION

Baseball

The city has a Texas League pro team, the San Antonio Missions, who are part of the L.A. Dodgers farm system. They play April-Aug. at Keefe Field, St. Mary's University (tel. 210-434-9311).

Basketball

The San Antonio Spurs are a winning NBA team, and the city's only national pro team of any kind. They play at the Convention Center Arena (tel. 210-224-9578) at HemisFair Park downtown between October and April.

Caving

Since San Antonio is right at the edge of the Hill Country, which is honeycombed with limestone caves, spelunking is a popular activity. The Alamo Regional Group of the Sierra Club (tel. 210-222-8195, P.O. Box 644, San Antonio, TX 78209) says there are 172 caves worth exploring within a 70-mile radius of the city, and they organize group caving trips throughout the year. Hard-core spelunkers will want to contact the Bexar Grotto of the Speleological Society (tel. 699-1388 or 377-3948) for a schedule of their weekend trips.

Cycling

Bicycle-riding is popular in and around San Antonio. The Alamo Regional Group of the Sierra Club (see "Caving" above for address and phone number) sells a guide called "Outdoor San Antonio And Vicinity" ($7) that contains several cycling maps for rides just outside the city. Another good source of information are the **San Antonio Wheelmen** (tel. 210-828-2717 or 696-4204, P.O. Box 34208, San Antonio, TX 78265), who meet monthly and organize group rides almost daily throughout the year. **B&J Bike Shop** (tel. 826-0177), 2445 Nacogdoches, is well stocked with cycling gear and they offer repair service; they also organize group cycle trips and teach bike repair.

Mexican Rodeo *(Charreada)*

Charreada, or Mexican-style rodeo, predates western rodeo and in fact traces its roots back to Spain's *vaquero* tradition. The **San Antonio Charro Association** (tel. 210-532-0693) performs frequently for city festivals throughout the year, most notably April's Fiesta, and is one of the state's premier *charro* (Mexican cowboy) organizations. The SACA practices most weekend afternoons at their *charro* ranch on Padre Drive, next to Mission County Park (near Mission San José), and visitors are welcome to watch. During warm weather, they hold full *charreadas* on Sunday afternoons (small admission fee).

Volksmarches

Group walking as a sport started with the International Volkssport Association in Germany in the '60s; this organization in turn sanctioned the founding of the American Volkssport Association in Fredericksburg, Texas, in the late '70s. Volks of all ages walk in the volksmarches and receive a patch or other symbol for each walk they complete. There's a registration fee for every volksmarche, but if you don't want the patch, it's free. In San Antonio, there are three chapters of the AVS: the Randolph Runners, the Selma Pathfinders, and the Texas Wanderers. For information and schedules, call the AVS at (210) 649-2112.

Parks And Gardens
Brackenridge Park (tel. 210-821-300) off Broadway and Hildebrand is the city's largest and most varied park, founded in 1899. Besides the San Antonio Zoo, the park's former rock quarry is the setting for the **Japanese Tea Gardens** (which were changed to the "Chinese Tea Gardens" during World War II, and later simply "Sunken Gardens"), a typical arrangement of paths, miniature bridges, and carp ponds.

Various paved roads traverse the 343-acre park, plus several hiking and equestrian trails, some of them along unspoiled sections of the San Antonio River. **Brackenridge Stables** (tel. 210-732-8881) offers horses for rent at $10 an hour. Two other modes of transport within the park are the **Skyride,** a cable-car system above the park (including aerial views of the zoo and the Japanese Tea Gardens) and the **Brackenridge Eagle,** a 3.8-mile miniature railway. Hours of operation for both cable cars and trains are Mon.-Fri. 9:30-6:30, Sat. and Sun. 9:30-7:30; fares for each are $1.75 adults, $1.25 children 3-12.

The 38-acre **San Antonio Botanical Center** (tel. 210-821-5115) at 555 Funston near Fort Sam Houston is a mixture of formal gardens and short bioregional trails. The trails emphasize three Texas biotic communities—the East Texas Piney Woods, the Hill Country, and the Southwest Texas plains—and display authentic early Texas houses appropriate to each region. Roughly a third of the area encompasses the formal gardens, including a section with medicinal and culinary herbs, a fragrance garden, and a biblical garden that features plants mentioned in the Bible.

In 1988 the center opened the $6.5-million **Lucile Halsell Conservatory,** which has since been cited for excellence by *Progressive Architecture* magazine. This 90,000-square-foot complex of underground and aboveground greenhouses is designed to work with the South Texas sun for the optimum benefit of the plantlife inside. Visitors enter the complex 16 feet below the ground, then are led through a series of conical pavilions climatically "tuned" to a variety of ecosystems, including a desert room, a palm room, a tropical room, and a citrus room ("orangerie"). The trapezoidal central pavilion forms a glass cone 100 feet wide and 55 feet high; a spiral ramp leads to a roof deck, with a view of the complex and surrounding area. Open Tues.-Sun. 9-6 (conservatory closes at 5); admission is $3 adults, $1.50 seniors, $1 children 3-13.

San Pedro Park (tel. 210-821-3000) at 1500 San Pedro, just north of downtown next to San Antonio College, is the oldest park in San Antonio

charreada, *San Antonio*

and the second oldest in the U.S. after Boston Commons. When built in 1852, it featured a museum, zoo, tropical garden, pavilion, and bathhouse, but its history goes back further since the San Pedro Springs were an important water source for early Spanish settlers (who dug the first *acequias* here in 1716 to irrigate their farmlands). In 1859, Governor Sam Houston held an anti-secession rally at the park. The pavilion stills stands, but the other facilities have been replaced by the 22-court McFarlin Tennis Center (tel. 732-1223), a municipal pool, and the San Pedro Playhouse, a performance venue for the San Antonio Little Theatre (tel. 733-7258).

About 12 miles northwest of the city off I-10 and Milsa Rd. is **Friedrich Park,** over 200 acres of virgin Hill Country wilderness. Part of the municipal park system, Friedrich offers several hiking and nature trails of varying difficulty, including one that climbs a valley ridge for a San Antonio vista. The park is forested with plum, oak, walnut, and cedar, and there are a few stone ruins of early frontier settlements. During the week you'll practically have the place to yourself.

INFORMATION

Tourist Offices
The San Antonio Convention and Visitors Bureau maintains a **visitor information center** (tel. 210-270-8748) across from the Alamo on Alamo Plaza. It's open daily 9-5:30. The mailing address for the CVB is P.O. Box 2277, San Antonio, TX 78298.

While not a tourist office per se, the San Antonio Conservation Society (tel. 224-6163) at 107 King William St. is a mine of information on historic sights in the city.

Mexico Information
San Antonio is a good starting place for a trip into Mexico. The office of the **Mexican Consulate General** (tel. 210-227-9145) is downtown at 127 Navarro. They can arrange visas and answer questions about customs regulations. **Sanborn's Mexican Insurance** (tel. 828-3587), 8107 Broadway, can arrange tourist cards, Mexican auto insurance, and currency exchange. Practically any travel agency in the city can also arrange tourist cards.

Foreign Exchange
NCNB Texas (tel. 210-229-2600) at 112 E. Pecan has the most complete international exchange services of any San Antonio bank, including foreign currencies other than Mexican pesos (and they don't levy service charges). Another bank that handles foreign exchange is Frost Bank (tel. 220-6561, 100 W. Houston).

Publications
The Paseo del Rio Association publishes the free monthly *Reflexiones,* which contains information on shops, services, and special events along the River Walk. Another tourist-oriented magazine is *Fiesta,* published monthly by the *San Antonio Light,* which features a dining guide, lists of museums and art galleries, an events calendar, and short descriptions of area attractions.

Current and *SA Weekly* are both free weeklies patterned after other American "free press" papers that contain a mixture of progressive politics, arts, and lifestyle features. Not quite the *Village Voice* or *Bay Guardian,* but trying hard.

The Hispanic Chamber of Commerce of San Antonio publishes a free, bilingual tourist monthly called *Welcome/Bienvenidos* in which all features and ads appear in Spanish and English.

Maps
The best single San Antonio map available is the AAA map. San Antonio's AAA office (tel. 210-736-4691) is at 323 Spencer Ln. and is open Mon.-Fri. 8:30-5, Sat. 9-1. Continental Maps, Inc. publishes one of lesser quality, but it's adequate.

Telephone
The area code for San Antonio is 210.

TELEPHONE AND EMERGENCY INFORMATION

Emergency (police, fire, medical)	911
Telephone Directory Assistance	1-411
National Weather Service	828-3384
Highway Patrol	533-9171
Amtrak (800) 872-7245 or	223-3226
Post Office Information	657-8300
Time/Temperature	844-4444
Western Union Telegraph	227-8311

SAN ANTONIO TRANSPORT

City Buses And Streetcars
VIA Metropolitan Transit Service (tel. 210-227-2020) offers 91 bus routes plus four downtown streetcar routes. The streetcars are particularly useful for downtown transportation since they stop at Market Square, the Alamo, the Spanish Governor's Palace, the King William district, and other downtown attractions; they're also very inexpensive (only 10 cents). The streetcars are actually built on regular bus chassis, but are replicas of the rail streetcars used in San Antonio until 1933 (even the brass bells on top were cast from an original S.A. streetcar bell). Since they re-

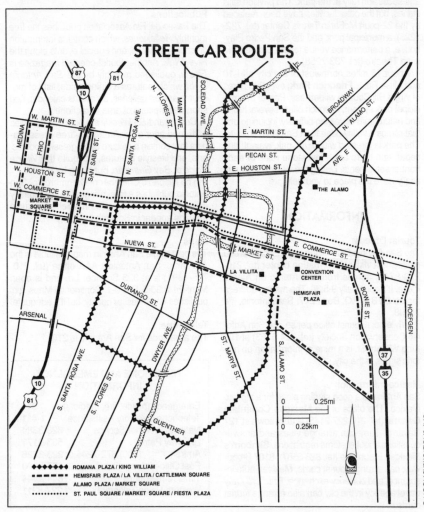

STREET CAR ROUTES

◆◆◆◆◆◆◆ ROMANA PLAZA / KING WILLIAM
■ ■ ■ ■ ■ HEMISFAIR PLAZA / LA VILLITA / CATTLEMAN SQUARE
▥▥▥▥▥ ALAMO PLAZA / MARKET SQUARE
⋯⋯⋯⋯ ST. PAUL SQUARE / MARKET SQUARE / FIESTA PLAZA

placed the El Centro downtown bus system in 1983, ridership has doubled (no doubt attracted by the authentic cast-iron and mahogany seats, brass railings, and leather grab-straps). All routes start at 7 a.m. Mon.-Fri. and 9 a.m. on weekends; service stops between 6:30 p.m. and 9 p.m. depending on the route. Houston St. is the best place to board the streetcars, since all four routes stop here (and none of the buses do, so there's less room for confusion). Regular bus transfers are accepted on the streetcars.

There are also special express buses from the downtown area to Sea World and Fiesta Texas.

River Taxis
Paseo del Rio Boats (tel. 210-222-1701) runs a fleet of flat-bottomed river taxis along the San Antonio River downtown. Their main ticket office is under the Commerce St. bridge (430 E. Commerce), or you can purchase tickets at boat stops. Tickets are $2 adults, $1 children 11 and under. Hours are 9 a.m.-10:30 p.m. from April through Oct., 10-8 from Nov. through March.

Car Taxis
Call **B&B Cab** (tel. 210-225-3345) or **Checker Cab** (tel. 226-4242) for 24-hour taxi service.

Interstate And Regional Buses
The **Greyhound Trailways Bus Terminal** (tel. 270-5824) is at 500 N. St. Mary's. The **Kerrville Bus Co.** (tel. 226-7371) runs a few buses back and forth between the city and the Hill Country.

Train
San Antonio's Amtrak station (tel. 210-223-3226), at 1174 E. Commerce, offers service three times weekly to/from New Orleans and Los Angeles and daily to/from Chicago.

San Antonio International Airport
This airport is conveniently located only eight miles from downtown, about 20 minutes by car. It's also the state's best looking airport—Terminal 1, in fact, won a prestigious American Institute of Architects award. Fourteen airlines provide service to 57 cities in the U.S. and Mexico. **Panchito's Cantina,** just inside Terminal 1's security check, makes fresh tortillas daily to wrap around their respectable, inexpensive fajitas. **Super Van** (tel. 210-344-RIDE) provides shuttle service between the airport and downtown hotels for $7 adults, $3.50 each additional passenger riding with one full-paying passenger. A taxi downtown costs $11-12.

Tours
As befits the state's number-one tourist destination, the city supports a number of bus tour companies. **Gray Line** (tel. 210-227-5371) offers 10 different itineraries, like a two-hour Mission Trail tour for $16.00 (children 5-11 $8.00). Other companies have similar itineraries and rates, including **San Antonio City Tours** (tel. 520-8687). **Fiesta City Fun Tours** (tel. 349-0989) operates half-hour tours of historic San Antonio for $6 pp ($1 discount for anyone carrying *Texas Handbook*). The trolleys leave frequently from in front of the Alamo. Fiesta operates a three-hour tour of San Antonio, with visits to Mission San Jose and the Lone Star Brewery for $28 pp. All-day bus tours to the Hill Country, including a tour of the Texas Whitehouse, a stop in historic Fredericksburg, and lunch for $69 pp. Fiesta also has an all-day shopping tour of Nuevo Laredo for $79 pp (lunch $10). (Readers receive a 10% discount on the above mentioned tours.) **St. Anthony Tours** (tel. 337-5017) does Hill Country and Mexican border trips for $45 each.

VICINITY OF SAN ANTONIO

CASTROVILLE

This town of 1,899 has one of the most distinctive local cultures in the state and is only 25 miles west of San Antonio via US 90. Many of the residents are direct descendants of the original Alsatian colonists who settled the area and have preserved hallmarks of their mother culture. The architectural heritage of the town is also well preserved.

History

Henri Castro, a Portuguese Jew born in Alsace, France, first visited Texas in 1842 as the French consul general to the Republic of Texas; shortly thereafter he received a million-acre land grant under the Texas *empresario* program. After Stephen Austin, Castro was responsible for bringing more immigrants to Texas than any other single *empresario*—700 between 1842 and 1844. A number of the Alsatians he recruited (mostly from Mulhouse, France) founded Castroville on the banks of the Medina River, west of San Antonio, in 1844. They started small farms and ranches and built their houses of native limestone and cypress in the Alsatian style. This close-knit community handed down a modified Alsatian way of life from generation to generation.

Today, many Castrovillians born before the 1950s still speak Alsatian (an unwritten Germanic dialect) as a first language. Since Alsatian is not formally taught in any of the public or private schools in Medina County or Castroville (the county seat), the language will probably be lost locally in another 30 or 40 years.

Economy

The local economy is still very much based on agriculture and ranching. Major farm products include corn, maize, wheat, oats, and vegetables. Much of the corn grown in the Castroville area is processed by the whole-kernel method for use in South Texas *tortillerias* and in the manufacture of corn chips. Beef cattle is the mainstay of livestock production, followed by dairy farming and sheep and goat raising.

Historic Buildings

Castroville's unique architecture is based on Alsatian designs that have been adapted to local

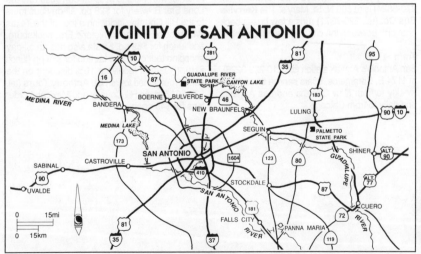

materials and Mexican building techniques. Simple four-square walls of stone and wood predominate, with roofs that slope forward over house fronts. Nearly a hundred buildings in town bear state historical plaques. The **chamber of commerce** (tel. 210-538-3142) at London and Naples (many of the streets in Castroville are named after European cities) distributes a free *Visitor Guide* that contains a walking tour map that covers over 50 historic structures. The **Castro Garden Club** (tel. 538-2298, P.O. Box 10, Castroville, TX 78009) can arrange tours of restored historic homes, which otherwise aren't open to the public.

The oldest standing building is the First St. Louis Baptist Church, on the corner of Angelo and Moye. This small 1846 Catholic church was the first church built in Medina County. A second, larger St. Louis Church was completed in 1870 in the Gothic style, with a tall stone bell tower and 150-foot-long base. Some of the stained-glass windows were imported from Europe while others were made locally. The latter structure is on Angelo between Paris and Madrid.

Landmark Inn State Historic Site

One of the first town mayors, Cesar Monod, built a single-story, Alsatian-style stone building on the Medina River around 1850 that he used as a home and general store. An Irish immigrant bought the place in 1853, added a second story, and turned it into a travelers' inn. Castroville was on the San Antonio-El Paso Rd. and the California gold rush brought a steady stream of travelers. Local entrepreneurs built a stone grist mill and dam on the river next to the inn in 1854. After that, the property changed hands twice more until it was donated to the state-park system by Ruth Curry Lawler, the last owner. (Lawler is a significant figure in the preservation of local culture, as everyone in Castroville will tell you.)

The state still runs the eight-room Landmark Inn as a country hotel—there are no telephones and no air conditioning. Ms. Lawler still lives on the property in a separate house (which is deeded to the state); the mill structures and inn are open to the public daily. Visitors may stay at the inn for a remarkably reasonable rate (see "Accommodations And Food").

The site is just past the Medina River as you enter the city from the direction of San Antonio on US 90. For further information, contact the Park Manager (tel. 210-538-2133), P.O. Box 577, Castroville, TX 78009.

Accommodations And Food

Rooms at the **Landmark Inn** (tel. 210-538-2133, off US 90) are furnished with 1930s antiques and only cost $28 s, $33 d. Since there are only eight rooms, reservations are usually mandatory—they'll take them up to a year in advance. Keep in mind that the inn is not air-conditioned (which is why it's usually easier to get rooms here in the summer). The **Best Western Alsatian Inn** (tel. 538-2262 or 800-528-1234) is about a half-mile west of the Landmark Inn off US 90 and is nicely situated on a hill, so some rooms have a view of the Hill Country to the north. Room rates are $43-59.

Traditional Alsatian cuisine lives on in a few local foods that all restaurants or bakeries carry. *Parisa* is an appetizer of ground beef, onions, and herbs that's spread on crackers, a popular accompaniment for beer. French bread is common, as are a number of sausage, noodle, and pickled vegetable dishes. Anise cookies are a favorite coffee snack. The Alsatian Inn's **Britsch's Restaurant** (tel. 210-538-3839) specializes in Alsatian dishes and is open daily 7 a.m.-10 p.m. San Antonio visitors favor **The Alsatian Restaurant** (tel. 538-3260) on Houston Square (open Mon.-Fri. for lunch and dinner, Sat. dinner only), which also offers Alsatian food. The locals' favorite is **Sammy's** (tel. 538-2204) at 202 US 90, which has been operated by the Tschirhart family since 1948. They do a few Alsatian dishes, but their fortes are chicken-fried steak and Mexican. **Haby's Alsatian Bakery** (tel. 538-2118) at 207 US 90 E is owned by the same family and features tasty apple fritters, strudel, *stollen,* homemade breads, pies, cookies, and coffee cakes; open Mon.-Sat. 5:30 a.m. to 6 p.m.

Another early opener in town is **El Charro** (tel. 210-538-3087) at 1005 US 90 W. They begin serving Mexican breakfasts at 4 a.m. and close at 3 p.m. (open till 8 p.m. Friday only).

Events

The Castroville event of the year is **St. Louis Day,** the feast day of the town's patron saint and a homecoming celebration for Castrovillians who have moved elsewhere. The main festivities are held on the Sunday nearest to August 25, St. Louis Day. A Sunday mass at St. Louis Catholic

Church kicks things off, followed by a public feast at Koenig Park on the river. As many as 10,000 residents and visitors show up for the event, so book early if you plan to spend the night. In addition to eating (the locals start preparing Alsatian-style sausage months in advance), activities include an outdoor auction, arts and crafts exhibits, games, music, and dancing. The Alsatian Dancers of Castroville perform traditional Alsatian folk dances, an art that has been reestablished in recent years (a dancing instructor from Strasbourg visited the town in the early '80s and revived the custom).

Castroville Regional Park

This park in southwest Castroville (take Athens St. south from US 90, then Lisbon St. west) covers 126 wooded acres along the Medina River. Facilities include an Olympic-size pool, picnic areas, tennis and volleyball courts, and camping areas. Bass fishing in the Medina River here is reputedly good. Day-use entry is $1 for adults, 25 cents for children. Tentsites cost $4 a night, while RV parking is $8 (weekly and monthly rates available). For information or campsite reservations, contact Castroville Regional Park (tel. 210-538-2224), P.O. Box 479, Castroville, TX 78009.

NEW BRAUNFELS

During the 1840s, thousands of Germans immigrated to Texas in hopes of escaping political and economic hardships. A group of 10 German noblemen (Mainzer Adelsverein) formed the Society for the Protection of German Immigrants in Texas (Verein zum Schutze deutscher Einwanderer in Texas), whose purpose was to purchase large plots of Texas land for German colonization. Prince Carl of Solms-Braunfel (one of Queen Victoria's cousins) was the society's commissioner-general. He led several thousand Germans to the port of Indianola, Texas, in 1844, at which point the teamsters who were supposed to transport them to their land in South Central Texas broke their contract (choosing more lucrative deals with the U.S. Army at the outbreak of the War with Mexico). Disease and lack of food meant that only a few hundred survived the overland trek to New Braunfels (named after Prince Carl's hometown), and the commissioner-general himself returned to Germany in 1845 to marry his fiancée

after less than a year at his newly founded colony.

The land the Germans had chosen at the intersection of the Comal and Guadalupe rivers was good to those who stayed, however, and by 1850 New Braunfels was one of the state's most prosperous farming towns. Today it's the Comal County seat and continues to prosper from the raising of cattle, sheep, Angora goats, sorghum, wheat, and oats. Tourism is also an important part of the local economy—the major attractions are the historic nature of the town itself and water recreation (fishing, tubing, and canoeing) in the two rivers.

Chili trivia: New Braunfels's Willie Gebhardt was the father of premixed chili powder and canned chili. He started with a small chili café in the back of the town's Phoenix Saloon in 1892, perfected the powder recipe by 1894, then moved to San Antonio and developed his infamous canned chili in 1908.

Museum Of Texas Handmade Furniture

During the mid- to late 19th century, New Braunfels became a minor furniture and cabinet crafting center. The Breustedt House (tel. 512-629-6504) at 1370 Church Hill contains 75 exemplary works from this period, plus collections of pewter and stoneware. Open from Memorial Day to Labor Day, Tues.-Sat. 10-4, Sun. 1-4, the remainder of the year Sat.-Sun. 1-4. Admission is $2 adults, $1 children 6-12.

Sophienburg Museum And Archives

This small museum (tel. 512-629-1572) is on the site that Prince Carl had chosen for his Sophienburg castle (named for his fiancée Sophia), which was never built. Displays chronicle the history of local German immigration and include a replica bakery, barbershop, and pharmacy. At 401 W. Coll; open Mon.-Sat. 10-5, Sun. 1-5. Admission is $2.50 adults, $1 18 and under.

Conservation Plaza

This collection of seven early New Braunfels structures was moved to one spot and restored by the New Braunfels Conservation Society. They include an impressive *fachwerk* house of cedar, cypress, and adobe, a log barn, a couple of stores, a school, and a music studio. A Folklife Festival is held here in early May. At 1300 Church Hill. Only the Baetge House is open to public entry, Sat. and Sun. 2-5 (daily 10-4 during Wurstfest).

Gruene Historic District

Pronounced "Green," this little ghost town four miles northwest of downtown New Braunfels was a cotton boomtown in the late 1800s and early 1900s. In 1925, boll weevils wiped the cotton business out and just about everyone left. In the 1970s, a few entrepreneurs from San Antonio and New Braunfels began moving and restoring the town for the burgeoning tourist trade. The main draw here is **Gruene Hall,** the oldest (or second-oldest, depending on whom you believe) dance hall in Texas. There's usually live music Thurs.-Sun., featuring anything from folk to country to roots rock performers. To get here, take FM 306 west off I-35 N to Hunter Rd., then turn left along Hunter to Gruene's main street.

Accommodations And Food

The **Faust Hotel** (tel. 512-625-8017) at 240 S. Seguin is a nicely restored 1928 hotel with antique-furnished rooms. Rates are $37-60 s, $37-63 d. A bit more expensive, but even more historic, is the restored 1898 **Prince Solms Inn** (tel. 625-9169), a bed-and-breakfast at 195 E. San Antonio with eight rooms, three suites ranging $50 to $75 during the week, $65-110 on weekends. For something modern and characterless, try the **Rodeway Inn** (tel. 629-6991) at 1209 I-35 S (exit 189). In nearby Gruene, the **Gruene Mansion Inn** (tel. 629-2641, 1275 Gruene Rd.) offers rooms in the main house, carriage house, and converted barns for rates starting at $75 a night including breakfast (best for small groups).

    Krause's Café (tel. 512-625-7581) at 148 S. Castell features inexpensive chili, stewed spareribs with dumplings and sauerkraut, various sausages, and other German-American fare (including *panna* and blood sausage in season— Nov.-March). Open Mon.-Sat. for breakfast, lunch, and dinner, except for the first three weeks in September when they close for a holiday. **Wolfgang's Keller** (tel. 625-9169) is in the cellar of the Prince Solms Inn and is a bit more formal, with American and continental dishes. Open Mon.-Sat. for lunch and dinner, Sun. dinner only.

    The **New Braunfels Smokehouse** (tel. 512-625-2416) specializes in smoked meats of all kinds, including sausages, chicken, turkey, ham, beef brisket, and ribs. They also have a few non-smoked dishes like chicken and dumplings. Huge breakfasts. At the junction of State 81 and State 46; open daily for breakfast, lunch, and dinner.

Campgrounds And RV Parks

There are at least 15 campgrounds and RV parks in the New Braunfels vicinity. Rates are around $5-10 for tent sites, $10-15 for RV sites with full hookup. **Whitewater Sports Campground and Canoe Livery** (tel. 512-964-3800) has 500 acres of camping areas and hiking trails along the Guadalupe, off FM 306 just before it crosses the river north of New Braunfels. Others in the area include **Guadalupe River Sports Campgrounds** (tel. 629-3009, 137 N. River Terrace), **Lakeside RV Park** (tel. 625-5494, 1671 Arndt Rd.), and **Stone Creek RV Park** (tel. 620-7759, 18905 I-35 N).

Guadalupe River State Park

Thirty miles west of New Braunfels off State 46 are 1,900 acres of unspoiled Guadalupe River and Hill Country terrain under state protection. The river flows through limestone cliffs and stands of bald cypress, pecan, sycamore, walnut, and willow. Higher park elevations feature oak and juniper woodlands. While not quite as rough as the Canyon Lake-New Braunfels run, canoeing is a popular activity here since there are four sets of rapids within the park boundaries.

    Facilities include picnic areas, a playground, and camping areas. Campsites are $7 on weekdays, $9 on weekends with water only, $10/12 with w/e. Park entry is $3 a day per vehicle, $1 for pedestrians and cyclists. For further information or camping reservations, contact the Park Superintendent (tel. 512-438-2656), Guadalupe River State Park, HC 54, Box 2087, Bulverde, TX 78163.

Natural Bridge Caverns

This is one of the most popular series of limestone caves found throughout South Central Texas. The entrance to the caverns is spanned by a 60-foot length of limestone that forms a natural bridge, hence the name. Different rooms within the caverns are named for the predominant rock formations in each: the Castle of White Giants features imposing limestone columns; the Chandelier has delicate, ribboned formation hanging from the ceiling; while the Sherwood Forest has tall, thin, tree-like formations. Guided tours take a leisurely hour and 15 minutes to complete the half-mile circuit through the various rooms open to the public.

Facilities outside the cave include a picnic area, snack bar, interpretive center, and gift shop. The caverns are located about halfway between San Antonio and New Braunfels, off FM 3009 west off I-35 (Garden Ridge-Schertz exit)—you can't miss the signs.

The caverns open at 9 a.m. daily and tours leave every half-hour till 6 p.m. June-August, till 4 p.m. the rest of the year. Admission is $6.25 adults, $4.75 children. For further information, call (210) 657-6101

Events

The 10-day **Wurstfest,** billed as "the best of the *wurst,"* is celebrated annually starting the Friday before the first Monday in November. This is New Braunfels's own rendition of Germany's Oktoberfest, with the focus on sausage-eating as well as beer-drinking. Local men dress in lederhosen, the women in dirndl. It started as a local one-day affair in 1960 and now draws over 130,000 visitors a year. Don't go expecting an authentically German atmosphere, though, as it's really an ersatz American version—almost a self-parody at times. Most events are held at Landa Park and include arts shows, music and dancing, historical exhibits, food vendors, and the Tour de Gruene Bicycle Classic, a 26-mile road race. There is also an antique bike show attended by antique bicycle clubs from around the state and beyond. The antique bike riders wear period dress—quite a spectacle if you've never seen it before. Music and dance performances are held in the park's Wursthalle and in large outdoor tents.

The second-largest affair of the year is the **Wasserfest,** which takes place the first weekend in June at Landa Park. Events include waterfront concerts, a volleyball tournament, Comal River tubing (tubes and shuttle service available), a kanube races (a "kanube" is a local canoe-inner tube hybrid), a floating parade, and a rock 'n' roll dance at the Wursthalle.

Recreation

Comal River: The 310-acre **Landa Park** on the Comal River features boat rentals and picnic areas. On weekends between Easter and Labor Day the park is closed to motor traffic (a brilliant policy that makes the park even more attractive). The park also has two large swimming pools, including one that's spring-fed, an 18-hole golf course, and a miniature train ride. Just below

Landa Park on the river is **Prince Solms Park,** which offers the **Tube Chute,** a forced-water canal that shoots tubers into the Comal.

Another place to enjoy whitewater excitement along the Comal is at the **Schlitterbahn,** across from Landa Park. It differs from the usual prefab water park in that the water used in the manmade chutes and slides comes directly from the Comal and is recycled back into the river. All but one of the rides were designed and constructed by the Henry family, owner-operators of the park. Most involve ordinary inner tubes, rather than fake logcars, so floaters have a degree of control over speed and trajectory. Probably the most exciting ride is the Whitewater Tube Chute, which rockets tubers through 1,600 feet of banked turns, twists, and spins, and into the river itself. Tubers then float down the river and arrive back at the park to start over. In addition to the four chutes, six water slides, and the Schlittercoaster (a two-story raft slide, the only ride not designed by the Henrys), there are three large hot tubs, a playground, picnic area, miniature-golf course, and three snack bars. The park is open daily Memorial Day-Labor Day, 10-8, on weekends in May and September, closed the remainder of the year. Admission is $17 for a full day, $11 a half day. Children 3-11 pay $14 for a full day, $9 half day.

Guadalupe River Running: The stretch of the Guadalupe River from Canyon Lake south to New Braunfels is the place for real whitewater canoeing, kayaking, and rafting. Most of it's negotiable by novices when water levels are moderate, and those rapids that are tricky (e.g., Hueco Springs and Slumber Falls) have easy portage along one side or the other. Trips can last anywhere from three to nine hours, depending on where you put in and what kind of craft you choose. Canoes typically rent for $30 a day, kayaks are $20, and rafts run from $30 for a two-person size to $120 for a raft that'll carry up to 10 people. These rates usually include paddles, life jackets, and river pick-up service. Some outfitters also rent large inner tubes for $3 a day, an economical way to shoot a few of the easier rapids. Because most of the land along the banks of the Guadalupe is privately owned, you can generally only put in or take out at designated points—many of the outfitters distribute maps.

Established outfitters include **Gruene River Co.** (tel. 512-625-2800, 1495 Gruene Loop Rd.), **Rainbow River Trips** (tel. 964-2227, River Rd.),

Rockin' R River Rides (tel. 629-9999, 1498 Gruene Loop Rd.), **Texas Canoe Trails** (tel. 625-3375, 131 Ruekle Rd.), and **Texas Homegrown** (tel. 629-3176, 1641 Hunter Rd.).

Shopping

The shops of New Braunfels cater to out-of-towners looking for country or Victorian antiques and German souvenirs. **Opa's Haus** (tel. 629-1191) at 1600 River Rd. carries a large selection of merchandise imported from Germany, Austria, and Switzerland—everything from clocks to lederhosen. The **Lace and Lavender Haus** (tel. 629-7106) at 273 Mill Rd. stocks lace and fabrics from the late 1800s and early 1900s, plus some antique furniture. Along San Antonio and Seguin roads are several antique stores, including ones that carry furniture made by the 19th-century New Braunfels cabinetmakers.

CANYON LAKE

Formed by the impoundment of the Guadalupe River by the Canyon Dam and Reservoir (completed by the U.S. Army Corps of Engineers in 1964), this is the major flood control facility in the San Antonio-New Braunfels area. It's also a major recreational spot, drawing a couple of million visitors a year who water-ski, sail, windsurf, fish, swim, and scuba dive within its 8,231-acre surface area and 80-mile shoreline. As the lake is only 14 miles off I-35, it's a popular overnight stop for winter Texans with campers or RVs on their way south.

The U.S. Army operates eight recreation areas along the shoreline, six of which (North Park, Canyon Park, Potters Creek Park, Cranes Mill Park, Comal Park, and Overlook Park) are open to public use. Four of the latter parks have campgrounds where basic tentsites cost $6 per night, sites with water and electricity are $8. All of the parks have boat ramps; there are also two commercial marinas on the lake, Canyon Park Marina and Cranes Mill Park Marina, where motorboats can be rented.

The lake is 48 miles northeast of San Antonio or 16 miles northwest of New Braunfels via I-35 N and FM 306. For further information, contact the Project Manager, Canyon Lake, Fort Worth District, Corps of Engineers, HC 4 Box 400, Canyon Lake, TX 78133.

UVALDE

The Spanish tried to settle the area around Uvalde in the 18th century without success. The Spanish governor of Coahuila (a colonial state in what is now northern Mexico), Juan de Ugalde, won a famous battle here against the Mescalero Apaches in which he commanded a combined force of Comanches, Wichitas, Tawakonis, and Taovayas. The river valley where the 1890 engagement occurred was named Cañon de Ugalde, which later became Uvalde. The town was first established in 1855 by Reading Black, who moved to Mexico during the Civil War because of his opposition to the Confederacy. By the 1880s, Uvalde was a wild West town on the San Antonio-El Paso Trail (now US 90). Corrupt lawman Pat Garrett moved here after shooting Billy the Kid in New Mexico.

The town has calmed considerably since the turn of the century but is still primarily a ranching and farming community, with a 70% Hispanic majority.

Sights

The **Grand Opera House** (tel. 210-278-4184) on 100 W. North St. at US 83 was erected in 1891. After a brief opera career, this three-story brick edifice was used as an office building, but in recent years it's been restored to a 390-seat live performance venue. There is also a small museum in the building. It's open for free guided tours Mon.-Fri. 9-4.

Franklin Delano Roosevelt's first- and second-term vice president, John Nance Garner, was born in Uvalde; after serving with FDR, he returned home and lived here until his death in 1967 at age 98. He had also served as a congressman and speaker of the House. Texans nicknamed him "Cactus Jack" because of his unsuccessful campaign to make a cactus the state flower. When his wife died in 1948, he presented their home to the city (he moved into a smaller house); it was made into the **Ettie R. Garner Museum** (tel. 278-5018, 333 N. Park), which contains memorabilia from Garner's political career.

For cowboy lore, gallop over to **Taylor Made Saddles** (tel. 278-5521) at 112 E. North. Western saddle prices here start at a reasonable $800 (many places in Texas start at $1000).

BOB RACE

Palmetto State Park

Accommodations And Food
The **Inn of Uvalde** (tel. 210-278-9173) at 810 E. Main has well-kept rooms for $26 s, $31 d and a pool. Rooms at the newer **Holiday Inn** (tel. 278-4511) at E. Main cost $42 s, $50 d. **Amber Sky Motel** (tel. 278-5602), 2005 E. Main St. is a classic Route 66-style motel with rooms for just $21 s, $23 d. There's also the **Best Western Continental Inn** (tel. 278-5671, 800-528-1234) at 701 E. Main St., where rooms cost $30 s, $35 d.

Jerry's Restaurant (tel. 278-7556) at 539 W. Main features a classic, small-town Tex-Mex menu; open Mon.-Sat. 6 a.m.-10 p.m. Other small-town culinary sensations can be found at **Evett's Bar-B-Que**, 310 E. Main, which locals claim has the best barbecue in Texas, and at the old-fashioned soda fountain at **Uvalde Rexall Drug**, 201 N. Getty, which serves hand-dipped Blue Bell ice cream.

Entertainment And Events
A large dance hall, **The Purple Sage** (tel. 210-278-1006), is five miles west of town on US 90. There are two levels with bars, live music, and dance floors on each. It's open weekends only, and minors are admitted. The **Cactus Jack Festival** is held at the County Fairgrounds (on US 90W) and other locations during the second weekend in October. Activities include a fiddler's contest, parade, barbecue cookoff, music and dancing, arts and crafts show, and an intercollegiate rodeo at Southwest Texas Junior College (FM 1023, off US 90E). Call the Uvalde Chamber of Commerce (tel. 278-3361) for information.

EAST OF SAN ANTONIO

The counties to the immediate east and southeast of San Antonio—Guadalupe, Gonzales, Karnes, DeWitt, and Lavaca—were mostly settled in the mid- to late 18th century by Germans, Czechs, and Poles who fled political and religious persecution in Central Europe (with Prussia, Russia, and Austria the main oppressors). Nearly all sailed to the port of Galveston, motivated by stories that Texas was a land of tolerance and opportunity. They were usually unprepared for the hardships they faced upon arrival, including lack of inland transport, hostile Indians, and disease in the low-lying coastal areas. Their common destination was South Central Texas, but many died between Galveston and San Antonio, while others gave up and settled in the most hospitable areas they found along the way.

Palmetto State Park
About 60 miles east of San Antonio near Luling is the Ottine Swamp, home to the dwarf palmetto

(Sabal minor). Palmetto State Park protects 263 acres of wooded swamplands where the palmetto grows profusely. The swamp is fed by an artesian spring and by overflow from the San Marcos River, which passes through the park. The "oxbow" lake near the picnic area is a former San Marcos tributary and is now a popular local spot for swimming, fishing, and boating. Other facilities include hiking and nature trails, an interpretive center, and three camping areas.

Campsites with water only are $6 a night weekdays, $8 weekends; sites with w/e are $9/11. Admission to the park is $3 per vehicle, $1 cyclists and pedestrians. The park is located a couple of miles south of Luling (which is on I-10 E) off State 183. For further information contact the Park Superintendent (tel. 672-3266), Palmetto State Park, Route 5, Box 201, Gonzales, TX 78629.

Shiner

This Czech-German town of just over 2,000 residents is off the beaten path, that is, well off I-10 between San Antonio and Houston. The main reason out-of-towners visit is to make a pilgrimage to the Spoetzl Brewery, home of Shiner beer. The town was founded in 1887 by a Luxembourgian named Henry Shiner as a trading center for local Czech and German farmers. In the late 1800s the town prospered from cotton grown in the sandy loam and black waxy soils of surrounding Lavaca County. The 1925 Central Texas boll weevil invasion forced the county to diversify, and ever since the economy has mostly rested upon livestock (cattle, chickens, and turkeys) and grain (hay, milo, and corn) production, although cotton remains an important crop.

Many of the older town residents still speak German or Czech as a first language. At the **Shiner Bar** on Ave. E (US 90 Alt.), in business since 1912, old-timers play dominoes and listen to polkas on the jukebox while drinking Shiner beer (on tap). The interior of the bar is decorated with rococo tin panels in Old World patterns. **Patek's Market** on the same road sells homemade sausage and polka records (some recorded by local bands).

Church: Saints Cyril and Methodius Catholic Church, built in 1922 in the majestic Romanesque Revival style, features a 142-foot domed tower with an octagonal, eight-story spire. Leaded-glass windows display saints above each side entrance and parts of the interior sport painted murals.

Brewery: Of the three major Texas beer labels, Shiner, Lone Star, and Pearl, Shiner is indisputably the best. The **Spoetzl Brewery** (tel. 512-594-3852) at 603 E. Brewery was founded in 1909 by Bavarian-born Kosmos Spoetzl, a graduate of the Augsburg Brewery Institute. After a career as a peripatetic brewmaster in Germany, Bohemia, Egypt, Canada, and California, Kos-

*Catholic church,
Panna Maria*

mos settled in Shiner and began producing only one beer, a dark malt lager called "Old World Bavarian Draft." It was sold only within a 70-mile radius of Shiner, in Czech- and German-dominated towns like Praha, Flatonia, Hochheim, Schulenburg, and Waelder. During Prohibition, he continued to make and distribute Shiner, reboiling the brew to remove the alcohol. After Prohibition, he changed the name of his beer to "Texas Special Export" and went after bigger markets like San Antonio and Austin (but even today, Shiner beer is difficult to find outside Central Texas). When Kosmos died in 1950, his daughter Cecilie managed the business until she sold to New Braunfels investors in 1966. They unfortunately lightened the traditional recipe to follow the trend among American beers, which were becoming less and less flavorful in general, and this became the "Premium" label. Beer connoisseurs stick to the heavier "Shiner Bock," which uses toasted malt and is said to be closer to the original recipe.

Although Shiner production is currently up to 70,000 barrels a year (virtually nothing compared to the average American label), it is still brewed by a staff of only 50 employees, using an all-natural process that requires no additives. Kegs are still bunged by hand (the tour guides boast that they have the smallest commercial brewing kettle in the nation, with only a 75-barrel capacity). The brewery offers free half-hour tours Mon.-Thurs. at 11 a.m. The hospitality room is open for free tasting Mon.-Fri. 9-4:30.

Accommodations and Food: Stay at the **Aljo Motel** (tel. 512-594-3335), 1016 N. Ave. E (US 90A) for $30-35 a night or **Old Kaspar House Bed & Breakfast** (tel. 594-3100), 219 Ave. C for $40-60 a night including continental breakfast.

The **Palace Cafe** on 7th St. has been in continuous operation since 1911. The menu includes burgers, stews, and chili, plus daily blue plate specials; it's open 9-4 daily. The **Half-Moon Saloon & Restaurant** at 522 N. Ave. E (US90A) is a full-service restaurant with Cajun chicken, Cantonese shrimp and calorific desserts like pecan praline cheesecake and bread pudding with butter brandy sauce. Open Tues.-Thurs. for lunch and dinner, Fri.-Sat. for dinner only.

Events: If you happen to be in the Shiner vicinity on the Sunday before Labor Day, drop by the American Legion Park on Ave. G for the **Shiner Catholic Church Picnic,** an event that's been held annually since 1897. It runs from noon to midnight and features the famous Shiner Picnic Stew dinner, polka and country music, a horseshoe-throwing tournament and other games, and an auction.

Getting There: Shiner can be hard to find on a Texas map. The quickest way to get here from San Antonio is to proceed east on I-10 about 28 miles, then take the US 90 Alternate exit for Seguin and continue east on US 90 Alt. (via Belmont and Gonzales) for another 58 miles to Shiner.

Panna Maria

In 1854 Father Leopold Moczygemba and 100 Catholic families fled religious persecution in Poland's Upper Silesia for brighter Texas horizons. On Christmas Eve of that year they arrived at the junction of the San Antonio River and Cibolo Creek after walking 200 miles from Galveston port, and named their new home Panna Maria, "Virgin Mary"—the first Polish settlement in the United States. The **Church of the Immaculate Conception,** built two years later, is still an active Polish Catholic church and stands in the center of the small village (less than a hundred current residents). Inside the church is a mosaic of the Black Madonna, a replica of the famous Black Madonna of Czestochowa, which President Lyndon Johnson presented to the town in 1966.

The first Polish school established in the U.S. (1868) now houses the **Panna Maria Historical Museum,** a modest collection of displays that chronicle local history. Panna Maria Elementary School is the successor to the original school and is operated by Felician Sisters. Many older town residents still speak a Silesian dialect. For local color, visit the **Snoga Store,** which was originally built as a barn in 1855.

Panna Maria is in Karnes County, about 55 miles southeast of San Antonio off US 181 and FM 81 (about halfway between San Antonio and Goliad).

BOB RACE

SOUTH TEXAS

South Texas begins below the San Antonio River where the Coastal and Rio Grande plains meet. Spain founded many of its earliest Texas settlements in this area and introduced cattle ranching to North America here (some of the direct descendants of the Spanish colonists still live on original colonial land grants). The first great cattle trail, the Shawnee Trail, stretched from Brownsville at the southernmost tip of South Texas to Kansas City in the 1840s.

Throughout early Texas history, Anglo and European immigrants were largely uninterested in South Texas, which remained a stronghold of Hispanic culture until well into the 20th century. Even today, most South Texas counties have Hispanic-majority populations. Ranching and agriculture are economic mainstays, along with winter tourism and hunting (primarily white-tailed deer, javelina, and wild turkey).

UPPER SOUTH TEXAS

GOLIAD

Founded in the early 1700s as Santa Dorotea, a colony of New Spain, Goliad has played a strategic role in the state's history. When a Spanish mission and presidio were moved here from the Gulf coast in 1749, the name was changed to La Bahía; then following the Mexican revolution of 1821, it was changed again to Goliad. Mission Espiritu Santo was the longest-running mission in Texas and during its 110-year tenure was responsible for Goliad's development into a cattle ranching center. Because the settlement was between the early Texas port of Indianola and San Antonio, it also became an important trade center. When Galveston replaced Indianola as the coast's major port, Goliad trade declined and the area economy reverted to ranching and agriculture.

The main attractions here are the restored Spanish presidio (the oldest fort in the Western U.S.) and mission. The **Courthouse Square Historic District** is also worth a tour—pick up a free, walking-tour map at Goliad's Chamber of Com-

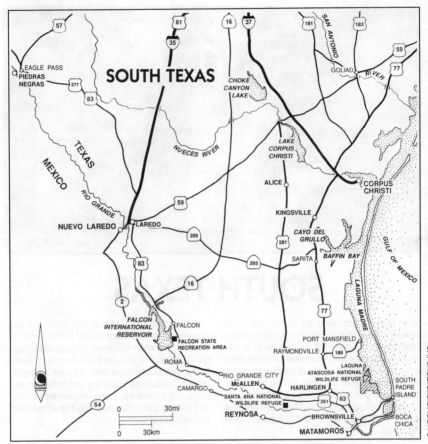

SOUTH TEXAS

EAGLE PASS
PIEDRAS NEGRAS

NUEVO LAREDO / LAREDO

FALCON INTERNATIONAL RESERVOIR

FALCON

FALCON STATE RECREATION AREA

ROMA

RIO GRANDE CITY

CAMARGO

McALLEN

SANTA ANA NATIONAL WILDLIFE REFUGE

REYNOSA

MATAMOROS

BROWNSVILLE

BOCA CHICA

SOUTH PADRE ISLAND

LAGUNA ATASCOSA NATIONAL WILDLIFE REFUGE

HARLINGEN

RAYMONDVILLE

PORT MANSFIELD

LAGUNA MADRE

SARITA

BAFFIN BAY

CAYO DEL GRULLO

KINGSVILLE

ALICE

LAKE CORPUS CHRISTI

CORPUS CHRISTI

GULF OF MEXICO

CHOKE CANYON LAKE

NUECES RIVER

GOLIAD

SAN ANTONIO RIVER

TEXAS

MEXICO

RIO GRANDE

0   30mi
0   30km

© MOON PUBLICATIONS, INC.

merce (tel. 512-645-3563) at 202 Market, at Franklin. In the same building is the **Market House Museum,** which features minor historical exhibits pertaining to Goliad history.

Presidio La Bahia

This fort was first established in 1721 among the ruins of France's Fort St. Louis on Matagorda Bay, hence the name La Bahia (The Bay). The full Spanish name for the fort was El Presidio Real de Nuestra Señora de Loreto de La Bahía del Espiritu Santo de Zuniga, as it was built to protect Mission Espiritu Santo de Zuniga. Both mission and presidio were moved to their present location on the lower banks of the San Antonio River in 1749. Pre-

sidio La Bahia is said to be the only completely restored Spanish colonial fort in the western hemisphere and the most fought-over fort in American history. Over a hundred-year period, the presidio was involved in six separate independence wars and flew nine different flags.

Spanish soldiers stationed at La Bahia participated in the American Revolution of 1779-82 when they defeated the British colonial forces at Baton Rouge, Natchez, Mobile, and Pensacola. Three unsuccessful battles against Spanish rule were later fought here, in 1812, 1817, and 1821. Following Mexican independence, the fort was turned over to Mexican troops and became an important Mexican outpost. General Ignacio

Zaragoza, born in Goliad and educated in Mexico, led the successful battle against the French invasion at Puebla, Mexico, from the fort on May 5, 1862 (now celebrated in Mexico and the American Southwest as Cinco de Mayo). For Texans, the most infamous incident here was the Goliad Massacre of 1836, when 300 Texican rebels under Colonel James Fannin surrendered to Mexican forces at nearby Coleto and then were executed at the presidio.

The presidio was restored to its original 1836 appearance in 1967. A museum in the presidio contains artifacts found during the restoration, including evidence of nine previous habitation eras. The presidio chapel still holds services on Sundays. A Living History Program re-creates various events in the fort's history on-site: the 1812-1813 siege/Magee-Gutierrez Expedition (January), the Goliad Massacre (March), the Spanish Nightwatch (June), Las Posadas and Our Lady of Loreto Festival (Christmas).

The presidio (tel. 512-645-3752) is about two miles south of Goliad off US 183. Open daily 9-5; admission is $2 adults, 50 cents children 6-12.

Goliad State Historical Park

This 178-acre park commemorates the 300 Texicans slain at the 1836 Goliad execution and contains the restored **Misión Espiritu Santo de Zuniga.** This mission was one of the most important in New Spain's province of Texas, with jurisdiction over all land between the Guadalupe and San Antonio rivers. The mission prospered and, at its peak, maintained as many as 40,000 head of cattle, which supplied beef to other Spanish settlements as far away as Mexico and Louisiana. It was secularized in the 1820s.

The mission buildings—a church, granary, *convento,* and workshop—have been restored and decorated with period furnishings. A museum displays colonial and Aranama Indian artifacts and interpretive exhibits, including an audio-visual history presentation.

Park flora represents a mosaic of four biotic communities: Tamaulipan, Texan, Balconian, and Austroriparian. The **Aranama Trail** (about a third of a mile long) forms a loop near the mission and takes visitors through transitional subtropical-brush country vegetation such as live oak, *huisache,* bluewood, honey mesquite, *chapotillo* (torchwood), prickly pear cactus, yucca, and blackbrush acacia. A trail system along the San

Misión Espiritu Santo

Antonio River passes through riparian woodlands of sycamore, pecan, cottonwood, Texas persimmon, and sugarberry.

The park has a wide selection of camping areas: primitive tentsites for $4 a night; tent/-camper sites with water or w/e for $6-9, full RV hookups for $10, and screened shelters for $15. Park entry is the usual $3 per vehicle, $1 for pedestrians and cyclists.

For more information, contact Goliad State Historical Park (tel. 512-645-3405), P.O. Box 727, Goliad, TX 77963.

La Bahia Downs

This track (tel. 512-645-8208), a mile north of town off US 183, features quarter-horse racing and pari-mutuel betting from Sept. to Nov. and in June and July.

Accommodations And Food

The family-owned **Antlers Inn** (tel. 645-8215) on US 59S is a standard-looking motel with rooms for $26-28 s, $31-33 d. **The Dial House** (tel. 645-

3366) offers bed-and-breakfast accommodation in a 1905 house at 305 W. Oak for $45-65. Another B&B, **White House Inn** (tel. 512-645-2701, 203 N. Commercial) has rooms for $45-55 including full breakfast.

La Bahia Restaurant (tel. 512-645-3651), on US 77 at Refugio Rd., serves Mexican food daily for lunch and dinner. **Hunter's Cafe** at the Antlers Inn is open daily 5 a.m.-10 p.m. and serves a variety of American standards.

RV Parks
Six miles west of Goliad on FM 1351, off US 59 W, is **Encino Grande RV Park** (tel. 512-645-3179), where full hookups are $10 a night (senior discounts are available for stays of more than one night).

Entertainment And Events
For an authentic Texas roadhouse experience, seek out **Schroeder Dance Hall** on FM 622, about 15 miles northeast of Goliad off US 183. Schroeder's green-oak dance floor has been hosting country dances every weekend since 1949.

On the weekend closest to May 5 (Cinco de Mayo), Goliad County hosts the **Fiesta Zaragoza** in honor of the Goliad-born Mexican general who defeated the French at Puebla in 1862. Festivities are held at the Goliad County Fairgrounds on US 183 (about a mile south of town) and include a barbecue, music, dancing, arts and crafts, and a carnival midway. A field mass is held at the Presidio La Bahia amphitheater on May 5.

CHOKE CANYON STATE PARK

This recently established 385-acre park is on a peninsula in Choke Canyon Lake, a 26,000-acre reservoir created by the impoundment of the Frio River. The rest of the shoreline (approximately 8,700 acres) comprises the James E. Daugherty Wildlife Management Area. Choke Canyon is the westernmost habitat for the American alligator.

Facilities
Park facilities are distributed among two recreational areas, the South Shore Unit and the Calliham Unit, and include swimming beaches, picnic pavilions, nature trails, boat ramps, a bait and tackle concession, gym, baseball field, park store, and tennis courts—in short, everything needed

for a long vacation. The plentiful campsites include water-only sites for $7 weekdays, $9 weekends, w/e for $10/12, and screened shelters for $15/18; trailer dump sites are also available.

Park entry is $3 weekdays, $5 weekends per vehicle, $1 for bicyclists and pedestrians. For further information, contact the Park Superintendent (tel. 512-786-3868), Choke Canyon State Park, Box 2, Calliham, TX 78007.

Getting There
Choke Canyon Lake is about 80 miles southeast of San Antonio off I-37, a little less than halfway to Corpus Christi on the Gulf coast.

KINGSVILLE

What started out as a ranch developed into a one-town county, with Kingsville (pop. 25,000) as the county seat of Kleberg County (pop. 30,000). Former Rio Grande riverboat captain Richard King stopped off at the abandoned Santa Gertrudis land grant in the Wild Horse Desert en route to the 1853 Lone Star Fair in Corpus Christi. He'd made a fortune supplying the U.S. Army during the War with Mexico and was seeking acreage for a cattle ranch. That same year he bought the Santa Gertrudis tract and eventually turned it into the largest ranch in the world before his death in 1885. His widow, Henrietta, along with son-in-law Robert Kleberg (a German immigrant), established the town of Kingsville in 1904 as a railhead for the newly founded St. Louis, Brownsville, and Mexico railroad.

Today, Kingsville is still mainly a ranching center that services the huge King Ranch, and it's also the home of Texas A & I University and the Kingsville U.S. Naval Air Station. Except for the ranch and the university's Conner Museum, however, there is little of interest in town. The **Sellers Market** is an arts and crafts cooperative housed in a hundred-year-old building at 205 E. Kleberg. The co-op sells its wares to the public Wed.-Fri. 10-5:30.

King Ranch
The largest privately owned ranch in the world covers over 1.2 million acres in four Texas counties, with the main tract of 825,000 acres (larger than the state of Rhode Island) in Kleberg County. The ranch employs over 500 employees to overlook its 2,000 miles of fences, 500 miles of

roads, 60,000 head of cattle, and 1,000 registered quarter horses. The ranch's multinational corporate extension controls over four million acres worldwide for the production of cattle, sugar cane, sorghum, rice, hay, and corn.

The King family has not only been skilled in multiplying ranch acreage, but in animal breeding as well. In seeking to produce a cattle breed that could thrive in the harsh South Texas climate, they came up with the highly successful Santa Gertrudis, a cross between the Indian Brahman and the British shorthorn—the first new cattle breed in the Western Hemisphere. They've also had luck with breeding champion quarter horses; when the American Quarter Horse Association was founded in Fort Worth in 1941, the number-one entry in the stud book was a King horse, Wimpy. The ranch has since produced several Derby winners among its world-class cutting horse stallions.

The **King Ranch Visitor Center** (tel. 512-592-8055) is off Hwy. 141 two miles west of US 77 in Kingsville. Guided van tours along a 12-mile road through the Santa Gertrudis division are available from the center Mon.-Sat. 10-3, Sun. 1-4. The cost is $6 per person for adults, $5 seniors, $2.50 children 5-12. The tour takes in cattle and horse pastures, feedlots, show pens, an auction ring, and various ranch buildings.

Also in town is the **King Ranch Museum** (tel. 512-592-0408), in the Henrietta Memorial Center at 6th and Lee streets. On display are photos documenting King Ranch life in the '30s and '40s as well as several vintage automobiles. One of the more amazing exhibits is the custom-built 1949 Buick Straight Eight hunting car, with triple rifle scabbards mounted on each fender and a bar in the rear. The museum is open Mon.-Sat. 10-2, Sun. 1-5. Admission $4 adults, $3 seniors, $2.50 children 5-12.

Robert Salas, the skilled saddlemaker for the ranch, has recently opened the **King Ranch Saddle Shop** (tel. 800-282-KING) at 6th and Kleberg in the restored 1909 Ragland Building. In addition to 100% handmade saddles, Salas and his assistants fashion gun cases, purses, briefcases, and other leather items, each emblazoned with the running-W ranch logo. The saddle shop is open Mon.-Fri. 9-6, Sat. 10-2. The current wait time for a custom saddle is about six weeks.

For further information on visitor operations contact the King Ranch (tel. 512-592-8055), P.O. Box 1090, Kingsville, TX 78364.

Texas A & I University
Founded in 1925 as South Texas State Teachers College, the school became Texas College of Arts and Industries in 1929 and assumed its current name and university status in 1967. The enrollment of 5,400 is 53% Hispanic; a strong program in bilingual education is offered through the doctoral level. Other large programs include animal science and engineering. Majors are divided into five colleges: Agriculture and Home Economics, Arts and Sciences, Business Administration, Education, and Engineering.

The **John E. Conner Museum** (tel. 512-595-2819) at Armstrong and Santa Gertrudis on campus features exhibits on the area's bicultural heritage, South Texas and northern Mexico natural history, and ranching history. The museum is open to the public Mon.-Fri. 9-5, Sun. 2:30-5; admission is free.

Kaufer-Hubert Memorial Park
This county park is about 25 miles south of Kingsville on Baffin Bay, a huge brackish lagoon off the Gulf of Mexico (16 miles south on US 77, then another nine miles east on FM 771). Facilities include two freshwater lakes, boat ramps, picnic areas, bait/tackle concessions, a restaurant, grocery, laundromat, bird-observation tower, horseshoe pits, soccer/softball fields, a beach, jogging trail, and a 12-station senior fitness course—in short, everything for the winter Texan. The **Seawind RV Resort** (tel. 512-297-5738) operates in conjunction with the park and offers 134 RV sites with full hookups, including telephone. Post office boxes are available. For further information, contact Kaufer-Hubert Memorial Park and Seawind RV Resort, Route 1, Box 67-D, Riviera, TX 78379.

Accommodations And Food
The **Best Western Kingsville Inn** (tel. 512-595-5657), on King Rd. at the US 77 bypass, has rooms for $37-45 a night. The nearby **Motel 6** (tel. 592-8133) has adequate rooms for $21.95 a night, plus $6 for each additional adult. Also inexpensive is the **Sage Motel** (tel. 592-4331) on US 77 Business, where rooms are $23 s, $30 d.

The Mexican family-owned **La Placita** restaurant (tel. 512-592-7581) at 801 N. 14th serves Tex-Mex, fresh catfish, and chicken-fried steak. At the edge of Cayo del Gruyo (a finger of Baffin Bay about 10 miles south on US 77, then east on FM 628 nine miles) is the **King's Inn** (tel. 297-4265).

Fresh seafood is the specialty here, including crab, oysters, shrimp, frogs' legs, and catch of the day.

Events
The **George Strait Team Roping and Concert** is held one weekend in June at the Northway Exposition Center in Dick Kleberg Park. Country singer/native Texan George Strait and his brothers compete in the roping competition along with other U.S. teams on Saturday and Sunday. Saturday night Strait performs. Call the Kingsville

Chamber of Commerce (tel. 512-592-6438) for further information.

Driving South
A word of caution to those driving south from Kingsville on US 77: for the 73-mile stretch between Kingsville and Raymondsville, there are no gas stations. This is ranch country, most of it belonging to the King Ranch. Be sure to fill up before you leave town.

RIO GRANDE VALLEY

THE LAND AND WILDLIFE

Three counties—Willacy, Cameron, and Hidalgo —make up the "Rio Grande Valley," which is not really a valley but a river delta. In spite of the fact that there are no nearby mountains to make it a valley, it's often referred to as simply "the Valley" (a name that goes back to the last century) by the local populace and by winter Texans. The topography represents a cross section of Gulf Coastal Plains and North Mexico Plains—a unique blend of humid, subtropical conditions and brush country. Ten biotic communities have been identified in the area: Chihuahuan thorn forest, upper valley flood forest, barretal, upland thorn scrub *(matorral)*, mid-delta thorn forest, mid-valley riparian woodland, woodland potholes and basins, coastal brushland potholes, Sabal palm forest, and loma (coastal clay) tidal flats.

These habitats together support over 115 unique vertebrate species, including four of the five remaining wild cats in the U.S.—cougars, bobcats, and the endangered **ocelot** and **jaguarundi** (50 years ago the Valley was also home to the jaguar and the margay cat, but these have since disappeared). These habitats also provide important nesting and migratory grounds for several hundred bird species, more birdlife than anywhere else in the United States (see "Birding" below).

The rich alluvial soils of the Rio Grande Plain were virtually ignored until the turn of the century when river levees and underground irrigation systems were developed. Before that, periodic floods made farming along the Rio Grande a risky proposition. Also, although the soils were intrinsically rich, the naturally high evaporation rate made it almost impossible to farm the Valley without irrigation. As a result of controlled watering and mild year-round temperatures, the area now enjoys a 330-day growing season and is an important truck-farming center. The land produces 56 varieties of fruits and vegetables, including citrus, sugar cane, onions, cucumbers, tomatoes, cabbage, and 99% of the aloe vera grown in the country.

Farming has brought a measure of prosperity to planters, landowners, and trucking companies but little to the Chicano- and Mexican-majority workers who pick and process Valley produce. To get a feel for the Rio Grande Valley that's not described in the tourist brochures, take a drive along the area's back roads, off the palm-lined main highways; the fields of citrus, aloe, and sugar cane are beautiful, but the poverty of La Frontera, "The Borderland," all too apparent.

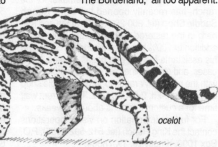

BOB RACE

ocelot

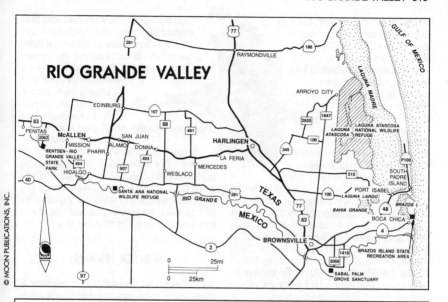

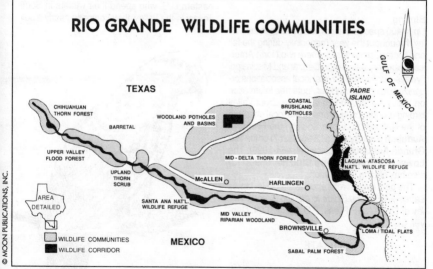

Wildlife Corridor

Because local farming contributes to an ever-increasing habitat loss, there are current local, state, and national efforts to create a "Wildlife Corridor" that would link several already-existing state parks and national wildlife refuges throughout the 10 identified habitats. Some of the lands included in the proposal are under private ownership while others are public; the plan is to allow these "missing links" in the corridor to return to their natural state, thus establishing a 107,000-acre protected strip extending from the Falcon Dam in Zapata County to the Gulf of Mexico (a distance of around 175 miles). Active participation in the lobbying and public education effort in favor of the proposed corridor has become a favored activity for a small number of winter Texans, since habitat loss affects everyone in the long run. For information on the project, contact the Wildlife Corridor Task Force (tel. 512-968-3275) or the Santa Ana/Lower Rio Grande Valley National Wildlife Refuges (tel. 787-7861), Route 2, Box 202A, Alamo, TX 78516. The staff at the Valley Nature Center (tel. 969-2475) at 301 S. Border Ave. in Weslaco are also involved in the Corridor project and are always looking for volunteers.

black-bellied whistling duck

TODD CLARK

Birding

Up to 400 species of birds can be seen in the Valley throughout the year (especially during the fall and winter), since this is where two North American migratory paths—the Central and Mississippi flyways—converge. Several local associations organize birding trips and distribute free information on Valley birdlife. To find out more about Valley birding groups, contact one of the local chapters of the National Audubon Society: the **Frontera Audubon Society** (tel. 512-968-3257) or the **Rio Grande Audubon Society** (tel. 464-3029). The **Lower Rio Grande Sierra Club** (tel. 969-2113) also has birding information.

The best written reference available is James Lanes's *A Birder's Guide to the Rio Grande Valley of Texas* (L&P Press, P.O. Box 21604, Denver, CO 80221).

CLIMATE

Most of the Rio Grande Valley is at the same latitude as the Florida Keys, which means mild winter temperatures. The average low temperature in Brownsville for January is 51° F, while the average high for the same month is 70°. In July, Brownsville temperatures range from 76° to 93° F. In general,

summer highs in the Valley are two or three degrees lower than in San Antonio or Austin. Average annual precipitation in the Valley is around 25 inches (about half the average rainfall in Miami). September is by far the wettest month, averaging around five inches. The hurricane season begins in May, peaks in August and September, and fades out by the end of October, but most of the Valley suffers little or no damage during tropical storms or hurricanes—just rain and high winds (there's only a one-in-seven chance of a hurricane striking this far south in any given year). With an eye to the weather, the best time of year for a visit is between October and May.

WINTER TEXANS

Winter Texans (or "snowbirds") are residents of snowy states in the upper midwestern and northeastern U.S. who spend their winters in South Texas; in the Valley, they comprise nearly a sev-

yellow-headed parrot

BOB RACE

enth of the population between November and April—as many as 125,000. They're drawn primarily by climate—the average year-round temperature is 76° F (see "Climate" above for more details)—and by the low cost of living (several points below the national average). Another major attraction is the Valley's unique position between the barrier islands of the Gulf of Mexico and Old Mexico itself. The vast majority of out-of-staters who winter in the Valley are retirees with time on their hands; the recreational opportunities provided by nearby South Padre Island, two national wildlife refuges, a state park, and the Mexican border towns of Matamoros and Reynosa add variety to what might otherwise be a mere escape from cold weather.

The average winter Texan spends up to three months in the Valley, which has made it the number-one destination in the state for visits of longer than 30 days.

Activities And Information

The main centers for winter tourism are Harlingen, Brownsville, and McAllen, followed by the smaller communities of Mission, San Juan, Weslaco, Mercedes, and San Benito. During the winter the average age of the local population climbs, with as many as 20% over 55 years. Most Valley towns have special centers that provide services for seniors and retirees, such as health screening and social events. Common organized activities include square, tap, clogging, and jazz dancing, arts and crafts classes, photography clubs, card games (bridge, poker, etc.), woodcarving, sewing, quilting, shopping trips to Mexico, tennis, fishing, and golf. The larger RV parks also offer group activities—some even have their own dance halls, shuffleboards, golf courses, or tennis courts (see "RV Parks" below).

Square and round dancing are particularly popular, and the Valley deservedly claims itself the square dance capital of the United States. Dances are announced weekly in Harlingen's *Valley Morning Star* (Monday), McAllen's *The Monitor* (Saturday), and Brownsville's *The Herald* (Saturday). The *Magic Valley Square And Round Dance Directory* is published twice per season (November-January, February-April) and provides information on dance locations, a caller and cuer directory, a list of dance clubs affiliated with the Magic Valley Square and Round Dance Association, a schedule of classes and workshops, and festival listings. Copies are freely distributed year-round (many clubs maintain a year-round schedule) throughout the Valley or are available by contacting the Magic Valley Square and Round Dance Directory (tel. 512-687-3931), 313 Nolan, McAllen, TX 78504.

A large number of out-of-state residents organize their own state-oriented picnics and potlucks in the Valley. Kansas, Minnesota, Oklahoma, Nebraska, Illinois, North Dakota, South Dakota, and Iowa are among the most active. The Rio Grande Valley Chamber of Commerce issues a seasonal schedule of events that includes listings for state-oriented activities. It's distributed free throughout the Valley or is available by mail for $1 from P.O. Box 1499, Weslaco, TX 78596.

Several educational institutions in the Valley offer adult or continuing education programs for winter Texans: **University of Texas-Pan American** in Brownsville and Edinburg, **Texas Southmost College** in Brownsville, and **Texas State Technical College** in McAllen and Harlingen (see individual destinations for addresses and phone numbers). Non-degree program offerings are diverse, ranging from Spanish language to local ecological studies.

The State Highway Dept. maintains one of its 12 state tourist bureaus on the outskirts of Harlingen, at the junction of US 77 and US 83. This office (tel. 512-428-4477) distributes free printed information on statewide travel with an emphasis on Rio Grande Valley material. The staff can answer just about any question regarding Valley tourism. It's open daily 8-5.

RV Parks

This is big-time RV country: over 500 RV parks are scattered throughout the valley, comprising as many as 66,000 RV sites. Rates are low, especially for long-term stays. The average monthly rate is $90-100, three months $200-225, six months as low as $420. A listing of all the RV facilities in the Valley is beyond the scope of this book, but Data File's *The Park Book* is available free at any state or town tourist office and contains up-to-date listings of all parks and RV dealers. It's revised annually and is also available by mail (include $1 for postage and handling) from Data File, Route 7, Box 508, Harlingen, TX 78552.

HARLINGEN

This town of approximately 55,000 is the unofficial capital of the Rio Grande Valley, mainly because Harlingen International Airport (also called Valley International) is the air-transport hub for the entire area. Harlingen was the second major settlement in the area after Brownsville. Founder Lon C. Hill developed the levee and irrigation systems that brought fertility to the Valley and a resultant influx of settlers. During the early 1900s it was dubbed "Six-Shooter Junction" because a large contingent of Texas Rangers and Border Patrolmen were headquartered here to quell Mexican bandit activity.

Harlingen straddles the intersection of two main Valley thoroughfares, US 77 and US 83. Although the downtown area is quite compact, the town spreads in all directions for several miles.

Rio Grande Valley
Historical Museum Complex

Several buildings at the intersection of Boxwood and Raintree in the Harlingen Industrial Air Park (three miles north of town) comprise the museum. The main building contains exhibits that interpret the history of the Valley from the time of the Karankawa and Coahuiltecan Indians onward. Other buildings include the 19th-century Paseo Real Stagecoach Inn and the 1923 Harlingen Hospital, both of which were moved here from their original locations and have been restored with period furnishings. A fourth building is the relocated Lon C. Hill home, built in 1905. Admission to all buildings is free (donations requested); open Tues.-Fri. 9-12 and 2-5, Sun. 2-5. For further information, call (512) 423-3979.

Aloe Vera Information Center

The naturally formed gel inside aloe vera is valued for its astringent, antibiotic, and coagulating properties. Virtually all of this subtropical succulent grown in the U.S. comes from the Valley, and 75% of it is cultivated by one enterprise, Harlingen's Forever Living Products. The company has established an information center in order to educate Valley visitors about aloe vera, and, less obviously, to expand sales. Admission is free, however, along with a video tour of the facilities and a 25-minute film that presents aloe's cultural and medicinal history. The center is a few miles west of Harlingen at US 83 and Altas Palmas Rd.; hours are Mon.-Fri. 9-4. Call (512) 425-2585 for information.

Accommodations

Sun Valley Motor Hotel (tel. 512-423-7222) is well located at the south edge of town (easy access to Brownsville and South Padre) at 1900 S. 77 Sunshine Strip. It offers separate duplexes from $30 a night, with senior and long-term discounts available. **Motel 6** (tel. 421-4200) is at 224 S. US 77 near the Tyler exit; rooms are $27.95 s plus $6 for each additional adult. Nearby at 1821 W. Tyler is the **Rodeway Inn** (tel. 425-1525), where rooms are $34 s, $38 d.

Over on US 83 is **La Quinta Motor Inn** (tel. 512-428-6888, 1002 US 83S), with rooms for $51-65. The **Holiday Inn** (tel. 425-1810) at 1901 W. Tyler is Harlingen's most expensive, at $55-74 s, $62-81 d. Both Holiday Inn and La Quinta offer airport transportation.

Food

Probably the most famous restaurant in Harlingen is **Mamacita's Mexican Cuisine** (tel. 512-421-2561, 521 S. 77 Sunshine Strip), where traditional Tex-Mex like *tacos al carbon* and *carne guisada* brings in the hungry droves. The *capirotada* (Mexican-style bread pudding) is a don't-miss. Open daily for lunch and dinner. The **Mesquite Tree** (tel. 425-3542, 803 S. 77 Sunshine Strip) serves all kinds of mesquite-broiled meats and chicken and is open Mon.-Sat. for lunch and dinner. Along the same boulevard is the popular **China Star Restaurant** (tel. 425-2991, 1801 S. 77 Sunshine Strip), with an extensive Chinese menu and inexpensive weekday lunch specials; open daily for lunch and dinner. There are many other restaurants along 77 Sunshine Strip, including the usual fast-food chains.

The **Vannie Tilden Bakery** (tel. 512-423-4062) at 202 E. Harrison downtown, is a good place for breakfast—both pastries and coffee and full country breakfasts. For lunch they serve chili, chicken-dumplings, sandwiches, and salads. Open Mon.-Saturday.

If you happen to be passing through Raymondville on the way into the Valley and are looking for a food stop, consider the **Valley Bakery & Restaurant** at 383 E. Hidalgo. The Mexican family that owns and operates the restaurant serves ac-

HARLINGEN

claimed *caldo de res* or rice soup, *migas,* and fajitas, as well as traditional Tex-Mex and chicken-fried steak. Open Mon.-Sat. for breakfast and lunch.

RV Parks

Data File's handy *The Park Book* (see "RV Parks" under "Winter Texans" above) lists 53 RV parks in Harlingen; if you want the full list, be sure to pick up a copy at the Harlingen Chamber of Commerce (tel. 512-423-5440, 311 E. Tyler) or from the Texas Tourist Bureau (tel. 428-4477, US 83 and US 77). Because there's so much local competition, rates start at a low $8-10 a night, with generous discounts for long-term stays.

The following parks are members of the chamber of commerce (and should, therefore, be reputable): Country Boy Mobile Home & RV Park (tel. 512-425-2540, 4506 N. Business 77); Dixieland Manor Mobile Home & RV Park (tel. 425-6707, 1325 Dixieland); Fair Park Estates (tel. 423-1948, 613 N. I St.); Palm Gardens Mobile Estate (tel. 423-7670, 3401 Business US 83); Posada del Sol (tel. 423-3534, Palm Dr. off US 83); Fig Tree RV Resort (tel. 423-6699, 8820 W. US 83); Lake Shore Estates (tel. 428-4733, 2601 Wilson); Lakewood RV Park (tel. 423-1170, 4525 Graham); Paradise Park (tel. 425-6881, 1201 N. US 77); Park Place Estates (tel. 428-4414, 5401 W. Business 83); Sunshine Country Club Estates (tel. 425-1420, 1 E. Michigan); and Sunshine RV Park (tel. 428-4137, 1900 Grace).

Events

February: The **Texas Square Dance Jubilee,** one of the Valley's largest square and round dance events, is held in mid-February at Lakewood RV Park (tel. 210-423-1170, 4525 Graham) and Fun 'N Sun RV Park (tel. 399-5125, Helen Moore Rd. off US 83, San Benito).

October: Riofest is held for three days in mid-April at the Fair Park, Valley Fair Boulevard. A tent city is erected that features arts and crafts exhibits, music, dancing, and food.

Recreation

Harlingen Parks and Recreation (tel. 512-427-8870) sponsors a **Harlingen Tourist Club** at the Community Center, 201 E. Madison, between November and April. For a flat fee of $25 per season, winter Texans can avail themselves of the 14,000-square-foot, air-conditioned tourist center, 25 outdoor and 10 indoor shuffleboard courts, a pool hall, and lawn bowling green. Other activities at the tourist center include arts and crafts classes, dancing, potluck dinners, card games, and various social events. The club is open Mon.-Sat. 9 a.m. to 10 p.m.

Golf: Harlingen has several golf courses, most of them private clubs. The municipal **Tony Butler Golf Course** (tel. 512-423-9913) is a 27-hole, par-70 course with a USGA rating of 69.6. It's located off M St., a half-mile south of US 77. The **Fairway Golf Course and Driving Range** (tel. 423-9098), at 2524 W. Spur 54 (off US 77 N), has a municipal nine-hole course.

Tennis: H.E.B. Tennis Center (tel. 512-428-8889) in Pendleton Park (take 77 Sunshine Strip north to Morgan Blvd. at Grimes) features 12 lighted municipal courts where reservations aren't necessary—it's first-come, first-served. You can pay by the hour or buy a six- to 12-month pass that allows unlimited play. Resident pros offer tennis lessons, and ball machines are available. **Victor Park** at M St. and US 77 has eight lighted tennis courts that are free.

The **Valley Greyhound Park** on south Ed Carey Dr. (just south of town off US 77/83) offers greyhound races and pari-mutuel betting year-round; highest payoffs run $20,000-30,000. The 80,000-square-foot, state-of-the-art spectator facility is fully air-conditioned and contains a clubhouse, bar, and restaurant. Races are held daily except Tues. and admission is $1 general, $2 clubhouse, plus $1-3 for parking.

Shopping

In addition to a small downtown shopping area centered around Jackson Ave. and 2nd St., **Valley Vista Mall** near the junction of US 77 and US 83 offers the usual assortment of department and specialty stores.

For custom boots, it's worth making the 23-mile trip north (along US 77) to **Raymondville.** Local history goes back to a 1790 Spanish land grant, and the town has been a bootmaking center since at least the turn of the century. Leo Torres's famous Rios Boot Co. has closed, but two heirs to his bootmaking prowess are **Armando's Boot Co.** (tel. 512-689-3521) at 169 N. 7th St. and **Torres Custom Boots** (tel. 689-3171) at 246 S. 7th Street. Both places offer just about the best prices for custom-made boots in the state, starting at around $250 for plain cowhide (similar boots in Austin or Dallas would fetch as much as $500-600).

Closer to Harlingen in the town of Mercedes (about 12 miles east on US 83) is **Amado's Boot Co.** (tel. 512-565-9641), 710 2nd Street. Boots here cost about the same as in Raymondville, but aren't quite as fine.

Valley International Airport

Located on the northeast edge of Harlingen, this airport hosts five airlines (American, Continental, Southwest, Conquest, and AeroMonterrey) with daily flights to 83 domestic and 19 international destinations (including Holland, Belgium, Germany, Switzerland, Great Britain, Spain, France, Australia, Japan, Canada, and Mexico). The airport has a restaurant, five auto rental services, and taxi/limousine services.

AeroMonterrey (tel. 800-531-7921) has non-stop 45-minute service on turboprops to Monterrey, Mexico. The fare is $98 roundtrip which includes free sandwiches and Tecate beer served en route.

LAGUNA ATASCOSA NATIONAL WILDLIFE REFUGE

Laguna Atascosa (Spanish for "Muddy Lagoon") is the southernmost wildlife refuge in the United States. It preserves a 45,000-acre chunk of the Rio Grande Valley as it was before farming and human habitation altered the topography, representing a transitional zone between semiarid brush country and subtropical wetlands. The terrain consists mostly of a series of estuaries, marshes, salt flats, and *resacas*, ox-bow lakes that were once tributaries of the Rio Grande.

Over 360 bird species visit the refuge during the year, attracted by mild temperatures, an abundance of food and water, and the protection from Gulf of Mexico tempests provided by South Padre Island and Laguna Madre (a large body of water between South Padre and the mainland). Fall and winter are the best times for waterfowl sighting, spring for songbirds. Among the commonly sighted species are loons, grebes, gannets, pelicans, cormorants, bitterns, herons, ibises, spoonbills, swans, ducks, geese, hawks, falcons, chachalacas, wild turkeys, pheasants, bobwhites, cranes, roadrunners, warblers, and pipits. The most common waterfowl is the redhead duck, since 80% of the continent's population spends winters here.

Mammals that inhabit the refuge include various bats (cave myotis, Brazilian freetail), armadillos, cottontail rabbits, Mexican ground squirrels, coyotes, gray foxes, raccoons, weasels, mountain lions, ocelots, jaguarundis, bobcats, javelinas, wild boars, white-tailed deer, and the occasional nonnative nilgai (a short-horned antelope from India —escaped from nearby game ranches).

Facilities
Two tour roads are open to the public: Bayside Dr. passes through dense brush, coastal prairie, and along Laguna Madre; Lakeside Drive winds through farm fields and over a *resaca* to the banks of 3,100-acre Laguna Atascosa.

You're more likely to see native wildlife if you hike on one or more of the six self-guided nature trails within the refuge. The best hiking times are around dawn or dusk, just after the refuge opens for public visitation or just before it closes. The 1.5-mile **Mesquite Trail** leaves from the visitor center parking lot and runs through a marsh area—good for watching waterfowl. The 1.5-mile **Lakeside Trail** starts at the Osprey Overlook and passes through dense brush along Laguna Atascosa (look for chachalacas, turkey, bobwhites); there are also a couple of short side trails that lead away from the lagoon. The **Paisano Trail** forms a one-mile loop off Bayside Dr. through dense brush.

The 2.2-mile **Moranco Blanco Trail** also starts off Bayside Drive. Part of it proceeds along a service road through cord grass flats next to a *resaca;* then it leaves the service road and continues through brush to the Laguna Madre (with chances of seeing several different bird species). The **Gunnery Range Trail** is a half-mile walk along an old railbed where WW II gunner trainees once practiced shooting. They fired at targets carried by a small automatic train that

once ran along the rails here. The best place to see larger mammals (deer and javelina —you're not likely to see cats in the daytime) is along the **White-tailed Trail,** which begins six miles from the visitor center off FM 106. It forms a 4.5-mile loop along Cayo Atascoso and winds through seven ponds among brush and grassland.

The visitor center features interpretive exhibits on natural history and standard national wildlife refuge literature. The NWR staff also lead occasional refuge tours; during the winter, local bird authority (and priest) Father Tom Pincelli leads special monthly birding tours—highly recommended. The center is open daily 10-4 from October to April, Sat. and Sun. 10-4 in September and May, closed June-August. The trails and tour roads are open daily 7-7, year-round.

Getting There
From Harlingen, take State 345 north off US 77/83 S to FM 106, then east to the refuge entrance—a total trip of around 26 miles.

From Brownsville, take FM 1847 north till it meets FM 106 and then proceed east to the refuge, about 30 miles total.

BROWNSVILLE

History
Sixteenth-19th Centuries: Along with San Antonio and Goliad, Brownsville is one of the most historic cities in Texas. In 1519, Spanish explorer Alonso Alvarez de Piñeda came upon the section of the Rio Grande that now passes between Brownsville and its Mexican

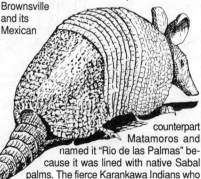

counterpart Matamoros and named it "Rio de las Palmas" because it was lined with native Sabal palms. The fierce Karankawa Indians who inhabited the area weren't amenable to Spanish settlement, however, so it wasn't until 1748

BROWNSVILLE / MATAMOROS

BROWNSVILLE TOURIST INFORMATION CENTER

VALLEY REGIONAL MEDICAL CENTER

802

RESACA DE LA GUERRA

RESACA DE LA PALMA BATTLEFIELD

77

83

CENTRAL BLVD.

BOCA CHICA BLVD.

TO SOUTH PADRE ISLAND, BOCA CHICA

4

RESACA DE LA GUERRA

TO AIRPORT

PALM BLVD.

GLADYS PORTER ZOO

SAMS MEMORIAL STADIUM

E. 6th

E. 7th

E. 12th

E. 14th

INTERNATIONAL BLVD.

SOUTHMOST RD.

E. ADAMS

E. WASHINGTON

E. ELIZABETH

E. LEVEE

HISTORIC BROWNSVILLE MUSEUM

HARRISON

VAN BUREN

BROWNSVILLE

STILLMAN HOUSE MUSEUM

CIVIC CENTER

TEXAS SOUTHMOST COLLEGE

UNIVERSITY OF TEXAS - PAN AMERICAN

RESACA

GATEWAY BRIDGE

MEXICO ST.

B&M BRIDGE

TEXAS

MEXICO

RIO GRANDE

HIDALGO

HERRERA

BUSTAMENTE

BRAVO

MARKET

PLAZA

GONZALES

MORELOS

SENDERO NACIONAL

AV. CUAHTEMOC

CALLE 7

CALLE 6

CALLE 4

CALLE UNO

ALVARO OBREGON

AV. TAMAULIPAS

AV. CO. DE MEXICO

CASA MATA MUSEUM

SANTOS DEGOLLADO

AV. LAURO VILLAR

AV. CANALES

TEXAS

MEXICO

RIO GRANDE

MATAMOROS

0   0.5mi

0   0.5km

© MOON PUBLICATIONS, INC.

that another Spaniard, José Escandón, was able to establish communities along the river's southern banks (by this time the nomadic Karankawas had left the area). One of the villages grew into a regional trade center known as Congregación de Nuestra Señora del Refugio or simply Villa del Refugio. The name was later changed to Matamoros in honor of Mariano Matamoros, a priest executed during the Mexican War of Independence in 1821.

The northern bank of the lower Rio Grande remained largely undeveloped until the Republic of Texas was annexed to the U.S. in 1845. The U.S. and Mexico disputed the border between the two countries—Mexico claimed it was the Nueces River while the U.S. claimed it was the Rio Grande—and this led to the establishment of Fort Taylor across the river from Matamoros, thus sparking the Mexican-American War. After Mexican troops attacked the post and killed its commander, Major Jacob Brown, it was renamed Fort Brown. Several other battles in this brief war were fought in the area, until Mexico surrendered its border claim a few months after the fort was established.

A New England businessman, Charles Stillman, planned the original town site that became Brownsville (named for Major Brown). Because it was protected by Fort Brown, many residents who had been living in Matamoros relocated across the river. They were joined by gold prospectors who arrived in Brownsville by boat via the Gulf of Mexico and who decided not to continue on to California.

During the Civil War, Brownsville/Matamoros made out very well by supplying Texas cotton to Europe via the Mexican Gulf port of Bagdad, southeast of Matamoros, thus avoiding the Union stockade along the Texas coast. Five weeks after Robert E. Lee's surrender at Appomattox, the last battle of the Civil War was fought at Palmito Ranch, east of town, when Union troops attacked from Brazos Island (they were defeated by Confederate soldiers under the command of Colonel Rip Ford).

Twentieth century: Around the turn of the century the town became embroiled in the Bandit Wars that plagued the Rio Grande Valley, as Texas Rangers and U.S. National Guardsmen struggled to bring a measure of law and order to the vicinity. In 1904 the St. Louis, Brownsville, and Mexico railhead was established at Brownsville and the town's importance as a trade center increased. The Brownsville/Matamoros area now

supports over 80 *maquilas*. A Union Pacific rail terminus connects with Mexico's national railway via the B&M Bridge over the Rio Grande; a 17-mile deep-sea channel in the Brownsville Navigation District links the area with the U.S. Inland Waterway System and the Gulf of Mexico. These transport systems allow Brownsville to act as a major shipping point for Valley agricultural products as well as Mexican and *maquila*-manufactured goods.

Winter tourism is also an important source of municipal income, and the chamber of commerce goes all out to make winter Texans feel welcome. For many Valley visitors, Brownsville is becoming a preferred destination because of its proximity to South Padre Island and Matamoros. It also has more of intrinsic interest than other Valley towns, with the Gladys Porter Zoo, a historic downtown, a strongly bicultural, bilingual community (pop. 95,000), a university and college, and the Sabal Palm Grove Sanctuary.

Downtown

Driving through Brownsville's downtown district, you might think you'd inadvertently crossed the border into Mexico—most signs are in Spanish or are bilingual. The town's original main avenue, Elizabeth St., has been opened up into a modern boulevard, but still runs through the town center; the most historic buildings are found along a street grid that straddles Elizabeth between Palm Blvd. to the west, E. Jackson St. to the north, International Blvd. to the east, and E. Fronton St. to the south. Common architectural styles include Spanish Colonial (e.g., the 1897 El Globo Nuevo, 1502 E. Madison or the 1928 Southern Pacific Depot, 601-641 E. Madison), Gothic (the 1859 Immaculate Conception Cathedral, 1218 E. Jefferson), Renaissance Revival (the 1883 Old Cameron County Courthouse, 1131 E. Jefferson), and simple frame houses with double gables and decorative fascia (the 1887 El Globo Chiquito, 1059 E. Monroe).

The Brownsville Convention and Visitors Bureau's detailed city map contains a list of 44 historic structures in town and is available free from their information center (tel. 210-541-8455) at the junction of US 77/83 and FM 802.

Museums

The **Historic Brownsville Museum** (tel. 210-548-1313) is housed in the restored Southern Pacific Railroad Depot at 601-641 E. Madison. Various exhibits provide a detailed account of early Spanish exploration, with lots of old maps, plus blow-by-blow descriptions of historic battles—including the Battle of Resaca de la Palma, the Battle of Palmito Hill, and the Bandit Wars of the early 1900s (see "History" above). Features of the restored depot itself form part of the display, including segregated water fountains (as a railroad structure, it was used between 1927 and 1952). Also on display is a huge portable altar that was once carried on a wagon for traveling Catholic masses. Outside the depot is an old Rio Grande Railroad steam engine and a caboose. The museum is open Tues.-Sat. 10-4:30, and Sun. 2-5; admission is $2 adults, 50 cents children.

The **Brownsville Art Museum** (tel. 210-548-1313) at 230 Neal Rd. is operated by the privately supported Brownsville Art League (headquartered next door in the historic 1850 Neal House). This is the center for the town's culture vultures and a host to traveling art exhibits, lectures, workshops, art classes, and films. A small permanent collection displays mostly Southwestern works. Open Mon.-Fri. 9:30-2:30; admission is free (donations accepted).

The **Stillman House** (tel. 210-542-3929) at 1305 E. Washington was built in 1850 by town founder Charles Stillman. It has been restored and turned into a museum that displays period furnishings and Brownsville memorabilia. Open Mon.-Fri. 10-noon and 3-5, Sun. 3-5; admission is $1 adults, 15 cents students, children under 12 free.

Gladys Porter Zoo

Zoo professionals named this zoo one of the country's 10 best in a recent poll. The considerable funds for the facility, which opened in 1971, were provided by the estate of Earl Sams, the president and board chairman of the J.C. Penney Co. for 33 years. His daughter Gladys Porter oversaw the zoo design and selection of animals and is largely responsible for the resulting high quality. The zoo's 31 acres are divided into four zoogeographic areas: Tropical America (which exhibits many local species as well as species from Central and South America), Indo-Australia, Asia, and Africa. Ancillary to the main design are a herpetarium, aquatic wing, children's zoo and nursery, bear grottos, and a free-flight aviary. Some of the more rare creatures on display include Przewalski's horse, the jaguarundi, the

Madagascan tortoise, spectacled bears, and various rare African and Asian deer, oryx, bushbuck, bongos, bonteboks, and duikers. There's also a good collection of monkeys, baboons, crocodiles, elephants, and giraffes; the mountain gorillas are particularly healthy-looking specimens.

The main walking path through the zoo is a one-mile circuit around the center; shorter paths branch out from the circle, like wheel spokes. A tour train runs through the zoo on Sundays 1:30-3:30 ($1 adults, 50 cents children under 14). Zoo facilities include a couple of snack bars and restaurants, plus tables and benches. One of the nicest things about this zoo is that it never seems to get crowded, even in the peak winter Texan season.

The zoo (tel. 210-546-7187) is located at Ringgold and 6th, between International and Palm. It's open daily 9-5, with extended weekend and summer hours (till sunset). Admission is $4.75 adults, $2.50 children 2-13. Wheelchairs and strollers are available for rent.

Fort Brown/ University of Texas-Pan American

All that remains of the 1846 fort that sparked the War with Mexico is the post hospital (now the administration building for Texas Southmost College, tel. 210-544-8200), the post headquarters, and the guard house (now a fine arts center). At different times during the Civil War, both Union and Confederate troops used the fort. Just below the fort buildings is the curved Fort Brown Resaca.

The upper-division branch of **University of Texas-Pan American** (tel. 210-982-8230) is on the campus of Texas Southmost College adjacent to Fort Brown. Both schools offer special continuing education and adult education classes specially oriented toward winter Texans.

Access to the fort/college/university complex is via International Blvd. off E. Elizabeth.

Sabal Palm Grove Sanctuary

To see what the environment along the Rio Grande looked like before it was under heavy cultivation, pay a visit to this National Audubon Society-sponsored preserve. Formerly part of the Rabb Plantation, the sanctuary protects the last remaining Sabal palm grove in the delta. The *Sabal texana* is the state's only native palm and was once prolific in the area (hence, the early Spanish name for the Rio Grande—Rio de las

Gladys Porter Zoo

Palmas)—it's now considered an endangered species. It's also found several hundred miles south in certain Mexican valleys, but is fast being eliminated there, too. *Micharos,* the fruit of the Sabal palm, is sometimes found in Matamoros markets and is considered a local delicacy.

Of the 172 acres protected by the sanctuary, only about 32 acres comprise a true *boscaje con las palmas* or palm grove. A walk along the trail leading through this dense forest conjures up visions of West Africa (in 1930 *Life Along the Delta,* an African hunting epic inspired by Frank Buck's *Bring 'Em Back Alive,* was filmed here). The tallest palm in the sanctuary, a national champion, extends 49 feet high, with a crown 12 feet across and a trunk 41 inches in diameter. The sanctuary consists of much more than the palm grove, however, and in fact preserves a unique ecosystem that includes coastal clay dunes (loma), wetlands, and old farm fields that are being allowed to return to their natural state. Other protected vegetation include Texas ebony, *tepeguaje,* anacua (anaqua), brasil, colima, *granjeño* or spiny hackberry, manzanita or Barbados cherry (in the U.S., this tree grows wild only in Cameron and Hidalgo counties, Texas), and two other endangered species, David's milkberry and Palmer's bloodleaf.

Birdwatchers flock to the sanctuary to catch glimpses of the rare green jay, as well as others on their lists such as the chachalaca (sometimes called "Mexican pheasant"), white-tipped dove, olive sparrow, *pauraque* (parakeet), buff-bellied hummingbird, least grebe, kiskadee flycatcher, and black-bellied whistling duck. Most of these birds are easily seen by the patient eye. The sanctuary is also one of the few spots in South Texas still inhabited by ocelots (five sightings since 1988) and jaguarundi (eight sightings since '88).

The **Sabal Palm Grove Nature Trail** makes a half-mile loop that starts and ends at the visitor center near the entrance. A trail guide is available at the center, with plant and animal descriptions that correspond to numbered posts along the trail. It's a good idea to bring insect repellent along, as bugs occur in some abundance year-round.

The sanctuary is open Thurs.-Mon. 8-5 from November to April and Sat. and Sun. 8-5 the remainder of the year. Admission is $2 adults, $1 children. For further information, contact the Refuge Manager (tel. 210-541-8034), Sabal Palm Grove Sanctuary, P.O. Box 5052, Brownsville, TX 78523.

Getting There: The sanctuary is located right on the Rio Grande off FM 1419. Probably the easiest way to find it is to take Boca Chica Blvd. (State 4) east from Brownsville, then turn right (south) on FM 3068 (which passes the Brownsville/South Padre Island International Airport) till it ends at FM 1419. Turn right (west) on FM 1419 and you'll come to a marked road on the left that leads down to the sanctuary. You can also get there by taking Southmost Rd. southeast off International Blvd. in town and following it (through several twists and turns) till it becomes FM 1419; the access road to the sanctuary will be on the right, about five miles from International Boulevard.

Accommodations

Motel 6 (tel. 210-546-4699), off US 77/83 at the FM 802 exit, has single rooms for $25.95 a night, plus $7 for each additional adult. The next least expensive motel is the nearby **Best Western Rose Garden Inn** (tel. 546-5501, 845 US 77/83 N), where rooms are $35-45 s, $45-55 d. The well-appointed **Sheraton Plaza Royale** (tel. 350-9191) is a bit farther north off US 77/83 (near the tourist information center) and has rooms for $70 s, $80 d.

Several resort hotels in town offer golf courses and tennis courts, and specialize in long-term room rentals—they're really more like resort condominiums. The **Fort Brown Hotel Resort** (tel. 210-546-2201), at 1900 E. Elizabeth (near Fort Brown), has rooms for $69 s, $77 d per night, cheaper for stays of a week or more (two lighted tennis courts, no golf). The upper-range **Ranch Viejo Resort** (tel. 350-4000), about 10 miles north of the town center off US 77/83, has one- to three-bedroom units ("villas") along a *resaca* and a 36-hole golf course. Nightly rates are $88-309 (up to six persons), with discounts for longer stays.

There are also a couple dozen apartment complexes in town that take winter Texans for a few weeks or months at a time (rates are lower than at the resort hotels). The Brownsville Tourist Information Center (tel. 210-541-8455) at US 77/83 and FM 802 maintains a list of these and can assist with reservations.

chachalaca

pauraque

Camping And RV Parks

Like the rest of the Valley, Brownsville is well equipped for RV and mobile-home drivers (43 listings in *The Park Book*). Most of the RV parks are scattered throughout an area east of town, off Boca Chica Blvd. and Minnesota Ave. (FM 313). Several reputable parks that belong to the Brownsville RV and MH Association (which represents approximately 1,900 RV spaces) include: Autumn Acres Trailer Park (tel. 210-546-4979, 5034 Boca Chica); Blue Bonnet Trailer Park (tel. 546-0046, 2404 Las Casas); Citrus Gardens Trailer Park (tel. 546-0527, 2225 S. Dakota); Crooked Tree Campland (tel. 546-9617, 605 FM 802); Four Seasons RV & MH Park (tel. 831-4918, 6900 Coffee Port); Los Amigos Trailer Park (tel. 542-8292, 3350 Boca Chica); Paul's Trailer Park (tel. 831-4852, 1129 N. Minnesota); Rio RV & MH Park (tel. 831-4653, 8801 Boca Chica); Stagecoach RV Park (tel. 542-7048, 325 FM 802); Tip-O-Tex (tel. 350-4031, 6676 N. Frontage); and Trailer Village (tel. 546-8350, 5107 Boca Chica). As elsewhere in the Valley, rates tend to be a uniform $10-12 nightly, $100 monthly, $200-225 for three months, $450 for six months.

The only tent-camping area in the Brownsville vicinity is **Brazos Island State Park** on the Gulf of Mexico, about 24 miles east of town via State 4. This park is completely undeveloped except for a few trash containers—you must bring in your own drinking water. On the plus side, you have the beach to yourself most of the time, the fishing's good, and there are no camping fees.

Food

Mexican and Tex-Mex are what Brownsville restaurants do best. Virtually every fast-food place in the city, even McDonald's and Dairy Queen, serves tacos of some kind. One classic local joint is **Maria's Better Mexican Food** (tel. 542-9819), nearby at 1124 Central. Everyone from elderly winter Texans to bilingual border patrol officers stop by for their great breakfast *gorditas,* made with thick, homemade flour tortillas (open daily 7 a.m.-5 p.m.). For sit-and-linger Tex-Mex meals, one of the best places in town is **Los Camperos Char Chicken** (tel. 546-8172), at 1440 International Blvd., where the house specialty is smoked, charbroiled chicken served with corn tortillas and red and green salsas.

Of course, you can cross over to Matamoros for a "real" Mexican meal, but the food isn't really so different since the two towns are such cultural twins. A popular Matamoros place at Avenida Alvaro Obregón and Anapolas, about six blocks south of Gateway International Bridge, is **Garcia's** (tel. 31566). It's a bit on the touristy side, with strolling *trovadores,* but the extensive menu includes seafood and quail as well as Mexican standards.

There are several Chinese restaurants in town. The best are **Lotus Inn** (tel. 210-542-5715, 905 N. Expressway, open daily for lunch and dinner) and **Peking Restaurant** (tel. 541-4621, 3503 Boca Chica, open daily for lunch and dinner). Both have extensive menus, pleasant dining rooms, and take-out service. For something different, try the "twice-fried noodles" at Lotus Inn.

Brownsville has plenty of fast-food franchises, including four **Church's Chickens,** three **Dairy Queens,** three **Whataburgers,** and two **McDonald's.** Most are clustered along Boca Chica Blvd. on the east side of town or off the expressway (US 77/83) on the north side.

Brownsville Winter Residents Club

This city-sponsored service for winter Texans issues a weekly schedule of organized events, including dancing (square, round, ballroom, and pattern), golf, bowling, arts and crafts workshops, cards, films, shuffleboard, picnics (state-oriented—for Iowa, Minnesota, Ohio, Indiana, Michigan, Missouri, Illinois, Wisconsin—and for Canadians), and other activities. Most of the indoor activities take place at the New Pavilion at Dean Porter Park on Camille Drive. The club is open October to April; seasonal dues are $8.50. For more information, call Brownsville Parks and Recreation at (210) 542-2064.

Entertainment

Brownsville has a pretty quiet nightlife. Turn on the TV and you'll find that most stations broadcast in Spanish or in a mixture of English and Spanish. Mexican television station XHAB broadcasts Spanish-language films and MTV Internacional. Bilingual DJs at radio station KIWW FM 96.1 play a hot selection of Tex-Mex and nuevo-wavo music.

Events

Charro Days is the Brownsville-Matamoros version of a pre-Lenten festival (à la Mardi Gras), held for three days in late February at various venues in each city. It's the area's oldest and biggest annual event and includes parades, costume balls, food, music and dancing.

Diez y Seis or Mexican Independence Day (Sept. 16) is also big in both cities; on the nearest weekend to the 16th they cooperate for **Fiesta Internacional,** a bicultural weekend of fireworks, parades, and *mucho* celebration. For scheduling details on either event, call the Brownsville Chamber of Commerce (tel. 210-542-4341).

Matamoros

Of the larger Mexican towns along the Texas-Mexico border (Nuevo Laredo, Matamoros, Reynosa, Ojinaga, and Juarez), Matamoros (pop. 350,000) is the most "Mexican," probably because its counterpart, Brownsville, is the least "American." Its history goes back to 1765, when it was settled as Congregación de Nuestra Señora del Refugio. Later renamed Matamoros in commemoration of Mexican independence hero Mariano Matamoros, it's one of only four cities in Mexico whose names are preceded by the honorific "H," which stands for the English equivalent of "Heroic, Loyal, and Unconquered" (this is why Mexican traffic signs in the area read "H. Matamoros").

The Gateway International Bridge joins Brownsville and Matamoros and leads to the main tourist strip, Avenida Alvaro Obregón, which is lined with bars, restaurants, and souvenir shops. To get a feel for non-tourist Matamoros, walk a few blocks down the Avenida and make a left at Calle 5 (Carranza) or 6, which lead to the **Plaza Hidalgo,** the main public square. As is typical for former colonial towns in Mexico, a Spanish cathedral faces the plaza. Day or night, this is the city's downtown heart.

Sights: The top cultural attraction in Matamoros is the **Museo del Maíz** or Museum of Maize (also called the Casa de Cultura). It's a short walk from the bridge at the corner of Calle 6 and Avenida Constitución. Exhibits detail the history of maize cultivation in Mexico from pre-Columbian times through the present, as well as traditional folkloric and medicinal uses of the maize plant. There's a strong underlying political message accompanying some of the displays, focusing on criticism of national land distribution policies (Mexico was self-sufficient in corn until 1965 and is now a net importer). The exhibits are fairly easy to follow even if you can't understand the Spanish-only labels. Open Tues.-Sun. 9:30-5; admission is free.

Another place of interest is **Casa Mata,** a fort that played a strategic (though losing) role in the Mexican-American War. A museum at the fort displays Mexican Revolution memorabilia and Indian artifacts, but very little concerning the Mexican-American War. It's located at the corner of Santos Degollado and Guatemala (take Calle 1 south to Santos Degollado and make a left). It's usually open Tues.-Sun. 10-4; admission is free.

Shopping: Most Texans come to Matamoros for quick south-of-the-border bargains. The shops along Avenida Alvaro Obregón are not the cheapest, since they cater to day tourists who don't venture very far into town, but some of their folk art is decent. **Barbara de Matamoros** at No. 40 is one of the better shops. Two large markets in town carry a wide selection of Mexican arts and crafts and are more susceptible to negotiation. **Mercado Juarez,** stretching across Abasolo and Matamoros between Calles 9 and 10 (about three blocks east of the plaza), is the biggest; a smaller version is on Bravo between Calles 8 and 9.

Liquor is much cheaper in Matamoros than on the U.S. side (about 50% lower). It's also duty-free, as long as you don't bring back more than a quart within a 30-day period.

Crossing The Border: You can walk across the bridge into Matamoros from International Blvd. on the Brownsville side in 15-20 minutes. Or take a "Maxi-Taxi" for only 25 cents. The Mexican government has a small tourist office at the end of the bridge on the Matamoros side, but they have very little printed information to offer. The staff at the customs and immigration post, also at the bridge, are very quick about letting visitors in for stays of under 72 hours. If you're planning to continue deeper into Mexico (or look like you are), you need a tourist card; the Matamoros immigration officers are notorious for soliciting *morditas* (small bribes—literally "small bites") from tourists at the border before they'll approve your papers.

Tours: Gray Line (tel. 210-542-8962) has a Brownsville/South Padre Island service that leads three-and-a-half-hour sightseeing/shopping tours of Matamoros for $12.50 per person. A local operation, **Bro-Mat** (tel. 544-6292), also does Matamoros tours ($15 per person).

Excursion Train To Monterrey: Mexico's national rail system has introduced a new first-class rail service *(primera especial)* between Matamoros and Monterrey (where the real bargains are) which is oriented toward overnight gringo shopping trips. The service, called *El Tamaulipeco,* has air-conditioned cars with reclining seats that can be reserved in advance through most travel agencies in Brownsville. The train leaves the Matamoros station (tel. 6-67-06), at Avenida Hidalgo and Calle 10 daily at 3 p.m., arriving in Monterrey at 7:50 p.m. In the reverse direction, it leaves Monterrey at 9:40 a.m. and arrives in Matamoros at 2:40 p.m. (These are Mexican departure times—remember that Mexican time doesn't change in the fall and spring to accommodate American Daylight Savings Time.) The fare for reserved tickets, purchased in Brownsville, is $45 roundtrip including a box lunch in each direction; if you book a *primera especial* ticket yourself at the Matamoros station, it costs less than half that (lunch also included).

Brownsville Information

Tourist Office: The **Brownsville Information Center** (tel. 210-596-3721, or tel. 800-626-2639 outside Texas), at the junction of FM 802 and US 77/83, has a very helpful staff and loads of free literature on what to see and do in the area. It's open Mon.-Fri. 8:30-5, Sat. 8-5, Sun. 9-4.

Telephone: The area code for Brownsville is 210. To call a Matamoros number from Brownsville (or anywhere else in the Rio Grande Valley), dial 011-52-891 before the local five-digit number.

Transport

Brownsville has two downtown bus terminals: the Trailways station (tel. 210-546-7171) at 1134 E. St. Charles at 12th, and the Greyhound/Valley Transit Co. (VTC) station (tel. 546-2264), at 1305 E. Adams. Greyhound and Trailways buses ply long-distance intra- and interstate routes, while VTC handles Rio Grande Valley and South Texas routes. From the Trailways station, you can also catch Mexico's Tres Estrellas de Oro buses (first class) to several destinations south of the border, including San Luis Potosí, Monterrey, Guadalajara, and Mexico City (only $21).

City buses run hourly between Brownsville International Airport and the city terminal on 12th St.; fare is 50 cents.

SANTA ANA NATIONAL WILDLIFE REFUGE

This 2,000-acre refuge is one of the smallest in the national wildlife refuge system, yet it contains one of the nation's most diverse biomes. Similar to the Sabal Palm Grove Sanctuary outside Brownsville, it preserves a chunk of the Rio Grande delta as it appeared before the land was cleared for cultivation.

A cross-section of temperate, tropical, desert, and coastal elements attracts over 370 bird

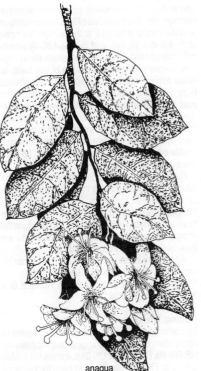

anaqua

LOUISE FOOTE

crested caracara

TODD CLARK

species, including a number of Mexican species rarely seen north of the border (black-bellied tree duck, *chachalaca, jacana,* red-billed pigeon, crested caracara, groove-billed ani, *pauraque,* rose-throated becard, and green jay to name a few). The densely forested interior of the refuge supports cedar elm, Texas ebony, anaqua, *granjeño* or spiny hackberry, *tepeguaje* or lead-tree, *huisache, guayacon, retama* or Jerusalem thorn, and mesquite. In patches of forest near Santa Ana Lake, the trees are thick with Spanish moss.

Mammals that inhabit the refuge include the endangered ocelot, a spotted cat around 30 inches long (up to 45 inches with tail), and the jaguarundi, which reaches 20-30 inches in length (up to 50 inches with tail) and has short reddish or gray-blue fur.

Facilities

The visitors center contains excellent interpretive displays that describe lower Rio Grande habitats and the flora and fauna that thrive here. It's open Mon.-Fri. 8-4:30, Sat. and Sun. 9-4:30. A seven-mile paved road (Refuge Dr.) bisects the refuge and passes trailheads to 12 miles of foot trails. To really experience the biological diversity offered here, you have to get out on the trails, which wind past three lakes (always full of diverse waterfowl species) and through various vegetational zones. Permanent photo blinds are situated at bird concentration points and are good places to watch birdlife even if you don't have a camera. The trails are open daily from sunrise to sunset.

Between late November and the end of April, the refuge offers an interpretive tram tour along Refuge Dr. that costs $2 for adults, $1 for children under 12. On certain days during the tram season, the tours are available only to environmental education groups. Refuge Dr. is closed to private vehicles from mid-January through mid-April.

Admission to the refuge is free. For further information, call or write the Santa Ana National Wildlife Refuge (tel. 210-787-3079), Route 2, Box 202A, Alamo, TX 78516.

Getting There

The refuge is about 12 miles south of Alamo (a small town between Harlingen and McAllen on US 83) via FM 907, at US 281. Instead of taking US 83 to FM 907, you can get here by following US 281 west from Brownsville along the border, an interesting drive that passes citrus groves, sugar cane fields, and small border towns. The vertical concrete pipes in the fields act as vents for the underground irrigation system.

MCALLEN

This town of around 84,000 was originally settled by Scotsman John McAllen in the mid-1800s but has a fairly undistinguished history. It's the center for the Valley's citrus industry, and has been dubbed "The City of Palms" because of the non-native Egyptian palm trees planted in and around the city. It's third behind Harlingen and Brownsville in the number of RV parks in the immediate vicinity (around 37), but the nearby towns of Mission, San Juan, Pharr, Edinburg, Alamo, and Palmview are also popular with

RVers, so McAllen has become a winter-Texan hub for this end of the Valley.

Eight miles from the center of McAllen across the Rio Grande is the Mexican city of Reynosa (pop. 375,000), a somewhat popular tourist destination for west Valley visitors.

McAllen International Museum

This is the only museum in the Valley accredited by the American Association of Museums. Galleries feature rotating exhibits of Mexican and American art (especially folk art), as well as exhibits on geology, archaeology, and natural history. There is also an ongoing schedule of special programs, including seminars, workshops, and cinema. At 1900 Nolana (at Bicentennial); open Tues.-Sat. 9-5, Sun. 1-5. Admission is $1 for adults, 25 cents for children 5-12; free on Sundays.

McAllen Botanical Gardens
And Nature Center

This 20-acre park (tel. 210-682-1517) features a sunken garden, waterfalls, and nature trails through various landscapes that are planted with South Texas flora. It's off US 83 about 2.5 miles west of town (past Ware Rd.). Open daily sunrise to sunset; admission is free.

Nearby Attractions

Top Tex Packing Co. (tel. 210-585-6662) is a citrus-packing operation that offers free self-guided tours through a greenhouse and citrus grove. Naturally, they hope you'll purchase some of their ruby red grapefruit or other products. It's on Shary Rd., off US 83 between McAllen and Mission; other packers and fruit-growers in this area sponsor similar activities.

The ferry at **Los Ebanos** is a local attraction since it's the last hand-pulled ferry on the Rio Grande. To get here, drive west from McAllen on US 83 to FM 886 (between Havana and Sullivan City), then turn left (south) until you hit the river. The ferry works by a system of cables and pulleys that are pulled by hand; it can carry two cars and a small number of pedestrians on each crossing. On the Mexican side, it's two miles to the nearest village, Diaz Ordaz.

Accommodations

Room rates at McAllen's **Motel 6** (tel. 210-687-3700), 700 US 83 (2nd or 10th St. exits), are among the highest Motel 6 rates in Texas:

$31.95, plus $6 for each additional adult; but then hotel/motel accommodations in McAllen tend to run the highest in the Valley. The **Red Carpet Inn** (tel. 787-5921), at US 83 and Jackson Rd., costs $36-39 s, $39-42 d. The **Imperial Motor Hotel** (tel. 686-0281), at 601 S. 10th, has decent rooms for $33 s, $37-39 double.

In the mid-range category in the **Holiday Inn Civic Center** (tel. 210-686-2471), 200 US 83 (2nd St. exit), where rooms are $58-78 s, $66-86 d. There are a number of other motels along nearby S. 10th St., including the **McAllen Airport Hilton** (tel. 687-1161, 2721 S.10th St., $54-68 s, $64-78 d) and the **Quality Inn McAllen** (tel. 682-8301, 1401 S. 10th St., $50s, $55 d). In this general price range, however the best choice is the restored **Casa de Palmas Hotel** (tel. 631-1101 or 800-4-COMPRI), a Spanish Colonial-style inn built in 1918. Nicely appointed rooms are $60-80 s, $70-80d.

Another atmospheric place is the **San Juan Hotel** (tel. 210-781-5339) at 125 Business 83 in nearby San Juan (east of McAllen). Built in the 1800s, it was restored by the Sigle family and now offers simple rooms for $20-30 s, $30-40 d.

Food

We're still in the Valley, where Mexican food rules. **The Hi-Way Inn Restaurant** (tel. 210-687-5945, 2017 US 83) packs them in for their *tacos de carne guisada;* on the weekends they serve barbacoa. Another McAllen budget classic is **La Casa del Taco** (tel. 631-8193, 1100 Houston), where you make your own tacos from "the Sombrero," a stack of homemade tortillas under a straw hat, piled on fajitas, *frijoles a la charra*, grilled onions, and peppers. Both of these restaurants are open daily for breakfast, lunch, and dinner.

If you happen to be in nearby San Juan and are looking for Tex-Mex, funky **Garza's Café** (tel. 210-787-9052) is the place. Their enchiladas (with homemade sauce), *chaupas*, and *carne guisada* are known throughout the west end of the Valley, and it's quite inexpensive. Open Tues.-Fri. for lunch only, Sat. and Sun. for lunch and dinner.

For Italian, try **Ianelli** (tel. 210-631-0666) at 321 S. Main, which serves pasta, pizza, chicken, and seafood; open Mon.-Sat. for lunch and dinner. McAllen has a branch of the Lotus Inn (tel. 631-2693) at 1120 N. 10th St., which has a mixed Chinese menu. Also good for Chinese are the **Chi-nese Inn North** (tel. 631-4705, 4000 N. 10th) and the **Chinese Inn South** (tel. 686-2328, 2001 S. 10th). All three Chinese restaurants are open daily for lunch and dinner.

The best steak in the area is probably across the border in Reynosa at **Sam's** (tel. 20034), on Allende at Ocampo. It's open daily for lunch and dinner; steak with all the trimmings is only about $8. Also in Reynosa, there are several good, fairly inexpensive restuarants serving Mexican and Continental food along Zaragosa and Allende streets in the Zona Rosa.

Pepe's On The River, off FM 1016 just south of Mission, is the only restaurant and bar built over the Rio Grande. Boaters can tie up at the restaurant's floating dock; it's also a favorite with winter Texans from Nov. to March, when the restaurant features live music in the afternoons.

RV Parks

RV sites in McAllen run about the same as in Harlingen and Brownsville: approximately $10 nightly, $100 a month, $250 for three months, as low as $450 for six months. A few listed with the McAllen Chamber of Commerce include: **Ashworth Trailer Park** (tel. 210-686-0112, Ash and 6th), **Casa De Mobile** (tel. 686-1836, 2022 11th, next to La Plaza Mall), **Citrus Valley RV Park** (tel. 383-8189, State 107 and Rooth), **Handke's Mobile Park** (tel. 686-3076, Taylor Rd.), **Sunlight Trailer Park** (tel. 682-7721, 4821 W. Business 83), and **VIP Motel & RV Park** (tel. 682-8384, 3501 US 83). There are dozens more RV parks in the nearby communities of San Juan, Mission, Pharr, Alamo, and Penitas—many of these have the lowest rates in the Valley.

Events

In nearby Mission, the **Texas Citrus Fiesta** is celebrated during the last two weeks of January with parades, arts and crafts shows, barbecues, costume shows, and the coronation of King Citrus and Queen Citrianna. All events feature citrus themes.

The **Texas Square Dance Jamboree,** possibly the largest square-dance festival in the state, is held the first Saturday in February at the McAllen Civic Center (at the junction of US 83 and S. 10th).

Early in March, McAllen and Reynosa sponsor a joint **Rio Grande Valley Music Festival** that focuses on folk and classical music. Performances are held at various venues on either side of the border.

For further information on these annual events, contact the McAllen Chamber of Commerce at 682-2871.

Reynosa

This Mexican border town was founded in 1749 as Villa de Nuestra Señora de Guadalupe de Reynosa. Its original location was about 12 miles from here, but an 1802 flood forced the townspeople to move to the current site. The small Texas town directly across the river is Hidalgo, which is about eight miles south of McAllen via State 336. There's a cheap parking lot here where you can leave your car and walk over the bridge to Reynosa (or you can take a Valley Transit Co. bus direct to Reynosa from the McAllen VTC terminal at 120 S. 16th St. for $1.50).

Reynosa's main square, market, and cathedral sit atop a small hill about a half mile from the bridge via Calle Zaragoza at Juarez. Between the bridge and the square along Zaragoza and Allende is a zona rosa or "pink zone" of tourist-ori-

Bentsen-Rio Grande Valley State Park

ented shops, restaurants, bars, discos, and hotels. The bar with the windmill out front on Zaragoza is **Dutch's,** an old gringo standby. More fun is the nearby **Hostelería del Bohemio** (also on Zaragoza), which features live Mexican music most evenings.

On Dec. 12 every year, the city celebrates the feast day of its patron saint, Our Lady of Guadalupe. Pilgrim processions begin the week before and folk dancers perform in front of the cathedral every afternoon.

McAllen Information

The **McAllen Convention and Visitors Bureau** (tel. 210-682-2871), at 10 N. Broadway, has printed information on local attractions in McAllen and Reynosa and can answer tourist-oriented questions.

To call Reynosa from McAllen, dial 196 before the local five-digit number.

BENTSEN-RIO GRANDE VALLEY STATE PARK

This protected 588-acre section of Rio Grande delta riparian woodlands and *matorral* (thorn scrub) is the second-largest such preserve on either side of the border after the Santa Ana National Wildlife Refuge. Much of the flora is similar, including cedar elm, *retama,* huisache, *guayacan,* the rare (for the U.S.) manzanita or Barbados cherry, Texas ebony, honey mesquite, *granjeño,* colima, anacua, and Spanish moss, plus *coyotillo,* lotebush, old man's beard, and desert olive. Unlike Santa Ana, it has overnight facilities, so there's more opportunity for experiencing both diurnal and nocturnal wildlife.

As with parks and refuges farther southwest along the river, the Bentsen-Rio Grande Valley State Park is a mecca for birders, with hundreds of species either permanently residing or passing through in the spring and fall. This is the northern limit of the habitat range for many bird species: the green jay, chachalaca, groove-billed ani, *pauraque,* and Lichtenstein's oriole. Other commonly seen winged residents are the great blue heron, snowy heron, turkey vulture, long-billed curlew, cactus wren, tropical parula, eight species of warblers, 16 species of duck, kites, six species of owl, hawks, falcons, and flycatchers.

Mammal residents are the same as for Santa Ana: the nine-banded armadillo, coyote, cottontail rabbit, bobcat, ocelot, jaguarundi, javelina, seven species of bats, weasel, and badger. Two amphibians unique to the area are the Rio Grande siren (an eel-like salamander with two small front legs only) and the Rio Grande leopard frog. Both are found in the shallows of the Rio Grande bordering the south edge of the park and in the two *resacas* on either side. About a dozen snake species normally live in the park, including the colorful Texas indigo snake and the sometimes large bullsnake—both are nonvenomous. The only poisonous reptile in the area is the coral snake, which is rarely seen.

Facilities

The park has two hiking trails. The **Rio Grande Hiking Trail** forms a two-mile loop from the camping area to the river and back, passing *matorral,* marshy areas next to the eastern *resaca,* and riverbanks festooned with willow and cattails. Numbered markers along the trail correspond to brief descriptions in a free trail guide available at park headquarters. The **Singing Chaparral Nature Trail** is a 1.5-mile loop that starts from the road between park headquarters and the camping area and leads to a wildlife waterhole. As with the Rio Grande Hiking Trail, there's a free interpretive booklet that identifies numbered areas along the way.

The camping area has tent/camper sites with water for $6 a night, full RV hookups for $10, a screened shelter for $12, and cabins for $25. The screened shelter is designed for group camping—when it isn't booked, individuals are welcome

green jay

to use it (the $12 fee is for one to 24 persons!). As with all Texas state parks, daily admission is $3 per vehicle, $1 for pedestrians or cyclists.

For further information, contact the Park Superintendent (tel. 512-585-1107), P.O. Box 988, Mission, TX 78572.

Getting There

The park is about five miles southwest of Mission via Loop 374 (west) and FM 2062 (south).

LOUISE FOOTE / 2

badger

LAREDO

INTRODUCTION

Los Dos Laredos ("The Two Laredos"—Laredo on the U.S. side of the Rio Grande, Nuevo Laredo on the Mexico side) form one of the region's most historic and culturally intriguing municipalities. Founded as the first nonmissionary, nonmilitary Spanish settlement in North America, Laredo has a current population of about 120,000 that is 90% Hispanic. Most Laredoans are bilingual, and they take great pride in the ways local culture, cuisine, and language distinguish Laredo from Texas-Mexico border areas to the east and west. This is also the most festive area along the border, where holidays as culturally distinct as Washington's Birthday and Mexican Independence Day are celebrated with equal fervor on both sides of the river.

Laredo is South Texas's main business center and Nuevo Laredo is the largest port of entry anywhere on the U.S.-Mexico border; consequently, tariff and customs revenues here are greater than at any other customs office in Mexico. The *maquiladora* industry that plays such an important economic role in other large border towns is here integrated into a more diverse area economy that includes import-export operations, transportation, oil production, cotton farming, ranching, and tourism. Banking is also an important industry—Mexicans keep billions of U.S. dollars on deposit in Laredo banks to escape the Mexican peso's downward-spiraling value relative to other world currencies. Because of this diversity, Laredo was one of the state's first cities to pull out of the oil-glut-induced slump of the early to mid-1980s.

History
In 1755, Spanish *empresario* Don Tomás Sánchez established a settlement on the north banks of the Rio Grande and named it Villa de San Agustín de Laredo (the hometown of his sponsor José Escandón was Laredo, Spain). It was the center of the Spanish colonial province of Nuevo Santander, which included parts of what are now South Texas and northern Mexico. San Agustín Plaza (now part of restored downtown Laredo) was the heart of the new settlement.

Laredo got caught between two wars of national liberation in the early 1800s, first Mexican independence from Spain (throughout which most Laredo residents remained Spanish loyalists) and then Texan independence from Mexico. When neither of the newly formed republics of Mexico and Texas would provide them with protection against marauding bandits and Indians, Laredo joined the north Mexican states of Tamaulipas, Nuevo Leon, and Coahuila in declaring their own Republic of the Rio Grande in 1840. Laredo was made the capital of the new republic, which only lasted 10 months before Mexican troops brought the area back under Mexican rule.

In 1845, when the Republic of Texas was annexed to the U.S., Laredo was again abandoned in a no-man's land between two countries, since the U.S. and Mexico disagreed over the boundary line between Texas and Mexico. The Treaty of Guadalupe Hidalgo, signed at the end of the Mexican-American War, established the Rio Grande as the boundary; those Laredoans who wanted to remain Mexican citizens moved across the river and established Nuevo Laredo in 1848.

During the American Civil War in the 1860s, Laredo prospered as a relay point for transshipment between the Confederate states and Europe (via Mexican ports). In the late 1880s, the founding of two new railroads made Laredo a major transportation link between the reunited U.S. and Mexico—the Texas-Mexican Railway connected the city with the deep-water port of Corpus Christi on the Texas Gulf coast, while the Missouri Pacific joined the midwestern U.S. with Mexico's national railway and Mexico City. In 1935, the Pan-American Hwy. was completed, establishing a continuous roadway between Laredo and the Panama Canal via Mexico and Central America. Tourism first came to the area during the U.S. Prohibition years, when Texas residents would slip over the border to the Cadillac Bar and other Nuevo Laredo watering holes for a legal drink.

The Land And Climate
The terrain around Laredo is mostly lowland *monte* or *montorral,* characterized by flat plains covered with dense scrub—mesquite, prickly

LAREDO / NUEVO LAREDO

© MOON PUBLICATIONS, INC.

pear, dwarf oak, huisache, huajillo, blackbrush, catclaw, and *cenizo*. Sparse willow woodlands are found along the Rio Grande in places, but most trees in Laredo are non-native, planted species.

Average temperatures in the Laredo area range from a pleasant 45-68° F in January to a stifling 76-99° F in July. It's not unusual for the thermometer to break 100° F on a typical July afternoon. Annual average precipitation is a moderate 20 inches, with May and September getting slightly more rainfall than other months. Any time besides June-August is good for a Laredo visit. If you come in the summer, it's best to stay indoors during the afternoon hours, as heat stroke is a very real threat to travelers who aren't used to temperatures in the high 90s and low 100s. The only town of any size in Texas that's hotter than Laredo in the summer is Presidio.

SIGHTS

Villa De San Agustín Historical District

San Agustín Plaza, bounded by Zaragoza, Flores, Agustin, and Grant streets (near International Bridge #1), is the site of the original 1755 Spanish settlement of Villa de San Agustín. At the east end of the plaza is **San Agustín Church,** built in 1872 on the foundation of two earlier churches. At

LA FRONTERA

Texas and Mexico share a thousand-mile border that has become more than just a political boundary. When residents on either side of the border refer to "La Frontera," they're talking about an area that extends as far as a hundred miles north and south from the Rio Grande. It's the center of a hybrid culture that's neither American nor Mexican; here First World meets Third World, and north European, Protestant capitalism meets south European, Catholic feudalism. Despite the fact that Mexico is the U.S.'s third-largest trading partner, La Frontera is one of the poorest areas in either country.

The burgeoning twin-plant *(maquila* or *maquiladora)* industry along the border, in which American technology and management exploits cheap Mexican labor, is said to be the hope of the future for the borderland. Goods produced at the plants are given special trade status since they're established in "export-processing zones" using U.S. capital. As the number of *maquilas* increases, more unemployed Mexicans migrate to northern Mexico in hopes of landing steady, though low-paying, jobs. Once they're on the border there's the imminent attraction of higher-paying work just over the river, so labor tends to flow back and forth. Human taxis even wade across carrying passengers on their backs (25 cents a trip) during "commute" hours. In spite of a multimillion-dollar U.S. Border Patrol budget, the border will probably remain effectively fluid far into the foreseeable future. After all, 150 years ago South Texas was still part of Mexico, and in the century before that, practically no one lived in South Texas.

Rolando Hinojosa, a Chicano writer born in Mercedes, Texas, has captured La Frontera spirit in his well-written, humorous book *The Valley* (Bilingual Press, Tempe, AZ), a fictional narrative obviously inspired by the lower Rio Grande Valley (with an imaginary "Jonesville-On-The-Rio" for Brownsville).

the south end on Zaragoza is the **Ortiz House,** which was begun in the 1700s and modified as late as 1870.

The small stone building on the plaza next to La Posada Hotel was built in 1830 and served as the capitol of the short-lived Republic of the Rio Grande. It now houses the **Republic of the Rio Grande Museum,** which displays memorabilia

from the separatist movement of 1840 (which went so far as to elect a president, appoint a presidential cabinet, and design its own flag), as well as three rooms decorated in period style. It's open Tues.-Sun. 10-noon and 1-5; admission is free.

El Mercado

This old market building, constructed in 1883, has recently been partially restored to its original function as a public marketplace (it also houses the City Hall). The surrounding city blocks, bounded by Flores, San Agustin, Hidalgo, and Lincoln streets, are also undergoing historic restoration so that the original cobblestone streets and Victorian buildings can join San Agustín Plaza in bringing a turn-of-the-century feel back to downtown Laredo.

Laredo State University

LSU (tel. 210-722-8001) shares a 196-acre campus with Laredo Junior College in West Laredo and is the most important institute of higher education in South Texas. Originally established as Texas A & I University in 1969, it was upgraded to state university status in 1977, and in 1989 became part of the Texas A & M University system. The total enrollment of 1,140 is about half graduate, half undergraduate. The most acclaimed LSU degree program is the MBA program in international trade, with an emphasis on Latin American trade; the bilingual education program is also highly reputable. LSU's Acculturation Project provides a unique community service by introducing Los Dos Laredos newcomers to the local bilingual-bicultural milieu.

ACCOMMODATIONS

Hotels And Motels

The most conveniently located hotel for Rio Grande crossings and downtown exploration is **La Posada** (tel. 210-722-1701), on Zaragoza St. at San Agustín Plaza. It's laid out in the classic Mexican colonial style around a courtyard and is a short walk from El Mercado, International Bridge #1, and downtown restaurants (and it has a parking garage). Rooms are $55-69 s, $69-79 d (senior discount available). Five blocks west of International Bridge #1 on S. Main Ave. is the **Howard Johnson Plaza Hotel** (tel. 722-2411), where rooms are $49-69 s, $59-89 d (senior discount available).

Most other hotels and motels in town are located in North Laredo off I-35. The **Fiesta Inn** (tel. 210-723-3603) is at the north end of San Bernardo Ave., just west of I-35; rooms rates are $54 s, $64 d during the week, $5 lower on weekends (senior and weekly discounts available). Also in this area is the **Holiday Inn Civic Center** (tel. 727-5800), at 800 Garden St. (exit 59 off I-35), where rooms are $65-80 s, $75-90 d (senior discount available).

Less expensive motels include the **Monterrey Inn** (tel. 210-722-7631, 4820 San Bernardo Ave., $30 s, $35-37 d) and the **Siesta Motel** (tel. 723-3661, 4109 San Bernardo Ave., $32-36 s, $36-46 d). **Motel 6** has two Laredo locations, one at 5310 San Bernardo Ave. (tel. 725-8187) and one at 5920 San Bernardo Ave. (tel. 722-8133); rates are $28.95 and $30.95 respectively for singles, plus $6 for each additional adult.

Camping And RV Parks

Lake Casa Blanca State Park (tel. 210-725-3826), just east of Laredo International Airport off US 59, has primitive campsites for $4 a night, wites with water for $6, and screened shelters for $15.

The next nearest campground is at Falcon State Recreation Area, about 80 miles south of Laredo off US 83 (see "Vicinity of Laredo"). **Casa Norte Mobile Home and RV Park** (tel. 210-722-3913), off I-35 N between Del Mar Blvd. and Mann Rd., rents RV sites with full hookups for $10 a night, $60 weekly, $220 monthly.

FOOD

Laredo has its own style of Tex-Mex cuisine that distinguishes it from San Antonio, El Paso, or even other border areas to the east and west. For one thing, they call Laredo-style breakfast tacos *mariachis;* local legend has it that the name (and style) originated at **Las Cazuelas** (tel. 210-723-3693, 303 Market St.) after a railroad worker in the 1930s made daily requests for a spicy breakfast taco that would make him shout like a *mariachi.* The recipe that finally satisfied his bent for chiles came to be called the *mariachi.* Practically every restaurant in the city that's open for breakfast has *mariachis* on the menu. Another region-

al variation on a familiar Tex-Mex theme is *panchos,* which are nachos loaded down with beef, cheese, and jalapeños (since this is cattle country, beef is a popular item on all menus). A strictly local specialty you might come across is *machito,* goat-tripe sausage.

With your Laredo menu vocabulary in hand, you might try some of these Tex-Mex restaurants: Near La Posada Hotel at 1108 Zaragoza is the inexpensive and authentic **El Paizzano** (tel. 210-722-4741), which is open daily for breakfast, lunch, and dinner. The Mexican breakfasts here are particularly good. **Cotulla Style Pit Bar-B-Q** (tel. 724-5747), at 4502 McPherson, specializes in a South Texas barbecue style that was created in the small town of Cotulla nearby—based on Mexican *carne asada* recipes. It's also well known locally for its *mariachis* and fajitas, served with fresh, homemade tortillas; open Tues.-Sat. 6:30-5:45, Sun. 6:30-2:45. **El Mesón del Rey** (tel. 722-2629) is popular for *carne asada, cabrito,* and *machitos.* For interior Mexican cuisine, try **El Mesón de San Agustín** (tel. 722-9727), at 908 Grant St., which specializes in Oaxaqueñan dishes.

The popular **Unicorn Restaurant and Pegasus Bar** offers a mixed menu of mesquite-grilled steaks, chicken-fried steak, *carne asada,* seafood, salads, soups, and appetizers (including *panchos* that ought to satisfy small groups who can't agree on what kind of food to eat). There are two locations: 3810 San Bernardo (tel. 727-4663) and 600 E. Calton Rd. (tel. 722-7978); both are open daily for lunch and dinner.

La Posada Hotel's **Main Dining Room** (tel. 722-1701) features different specialties every evening as well as lunchtime buffets during the week that change daily (e.g., Mexican buffet on Wednesdays) and a Sunday brunch buffet. The regular menu offers a wide variety of Mexican and American dishes; open daily for breakfast, lunch, and dinner. The hotel's **Tack Room Restaurant & Bar** (same phone number as above) has character and style (and prices to match), and is situated upstairs in a 1916 building that served as a home, high school, and telephone exchange before the hotel acquired it. It's open Mon.-Sat. for dinner only; the bar features happy hour Mon.-Fri. 5-8 p.m.

Nuevo Laredo has some excellent restaurants too—see "Nuevo Laredo" below.

ENTERTAINMENT

Music Halls

Laredo is one of Texas's three main centers for Tejano music (the other two are San Antonio and Corpus Christi). Most weekends the Civic Center (tel. 210-722-8143) at 2400 San Bernardo hosts live Latino, Tejano, and *conjunto* performances. **Roli's Music Hall** (tel. 722-2453), at 100 E. Taylor near McClellan, also frequently features Tejano and *conjunto*. During the Jalapeño Festival in February, Laredo holds a Tejano music festival (see "Events" below). A good local group to look out for is Borderline.

Hotel Clubs

Ordinarily this author wouldn't recommend hotels for local entertainment, since most hotel/motel clubs across the U.S. offer the same sort of mainstream pop. In Laredo, however, several hotels support local sounds. The **Crystal Palace** (tel. 210-722-2441), in La Hacienda Hotel at 4914 San Bernardo, features live Tejano bands Tues.-Sun. nights until 2. Holiday Inn's **The Covey** and Howard Johnson's **Windows on the Rio** also have occasional Tejano music, either live or on disk (see "Accommodations" above for addresses).

EVENTS

February

George Washington's Birthday: In spite of the fact that George's birthday has been subsumed under "Presidents' Day" on a national level, it's a 10-day festival in Laredo/Nuevo Laredo that's been celebrated since 1898. In these twin cities, it really combines a traditional Mexican pre-Lenten festival with a commemoration of the signing of the U.S. Constitution. The schedule varies from year to year, but usually kicks off on the second Friday in February with a Tejano music presentation at the Civic Center Auditorium, followed by the Princess Pocahontas Pageant on Saturday, also at the Civic Center. On Sunday there are fireworks and a band concert at Casa Blanca Lake, and during the week are more parades, a masquerade ball, and various smaller events.

On the second weekend, the festival divides in two: for the older, society-oriented population,

there's the Colonial Pageant (which features the Society of Martha Washington Debutante Presentation) and Ball (which reenacts the signing of the Constitution with two members of the community portraying George and Martha Washington), and for the younger, Tejano-oriented crowd, there's the **Jalapeño Festival,** which used to be held separately but has been combined with the George Washington's Birthday schedule. The Society of Martha Washington events are held at the Civic Center. Activities for the Jalapeño Festival take place at various venues around town and include the coronation of Miss Jalapeño, a jalapeño-eating contest (the winner is crowned "King Chile"), Tejano music, and a water race on the Rio Grande.

On the final Saturday, there's a binational friendship ceremony on International Bridge #2, followed by a parade across the bridge. On the last day of the festival, Sunday, a "Farewell Fiesta" takes place in San Agustín Plaza with plenty of food, music, and dancing.

April

The week preceding Easter Sunday is **Semana Santa** or Holy Week for Catholics on both sides of the river. Religious events center around Holy Redeemer Church on Main Ave., but you'll also notice that cafés and bakeries offer special *buñuelos* (fried sweet bread) and *capirotada* (Mexican bread pudding with raisins and papayas) for the occasion.

May

The 3rd of May is **Day of the Holy Cross** in Mexico and is celebrated in Laredo by a *matachine* procession (see "December" below).

Cinco de Mayo is a Chicano-Mexican cultural festival that commemorates the Battle of Puebla in 1862. Events include a special bullfight and *charreada* at La Fiesta Bullring in Nuevo Laredo.

July

Borderfest is a folklife festival held Fourth of July weekend at the Laredo Civic Center. The three-day event features arts and crafts exhibits, local music and dancing, and food vendors.

September

The event of the month is the Laredo International Fair and Exposition, held at the L.I.F.E. grounds on US 59, east of the airport, around mid-month (coinciding with Mexican Independence Day, September 16). The show includes a rodeo, livestock exhibits, music and dancing, food booths, and quarter-horse racing.

December

The 12th of the month is the feast day of the Virgin of Guadalupe, which in Laredo is celebrated by a unique *matachine* procession to Holy Redeemer Church on Main Avenue. *Matachine* is an inherited local variation of an ancient pre-Columbian Indian folk dance (the word comes from the Aztec for dance, *matlaxin)* that fulfills a variety of religious, social, and cultural functions. The musical ensemble that accompanies the dancers includes a drum, violin, accordion, and sometimes guitar, while the dancers dress in velveteen coats hung with reed ornaments and bells. Someone at the head of the procession carries a flower-decorated eight-foot cross and small altars are erected along the procession route.

The *matachine* tradition is said to be stronger in Laredo than anywhere in Mexico or the Southwest and preserves the *la flecha* ("arrow") style movements lost elsewhere—several local groups practice throughout the year (the most authentic is said to be Los Matachines de la Santa Cruz de Ladrillera, while the most visually striking is Aztecas Matachines). Many Mexican observers visit Laredo to view this rare Guadalupe Day procession.

SPORTS AND RECREATION

La Casa Blanca State Park

This 1,600-acre impoundment of San Ygnacios and Chacon creeks has facilities for water recreation (swimming, boating, fishing, and water-skiing), picnicking, and camping. It's just east of Laredo International Airport off US 59 E. Entrance to the park is $3 per vehicle, $1 for pedestrians and cyclists. Nearby is the 18-hole **Casa Blanca Golf Course** (tel. 210-727-9218), off Casa Blanca Lake Rd., which is open to the public.

L.I.F.E. Downs

This horse-racing track and rodeo arena is on the Laredo International Fair and Exposition grounds east of Casa Blanca Lake, off US 59. Quarterhorse races, livestock shows, and rodeos are held here during the yearly L.I.F.E. schedule and

occasionally during other times of the year; call 722-9948 for information.

Beisbol Liga Mexicana

The two Laredos field their own professional AAA baseball team in the Mexican League, the Tecolotes ("Tecos" for short). Home games are played at West Martin Field (tel. 210-722-8143) at 2200 Santa Maria on the Laredo side. The season starts in mid-March and ends in September.

SHOPPING

Laredo's **Mall del Norte** (off I-35 N between Mann and Hillside) claims to be the largest shopping center on the U.S.-Mexico border; it even has its own 5,000-square-foot Catholic church, decorated in the Spanish colonial style, for Sunday visitors. Over 130 stores in the mall attract Mexican as well as local shoppers. The smaller **Riverdrive Mall** is off Zaragoza St. three blocks west of International Bridge #1. **El Mercado** at Hidalgo and Flores downtown has a few specialty and craft shops. **Oscar's Antiques** (tel. 210-723-0765) at 1002 Guadalupe carries Mexican, European, and American antique furniture, including salvaged architectural items like Spanish colonial doors. **Blue Gate Antiques** (tel. 727-4127) at 719 Corpus Christi specializes in antique china, silver, jewelry, and crystal.

LAREDO INFORMATION

Tourist Offices

The main office of the **Laredo Convention and Visitors Bureau** (tel. 210-722-9895 or 800-292-2122 outside Texas) is located in the Laredo Civic Center at 2310 San Bernardo Avenue. They produce and distribute printed material on what to see in Laredo and Nuevo Laredo and can answer questions on area travel; open Mon.-Fri. 8-5. They also maintain an information center in El Mercado at Flores and Hidalgo, near San Agustín Plaza.

The State Highway Dept. operates one of its Texas Tourist Bureaus (tel. 210-722-8119) off I-35, six miles north of town. They hand out free maps and tourist literature for the entire state, as well as for Laredo and South Texas; open daily 8-5.

souvenir shop,
Nuevo Laredo

Telephone

The area code for Laredo is 210. To call numbers in Nuevo Laredo from Laredo, dial 011-52-871 before the local five-digit number.

TELEPHONE AND EMERGENCY INFORMATION

Emergency (police, fire, medical)	911
Telephone Directory Assistance	411
Highway Patrol	727-2145
National Weather Service	722-8119
Post Office Information	723-2043
Western Union Telegraph	722-4321

TRANSPORT

City Buses

Laredo's municipal transit system is called "El Metro," but for getting around downtown walking is easiest. El Metro does have special shuttle services, however, between most hotels and the Mall del Norte or Nuevo Laredo Downs.

Inter-city And International Buses

The Greyhound-Trailways Bus Depot is at Matamoros and San Bernardo Ave. in downtown Laredo. Greyhound operates buses to other major cities in Texas as well as to other states.

You can also catch buses from this station to cities in interior Mexico. Transportes del Norte runs several first-class buses a day from the Greyhound station, while Transportes Frontera runs second-class buses from the Trailways station. Fares from Laredo include a $2 surcharge for crossing the border; first-class fare to Mexico City (there is no second-class direct service to Mexico City) is $16.50, to Monterrey $5.

City Taxis

Call **Garza's Taxi** (tel. 210-723-5313).

Tours

Olé Tours (tel. 210-726-4290) and **Fiesta Time Tours** (tel. 726-4290) provide half-day van or bus tours of Laredo and Nuevo Laredo for around $12 per person (half for children under 12). They also offer overnight tours to Monterrey and, during bullfighting season, special Nuevo Laredo bullfight tours.

The **Webb County Heritage Foundation** (tel. 210-727-0977) arranges walking and bus tours of Laredo's historic downtown, by appointment only.

NUEVO LAREDO

This is the quintessential Texas-Mexico border town, since more tourists enter Mexico via this city than any other place along Mexico's entire frontier with the United States. For Laredo residents and nearby South Texans, it's a place to shop and party on weekends or holidays. Most foreign visitors never get farther than a few blocks down Avenida Guerrero, the main tourist strip that runs directly south from the bridge.

If you're just going for the day, it's easy to walk over International Bridge #1 from downtown Laredo, near La Posada Hotel (you can park your car in the free lots off Zaragoza St., below Riverdrive Mall). If you must drive across (finding parking in downtown Nuevo Laredo can be very difficult), you can use either International Bridge #2, which crosses the river from the south end of I-35 and joins Mexico 85 in downtown Nuevo Laredo, or bypass Nuevo Laredo altogether by crossing at the Colombia Bridge north of Laredo. Bridge tolls are $1 for cars, 25 cents for pedestrians (it's a bit less in the reverse direction due to the weak peso).

Sights
Morelos Parque, three blocks east of International Bridge #1 between Calle de Bravo and 15 de Junio, exhibits 50 replicas of historical artwork from Mexico City's famous Museum of Anthropology as well as the Mayan ruins of Chichen Itza and Teotihuacan. The works represent seven pre-Hispanic cultures in Mexico and Central America. Seven blocks down Avenida Guerrero is the **main plaza** and municipal palace, a popular outdoor gathering place.

Restaurants And Bars
Nuevo Laredo has been a favorite eating and drinking spot for South Texans since Prohibition in the 1920s. The most famous border joint of all, the **Cadillac Bar** (tel. 20015), has been in business since 1926 and is still a favorite gringo rendezvous. While it may have seen better days, it still offers a tasty Ramos gin fizz (invented here) and classic border/gulf cuisine like *cabrito,* braised frogs' legs, roast quail, and red snapper *papillote,* plus Tex-Mex standards like huevos rancheros. Another specialty drink here is the "popper," a savory tequila concoction served in a large shot glass with a loud flourish—in which a white-jacketed waiter slams the glass onto the bar (or table). (Somehow, the drink's name has been transformed to "slammer" in the Austin, Houston, San Antonio, and San Francisco versions of this restaurant.) On New Year's Eve and during the Jalapeño Festival on Washington's Birthday, the Cadillac is filled to overflowing—regulars adjourn to the nearby **Gomez Bar.** The

Cadillac is at the corner of Ocampo and Belden (walk two blocks south of the bridge and make a left on Belden) and is open daily 10 a.m.-11 p.m.

Around the intersection of Victoria and Matamoros, only a block from the bridge, is a cluster of more upscale, tourist-oriented restaurants with international menus. Seafood fans swear by **Mariscos Mandinga** at 1307 Obregón. The **Winery Pub & Grill** (tel. 20895) at Matamoros No. 308 is quite popular, also, and features live Latin music nightly after 9. Both are open daily for lunch and dinner.

The moderately priced **La Palapa** at 3301 Reforma (Mexico 85) specializes in mesquite-grilled fajitas, sold by the kilo. It's open daily for dinner only. Another good place for fajitas (also *queso flameado)* is **Las Tablitas** at H. Nacataz and Degollado near the Nuevo Laredo City Hall; open daily for lunch and dinner. For authentic food and a funky, local atmosphere, try the family-run **Café Almanza,** near the plaza at Ocampo and González. Mexican breakfasts, *caldos,* and seafood are quite inexpensive here, and it's open daily 7 a.m.-midnight.

Entertainment
Nuevo Laredo Downs (Hipódromo-Galgódromo) (tel. 210-726-0549 in the U.S., 23802 in Mexico, 800-292-5659 in Texas only) is seven miles south of town off Mexico 85 at 2829 Venustiano Carranza and offers greyhound and horse racing every Saturday and Sunday (yes, you can bet with US dollars). There are also occasional dog races Wed.-Friday. Laredo's "El Metro" bus service (tel. 722-0951) runs a shuttle service between downtown Laredo hotels and Nuevo Laredo Downs. The rustic **Nuevo Laredo Turf Club** at Bravo and Ocampo (one block left from the bridge) offers off-track betting on U.S. and Mexican races; open daily.

La Fiesta Bullring (Plaza de Toros La Fiesta) on Mexico 85 just past the Nuevo Laredo airport, features Sunday bullfights between Washington's Birthday and early September. Call the Laredo Chamber of Commerce for the latest schedule (tel. 722-9895).

Nuevo Laredo's discos are crowded with bouncing bodies on weekends. A few blocks down Guerrero and over one street, on parallel Matamoros (next to The Winery Pub & Grill) is the **Lion's Den,** a disco that's popular with tourists. **Vivanti's,** across from the El Rio Motel on Mexico 85, and Firenze's, two blocks down from Vivanti's, get a mix of young people from both sides of the border. All three are open Wed.-Sun. till 2 a.m.

Shopping

Tourist-oriented gift shops line the north end of Avenida Guerrero near the bridge. Unless you're buying liquor and cigarettes (which cost about the same everywhere in Nuevo Laredo), the prices aren't that good. **Marti's** (tel. 23137) at Guerrero and Victoria is a boutique that carries unique clothing, furniture, and arts and crafts—at boutique prices. **La Casa del Café** at Matamoros and Hidalgo sells whole or fresh-ground coffee beans by the kilo at excellent prices. The two-story **Nuevo Mercado de La Reforma** at Guerrero and Belden houses a collection of shops where bargaining (which is expected) can result in occasional good buys. **Mercado M. Herrera** at Hidalgo and Ocampo is another market nearby. Near the plaza are a couple of smaller markets frequented by locals.

Information

The Mexican tourist office at the end of International Bridge #1 has tourist brochures on Nuevo Laredo and Mexico and a helpful staff; it's usually open Mon.-Sat. 9-3. There's an American Consulate (tel. 40512) at Avenida Galeana (one block east of Avenida Ocampo) and Calle de Madero, about 12 blocks south of the bridge.

Transport

For $2 you can take a Transportes del Norte or Transportes Frontera bus from the Laredo Greyhound station to Nuevo Laredo's bus terminal (about two miles south of the bridge) to connect with buses going into the interior of Mexico. This the cheapest way to ride buses onward into the country, but you can also get buses to various Mexican destinations direct from the Greyhound station (at higher ticket prices)—see "Laredo—Transport."

The Nuevo Laredo railway station is at Avenida César López de Lara and Calle Gutiérrez de Lara, east of Guerrero. The first-class *El Regiomontano* train runs between here and Mexico City via Monterrey, Saltillo, and San Luis Potosí. Reserved seats, if you book them yourself in Nuevo Laredo, are $19 to Mexico City (19 hours) or $4 to Monterrey (four hours). Sleeping cabins to Mexico city are $25s, $28d. Tickets for El Regiomontano trains can be booked in advance at Laredo travel agencies, but they will add a surcharge to the Mexican fare. The Nuevo Laredo railways station is on Calle Cesar López de Lara de Mina.

A new 53-mile, four-lane toll highway from Nuevo Laredo to Monterrey is only nine miles shorter than the old road but shortens the drive from an hour and a half to about an hour. The speed limit is 68 mph, one of the highest in Mexico. The toll is also a record-breaker—$12 each way.

VICINITY OF LAREDO

Laredo is really in the middle of nowhere, so that "in the vicinity" means within a 150-mile radius. Zapata is 49 miles southeast along US 83, followed by Roma (89 miles) and Rio Grande City (109 miles). This stretch of Texas border towns is held together by a common historical and cultural thread, since all were settled by Spanish colonists in the mid-18th century as part of the famous José Escandón land grant. The area between Falcon and Rio Grande City makes an especially interesting road trip if you zig-zag back and forth across the border at various small crossings: US 83 and Mexico 2 run parallel on either side of the border here.

Eagle Pass is 126 miles in the opposite direction, almost as far northeast as Del Rio, where South Texas meets West Texas.

Zapata

The original settlement that became Zapata was founded in 1750 by Spaniard José Vasquez Borrego. It was later renamed for legendary Indian fighter Antonia Zapata. When the Rio Grande was dammed to create Falcon International Reservoir, old Zapata was completely submerged and a new Zapata was built on higher ground. To see what old Zapata looked like, visit the **La Paz Museum** in a 200-year-old house near Benavides Elementary School in San Ygnacio, about 25 miles northwest on US 83. The museum contains old photos of the original Zapata, local ranch and farm implements, and antiques. It's open from September to May, Mon.-Fri. 8-3; admission is free.

Falcon State Park

Falcon Dam was constructed across the Rio Grande in 1953 in order to create the 87,210-acre Falcon International Reservoir. Both the U.S. and Mexico utilize the dam and reservoir for hydroelectric power, flood control, and recreation. The Falcon State Park is at the southeast shore of the lake, off US 83 north of Roma (via FM 2098 and Park Rd. 46). The fishing is said to be outstanding here, particularly for black and white bass, stripers, catfish, and crappie.

Approximately 572 acres of typical Rio Grande brush country are protected by the park along the lake shores. Facilities include shaded picnic area, a boat ramp, fish-cleaning shelter, and four camping areas. Tent-camper sites with water are $6 a night, with w/e $9. Full hookup RV sites are $10 a night; screened shelters are available for $15. Park entry is $3 per vehicle, $1 for pedestrians and cyclists.

For further information, contact the Park Superintendent (tel. 210-848-5327), Falcon State Park, P.O. Box 2, Falcon Heights, TX 78545.

Other RV Parks: The **Oso Blanco RV Park** (tel. 210-765-4339) is about 10 miles north of Falcon State Recreation Area off US 83; full hookups are $10-12 a night; facilities include a boat ramp and docks. Thirty miles farther north off US 83 in Zapata is the larger **Bass Lake RV Park** (tel. 765-4961), with the same rates as Oso Blanco; facilities include boat ramps, docks, and a spa.

Roma

This atmospheric little town was founded under a Spanish land grant in 1765. Before the railways arrived in South Texas in the late 1800s, it was an important riverboat terminal on the Rio Grande for transshipment to and from the Gulf of Mexico (of course this was long before they dammed the river to the north). Unlike most Rio Grande border towns, Roma is situated in hilly terrain, a setting which shows off its historic buildings to good advantage. To see these mostly unrestored buildings, walk or drive through the streets on the river (west) side of town. Some of the more impressive structures around the *plazita* (dating from the 19th cen-

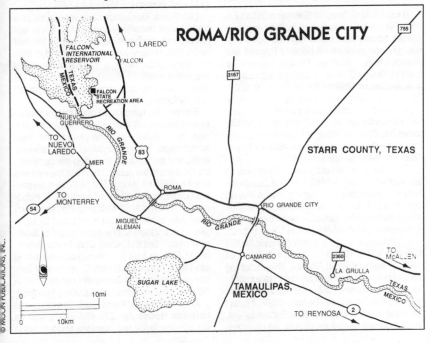

ROMA/RIO GRANDE CITY

TODD CLARK

Capilla San Juan

tury) were built by Spanish-German architect Enrique Portcheller. His trademark building design includes double doors and high windows with wrought-iron grillwork—a blend of Spanish and French Creole influences. The bell tower of Our Lady of Refuge Church, at Convent and Estrella, was erected in 1854 by Father Pierre Keralum. The *convento* across the street is a Portcheller design, as is the Manuel Guerra Store at Convent and Portcheller streets. The **Roma Historical Museum** (tel. 210-849-1535), at Estrella and Lincoln, contains exhibits chronicling local history; it's open Mon.-Fri. 9-4 or by appointment.

Of further historical note: Roma was chosen as an outdoor set for the 1952 film *Viva Zapata* (directed by Elia Kazan and starring Marlon Brando and Anthony Quinn—who won an Academy Award for his performance) because it so perfectly resembles a turn-of-the-century Mexican town.

A suspension bridge (the only one over the Rio Grande) built in 1927 links Roma with the small Mexican town of **Miguel Aleman**. There's nothing much to see in Miguel Aleman, but 11 miles northwest of here via Mexico 2 is the historic Mexican town of **Mier**. Founded in the early 1750s, it hasn't changed much since the Nuevo Santander era, with its narrow sandstone streets, old churches,

and plazas. **Capilla San Juan,** off Mexico 2 just before Mexico 54 south to Monterrey, is a nicely restored 1752 Catholic chapel. A larger church, built in 1798, is next to the main plaza and features a Portcheller-designed clock tower.

Rio Grande City

As part of the same land grant as Roma, this early Spanish town was founded as Carnestolendas in 1768. The hilly, brush-country terrain is similar to that around Roma. During the War with Mexico in 1848, the U.S. Army established Fort Ringgold nearby as a front line of defense, and it became an important steamboat terminal for supplying the fort. In the early 1850s, after the Rio Grande had been designated as the U.S.-Mexico border, the town was made the new Starr County seat and renamed Rio Grande City. An army of Mexicans and Americans who were dissatisfied with both national governments convened in Rio Grande City in 1852 and led an unsuccessful attack against Mexican troops in nearby Camargo in an attempt to establish a "Republic of the Sierra Madre" in northern Mexico.

Like Roma, Rio Grande City's importance as a trade center lessened considerably as the railroads came into South Texas during the last half of the 19th century. An international bridge links the city with Camargo, a Mexican town with a population of around 10,000, so import-export still plays a role in the local economy, along with Starr County farming and ranching.

Sights: The remaining **Fort Ringgold** buildings—barracks, officers quarters, storerooms, stables, and bakery—are now used by the local school district. During after-school hours, on weekends, and on holidays (including the summer), they're open to the public. They're at the east end of town off US 83. Along Main St. in town are several buildings constructed in the late 1800s, including the restored 1899 **LaBorde House,** now a hotel (see below). Another good street for sightseeing is Mirasoles, one block south of Main, where you'll find the **Henry Clay Davis House,** built in 1848, and several others built in the mid- to late 1800s. Next to the County Courthouse at Second and Britton is the **Grotto of Lourdes,** built in 1928 as a replica of the famous shrine in France.

Accommodations and food: The renovated **LaBorde House** (tel. 210-487-5101), with its wrought-iron fence and hurricane shutters, looks like it's been plucked from New Orleans' French Quarter. The original owner, Francoise LaBorde, was a New Orleans native who had his Rio Grande City home designed by Parisian architects in the 1890s. It's now listed with the National Register of Historic Places, which means that restoration was carried out under U.S. Department of Interior guidelines. Replacement bricks, where needed, were handmade at the same Camargo, Mexico, brick foundry as the originals. The eight original rooms, at 601 E. Main, are furnished with Victorian antiques and cost $59; modern rooms in back of the historic building are $40.

The newer **Fort Ringgold Motor Inn** (tel. 487-5666) at 4350 US has 83 rooms for $35-45 s, $45-50 d.

The family-run **Caro's** (tel. 210-487-2255), at 205 N. Garcia, is an inexpensive northern Mexican-style café with a statewide reputation; the corn for their tortillas is ground fresh daily, as are the Mexican spices (open daily for lunch and dinner). **Che's Restaurant and Bar** (tel. 487-5101) in LaBorde House also offers good border cooking, plus fresh Rio Grande catfish (open daily for breakfast, lunch, and dinner).

Ciudad Camargo: Across the river from Rio Grande City is the small Mexican town of Camargo (pop. 10,000). This was José Escandón's first Nuevo Santander settlement, dating from 1749. The oldest building in town is a Catholic church with one bell tower on Calle Libertad, which was built in the early 1750s. The town square **Plaza Hidalgo** has a *kiosco* or gazebo where musical groups and dancers perform during festivals. Sixteen miles southwest of Camargo via Mexico 2 is **Sugar Lake,** which is part of Parque Nacional Camargo (Camargo National Park). The lake has facilities for fishing, boating, and camping, plus a restaurant that serves Mexican food and freshwater fish under outdoor *palapas* (thatched umbrellas).

Eagle Pass

Few tourists ever make it to Eagle Pass, a sleepy Tex-Mex town of 24,000 on an isolated section of the Texas-Mexico border. The town was founded in 1850 by San Antonio banker John Twohig and named for a nearby river ford called Paso del Aguila by the Mexicans. The town became the Maverick County seat in 1856, named for rancher Sam Maverick, who was one of the signers of the 1836 Texas Declaration of Independence. His name also has a permanent place in American vocabulary: So that he could say that any unbranded cattle on the range belonged to him, he didn't brand his cattle. This was such a unique scheme that the word "maverick" came to refer to any person with especially new, independent ideas (in ranching, it still refers to unbranded stock).

About the only reason to come to Eagle Pass is for a visit to **Piedras Negras** (pop. 120,000) on the other side of the Rio Grande, since it's the closest border town to San Antonio (142 miles away via US 57/I-35—about two to three hours by car). It's really only 10 miles closer to San Antonio than Laredo, but the town is somewhat less touristed. Eagle Pass is in many ways a "suburb" of Piedras Negras; the main newspaper in the area is the *Zócalo*, which is published in Spanish on the Mexican side of the border but contains an Eagle Pass section.

The international bridge is a short walk from downtown Eagle Pass (the chamber of commerce parking lot at 400 Garrison offers free parking for Piedras Negras day visitors). Just across the international bridge at Hidalgo and Abasolo is **La Estrella**, a government-sponsored arts and crafts shop, as well as a number of other shops and restaurants. A central *mercado* is a block west on Zaragoza, and the **Plaza de Toros** on Avenida Lopez Mateos features bullfights on Sundays between June and September.

The Kickapoos: About eight miles south of Eagle Pass off FM 1021 is a small Kickapoo Indian reservation, for the most part used during the summer months only. The rest of the year they reside at El Nacimiento, Mexico, about 90 miles southwest of Piedras Negras off Mexico 57 S and 53 N. The Kickapoos originally hail from Wisconsin and Michigan, but were driven south in the 18th and 19th centuries. In 1775, Spain's Charles III gave them permission to settle in the Mexican colonial province of Coahuila y Texas in return for defending the area against Comanche and Apache raids. By the late 1800s, many of those on the Texas side were banished to Oklahoma reservations. Some were able to flee to northern Mexico and were given land by the Mexican government (like the Seminoles, a number of Kickapoos came north again to serve as scouts with the U.S. Cavalry in Texas). The Kickapoos have maintained a strong sense of cultural identity and have preserved their language, religion, and many of their traditional customs (such as keeping a sacred fire burning year-round in each home). Both the U.S. and Mexican governments have given them special permission to cross the border at will and to reside in either country.

Accommodations And Food: The **Eagle Pass Inn** (tel. 210-773-9531), four miles north of town on US 277, has rooms for $28-35 s, $35-40 d (senior discount and weekly rates available). **La Quinta Motor Inn** (tel. 773-7000), 2525 Main St.,

has slightly larger rooms for $47-53 s, $54-60 d (senior discount available).

Both Eagle Pass and Piedras Negras offer the usual assortment of border-style cafes and restaurants. Nachos—tortilla chips topped by jalapeños and melted cheese—were reportedly invented by Ignacio "Nacho" Anaya, a cook at the Victory Club (now the Moderno Restaurant) in Piedras Negras.

GULF COAST
INTRODUCTION

America's "third coast" stretches for over 360 miles (over 600 miles if you count the ins and outs of every bay and inlet) along the Gulf of Mexico, the world's largest gulf, and is unparalleled in its variety of beaches, dunes, islands, lagoons, and saltwater marshes. Flashy tourist brochures call it the "Texas Riviera" or the "Texas Gold Coast," but the truth is that you won't find anyplace comparable to St. Tropez or Miami Beach here. Instead, you'll find a rich mixture of laid-back fishing towns, seashore parks, wildlife refuges, a smattering of high-rise condo developments, and only one city of any size (Corpus Christi, which hardly disturbs the coast since it's on an inland bay).

THE LAND AND SEA

A basic topographic pattern is repeated along the coast's full length. Long, narrow barrier islands and peninsulas are separated from an inner shoreline by a series of wide, shallow lagoons. The lagoons are fed by a mixture of Gulf saltwater and freshwater rivers, and wash against salt marshes and other coastal wetlands. Farther inland, the marshes and wetlands blend with coastal grasses to form the Gulf Coast Plains. This layered coastal barrier not only protects inland Texas from the full force of tropical cyclones and hurricanes that originate in the Gulf, but also provides an unusually diverse concentration of habitats that harbor wildlife of all kinds, from tiny fawn-breasted hummingbirds to giant manta rays. The Gulf itself contributes some $175 million to the state's economy annually in receipts from harvested seafood—shrimp, crab, oysters, flounder, red snapper, and a variety of other shell- and finfish.

The entire shoreline can be divided into three sections according to the climate and terrain typical to each. The upper coast, extending from the northern end of the Bolivar Peninsula to Matagorda Island, is the most humid and receives the most precipitation; the inner shoreline is thick with *spartina* or salt grass (this is also the state's main rice-producing region). The central coast, from Matagorda Island to Corpus Christi, is a transition zone between the upper and lower coasts, with a mixture of grasslands, marshes, live oak, and scrub vegetation. The lower coast, from Corpus Christi to the Mexican border, is much more arid, with fewer marshes and grasslands, more scrub country and sand dunes. This last section of Texas shoreline, which includes North and South Padre Island, was recently named as one of the country's 10 most ecologically pristine coastal areas by the Coast Alliance and by the University of Maryland's Coastal Research Laboratory.

Preservation Versus Development

The most developed areas of the Texas shoreline are along the Upper Coast between Galveston and Port Arthur, where inland oil refineries are located near large ports for out-of-state shipment of petroleum products. The Central and Lower coasts have, for the most part, been spared this intensive assault on coastal resources, but are contending instead with the slower-growing menace of urbanization. One aspect of human intervention that affects all parts of the coast is the Gulf Intracoastal Waterway, a series of channels that connect lagoons and bays so that boats can navigate the Gulf coast's entire length from Brownsville, Texas, to St. Marks, Florida. It's difficult to say what the long-term effects of these channels will be on the natural coastal system (except where they have obviously been cut through wetlands and salt marshes); for the moment, only the waterways around Galveston, Port Arthur, and Corpus Christi are heavily trafficked.

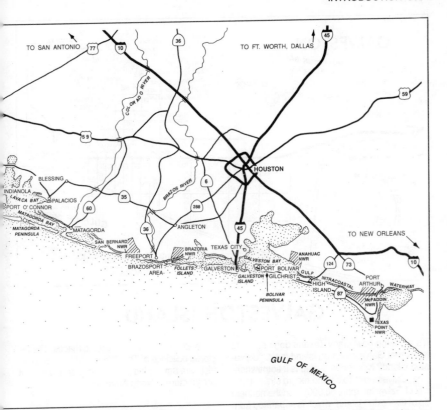

TO SAN ANTONIO 77 10

36

TO FT. WORTH, DALLAS 45

59

COLORADO RIVER

59

HOUSTON

BLESSING

INDIANOLA

LAVACA BAY PALACIOS

PORT O' CONNOR

60

35

BRAZOS RIVER

6

288

MATAGORDA BAY

MATAGORDA

36

ANGLETON

45

MATAGORDA PENINSULA

SAN BERNARD NWR

TEXAS CITY

BRAZORIA NWR

ANAHUAC NWR

TO NEW ORLEANS

FREEPORT

BRAZOSPORT AREA

FOLLETS ISLAND

GALVESTON BAY

PORT BOLIVAR

GULF

124 73

10

GALVESTON

GALVESTON ISLAND

GILCHRIST

HIGH ISLAND

INTRACOASTAL

PORT ARTHUR

WATERWAY

87

BOLIVAR PENINSULA

McFADDIN NWR

TEXAS POINT NWR

GULF OF MEXICO

From Corpus Christi south, the Gulf Intracoastal Waterway (part of Laguna Madre) seems to be mainly used by pleasure craft and the occasional Brownsville ship (total reported tonnage shipped in 1987 between Corpus Christi and the Mexican border was only about two percent of that shipped between Port Arthur and Galveston).

State and federal authorities have so far set aside nine undeveloped areas as wildlife refuges along the coast to preserve the land and its native inhabitants; in addition, the Coastal Barrier Resources System Act of 1982 protects another 200,000 acres of Texas coast. Many Texans are actively involved in ongoing efforts to preserve what remains of the unprotected virgin dunes, beaches, islands, wetlands, and salt marshes between Galveston and Boca Chica (the southernmost beach in Texas). If you'd like to join them in their mission (this is a great way to learn more about the Texas coast), contact one of these organizations: Coast Alliance (tel. 202-265-5518), 1536 16th St. N.W., Washington, D.C. 20036; Lone Star Chapter of the Sierra Club (tel. 512-476-6962), 1104 Nueces, Suite 2, Austin, TX 78702; South Bay Taskforce (tel. 512-943-5571), 300 Garcia St., Port Isabel, TX 78578.

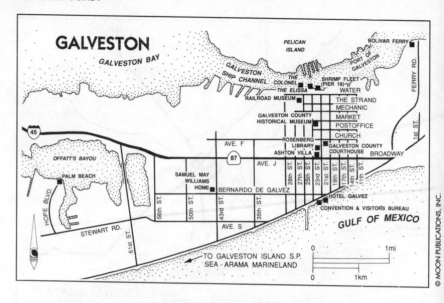

GALVESTON ISLAND

It's amazing how many Texans don't seem to know that Galveston is an island town. "Galveston Island? Never heard of it. Is it somewhere near Galveston?" To set the record straight: the city of Galveston (pop. 60,000) is on the northern tip of Galveston Island, which is separated from the Texas mainland by Galveston Bay; it's also the seat of Galveston County, which encompasses the island plus a wedge of mainland around Texas City, southeast of Houston and Pasadena, and the Bolivar Peninsula (just northeast of Galveston across the mouth of Galveston Bay).

Once the state's largest city (and the state's first to get each of the following: national bank, post office, locomotive, telephone service, hospital, public library, streetcars, and electric lights), the island is now mostly a vacation spot that draws weekend, holiday, and summer tourists to its 32 miles of beaches and 19th-century historic districts. The beaches aren't the state's best, but they're very accessible (only 51 miles from Houston) and the county does an admirable job of keeping them clean. The historic districts are splendid, however, encompassing over 1,500 19th-century structures, 550 of which are listed on the National Register of Historic Places. The restored buildings of The Strand and East End districts are among the finest examples of Victorian architecture in North America.

HISTORY

Pirates And Indians

Not much is known about the early history of human habitation on Galveston Island, mainly because periodic hurricanes have made it difficult if not impossible to obtain reliable evidence from archaeological excavations. At one time the Karankawa Indians, who had a reputation for fierceness (some histories claim they practiced ritual cannibalism), held domain over the region. When famous Spanish explorer Cabeza de Vaca was shipwrecked here in 1528, he and his crew were rescued and taken prisoner by the Karankawas, with whom they lived for several years (de Vaca finally made it to Mexico City in 1536, after a series of adventures among a number of Texas Indian tribes, who tended to regard him as a great medicine man).

The Spanish returned in the mid-18th century and set up a short-lived presidio named for the Spanish governor of Louisiana, Bernardo de Galvez. They left the island to the French after Franco-Spanish relations in East Texas grew tense; by the end of the century, the French had abandoned their American colonies, too. Mexican revolutionaries stationed themselves here for a short time in the early 1800s, then left.

In 1817, buccaneer Jean Lafitte established a pirate colony called Campeachy on the island. After a run-in with an American gunboat, Lafitte was forced to leave in 1821, but he left behind a small but growing community that Anglicized the original Spanish name as "Galveston." Treasure-hunters still speculate about the likelihood of buried loot somewhere on the island.

Galveston banker Samuel May Williams poured loot of his own into the Texas revolution against Mexican rule in the late 1830s. Texas Navy ships stationed at Galveston also held off a Mexican blockade of the coast here and the town was made a temporary capital of the aspiring republic. Once independence was won, plans for a new town were laid as Galveston geared up to become the new republic's chief port.

Civil War, The 1900 Hurricane, And Renewal

During the state's 10-year status as a sovereign nation, the port of Galveston grew slowly as the Texan economy started and sputtered. Once Texas was annexed to the U.S., things looked rosy for the town—until its strategic position made it a focus for the Civil War in the 1860s. Union troops were able to capture the port in 1862, but the Confederates soon regained control and kept it till the end of the war. A Union naval blockade prevented any goods from coming in or out of the port, however, so the local economy stagnated along with the rest of the state.

After the war ended, Galveston prospered. By the late 1800s, it was the biggest and most modern city in the state, the third-largest port in the nation, and a banking center for the Southwest. The island town's destiny was forever altered, however, by the hurricane of 1900, which is still listed as the worst natural disaster in American history. Tides up to 20 feet high engulfed the entire island, speeded by 100-mile-an-hour winds; at least 6,000 people died and hundreds of buildings were flattened.

To protect the island from future hurricanes, Galvestonians constructed a massive seawall and raised the city 17 feet higher in some places, but Galveston never regained its former glamour. A new ship channel was constructed between nearby Houston and Trinity Bay that all but finished the port of Galveston. In the '30s and '40s the island became a gambling haven, but a legal crackdown in the 1950s ended that experiment. In the '60s and '70s, Galveston began making a comeback as a port by specializing in different commodities than its neighbor Houston (importing bananas and plantains and exporting wheat, sorghum, and rice rather than the import/export of petrochemicals and building materials) and by developing an especially efficient port system that has earned it a reputation as the "Port of Quickest Dispatch"; it's now the seventh-most important of the state's 27 Gulf ports.

About 25 years ago, the island's beaches began attracting tourists from North and East Texas. Major historical restoration efforts by the Galveston Historical Foundation have made the city even more of a holiday destination, so that tourism and conventions are now second to shipping and agriculture (mainly rice grown on the mainland section of the county) in economic importance to Galveston County.

SIGHTS

Seawall Boulevard

Most visitors arrive on the island via I-45 over the Galveston Causeway, which eventually becomes Broadway. Broadway in turn ends at Seawall Blvd., which runs for 10 miles along the seaward side of the island. Below the seawall is a beach of sorts (better beaches are farther south beyond the seawall), and between 10th and 61st streets are 14 jetties made of huge granite blocks. A wide sidewalk runs the entire length of the seawall, making it one of the longest beach promenades in the country. On the inland side of the boulevard are rows of hotels, restaurants, beach condos, beachwear and souvenir shops, and recreational equipment rental services (for surfboards, sailboards, skateboards, skates, etc.). See "Recreation" below for descriptions of specific beaches and beach activities.

Museums

The **Galveston County Historical Museum** (tel. 409-766-2340), jointly sponsored by the county and the Galveston Historical Foundation, is housed in a 1919 former bank building at 2219 Market (Ave. D). Permanent exhibits on the first floor recount Galveston history, including early Karankawa Indian habitation, the exploits of pirate Jean Lafitte, and the 1900 hurricane. The mezzanine floor features rotating exhibits which deal with more arcane facets of local history. The museum also offers a lecture series. Open Memorial Day to Labor Day Mon.-Sat. 10-5, Sun. noon-5; the remainder of the year it's closed on Sunday. Admission is free (donations accepted).

The **Railroad Museum** (tel. 409-765-5700) is appropriately located in the old Galveston Railway Station, an art deco structure that's been restored to its original 1932 condition. Thirty-nine life-size plaster sculptures of "passengers" are sitting and standing in the former waiting room; headphone stations near each group of sculptures allow visitors to listen in on dramatized conversations. Other rooms in the station feature a working HO-scale model of the Port of Galveston and audiovisual displays that explain Texas rail development. Out on the tracks are collections of restored steam locomotives and passenger cars, including 1920s-era Pullman sleepers and a 1922 Santa Fe engine (#555). Two restored dining cars contain a full-service restaurant, Dinner On The Diner (see "Food" for details). The museum is at 25th and The Strand, at the west end of The Strand historic district. It's open daily 10-5; admission is $4 adults, $3 seniors, $2 children 4-12.

Historic Buildings

Galveston is full of late 19th-century homes built in the Victorian and Greek Revival styles. The most impressive is undoubtedly **The Bishop's Palace** (tel. 409-762-2475) at 1402 Broadway. It was designed for Colonel Walter Gresham by renowned Galveston architect Nicholas Clayton and completed in 1886 for a cost of $250,000; current appraisals estimate its value at $5.5 million. The local Catholic Diocese purchased it in 1923 for Bishop Byrne, who lived here until 1950. The 24-room mansion is listed with the Library of Congress as one of 14 structures in the U.S. most representative of the Victorian age of architecture, while the American Institute of Architects counts it as one of the 100 most significant buildings in the country.

The exterior is constructed of red sandstone, white limestone, and pink granite. Inside are 14 magnificent fireplaces, plus wood paneling and archways of black walnut burl. One of the most stunning interior features is a spiral staircase which took 61 craftsmen three years to build, using oak, maple, white mahogany, rosewood, satinwood, and other fine hardwoods. All rooms are fully restored and furnished in period antiques. It's open Memorial Day to Labor Day daily 10-5, the remainder of the year Wed.-Mon. noon-4. Tours leave every 30 minutes; admission is $3

Bishop's Palace

adults, $1.50 for children 13-18, 50 cents for children under 13.

The **Ashton Villa** (tel. 409-762-3933), at 24th and Broadway, is a three-story, Victorian Italianate brick villa that was built in 1859 for Colonel James M. Brown. It was restored by the Galveston Historical Society, which offers a one-hour tour of the mansion and carriage house that includes an audio-visual presentation on the 1900 hurricane. It's open Memorial Day to Labor Day daily 10-5, the remainder of the year Mon.-Fri. 10-4, Sat. and Sun. 10-5; admission is $3 adults, $2.50 seniors and children 12-18, $1.50 children 6-11.

One restored example of Greek Revival architecture in Galveston is open to the public year-round. **John Sydnor's 1847 Powhatan House** (tel. 409-763-0077) is a two-story mansion with 24-foot-high Doric columns and period furnishings at 3427 Ave. O. It's maintained by the Galveston Garden Club, who open it to self-guiding tours on weekends (1-5). Admission is $2 adults, $1 for students and seniors.

The **Samuel May Williams Home** (tel. 409-765-1839), at 3601 Bernardo de Galvez (Ave. P), is considered the town's oldest residence. A modest New England-style house crowned by a widow's walk, it was originally built in Maine, then disassembled and moved to Galveston, where it was reassembled piece by piece. Williams was an important local figure who started Texas banking, recruited volunteers for the Texas Revolution, and built ships for the Texas Navy. The Galveston Historical Society leads tours of the home Memorial Day to Labor Day Mon.-Sat. 10-5, Sun. noon-5; the remainder of the year it closes at 4 p.m. on the same days. Admission is $3 adults, $2.50 children and seniors.

The Victorian-era **Grand 1894 Opera House** (tel. 409-765-1894), at 2020 Postoffice, has recently been restored to its original 1894 splendor, in which no seat is more than 70 feet from the stage. Such artists as Anna Pavlova, Al Jolson, Sarah Bernhardt, John Philip Sousa, and the Marx Brothers performed here in its heyday. Today it serves as a performance venue for everything from grand opera and symphony to rock and jazz concerts. It's also open to the public for self-guided tours Mon.-Sat. 9-5, Sun. noon-5; admission is $2 adults, children under six free.

The **Tremont House** (tel. 409-763-0300), 2300 Mechanic St. (Ship Mechanic's Row), is Galveston's most historic hotel. The original, built in 1839, hosted such famous guests as Sam Houston, Ulysses S. Grant, Clara Barton, and Anna Pavlova, but burned down in 1865. A replacement was erected in 1872, but was abandoned and leveled 56 years later. The latest incarnation, near the original site, is housed in a huge 1879 building which has been totally renovated and outfitted with Victorian-era furnishings. Wrought-iron bridges connect the upper floors, which are reached by old-fashioned birdcage elevators; most of the 111 guest rooms have 14-foot ceilings and 12-foot windows. Even if you can't afford to stay here, drop by the **Toujouse Lounge** for a drink at the 1860s rosewood bar.

Established in 1902, the **Rosenberg Library** (tel. 409-763-8854) at 23rd and Sealy (Ave. I) is the oldest continually operating public library in Texas. Besides offering the usual book collection and lending services, the library houses the Galveston Art League Gallery and several historical displays that recount different aspects of local and state history. It's open to the public Mon.-Thurs. 9-9, Fri. and Sat. 9-6.

Elissa: A Tall Ship For Texas
This 150-foot, square-rigged iron barque is the third-oldest ship afloat (next to England's *Cutty Sark* and San Diego's *Star of India*) and possibly the only fully operational 19th-century vessel in the world. First launched in Scotland in 1877, the *Elissa* made calls at Galveston in 1883 and 1886. When the Galveston Historical Foundation was seeking a 19th-century sailing ship connected with Galveston history, it found the *Elissa* rusting in a Piraeus, Greece, shipyard in 1974. It has since been fully restored to form and function (at a cost of $3.6 million) and makes yearly voyages along the Gulf coast and beyond. In 1986, she sailed up the Atlantic coast to participate in the Parade of Sail in New York Harbor.

Most of the year, she's moored at Pier 19, near 22nd and Water on the Galveston Ship Channel (an easy stroll from The Strand Historic District). Visitors are welcome to tour the ship and the various seafaring exhibits on board. When in port, she's open daily 10-5; admission is $4 adults, $3.50 for students and seniors, $3 for children 6-12. For further information, call (409) 763-1877.

Historic Districts
The Strand Historic District, a 12-block area along Water, Mechanic, and The Strand between

The Strand

20th and 25th streets, represents one of the finest collections of iron-front (actually a mixture of brick, stucco, and cast iron) Victorians in the country. The centerpiece of the district is The Strand, which was modeled after London's street of the same name in the late 1800s. For a while it was the most important financial center between San Francisco and St. Louis and it became known as "the Wall Street of the Southwest"; although the buildings survived the 1900 hurricane, the port's general decline thereafter led to the district's virtual abandonment. Fortunately, the city chose to preserve the old storefronts here rather than tear them down or alter their appearance, and today the buildings are owned or leased by restaurants, shops, and other small businesses, most of them tourist-oriented. A few iron-fronts have been turned into residential apartments and lofts. Galveston's two biggest annual events are held on The Strand—Mardi Gras in February and "Dickens On The Strand" in December (see "Events" for details).

The **East End Historic District** is a 40-block area bounded by 11th, 19th, Market, and Broadway. Most of the homes here were built between 1875 and 1900, when this was an upscale residential district. The entire district is listed on the National Register of Historic Places. A driving and walking tour map of the district is available from The Strand Visitors Center, 2016 The Strand.

Several homes in the smaller **Silk Stocking Historic District,** along 24th and 25th between avenues L and O, are listed with the National Register of Historic Places or the Texas Historical Commission. The district's name is an early political label that referred to the fact that only ladies living in this part of town could afford silk stockings. Nicholas Clayton, the architect of the Bishop's Palace (see "Historic Buildings" above), also designed the **Sweeney-Royston House** at Ave. L and 24th. It's not open to the public except during the Historic Homes Tour in May (see "Events").

Lone Star Flight Museum

Recently opened in a custom-designed hangar at Scholes Field, 2002 Terminal Dr. (south of Galveston Municipal Airport and Offats Bayou), this is Galveston's newest tourist attraction. The museum's collection of 32 historic planes includes a number of WW II-vintage military aircraft, a Vietnam-era A-37 Dragonfly, a Republic P-47 Thunderbolt (one of only six operational Thunderbolts in existence), an F7F Tigercat, a P-38 Lightning (the best surviving example in the world), a 1836 Beech Staggerwing, and a Boeing B-17G. The museum (tel. 409-740-7722) is open daily 10-5; admission is $5 adults, $2.50 for seniors and children 2-13.

GALVESTON ACCOMMODATIONS

Hotels, Motels, And Condominiums

Galveston has a large selection of places to stay, most of which are along Seawall Blvd. or farther down along the southwest beaches. Naturally, the cheapest hotels and motels are those without a sea view (most places on Seawall Blvd., however, are constructed so that all rooms face the Gulf). If you want a sea view, be sure to request one when making reservations.

Beach condos in Galveston usually cost between $65 and $200 a night, depending on the number of bedrooms. Since they're equipped with full kitchens, it's generally less expensive to stay in condos rather than hotels or motels if you'll be there for several days or more. A few offer weekly or monthly rates (though beach home rentals are a better bargain for stays of a week or longer). For further details, see the "Galveston Hotels, Motels, And Condominiums" chart on next page.

Beach Homes

Several local real estate agencies handle beach home rentals, which start at around $300 a week ($150 and up for a weekend) for a basic one- or two-bedroom place. Most are located west of 100th St. and provide maid and linen service. Contact one of these realtors for further information: Grover & Associates (tel. 409-737-2663, Rte. 1, Box 162, Galveston, TX 77551); Menotti Properties (tel. 737-4700, Rte. 1, Box 150-A1); Sand 'N Sea Properties (tel. 737-2556, P.O. Box 5165); or Wolverton & Associates (tel. 737-1430, P.O. Box 5255).

Bed And Breakfasts

Galveston has around a dozen bed-and-breakfast inns, most of them in restored Victorian homes. The Strand Visitors Center distributes brochures from local B&Bs and Bed & Breakfast Reservations (tel. 409-762-1668, P.O. Box 1326, Galveston, TX 77551) can assist with bookings. Rates are in the $65-150 range.

Several places will take reservations directly, including The Gilded Thistle (tel. 409-763-0194) at 1805 Broadway, an 1893 house with three rooms for $110-130 a night, including full breakfast and complimentary wine and cheese in the evening. The Inn On The Strand (tel. 763-0806), at 2021 The Strand, has four large rooms and two suites in a restored 1856 warehouse. Rates are $60-160 a night with continental breakfast and evening champagne. The White Horse Inn (tel. 762-2632), at 2217 Broadway, has two rooms in the 1885 main house for $100 a night and four rooms in the carriage house for $80; rates include full breakfast. Michael's (tel. 763-3760), a 1916 brick house at 1715 35th, has rooms for $85 a night (shared bath only) including full breakfast. Galveston's first B&B was the The Victorian Inn (tel. 762-3235), a massive colonial-style home at 511 17th, within walking distance of The Strand. The four rooms cost $65-125 a night (only the most expensive has a private bath), including continental breakfast and evening hors d'oeuvres.

Camping And RV Parks

Tent camping and RV parking are permitted at Galveston Island State Park at Seawall and 13 Mile Rd. (see "Recreation" for details). Dellanera RV Park (tel. 409-740-0390), at 10901 San Luis Pass (just west of Sea-Arama and Six Mile Rd. off Seawall), is a city-operated facility with 50 full hookups, showers, laundry, grocery store, and beach area. Sites are $15 nightly, $84 weekly, and $300 monthly during the spring and summer, somewhat less during the fall and winter. Rates are similar at Bayou Heaven (tel. 744-2837, 6310 Heards Ln.) and Texas Campgrounds (tel. 737-2861, 4417 Antigua).

FOOD

The highest concentration of restaurants in Galveston is along Seawall Boulevard. Another restaurant area is The Strand Historical District, where meals are generally more expensive. You'll find several grocery stores along Seawall; if you're staying at the west-end beaches (Jamaica Beach, Dellanera RV Park, or Galveston Island State Park), the nearest grocery store is Seven Seas Grocery (tel. 409-737-1152), also known as Red's. Besides groceries, gas, and fishing tackle, Red's also offers a video rental service.

American

$$$ Dinner On The Diner: Two restored dining cars at the Railroad Museum offer fixed-price menus with choice of beef or veal, seafood, and fowl entrees. At 25th and The Strand (tel. 409-763-4759); open Mon.-Sat. for lunch and dinner, Sun. for brunch.

$ Country Morning Bakery: This is a great place to start off the morning with good coffee and fresh poppyseed kolaches, apple-pecan strudel, muffins, or other baked items. Just off The Strand at 21st (tel. 763-1617); open Tues.-Fri. 8-4, Sat. and Sun. 9-5.

$$ Yaga's: A Tropical Cafe: The Caribbean theme here carries over to the menu, which features tropical drinks and tasty "Rasta Pasta"—shrimp, crab, and pasta in a mildly spiced mayonnaise—as well as burgers, chicken, and fresh seafood. On weekends there's live music, usually reggae. At 2314 The Strand (tel. 762-6676); open Mon.-Thurs. 11:30-10, Fri. and Sat. 11:30 a.m.-2 a.m., Sun. noon-10.

GALVESTON HOTELS, MOTELS, AND CONDOMINIUMS

Ranges given are for the peak season (spring-summer) and reflect both weekday and weekend rates. Fall and winter rates are usually less. Add 11% tax to all hotel rates. Area code: 409

NAME	ADDRESS	PHONE	RATES	FEATURES
By The Sea Condominiums	7310 Seawall	744-5295 or (800) 666-0905 (outside TX)	$70-105	pool, tennis court
Casa del Mar Hotel Condominiums	6102 Seawall	740-2431 or (800) 392-1205 (in TX)	$65-129	1-bedroom suites w/kitchens, sea view, pool, coin laundry
Commodore On The Beach	3618 Seawall	763-2375, or (800) 543-0074 (800) 231-9921 (outside TX)	$64-90	all rooms w/sea view, pool, airport shuttle
Days Inn	6107 Broadway	740-2491	$35-75	pool, weekly rates
EconoLodge	2825 61st	744-7133	$40-60	pool
The Flagship Hotel	2501 Seawall	762-9000 or (800) 392-6542 (800) 231-7128 (outside TX)	$79-109	on private pier, pool, fishing, weekly rates
Gaido's Seaside Inn	3828 Seawall	762-9625 or (800) 525-0064 (outside TX)	$40-70	pool, sea view, wkly. rates
Galleon Suites Resort Hotel	9520 Seawall	744-2244	$79-135	1-2 bedroom suites with kitchen, pool, fitness center, comp. cont. brkfst.
Galveston Resort Inn	600 The Strand	765-5544	$55-85	pool, next to Galveston Yacht Basin, wkly. rates
Galvestonian Condominiums	1401 East Beach	765-6161	$120-325	sea views, lighted tennis courts, heated pool, Jacuzzi,
Harbor View Inn	928 Ferry	763-2888	$39-75	pool
Holiday Inn On The Beach	5002 Seawall	740-3581	$89-119	sea view, pool, coin laundry
Hotel Galvez	2024 Seawall	765-7721, or (800) 392-4285	$90-120	historic (est. 1911), sea view, pool, senior discount
Islander East Condominiums	415 East Beach	765-9301	$65-190	pool, tennis courts

GALVESTON HOTELS, MOTELS, AND CONDOMINIUMS

Ranges given are for the peak season (spring-summer) and reflect both weekday and weekend rates. Fall and winter rates are usually less. Add 11% tax to all hotel rates. Area code: 409

NAME	ADDRESS	PHONE	RATES	FEATURES
Key Largo Resort Hotel	5400 Seawall	744-5000, or (800) 833-0120	$55-110	sea view, pool
La Quinta Motor Inn	1402 Seawall	763-1224, or (800) 531-5900 (outside TX)	$57-99	sea view, pool, senior discount
Manor House	2300 Seawall	762-1166	$59-85	sea view, pool
Motel 6	7404 Ave. J	740-1261	$23.95 + $6 ea. add.	pool
Ramada Inn	5914 Seawall	740-3794 or (800) 228-2828	$45-75	pool
Sandpiper Motel	2nd & Seawall	765-9431	$40-80	pool
San Luis Hotel	5222 Seawall	744-1500, or (800) 392-5937 (800) 445-0090 (outside TX)	$85-166	sea views, pool, sauna, tennis courts
Seascape Condominiums	10811 San Luis Pass	740-3561, or (800) 666-3561	$94-164	beach, heated pool, spa, tennis court
Seaside Point All-Suite Resort	7820 Seawall	740-3030, or (800) 992-1187	$52-155	suites w/sea view and kitchen, comp. cont. breakfast, pool, spa,tennis court, volleyball court
The Tremont House	2300 Ships Mechanic Row	763-0300, or (800) 874-2300	$100-150	historic, near The Strand, senior discount, special mid-week rates
The Victorian Condo Hotel	6300 Seawall	740-2555, or (800) 392-1215 (800) 231-6363 (outside TX)	$49-169	1-2 bedroom suites w/sea view, kitchens, heated pool, tennis courts, weekly and monthly rates

$ **Star Drug Store:** This is the oldest continually operating drugstore in the state; the neon Coca-Cola sign out front is said to be the "oldest in existence." The antique soda fountain offers sandwiches, ice cream, fountain drinks, and phosphates. At 510-512 23rd (tel. 762-8658); open 7 a.m. till sunset.

Chinese
$$ **Hunan Restaurant:** The extensive menu here emphasizes fresh seafood prepared in the spicy, hybrid Szechwan-Hunan style that America knows as "Hunan." Next to the Holiday Inn, at 4918 Seawall (tel. 409-765-5955); open daily for lunch and dinner.

Continental
$$ to $$$ **Cafe Torrefie:** The menu here actually offers a mix of continental dishes like crepes and quiche and Texan food like grilled steaks, prime rib, and jalapeño-stuffed shrimp. During the week they have a 4-8 p.m. happy hour and on

weekend evenings there's live music. At 22nd and The Strand (tel. 409-763-9088); open Mon.-Sat. for lunch and dinner.

$$$ Nash D'Amico's Pasta And Clam Bar: This recently opened, casual-but-classy restaurant on The Strand (in the 1895 Hutchings-Sealy Building) is a branch of the well-known Houston eaterie. The menu's primary focus is Italian, and the clams used in the restaurant's namesake are flown in fresh daily from Boston. At 24th and The Strand (tel. 763-6500); open daily for lunch and dinner.

$$$+ The Wentletrap: Named for a rare Texas seashell, Galveston's most elegant restaurant is housed in the restored 1871 League Building on The Strand, with a three-story atrium in the center. The menu changes periodically, usually featuring a short but varied selection of beef, seafood, and fowl. Men are required to wear coats after 6 p.m. At The Strand and Tremont (tel. 765-5545); open Mon.-Sat. for lunch and dinner, Sun. for brunch and dinner.

Mexican

Galveston has several funky Tex-Mex places that offer a cheap and tasty alternative to seafood.

$ Apache Tortilla Factory & Mexican Food: Good Mexican breakfasts and Tex-Mex standards, along with daily specials. At 511 20th (tel. 409-765-5646); open Tues.-Sat. for breakfast, lunch, and dinner, Sun. breakfast and lunch only.

$ El Nopalito: This family-run cafe is another classic Tex-Mex breakfast-and-lunch place. At 614 42nd (tel. 763-9815); closed Wednesday.

$ The Original Mexican Café: Claims to be Galveston's first; similar to the above café. At 1401 Market (tel. 762-6001); open daily for lunch and dinner.

Seafood

Seafood is naturally Galveston's strong suit. Many Cajuns have settled on the island over the years, so there's a strong Cajun influence in the way seafood is prepared locally. The "Mosquito Fleet," the island's shrimp boats, are anchored at Pier 19; you can sometimes buy fresh shrimp direct from the boats.

$ Benno's: This is one of several casual seafood places at the east end of Seawall. They're experts at preparing tasty Cajun-style shrimp, oysters, crab, and crawfish, plus Cajun standards like gumbo and red beans and rice, at great prices—eat in or take out. At 12th and Seawall (tel. 409-

762-5950); open daily from 11 a.m. till late.

$$ Christie's Beachcomber: Very popular, with inside and outside seating. At 4th and Seawall (tel. 762-8648); open daily 11-9.

$$ to $$$ Clary's: Located on Offatt's Bayou, this is one of the better choices for more formal seafood dining (reservations suggested). Besides a variety of fresh seafood specials, they serve steak. At 8509 Teichman, off I-45 (tel. 740-0771); open Mon.-Fri. for lunch and dinner, Sat. dinner only (closed the last two weeks of November).

$$ Gaido Seafood Restaurant: This family-owned and -operated place has been a local favorite for over 70 years. The menu features catch-of-the-day and there's usually a choice between grilled, fried, or broiled entrees. At 39th and Seawall (tel. 762-9625); open daily for lunch and dinner.

$$ to $$$ Landry's: This is a branch of a famous Corpus Christi restaurant that specializes in fresh seafood specials and large combo seafood platters. At 1502 Seawall (tel. 762-4261); open daily for lunch and dinner.

ENTERTAINMENT

Live Music

The majority of Galveston visitors are interested in sun, sand, and sea rather than late-night entertainment, so the island closes down early for the most part (the major exception is during spring break in March, when hundreds of college students flock here for round-the-clock partying). During the summer, the **Beach Club** (tel. 409-765-5922) at Stewart Beach Park has live music on weekends and DJs during the week, and it's open till 2 a.m. **Cafe Torrefie** and **Yaga's**, both on The Strand, have live bands year-round on weekends, sometimes during the week. The larger hotels also often feature live music on weekends.

On Sunday 1-5 p.m. **Club 23** (tel. 409-763-9393), at 2009 23rd St., features live Cajun music. The show is always broadcast on local radio station KGBC AM 1540, so if you can't make the club, tune in.

Galveston Island Outdoor Musicals

The 1,800-seat Mary Moody Northern Amphitheater (tel. 409-737-3440 or 800-992-8000), at Galveston State Park, features three alternating musicals throughout the summer. One of them is always *The Lone Star*, a musical dramatization of the Texas Revolution with a 100-person cast; others have been *Hello Dolly!, South Pacific,* and *Oklahoma,* but they change from year to year. Tickets are usually around $8-10 for adults, $3-5 for children.

The Strand Street Theatre
This 110-seat theater at 2317 Ships Mechanic Row hosts the island's only professional theater group for seven or eight shows a year. Performances are on weekends only, including a Sunday matinee. Call (409) 763-4591 for further information.

EVENTS

January-February
Mardi Gras: This pre-Lenten festival has been celebrated in Galveston since the mid-1800s, although until recently it had all but died out. It's now on its way to becoming the island's biggest annual celebration, drawing around 200,000 party-goers during the week before Ash Wednesday in February. Local events start in early January with a Miss Mardi Gras pageant, followed by mask-making workshops and parties later in the month (at Galveston Arts Center, 2127 The Strand). During Mardi Gras week, there's a Mardi Gras Ball at the Grand 1894 Opera House (2020 Postoffice), the arrival of King Neptune at the tall ship *Elissa* pier, and six parades. The final Grand Night Parade is held on the Saturday before Ash Wednesday and proceeds from Seawall Blvd. to The Strand. New

Orleans celebrities like Fats Domino, Pete Fountain, and Al Hirt are usually in the parade. If you plan to arrive in Galveston during Mardi Gras week, you'd better book your accommodations at least a month or two in advance. For scheduling information, call the Galveston Convention and Visitors Bureau (tel. 409-763-4311).

March
Galveston Film Festival: This is a four-day event sponsored by the Motion Picture Producers of Texas, the Texas Film Commission, and the Houston Film Commission. Texas film screenings and panel discussions are held at the Galveston Arts Center (tel. 409-763-2403), 2127 The Strand.

April
Blessing Of The Shrimp Fleet: Usually held on the first weekend following Easter, this two-day festival centers on the Cajun shrimper tradition of calling in Catholic priests to bless the shrimp trawlers for the spring harvest. As part of the celebration, the shrimper crews decorate their boats with streamers and flowers and cruise up and down the Galveston Ship Channel. On the waterfront (near Pier 19) are arts and crafts exhibits, food vendors, and entertainment.

May
Historic Homes Tour: During the first two weekends of May, around 10 historic Galveston homes that aren't usually open to the public offer guided tours (Sat. 10-6, Sun. noon-6). The Galveston His-

Dickens on The
Strand Festival

torical Foundation (tel. 409-762-TOUR) sells tickets for the tours: $9 before March 1, $10 before May 5, and $12 thereafter (GHF members get a discount).

June

Crawfish Fest: This rather recent annual event is usually held on the first or second weekend of the month. It's a serious crawfish cook-off in which such celebrated Louisiana Cajun/Creole chefs as Alex Patout and Enola Prudhomme compete against their Texas counterparts. Prizes are awarded for best-tasting crawfish dish, best presentation, and most original recipe, as well as biggest, fastest, and longest "bugs" (Cajun slang for crawfish). Check with the Galveston Convention and Visitors Bureau (tel. 409-763-4311) for the latest schedule and venue.

November

Galveston Island Jazz Festival: Local, state, and national jazz acts convene for a weekend of free afternoon concerts, music cruises, and night performances at the Grand 1894 Opera House. It's usually held on the second weekend of the month. For further information, call the Galveston Convention and Visitors Bureau (tel. 409-763-4311).

December

Dickens On The Strand: The Strand Historic District is the perfect setting for this Victorian-style Christmas celebration on the first weekend of December. This annual event, sponsored by the Galveston Historical Foundation, began in 1974 and emphasizes a Charles Dickens theme (avowedly because of the town's historic maritime ties with England and London's own Strand). The entire district comes alive with Victorian-costumed entertainers—jugglers, musicians, magicians, carolers, handbell choristers, dancers, and mimes—who perform on street corners and on six stages placed throughout the 12-block area. Restaurants and street vendors along The Strand serve roasted chestnuts, bangers (British sausages), baked oysters, plum pudding, hot cider, and other evocative food and drink.

In recent years, Dickens's great-grandson Cedric Dickens has made public appearances at the event, reading from his own writings and those of his great-grandfather. Dickens's *A Christmas Carol* is also performed several times at the Grand 1894 Opera House during the weekend. One

event held outside of The Strand district is the **Morning Tea** at Ashton Villa, 2328 Broadway (Sat. 9-1, Sun. 9-noon), which features tea, scones, fresh fruit, and a tour of the historic mansion.

As with Mardi Gras, it's a good idea to book accommodations well in advance if you plan to attend the festivities. For further information, contact the Galveston Historical Foundation at (409) 765-7834.

RECREATION

Beaches

Finding a spit of sand to call your own for the day isn't difficult—just drive, bike, or hike the 32 miles along the seaward side of the island till you find something that suits you. All beaches on the island are open to beach driving except between March 15 and Sept. 15, when you must park along the road or in designated lots.

The city of Galveston operates four public beaches along FM 3005 (Seawall Blvd.). The most popular (and most crowded during the summer) is **Stewart Beach Park** (tel. 409-765-5023), which is right in front of the intersection of Broadway and Seawall. Facilities include a bathhouse, restaurant and food concessions, nightclub, roller skate rentals, and a small amusement park. Farther east near the intersection of Seawall and Boddecker is the **R.A. Apffel Park** (tel. 763-0166), with 800 acres of wide, sandy, dune-backed beach, plus a boat launch, fishing jetty, and an 11,000-square-foot recreation center with bathhouse and concessions. **Seven Mile Park** is at Seven Mile Rd. and has restrooms and a boardwalk only. The fourth is the much less frequented **Dellanera RV Park** (tel. 740-0390), west off Seawall near San Luis Pass Rd., which is open for day use as well as to RVers. There is no entry fee for use of these parks, although the parking lots closest to Apffel and Stewart charge parking fees.

The county operates three "pocket parks," one off Seawall at 7 Mile Rd., one at 9 Mile Rd., and one at 11 Mile Road. Each has a bathhouse, food concession, and beach boardwalk, and they're all closed Oct. 15 to March 15; when they're open, there's a $3 entry fee per vehicle.

Palm Beach At Moody Gardens (tel. 409-744-PALM) is a pre-fab beach made of imported white sand that overlooks Offatt's Bayou at the end of Hope Blvd., not far from the airport. Two manmade freshwater lagoons provide a pseudo-tropical atmosphere. Admission is $3.50 for adults, $2.50 for children, free for seniors and the disabled.

Galveston Island State Park

This 2,000-acre park spans the island from the Gulf of Mexico to West Galveston Bay, about six miles southwest of the city of Galveston. The Gulf side of the park features a 1.6-mile sandy beach; the inland section has coastal prairie, salt marshes, bayous, and tidal flats. Four miles of nature trails lead through coastal dunes and along the Jenkins and Butterowe bayous to observation platforms, bird blinds, and boardwalks over wetland areas. Fishing is permitted anywhere there's water, including the bayous and bay (for sea trout) and the Gulf (for flounder and red drum).

Park facilities include bathhouses, fish-cleaning shelters, picnic areas, campgrounds, and the Mary Moody Northern Amphitheater (see "Entertainment"). Multi-use campsites with w/e cost $10 weekdays, $12 weekends, while screened shelters are $15/18. Admission to the park is $3-5 per vehicle, $1 for cyclists or pedestrians. For further information or campsite reservations, contact Galveston Island State Park (tel. 409-737-1222), Route 1, Box 156-A, Galveston, TX 77554.

Fishing And Boating

Anglers have a choice of surf, bay, freshwater, and deep-sea fishing, plus crabbing, gigging, and seining. A state fishing license is required and is available from most bait and tackle shops on the island or from the Galveston County Courthouse (tel. 409-762-8621), 722 Moody. Several free public piers extend into the Gulf from the seawall. Commercial fishing piers, which charge a user fee of around $2, include the **Flagship Pier** at 25th and Seawall, the **61st Street Pier** at 61st and Seawall, the **Gulf Coast Fishing Pier** at 90th and Seawall, and **San Luis Pass Fishing Pier** at FM 3005 and San Luis Pass.

Fishing boats can be chartered at Pier 19 on the ship channel or at the Galveston Yacht Basin, Holiday Dr. and Wharf St. near the Port of Galveston. Fishing trips start at around $15 per person for a four-hour trip and go up to $85 for a deluxe all-day affair. Pleasure boats can also be chartered at Pier 19 and at the Yacht Basin.

The *Colonel*

This restored paddlewheeler and floating museum (tel. 409-763-4666), docked at Pier 22, offers two-hour scenic cruises of Galveston Bay at noon and 3 p.m. daily between April 1 and Labor Day. The fare is $10 for adults, $5 for children 4-12. There's also a dinner/dance cruise that leaves Thurs.-Sat. nights at 8; the fare is $27.50 per person including the buffet dinner; without dinner, it's the same as for the day cruise. On Saturday nights only, from 11 p.m. to 1 a.m., the *Colonel* does a moonlight cruise for $10, adults only.

During the rest of the year the *Colonel* sails only on weekends—Fri.-Sun. for the day cruises (same departure times as in the summer), Sat. night for the dinner/dance cruise—and there are no late-night cruises.

Surfing

Galveston is popular among Texas surfers for the seawall breaks; surfing is permitted wherever there are signs that read No Swimming. The best surf generally breaks along the granite jetties. Experienced hodads say the 61st St. jetty usually gets the top waves, but it varies from day to day. Shops along the east end of Seawall Blvd. rent boards by the hour or by the day.

Scuba Diving

Galveston Island and the immediate vicinity offer little of intrinsic interest for divers but within a 50-mile radius is a collection of abandoned oil rigs and sunken tankers that present challenging dive possibilities. **The Deep** (tel. 409-765-9746), a dive shop at 4104 Seawall, offers one-day diving trips in the late spring and during the summer for $75-90 a day. They also provide diving instruction and equipment sales/ rentals.

Reef Dives: About 110 miles southeast of the island are two huge, pristine reef communities known as the **Flower Gardens.** The **East Flower Garden Bank** is three miles in diameter and rises within 52 feet of the Gulf surface.

TODD CLARK

manta ray

At its crest, the total area is an incredible 400 acres. Twelve miles west is the **West Flower Garden Bank,** which is about seven by five miles in diameter and crests 66 feet below the water surface with an area of approximately 100 acres. The Flower Gardens are unique in that they're more than 300 miles from the tropics and 500 miles from the next nearest major reef system (Tampico, Mexico).

This is the most ecologically complex area of the Texas-Louisiana continental shelf, with 253 macro-invertebrate species, 175 fish species, and 18 coral species (including mountainous star, smooth brain, cavernous star, giant brain, mustard hill, blushing star, stinging millepora, knobby brain, large flower, and solitary disk corals). Manta rays *(Manta birostris)* that measure up to 20 feet across and weigh 3,500 pounds are commonly seen; the mantas like to be stroked and even allow divers to hitch rides by holding onto their horn-like pectoral fins.

Because these reefs are so remote (Galveston is the nearest port) and so few divers visit them, they're among the healthiest in the entire Gulf of Mexico or the Caribbean. Visibility extends up to 125 feet (100 feet is average) since the area is far from shore debris and suspended sedimentation. The U.S. Department of the Interior has enacted a "zone of no activity" over the reef system to protect it from Gulf oil and gas exploration and has placed it on an evaluation list for possible designation as a national marine sanctuary. In the meantime, one boat docked near Galveston Island operates regular trips to the Flower Gardens: *The Fling* (tel. 713-893-3922) in Freeport (about 35 miles southeast of downtown Galveston via FM 3005). The boat proprietors operate two- and three-day trips to the reefs from late June to late October. All trips visit the East Flower Garden Bank (four or five dives, including one night dive), an abandoned oil rig, and the separate Stetson Bank, a massive brain coral formation; the three-day trip includes four or five dives at the West Flower Garden Bank as well. Rates are $275 and $375 respectively and include all meals and accommodations aboard the boat, plus unlimited air refills (divers must bring full tanks at the beginning of the trip).

SHOPPING

Shops in The Strand Historic District offer everything from cheap beach souvenirs to expensive designer clothing. Of special note is the **Hendley Market** (tel. 409-762-2610), at 2010 The Strand, which sells antiques and folk art. Another antique place is the **Peanut Butter Warehouse** (tel. 762-8358), at 20th and The Strand, which also has homemade peanut butter, cookies, and candy. **Col. Bubbie's Strand Surplus Senter** (tel. 762-7397), at 2202 The Strand, has a huge selection of military surplus items from around the world.

GALVESTON INFORMATION

Tourist Offices

The **Galveston Convention and Visitors Bureau** (tel. 409-763-4311, 800-351-4236 in Texas, 800-351-4237 outside Texas) is on the ground floor of Moody Civic Center, 2106 Seawall. The staff are knowledgeable and helpful, and they have loads of brochures and information handouts (including a list of accommodations with current rates). It's open daily 9-5:30. The Galveston Historical Foundation operates **The Strand Visitors Center** (tel. 765-7834) at 21st and The Strand. It's open daily for roughly the same hours and has a lot of the same information, plus historical displays and a free 11-minute island orientation film.

Telephone

The area code for Galveston Island and vicinity is 409.

TELEPHONE AND EMERGENCY INFORMATION

Emergency (police, fire, medical)	911
Telephone Directory Assistance	1-411
Local Weather	765-9479
Department of Public Safety	740-3239
National Weather Service	763-4681
Coast Guard	766-3687

Publications

The *West Beach Sun* is a free monthly newspaper that contains a map of the town and island, as well as information on fishing, dining, and entertainment from Galveston southwest to Freeport. The *Galveston Daily News,* the only daily newspaper published on the island, offers up-to-the-minute information on local activities and events.

GALVESTON TRANSPORT

Galveston Island Trolley

Galveston's original trolley system ran between 1866 and 1938. A new system has partially revived the service, with 4.7 miles of track (about one-tenth the original track mileage) between the east beachfront and downtown areas, including The Strand and Silk Stocking Historic Districts. Along the new track run four trolley cars, vintage replicas with interiors of solid cherry, oak, and mahogany that cost $495,000 each to build.

There are 25 stops along the route and two terminals, one on The Strand and one on Seawall, where full trolley information is available. Operating hours are 10-9 (extended during special events like Mardi Gras and Dickens On The Strand) and trolleys usually pass about once every 30 minutes; a round-circuit trip takes about an hour. The city plans to add more cars to the system as ridership increases, so waits may become shorter in the future. Fares are $2 roundtrip for adults, $1 for seniors and children 6-12. Discounted frequent rider and one-day passes are available.

The trolley connects with the **Island Transit** city bus system on 20th between Market and Postoffice (free transfers are available).

Airport Limousine

Galveston Limousine (tel. 409-765-5288/744-0563) operates a shuttle service between Galveston hotels and Houston's Hobby (one hour, $15) and Intercontinental airports (two hours, $18). Door-to-door service from the airports to beach homes or condos is an additional $3.

Tours

The **Galveston Sightseeing Train** (tel. 409-765-9564) does a one-hour, 17-mile auto-train tour of the town that leaves from Moody Center at 21st and Seawall. The number of tours per day varies, from two departures a day March to May, to nine tours a day in the summer; no tours are given in January and February. The fare is $4.30 for adults, $3.75 for seniors, $2.50 for children 3-12.

Classic Carriage Tours (tel. 409-762-1260) operates horse-drawn carriage rides through The Strand and other historic districts. The rates depend on where you're going, length of the tour, and the number of passengers. You can contact the carriage drivers directly on The Strand (in front of the visitor center) or in the parking lot of the Hotel Galvez on Seawall Boulevard.

VICINITY OF GALVESTON

BOLIVAR PENINSULA

This 50-mile-long strip of sparsely populated beaches, marshes, lagoons, and bayous is northeast of Galveston Island, across the mouth of Galveston Bay. Many who find Galveston too touristed these days find that the Bolivar (locally they say "BALL-i-ver") Peninsula is just their cup of tea. Fishing (sea trout, redfish, croaker, flounder, and a variety of shellfish) and hunting (duck and goose) are the main local attractions, though many Texans have built beach houses along the southern end of the peninsula near the small town of **Crystal Beach,** where the beaches are widest.

The best fishing is at **Port Bolivar** and at **Rollover Pass,** a narrow canal that cuts across the peninsula near Gilchrist, joining East Galveston Bay and the Gulf of Mexico. Rollover Pass is the narrowest section of the peninsula; it was named thus because Jean Lafitte and his pirates would roll supply barrels across the peninsula to and from boats anchored in the Gulf here. Near Port Bolivar on the southern tip of the peninsula is the **Bolivar Point Lighthouse,** which was first erected of cast iron in 1852; the Confederates disassembled it for

Bolivar Point Lighthouse

scrap during the Civil War but it was rebuilt in 1872 and remained in service till 1933. The only other towns on the peninsula include the equally minuscule fishing villages of **Gilchrist** and **High Island.** North of Crystal Beach the beaches are more narrow, virtually disappearing with high tides. State 87 runs the entire length of the peninsula, eventually leading to Port Arthur at Sabine Pass (see "Port Arthur" under "East Texas").

Galveston-Port Bolivar Ferry

A free 24-hour ferry service (tel. 409-763-2386) carries vehicles and passengers across the bay mouth in about 15 minutes. The Galveston ferry pier is at the end of Ferry Rd., off the east end of Seawall Blvd.; on the other side of the channel the pier is at Bolivar Point, the end of State 87. On summer weekends and holidays the wait at either end can be as long as an hour; at other times there's a wait of up to 20 minutes or so (or no wait if you happen to drive up to the pier right when they're loading).

Wildlife Refuges

The Texas Point and McFaddin national wildlife refuges straddle the peninsula, while Anahuac National Wildlife Reserve is just opposite Gilchrist across East Galveston Bay on the Chambers County line. All three permit waterfowl hunting (in season), fishing, and crabbing.

McFaddin NWR is the largest of the three, covering 41,682 acres of beach, salt marshes, and coastal prairie, and is a major winter habitat for migratory waterfowl, including the mottled duck, wood stork, least tern, roseate spoonbill, pelicans, herons, egrets, and several varieties of geese. Small fur-bearing animals—mink, raccoon, nutria, river otter, muskrat, gray fox, and bobcat—inhabit the refuge year-round. American alligators are also abundant here in the marshes and bayous but they're hard to see unless you hike or boat well into the refuge. Bayous feed into two small lakes, Clam Lake and Star Lake. Free camping is permitted along the 12-mile beach facing the Gulf at the edge of the refuge; however, for day visitors the refuge is only open weekdays 7 a.m.-3:30 p.m. Other facilities include eight miles of interior roads, three boat ramps, nature trails, and a beach picnic area. Access is via

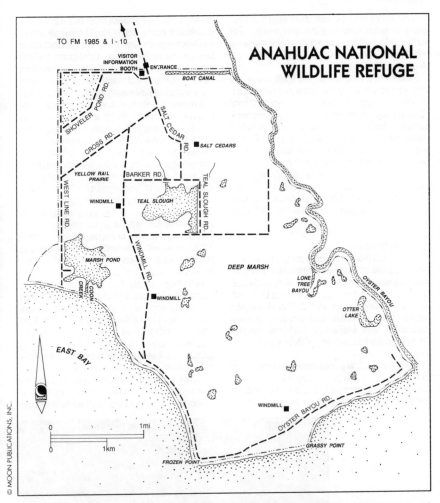

ANAHUAC NATIONAL WILDLIFE REFUGE

TO FM 1985 & I-10

VISITOR INFORMATION BOOTH

ENTRANCE

BOAT CANAL

SHOVELER POND RD.

CROSS RD.

SALT CEDAR RD.

SALT CEDARS

YELLOW RAIL PRAIRIE

BARKER RD.

WEST LINE RD.

WINDMILL

TEAL SLOUGH

TEAL SLOUGH RD.

MARSH POND

WINDMILL RD.

DEEP MARSH

LONE TREE BAYOU

OYSTER BAYOU

COON CREEK

WINDMILL

OTTER LAKE

EAST BAY

MOON

0   1mi

0   1km

WINDMILL

OYSTER BAYOU RD.

GRASSY POINT

FROZEN POINT

© MOON PUBLICATIONS, INC.

State 87. For further information, contact Mc-Faddin National Wildlife Refuge (tel. 409-971-2909), P.O. Box 609, Sabine Pass, TX 77655.

Anahuac NWR is the second largest, with 28,240 acres of fresh- and saltwater marshes, bayous, and rolling coastal prairie along the shore of East Galveston Bay. It's the most visited of the three refuges because it's open 24 hours and has easy road access deep into the center (via 12 miles of shelled and gravel roads). From the Bolivar Peninsula, take State 124 north off State 87 at High Island to FM 1985, then proceed west to the refuge entrance. Anahuac shelters many of the same wildlife species as McFaddin, plus the endangered southern bald eagle and peregrine falcon. Snow geese concentrations run to 50,000 between October and March. Alligators are easily viewed at Shoveler Pond in the northwest corner of the refuge, especially in the spring. The only facilities here are a refuge office, restrooms, and a few trails; primitive camping (bring your own water) is permitted along the bayshore (three-day limit, no charge). Boating is allowed only on the designated boat canal (which feeds into Oyster

Bayou; boats may be launched from the bay-shore or at the ramp near the refuge office. For further information, contact Anahuac National Wildlife Refuge (tel. 409-267-3337), Box 278, Anahuac, TX 77514.

Texas Point NWR preserves 8,952 acres and also protects many of the same species as Mc-Faddin. Although it's located just off State 87 near Sabine Pass, there are no parking facilities here; access is by foot or boat (via a private launch at Texas Bayou in Sabine Pass) only. Texas Point is visited mostly by anglers and hunters—bird-watchers find either McFaddin or Anahuac much more to their liking. Like McFaddin, it's only open weekdays 7 a.m.-3:30 p.m. For more information, contact Texas Point National Wildlife Refuge (same phone number and address as McFaddin NWR above).

Sea Rim State Park

This is one of the state's most unique parks, with 15,109 acres of beach, salt marshes, sloughs, bayous, dunes, and lakes. The park is divided into two sections, the huge Marshlands Unit north of State 87 and the smaller D. Roy Harrington Beach Unit south of this road. The park shares a boundary with McFaddin National Wildlife Refuge, at the northern end of Bolivar Peninsula, near Sabine Pass

Beach Unit: The park's shoreline extends for 5.2 miles along the gulf; three miles of this is sandy beach separated from the marshlands by small dunes, while 2.2 miles is rare "sea rim

marsh," where marshlands meet Gulf waters. The **Gambusia Trail** is a 3,640-foot boardwalk nature trail that winds through the sea rim marsh about two feet above the surface. Cord grass and salt grass comprise the marsh's primary vegetation. Several ponds in the marsh attract small mammals (including fur-bearing nutria, muskrat, mink, and raccoon), waterfowl, and various smaller reptiles and amphibians. In the spring and fall, birds are abundant and birdwatchers have an opportunity to view some 289 winged species, including the great blue heron, the American bittern (which camouflages itself by sticking its beak straight up and swaying with the grass), American coot, and a wide variety of loons, grebes, ducks, geese, terns, cormorants, egrets, hawks, gulls, ibis, and songbirds. However, to see the greatest variety you must venture into the park's marshlands unit (see below). Facilities at the beach unit include a visitor center with excellent interpretive exhibits, first-aid station, observation deck, food concessions, bathhouse, and camping area.

Marshlands Unit: This section of the park is for visitors who want a more in-depth experience of these extraordinary coastal marshlands. Alligators (one to 14 feet in length) are a common sight along the unit's shallow lakes, sloughs, and bayous, especially in the summer when they sun themselves. The best way to explore the area is by boat along these waterways. Some routes are navigable only by airboat or mud boat, others only by pirogue or canoe. Between March and October, park rangers operate half-hour airboat

campground,
Sea Rim State Park

tours for around $7 per person. Canoes can be rented year-round at a store called **Breeze Inn Again** on State 87 just east of the park.

Crabbing is excellent throughout the marshlands, but especially in the lakes and ponds. The tasty blue crab is the most common and reaches about nine inches across its body shell. Crawfish are also abundant. Five camping platforms and four observation platforms (with blinds) are located throughout the marshes and are only accessible by boat.

Camping: The beach unit has 20 tent/camper sites with w/e (dump station available) for $8 a night on weekdays, $9 weekends. Tent camping is permitted on the beach for $4 a night. The camping platforms in the marshlands unit are suitable for tent camping only and are $4 a night on weekdays, $6 on weekends. The park entry fee is $3 per vehicle or $1 per person for cyclists and pedestrians. Be sure to bring plenty of insect repellent. For further information or campsite reservations, contact the Park Superintendent (tel. 409-971-2559), Sea Rim State Park, P.O. Box 1066, Sabine Pass, TX 77655.

Motels

Two motels off State 87 in Crystal Beach offer rooms for around $30-35 a night, some with kitchenettes (rates are lower for stays of a week or more): **Crystal Palace Resort** (tel. 409-684-6554) and **Joy Sands Motel** (tel. 684-6152). A bit farther north in Gilchrist is the similarly priced **Ocean View Motel** (tel. 286-5864), also with kitchenettes.

Beach Home Rentals

The following realtors can arrange weekend, weekly, and monthly beach-home rentals in Crystal Beach: **Cobb Real Estate** (tel. 409-684-3790), **Hamilton Real Estate** (tel. 684-3792), **Mike Olsten Real Estate** (tel. 684-0012), and **Thompson Real Estate** (tel. 684-0363). Rates start at around $150 a weekend for a basic one- or two-bedroom home.

RV Parks

Gilchrist has two RV parks, both on State 87: **Hazel's** (tel. 409-286-5228) and **Las Palmas** (tel. 286-5612). Crystal Beach has one, the **Crystal Beach RV Park** (tel. 684-5723), also on State 87. All three parks charge around $12 a night for full hookups and have discounted weekly and monthly rates.

Food

The **Stingaree Restaurant** (tel. 409-684-2731) in Crystal Beach (south side of State 87) is one of the better seafood places on the peninsula and is open daily for lunch and dinner. Also off State 87 in Crystal Beach is **Mama Theresa's Flying Pizza** (tel. 684-3507), with pizza and Italian food (open Tues.-Sun. for lunch and dinner). The **Corner Cafe** (tel. 286-5683) in Gilchrist serves simple American fare, including homemade bread, Mon.-Sat. for breakfast, lunch, and dinner. Three wholesale/retail seafood stores in Crystal Beach sell fresh fish, shrimp, crab, and oysters to the general public: **Falcon Seafood** (tel. 684-3838), **J. B.'s Seafood** (tel. 684-6464), and **Seafood Warehouse** (tel. 684-6270).

Information

The **Bolivar Peninsula Chamber of Commerce** (P.O. Box 1421, Crystal Beach, TX 77650) sends out a couple of information brochures on request and can answer specific questions about Bolivar visits.

BRAZOSPORT

"Brazosport" (meaning "Port of Brazos" with reference to the Brazos River) is not a town name but rather a chamber of commerce term for the loose conglomeration of Brazoria County communities south of Galveston Island, including the beach towns of Surfside and Quintana as well as the industrial town/fishing port of Freeport and its satellites Clute, Oyster Creek, Lake Jackson, Richwood, and Jones Creek. The beaches are few and they aren't great, but the worst thing about the area is that chemical manufacturing plants provide an unsightly nine-mile backdrop.

Beauty is in the eye of the beholder, however, and inside the Dow Chemical-owned facility some of the most technically sophisticated research in the world is conducted on products people use everyday. Dow (tel. 409-238-9222) offers free tours of the facility each Wednesday at 2 p.m. for those interested in seeing the largest chemical facility in the country.

The 60-foot, 40-ton shrimp trawler *The Mystery* is enshrined on Brazosport Boulevard in Freeport. In her day she was the undisputed champion of Gulf shrimping, having netted an estimated 3.5 million pounds of pink crustaceans before retirement. The **Bridge Harbor Yacht**

Club at the west end of Surfside Bridge is a sailing resort with over 300 deep-water slips. About the only other sight of renown is **Girouard's General Store,** said to be the only grocery store in the country that's also a certified government agent for marine charts. The store slogan is "If we don't have it, you don't need it," and they proffer everything from fresh meat to passport photos.

Center For The Arts And Sciences
The **Museum of Natural Science** (tel. 409-265-7831) at Lake Jackson's Center for the Arts and Sciences, 400 College Dr., houses the Hall of Malacology with one of the finest seashell collections in the country. The museum also contains exhibits on archaeology, mineralogy, and wildlife. Hours are Tues.-Sat. 10-5 and Sun. 2-5; admission is free.

The Center also serves as a meeting place for the Brazosport Birders, a group of avid local birdwatchers. Year after year, Freeport's Christmas Count leads the U.S. in numbers of bird species identified within a 24-hour interval. For information on the club's year-round activities, call the Museum of Natural History (phone number above).

A self-guided nature trail along Oyster Creek, adjacent to the Center, introduces visitors to the over 200 species of Texas river-bottom vegetation.

Beaches
The next link in the barrier island chain moving down the Texas coast is **Follets Island,** where Brazosport's Gulf beaches are located. Farm-to-Market 3005's south terminal is at **Surfside Beach,** a favorite among young Texans (Houston is only 60 miles away) who come here to swim, surf, and party on summer weekends. At one time Surfside had a reputation for attracting rowdy crowds, but since the summer of 1982, when the small town instituted roadblocks to flush out drunk drivers, the scene has calmed down somewhat. Driving is still permitted on the beach here, but you must purchase a beach driving permit ($6 annual fee, available at most local stores). The beachfront is lined with small shops offering fast food, beachwear, and surfboard rentals.

Next south is the small **Quintana Beach,** which has a bathhouse, a boardwalk, a fishing pier, and camping facilities. At the south end of the island (which would be a peninsula if it weren't for the cut made by Brazos River as it meets the Gulf) is the 878-acre **Bryan Beach State Recreation Area.** Since the road south from Quintana (FM 1495) ends well before the park, the only way to get here is to drive along the beach, walk, or take a boat in. Driving and walking along the beach can be tricky because of incoming tides. Bryan Beach is undeveloped except for a few trash receptacles; primitive camping is permitted (no fee; bring your own water). The surf fishing here is good, as the Brazos River mouth is a feeding grounds for native fish. Birders can view a wide variety of shorebirds.

Wildlife Refuges
Freeport usually ranks first in the National Audubon Society's annual winter bird census and holds the all-time U.S. record for number of species counted in 24 hours within a 7.5-mile radius: 226. The reason Freeport is such a good birding area is because it's between two national wildlife refuges established as winter habitats for migratory birds: **Brazoria National Wildlife Refuge** (12,000 acres) to the north and **San Bernard National Wildlife Refuge** (24,500 acres) to the south. Among the more notable common birds at both are great blue herons, white ibis, mottled ducks, snow geese, sandhill cranes, and roseate spoonbills.

Access to marshy Brazoria for fishing and waterfowl hunting is by boat only (via Big Bayou or the Gulf Intracoastal Waterway). During the first weekend of every month, the refuge is open to daytime drive-through visitors. For information, contact the Refuge Manager (tel. 409-849-6062), Brazoria National Wildlife Refuge, P.O. Box 1088, Angleton, TX 77515.

The much larger San Bernard covers a wide range of habitats, including coastal prairies, salt flats, potholes, and both fresh- and saltwater ponds. Access is via State 36 west from Freeport to FM 2611, then south to FM 2918, and east to the refuge entrance. For information, contact the Refuge Manager, San Bernard National Wildlife Refuge (same address and phone number as Brazoria above).

Guided Fishing Trips
Several charter boats operate fishing trips out of Freeport (including deep-sea trips). **Captain Elliot's** (tel. 409-233-1811) at 1010 W. 2nd in Freeport offers group deep-sea trips for around $50 per day.

Scuba Diving
The Fling, a 100-foot boat docked in Freeport, offers two- and three-day diving trips to the magnificent Flower Garden reef system, 110 miles east in the Gulf. For details, see "Scuba Diving" under "Galveston Island" pp. 365-366.

Brazosport Hotels And Motels
Most of the chain accommodation is concentrated a few miles inland along State 332 in Clute and Lake Jackson. The **Motel 6** (tel. 265-4764) at 1000 State 332 has rooms for $21 s, $6 for each additional adult. Also in Clute is the nearby **La Quinta Inn** (tel. 265-7461) at 1126 State 332, where rooms are $41-52. Farther west at 925 State 332 in Lake Jackson is the **Brazosport Hilton Inn** (tel. 297-1161) with rooms for $50-80. The **Best Western Lake Jackson Inn** (tel. 297-3031) at 915 State 332 has rooms for $42-45.

Beach Home Rentals
A couple of hundred beach homes in the Surfside Beach area are for rent year-round. Most rates are based on weekly rentals, with the average being $450-800 a week for two or three bedrooms during the summer. A very basic one-bedroom place can be had for as low as $200 a week in the winter. The following realtors handle beach home rentals (all box numbers are followed by Route 2, Surfside Beach, TX 77541): **Resort Rentals** (tel. 409-233-6734), Box 1195; **Sand Castle Rentals** (tel. 233-7879), Box 1155; **Brannan Realty** (tel. 233-1812), Box 1115; and **Haygood Properties** (tel. 233-6734), Box 1087.

Brazosport Information
The **Brazosport Visitors and Convention Council** (tel. 409-265-2505) is at 420 State 332 in Clute. They handle all queries on attractions in the Brazosport area.

CENTRAL COAST

The state's earliest ports were in the central coast area between Freeport to the north and Corpus Christi to the south, clustered around Matagorda and Lavaca bays: Indianola, Matagorda, Port Lavaca, Palacios, Point Comfort, and Port O'Connor. Because of their vulnerability to tropical storms and hurricanes, however, none of these grew into a current major port like Corpus Christi or Galveston. Today they are for the most part sleepy backwaters supported by a combination of fishing, light industry, and agriculture (primarily rice-growing). Except for the gulfward side of Matagorda Island, the beaches along the central coast are unmemorable, though some Texans favor the area because of the laid-back and uncrowded atmosphere.

MATAGORDA BAY

Matagorda
The name "Matagorda" (Spanish for "Dense Cane") is attached to a town, county, bay, island, and peninsula. The town itself (pop. 700) was founded in 1829 as a port for Stephen Austin's colony because of its strategic location at the junction of three waterways: the mouth of the Colorado River, Matagorda Bay, and East Matagorda Bay (Matagorda Peninsula separates the two bays).

Of historical interest in Matagorda is **Christ Episcopal Church** at Cypress and Lewis, which was built in 1841, destroyed by an 1854 hurricane, and rebuilt in 1856 using the salvaged cypress timbers. It's the state's oldest Episcopal church and services are still held regularly. Several other buildings in town date to the late 1800s.

Palacios
This town of around 4,000 inhabitants is on a smaller bay off Matagorda called Tres Palacios Bay. The bay and town were named after José Felix Trespalacios, the local governor when Stephen Austin established his first colony in the early 1800s. Fishing, both commercial and sport, is the main local source of livelihood. The largest blue crab processing plant in the country has its home here, as well as a 300-boat shrimp fleet. Guided fishing trips can be arranged at the Palacios waterfront.

Hotel: The stately **Luther Hotel** (tel. 512-972-2312) at 408 S. Bay Blvd. was built in 1903 entirely of cypress wood in the Greek Revival style. Commanding a view of Tres Palacios Bay, this classic Gulf coast hotel has the feel of an antebellum mansion, the very epitome of Southern indolence. Many of the rooms have been converted to apartments that rent by the month or by the week; around 15 rooms are available on a nightly basis for $35-55. Suites with kitchens are available for $75 a night. There are no telephones or TVs in the guest rooms (proprietor Mrs. Luther says, "I don't want people to come here to watch television") but the lobby has a TV.

Food: The most popular eating place in town is **Petersen's Restaurant** (tel. 512-972-2413) at 416 Main, which has been serving fresh seafood, burgers, steaks, chicken, and homemade pies since 1944. They're open daily for breakfast, lunch, and dinner.

Blessing

About eleven miles north of Palacios via State 35 is this small town of 600 with no beach and nothing else to recommend it except for another Gulf coast accommodation classic, the **Hotel Blessing** (tel. 409-588-9579) at 10th and Ave. B (FM 616). Built in 1906 by Jonathan Pierce, brother of famous cattle baron "Shanghai" Pierce, the hotel is constructed in the Spanish mission style of wood (instead of the usual stone or stucco), and is listed with the National Register of Historic Places. Rooms cost only $20-25 a night, depending on whether they come with private or shared baths; discounted weekly and monthly rates are available. Locally, the hotel is known for its downhome coffee shop (tel. 588-6623), which is open daily for breakfast and lunch. During lunch, diners help themselves from pots of food in the kitchen—specialties include barbecued chicken, cream gravy, corn bread, vegetables, and lots of rice (on Sundays, turkey and ham are served).

LAVACA BAY

Port Lavaca

The largest Calhoun County town (pop. 12,000) and county seat is named for *la vaca*, "the cow" in Spanish, because at one time it was a major shipping point for exported cattle and cattle products. The current town was founded in 1840. Commercial and sport fishing are the main local industries; many Port Lavaca residents also work in the Alcoa bauxite refinery (for the manufacture

of aluminum), the country's largest, in nearby **Point Comfort.**

Nearby **Indianola** (about 10 miles southeast of Port Lavaca at the end of State 316) was once the chief Texas port—everything from African slaves to camels to European immigrants arrived by ship here in the early 1800s. Three major hurricanes between 1866 and 1886 turned the prospering port into a virtual ghost town. A 22-foot-high granite monument alongside State 316 commemorates French explorer LaSalle (René Robert Cavalier), who landed here in 1685 and established Fort Saint Louis nearby. LaSalle was killed by one his men two years later and Karankawa Indians burned the settlement. A cluster of fishermen's houses and an old courthouse foundation comprise what remains of Indianola.

The most popular local recreation spot is undoubtedly the **Port Lavaca State Fishing Pier** at the west end of the Lavaca Bay Causeway (State 35 N). The 3,200-foot pier is open 6 a.m. to midnight (it's lighted at night) and is a good place to drop a line or two during redfish, flounder, or speckled trout runs. The pier bait shop issues daily fishing permits for $1 per fishing device. At the base of the pier is **Port Lavaca City Park,** with a boat ramp, picnic area, swimming pool, and waterfront RV park with two-way hookups ($7.50 a night with picnic tables, $6.50 without).

Accommodations And Food: The **Days Inn** (tel. 512-552-4511) at 2100 State 35 N Bypass has rooms for $40-45 s, $46-51 d, with weekly and monthly rates (and rental refrigerators) available. Right at the start of the State 35 causeway, facing the bay, is the **Shell Fish Inn** (tel. 552-3393), with rooms for $30 s, $33-37 d; refrigerators are available on request, as are weekly and monthly rates. For fresh seafood, your best bet is the **Ocean Inn** (tel. 552-7650) at 116 Commerce, where portions are generous and not everything comes fried; open daily for breakfast, lunch, and dinner (oyster bar open in the evenings only). **El Patio** (tel. 552-6316) at 534 W. Main serves standard Tex-Mex daily for breakfast, lunch, and dinner.

Port O'Connor–Seadrift

This area was first mapped by Spaniard Alonso Alvarez de Piñada in 1519, when he named the mainland "Amichel." Today it's mostly a home port for commercial fishing boats and shrimp trawlers, as well as charter boats for deep-sea fishing trips and shuttle service to nearby Matagorda Island. Strategically situated at the intersection of Matagorda Bay, Espiritu Santo Bay, and the Gulf of Mexico, Port O'Connor has some of the best saltwater fishing on the coast (with redfish, drum, flounder, speckled trout, pompano, bonito, croakers, tarpon, and others in abundance).

The Matagorda Island State Natural Area headquarters (tel. 512-983-2215) is in Port O'Connor at S. 16th and Maple. Ferry transport to the island and permits for camping are available here (see "Matagorda Island National Wildlife Refuge and State Natural Area" below for details).

Accommodations and Food: The **Tarpon Motel** (tel. 512-983-2606) at 14th and Maple has rooms for $35-55 a night, apartments for $40-100 a night (less for stays of a week or more), and RV sites with full hookups for $10 a night. A pool and grocery store are on the premises as well. There are also a few beach homes for rent through the Port O'Connor Chamber of Commerce (tel. 983-2898). **Port Motel** (tel. 983-2724) and **Verna's Motel** (tel. 983-2395) have rooms in the $25-30 range. In addition to the park adjacent to the Tarpon Motel, three other RV parks offer full hookups for US$10-12 a night: **Lots O Luck** (tel. 983-2869), **Canal** (tel. 983-2621) and **Sea Isle** (tel. 983-2305).

In the small port town of Seadrift, at the west end of the peninsula on San Antonio Bay, is the historic **Hotel Lafitte** (tel. 512-785-2319, 302 Bay Avenue). Originally built as a railroad hotel in 1909, the restored three-story inn offers a range of rooms for $55-95 a night including a full breakfast for two, plus complimentary wine in the afternoons. For more information, call or write Hotel Lafitte, P.O. Box 489, Seadrift, TX 77983.

In Port O'Connor, **Beachcomber Restaurant** (tel. 512-983-2992) and **Stryker's Cafe** (tel. 983-288) serve daily fresh seafood specials. If you have the use of a kitchen, you can buy fresh fish from several local seafood dealers who sell direct to the public, including **Clark's, Raby's**, and **Shotsie's**. Mexican food is available at **Josie's** (tel. 983-4720).

Matagorda Island National Wildlife Refuge And State Natural Area

Once a haven for 18th-century freebooters and smugglers (including pirate Jean Lafitte), 38-mile-long, 56,669-acre Matagorda Island, has recently come under the full stewardship of the state and federal government. Besides the occasional park staff, the only inhabitants are white-tailed deer, feral hogs, waterfowl, and other wildlife, including at least 19 state or federally listed endangered animal species, (e.g., American alligators, Texas horned lizards, Kemp's ridley, hawksbill, loggerhead, and green sea turtles, brown pelicans, peregrine falcons, piping plovers, and whooping cranes). Bottle-nosed dolphins are common along the gulf and bay shores of the island.

Birding and shell-collecting are superb here,

alligator, Aransas National Wildlife Refuge

and when the Gulf surf is pumping, Matagorda provides surfers with unparalleled Gulf Coast wave action. Fishing is also excellent on both sides of the island, and off-road cyclists and hikers can make use of 80 miles of beach and island trails. Hardy local surf anglers combine fishing with cycling, pedaling around the island with rod and tackle in backpacks or panniers. Common game fish include red drum, spotted seatrout, tarpon, shark, flounder, and mackerel.

The state park headquarters in Port O'Connor on the mainland offers a regular ferry service to the island on weekends and some holidays. The first ferry leaves from the park pier at 16th and Maple at 8 a.m.; the last leaves Matagorda Island at 4 p.m. The roundtrip fare is $8 for adults, $4 for children 12 and under; reservations are required. On the island itself, the park service also operates a shuttle between the park pier and the beach for $2 roundtrip for adults, $1 for children under 12. Holders of the Texas Conservation Passport can

also sign up for birdwatching, beachcombing, and natural/cultural history tours with park staff for nominal fees (write for a schedule).

A few fishing boats in Port O'Connor also offer drop-off and pick-up service to the island; call **Red's Coastal Charter** (tel. 512-983-2937), Robby Gregory (tel. 983-2862), or Jimmy Crouch (tel. 983-2897) for arrangements or the chamber of commerce (tel. 983-2898) for other possibilities. The standard rate is $75 roundtrip for one to three people, plus $25 for each additional person.

Facilities at the park include primitive campsites along two miles of beach, dockside campsites, outdoor showers, and pit toilets. Camping is $4 per four-person site, with a 14-day limit. You must bring your own food and water. For further information, contact the park staff at their Port O'Connor office (tel. 512-983-2215), 16th and Maple (mailing address: Matagorda Island State Park, P.O. Box 117, Port O'Connor, TX 77982).

CORPUS CHRISTI

INTRODUCTION

The Corpus Christi area is the closest the Gulf coast comes to living up to the fanciful "Texas Riviera" image marketed so widely. Day or night, a drive south over the Harbor Bridge meets with a sparkling city and bay vista, where sailboat masts mix with downtown skyscrapers. Although central Corpus itself (Texans usually dispense with "Christi") has only a few meager bay beaches, nearby Mustang and Padre islands offer well over a hundred miles of sandy Gulf beaches (see "Vicinity of Corpus Christi," p. 390)—the best anywhere along the Texas coast. Parts of North Padre are actually within Corpus Christi city limits.

Although the main attractions are sun, sky, sea, and sand, Corpus doesn't go to sleep as soon as the sun goes down. The old adage about "a big city with a small town feel" should really be modified in this case; with a population of just over a quarter million, Corpus is a medium-sized port town with urban pretensions, which is perfect for visitors who want to do more than just fish and lie on the beach. As a corner of the "South Texas Triangle" (including San Antonio and Laredo), it also reflects the Hispanic-majority nature of the regional culture, which sets it apart from coastal towns farther north.

Land And Climate

Corpus Christi lies in a transition zone between the central coast and lower coast, which means that the usual Gulf Coast characteristics are somewhat tempered by Rio Grande Plain influences. Humid coastal plains meet arid northern Mexico plains to form a semiarid, subtropical zone that produces a wide variety of dense scrub intermixed with coastal grasses. The Nueces River feeds into the Gulf here, providing a riparian habitat that further contributes to geographical and biological diversity.

The average temperature range in January is 46° to 67° F, while in July it's 76° to 94° F. Average annual precipitation is a moderate 30 inches (five inches more than the Rio Grande Valley). September is by far the wettest month, generally speaking, logging an average of six inches of rain; the next wettest month is August, with 3.5 inches, followed by May, June, and October, each receiving a little over three inches per month on average. The average relative humidity in July at 6 p.m. is 63%.

The Corpus Christi area is one of the most consistently windy areas in the country, with an average year-round wind speed of 12 miles per hour. Winds are highest in April when the average is 14 miles per hour, classified on the Beaufort wind scale as a "moderate breeze." Because of the abundance of water and wind, windsurfing magazines often rate Corpus Christi Bay and the nearby Laguna Madre among the top-10 windsurfing spots in the world (for details, see "Recreation").

Over the last 90 years only two hurricanes have struck Corpus, one in 1919 and one in 1970 (Hurricane Celia, which reached maximum wind velocities of 130 m.p.h. and caused 11 deaths and an estimated $453 million in damages). In any given year, the odds of a tropical cyclone (hurricane or tropical storm) striking the Coastal Bend area (Baffin Bay to Aransas Bay, including Corpus) are one in eight.

History

As with other points along the central and lower coasts, Corpus Christi was first mapped in 1519 by Spanish explorer Alonso Alvarez de Piñeda, who named the bay in honor of the feast day of the body of Christ (the day his ship landed here). For the next three centuries, the area lay undeveloped; then Colonel Henry Kinney established a trading post on the bay in 1839. Until the War with Mexico, Kinney's settlement prospered on contraband trade between Texas and Mexico, since Corpus Christi was just below the Nueces River (which Mexico recognized as its northern border), yet above the Rio Grande (which the Republic of Texas, and later the United States, recognized as its southern border).

During the War with Mexico, the town further developed as a supply post for the U.S. Army (in 1848, of course, Mexico and the U.S. agreed that henceforth the Rio Grande would serve as the undisputed border). Immediately thereafter, the

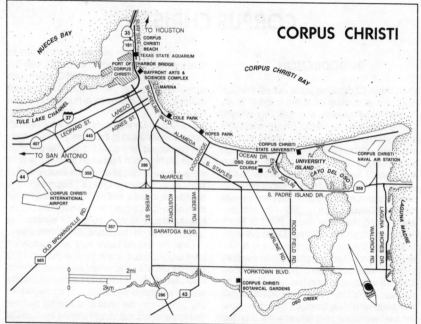

CORPUS CHRISTI

© MOON PUBLICATIONS, INC.

town's fortunes waned until the 1920s, when the federal government authorized the dredging of the bay and ship channel, thus turning Corpus into a deep-water port. This attracted industry to the area almost immediately, followed by the military (which established a naval air station and Army depot at the bay's east end).

Economy

In terms of tonnage handled, the Port of Corpus Christi is now the sixth-largest port in the country and the second largest in Texas (after Houston). Other major economic contributors in surrounding Nueces County include the petrochemical industry, tourism, military bases, ranching, and agriculture (cotton, corn, wheat, and grain sorghum). Nearby Ingleside, in San Patricio County on the north side of Corpus Christi Bay, has recently been made a home port for several U.S. Navy reserve vessels and mine-sweepers. Though not all Corpus residents condone the city's dependence on military-industrial revenues, such diversity has given Corpus a higher overall growth rate than

most other Texas cities in recent years.

The downtown area underwent a micro-depression in the '60s and '70s, however, as retail businesses moved out of central Corpus to suburban malls and business parks. The Heart of Corpus Christi, an urban revitalization group, has made great strides in bringing businesses back downtown, which, along with new office buildings, high-rise hotels, and a thriving marina, have made the Corpus waterfront the most visually striking city profile in the South Texas triangle.

Attracted by Corpus Christi's overall cultural appeal and mild climate, increasing numbers of "snowbirds" have been settling in the area for the winter as an alternative to the Rio Grande Valley. Corpus has welcomed them with open arms, responding quickly to the need for more RV parks and other facilities that cater to winter Texans. In 1989, the city earned *Trailblazer* magazine's Snowbird Award for best place in the U.S. to spend the winter (tying with Yuma, Arizona, and Sarasota, Florida).

SIGHTS

Downtown Waterfront

Mount Rushmore sculptor Gutzon Borglum designed the two-mile downtown seawall that runs along Shoreline Blvd., with a walkway and benches along the top and wide steps leading down to the water. The adjacent marina consists of three manmade peninsulas named for their shapes and for the downtown streets that meet them. The **Peoples Street T-Head** is the farthest north and is reserved for working boats (including charter and party boats, cruise boats, and shrimpers) and recreational equipment rental (water trikes, sailboats, paddleboats, sailboards, and Jet Skis).

The **Lawrence Street T-Head** and **Cooper's Alley L-Head** (usually just called "the L-Head," since there's only one) are reserved for privately owned pleasure craft. Visiting boats are welcome; see "Recreation" for details on slip rental and transient use facilities. Every Wednesday around sunset, local sailors compete in informal sailing regattas. Both T-heads have restaurants open to the public (see "Food").

As you drive east, Shoreline Blvd. eventually becomes **Ocean Drive**, a long bayfront residential avenue of large, older homes with the best views in town.

Harbor Bridge

Spanning the ship channel between the downtown area and Corpus Christi, this immense cantilever bridge is 620 feet long and 250 feet high. It was built in 1959 (at a cost of $20 million) and features a pedestrian walkway with a great view of the marina and city skyline.

Texas State Aquarium

Opened in 1990, this new attraction at Corpus Christi Beach will be the largest seashore aquarium in the country when all four phases are completed (over an estimated five- to 10-year period). The focus is on marinelife native to the Gulf of Mexico and the Caribbean; a unique "touch pool" allows visitors to become acquainted with crabs, starfish, and sea urchins. Together with other underwater habitat exhibits, the aquarium currently displays over 2,000 marine animals in 350,000 gallons of seawater. The biggest tank is the 132,500-gallon "Islands of Steel," which replicates the type of Gulf of Mexico reef habitat created by huge steel-legged oil rigs. A six-foot inset in the Lucite walls allows visitors a 180-degree wraparound view of the fish. It's rumored that the aquarium may eventually lead diving tours of the magnificent Flower Gardens reef system, some 220 miles distant in the Gulf (see "Scuba Diving" under "Galveston Island," p. 365, for more details on the reefs). Hours are Mon.-Sat. 9-5, Sun. 11-5; admission is $7 for adults, $5 for seniors, military, and college students, and $3.75 for children 4-17. For further information, call (512) 881-1300 or (800) 477-4853.

Bayfront Arts And Sciences Park

This complex on the bay, at the north end of Shoreline Blvd., serves as a combination arts and museum district, municipal park, and convention center. The park is roughly equivalent in area to eight city blocks, so all attractions are within walking distance of one another.

The **Art Museum of South Texas** (tel. 512-884-3844) at 1902 N. Shoreline hosts traveling exhibits of painting, sculpture, photography, and folk art, but they're also developing a small permanent collection. The stark-white, cast-concrete museum building was designed by renowned New York architect Philip Johnson. It's open Tues.-Fri. 10-5, Sat. and Sun. noon-5; admission is $2 (free on Sat. 10-noon).

The **Corpus Christi Museum** (tel. 512-883-2852) at 1900 Chaparral is primarily devoted to natural history exhibits, along with some local history. A new wing houses an exhibit of artifacts from three Spanish galleons that wrecked on nearby Padre Island in 1554, including a replica of one of the ships. It's open Tues.-Sat. 10-5, Sun. noon-5; admission is $2.

Also in the park complex are a community theater, water gardens (with 150 four-foot fountains), municipal auditorium, and convention center.

Heritage Park

Various nonprofit organizations in Corpus Christi (e.g., Camp Fire, Inc., the Junior League, Creative Arts Center, and League of United Latin American Citizens) have brought a collection of eight historic local homes together into one area along N. Chaparral between Fitzgerald and Hughes (near the Bayfront complex). Each organization has taken responsibility for restoring one

DOWNTOWN
CORPUS CHRISTI

TO HOUSTON

35
181

PORT OF CORPUS CHRISTI

TEXAS STATE
AQUARIUM

INDUSTRIAL CANAL

HARBOR
BRIDGE

PORT OF CORPUS CHRISTI

CORPUS
CHRISTI
MUSEUM

ART MUSEUM
OF SOUTH TEXAS
WATER GARDEN
AUDITORIUM

HARBOR PLAYHOUSE

CONVENTION
CENTER

CORPUS CHRISTI BAY

BREWSTER

HUGHES

HERITAGE
PARK

FITZGERALD

POWER

N. WATER

N. SHORELINE BLVD.

N. CHAPARRAL

N. MESQUITE

PORT AVE. E

CONVENTION AND
VISITORS BUREAU

MAIN

TAYLOR

STARR

N. LOWER BROADWAY

TRAILWAYS -
GREYHOUND
BUS TERMINAL

PEOPLES ST.
T - HEAD

POST
OFFICE

PEOPLES

SCHATZEL

LAWRENCE

LAWRENCE ST.
T - HEAD

WILLIAM

LAGUNA

COOPER'S ALLEY

L - HEAD

N. STAPLES

TO SAN ANTONIO

37

LEOPARD

407

LIPAN

N. UPPER BROADWAY

ALAMEDA

286

LAREDO

AGNES

S. STAPLES

S. SHORELINE BLVD.

S. WATER

MEMORIAL
COLISEUM

MAGEE
BEACH

0   0.25mi

0   0.25km

© MOON PUBLICATIONS, INC.

structure for historical and educational purposes (in return, they're allowed to use the homes for group functions). Four of the homes, including one owned by the city, are open to public tours.

The most spectacular restoration is the **Sidbury House** (tel. 512-883-9351), which was built in 1893 in the Queen Anne (or High Victorian) style and is listed with the National Register of Historic Places. The first floor is furnished in period style, including hand-printed European wallpaper. It's open Tues.-Thurs. 9:30 a.m.-12:30 p.m. The two-story, Colonial Revival-style **Galvan House** (tel. 883-0639) was built in 1908 and houses the city-sponsored Multicultural Center (no period furnishings); it's open to the public Mon.-Fri. 10-4, Sat. 10-2. The smaller 1873 **Lichtenstein House** (tel. 888-5692), also designed in the Colonial Revival style and listed with the NRHP, is sponsored by the Creative Arts Center, which offers various community programs in the arts; open Mon.-Fri. noon-4. The front rooms of the 1882 Late Victorian-style, NRHP-listed **Guggenheim House** (tel. 887-1601) are furnished in period fashion; open Mon.-Fri. 10-4. Admission to all the Heritage Park homes is free.

Centennial House

The oldest existing house in Corpus Christi (tel. 512-992-6003, 411 N. Upper Broadway), built in 1849, was used as a hospital by both Union and Confederate forces in the Civil War. Its name comes from the fact that it was awarded a Texas Historical Commission plaque during the Texas Centennial and it is now listed with the National Register of Historic Places as well. Restored and furnished in early American Empire style, it's open to visitors Wed. 2-5 p.m.; admission is $2 adults, $1 students.

International Kite Museum

There's always a kite or two flying somewhere in Corpus. This unique little museum at the Best Western Sandy Shores Resort (tel. 512-883-7456) on Corpus Christi Beach (at the north end of the Harbor Bridge) celebrates the kite; exhibits trace the history of the device from its invention in China to its use in the Wright Brothers' experiments. Naturally, an attached shop sells a variety of new kites. The museum is open daily 10-5 and is free.

Museum Of Oriental Cultures

Exhibits in this small museum at 418 Peoples St.

(tel. 512-883-1303) focus mainly on East Asian (Chinese, Japanese, and Korean) arts and culture. The Japanese *hakata* doll collection is one of the largest in the United States and a diorama presents 20 scale-model scenes from traditional Japanese life. Occasional traveling exhibits are on display as well, such as the recent "Talismans of the Far East," a collection of 60 framed folk and religious talismans (woodblock prints, temple rubbings, small sculpture) from Japan, Taiwan, Korea, and Southeast Asia. Open Tues.-Sat. 10-4; admission is $1 for adults, 50 cents for seniors and children 5-12.

Colleges And Universities

Del Mar College (tel. 512-886-1200) is a two-year community college with an approximate enrollment of 10,000 and a broad range of academic and technical study programs. There are two campuses, the East Campus on Old Brownsville and Airport, and the West Campus at Baldwin and Ayers.

Corpus Christi State University (tel. 991-6810) is much smaller in enrollment (3,700) but much larger in physical size—it occupies an entire 250-acre island near the east end of Ocean Dr., with Corpus Christi Bay on one side and Cayo del Oso on the other. It's for upper-division undergraduate and graduate students only, but will enroll its first freshman class in 1994, when it becomes Texas A & M University of Corpus Christi. One of the more unusual program offerings is the National Spill Control School, which teaches techniques for handling hazardous material spills. The physical education department features sailing and windsurfing classes. The university also has music, film, and lecture series open to the public.

Corpus Christi Naval Air Station

This is the headquarters for the U.S. Naval Air Training Command, the next step for multi-engine pilots who have graduated from primary naval flight training in Pensacola, Florida. Also on base are the largest Army helicopter repair depot in the country and a Coast Guard search-and-rescue unit. The air station is closed to the nonmilitary public except on Wed. at 1 p.m., when free tours are given from the north gate at the east end of Ocean Drive. For further information, call (512) 939-2568.

CORPUS CHRISTI ACCOMMODATIONS

Hotels, Motels, And Beach Condominiums
Corpus has just about every kind of accommodation except a youth hostel. They're clustered in four areas: downtown along Shoreline Blvd. facing the marina (or one block back on Water St.), to the west of town near the airport, on Corpus Christi Beach at the north end of the Harbor Bridge, and on the Gulf side of North Padre Island. See "Corpus Christi Hotels, Motels, And Condominiums" chart for details.

Bed And Breakfast Inns
Sand Dollar Hospitality Bed & Breakfast (tel. 512-853-1222, 3605 Mendenhall, Corpus Christi, TX 78415) maintains a register of around 15 bed- and-breakfast homes in Corpus Christi. Rates are $30-60 s, $35-70 d per night including full breakfasts.

Campgrounds And RV Parks
The nearest public campground is at the county-operated **Padre Balli Park** (tel. 512-949-8121) on North Padre Island off Padre Island Drive. Beach or hard-top camping is $4 a night, $10 with w/e, and there is a three-day limit. You can also camp at Padre Island National Seashore (see p. 401).

Although Corpus Christi doesn't have nearly as many RV parks as the Rio Grande Valley farther south, it has enough spaces to meet the current demand. Rates are similar among all the Corpus Christi area facilities: around $10-11 nightly, $55-60 weekly, and $125-150 monthly ($90 a month at places where RVers pay for their own electricity at 8 cents per kilowatt-hour). Among the largest parks is **Colonia Del Rey RV Park** (tel. 512-937-2435) at 1717 Waldron (off Padre Island Dr. between Cayo del Oso and Laguna Madre), which has a swimming pool, horseshoe pit, rec hall, and laundromat. Farther south on the same road is the smaller **Shady Grove Mobile Home and RV Park** (tel. 937-1314) at 2919 Waldron. Another big one at this end of town is **Anchor Harbor Mobile Home and Travel Trailer Park** (tel. 991-3292) at 8100 S. Padre Island Dr., which has a pool, club room, and laundromat. A bit farther north, near the Naval Air Station, is **Marina Village RV and Mobile Home Park** (tel. 937-2560) at 229 N.A.S. Dr.;

facilities include laundromat, pool, and rec hall. **Padre Palms Travel Park** (tel. 937-2125) is in the same area, at 131 Skipper Ln. (off N.A.S. Dr.).

Over on the west side of town is the conveniently located **Hatch RV Park** (tel. 512-883-9781) at 3101 Up River Rd. (exit 2 off I-37), just a couple of miles from the downtown area. **Gulley's RV Park** (tel. 241-4122) at 8225 Leopard is farther out I-37 off the Tuloso Rd. exit (#7).

The city has plans to build a new RV park at the north end of Corpus Christi Beach within the next couple of years. Call the Corpus Christi Area Convention and Visitors Bureau (tel. 512-882-5603) for the latest information.

FOOD

With Corpus Christi Bay, Cayo del Oso, Laguna Madre, and the Gulf of Mexico nearby, you'd better enjoy fresh seafood. Virtually every restaurant in town, outside of the chain burger joints, offers seafood specials on their menus. You can buy your own fresh shrimp and fish directly from the commercial boats docked at the Peoples Street T-Head at the marina.

American
$ to $$ **Black-Eyed Pea:** Down-home food including chicken-fried steak. At 4801 S. Padre Island Dr. (tel. 512-993-4588); open daily for lunch and dinner.
$ to $$ **Elmo's City Diner and Oyster Bar:** Features a '50s diner-style decor with excellent Cajun, Texan, "blue plate specials," and seafood dishes. At 622 N. Water (tel. 883-1643); open Mon.-Sat. for lunch and dinner.

Barbecue
$ to $$ **County Line:** Another branch of the state's best barbecue franchise, with the usual brisket, links, and ribs, plus chicken, duck, and turkey. At 6102 Ocean Dr. (tel. 512-991-7427); open daily for lunch and dinner.
$ **Joe Cotten's Barbecue:** This one's actually in Robstown, about eight miles southeast of the city limit on US 77. Barbecue aficionados swear this is the best in South Texas—and they crowd the place to prove it. On US 77 business (tel. 767-9973); open Mon.-Sat for lunch and dinner.

CORPUS CHRISTI HOTELS, MOTELS, AND CONDOMINIUMS

Ranges given are for the peak season (spring-summer) and reflect both weekday and weekend rates. Fall and winter rates are usually less. Add 11% hotel tax to all rates. Area code: 512

NAME	ADDRESS	PHONE	RATES	FEATURES
CORPUS CHRISTI BEACH				
Best Western Sandy Shores	3200 Surfside	833-7456 or (800) 528-1234	$49-109	rooms with bay view, heated pool, saunas, coin laundry
Gulf Beach II	3500 Surfside	882-3500 or (800) 882-3502	$45-70	rooms with bay view, coin laundry, weekly rates
Koronado Motel	3615 Timon	883-4411	$35-58	rooms with bay view, pool, coin laundry, kitchens available (add $10)
Sea Shell Inn	202 Kleberg	888-5391	$53-69	rooms with bay view, heated pool, coin laundry, wkly. and monthly rates (off season only)
Villa Del Sol	3839 Surfside	883-9748 or (800) 242-3291	$71-115	all rooms with bay view, kitchenettes avail., heated pool, coin laundry, weekly rates, senior discount, weekend discount
DOWNTOWN (SHORELINE BOULEVARD)				
Ashford Inn	411 N. Shoreline	884-4815	$39-55	all rooms with bay view, pool
Corpus Christi Marriott Bayfront	900 N. Shoreline	887-1600 or (800) 874-4585	$120-140	bay views, heated pool, saunas, racquetball courts, airport shuttle
Holiday Inn Emerald Beach	1102 S. Shoreline	883-5731 or (800)-HOLIDAY	$66-125	private beach, airport shuttle
Quality Hotel Bayfront Royal Nueces	601 N. Water	882-8100 or (800) 688-0334	$69-79	1 block from marina, atrium, pool, airport shuttle
Radisson Marina Hotel	300 N. Shoreline	883-5111 or (800) 333-3333	$61-83	bay views, pool, sauna, tennis courts, airport shuttle
Ramada Inn Bayfront	601 N. Shoreline	883-7271	$50-55	pool, senior discount

(continued)

CORPUS CHRISTI HOTELS, MOTELS, AND CONDOMINIUMS

Ranges given are for the peak season (spring-summer) and reflect both weekday and weekend rates. Fall and winter rates are usually less. Add 11% hotel tax to all rates. Area code: 512

NAME	ADDRESS	PHONE	RATES	FEATURES
DOWNTOWN (SHORELINE BOULEVARD) (continued)				
Sheraton Corpus Christi Bayfront	707 N. Shoreline	882-1700	$75-85	marina views, heated pool, sauna, airport shuttle
AIRPORT				
Comfort Inn Airport	6301 I-37 (exit 5)	289-6925	$37-43	pool, coin laundry, airport shuttle
Days Inn	901 Navigation (I-37 exit 3A)	888-8599 or (800) 325-2525	$39-54	pool, coin laundry weekly rates
Drury Inn	2021 N. Padre Island (I-37 exit 4A)	289-8200 or (800) 325-8300	$42-55	pool, senior discount comp. eve. beverage
Holiday Inn Airport	5549 Leopard	289-5100 or (800)-HOLIDAY	$69-75	heated pool, saunas, airport shuttle, weekend discount
La Quinta Motor Inn North	5155 I-37 N (exit 3A)	888-5721 or (800) 531-5900	$47-55	pool, senior discount
Motel 6	845 Lantana (I-37 exits 3B/4B)	289-9397	$22.95 + $6 ea. add.	pool
NORTH PADRE ISLAND				
Holiday Inn North Padre Island Resort	15202 Windward	949-8041 or (800)-HOLIDAY	$66-135	beach, pool, weekly rates (off season only)
Puente Vista Condominium Apartments	14300 Aloha	949-7081	$105-130	2-3 bedroom units, w/full kitchens, beach, pool, coin laundry, sauna, boat dock, weekly rates
Surfside Condo	15005 Windward	949-8128 or (800) 548-4585	$75-95	2-bedroom units w/full kitchen, beach, pool, coin laundry, wkly. and monthly rates

European

$ to $$ **Che Bello:** A downtown eatery that may appease homesick New Yorkers or San Franciscans with its espressos, pastries, sandwiches, and gelatos. At 320-C William, Water Street Market (tel. 512-882-8832); open Mon.-Thurs. 7:30 a.m.-10 p.m., Fri. 7:30-midnight, Sat. 10-midnight, Sun. 10-10.

$$ **Luciano's:** An old, established Italian restau-

rant that serves pasta standards, homemade Italian sausage, espresso drinks, and Italian desserts. At 1618 S. Staples (tel. 884-1832); open Tues.-Fri. for lunch and dinner, Sat. and Sun. dinner only.

Mexican

$ to $$ **Kiko's Mexican Food:** This Tex-Mex

place is located in the Mercado, a local Mexican curios market. The menu features fajitas, taquitos, enchiladas, *almuerzo,* and other South Texas favorites. At 5520 Everhart (tel. 512-991-1211); open Mon.-Sat. for breakfast, lunch, and dinner, Sun. for breakfast and lunch only.

$ to $$ Old Mexico: The same family has run this simple restaurant for the last 35 years. Often cited as the city's best all-around Mexican restaurant, they serve an especially good puff taco. At 3329 Leopard at Nueces Bay Blvd. (tel. 883-6461); open Tues.-Sat. for lunch and dinner.

$ Ray's: Another old Tex-Mex standby with a loyal Corpus following. At 920 Louisiana (tel. 883-1413); open Mon.-Sat. for lunch and dinner.

Seafood

$$ Baja Coast Seafood Grille and Oyster Bar: You can watch the cooks grill fresh seafood over mesquite coals from your table here, since the dining tables are arranged in tiers above the cooking area. The menu is extensive and includes catch-of-the-day specials. There's a fish market in the front of the building. At 5253 S. Staples (tel. 512-992-3474); open daily for lunch and dinner, Sunday brunch.

$ to $$ Catfish Charlie's: Although the only seafood on the menu are shrimp, oysters, and catfish, low prices and Cajun cooking make this restaurant noteworthy. An all-you-can-eat platter of catfish fillets, hush puppies, cole slaw, and country-fried potatoes is $7.95. Gumbo, shrimp creole, and red beans and rice are also served. At McArdle and Airline, Crossroads Center (tel. 993-0363); open daily from 11 a.m. through dinner.

$$ to $$$ Landry's Seafood: A restored 1939 barge is the setting for this floating restaurant at the city marina which serves steak, smoked chicken, and fresh Gulf seafood. Monday-Sat. 5-7 and all day Sunday they offer economical "early-bird" specials; during the week there's a "Chill Out Hour" 4:30-7:30 when beer and margaritas are $1, oysters on the half-shell are 25 cents each, and a half-pound of boiled shrimp is $6. At the end of the Peoples Street T-Head (tel. 882-6666); open daily for lunch and dinner.

$$ to $$$ The Lighthouse Restaurant and Oyster Bar: Another marina restaurant, this one's built on solid ground and has the best bay view. The menu features fresh seafood, beef, and chicken. It can get crowded on Wednesdays early in the evening when people come to watch the sailboat races. At the end of the Lawrence Street T-Head (tel. 883-3982); open daily for lunch and dinner.

$ to $$ Snoopy's: One of two popular seafood places located under the JFK Causeway between Corpus and Padre Island (the other, **Frenchy's,** is also good), Snoopy's serves only locally caught fish and shellfish, fried or broiled to order. At 10875 South Padre Island Dr. (tel. 949-8815); open daily for lunch and dinner.

$$ Water Street Oyster Bar: Specializes in mesquite-grilled and Cajun-style seafood, including blackened redfish and blackened shark. At 309 N. Water St. (tel. 881-9448); open daily for lunch and dinner.

$$ Water Street Seafood Company: A larger version of the above with a more extensive menu. Same address (tel. 882-8683); open daily for lunch and dinner.

$$ to $$$ The Yardarm: French-influenced seafood *(coquilles St. Jacques,* red snapper papillote, sauteed frogs legs) served in one of Ocean Drive's stately bayfront homes. At 4310 Ocean Dr. (tel. 855-8157); open Wed.-Sun. for dinner only, closed November-February.

ENTERTAINMENT

Live Music

Cantina Santa Fe (tel. 512-883-7204) at 1011 Santa Fe in central Corpus features live rock and jazz groups several nights a week. For straight-ahead rock 'n' roll check out **Elizabeth's** (tel. 887-1953) at 902 N. Chaparral or **Rum Boogie Bar** 709 N. Chaparral. For the urban-country crowd, there's **Dallas** (tel. 952-8088) at 24 Parkdale Plaza and **Booters** (tel. 991-6091) at 5700 S. Staples.

Comedy

Corpus has one comedy club, **High Tides** (tel. 887-1600) in the Corpus Christi Marriott, 1900 Shoreline. Comedians perform Tuesday-Saturday at 8:30.

Radio

Radio station KKED 90 FM, the local National Public Radio affiliate, broadcasts a variety of locally produced jazz and classical music shows. "Magic 105" (105.1 FM) is a good bilingual Tejano radio station that plays an upbeat mix of local and international styles.

EVENTS

April

Buccaneer Days, formerly "Splash Days," is a 10-day festival commemorating the 1519 European "discovery" of Corpus Christi Bay is usually held the last two weeks of the month. Festivities include a beauty pageant, bayfront fireworks, downtown parades, music, sailing regattas, and a carnival.

July

The **Texas Jazz Festival** is a growing festival featuring three days (around July 4th) of jazz performances, including concerts, cruises, jam sessions, and free workshops. The artists who appear are a mixture of state, local, and national names.

September-October

Bayfest, originally held for the Bicentennial, has become an annual fall festival at the Bayfront Arts and Science Park and is usually on the last weekend in September or first weekend in October. Activities include music, food vendors, arts and crafts, shows, and boat races.

December

On the first Saturday of the month, **Harbor Lights** celebrates Christmas Corpus Christi-style with a bayfront parade and the lighting of boats moored at the marina.

RECREATION

Beaches

Corpus Christi has five beaches within or contiguous with the city limits—three on Corpus Christi Bay and two on the Gulf. The oldest and most popular with tourists is **Corpus Christi Beach** at the north end of the Harbor Bridge. In the '30s casinos were lined up along the 1.5-mile beach (it was called "North Beach" then) and it carried an unsavory reputation for a long time thereafter. The U.S. Army Corps of Engineers restored the beach in the '70s and it's now chock-a-block with motels and beach condos.

Magee Beach is only 250 yards long but is close to the city marina, across from the coliseum off Shoreline Boulevard. Besides the beach, there's a pier, a quarter-mile-long breakwater,

food concession (open Memorial Day to Labor Day), and showers.

Farther east, off Ocean Dr. (2000 block) is **Cole Park,** which features a small beach, fishing pier, picnic area, and restrooms. This is a favorite local windsurfing spot (see "Windsurfing" below). During the summer, the amphitheater here hosts Sunday evening concerts.

Padre Balli County Park is on the Gulf of Mexico, about 15 miles from downtown Corpus via Padre Island Dr. across the JFK Causeway. It's the closest Gulf beach to the city, so it gets crowded on summer weekends. Facilities include a 1,200-foot-long lighted fishing pier, picnic areas, bathhouse, and a campground (see "Campgrounds And RV Parks" above for rates).

Just north of North Padre's condo strip is the **J.P. Luby Youth Park,** a beach developed especially for surfers. The main feature here is a 600-foot row of pier pilings that extend into the surf to enhance wave action for surfing.

Parks And Gardens

Corpus Christi Botanical Gardens (tel. 512-993-7551) is on Oso Creek, at Staples and Yorktown in the southwest part of the city, and is being opened a section at a time (when completed it will cover 100 acres). A nature trail leads through small native subtropical gardens and flower and vegetable displays. Facilities include an information center, gift shop, and picnic area. Open Tues.-Sun. 9-5; admission is $1.

Hans Suter Wildlife Refuge, a 22-acre park on Cayo del Oso (Oso Bay) off Ennis Joplin Rd., is the best birding spot within the city limits. Facilities include an 800-foot boardwalk across a preserved saltmarsh, an observation tower, and hiking trails. It's open dawn to dusk and admission is free.

Boating

Launching/Berthing: The downtown marina/yacht basin is the city's pleasure-boat center, offering boat-launching facilities, slip rentals, boat rentals, charter boats, and excursion boats. If you plan to sail into the bay on your own craft, call ahead to the marina office (tel. 512-882-7333, or fax 883-4778) to reserve a guest slip. Guest sailors pay a daily rate of 50 cents per foot per boat or, for longer stays, flat rates of $89 a week, $330 a month. Permanent slips are $2.65 per foot per month. Marina facilities include restrooms, laundry, and hot showers.

city marina

Smaller boat launching facilities are available at the end of Ocean Dr. on Oso Bay and at the end of Rincon Rd. beneath the Nueces Bay Causeway.

Sailing Instruction: Corpus Christi Bay and Laguna Madre are excellent places to learn how to sail; the **International School of Sailing** (tel. 512-881-8503) on the marina's L-Head offers a weekend sailing school (all day Sat. and Sun.) for $135. For more intensive instruction, consider the three-day or five-day "live-aboard" courses for $390 and $750 respectively, which include all boat accommodations, meals, and instruction.

Charters: The L-Head's **Charter Boat Associates** (same phone number as above) can arrange yacht charters ranging from $160 for an eight-hour bareboat 31-foot Allmand charter to $2225 for a week-long captained Oyster 41-foot trip.

Sightseeing Boats: The *Flagship* and the *Gulf Clipper,* both docked at the Peoples T-Head (tel. 512-643-7128), take passengers on one-hour harbor tours for $5.25 adults, $3.25 children 4-11. During the summer, the tours leave three times a day; the rest of the year, they only leave once a day (except Tuesday, when they're closed). On Friday and Saturday nights, they offer night tours of the harbor and bay, with live music, for $6.75 (7:30-9) and $7.50 (9:30-11, summer only).

One of the more unusual charter-boat operations at the Nueces Bay Causeway is the **Dolphin Connection** (tel. 512-882-4126), which makes trips into the bay to visit four pods of At-lantic bottlenose dolphins. The boat leaves daily at 8:30 a.m. and 10:30 a.m. March-October for the one-hour trip and costs $15 per person.

Fishing

Anglers can choose among several fishing options in Corpus Christi Bay, Cayo del Oso (Oso Bay), Laguna Madre, and the Gulf of Mexico. Shore fishing is possible just about anywhere there's water, since there always seems to be a pier, breakwater, or wharf nearby. In the bays you can fish for speckled trout, redfish, sand trout, sheepshead, golden croakers, skipjack, drum, and flounder. In the Gulf inshore areas, there're also tarpon, mackerel, ling, pompano, jackfish, jewfish, and blue runner. Farther out in the Gulf is almost everything previously listed, plus kingfish, dolphin, bonito, sailfish, marlin, and barracuda. Deep-sea anglers who make it to Snapper Banks, 40-60 miles out, have a shot at red snapper, grouper, amberjack, and warsaw. The Corpus Christi Area Convention and Visitors Bureau (tel. 512-882-5603) issues an excellent fishing calendar that lists the best seasons for each species.

Piers And Jetties: Fishing is allowed at the **marina** from the T-heads or from the seawall. The lighted breakwater jetty between the marina and Magee Park is open for fishing 24 hours. The pier at **Cole Park,** 2000 block of Ocean Dr., is also lighted and open 24 hours. All of the foregoing piers and jetties are free. The lighted, 24-hour **Nueces Bay Pier** at Corpus Christi Beach (Hull St.) charges a small daily fee for fishing, as does the long **Bob Hall Pier** at Padre Balli Park on North Padre Island.

Fishing Boats: Several boats docked at the marina's Peoples Street T-Head offer bay fishing trips (for Gulf fishing trips, Port Aransas is a better choice; see "Vicinity of Corpus Christi"). The 65-foot **Captain Clark** (tel. 512-884-4369) takes visiting anglers on three four-hour trips per day (7:30 a.m., 2 p.m., and 8 p.m.). The fee is $12 for adults, $6 for children 4-11, and includes bait (bring your own rod and reel or rent them for $3). Food and beverages are sold onboard. The **Star Trek** (tel. 883-5031) offers the same arrangements and departures.

Windsurfing

Because of the steady breezes and long expanses of open water in the bay and in Laguna Madre (sheltered from high winds by barrier islands), Corpus is consistently rated among the world's top-10 windsurfing centers. In 1989, the U.S. Open Pro Am and the Mistral World Championship windsurfing tournaments were both held on Corpus Christi Bay. (Mistral, a major sailboard manufacturer, will probably make Corpus the tournament's permanent home.) The state's own sailboard manufacturer, Westwind, will move operations here from Galveston in the near future.

The semicircular geography of the "Coastal Bend" means that the wind is always blowing somewhere around the bay (usually everywhere). The most popular windsurfing spot within the city limits is **Oleander Point** at the southern end of Cole Park (2000 block of Ocean Dr.). Farther east along Ocean Dr. are **Ropes Park** (3500 block) and **Poenisch Park** (5000 block), also good places to launch a sailboard. Corpus Christi Beach (at the north end of Harbor Bridge) gets its share of windsurfers, too, both novice and experienced.

Windsurfing equipment can be rented at the Peoples Street T-Head, at Corpus Christi Beach, and at **M.D. Surf-N-Skate** (tel. 512-854-SURF) at 3821 S. Staples. Surf-N-Skate also offers windsurfing equipment sales, service, and instruction. An introductory course (four hours) costs $48, while a full certification course (eight hours) is $85; all equipment is included.

Other shops in town offering instruction, rentals, and sales include **Mastercraft of Corpus Christi** (tel. 512-992-4459, 6425 S. Padre Island Dr.) and **Wind & Wave Water Sports** (tel. 937-9283, 10721 S. Padre Island Drive).

Scuba Diving

Various jetty complexes in Aransas Bay and farther south at Port Mansfield and South Padre Island offer artificial reef viewing, as do offshore oil rigs. For information on guided trips or equipment rental/service, contact **The Dive Shop** (tel. 512-991-2760), 6341 S. Padre Island Dr., or **Padre Island Dive Shop** (tel. 993-6000), 6901 S. Padre Island Drive. It's possible to arrange overnight dive trips to the magnificent Flower Gardens reef system, 220 miles northeast in the Gulf, but Freeport is a much more convenient departure point since it cuts the total mileage in half (see "Scuba Diving" under "Galveston Island," p. 365). The Texas State Aquarium (tel. 881-1300) may begin offering dive trips to the Flower Gardens in the near future.

Golf

The city-operated **Oso Beach Golf Course** (tel. 512-991-5351) at 5600 S. Alameda (at Glenmore) is an 18-hole, par-70 course near Oso Bay. Green fees are $6.95 on weekdays, $8.45 weekends. **Gabe Lozano Sr. Golf Center** (tel. 883-3696) is an 18-hole, par-72 public course with the same greens fees as the Oso Beach course.

Tennis

Corpus Christi operates two municipal tennis centers: **H.E.B. Tennis Center** (tel. 512-888-5681) at 1520 Shely (H.E.B. Butt Park) and **South Bluff Center** (tel. 888-6942) at 502 King. At either, court fees (hour-and-a-half limit) are $2 days, $3 nights.

LOUISE FOOTE

CORPUS CHRISTI
INFORMATION

Tourist Offices

The **Corpus Christi Area Convention and Visitors Bureau** (tel. 512-882-5603) at 1201 Shoreline is open Mon.-Fri. 8:30-5. The staff are very helpful and they have tons of free brochures on local attractions, accommodations, and recreation. The CCACVB also maintains a 24-hour toll-free line that visitors can call to order a free packet of information through the mail (800-766-BEACH). Similar information, though not as extensive, is available at the **Corpus Christi Tourist Information Center** (tel. 241-1464), at Nueces River Park (junction of US 77 and I-37), and at the **Corpus Christi Visitor Bureau** (tel. 937-6711), 9405 S. Padre Island Drive.

Publications

The convention and visitors bureau publishes an annual *Corpus Christi Bay Area Visitors Guide* in magazine format that contains a variety of short features on local attractions, recreation, and events (plus loads of advertising). Miller Publications's *Visitors Guide* is somewhat similar but focuses more on dining, shopping, and cultural events. The *Island Sun* is a free weekly newspaper with up-to-date information on fishing, tides, and TV listings that cover the entire Coastal Bend (Padre Island to Rockport).

Maps

A good Corpus Christi area map is crucial for exploring the area, with all its bays, ship channels, and lagoons. The best all-around map is the one published by the city's own **Zdansky Map Store** (tel. 512-855-9226), 5230 Kostoryz, available throughout the city at shops that carry maps. Besides a large city map (with downtown inset), it features inset maps for North Padre Island, Robstown, Portland, Mustang Island, Port Aransas, and Nueces County. The one drawback of the Zdansky map is that it doesn't show street numbers; if you need street numbers, get the smaller Rand McNally Corpus Christi map.

Telephone

The area code for Corpus Christi and vicinity is 512.

TRANSPORT

City Buses

The **Regional Transportation Authority** (tel. 512-882-1722) operates the city bus system. Visitors will probably be most interested in three of the RTA's "B-Lines." The "B Trolley Scenic Trail" uses buses that have been modified to look like trolley cars (as in San Antonio) and runs along the downtown waterfront between Brewster and Buford, stopping at Heritage Park, the Bayfront Arts and Sciences Park, and the marina T-heads. Hours of operation are Mon.-Fri. 1:45-9:45, Sat. 11-10:15. These buses come by every half-hour during the week, every 15 minutes on Saturday; a roundtrip circuit only takes 30 minutes. The fare is 25 cents Mon.-Fri., 10 cents on Sat. (children under six ride free).

The "B Trolley Shopping Trail" runs a longer circuit between the bayfront and the city's two major malls, Sunrise and Padre-Staples, also stopping at Cullen Mall, Town and Country Center, The Village, and several other shopping centers. Hours of operation are Mon.-Sat. noon-8:38. The schedule is the same all week, with buses beginning the circuit every 65 minutes; a roundtrip circuit takes about an hour. The fare is 25 cents all week; children under six ride free.

The third line of general interest to visitors is the #10 Flour Bluff-Island Express, which runs from Padre-Staples Mall to Port Aransas via Mustang Island State Park. This line runs two buses a day, Mon.-Fri. only, starting at Padre-Staples at 7:33 a.m. and 2:28 p.m. The second bus leaves Port Aransas for the return trip at 3:30 p.m. Large luggage compartments hold beach chairs, sailboards, coolers, and other beach equipment. Fares are $1 adults, 50 cents seniors, disabled, and children 6-

---

TELEPHONE AND EMERGENCY
INFORMATION

Emergency (police, fire, medical)	911
Telephone Directory Assistance	1-411
National Weather Service	289-1861
Beach and Surf Conditions	949-8175
Time/Temperature	884-8463

12. Transfers from other bus lines in the RTA system may be applied to the fare for 50 cents.

Taxis
Call **Star Cab** (tel. 512-884-9451) for 24-hour taxi service.

Corpus Christi International Airport
This airport is conveniently located about 15 minutes southwest of downtown Corpus via Agnes Street. Five commercial airlines (American, Conquest, Continental, Delta, and Southwest) oper-

ate daily flights to six other Texas cities as well as 18 destinations in the U.S. and Mexico. The terminal's one restaurant, **Riviera Red's** (tel. 512-289-5418), serves decent seafood.

A limousine from **Texas Riviera Transportation** (tel. 512-289-0191) costs $7 between the airport and the downtown area.

Intercity Buses
The **Trailways-Greyhound Bus Terminal** (tel. 512-884-9474) is downtown at 702 N. Chaparral near Starr.

VICINITY OF CORPUS CHRISTI

East of Corpus Christi are the barrier islands of Mustang and Padre, which really function as one island since the narrow channel that once separated them has silted up on the Gulf side. Padre Island runs 113 miles from its north end at Corpus Christi Pass to the south end at the Mansfield Cut (Mansfield Channel), while Mustang Island is only 18 miles long. To the north of Mustang Island are the Rockport-Fulton Peninsula, Aransas Bay, Copano Bay, St. Charles Bay, and the Aransas National Wildlife Refuge.

PORT ARANSAS

Perched at the northern tip of Mustang Island, this is one of America's few remaining old-fashioned beach towns, the kind with funky motel courts instead of Holiday Inns. Until the 1950s, it was rather difficult to reach Port Aransas; two ferry crossings were necessary, one from the mainland to Harbor Island, then another from Harbor Island to Mustang Island, and there wasn't even a road leading to the mainland ferry terminal (you had to take a train from Aransas Pass). As the Port of Corpus Christi superseded Port Aransas, no one seemed to be in any hurry to improve island access. But finally in 1954 the Mustang Island Highway (State 361) and south causeway was built to connect the south part of the island with Corpus Christi and in 1960 another causeway linked the mainland with Harbor Island. The ferry service between Harbor Island and Port A (as it's known locally) is still the only way to avoid coming through Corpus Christi, however.

State 361 now leads, via the north causeway, to the Harbor Island ferry landing. The ferry service to Port A operates 24 hours a day, takes about five minutes to complete the crossing, and is free of charge. The usual waiting time to get on the ferry is five to 15 minutes. During summer weekends and spring break, however, the wait can be as long as two hours; when it's that backed up, it's best to drive around through Corpus to Padre Island, and from there north to Port A (a trip of about 80 minutes in normal traffic conditions). Along this route, a low bridge carries drivers over the silted Corpus Christi Pass that once separated Padre from Mustang.

Whichever way you choose to come to Port A, the accessibility issue tends to deter the average weekend beachgoer, a situation that's a major plus for those seeking a more tranquil seaside setting than is available in Galveston or Corpus Christi. In spite of the condo developments coming up at the south edge of the city limits, the permanent population here is still just over 2,000 and the atmosphere remains that of a 1950s fishing village. From here all the way down to just above the Mexican border (where Padre Island is separated from South Padre Island by an artificial channel), the beaches are wide open.

The one time of year to avoid Port Aransas, unless you know what you're in for, is "spring break," a three-week period overlapping the end of March and beginning of April. Spring break brings thousands of college and university students to the island and town facilities are taxed almost to their breaking point. During this period, spring-breakers can outnumber locals 50 to one or more (many locals clear out of town till it's over).

History

The first known Mustang Island inhabitants were Karankawa Indians, who were wiped out by Comanches, disease, and European colonists by the 1800s. Gulf pirates visited the area regularly, but the first European settler was Englishman R.L. Mercer, who brought his family to Mustang Island (named for the wild horses that once roamed here) in the 1850s to fish and raise cattle. The town that grew up around the Mercer settlement became known as Tarpon, after the fish of the same name that were once plentiful in nearby Gulf waters. As it developed into a ship-service stop for Aransas Pass, the name was changed to Port Aransas.

Economy

Commercial and sport fishing have kept Port Aransas (and its nearest mainland neighbor, Aransas Pass) alive over the years. As in Corpus Christi, a variety of fishing possibilities (flats, bays, and surf fishing) lure anglers from all over the state and beyond. Port Aransas, however, has the added pull of deep-sea fishing, since it has the easternmost harbor in the center of the Coastal Bend. This means that anglers in Port Aransas spend much less time boating out to the offshore fishing grounds than their Corpus counterparts, hence deep-sea charter trips are more time- and cost-effective. Not all tourism is fishing-related, however; many South Texas beachgoers come to Port Aransas to avoid the summer crush in nearby Corpus Christi, bringing additional revenues. A smattering of winter Texans have found their way to the island as well.

Sights

Besides the beaches and wildlife, there's not a lot to see around town. The **Civic Center Historical Exhibit** (tel. 512-749-4111) at Cut-Off Rd. and Ave. A has a display of locally collected items, including gold coins and a lens from an old lighthouse, that provides a pieced-together history of the island. The exhibit is open Mon.-Fri. 8-5; admission is free.

More interesting is the visitor center at the **University of Texas at Austin Marine Science Institute** (tel. 512-749-6729), which is an 80-acre facility at the end of Cotter St. across from Nueces County Park. The institute conducts laboratory and field research in ecology, marine chem-

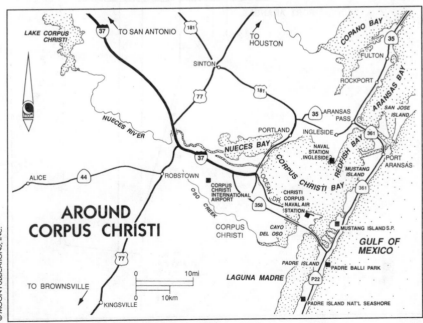

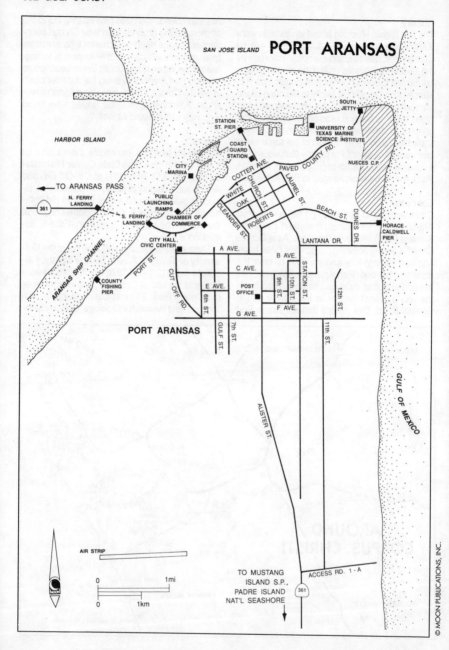

SAN JOSE ISLAND **PORT ARANSAS**

HARBOR ISLAND

TO ARANSAS PASS ←

361

N. FERRY LANDING

S. FERRY LANDING

ARANSAS SHIP CHANNEL

COUNTY FISHING PIER

PORT ARANSAS

STATION ST. PIER

COAST GUARD STATION

CITY MARINA

PUBLIC LAUNCHING RAMPS

CHAMBER OF COMMERCE

CITY HALL, CIVIC CENTER

SOUTH JETTY

UNIVERSITY OF TEXAS MARINE SCIENCE INSTITUTE

NUECES C.P.

PAVED COUNTY RD.

COTTER AVE.

WHITE

OAK

CHURCH ST.

LAUREL ST.

ROBERTS

OLEANDER ST.

BEACH ST.

DUNES DR.

HORACE CALDWELL PIER

LANTANA DR.

PORT ST.

A AVE.

B AVE.

C AVE.

CUT-OFF RD.

E AVE.

6th ST.

POST OFFICE

9th ST.

10th ST.

STATION ST.

12th ST.

F AVE.

G AVE.

GULF ST.

7th ST.

11th ST.

GULF OF MEXICO

AIR STRIP

0   1mi

0   1km

ALISTER ST.

TO MUSTANG ISLAND S.P., PADRE ISLAND NAT'L SEASHORE

ACCESS RD. 1-A

361

© MOON PUBLICATIONS, INC.

istry, biological oceanography, mariculture, marine botany, and several other fields related to marine environments. The visitor center contains seven aquaria that represent microcosms of local marine habitats, from mangrove marshes to offshore reefs. Other exhibits display information on past and current research projects, as well as preserved or photographed marine specimens. The center is open Mon.-Fri. 8-5; admission is free. An auditorium in the complex hosts free film and video presentations on such topics as the Kemp's ridley turtle, intertidal zones, or barrier-island ecosystems, Mon.-Thurs. at 11 and 2.

Nueces County Park

Also called Port Aransas Park (or just "the beach"), this beach park is on the northeast corner of the island near the South Jetty. The beach here is okay, but not as pristine as those farther south. Surfing is allowed except within 300 feet of the pier (best surf action is in the winter). Facilities include showers, restrooms, food concessions, the Horace Caldwell Pier (see "Fishing" below), and a campground. Tent camping is $4 a night and two-way RV hookups are $10 (14-day maximum stay).

Mustang Island State Park

This 3,703-acre park spans the southern quarter of Mustang Island (about 14 miles south of Port Aransas) between Water Exchange Pass to the north and Corpus Christi Pass to the south, and from Corpus Christi Bay to the Gulf. On the Gulf side is 5 1/2 miles of beach, separated from the interior of the island by coastal ridge dunes that reach as high as 35 feet.

Vegetation is sparse on the seaward side of the dunes but becomes thicker on the inland side, which gives way to troughs, grassy flats, and secondary dunes. Farther west, on the bay side of the park, are tidal flats and marshes. Wildlife protected by the park includes jack rabbits, cottontail rabbits, opossums, raccoons, armadillos, coyotes, shorebirds, and a variety of waterfowl that changes with the seasons.

Facilities: At the north end of the beach is a day-use area with a parking lot, toilets, showers, a fish-cleaning shelter, and an area designated as the main swimming beach. The next 7,000 feet of beach south of the day-use area is set aside for beach camping ($5 weekdays, $7 weekends); "convenience stations" with toilets, showers, and a water supply are set up every thousand feet.

The park headquarters is back from the beach a bit between the day-use and beach-camping areas. Next to it is a multi-use camping area with two-way hookups ($10 weekdays, $12 weekends), shade shelters, picnic tables, cooking grills, and hot showers.

As at most state parks, there's a $3 weekdays, $5 weekends admission fee per vehicle per day, $1 for cyclists or pedestrians. For further information, contact the Park Superintendent (tel. 749-5246), P.O. Box 326, Port Aransas, TX 78373.

San José Island

"Saint Joe," as everyone calls the island locally, is just across the Aransas Pass Channel to the north of Port Aransas. The island is privately owned and has no facilities whatsoever except for the North Jetty—perfect for anglers and beachcombers who find even Port Aransas too civilized. Beach camping is permitted at the south end near the jetty but you must bring over all your own food and water by boat or ferry. The only public ferry is from **Woody's Boat Basin** (tel. 512-749-5252), off Cotter St. near the Station St. Pier. There are 10 departures a day between 6:30 a.m. and 6 p.m.; the crossing takes 15 minutes and costs a whopping $7.50 for adults, $4 for children.

Port Aransas Accommodations

Cottages And Motel Courts: The Port Aransas Chamber of Commerce reports 26 different places in this classification. Most are a few blocks off the beach along Station, Alister, Cotter, 9th, 10th, 11th, or Ave. G. The typical cottage (or motel court—more than two or three cottages in a group) has two or three bedrooms with air conditioning, kitchenette, and TV, but little else (no separate living room). They're great values, however; a two-bedroom place averages around $30-35 while a three-bedroom goes for about $40 (not including 12% state and local tax). A complete list is available at the tourist information center (421 W. Cotter; also see "Information" below). A few established cottages/motel courts include: **Anchor Courts** (tel. 749-5340, 403 S. 10th); **Angler's Courts** (tel. 749-5327, 403 N. Alister); **Captain Dan Motel** (tel. 749-6577 S. Station); **Gibbs Cottages** (tel. 749-5452, 400 N. Alister); **Gulf Beach Courts** (tel. 749-5416, 506 E. Ave. G); **Haney's Cottages** (tel. 749-5792, 225 E. Oaks); **Harbor**

View Motel (tel. 749-6391, 111 W. Cotter); King Fish Courts (tel. 749-5527, 1648 E. 11th); Lone Palm Motel (tel. 749-5450, 316 S. Alister); Malibu Motel & Cottages (tel. 749-5531, 803 S. 9th); Marine Courts (tel. 749-5509, 411 N. Alister); Paradise Isle Motel (tel. 749-6993, 330 Cut-Off Rd.); Seahawk Motel (tel. 749-5572, 105 N. Alister); Sunrise Courts (tel. 749-5366, 302 E. Ave. C); and Tropic Island Motel & Apartments (tel. 749-6128, 303 Cut-Off Rd.).

Hotels And Motels: The Tarpon Inn (tel. 512-749-5555) at 200 E. Cotter is the oldest place to stay on Mustang Island and is listed with the National Register of Historic Places. It was first built in 1886 by an assistant lighthouse keeper who used surplus lumber from a Civil War barracks. It burned down in 1900 and was replaced by two inn buildings in 1904; a 1919 hurricane destroyed one of the buildings and damaged the other. The damaged building was repaired and reinforced with pier pilings, set in concrete, that extend from the ground through the attic. Over 7,000 signed fishing scales decorate the lobby walls, including one signed by President Franklin Delano Roosevelt, who stayed here in 1937. All rooms open onto a shaded terrace and have private baths, but none have TVs or telephones (there is a phone in the lobby, however). Rooms are $30-40 October-February, $45-65 March-September.

The Seaside Inn (tel. 512-749-4105) at Sand Castle and 11th has standard rooms for $35-40 s, $40-45 d, $65-75 for suites.

Condominiums: Port Aransas has nearly as many condo developments as motel courts, but they're spread thinly toward the south edge of town and just south of the city limits, off the Gulf

jackrabbit

LOUISE FOOTE

side of Mustang Island Highway. Condo units are more spacious and modern than Port Aransas cottages and common facilities include swimming pools, spas, and tennis courts. Average nightly rates range from as low as $45 for a one-bedroom condo during the winter to $200 for a two-bedroom in the summer (utilities included). Weekly and monthly rates are always available; some condos have a two-night minimum. Some complexes nearly went bankrupt during the state recession of the early '80s and are fighting to keep going—this means you can often negotiate the rates.

The chamber of commerce lists 22 condo developments. Each complex may have up to 100 units or more, so you can usually find a place even in the summer. One of the best run and located is the Aransas Princess (tel. 512-749-5118) on Access Rd. 1A, off the highway close to town. Two-bedroom units here start at $110 in the winter and run to $250 for a three-bedroom penthouse in the summer, a steal. Other possibilities in the same vicinity off Mustang Island Hwy. (with similar or lower rates) include: Gulf Shores Condominiums (tel. 749-6257); The Courtyard (tel. 749-6257); Executive Keys (tel. 749-6272); El Cortes Villas (tel. 749-6206); Mayan Princess (tel. 749-5183); Sandpiper Condominiums (tel. 749-6251); Mustang Towers (tel. 749-6212); and Lost Colony Villas (tel. 749-6314).

RV Parks

Port A has around 20 RV parks sprinkled throughout the town. Facilities at most are limited to three-way hookups; a few have LP gas and most have fish-cleaning shelters. Only one has a pool—Tropic Island Motel & RV Park (tel. 512-749-6128) at 303 Cut-Off. Rates are generally a little lower than elsewhere on the Texas coast: around $8-10 nightly, with weekly rates of $40 and monthly rates of $90-100 (if RVers pay for electricity). Several centrally located places include: Beachway RV (tel. 749-6351, 223 N. Station); Bomarito's RV Park (tel. 749-5447, 312 S. 10th); Buccaneer Courts RV Park (tel. 749-5566, 715 Park 53); Gulf Breeze (tel. 749-5691, 319 Trojan); Island RV Resort (tel. 749-5600, 700 6th); Mayfield Trailer Park (tel. 749-5505, 300 E. Ave. M); Mustang RV Park (tel. 749-5343, 300 E. Cotter); Texsun Cottages/RV (tel. 749-5304, 107 E. Ave. G).

Nueces County Park and Mustang Island State Park also have RV parking facilities (two-ways only)—see separate entries above.

Food

The emphasis in Port A restaurants is naturally on fresh seafood. Business hours can be spotty; in the summer most are open every day, while during the winter they may close down for a day or two each week or even take several weeks off. At the north end of Alister St. near the marina are two waterfront restaurants that are quite popular with tourists: **Tortuga Flats Oyster Bar** (tel. 512-749-5255) and **Quarterdeck** (tel. 749-4449). Both specialize in fresh, locally caught fish and are open daily for lunch and dinner until late. **Yankee Betty's Seafood Galley** (tel. 749-4869) at 417 Alister also serves local fish—baked, broiled, or grilled to order—with an added twist: they'll cook fish you bring in for $3.50 a pound (you have to clean and fillet them first, though). They also have a selection of Gulf fish, shrimp, oysters, and "Alaskan white" on hand for those who don't bring their own, as well as pizza. **Pelican's Landing** (tel. 749-6405) at 437 Cotter is popular among locals as well as tourists. The extensive menu includes steak and beef teriyaki in addition to a complete selection of fresh seafood.

For something different, try the **Crazy Cajun** (tel. 512-749-5069) at Alister St. Square. They've got crawfish (in season), plus delicious seafood gumbo, jambalaya, Dixie beer, and a $12 Cajun seafood platter for two that includes shrimp, crab, and gumbo (half orders are available), all served on butcher paper. They're open Tues.-Sun. from 4 p.m. Another good value is the **Island Cafe & Smokehouse** (tel. 749-6602) at 224 W. Cotter, which serves steak, seafood, and a few Tex-Mex dishes. Open daily for à la carte breakfast, lunch, and dinner, the Island Cafe also has lunch specials Monday-Friday.

Finding a place to eat breakfast can be a problem in Port Aransas. The **Village Bake Shoppe** serves coffee, donuts, pastries, and other baked goods daily except Tues. from 5:30 a.m. to 1:30 p.m. The only other places that seem to be open for breakfast are the Island Cafe (mentioned above) and **Grandma's Kitchen** at 320 N. Alister.

Across from the Village Bake Shoppe is an IGA grocery store that's open daily. You can buy fresh fish and shrimp from the docks off W. Cotter Street.

Entertainment And Events

Tortuga Flats Oyster Bar (tel. 512-749-5255) at the end of Alister on the harbor, has live rock and R&B on weekends, as does **Billy's Place** (tel. 749-5009) at 203 N. Alister. **Bobby Ray's Spring Creek Saloon** (tel. 749-8098) at 503 S. Alister and **Gaff** (tel. 749-5970) at 319 E. Beach feature country and western bands on weekends. During the week, Billy's is reputed to have the best jukebox. **Shorty's** (tel. 749-5966) on Tarpon St., between the Tarpon Inn and the harbor, is the island's oldest watering hole; the dart boards and pool tables attract a mostly local crowd.

Most annual events in Port Aransas are centered around fishing tournaments—the chamber of commerce lists five in June, five in July, three in August, and two in October. The oldest and biggest is the **Deep-Sea Roundup**, held the first full week of July. It's the state's oldest fishing competition, having begun as the "Tarpon Roundup" in 1932.

Recreation

Fishing: This is what most people come to Port A for. Depending on the time of year, bay and pier anglers may hook redfish, flounder, speckled trout, or black drum, while surf casters can pull in these same species plus sand shark, pompano, croaker, and mackerel. The more challenging sport fish are found in offshore Gulf waters, including the popular kingfish, red snapper, amberjack, barracuda, yellowfin and blackfin tuna, bonito, jackfish, ling, blue and white marlin, sailfish, wahoo, and several varieties of shark.

Popular onshore fishing spots include the **North Jetty** at the entrance to the Aransas Pass Channel (free), **Horace Caldwell Pier** at Nueces County Park (lighted, open 24 hours, $1.50 fee), **J.P. Luby Pier** at Point Park across from the municipal marina (free), **Ancel Brundrett Pier** (also called Station St. Pier) at the north end of Station St. (free), and the **Nueces County Pier** at the end of Port St. across from Harbor Island (free).

Party and charter boats for offshore bay and deep-sea fishing trips are docked at the harbor area along W. Cotter. Half-day party-boat trips start at around $17 per person for bay fishing, $25 for Gulf trips. Longer trips—six to 12 hours—are charter only and cost up to $300 for one to six persons. Rates always include bait and tackle, but not food and beverages. One of the larger operations, **Dolphin Docks** (tel. 512-749-6624), also offers 40-hour "snapper safaris." Other Cotter St. operations include **Fisherman's Wharf**

surfers, Port Aransas

(tel. 749-5448), **Deep Sea Headquarters** (tel. 749-5597), and **Woody's** (tel. 749-5271). An association of local fishing guides, **Port Aransas Boatmen** (tel. 749-6339), has its own dock at the municipal marina (east of the ferry landing) where custom fishing trips can be arranged.

Boating: For sailboat or powerboat charters, go to the **Island Moorings Marina** (tel. 512-749-4983) south of town off State 361, near the airfield. Both crewed and bareboat charters are available.

Surfing: Surfing is allowed anywhere along Mustang Island's Gulf shore except within 300 feet of Horace Caldwell Pier. The best surf action is usually near the jetties on either side of the channel (the South Jetty on the Mustang side, or the North Jetty on the San José Island side). The beach off Ave. G is also decent in the winter. Tropical depressions coupled with hard south winds mean big surf anytime of year. Beach shops in Port A rent surfboards and boogie boards.

Horseback Riding
Mustang Riding Stables (tel. 512-749-5055) rents horses for $15 an hour for beach riding. The stables are located on the Gulf side of Mustang Island Hwy. just north of Mustang Island State Park (about 12 miles south of Port Aransas).

Information
The **Port Aransas Chamber of Commerce** (tel. 512-749-5919, or 800-452-6278) at 421 W. Cotter distributes free information on Port A ac-

commodations and recreation. The office is open Mon.-Sat. 9-5.

The daily *Port Aransas South Jetty* newspaper covers local events that aren't usually of interest to the casual visitor, but the publishers also produce a semi-annual *Port Aransas/Mustang Island Visitors' Guide* (free) that's packed with information, including extensive tips on local fishing.

ROCKPORT-FULTON

These two adjacent towns on Aransas Bay, with a combined population of around 6,000, are protected from Gulf tempests by San José Island. Rockport is the older of the two, having been founded in 1867 by New York's Morgan Steamship Co. as a transshipment point for cattle products destined for the eastern United States. Fulton developed next to it as a cattle-processing town. Both towns almost died with the 1880s arrival of Texas railroads, which established faster and less expensive means of overland transport. But the area was too scenic and the fishing too good for people to abandon it completely, and Rockport-Fulton eventually evolved into a sportfishing and resort center.

Today Rockport-Fulton is mostly residential, with small beach homes mingling with windswept live oaks. It's also something of an art center and claims the highest per-capita concentration of artists in the state.

Sights

The recently opened **Texas Maritime Museum** (tel. 512-729-1271) is at Rockport Harbor next to the Rockport Art Center. Museum displays provide an overview of Texas maritime history through a variety of photographic and hands-on exhibits. Souvenirs and books on the Texas coast are available in the gift shop. The museum is open Wed.-Sat. 10-4, Sun. 1-4; admission is $2.50 adults, $1 children 4-12.

The **Fulton Mansion State Historical Structure** (tel. 512-729-0386), on Fulton Beach Rd. at Henderson in Fulton, was built in the 1870s by cattle baron George Fulton. The three-story, French Second Empire house was considered state-of-the-art architecture in its time, since it was equipped with a water-cooled larder, central heat, shellcrete (crushed-shell concrete) insulation, gas lights, and flush toilets. To withstand hurricane-force gales, the upper walls were built of one- by five-inch pinewood planks, stacked horizontally and spiked together. Rooms are trimmed in walnut and cypress paneling, with English-tile floors in the halls and dining room. The Texas Parks and Wildlife Dept. has restored the mansion and furnished it in period style. Guided tours are given every half-hour Wed.-Sun. 9-noon and 1-4. Admission is $3 adults, $1.50 for children 6-12.

To see some of the art that Rockport's known for, visit the **Rockport Art Center** (tel. 512-729-5519) on Broadway at Rockport Harbor. Housed in the 19th-century Bruhl-O'Connor home, it features four galleries with rotating exhibits and three art studios. Art classes are open to public enrollment. The galleries are open Tues.-Sat. 10-5, Sun. 2-5; admission is free.

Rockport Beach Park

This manmade beach park is on a small peninsula extending from Rockport Harbor. The beach itself is about a mile and a quarter long and includes a bay swimming area as well as a saltwater pool. One end of the beach side of the peninsula is reserved for water-skiing, another for sailboats. The opposite side has a Jet Ski area, boat-launch ramps, and a paddleboat area (equipment is available for rent in the park). Other facilities include an 800-foot lighted fishing pier, two small islands with bird sanctuaries, an observation tower, picnic cabanas, and a park store with refreshments and beach supplies. Although the park is

open year-round, lifeguards are on duty only Memorial Day through Labor Day. The rest of the year it's "swim-at-your-own-risk"; the park store and equipment rentals are also closed then. Park hours are daily 5 a.m.-11 p.m. Admission is free but there's a nominal parking fee for vehicles.

Rockport-Fulton Accommodations

Cottages And Motel Courts: Like Port Aransas, much of the accommodation here is in the form of inexpensive cottages and motel courts. An added advantage is that many of the Rockport motels and cottages have their own private piers (however rickety) over Aransas Bay. Rates run a little higher than in Port A: around $35-45 a night for a basic two-bedroom cottage with kitchenette, $45-55 for a three-bedroom. In Rockport are: **Anchor Motel** (tel. 512-729-6262, 1114 E. Market); **Balboa Courts** (tel. 729-2517, 1408 Church); **Bayfront Cottages** (tel. 729-6693, next to Fulton Mansion); **Days Inn** (tel. 729-6379, 1212 Laurel); **Holiday Lodge Motel** (tel. 729-3433, 1406 Raht); **Hunt's Courts** (tel. 729-2273, 901 S. Water); **Rockporter Inn** (tel. 729-9591, 813 S. Church); **Surf Court Motel** (tel. 729-3249, 1204 Market); and **Surfside Motel** (tel. 729-2348, 1809 Broadway).

Houses And Condominiums: Condos are springing up like toadstools in Rockport. One of the more interesting developments is **Key Allegro Island,** a complex of streets and canals opposite Rockport Harbor. Virtually every unit is situated either on a canal or on Aransas Bay. Many are privately owned and available only when the owners aren't in town (which is most of the year for many owners). **Key Allegro Condos & Home Rental** (tel. 512-729-2772) at 1809 Bayshore handles rentals on the island. Rates range from $65 a night for a one-bedroom unit with kitchen and living room in the winter (Sept. 10 to May 15) to $85 a night for a two-bedroom unit with kitchen and living room in the summer (May 16 to Sept. 9). Weekly rates run $455-745, monthly $610-1035. For the names of other condo developments in the area, contact the Rockport-Fulton Chamber of Commerce (tel. 729-9952) at 404 Broadway.

RV Parks: Rockport has several RV parks within the city limits. All run about $8-10 a day for a three-way hookup, $40-50 weekly, $90-100 monthly. A few that are convenient to the harbor and Rockport Beach include: **Taylor Oak RV &**

Trailer Park (tel. 512-729-5187, 707 S. Pearl); **The Quiet One Travel Trailer Park** (tel. 729-2668, 500 W. James); **Woody Acres RV Park** (tel. 729-5636, off State 35 N at Mesquite); **Anderson Trailer & RV Park** (tel. 729-9651, FM 1781 at FM 2165); and **Trailer Inn By The Bay** (tel. 729-5608, State 35 and Fulton Beach Rd.).

Food

The Rockport-Fulton area has a nice variety of restaurants and cafes to choose from. Right in downtown Rockport is the **Austin St. Pub & Eatery** (tel. 512-729-4050), at 415 S. Austin, which offers a reasonably priced selection of sandwiches, chicken-fried steak, seafood, fajitas (beef, chicken, and shrimp), and daily specials like taco salad, meatloaf, and lasagna, plus homemade pies. It's open for lunch Mon.-Sat., for dinner Mon., Tues., and Thurs.-Saturday. **The Boiling Pot** (tel. 729-6972) on Fulton Beach Rd. specializes in Cajun-style blue crab, crawfish (in season), shrimp, and gumbo, and is open Mon.-Thurs. for dinner, Fri.-Sun. for lunch and dinner.

In spite of the name, seafood is the specialty at the **Duck Inn** (tel. 512-729-6663) at 705 Broadway; open daily for lunch and dinner. The only seafood place in town that overlooks the water is the **Sandollar Pavillion** (tel. 729-9589) at Fulton Beach Rd.; open daily 7 a.m.-10 p.m. If you're hankering for some barbecue, there's **Max's BBQ** (tel. 729-9388) at 815 E. Market; open Mon.-Sat. for lunch and dinner. For coffee-and-pastry breakfast, **Rockport Bakery** (tel. 729-5044) at State 35 N and Broadway is a good choice; open Mon.-Sat. 7-5.

Events

March: The **Fulton Oysterfest** is held the first weekend of the month at Fulton Park, Fulton Beach Road. The two-day festival features a raw oyster-eating contest, oyster-shucking contest, seafood vendors, and outdoor concerts.

July: Sponsored by the Rockport Art Association, the **Rockport Art Festival** is held the nearest weekend to the 4th of July at the festival grounds near the Rockport Art Center. A tent village displays paintings, sculpture, woodwork, pottery, and other artwork by Rockport-Fulton artists as well as by other artists from throughout the Southwest. Most work is for sale.

October: The **Rockport Seafair,** held on the weekend preceding Columbus Day at the Rockport Harbor, features sailing regattas, arts and crafts shows, crab races, a gumbo cook-off, beauty pageant, parades, music, and lots of seafood booths.

Fishing

Sportfishing in the Rockport-Fulton area is not quite as serious an undertaking as in Port Aransas, but plenty of fishing opportunities are available. In Rockport, many motels have their own private fishing piers (ask if you're in doubt).

One of the best public spots in the area is the **Copano Bay Causeway State Park Fishing Pier,** a 2.5-mile-long abandoned bridge that's been converted to a pier (a section in the middle is missing, so there's actually only about 1.5 pier miles). It's parallel to the Copano Bay Causeway (which joins the Rockport-Fulton Peninsula with the Lamar Peninsula to the north) and allows anglers to dangle their lines into the intersection of Copano and Aransas bays. At either end of the pier is a bait and tackle shop, snack bar, and restrooms. There's an entry fee of $1 per rod and reel.

You can also fish from the public pier (free) at Fulton Navigation Harbor or join a party or charter boat from the same harbor for trips out into one of the bays ($16-25 for a half-day trip).

Another good fishing spot is the pier at Goose Island State Recreation Area (see below).

Goose Island State Recreation Area

This 314-acre park is at the southernmost tip of the Lamar Peninsula, at the junction of the Aransas, Copano, and St. Charles bays, about 12 miles northeast of Rockport via the Copano Bay Causeway. The 174-acre mainland section of the park consists of live oak and redbay woodlands, coastal prairies, and wet inland meadows. Goose Island, just offshore, is 140 acres of tidal saltmarsh, salt flats, and grasslands. This is one of the Lower Coast's prime spots for viewing waterfowl, including great blue and Louisiana herons, common and snow egrets, killdeer, sandpipers, willets, terns, blue-winged teals, and many other species.

Facilities: The park has a 1,620-foot-long lighted fishing pier, boat launch, picnic areas, nature trails, bathhouses, and camping areas. Open shade shelters along the south shore of Goose Island, equipped with w/e, picnic tables, and cooking grills, cost $9 a night on weekdays, $11 weekends. In the mainland park unit, in wooded areas, are tentsites with water nearby for $6/8 and tent/camper sites with w/e for $9/11. The entry fee for day use only is $3 per vehicle, $1 for cyclists and pedestrians. For further information, contact the Park Superintendent (tel. 512-729-2858), Goose Island State Recreation Area, Star Route 1, Box 105, Rockport, TX 78382.

The Big Tree: Also known as the Lamar Oak, Bishop's Oak, and Goose Island Oak, this state-champion live oak grows just north of the park (take Palmetto Rd. north off Park 13 and follow the signs). Over a thousand years old, the tree is thought to have been used as a council tree by the Karankawa Indians and later as a hanging tree around the turn of the century. Its venerable trunk measures 35 feet in circumference, the total height is 44 feet, and the crown has a spread of 89 feet.

Rockport-Fulton Information

The **Rockport-Fulton Area Chamber of Commerce** (tel. 512-729-6445, 800-826-6441), next to Rockport Harbor off Broadway, is open Mon.-Fri. 9-5, Sat. 9-1. They sell an excellent map of the area for $1 that includes a nautical map of Aransas and Copano bays. For birders, another worthwhile $1 investment at the chamber is the *Birder's Guide to Rockport-Fulton,* a full-color booklet that features a driving guide to the area, bird sketches for identification, a bird checklist, and a comprehensive list of birding references and local resources. Also available for $1 is the 20-page *Fishing Guide to Rockport-Fulton,* which contains names of local fishing guides, tide tables, and pier and marina locations.

Twice a year the daily *Rockport Pilot* newspaper issues a *Visitor's Guide* supplement that contains comprehensive information on attractions, accommodations, fishing, and dining in Rockport-Fulton (available free at the chamber of commerce).

ARANSAS NATIONAL WILDLIFE REFUGE

This is one of the crown jewels of the U.S. national wildlife refuge system. Founded in 1937 by President Franklin Delano Roosevelt as a refuge for the dwindling whooping crane population, it now protects over a dozen other endangered species as well, including the brown pelican, least tern, Attwater's prairie chicken, the bald eagle, peregrine and aplomado falcons, the Eskimo curlew, gray wolf, red wolf, jaguarundi, and coati.

Geography

The refuge covers 54,829 acres of the Blackjack Peninsula (named for the native blackjack oak), which is surrounded by the Aransas, San Antonio, and Mesquite bays. Habitats encompassed by the refuge include wooded sand dunes, brushland, live oak and redbay oak motts, cord grass prairies, tidal marshes, freshwater ponds, and marine bays.

Whooping Cranes

This is the refuge's most famous seasonal resident. The largest bird in North America, an adult whooper stands five feet tall with a 7 1/2-foot wingspread. Its name comes from the loud whooping call produced by its long, convoluted windpipe (John James Audubon, the Audubon Society's namesake, claimed he could hear a whooper's call from three miles away). Its mating ritual is equally impressive, consisting of whooping, wing-flapping, head-bobbing, and huge leaps through the air. The birds mate for life and migrate in family groups of two to seven.

Whooping cranes were once prolific in North American skies, but hunting and human-induced habitat loss meant that by 1938 only 10 adult whoopers and four youths were left on the entire continent. Through the dual efforts of U.S. and Canadian wildlife authorities (the bird's summer home is Woods Buffalo National Park in Alberta, Canada), Aransas whooper sightings in 1989 reached a record 146, a tenfold increase since the refuge was established.

Whooping cranes inhabit the refuge between November and March, after completing the 2,500-mile, 30-day journey from Canada. They can sometimes be seen at Mustang Lake from the observation tower (equipped with telescopes), about 4.5 miles from the refuge entrance, or you might glimpse a few flying overhead elsewhere in the park. Visitors often mistake other birds for the whooper, including sandhill cranes, snow geese, white pelicans, swans, and assorted herons. When these birds are standing in the water at some distance, the lighter-feathered species can be very difficult to tell apart. In flight, however, the whooper is easily distinguished by its black wing tips, long, straight neck, slow wing beat, and, most significantly, by the fact that it's feet extend well

whooping crane

BOB RACE

beyond the tail (the sandhill crane also has feet that extend beyond its tail, but lacks black wing tips and often flies alone or in larger flocks, rather than in the two-to-seven group).

The best way to see whooping cranes (as well as other waterfowl) during this time of year is to sign up with one of the several tour boats that cruise from Rockport-Fulton across Aransas Bay to San Antonio Bay along the refuge shores. **Captain Ted's Whooping Crane Tours** (tel. 512-729-9589 or 800-338-4551) is the oldest operation and they guarantee whooper (and other wildlife) sightings or your money back. Captain Ted's M.V. *Skimmer* is docked next to the Sandollar Pavilion in Fulton and does two trips daily, 7:45-noon and 12:45-4:30. The cost is $25 per adult, $15 per child under 12. (The Sandollar Pavilion is open for breakfast at 7 a.m. for those who choose the early tour.)

Other Wildlife

Birds: Aransas NWR attracts over 350 known bird species simply because its mild winters and tidal marshes produce an abundant, varied supply of food (vegetation, insects, fish, and shellfish) and water. Besides the magnificent whooping crane, the refuge is a temporary or permanent home for a variety of loons, grebes, pelicans, cormorants, frigate birds, bitterns, herons, ibises, spoonbills, storks, ducks, swans, geese, vultures, kites, hawks, falcons, the crested caracara (Mexico's national bird), wild turkey, plovers, sandpipers, gulls, terns, skimmers, doves, owls, goatsuckers, hummingbirds, woodpeckers, flycatchers, larks, swallows, jays, titmice, wrens, vireos, thrushes, thrashers, warblers, tanagers, sparrows, blackbirds, finches, and many other related species. A complete bird list is available at the refuge visitor center.

During the late spring, summer, and early fall, tour boats (see "Whooping Cranes" above) take visitors on tours of various rookeries (bird colonies) along Aransas and Mesquite bay shores, including Blackjack Peninsula, San José ("St. Joe") Island, Matagorda Island, and a number of smaller islands. Times and rates are the same as for the whooping crane tours.

Mammals: Among the 80 mammalian species found in the refuge, the largest are white-tailed deer, feral hogs (descendants of domesticated American hogs and European wild boar introduced to the area in the '30s and '40s), javelinas, the occasional axis deer (who wander in from nearby game ranches), coyotes, red wolves (usually part coyote rather than purebred), and gray fox. Smaller mammals include ringtails, raccoons, coatis (rare), mink, long-tailed weasels, badgers, bobcats, cougars, three species of skunk, five species of bat, armadillos, blacktail rabbits, cotton-tailed rabbits, swamp rabbits, and opossums. Atlantic bottlenose dolphins are also common in the surrounding Aransas, Mesquite, and San Antonio bays.

Reptiles: The most popular reptile in the refuge (among visitors) is the American alligator, which is commonly seen in the lakes, sloughs, rivers, and marshes of the refuge (there are usually several loafing in Thomas Slough near the visitor center). Annual counts indicate there are about 250 gators living in the refuge, most in the four- to 10-foot-long range, with several individuals reaching 12-13 feet long. (You can estimate a gator's length even if all you can see above water are its eyes and nostrils. Gauge the distance in inches between its eyes and nostrils, then transpose inches to feet and you'll know its approximate length.) When provoked, gators make a hissing sound. During mating season bull gators utter a loud roar and females reply with a groaning sound; baby gators make amusing burping and chirping sounds.

Though you're not very likely to see them, the refuge harbors at least 31 species of snakes. Six are venomous: the Texas coral snake, broad-banded copperhead, western cottonmouth, western massasauga, western pygmy rattlesnake, and western diamondback rattlesnake. Take care when walking in grassy areas.

Most of the sea turtles that turn up on the refuge shores are dead, having been killed by Gulf fishing nets. The hawksbill sea turtle visits occasionally (alive) and there are five other turtle species found in the marshes and freshwater ponds farther inland.

Facilities
The Wildlife Interpretive Center near the refuge entrance is open daily 8-4:30 and features a variety of displays, including taxidermic exhibits and an audio-visual program about the whooping crane. A 16-mile paved road makes a loop through the refuge and passes six different trailheads for nature trails of 0.2 to two miles in length. An observation tower overlooks Mustang Lake at the loop's 4.5-mile mark.

If you have a boat and want to navigate San Antonio Bay along the refuge shores on your own, you can use the private boat ramp (for a fee) at Harper's Landing, about two miles from the refuge entrance off FM 2040.

Practicalities: No camping is allowed in the refuge, but there's a picnic area near the Bay

Overlook, about two miles from the entrance. No food or gas are available at the refuge; the nearest service stations are in Austwell (seven miles) and Tivoli (14 miles). Insect repellent is recommended year-round for hikers

Visiting hours are sunrise to sunset; admission is $2 per vehicle.

Getting There
From the Rockport-Fulton area, take State 35 north to FM 774, then zigzag east on FM 774 (watch the curves—they're only slightly banked) to FM 2040, which leads southeast to the refuge entrance. Driving time from Rockport is 40-50 minutes. No public transport is available.

For further information, contact the refuge manager (tel. 512-286-3559), Aransas National Wildlife Refuge, P.O. Box 100, Austwell, TX 77950.

PADRE ISLAND NATIONAL SEASHORE

Padre Island is the longest coastal-barrier island in the world, 113 miles from Corpus Christi Pass (which once separated it from Mustang Island to the north) to Mansfield Channel (which separates it from South Padre Island to the south). Eighty miles of its length are under the protection of the National Park Service; the remaining portions (North Padre) belong to Corpus Christi or Nueces County.

shrimp trawler

Geography

The Island: The entire length of the Gulf side of Padre Island is sandy beach—one of the longest undeveloped beaches in North America. The beach is backed by a coastal dune ridge, held in place by salt-tolerant vegetation. On the Laguna Madre side of the dunes is a section of coastal grasslands that vary in width; in some places, the dunes extend all the way across the island. In other places, the land behind the dune ridge is submerged by washover channels. Beyond the grasslands, marshy tidal flats extend from the island's east edge into Laguna Madre.

Laguna Madre: Separating Padre Island from the mainland, this shallow, salty body of water covers an area of 609 square miles; the national seashore boundary runs well into the lagoon, protecting around 20,000 surface acres. The average natural depth is about 2 1/2 to three feet (in some places it's only a few inches deep). The Gulf Intracoastal Waterway at the lagoon's midline, however, reaches a depth of 14 feet, with a width of around 225 feet. The waterway was constructed in 1949 and forms a 1,116-mile link between Brownsville, Texas, and St. Marks, Florida. The sand and silt ("spoil") that were dredged during construction of the waterway have been allowed to form islands called "spoil banks" that have since taken on local vegetation; some have even become bird nesting grounds.

No major rivers flow into Laguna Madre, so salinity is quite high. Tides are largely wind-controlled. Because of the lack of riverine (and Gulf) interference and the absence of human population centers, the middle and lower sections of the lagoon, between Baffin Bay and Port Mansfield, are virtually free of pollution.

Wildlife

Fish, Mollusks, and Crustaceans: The aquatic interplay of lagoon, tidal flats, washover channels, and Gulf waters produces a perfect environment for the spawning, foraging, and nursing of fish and shellfish species. Many local species spawn in one area, nurse in another, and forage in yet another, participating in a cycle that wouldn't be viable anywhere else. Redfish, for example, spawn in the Gulf but spend most of their lives in Laguna Madre; young shrimp nurse in the Laguna but move to the Gulf as adults.

Fishing, within state legal limits, is permitted in the park. On the lagoon side, flounder, sheeps-

---

JELLYFISH

Seven species of jellyfish are commonly seen near Padre Island shores. Only two carry a sting powerful enough to bother humans. The Portuguese man-of-war *(Physalia physalia)* is a pretty, translucent blue blob with see-through tentacles up to 40 feet long; the tentacles are loaded with a venom that can cause a severe stinging sensation upon contact, even when the man-of-war is shriveling on the beach. (The venom is actually 75% as strong as cobra venom, but humans rarely receive a high-enough dose to cause serious injury or death.) The man-of-war is a hydrozoan, meaning it doesn't move laterally under its own power but merely drifts with sea currents (it can move vertically by regulating internal gases, however), so if you see one in the water, don't assume it's coming for you! They can turn up anytime of year but are most common in the spring when Gulf currents are changing directions.

The other one to avoid is the sea nettle *(Chrysaora quinquecirrha)*, a bell-shaped creature with long tentacles around the bell's edge and four very long oral arms extending from the center underside of the bell. The tentacles vary in color from clear to pink to rust-brown. They're most commonly encountered in Laguna Madre during the summer.

The park staff at Malaquite Beach Visitor Center and at the ranger station (a mile north of Malaquite Beach) are adept at treating jellyfish stings. If you plan to be in a remote part of the park, especially in the spring, bring along a supply of unseasoned meat tenderizer (make sure it contains papain, an enzyme derived from papaya). To treat a sting, rub the affected area with alcohol, then make a paste of tenderizer and alcohol and rub it gently into the area. Papain neutralizes the proteins in jellyfish venom almost immediately on application, bringing welcome relief.

Not all jellyfish that end up at Padre Island are bothersome. One intriguing hydrozoan, the by-the-wind sailor *(Velella velella)*, looks like a Frisbee with a miniature sail on top. The plastic-like disk floats on the water surface and the little sail helps to speed it on its way. Different polyps along the edge of the disk specialize in reproduction, feeding, and stinging (not humans). Look for them in spring when they get blown onto the beach (usually minus their polyps).

---

head, black drum, redfish, skipjack, striped mullet, and speckled trout are common; on the Gulf side are sand trout, pompano, mackerel, tarpon, and, farther offshore, grouper, bonito, kingfish, red snapper, marlin, and sailfish.

A variety of oysters and crabs make their home among the island's intertidal zones. Crabs are especially plentiful; over 20 species are commonly seen, including the blue crab, the hermit crab, and a type of sand crab called "ghost shrimp" for its resemblance to shrimp.

Mammals: The most common mammals on Padre Island are rodents—squirrels, gophers, and moles—including one species that evolved here, the Padre Island kangaroo rat. Black-tailed jack rabbits, raccoons, and coyotes are also common. White-tailed deer, javelina, and nilgai (an African antelope introduced to nearby game ranches) occasionally visit from the mainland, wading across tidal flats. Three species of dolphin frequent nearby waters: the Atlantic bottlenose dolphin, the Atlantic spotted dolphin, and the bridled dolphin.

Reptiles: Five sea turtle species occasionally turn up on Padre beaches: Kemp's ridley, loggerhead, hawksbill, Atlantic green, and leatherback. All five have threatened or endangered status, the most endangered being the Kemp's ridley. In 1947, its numbers were estimated at 162,000; now there are fewer than 2,000 adults left in the world. Their main hatching ground is a 16-mile beach at Rancho Nuevo, Tamaulipas, Mexico; international efforts are underway to induce younger turtles to use Padre Island for nesting, since the Mexican market for sea turtle eggs, meat, skin, and shells makes protection at Rancho Nuevo very difficult. (In the U.S., taking any sea turtle into possession is a felony punishable by fines up to $20,000.)

Approximately 32 species of snake are known to inhabit the island; the most commonly seen are the western coachwhip, Mexican milk snake, Gulf coast ribbon snake, and checkered garter snake—all of which are harmless to humans. Two venomous species, the western diamondback and the western massasauga, have been sighted but are considered "uncommon."

Facilities
Malaquite Visitor Center: About a mile past the national seashore entrance is **Malaquite Beach,** the only beach area on the island with lifeguards on duty (summer only). Swimming is permitted anywhere along the Gulf shoreline, however. Next to the beach is the recently reconstructed visitor center, comprised of an interpretive center, observation deck, snack bar, gift shop, and bathhouse. The interpretive center has several books, brochures, and handouts on Padre Island attractions and activities. Most are distributed free, but one that's worth purchasing is *Padre Island National Seashore: A Guide to the Geology, Natural Environments, and History of a Texas Barrier Island,* published by the University of Texas. The staff is also quite knowledgeable. The visitors center is open 9-6 during the summer, 9-4 the rest of the year.

Camping: A paved campground is situated a half mile north of Malaquite Beach and provides a freshwater supply, cold showers, restrooms, picnic tables, and a dump station. No RV hookups are available. Cooking grills aren't provided, but campfires are allowed anywhere on the beach between the dunes and the water (this policy is the same for the entire island, except that no fires are allowed on Malaquite Beach). Camping fees are $5 a night ($2.50 for seniors). During the summer, park rangers present campfire programs at Malaquite Campground every evening; during the winter (Jan.-May), the programs are

dunes, Padre Island National Seashore

held on Friday and Saturday nights only. Rangers also lead seashore walks on weekends. A schedule of topics is available at the center.

At **Bird Island Basin,** opposite Malaquite Beach on the Laguna Madre side of the island, is a no-fee primitive camping area suitable for tents or campers; chemical toilets are provided. Farther south at **Yarborough Pass** (milepost 15), also on the Laguna Madre side, is another no-fee primitive camping area with chemical toilets (this one also has tables); to reach the area, however, you must hike or drive a four-wheel-drive vehicle.

No-fee primitive camping is also permitted anywhere on the Gulf side of the island. Camping is allowed on the beaches only, not on the dunes or in the grasslands.

Beach Driving

The paved road into the park ends just after the visitor center. Beyond this point, driving is permitted on the beach only. For the first five miles, beach conditions are usually suitable for any kind of vehicle; after that, a four-wheel-drive or other off-road vehicle is necessary because the sand becomes too loose and full of shells. Four-wheel-drive vehicles are available for rent in Corpus Christi for around $75 for 24 hours (try Advantage Car Rental, tel. 512-289-5364, at Corpus Christi International Airport).

Even with a powerful four-by-four, careful preparation is necessary if you want to proceed beyond milepost 5 and make it back in one piece. The National Park Service recommends that drivers carry extra fuel, extra water, a car jack, a basic tool kit, a long-handled shovel, a tow rope, and a few loose boards to use for traction if your vehicle gets stuck. To this list, add extra food, a tent, and a flashlight with extra batteries if you plan to camp overnight.

Just past milepost 5 is Little Shell Beach, named for the shell types commonly found here —mostly coquina clams. The shells pile up to one side of the beach to form shell banks. The trick in driving through here and across the next stretch (Big Shell Beach) is finding the right driving line between the deepest shell banks on the right and the softest sand on the left—it's very easy to get bogged down in either. Follow other vehicle tracks when they're visible. Big Shell Beach has coarse sand mixed with shells that make it even more difficult to navigate without getting stuck.

After 10-15 miles, Big Shell Beach gives way to conditions similar to Little Shell Beach again, which continue to the island's end at Mansfield Channel—a distance of about 60 miles from the Malaquite Beach Visitor Center.

Backpacking

Only the very hardy should attempt to hike the seashore's entire length. No fresh water and no shade are available along the way. Hiking is only allowed on the beach, and progress is slow (10 miles a day maximum, which means six days to reach Mansfield Channel). A more reasonable goal might be to hike to Yarborough Pass at milepost 15 (where there's a primitive campsite with toilets), or to Cuba Island (a small offshore island on the Laguna Madre side) at milepost 21. Backpacking prerequisites for Padre Island include plenty of sunscreen, insect repellent, a broad-brimmed hat, sunglasses, a backpacking stove, a tent, food, and at least a gallon of water per person per day. A rod and reel might make a handy addition, too—you can catch sand crabs to use as bait along the way. The most popular backpacking season on the island is winter, since the weather's cooler.

Boating And Windsurfing

The park has one boat launch at Bird Island Basin on Laguna Madre. This is also a popular spot for dedicated windsurfers looking to avoid the crowds in Corpus Christi.

Entry Fee

Admission into Padre Island National Seashore is $3 per vehicle or $1 per person (for pedestrians) for a seven-day pass.

Information

For further information, contact the Park Superintendent (tel. 512-937-2621), Padre Island National Seashore, 9405 S. Padre Island Dr., Corpus Christi, TX 78418.

SOUTH PADRE ISLAND AND PORT ISABEL

If the Mansfield Channel hadn't been constructed in 1964, South Padre Island would still be attached to Padre Island. It has all the same geographic features as its progenitor, but since it's not part of the national seashore, it has all the amenities of a modern beach resort. Although we've placed it under "Vicinity of Corpus Christi" for convenience, South Padre is over 150 miles by road from Corpus and might best be combined with a visit to Brownsville in the Rio Grande Valley.

Port Isabel is just across Laguna Madre from South Padre. Linked by a causeway, the two communities function together as a sort of twin-tourist destination—Port Isabel provides history (and a casino cruise ship) while South Padre has the beaches.

History
In the 16th and 17th centuries, Spanish colonists called what is now Padre (and South Padre) Island a variety of names, including Isla Santiago, Isla Corpus Christi, and Islas Blancas. They largely ignored the island, however, since it had a bad reputation among ship captains (at least 20 Spanish galleons ran aground here in the 16th century) and was also an area frequented by pirates who raided Spanish ships. In 1800, Catholic priest Padre Nicolas Balli applied for and received a Spanish land grant to establish Rancho Santa Cruz about 26 miles from the island's southern end. He raised cattle, sheep, and horses here until his death in 1829, and the island was afterward renamed to honor him.

The island remained abandoned until John Singer, of sewing machine fame, and his wife built a driftwood home on the site of Balli's ranch in 1847. When the Civil War broke out, they buried $62,000 in jewelry and gold coins among the sand dunes and fled. When they returned after the war to retrieve their treasure trove, the dunes had shifted; they never found it and the loot remains undiscovered to this day.

Throughout the remainder of the 1800s and most of the 1900s, Padre Island remained virtually untouched. The nearest mainland point, Port Isabel (originally named El Fronton de Santa Isabela by Mexican settlers in the 1830s), became an important transshipment port during the mid-1800s, but with the arrival of the railroads in South Texas, it quickly declined into a small fishing port. The only access to Padre Island was by boat until a causeway was built from Port Isabel in 1954. In 1964, South Padre was lopped from Padre Island 34 miles from the southern end to form the Mansfield Channel (also called the Mansfield Cut). By this time, South Padre was

beginning to attract a small contingent of avid anglers and nature-lovers, but there were few facilities available for long-term stays. The hotel-motel industry wasn't anxious to build on the island because very few insurance companies would insure property in the hurricane zone.

Things changed in the '70s when a state law was passed that required insurance companies to provide hurricane coverage. Motels and condominiums began appearing one by one, and a 2.6-mile, four-lane bridge (the Queen Isabella Causeway, the state's longest) was built to replace the earlier span. Today, only the southernmost five miles or so of the island are developed. Padre Blvd. (Park 100) runs up the center of the island another 10 miles; beyond this, the northern 20 miles remain completely undeveloped.

Sights—Port Isabel
Point Isabel Lighthouse State Historic Structure: This Parks and Wildlife-administered lighthouse at the intersection of State 100 and Taravana (at the causeway) is the only one of 16 such structures along the Texas coast that's open to the public. Because Port Isabel had become an important port for vessels coming through the Brazos Santiago Pass (which links the Gulf of Mexico and Laguna Madre between South Padre Island and Brazos Island to the south), the U.S. government funded the construction of the lighthouse in 1851-53. It was originally crowned with a light that could be seen 16 miles away. During the Civil War, the beacon was extinguished and both the Confederate and Union troops used it as an observation tower. After the war, it was relit and continued to operate as a lighthouse intermittently until 1905 when it was abandoned.

The State Parks and Wildlife Dept. acquired the structure in 1950 and had it restored by 1970, when it was opened to the public. Although the current mercury-vapor light is not as powerful as the original beacon, the tower is still marked on nautical charts as a navigation aid.

At the top of the 53-foot-high lighthouse is a rewarding view of Port Isabel, South Padre Island, Laguna Madre, and the Gulf. It's open daily 10-5; admission is $1 adults, 50 cents children 6-12.

The *Lady Bea* Shrimp Boat: Near the lighthouse in Beulah Lee Park, this restored trawler provides a close-up look at the outriggers, nets, and winches that are used in the shrimping industry. It's open 24 hours a day and is a first phase in the Laguna Madre Museum Foundation's effort to establish a permanent maritime museum in the park. When the museum facility is complete, it will contain photos, artifacts, and memorabilia related to local history, plus a souvenir shop. Free admission.

Sights—South Padre Island
Pan American University Coastal Studies Laboratory: This university research facility, located in Isla Blanca Park at the south end of the island, focuses on the coastal ecosystems of South Texas and North Mexico, particularly the marine biology of Laguna Madre and the Gulf. It's also an important participant in the Texas Marine Mammal and Sea Turtle Stranding and Salvaging Network, which works to save marine mammals (whales and dolphins) and sea turtles that become stranded along the coast. A public education area features aquarium exhibits and displays of local flora. Open Sun.-Fri. 1:30-4:30; admission to the lab is free, but Isla Blanca Park charges a $1.50 vehicle fee. For further information, call (512) 761-2644.

Isla Blanca Park: In spite of the fact that the northernmost 20 miles of South Padre offer acre after acre of virtually deserted beaches, this park at the southern tip of the island has the most popular beach. That's because it's the only beach on the island with a bathhouse, food concession, equipment rental, and other beach-going amenities, as well as a marina, campground, RV park, fishing jetty, cabins, a shaded pavilion, and various civic facilities. (See "Campgrounds And RV Parks" below for camping/RV/cabin rates.) Admission to the park is $1.50 per vehicle per day.

Sea Turtles, Inc. ("The Turtle Lady"): Ila Loetscher, known as "The Turtle Lady," is the founder of a nonprofit organization whose main purpose is the preservation of the endangered Kemp's ridley sea turtle. Ila's home at 5805 Gulf Blvd. has been turned into a sea turtle rehabilitation center where people bring stranded turtles. Ila and her assistants care for them until they can be released into the open sea again.

To support the organization, Ila offers "Meet the Turtles" programs Tues.-Sat. at 9 a.m. (May-August)

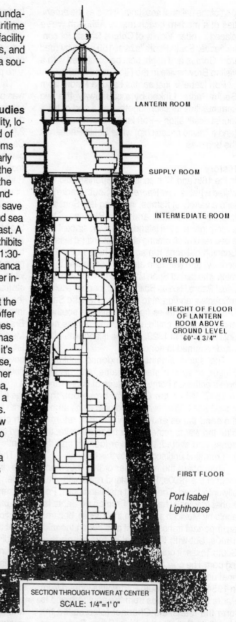

LANTERN ROOM

SUPPLY ROOM

INTERMEDIATE ROOM

TOWER ROOM

HEIGHT OF FLOOR OF LANTERN ROOM ABOVE GROUND LEVEL 60'-4 3/4"

FIRST FLOOR

Port Isabel Lighthouse

SECTION THROUGH TOWER AT CENTER
SCALE: 1/4"=1' 0"

or 10 a.m. (September-April). Visitors are shown turtles in rehabilitation, including the Kemp's ridley, and she sometimes even has performing turtles in costume. She asks for a donation of $1 (or more) per person at the door.

Hotels, Motels, And Condominiums

The South Padre Convention and Visitors Bureau lists 53 places to stay along the gulf shore, 16 along Laguna Madre ("the bay"), and 19 in the middle of the island ("inner island"). Gulf hotels, motels, and condos generally cost more than inner island and bay locations.

See "South Padre Island Hotels, Motels, And Condominiums" chart for information on selected locations. Contact the South Padre Convention and Visitors Bureau for information on rental agencies that handle reservations for condos not listed.

Campgrounds And RV Parks

No-fee primitive camping is permitted at county-operated **Andy Bowie Park,** 3.5 miles north of the causeway on the beach (Gulf side). An open pavilion and trash receptacles are the only facilities; no stay limit.

The only other legal place to camp on the island is **Isla Blanca Park** (tel. 512-761-5493) at the south end of Park 100. Tent camping is $8.50 a night. Two-way hookups are $11 a day, $50 a week, $165 a month, and $900 for six months; three-way hookups are $12 a night, $60 a week, $180 a month, and $1,000 for six months. There are also 18 screened cabins available, each with two double bunk beds, refrigerator, and stove (no linens or utensils) for $25 a night. Other facilities at the park include a marina with 65 slips ($6-12 per day) and two boat ramps, restrooms and showers, a grocery store, laundry, dump station, nondenominational chapel, and civic center. For cabin or campsite reservations, contact Isla Blanca Park (tel. 761-5493), P.O. Box 2106, South Padre Island, TX 78597.

Food—South Padre

For such a small community, South Padre has loads of restaurants and cafes. This means business competition is keen, so prices stay at a very reasonable level.

Rossi's Italian Ristorante (tel. 512-761-9391), 2412 Padre Blvd., is one of the better bar-

gains. The menu includes seafood and Italian standards such as eggplant parmigiana, fried oysters, manicotti, and flounder primavera. Dinner specials are under $6, lunch specials are under $4, and breakfast specials are as low as $1 (two eggs, hash browns, and toast). Popular **Blackbeard's** (tel. 761-2962), 103 E. Saturn, serves steaks, fresh seafood, and assorted sandwiches daily for lunch and dinner. **Jake's** (tel. 761-5012), 2400 Padre Blvd., has seafood, steak, and Mexican; open daily for lunch and dinner. A more extensive Tex-Mex menu is available at **Jesse's Cantina & Restaurant** (tel. 761-4500), 2700 Padre Blvd., including fajitas, *carnitas, camarones rancheros, pollo guisada, picadillo,* enchiladas, and flautas; open daily for lunch and dinner.

La Jaiba (tel. 512-761-9878), 2001 Padre Blvd., specializes in fresh Gulf seafood only, at reasonable prices; open Tues.-Sun. for lunch and dinner. **Dolphin Cove Oyster Bar** (no phone), a grass shack overlooking Brazos Santiago Pass in Isla Blanca Park, serves only fresh-shucked oyster and you-peel-'em shrimp.

The **IGA Blue Marlin Supermarket** at 2216 Padre Blvd. sells fresh seafood, produce, and other groceries; open daily.

Food—Port Isabel

Port Isabel restaurants have a better overall reputation, perhaps because they're more established and less tourist-oriented than those on South Padre Island (they're also more expensive). The town's most renowned restaurant is the **Yacht Club** (tel. 512-943-1301) at 700 Yturria. First opened in 1929 as a private club, the restaurant has been public for many years now and serves excellent seafood, including blue crab-stuffed jalapeños, red snapper (choice of broiled, blackened, meunière, and "Amsterdam-style," topped with shrimp, *beurre blanc,* and caviar), ceviche, and various combination platters, plus a few beef and chicken dishes. It's open Thurs.-Tues. for dinner only and is moderately expensive.

Cappuccino's (tel. 512-943-4201) is housed in the town's oldest commercial structure, the 1899 Champion Building (317 E. Railroad), which has been a general store, customs house, and post office. The exterior of the building still displays pictures of fish painted in 1905 by a one-armed, four-fingered artist named Juan

SOUTH PADRE HOTELS, MOTELS, AND CONDOMINIUMS

Ranges quoted are for the peak season (Memorial Day to Labor Day). Spring, fall, and winter rates are typically 30-60% less and discounts are usually offered for two-night and weekly stays.
All condominiums listed have kitchens. Add 13% hotel tax to all rates. Area code: 512

NAME	ADDRESS	PHONE	RATES	FEATURES
Bahia Mar Resort	6300 Padre	761-1343 or (800) 292-7502	$140-175	pool, tennis courts
Bay Breeze Condominiums	201 W. Red Snapper	761-7281	$75	inner island
Best Western Fiesta Isles Hotel	5701 Padre	761-4913	$82-108	inner island, pool
Castaways Condominiums	3700 Gulf	761-1903 or (800) 221-5218	$125	pool
Continental Condominiums	4908 Gulf	761-1306	$105	pool
Days Inn South Padre	3913 Padre	761-7831	$78	inner island, pool
Fisherman's Wharf	211 W. Swordfish	761-2303	$55	bay
Gulf I & II Condominiums	250-260 Padre	761-5910	$90-190	inner island, pool, tennis courts
Holiday Inn Beach Resort	100 Padre	761-5401	$60-100	pool, tennis courts
Island Inn	5100 Gulf	761-7677	$65-180	pool
La Internacional Condominiums	5008 Gulf	761-1306 or (800) 221-5218 (in TX)	$75	pool
Laguna Motel	201 W. Swordfish	761-2550	$35-65	inner island
Landfall Tower Resort Condominiums	6402 Padre	761-4909 or (800) 683-1930	$82-160	bay, pool, tennis courts
Las Brisas Condominiums	227 W. Morningside	761-5111 or (800) 241-5111	$85-145	bay, pool, tennis courts
Padre South Resort	1500 Gulf	761-4951	$120	pool
Radisson Resort South Padre Island	500 Padre	761-6511 (800) 333-3333 (outside TX)	$119-139	pool, tennis courts
Sand Castle Condominiums	200 W. Kingfish	(800) 221-5218 (in TX)	$48-66	bay, pool
Sea Grape Motel	120 E. Jupiter	761-2471	$55	inner island, pool
Seaside Apartments	3201 Gulf Blvd.	761-7035	$65-85	inner island
Sheraton South Padre Island Resort	310 Padre	761-6551	$120-230	pool, tennis courts

SOUTH PADRE HOTELS, MOTELS, AND CONDOMINIUMS

Ranges quoted are for the peak season (Memorial Day to Labor Day). Spring, fall, and winter rates are typically 30-60% less and discounts are usually offered for two-night and weekly stays. All condominiums listed have kitchens. Add 13% hotel tax to all rates. Area code: 512

NAME	ADDRESS	PHONE	RATES	FEATURES
South Padre Marina Condominiums	6201 Padre	761-7476 or (800) 637-9365	$95-120	bay, pool, tennis courts
Surf Motel	2612 Gulf	761-2831	$65	pool
Tiki Condominium Hotel	6608 Padre	761-2694 or (800) 879-8454	$98-125	pool, tennis courts, kitchens available
Vista Del Mar Condominiums	102 E. Pompano	761-2766	$83	inner island

Morelos. Cappuccino's serves fresh Gulf seafood (including blackened redfish) and a variety of Italian veal, chicken, and pasta dinners; prices are moderately expensive. It's open Mon.-Sat. for dinner only.

A less expensive seafood place here is **Pelican's Pouch Restaurant & Pub** (tel. 512-943-8923) at 823 Garcia. It's open Mon.-Fri. for lunch and dinner, Sat. for dinner only; the menu features all-you-can-eat lunch buffets Mon.-Fri. and dinner specials Mon.-Saturday.

For Mexican-style seafood, try the inexpensive **Mexiquito** (tel. 512-943-6106) at 814 S. Garcia; open daily for lunch and dinner (all-you-can-eat dinner specials on Wed. and Fri. evenings). You can buy fresh seafood to cook yourself at Port Isabel's **B&A Seafood Market** (tel. 943-2461) or **Quik Stop** (tel. 943-1159), both on State 100. The **IGA Val-U-Fest** at Las Palmas Plaza on State 100 is Port Isabel's only full-service grocery.

Entertainment

The larger South Padre hotels have clubs with live music, but it's pretty middle-of-the-road stuff. The **Third Coast** (tel. 512-761-6192, 5908 Padre Blvd.) features live country music most nights and has a few pool tables. **Kokomo** (tel. 761-1540, 2500 Padre Blvd.) plays recorded reggae. During the summer, open-air bars are popular, including **Parrot Eyes Island** (tel. 761-9457, 6101 Padre Blvd.) and **Tequila Sunset** (tel. 761-6198, 2300 W. Pike).

Events

College/university **spring break** brings tens of thousands of revelers to the island around the second or third week in March; the stragglers are usually gone by the end of the first week in April.

A variety of sailing regattas and fishing tournaments are held on the island from June to August. The biggest event, held the first week of August at various South Padre and Port Isabel locations, is the **Texas International Fishing Tournament** (the second-oldest state fishing event after Port Aransas's Deep-Sea Roundup). Trophies and cash prizes are awarded in a variety of categories, including both bay and offshore fishing.

Windsurfing competitions take place around the beginning of May. Call the South Padre Visitor and Convention Bureau (tel. 512-761-6433) for the latest schedule information.

Le Mistral

This 450-passenger, Panamanian-registered vessel (originally designed as a Sweden-Denmark ferry), docked at Port Isabel, offers six- to eight-hour cruises in the Gulf. Because the cruises reach international waters, passengers are permitted to gamble in the shipboard casino. The ticket price of $38 includes an all-you-can-eat buffet and free use of all of the ship's facilities, including a lounge with live music, the casino, and a sun deck.

Le Mistral (tel. 512-761-SHIP) is moored at 1250 Port Rd. in Port Isabel. Departures and rates tend to change from year to year. The ship usually departs at 11 a.m. on Wednesdays, at 7 p.m. Tues.-Sat., and at 1 p.m. on Sundays.

Fishing

Piers And Jetties: The recently opened **Captain Murphy's Fishing Pier** (tel. 512-943-7437) at Purdy's Point (just north of the foot of Queen Isabella Causeway) in Port Isabel is a lighted pier open 24 hours. The pier store offers snacks, tackle, fishing licenses, and bait; rental tackle is also available. The fee for using the pier is $2.25 per rod for a 12-hour period; non-fishing spectators pay 75 cents. A variety of Laguna Madre take the hook here, including flounder and redfish.

The jetties at Isla Blanca Park are also suitable for fishing ($1.50 vehicle entry fee).

Bay And Surf: Wade-fishing in the Laguna Madre "flats" (shallow sand flats) is popular and free—look for flounder, sheepshead, and croaker, plus occasional redfish and speckled trout. Surfcasting (on the Gulf side) is a bit more difficult but offers a wider variety of redfish, speckled trout, black drum, whiting, and sand trout.

Crabbing: Laguna Madre is full of crabs; all you need for a crabbing expedition (best in shallow areas—from piers or flatbottom boats) is a length of twine equal to the water's depth, crab bait (chicken meat is recommended), and a hand-net; net the crab *before* you pull it from the water or it'll let go of the bait.

Fishing Boats: Jim's Pier (tel. 512-761-2865) at 209 S. Whiting (north of the causeway, Laguna Madre side) operates party and charter boats for both bay and deep-sea fishing. A four-hour bay trip is $14 per person, bait included. All-day red snapper expeditions cost $60 per person. including all tackle and bait. Deep-sea trolling for kingfish, wahoo, ling, dolphinfish, and yellowfin tuna runs $350 for a five-hour trip taking up to four anglers (add $25 for each additional person). Marlin and sailfish charters are also available starting at $900 a day for up to four persons. Jim's also has a boat launching facility for privately owned boats, a bait and tackle shop, and a Shamrock gas station.

One block up, off Swordfish St., is **Fisherman's Wharf** (tel. 512-761-7818) with similar facilities. South of the causeway near the entrance to Isla Blanca Park, at Sea Ranch Marina, is **Captain Murphy's Charter Services** (tel. 761-2764), which specializes in red snapper expeditions.

Boating And Windsurfing

Island Sailboat Rentals (tel. 512-761-5061) at 212 W. Dolphin rents catamarans and sailboards by the hour or by the day. They also offer instruction for either.

Scuba Diving

American Diving (tel. 512-761-2030), at 401 State 100 in Port Isabel, has a 60-foot boat that takes divers out for offshore oil rig and shipwreck exploration. They also offer NAUI-certified instruction and equipment rental.

South Padre Island
And Port Isabel Information

Tourist Offices: The **South Padre Island Convention and Visitors Bureau** (tel. 512-761-6433, 800-343-2368 in the U.S. and Canada), at 600 Padre Blvd., across from the causeway, has a full-service information desk that's open Mon.-Fri. 9-6, Sat. and Sun. 10-5. The **Port Isabel Chamber of Commerce** (tel. 943-2262 or 800-527-6102 in TX), at 213 Yturria, also has information on the area; their office is open Mon.-Fri. 9-4.

Publications: The free monthly *South Padre Parade* newspaper-magazine is full of information on attractions and activities in the Port Isabel-South Padre area, plus the latest restaurant and happy-hour specials. You can pick it up at the convention and visitors bureau or at any one of 150 other locations around the island and in Port Isabel.

Telephone: The area code for the South Padre and Port Isabel area is 512.

Transport: The nearest full-service airport to South Padre/Port Isabel is **Valley International** in Harlingen (see "Valley International Airport" under "Harlingen," p. 324), 40 minutes away by car or taxi. Nearby Brownsville has a smaller airport. South Padre's **B.B.'s Taxi** (tel. 512-761-2851) operates a 24-hour taxi service, including transport to Valley International Airport and to Matamoros, Mexico.

Bicycles (also cars) can be rented at **Carport Car Rentals** (tel. 512-761-1313), 3200 Padre Boulevard.

Port Mansfield

This town didn't exist until the 1940s when Willacy County officials convinced the King Ranch to sell them 2,500 acres of coastal ranchland to build a fishing port. It's still surrounded by ranches; the nearest town of any substance is Raymondville, 24 miles west. The port is opposite the Mansfield Channel, which severs South Padre Island from Padre Island proper. Because of the co-mingling of Gulf and Laguna Madre fishes at this point and the area's isolation from large human populations, the fishing here is some of the best along the Texas coast. Port Mansfield is also the only "wet" town (where mixed drinks can be sold) in an otherwise dry Willacy County.

Fishing: This is Port Mansfield's solitary attraction. At **Fred Stone County Park** at the north end of town is a lighted public pier that's open 24 hours. Many of the local beach houses also have private piers. If you can get there (you need a boat), the jetties on either side of the channel are good fishing spots.

The **Port Mansfield Guides Association** (tel. 512-844-2528, P.O. Box 148, Port Mansfield, TX 78598) maintains a roster of experienced fishing guides for bay or Gulf trips. Besides the usual party and charter fishing boats offered in other coastal towns, the association maintains fishing barges which are anchored in Laguna Madre near prime fishing grounds (they're moved to follow seasonal runs). The barges are equipped with bunkhouses; the owners ferry their clients out to the platforms for overnight fishing trips (about $30 per person per night).

The association can also arrange boat transport to Padre Island National Seashore, directly opposite, for about $40 roundtrip.

Accommodations: Beach houses rent for $35-100 a night. The Port Mansfield Chamber of Commerce (tel. 512-944-2354, P.O. Box O, Port Mansfield, TX 78598) or Glaze Realty (tel. 944-2355, 701 Bayshore) can assist with reservations.

Fisherman's Inn (tel. 944-2882), **Casa de Pescadores** (tel. 944-2333), and **Harbor House Inn** (tel. 944-2888) rent rooms and efficiency apartments for $30-75 a night. The **Bay-View RV Park** (tel. 512-944-2253) and **R&R RV Park** (tel. 944-2253) have full hookups and other amenities for $8-10 a night.

EAST TEXAS
INTRODUCTION

Culturally and geographically, this part of the state is more linked to the American Southeast than the American Southwest. On a green, languid summer day in East Texas, you could easily think you're in Louisiana or Mississippi. It's more than geographic appearance; in rural areas at least (all bets off for Houston) lifestyles here are similar to those of other states in the Collard-Green Belt. The locals speak more slowly than their counterparts elsewhere in Texas; if you stop to ask directions, a little patience is in order. East Texans like to sit and chat for a spell when they get the chance (unlike the average tight-lipped West Texan).

THE LAND

The reason East Texas is so much greener than the rest of the state is that it rains more here, from 43 inches a year in Tyler to 59 inches a year in Orange. The heart of the region is what's called the "Piney Woods," a western extension of the

Pine Belt that stretches from here to Georgia. The pine forests are interspersed with various hardwoods and the lumber industry is the main economic staple for many counties. Vast oil fields, another East Texas economic resource, lie beneath Gregg, Rusk, and Smith counties. Morris County harbors significant iron deposits, adding to the area's array of marketable natural resources.

Parts of East Texas are also in the Post Oak and Blackland belts, where the pine forests thin out and the sandy, black-clay alluvial soils are especially well suited to farming. Cotton is the traditional crop in these sections, along with a variety of grains, fruits, and vegetables.

The southern extremes of East Texas, including Houston, Port Arthur, and Beaumont, belong to the state's coastal prairies. Grasslands are plentiful from the coast to as far as 30-60 miles inland, so cattle ranching is one of the principal economic activities. In irrigated areas rice is a major crop, followed by grain sorghum and various truck crops.

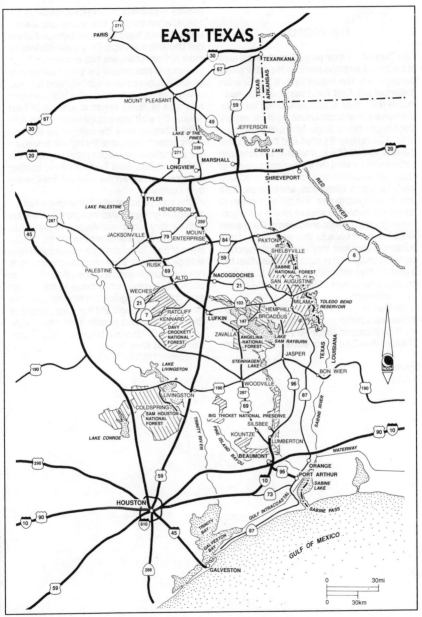

EAST TEXAS

THE PEOPLE

East Texas is the most polyglot, multicultural area of the state, though this condition is a rather recent development. The original French and Spanish dalliances with East Texas were brief and inconclusive due to their relative remoteness from colonial centers. Significant colonizing of the territory didn't begin until the Anglo-American immigration of the 19th century. It's often said that this part of the state attracted the less adventurous American settlers who crossed the Mississippi in search of cheap land—dirt farmers from Tennessee, Kentucky, Louisiana, Mississippi, and Georgia. But it also brought woodsmen who wouldn't dream of advancing beyond the western treeline to the godforsaken, open prairies and plains of Central and West Texas, not because they were afraid of new frontiers but because they viewed cattle-ranching as a lazy, undignified occupation. In less than half a century, they established what the Europeans couldn't achieve over a 200-year period—permanent settlements.

As East Texas farmers prospered, they began to develop a plantation economy based on models in Southeastern states—created on the backs of slave labor. East Texan slaveholders were the primary supporters of Texas secession in the 1860s; when the Civil War ended and slavery was outlawed, freed blacks became part of the civil population at large. They were followed by more African-Americans who migrated to Texas in search of jobs around the turn of the century when the state economy was beginning to surge.

When oil was discovered in the 1930s, a whole new type of Texan began to emerge in East Texas—the wildcatter and the investor. Get-rich-quick schemes were the order of the day and many farmers sold out to the highest bidder. As the petrochemical industry developed in the 1940s and '50s, East Texas received another large influx of non-Anglos—Cajuns and Creoles from Louisiana.

The population became further diversified following the growing Asian immigration of the late 20th century. Southeast Asians, in particular, have discovered a familiar climate in the coastal areas of East Texas and have concentrated here in large numbers. In general, the communities nearest Houston and the Gulf coast are the most ethnically diverse, while those farthest north around historic Longview and Marshall are more homogeneously Anglo and European. In spite of East Texas's relative plurality, it has never exhibited as much Hispanic influence as in South, Central, and West Texas.

HOUSTON

THE CITY

Chamber of commerce publications often boast that Houston is the state's largest city and the fourth-largest city in the U.S.; but with city limits that encompass over 500 square miles, a numerical comparison based on strict municipal boundaries (in a city notoriously lacking in city regulation) hardly gives an accurate picture. The reality is that when compared with other consolidated metropolitan statistical areas (a more practical way to measure population centers), Houston ranks ninth (total population 3.7 million) in the U.S., between Dallas-Fort Worth (eighth) and San Antonio (10th).

What really distinguishes this city from Dallas and San Antonio is not its size but its atmosphere of relative newness and lack of tradition. Houston has been a maverick town since brothers John and Augustus Allen first set up a trading post on the Buffalo Bayou in 1836 to capitalize on Texas' new status as a republic. They then boasted that Houston would become the next New Orleans. When cotton was king, Houston did well trading with the eastern U.S. and abroad. The Civil War took much of the wind out of the city's sails, though, and the Allens' prediction rang hollow until the coming of the railroads in the late 1800s. When oil was discovered at nearby Spindletop in 1901, another breed of entrepreneurs moved in to make the most of the new commodity. During WW II, Houston got another large boost when it became a wartime center for steel manufacturing, ship-building, and petrochemical production.

By the 1970s, Houston had become a national capital for the nouveau riche, but the wealth was still about 35% oil-dependent. In the '80s, following the drastic decline in world oil prices, downtown Houston threatened to become the country's largest ghost town. The local economy has since turned itself around to a certain extent by diverting focus to other industries—primarily medical research, aerospace technology, education, shipping, international banking, and high-tech manufacturing. The city's traditional theme of boom/bust cycles dependent on local commodities is giving way to an expanded international

role, with a consular corps of over 50 nations—the largest in the South or Southwest—and the country's largest multi-site foreign trade zone. As befits its maverick reputation, Houston remains a relatively young city with a median age of 29.

You won't find many Texans without an opinion about Houston. They either love the city for all it has to offer (museums and galleries, first-class ballet, symphony, and opera companies, a variety of exotic cuisines) or hate it for what it lacks (reasonable zoning laws, traffic control, clean air, a pleasant climate). Both sides are right, but both sides exaggerate their cases. Neither the traffic nor the pollution are as bad as in Los Angeles, for example. Nor are the museums and restaurants on a par with New York's or Washington's. Houston is still Texas, and at the same time Houston is its own city.

THE CLIMATE

Houston vies with Amarillo for having the state's worst climate for a large city. Whereas Amarillo is dry, windy, and cold much of the year, Houston is humid and hot. On top of all this, it's given to torrential downpours, with an average annual precipitation of 45-50 inches (in 1981 it received 82 inches, the wettest point in the state that year). At an elevation of only 49 feet above sea level, this means occasional flooding, usually in May and September when rainfall is heaviest. The months with the highest probability for sunshine are June and July (67% chance each).

The highest average relative humidity comes in October (93% at 6 a.m.), the lowest in July

SELECTED MONTHLY AVERAGE MAXIMUM/MINIMUM TEMPERATURES

Month	Max. (°F)	Min. (°F)
Jan.	62	41
March	72	50
May	85	65
July	94	73
Sept.	89	68
Nov.	72	49

HOUSTON

© MOON PUBLICATIONS, INC.

(58% at midnight). On the plus side, temperatures rarely reach freezing in the winter, and at the height of the summer, temperatures don't often climb above the 90-95° F range (of course, 90° F at even 70% relative humidity means a perceived temperature of 101° F). When President Jimmy Carter tried to require all federal offices nationwide to set summer thermostats at 80° F during his administration, federal employees in Houston reacted strongly and an exception was made for that city. (Expect air-conditioned buildings in Houston to be cooler than average—even cold at times—in the summer.)

SIGHTS

Art Museums

Houston has nearly 20 museums and galleries (several of which are on its university campuses—see "Colleges And Universities" below). The principal ones are centrally located in the "museum district" near the intersection of Montrose Blvd. and Bissonnet Street. The **Museum of Fine Arts** (tel. 713-526-1351) at 1001 Bissonnet (between Montrose and S. Main), established in 1924, houses the city's most comprehensive art collection: some 18,000 works of American, European, Latin American, North American Indian, African, and Asian/Pacific provenance (the Renaissance and impressionist collections are among the more noteworthy). The museum's Hirsch Library has an extensive collection of books on art history; across the street, the affiliated Alfred C. Glassell Jr. School of Art (5101 Montrose) offers a full range of art classes. The museum also sponsors an ongoing film and lecture series, a museum store, and a cafe. Open Tues.-Sat. 10-5 (Thurs. till 9 p.m.), Sun. noon-6; admission is $3 for adults, $1.50 for seniors and students (under 19 free), except on Thursdays, when admission is free.

The Menil Collection (tel. 713-525-9400) at 1515 Sul Ross (between Mandel and Mulberry), the legacy of John and Dominique de Menil, features rotating displays of their 10,000-piece collection and occasional traveling exhibits. The cypress-wood building was designed by architect Renzo Piano, co-creator of Paris's Pompidou Art Center, and usually contains a compelling mix of African, Oceanic, Byzantine, Coptic, surrealist, and contemporary works. Open Wed.-Sun. 11-7; free admission.

A bit farther east on Sul Ross at Yupon is the **Rothko Chapel** (tel. 713-524-9839, 1409 Sul Ross), an octagonal brick structure built to house 14 paintings by abstract expressionist Mark Rothko which were commissioned by the de Menils. The Menil Foundation-sponsored facility hosts a variety of ecumenical colloquia on religion, human rights, and cross-cultural studies (e.g., "Traditional Modes of Contemplation and Action," "Toward a New Strategy for Development," and "Processes of Inter-Ethnic Relations in Latin America, Southeast Asia, and the Pacific"). Any religious group can book the chapel for services; it's also open to individuals who want to pray or meditate independently. Open to the public daily 10-6; admission is free.

The city's boldest museum is undoubtedly the **Contemporary Art Museum** (tel. 713-526-0773 for general information, 526-3129 for a recorded listing of current exhibits and events) at 5216 Montrose (across from the Museum of Fine Arts). Inspired by the European art hall (Kunsthalle) tradition, the emphasis is on art presentation rather than on collection and maintenance. The museum's two galleries (a large upstairs space for "pivotal" one-person or group exhibitions, a smaller downstairs space for mixed presentations by emerging artists) display only art created since 1945; since there is no permanent collection, new shows open approximately every six weeks year-round. The CMA also hosts a series of films, lectures, and gallery talks. Open Tues.-Fri. 10-5, Sat.-Sun. noon-5; free admission. Free guided tours are conducted every Sunday at 3.

Bayou Bend (tel. 713-529-8773), a 28-room Greek Revival-style mansion surrounded by 14 acres of gardens along Buffalo Bayou (at 1 Westcott St., off Memorial Dr.), was built in the 1920s by the late Ima Hogg, daughter of former Governor Jim Hogg. In 1966 it was converted into an American decorative arts museum under the auspices of the Museum of Fine Arts. Miss Hogg's extensive private collection (expanded by the MFA) includes 18th- and 19th-century furniture, paintings, silverwork, textiles, ceramics, glass, and folk art.

In 1991 the Bayou Bend mansion closed for renovations; it is due to reopen in September 1993. The 14 acres of formal and woodland gardens will remain open to the public during the renovation period Wed.-Sun. 10-5, Sun. 1-5. Admission is free. Four hundred pieces from the Bayou

Bend Collection have been moved from the mansion to the new **Bayou Bend Museum of Americana at Tenneco** (tel. 659-3800), at 1010 Milam in downtown Houston. The museum is open Mon.-Fri. 11-6, Sat. 11-5, and Sun. 1-5; admission is $2 for adults, $1 seniors, free for children under 12. Admission is free for everyone every Thurs. and third Sun. of each month.

Outdoor Art: Houston's commitment to art is perhaps most visible in the dozens of outdoor sculptural and mural works around the city commissioned by various private and public organizations. The greatest proliferation of outdoor artwork is found in the downtown area, where there were some 28 pieces at last count. Another 25 or so

are in the museum district and around Rice University, and another 14 are scattered around the University of Houston.

Science Museums

The **Museum of Natural Science** (tel. 713-526-4273) at 1 Hermann Circle in Hermann Park (opposite Rice University) opened in 1909 (it moved to its present location in 1929) and contains exhibits pertaining to several scientific disciplines relevant to Houston's high-tech history, from astronomy to petroleum science. It's open Mon.-Fri. 9-5, Sat. 9-6, Sun. noon-6. On the second floor is the **Museum of Medical Science,** which features a standard array of anatomical displays.

Hours for this museum are Mon.-Sat. 9-5, Sun. noon-5 from May to Sept.; Tues.-Sat. 9-4:45, Sun. and Mon. noon-4:45 the rest of the year. Admission to both floors is $2.50 adults, $2 seniors and children. Also in the park is the domed **Burke Baker Planetarium;** shows are presented Mon.-Fri. at 1 and 2, Sat. and Sun. every half-hour 1-3:30, May-Sept.; Wed.-Fri. only the rest of the year. Admission is $3 for adults, $1.50 for children under 12.

Historic Spots

Sam Houston Park (tel. 713-655-1912), downtown at 100 Bagby, is Houston's oldest park. It's sponsored by the Harris County Heritage Society, which maintains eight restored historic structures built in the mid-1800s. Guided tours of the buildings are conducted hourly Tues.-Sat. 10-4, Sun. 1-5; admission is $4 for adults, $2 for students, and $1 for children 6-11.

The **Market Square Historic District,** bounded by Congress, Preston, Travis, and Milam downtown, is flanked by 53 historic buildings—Houston's original business district.

The small **Allen's Landing Park** at Main and Commerce, on Buffalo Bayou, is the site where the Allen brothers first stepped off their boat and started their trading post in 1836.

San Jacinto Battleground Historical Park (tel. 713-479-2421), 15 miles east of the city via State 225 and State 134, commemorates the 1836 battle in which Texan revolutionary forces defeated Santa Anna's Mexican army and won independence. The **San Jacinto Monument** marks the battle site itself; the 570-foot obelisk is said to be the tallest masonry monument in the world. An elevator takes visitors to the top for a bird's-eye view of the Gulf coast, ship channel, and Houston skyline (if the industrial haze isn't too thick). The monument is open daily 9-6; the elevator ride costs $2 for adults, $1 for children.

The **San Jacinto Museum of History** (tel. 713-479-2421) contains exhibits which chronicle regional history from Indian habitation through statehood. A new theater in the battleground's museum presents *Texas Forever!* a 30-minute, multi-media documentary of the Battle of San Jacinto narrated by Charlton Heston. Admission is $3.50 for adults, $2 for seniors and children.

On the ship channel near San Jacinto Battleground Historical Park is the battleship *Texas,* a veteran of both WW I and WW II. The ship is permanently moored here to serve as a naval museum, containing exhibits that recount the ship's wartime involvement. Open daily 10-5; admission is $3 adults, $1.50 children.

Houston Zoological Gardens

This 50-acre zoo (tel. 713-525-3300) in Hermann Park has recently been upgraded and, for the first time in 65 years, has begun to charge admission. It's very well kept throughout and features a mammal marina, education center, gorilla habitat, tropical bird house, deep-sea aquarium, and reptile house (which houses a rare 17$1/2$-foot Burmese python). Open Tues.-Sun. 10-6; admission is $2.50 for adults, $2 for seniors, 50 cents for children.

National Aeronautics And Space Administration (NASA)-Johnson Space Center

This is the center for the country's manned spaceflight program and the number-three tourist destination in the state, averaging 1.5 million visitors a year. At this writing, facilities open to the public include: the visitor center (Bldg. 2), which displays a variety of space hardware, astronaut suits, moon rocks, and short films; the Skylab trainers hall (Bldg. 5); the space shuttle orbiter training facility (Bldg. 9A); Mission Control Center (Bldg. 30); and the lunar sample building (Bldg. 31A), where 800 pounds of lunar material are stored and tested—visitors must obtain a free ticket for this 30-minute tour from the visitor center. The cafeteria (Bldg. 3), where visitors and NASA employees dine, has a gift shop selling NASA souvenirs. The visitor center is open daily 9-4. There is no admission charge for any of these facilities.

A new facility specifically designed for visitors, **Space Center Houston,** is expected to open the end of 1992. The 123-acre, $50 million complex is being designed by a team made up of engineers from NASA and Walt Disney Imagineering. Exhibits will include retired spacecraft—Skylab, Apollo 17, Gemini 5, and Mercury Faith 7—as well as hands-on spaceflight simulation training devices and interactive simulation exercises.

Call (713) 483-4321 for further information on NASA visitor facilities.

Getting There: Johnson Space Center is 25 miles southeast of Houston via I-45 S, on NASA Road.

DOWNTOWN HOUSTON

© MOON PUBLICATIONS, INC.

*Johnson Space
Center*

Astrodome

This 76,000-seat sports facility (tel. 713-799-9544) at 8400 Kirby (at Loop 610 S) is home to the Houston Astros (pro baseball) and the Houston Oilers (pro football) teams, as well as the Houston Livestock Show and Rodeo and other large-scale events. Daily tours of the stadium, conducted at 11 a.m., 1 p.m., and 3 p.m. (except when preempted by scheduled events), take visitors onto the Astroturf field, to the owner's lounge, and to the radio/TV broadcasting areas. Prices are $4 for adults, $3 for seniors and children 4-11.

The Orange Show

This urban folk-art park has got to be seen to be believed. The brainchild of Jeff McKissack, an ex-postman who for 25 years assembled a collection of found objects to create a fanciful monument to the orange, the part-Alexander Caldwell, part-Rube Goldberg design represents McKissack's personal testament to wisdom and good health. When McKissack died in 1980 at the age of 77, a group of Houston artists and city arts representatives formed The Orange Show Foundation to preserve the complex, which consists of several enclosed rooms, two small arenas, and two rooftop observation areas, all bedecked with hardy orange (and sometimes blue) displays. The dominant motif is the wheel—many of the sculptures consist of iron buggy wheels and tractor seats. Nearly every wall, pillar, and door is inlaid with tile messages like "Oranges for energy," "Love me, orange please love me," or "Be alert." Beneath a huge circular clown face is a sign that reads "The clown said I am alert. I take care of myself every hour every minute of every day. You can too if you will. Clowns never lie."

The Orange Show is at 2410 Munger St., southeast of central Houston off the Gulf Freeway (take I-45 S to the Telephone Rd. exit, then north on the access road to Munger). The complex is open to visitors daily noon-5 from Memorial Day to Labor Day and on weekends from Labor Day to mid-December and mid-March to Memorial Day. Admission is $1 adults, free for children under 12. The Orange Show Foundation uses the site not only as an exhibit in itself but as an educational and cultural community resource to host children's theater, poetry workshops, art shows, and musical performances. Call (713) 926-6368 for more information.

Colleges And Universities

The city's two major universities are the **University of Houston** and **Rice University.** The state-supported University of Houston (tel. 713-749-2937) has a total enrollment of 31,000, which includes an open-admissions undergraduate division, graduate schools in engineering, pharmacology, and optometry, as well as Bates College of Law and the Hilton School of Hotel and Restaurant Management. The central campus is south of the downtown area off I-45, Calhoun exit; there is also a downtown campus on Main. The **Blaffer Gallery** (tel. 749-1329), on the central campus, and the **O'Kane Gallery** (tel. 221-8042), downtown, feature changing local and national art exhibits.

artist's conception of Space Center Houston, expected to open in late 1992

COURTESY NASA - JOHNSON SPACE CENTER

Rice University (tel. 713-527-8101) is a private, liberal arts school with a scenic campus southwest of downtown and a total enrollment of approximately 4,000 (about one-third graduate, two-thirds undergraduate). The **Rice Media Center** (tel. 527-4894) hosts local, national, and international photography exhibitions and also screens classic and contemporary cinema. The university's **Farish Gallery** (tel. 527-4870) in the School of Architecture is devoted to changing architectural exhibits.

Other tertiary schools include the sectarian **Houston Baptist University** (tel. 713-774-7661, 7502 Fondren) and **University of St. Thomas** (tel. 522-7911, 3812 Montrose), and the state-supported **Texas Southern University** (tel. 527-7011, 3100 Cleburne). Two major medical schools, **Baylor College of Medicine** and the **University of Texas Medical School at Houston,** are located at the Texas Medical Center.

Texas Medical Center
The TMC is a conglomerate of 39 member institutions (hospitals, research institutes, nursing and medical schools) that cover a 580-acre area adjacent to Hermann Park and, as a group, comprise the city's largest employer. Among the care facilities is the Versailles of free-enterprise heart surgery, Michael DeBakey's Methodist Hospital, where incisions start at $25,000; luxury suites here cater meals from Jamail & Sons, a highbrow Houston deli. In other words, it's where state-of-the-art medical techniques meet 18th-century social values (doctors like to work here because there's no state income tax).

Free tours of the grounds and some of the facilities are conducted daily at 10 a.m. from the TMC Assistance Center (tel. 713-790-1136), which is on the first floor of TMC parking garage No. 2, at Bertner and Holcombe.

Port Of Houston
This port is the third largest in the U.S. (over 4,800 ships a year call here) and a linchpin of the local economy. The inspection boat *Sam Houston* (tel. 713-225-4044) takes visitors on free tours of the ship channel Tues., Wed., Fri., and Sat. at 10 a.m. and 2:30 p.m., Thurs. and Sun. at 2:30 only. The tour is free but you usually have to make reservations at least a month in advance to get on. The boat docks at Gate 8, 7300 Clinton Drive.

ACCOMMODATIONS

Houston Hotels And Motels

Hotel and motel accommodations are concentrated in five major areas: central Houston (including downtown), the west side (near the junction of US 59 and Loop 610), the S. Main/Astrodome area, near Houston Intercontinental Airport, and near Hobby Airport. See "Houston Hotels And Motels" chart for details.

Bed And Breakfast Inns

Houston's **Bed & Breakfast Society of Texas** (tel. 713-771-3919, 8880-B2 Bellaire #284, Houston, TX 77036) maintains a registry of 24 B&Bs in Houston, many of them in the historic Heights district. Rooms with private bath start at $25 s, $35 d.

Houses that accept direct bookings include **Durham House Bed & Breakfast** (tel. 713-868-4654) at 921 Heights, a large Victorian listed with the National Register of Historic Places. All rooms are furnished with antiques and have private baths; rates are $40 s, $50 d. Another is **Sara's Bed & Breakfast Inn** (tel. 868-1130) at 941 Heights, a Victorian where double rooms (all with shared bath) are $46-52 (weekly rates available).

The Downtown YMCA Residence

This conveniently located downtown Y (tel. 713-659-8501) at 1600 Louisiana welcomes men and women for an unbeatable $16.35 in the older rooms, $21.80 for new rooms. All rooms have air-conditioning and TV (shared bath only). Weekly rates are $72-109.

Houston International Youth Hostel

Also called Perry House (tel. 713-523-1009, 5302 Crawford St.), this large converted home, in a residential area about three miles southwest of downtown Houston, has dorm beds for $10.25 a night for AYH-cardholders, $13.25 for nonmembers. Cyclists note: next door is Daniel Boone Cycles, one of the city's best bike shops.

Metro buses #1, #2, #4, and #22 stop at the nearby intersection of Main and Southmore; from here it's a six-block walk east to Crawford, then right (south) one block.

Campgrounds And RV Parks

Alexander Deussen County Park (tel. 713-454-7057), a 309-acre wooded park about 20 miles northeast of the city on Lake Houston's southwest side, has camper/RV sites with two-way hookups for $4 a day (14-day limit). Tent camping is permitted only on weekends, no charge. Facilities include bicycle trails, boat ramps, a dump station, restrooms, picnic shelters, cooking grills, a snack bar, and a grocery shop.

On the south tip of Lake Houston is the 1,005-acre **Dwight Eisenhower Park** (tel. 713-456-0973), where no-fee camping is permitted (one-night limit Mon.-Thurs., no limit on weekends). Another camping area is at **Spring Creek Park** (tel. 447-3619), 12 miles northwest of FM 1960 off FM 149, on Spring Creek. Tent/camper sites

*Houston International
Youth Hostel*

HOUSTON HOTELS AND MOTELS

Add 15% hotel tax to all rates. Area code: 713

NAME	ADDRESS	PHONE	RATES	FEATURES
CENTRAL				
Days Inn Downtown	801 Calhoun	659-2222	$45-75	heated pool, sr. disc., wknd. rates
Doubletree at Allen Center	400 Dallas	759-0202	$110-140	wknd. and weekly rates available
Four Seasons Hotel Houston Center	1300 Lamar	650-1300	$170-245	heated pool, saunas wknd. rates
Hyatt Regency Houston	1200 Louisiana	654-1234	$100-200	pool, senior discount, wknd. rates
La Colombe D'Or	3410 Montrose	524-7999	$150-225	historic
The Lancaster	701 Texas	228-9500	$140-185	suites, wknd. rates
The Wyndham Warwick	5701 Main	526-1991	$135-150	historic, pool, sauna, wknd., weekly, and monthly rates
WEST				
Days Inn Sharpstown	6060 Hooton (Southwest Fwy., Hillcroft exit)	777-9955	$42-58	pool, sauna, wknd., wkly., and monthly rates
Doubletree Hotel Galleria	2001 Post Oak	961-9300	$120-160	pool, sauna
The Hilton Southwest	6780 Southwest Fwy. (Hillcroft exit)	977-7911	$89-107	pool, senior discount wknd. and monthly rates
Holiday Inn Crowne Plaza	2222 W. Loop 610 (San Felipe exit)	961-7272	$79-159	heated pool, sauna coin laundry, wknd. rates
Holiday Inn Galleria	3131 W. Loop 610 (Westheimer/ Richmond exits)	621-1900	$60-78	pool, coin laundry, senior discount, wknd. rates
Holiday Inn Greenway Plaza	2712 Southwest Fwy.	523-8448	$49-86	pool, saunas, wknd. rates
Holiday Inn I-10	7611 Katy Fwy. (west at Silber)	688-2221	$46-52	pool, coin laundry senior discount, wknd. rates
The Houstonian Hotel	111 N. Post Oak	680-2626	$120-150	heated pool, health cntr., bicycle rentals, airport shuttle, wknd., wkly., and monthly rates

HOUSTON HOTELS AND MOTELS

Add 15% hotel tax to all rates. Area code: 713

NAME	ADDRESS	PHONE	RATES	FEATURES
WEST (continued)				
J.W. Marriott Houston Galleria	5150 Westheimer	961-500	$139-149	heated pool, tennis and racquetball courts, health cntr., senior discounts, monthly rates
La Quinta Motor Inn Greenway Plaza	4015 Southeast Fwy.	623-4750	$59-65	pool, coin laundry, senior discount
Motel 6	9638 Plainfield (US 59, Bissonett exit)	778-0008	$28.95 + $6 ea. add.	pool
Quality Inn Greenway Plaza	4020 Southwest Fwy.	623-4720	$45-50	pool, sauna
Ramada Hotel Galleria	7787 Katy Fwy.	681-5000	$65-81	pool, wknd. and weekly rates
The Ritz-Carlton	1919 Briar Oaks (San Felipe exit)	840-7600	$155-265	heated pool, wknd. rates
Rodeway Inn SE Fwy.	3135 Southeast Fwy.	526-1071	$34-45	pool, senior discount
The Sheraton Grand Hotel	2525 W. Loop 610 (Westheimer exit)	961-3000	$109-159	pool, senior discount weekly rates
Stouffer Presidente Hotel	6 Greenway Plaza	629-1200	$109-144	pool, sauna, tennis courts, health club, sr. disc., wknd. rates
The Westin Gallerria	5060 W. Alabama	960-8100	$150-180	heated pool, sauna, tennis courts, sr. disc., wknd., wkly., and monthly rates
The Westin Oaks	5011 Westheimer	960-8100	$160-215	heated pool, sauna, wknd. rates
SOUTH MAIN (near Texas Medical Center and Astrodome)				
The Grant Motor Inn	8200 S. Main	668-8000	$26-39	pool, coin laundry, sr. disc., wkly. rates
Harvey Suites Medical Center	6800 S. Main	528-7744	$64-159	pool, medical center, shuttle
Holiday Inn Medical Center	6701 S. Main	797-1110	$69-89	pool, medical center shuttle, wknd. rates
Houston Marriott Astrodome	2100 S. Braeswood	797-9000	$59-109	pool, coin laundry
Houston Marriott Medical Center	6580 Fannin	796-0080	$114-129	heated pool, saunas, health center, sr. disc.,wknd. rates

HOUSTON HOTELS AND MOTELS

Add 15% hotel tax to all rates. Area code: 713

NAME	ADDRESS	PHONE	RATES	FEATURES
SOUTH MAIN .(continued)				
Houston Plaza Hilton	6633 Travis	524-6633	$87-97	heated pool, saunas, health center
Houston Villa Motor Hotel	9604 S. Main	666-1411	$27-37	pool
La Quinta Astrodome	9911 Buffalo Speedway	668-8082	$56-68	pool, coin laundry, airport shuttle
Main Street Inn	7905 S. Main	667-8200	$31-36	pool, sr. disc.
Park Inn International	6700 S. Main	522-2811	$38-43	pool, sr. disc.
Radisson Suite Hotel	1400 Old Spanish Trail	796-1000	$79-89	kitchenettes in all units, pool, sauna, coin laundry, sr. disc.
HOUSTON INTERCONTINENTAL AIRPORT				
Best Western Greenspoint Inn	11211 I-45 N (exit 60)	447-6311	$35-40	pool, airport shuttle
Comfort Inn North	12500 I-45 N (exit 61)	876-3888	$34-45	pool, coin laundry, sr. disc., airport shuttle
Days Inn Airport	17607 Eastex Fwy.	446-4611	$37-43	pool, coin laundry, airport shuttle
Doubletree Hotel	15747 JFK	442-8000	$109-119	pool, refrigs. avail., airport shuttle, wknd. rates
Holiday Inn Houston Intercontinental	3702 N. Sam Houston Parkway E	449-2311	$49-79	pool, saunas, tennis courts, coin laundry, airport shuttle
Houston Airport Hilton	500 N. Belt	931-0101	$61-105	heated pool, saunas, coin laundry, airport shuttle
Houston Airport Marriott	Airport Terminal	443-2310	$135	suites, pool, coin laundry, airport shuttle, wknd. rates
Houston Marriott North	255 Sam Houston Parkway E	875-4000	$115	suites, heated pool, saunas, airport shuttle, wknd. rates
La Quinta Inn Intercontinental Hotel	6 N. Belt	447-6888	$53-65	pool, airport shuttle, senior discount
Sheraton Crown Hotel	15700 JFK	442-5100	$85-105	suites, heated pool, coin laundry, airport shuttle

HOUSTON HOTELS AND MOTELS

Add 15% hotel tax to all rates. Area code: 713

NAME	ADDRESS	PHONE	RATES	FEATURES
HOUSTON INTERCONTINENTAL AIRPORT .(continued)				
Super 8 Motel	15350 JFK	442-1830	$35-44	pool, sauna, airport shuttle, senior disc., weekly rates
Wyndham Greenspoint	12400 Greenspoint	875-2222	$99-129	pool, sauna, racquetball courts, airport shuttle, monthly rates
HOBBY AIRPORT				
Days Inn Hobby Airport	8611 Airport	947-0000	$60-75	pool, airport shuttle
Hobby Airport Hilton	8181 Airport	645-3000	$88-128	pool, airport shuttle, wknd. rates
Holiday Inn Hobby Airport	9100 Gulf. Fwy.	934-7979	$85-109	heated pool, sauna, airport shuttle
Hotel Concord Hobby Airport	7777 Airport	644-1261	$39-43	pool, airport shuttle weekly rates
La Quinta Motor Inn Hobby Airport	9902 Gulf Fwy.	941-0900	$58-70	pool airport shuttle senior discount
Quality Inn Hobby Airport	1515 College	946-5900	$44-56	pool, airport shuttle wknd. & wkly. rates

with w/e are free, with a two-night limit (call in advance to see if there are sites available).

KOA has four campgrounds on the city outskirts. The **KOA Houston Central** (tel. 442-7700) is at 1620 Peachleaf, 12 miles north of downtown via US 59 N and FM 525 (west to Aldine-Westfield, south to Peachleaf). Tentsites are $14.50, two-way hookups are $15.50, and three-ways are $17.50. The **KOA Houston West** (tel. 934-4545) is actually 38 miles west of the city in Brookshire (I-10 W exit 731). Rates are $13 for tents, $16 two-way, $18 three-way. **KOA Houston East** (tel. 383-3618) is 33 miles east in Baytown off I-10 (exit 798); rates here are $12, $16, and $17.

Houston Leisure Park (tel. 713-426-3576) is a huge RV facility that's 19 miles east of the city off I-10 (exit 787) near San Jacinto State Park; rates are $10 for tents, $12-15 for full hookups, with weekly and monthly rates available. **Red Dot RV Park** (tel. 448-3438) is 12 miles north off I-45 (Aldine-Bender exit) at 15014 Sellers. Rates are $12.25 for full hookups, weekly and monthly rates available. The small **Travel Trailer Lodge** (tel. 694-2892) is only five miles north off I-45 on Tidwell (exit 54A/54B). Full hookups are $12. **Traders Village Campground** (tel. 890-5500) has four wooded acres at 7979 N. Eldridge off US 290 (northwest of Houston); full hookups cost $12 a night.

FOOD

San Antonio for Tex-Mex, Dallas for Southwestern, and Houston for Cajun is the usual refrain, only Houston's reputation really ought to be broadened to include Asian cuisine as well. With the highest percentage of Asians among the state's big three (and the only one with a "Chinatown"), Houston has more Asian restaurants—Chinese, Japanese, Thai, Vietnamese, Indian, Indonesian—than any other Texan city.

Most of the chain restaurants are located along Westheimer Rd. outside Loop 610, but there are also a few independent gems tucked away here and there in the endless series of soulless shopping centers.

American

$$ Ashland House: This converted two-story Victorian serves traditional American entrées like pot roast served with fresh vegetables and home-made yeast rolls (or cornbread). At 1801 Ashland (tel. 713-863-7613); open Mon.-Sat. for lunch, Thurs.-Sat. for dinner.

$$$+ Café Annie: A chi-chi restaurant that's considered one of the state's foremost exponents of Southwestern/new-American cuisine. The menu varies but is guaranteed to impress (e.g., cream of mussel soup seasoned with serrano chiles and cilantro, crabmeat tostadas). At 1728 Post Oak (tel. 840-1111); open Mon.-Fri. for lunch and dinner, Sat. dinner only.

$$ Hard Rock Café: Part of a chain with outlets in London, Tokyo, New York, Los Angeles, and Dallas to name a few. The main attraction here is the decor—electric guitars, gold records, a Harley, a T-Bird, and other symbols of rock 'n' roll culture—but the burgers aren't bad either. At 2801 Kirby (tel. 520-1134); open daily for lunch and dinner.

$$$+ Tony's: One of the hubs of Houston's so-cial scene for over a decade now, this red-walled eatery is usually classified "continental," but en-trées like veal medallions in a pecan-bourbon sauce, red snapper in a walnut-herb sauce, and chicken breast over grilled mangoes with chile sauce make it a hybrid nouvelle American. Men must wear jackets for lunch, coat and tie for din-ner—even in July. At 1801 Post Oak (tel. 622-6778); open Mon.-Fri. for lunch and dinner, Sat. dinner only.

Barbecue

$ to $$ Goode Company Bar-B-Q: Often cited as the best barbecue place in the city, Jim Goode's original restaurant (he also has seafood and burger spinoffs) features a menu that goes beyond the standard brisket and links to include crisp-skinned duck, Czech sausage-and-ribs with "dirty rice," and jalapeño-cheese bread. At 5109 Kirby (tel. 713-522-2530); open daily for lunch and dinner.

$ to $$ County Line Barbeque: Yet another in the statewide chain that started in Austin, this '40s-style roadhouse is in a pleasant pinewood setting in northwest Houston; menu includes smoked duck and chicken. At 13850 Cutten, a mile north of FM 1960 (tel. 537-2454); open daily for lunch and dinner.

$ to $$ Luther's Bar-B-Q: A very popular Hous-ton-based chain specializing in slow-smoked bar-becue brisket, pork ribs, links, and chicken. At 8777 S. Main (tel. 432-1107) and 11 other loca-tions; open daily for lunch and dinner.

Cajun/Creole

Houston shines in this category, as there's a sub-stantial portion of Cajuns and Creoles among the local population. You might find more authentic cooking in Port Arthur or Beaumont (or farther east in Louisiana, of course), but you'd be hard-pressed to find this much variety. Crawfish are in season late October to May.

$$$ Alex Patout's Louisiana Restaurant: Most Houstonians say Alex's has the city's best Creole kitchen. The menu offers black-bean soup, crab-crawfish cakes, eggplant fritters with a cream crawfish topping, and other innovative Creole stylings, as well as standard dishes; prices are moderate considering the chef's magic touch. Jackets are required at dinner for men. At 615 Stuart (tel. 713-520-5081); open Mon.-Fri. for lunch, Mon.-Sat. for dinner, and Sun. for brunch.

$$$+ Brennan's: A branch of the famed New Orleans Brennan's, this one has added a few Texas/Southwestern dishes, such as oysters in a chile-corn salsa, to its mostly Creole menu. As in New Orleans, men are required to wear jackets for dinner. At 3300 Smith (tel. 522-9711); open Mon.-Fri. for lunch, daily for dinner, Sat. and Sun. for brunch.

$$ Louisiana Don's: This long-established restaurant (originally started in Lafayette, Louisiana, in 1934) specializes in Cajun seafood—gumbos, bisques, jambalaya, stuffed red snapper, fried oysters, soft-shell crab, and frogs' legs. On Friday nights they have live Cajun and zydeco bands. At 3009 Post Oak (tel. 629-5380); open daily for lunch and dinner.

$ to $$ Pe-Te Cajun: This honky-tonk restau-rant is a few miles southeast of town on Old Galveston Rd. (State 3) toward the NASA center, but it's worth the drive on Saturday afternoons when they feature Cajun or zydeco bands along with gumbo, boudin (rice and pork sausage), al-ligator stew, red beans and rice, hog cracklins, and other down-home Cajun dishes. At 11902 Old Galveston Rd. (tel. 481-8736); open Mon.-Thurs. 9-7, Fri. 9-8, Sat. 10:30-6:30 (except the third Sat. of the month when they're open till mid-night for "double dances").

$ to $$ **Ragin' Cajun:** Despite the lame name, this funky cafe does some of the best Cajun cooking in the city. Dishes include crawfish pie, fried rabbit, and étouffée. At 4302 Richmond (tel. 623-6321); open Mon.-Sat. for lunch and dinner.

$$ **Treebeard's:** The place to go if you're looking for a downtown lunch spot for Cajun/Creole. At 315 Travis (tel. 225-2160); open Mon.-Fri. for lunch.

Caribbean

$$ **Calypso:** This place covers the territory with everything from Jamaican curries to Cuban black-bean soup, in a '50s Miami setting. Live music on some evenings. At 5555 Morningside (tel. 713-524-8571); open Mon.-Sat. for lunch and dinner.

$$ **Caribbean Cuisine:** This one serves mostly Jamaican dishes, including chicken curry and oxtail stew. At 7433 Bissonnet (tel. 774-7428); open Mon.-Sat. for lunch and dinner.

Chinese

Houston's many Chinese restaurants seem to come in two varieties—flashy, expensive places full of *gwailos* (non-Asians), usually set in shopping centers or malls, and inexpensive, no-interior-design places in Chinatown (mostly along St. Emanuel and Chartres, east of downtown), where the local Chinese tend to eat.

$$ to $$$ **Dong Ting:** The owner is a native of China's Hunan Province, so spicy Hunan cuisine is the focus, along with a mix of other regional dishes. House specialities include smoked duck and crab in black-bean sauce. *USA Today* named this one of the best nine Chinese restaurants in the country. At 611 Stuart (tel. 713-527-0005); open Mon.-Sat. for lunch and dinner.

$ **Hung Kee Restaurant:** In the heart of Chinatown, this place specializes in fresh egg noodles and Mandarin cuisine. At 902 St. Emanuel (tel. 225-9401); open daily 11 a.m.-10 p.m.

$ to $$ **New Grand Palace:** The main draw of this Chinatown restaurant is the dim sum, including nearly 40 varieties of dumplings, served 10-3 daily. At 1613 St. Emanuel (tel. 223-2939); open daily for lunch and dinner (plus as noted for dim sum).

$$$+ **Uncle Tai's:** A branch of the New York Uncle Tai's and arguably the best (inarguably, the most expensive) Chinese restaurant in the city. The menu is extensive, with a preponderance of Hunan dishes. At 1980 Post Oak (tel. 960-8000); open daily for lunch and dinner.

Down-home

This is East Texas, state stronghold of "down-home" or Southern cooking. Then again, this is Houston, so expect some urban variations.

$$ **The Black-Eyed Pea:** Down-home-style specialties here include pot roast, meatloaf, and fresh catfish, along with fried okra, baked squash, and cornbread. At seven locations throughout the city, including 4729 Calhoun, near the University of Houston (tel. 713-748-0471); open daily for lunch and dinner.

$ to $$ **This Is It:** An independent, funky place that's been serving soul food for over 25 years—ham hocks, chitlins, smothered steak, cabbage, cornbread, rice, sweet potatoes, pinto beans, and many other classics, depending on what's in the steam table. At 239 W. Gray at Genessee (tel. 523-5319); open Mon.-Sat. for breakfast, lunch, and dinner (till 3 a.m. Fri. and Sat.).

Health Food

$$ **Rich's Café:** Conveniently located in Ye Seekers Natural Foods and Supermarket (tel. 713-461-0858), 9336 Westview; open Mon.-Sat. for lunch and dinner, Sun. for lunch only.

Indian

The city has several adequate Indian restaurants, all serving similar North Indian, tandoori-based cuisines. The muggy, almost equatorial climate is begging for a good South Indian place, but so far no one's taken that adventurous step.

$ to $$ **Bombay Palace:** This restaurant is easy to find and has an all-you-can-eat lunch buffet Mon.-Friday. All the usual chicken, lamb, and beef dishes, grilled or in curries. At 3901 Westheimer (tel. 713-960-8472); open daily for lunch and dinner.

$$ **India's Restaurant:** One of the few Indian restaurants in the city that isn't afraid to bring dishes more in line with authentic recipes by adding a little chile to them. At 5704 Richmond (tel. 266-0131); open daily for lunch and dinner.

$$ **Shiva:** North Indian again, focusing on tandoori. At 2514 Times (tel. 523-4753).

Italian And Pizza

$$ to $$$ **Damian's Cucina Italiana:** A city favorite with standard pasta dishes as well as more trendy entrées like grilled chicken with sun-dried tomatoes and goat cheese. At 3011 Smith (tel. 713-522-0439); open Mon.-Fri. for lunch and dinner, Sat. dinner only.

$$ Carrabba's: The woodburning oven here turns out some of the best pizza in town; there's homemade pasta, too. At 1399 S. Voss (tel. 468-0868) and 3115 Kirby (tel. 522-3131); open daily for lunch and dinner.

$$ Nash D'Amico's Pasta & Clam Bar: Like the name suggests, clams and pasta are the focus here; other fresh seafood is available as well. The menu was created with the help of the American Heart Association and a registered nutritionist, so the choices are made as guilt-free as possible. At 2421 Times Blvd. in the Village (tel. 521-3010) and 5640 Westheimer (tel. 960-1230); open Mon.-Fri. for lunch and dinner, Sat. and Sun. for dinner only.

$$ to $$$ Rao's: This is another Italian place with a light, low-calorie touch. One of the house specialties is *ossobuco* with *risotto*, along with grilled seafood and pastas. At 3700 Richmond (tel. 622-8245); open Mon.-Fri. for lunch and dinner, Sat. for dinner only.

$$ Pizzeria Uno: A branch of the famous Chicago pizza parlor, known for its deep-dish-style pizzas. At 7531 Westheimer (tel. 780-8866); open daily for lunch and dinner.

$ to $$ Star Pizza: This is a favorite among Houston students because the pizza is quick, tasty, and inexpensive. At 2111 Norfolk, off Montrose (tel. 523-0800); open daily for lunch and dinner.

Japanese

$$ Tokyo Gardens: Houston's longest-running Japanese restaurant and sushi bar; classical Japanese dancing nightly. At 4701 Westheimer (tel. 713-622-7886); open Mon.-Fri. for lunch and dinner, Sat. and Sun. for dinner only.

$$ Miyako Japanese Restaurant & Sushi Bar: Extensive sashimi selection, tatami dining rooms. At 6345 Westheimer (tel. 781-6300) and 2444 Times Blvd. (tel. 520-9797); open daily for lunch and dinner.

$$ Yoshida-Ya: Blond-wood paneling brings a reasonable facsimile of modern Tokyo to Houston; the sushi and traditional Japanese dishes are also authentic. At 855 Frostwood (tel. 464-3449); open Mon.-Sat. for lunch and dinner, Sun. dinner only.

Mexican

Mexican food in Houston is better than in Dallas, but not quite as good as in San Antonio, Austin, or El Paso (and there's a definite lack of places with Mexican breakfasts).

$ to $$ Amalia's: Some Houstonians say Amalia's has the city's best chicken and beef fajitas. Their salsas—an avocado-based green one and a garlic-infused red one—also get raves. At 6802B Southwest Fwy., between Hillcroft and Bellaire Blvd. (tel. 785-4533); open daily for lunch and dinner.

$$ to $$$ Armando's: This is the city's most upscale Mexican place and one of the most authentic (e.g., they use white Mexican cheese rather than orange American). At 1811 S. Shepherd (tel. 521-9752); open daily for lunch and dinner.

$$ Cadillac Bar: Yet another clone of Nuevo Laredo's 1920s border classic. Some of the menu items, like *cabrito,* roast quail, and frogs legs, are the same as the south-of-the-border Cadillac; others are Houston additions. At 1902 Shepherd (tel. 862-2020); open daily for lunch and dinner.

$ Cortés Meat Market & Deli: This homey hole-in-the-wall is recommended for aficionados of bean-and-cheese and bean-and-rice tacos; available enhancers include a mind-bending green salsa, fresh guacamole, and *pico de gallo.* They also serve fajitas rancheras, ceviche, and Mexican breakfasts. At 2404 W. Alabama (tel. 522-7771); open daily for breakfast and lunch.

$$ Cyclone Anaya: Very popular for its giant frozen margaritas; the food is classic Tex-Mex, with fajitas and soft tacos prominently featured. Named for a pro wrestler. At 1015 Durham (tel. 862-3209); open daily for lunch and dinner.

$ to $$ Doneraki's: A Greek family owns this authentic Tex-Mex restaurant that features Laredo-style *machitos* (goat-tripe sausage), *tacos al carbon, molcajete,* and fajitas. At 2836 Fulton (tel. 224-2509); open daily for lunch and dinner, weekends till 3 a.m.

$$ Merida Restaurant: Great Yucatecan specialties, including *cochinita pibil* (marinated, pit-cooked pork), which can be ordered in *panuchos* (Yucatecan-style tacos with extra-thick corn tortillas and black beans). At 2509 Navigation (tel. 227-0260); open daily for lunch and dinner.

$ Taquería Mexico: An urban *taquería* with a good selection of fillings, including *milanesa, pollo guisada,* and *barbacoa,* plus coconut *horchata,* a traditional Mexican beverage that's not commonly found in Texas. At 7626 Clarewood (tel. 713-271-0174); open Sun.-Thurs. for breakfast, lunch, and dinner, Fri. and Sat. 24 hours.

Seafood

$ Captain Benny's: Benny's has four locations, all small and designed to look like boats. The oysters, crab, catfish, shrimp, and gumbo are quick, fresh, cheap, and tasty. At 8018 Katy Fwy. (tel. 713-683-1042); open Mon.-Sat. for lunch and dinner.

$$ Christie's: A Houston institution since 1917, Christie's has a friendly, family atmosphere and no-frills, simply prepared seafood that's mostly fresh from the Gulf. At four locations, including 6029 Westheimer (tel. 978-6563) and 3512 S. Main (tel. 522-5041); open daily for lunch and dinner.

$$ Goode Company Texas Seafood: A successful spinoff of Goode's barbecue restaurant that specializes in mesquite-grilled seafood. At 2621 Milford (tel. 523-7154); open daily for lunch and dinner.

$$ Pappas Seafood House & Oyster Bar: Probably the most popular seafood restaurant in the city, Pappas serves fresh Gulf fish and shellfish fried, blackened, or pan-broiled. At five locations, including 6894 Southwest Fwy. (tel. 784-4729) and 12010 I-10 E (tel. 453-3265); open daily for lunch and dinner.

$$ to $$$ Shanghai Red's: People come here for the nighttime view of the Houston Ship Channel. Offers a variety of fresh seafood. At 8501 Cypress (tel. 926-6666); open daily for lunch and dinner.

$$ Tony Mandola's: Fresh seafood with an Italian slant, including crawfish ravioli (in season). At 1962 W. Gray (tel. 528-3474); open Mon.-Sat. for lunch and dinner, Sun. for dinner only.

Steak

$$ Cattleguard: A macho, ranch-style steakhouse that serves large portions of Mexican and Cajun as well as steak. At 2800 Milam (tel. 713-520-5400); open daily for lunch and dinner.

$$$ Lynn's Steakhouse: Prime beef (filet, strip, ribeye, and porterhouse) is cut to order here. At 955 Dairy Ashford (tel. 870-0807); open Mon.-Sat. for lunch and dinner.

$$$ Ruth's Chris Steak House: A transplant from the Panhandle (Amarillo and Lubbock) that serves only USDA prime beef, plus lamb, veal, and seafood. At 6213 Richmond (tel. 789-2333); open daily for lunch and dinner.

Thai

$$ Paddy Thai Cuisine: A small, intimate restaurant where the Thai menu changes nightly. At 6018 Westheimer (tel. 713-782-4849); open Mon.-Fri. for lunch and dinner, Sat. for dinner only.

$$ Patu Thai: New owners have taken over the old location of Renu's Thai Village, Houston's oldest Thai restaurant. Good bets on the menu include *yam makheua* (roasted egplant salad), chicken *panang* (a savory curry), and *pad voon sen* (spicy bean thread noodles with chicken and shrimp).

$$ Thai Pepper: Houston's most authentic Thai restaurant (many fewer Chinese menu items) uses fresh herbs and spices, and no MSG. The *yam* ("lime salads" on the menu) are especially good. At 2120 Post Oak (tel. 963-0341); open Mon.-Fri. for lunch and dinner, Sat. for dinner only.

Vietnamese

$ to $$ Van Loc Restaurant: The menu here encompasses 140 reasonably priced Vietnamese and Chinese dishes. At 3010 Milam (tel. 713-528-6441); open daily for lunch and dinner till midnight, on weekends till 3 a.m.

$ to $$ Vietnam Restaurant: Standard Vietnamese specialties; lunch buffet weekdays. At 3215 Main at Elgin (tel. 526-0917); open daily for lunch and dinner till midnight, on weekends till 3 a.m.

ENTERTAINMENT

Live Music

Houston's black wards (especially the 4th and 5th wards) were very influential in the early Texas blues scene and the city is still very much a blues and R&B town, with a little zydeco and country thrown in for good measure. The *Houston Post Calendar* appears every Sunday with a fairly complete listing of the more popular clubs. More complete is the one compiled weekly by *Coors Light Music News* and distributed at local clubs and music shops.

Several clubs in the Heights district, north of Buffalo Bayou, book a mix of local, regional, and national acts, mostly (but not limited to) roots rock, blues, and R&B: **Bon Ton Room** (tel. 864-0001, 4216 Washington), **Black Forest Tavern & Gardens** (tel. 713-861-2968, 3426 Feagan at Waugh), **Fitzgerald's** (tel. 862-7580, 2706 White Oak), **Reddi Room** (tel. 868-6188, 2626 White Oak), and **Rockefeller's** (tel. 861-9365, 3620 Washington). In a similar vein but just northeast of downtown is the **Last Concert Cafe** (tel. 226-8563, 1403 Nance). **Zelda's** (tel. 862-7469, 2706 White Oak) is in the Heights but features pop and modern-rock bands. North of the Heights but just inside the loop is **Dan Electro's Guitar Bar** (tel. 862-8707, 1031 E. 24th), where Mon. night is blues night, Tues. and Wed. are open-mike nights, Thurs.-Sat. mostly rock 'n' roll (the name comes from the decor—on the walls hang a number of guitars, including some rare Danelectros). **Etta's Lounge** (tel. 528-2611, 5120 Scott), south of downtown, features mostly blues—one of the last of the city's great blues bars that were so common in the '30s and '40s.

Probably the best place to hear zydeco in Houston is at Catholic church dances—there's usually at least one Creole parish holding a zydeco dance on any given weekend (12 or 13 of them rotate by month, including St. Nicholas, St. Francis, St. Peter the Apostle, Our Lady Star of the Sea, St. Anne, and St. Gregory the Great). Three clubs book zydeco acts on weekends as well: **Zydeco Cha-Cha Lounge** (no phone, 5115 Hirsch), the **Continental Lounge** (tel. 713-229-8624, 3101 Collingsworth), and the **Silver Slipper Club** (tel. 673-9004, 3717 Crane). None of these clubs are in so-called "good" neighborhoods, so it's best to check them out in the daytime first to see if they're your cup of tea or not. Somewhat tamer are the several Cajun restaurants that feature Cajun and zydeco bands on the weekends, including **Pe-Te Cajun** (see "Food" above for addresses). The Black Forest (mentioned above) also frequently books zydeco bands.

For jazz, a longtime Houston favorite is **Cody's** (tel. 713-522-9747, 3400 Montrose), which also has a nighttime view of the city. Most other jazz in the city is of the piano-bar variety.

Oddly enough, considering the setting, British-style pubs are fashionable in Houston. Several of them book local rock and folk bands, including the **Pig n' Whistle I** (tel. 713-522-0706, 2150 Richmond), the **Pig n' Whistle Live** (tel. 952-9607, 6333 Richmond), the **Ale House** (tel. 521-2333, 2425 Alabama), the **Red Lion** (tel. 795-5000, 7315 S. Main), **Sherlock's Baker St. Pub** (tel. 977-1857, 10001 Westheimer, in Carillon Center), and the **Black Labrador Pub** (tel. 529-1199, 4100 Montrose). For low-key, singer-songwriter-type gigs, there's the established **Anderson Fair** (tel. 528-8576, 2007 Grant St.), **Ovations** (tel. 522-0706, Times Blvd. at Kirby), and **Wunsche Bros. Cafe** (tel. 350-1902, 103 Midway in Old Town Spring).

The Axiom (tel. 713-224-1420, 2524 McKinney) belongs in its own category: Texas avant-garde—punk, sub-metal, poetry, and performance art.

Of the many country-music venues in and around the city, the most popular are **The Chip Kicker** (tel. 713-440-8882, 3225 FM 1960), **Bullwhip** (tel. 778-1200, 7011 Southwest Fwy. between Hillcroft and Bellaire), and **Eddie's Country Ballroom** (tel. 489-8181, State 288, Manvel). The **City Auditorium** (tel. 331-9382, Lewis Ln. at FM 1128) in nearby Manvel (just south of Houston) also books occasional country shows, like the Southern Opry, as does the **Sons of Hermann Skyline Ballroom** (tel. 862-0018, 147 Heights).

Comedy

Houston has four, count 'em, four comedy clubs. Two are in hotels, **A Good Humor Bar** (tel. 713-444-4312, Holiday Inn North, 17610 North Fwy.), which usually features performances on weekends only, and **The Punch Line** (tel. 960-0111, Marriott Hotel, Loop 610 at San Felipe), with Tues.-Sun. performances. **The Comedy Showcase** (tel. 481-1188, 12547 Gulf Fwy. at Fuqua) and **The Laff Stop** (tel. 524-2333, 1952 W. Gray) book touring as well as local acts, Wed.-Sunday.

The **Radio Music Theater** (tel. 713-522-7722) at 1840 Westheimer is a unique comedy repertory group that performs skits inspired by different radio-show styles. Performances (some of which are recorded for a nationally syndicated radio broadcast) are Thurs.-Sat. nights.

Wortham Center

This 437,000-square-foot, $70.5 million performing arts center is a city showpiece. A variety of events are scheduled here throughout the year, but its main function is as a home for the **Houston Ballet** and the **Houston Grand Opera,** each with separate theaters within the center. The Houston Ballet (tel. 713-523-6300) is a first-rate company that tours the U.S. and abroad regularly.

The Wortham Center is open for tours Mon.-Fri. 10-3 and Sat. 10-11; admission is $2 for adults and $1 for children 6-18.

Radio

Houston has radio stations for practically every taste. Rockers listen to KLOL FM 101.1, kickers (country music fans) to KIKK FM 95.7, and for public radio fans it's KTSU FM 90.9 (which broadcasts a broad variety of jazz, blues, and gospel; listen for the all-night blues show every Monday). KMJQ FM 102 plays jazz and R&B while KCOH AM 1430 plays straight R&B. KYST AM 920 plays a mix of rock, dance tunes, and Tejano music; KLAT AM 1010 plays Latin and Tejano music 24 hours a day. The only station that plays music by local bands (mixed in with Top 40) is KRBE AM 1070.

EVENTS

February
Chinese New Year Festival: The timing for this festival varies according to the Chinese lunar calendar (call 713-780-8112 for current scheduling). Activities include fireworks, lion parades, food vendors, and music. At McKinney and St. Emanuel in Chinatown.

February-March
Houston Livestock Show And Rodeo: Usually held the last 10 days in February and first week of March at the Astrodome (Kirby and S. Loop 610) and adjacent Astrohall and Astroarena. The rodeo ranks as a top-five event, with a payout of over $325,000.

April
Houston International Festival: An arts and culture festival that celebrates Houston's ethnic diversity and brings in artists and performers from abroad as well. Events include outdoor music, dance, and theater performances, arts and crafts shows, food presentations, and the Houston International Film Festival. Held for 10 days beginning the third week of the month at various locations throughout the city.

May
Cinco De Mayo: A celebration of Mexico's victory over the French navy in 1862, featuring food vendors, music, and dancing. At the Brown Convention Center on the nearest weekend to May 5th.

Heights Home Tour: During Mother's Day weekend several historic homes in the Heights district are open for tours. Call the Greater Houston Convention and Visitors Council (tel. 713-523-5050) for information.

June
Juneteenth: Houston's biggest annual celebration commemorates the June 19, 1865, announcement in Galveston that slavery was abolished. Activities are mostly based around music, starting off with the Juneteenth USA Gospel Festival and the Juneteenth Blues Festival at Miller Outdoor Theater on the weekend before Juneteenth weekend. Then on the weekend nearest to June 19, the National Emancipation Association sponsors a Juneteenth Freedom Festival, also at Miller Outdoor Theater. In between the two weekends are various other cultural events celebrating Houston's African-American heritage.

September
Fiestas Patrias: A celebration of Mexican Independence Day (Sept. 16) that features a downtown parade, beauty pageant, ball, music and dance festivals, and civic awards ceremonies held at various locations throughout the city.

October
Italian Parade And Festival: Three days of food, music, and parades, held on the nearest weekend to Columbus Day at St. Anne's Catholic Church on Westheimer.

Alamo Challenge Bike Trek: A two-day, 160-mile bicycle race between Houston and San Antonio, sponsored by the American Lung Association and held on the second weekend of the month. Call (800) 252-5864 for information.

Asian-American Festival: A weekend of Asian arts, music, dance, food, and cultural exhibits at Miller Outdoor Theater, on the third weekend of the month.

October-November
Texas Renaissance Festival: This popular theme festival is held 45 miles northwest of the city off FM 1774 between Plantersville and Magnolia every weekend between Oct. 1 and Nov. 15. The food, entertainment, costumes, arts and crafts, and setting attempt to re-create the atmosphere of Renaissance England.

November
Foley's Thanksgiving Day Parade: A classic American-style parade that starts downtown in front of Foley's department store (1110 Main).

SPORTS AND RECREATION

Baseball
The hometown pro team is the **Houston Astros** (tel. 713-799-9555 for tickets), who play home games April-Oct. at the Astrodome.

Basketball
The **Houston Rockets** (tel. 713-627-0600 for tickets) play Oct.-April at The Summit (Greenway Plaza, Southwest Fwy.).

Football
The underdog **Houston Oilers** (tel. 713-797-1000 for tickets) play Sept.-Dec. at the Astrodome.

Bicycling
Houston has a very active cycling community, probably because the city and surrounding area are so flat. The **Houston Bicycle Club** (tel. 713-529-9709, Box 52752, Houston, TX 76101) has information on local cycling events. Alexander Deussen County Park (see "Campgrounds And RV Parks" above) has several miles of bicycle trails, as does Brazos Bend State Park southwest of Houston (see "Brazos Bend State Park" below).

Alkek Velodrome (tel. 713-578-0858) is a unique facility operated by the city Parks and Recreation Dept. in Cullen Park, 19008 Saums Road. This Olympic-standard bike arena (333 meters long with a 33° incline) is open for general recreational use as well as serious training. Races are held on Sat. evenings; racing instruction is available.

Golf
Seven municipal 18-hole golf courses are open to the public: **Brock** (tel. 713-458-1350, 8201 John Ralston Rd.), **Glenbrook** (tel. 644-4801, 8101 Bayou Dr.), **Hermann** (tel. 526-0077, 6110 Golf Course Dr.), **Memorial** (tel. 862-4033), **Sharpstown** (tel. 988-2099, 6600 Harbor Town), and **Wortham** (tel. 921-3227, 7000 Capitol). Hours are daily 6-6 in the winter, 7 a.m.-8:30 p.m. in the summer.

Tennis
Many of the public parks in Houston have tennis courts where play is conducted on a first-come, first-served basis. The city also operates three tennis centers that take reservations: **Homer L.**

Ford Center (tel. 713-747-5466, 5225 Calhoun, 16 lighted courts), **Memorial Tennis Center** (tel. 861-3765, 6000 Memorial Loop Dr., Memorial Park, 18 lighted courts), and **Southwest Tennis Center** (tel. 772-0296, 9506 Gessner, 26 lighted courts). Rates are the same at all three: $3.50 per hour-and-a-half before 5:30 p.m. on weekdays, $5.50 per hour-and-a-half after 5:30 and on weekends.

Parks And Gardens
The **Armand Bayou Nature Center** (tel. 713-474-2551), off I-45 S at 8600 Bay Area, is an 1,800-acre preserve with woodland, marsh, and prairie nature trails, plus a working turn-of-the-century farm. The bayou, which feeds into Clear Lake, is popular for boating. Free guided tours are given on weekends. Open daily 9-5; admission is $2.50 for adults, $1 for seniors and children 5-17.

Mercer Arboretum and Botanic Gardens (tel. 713-443-9731), off Aldine-Westfield Rd. in Humble (a small township next to Houston Intercontinental Airport), features 214 acres of formal gardens displaying local flora, five miles of nature trails, and a Big Thicket-style arboretum with a picnic area. Open daily 8 a.m.-7 p.m. during Daylight Saving Time, 8-5 Standard Time; free admission. **Houston Arboretum and Nature Center** (tel. 681-8433), in Memorial Park (off I-10 at Woodway), is similar but smaller, though there are five miles of trails through native woods and prairies. Open dawn to dusk; free admission.

Buffalo Bayou
Houston got its start as a trading post on Buffalo Bayou and owes its preeminence as a port to the dredging of the bayou to create the Houston Ship Channel and Port of Houston. There's still a lot of bayou left, however; it bisects the city, beginning in rural west Harris County at Barker Reservoir (an impoundment of the bayou for flood control) and meanders 50 miles east through suburbs, downtown business districts, and parks to the ship channel, which feeds into a series of small bays off Galveston Bay. The most scenic section is in lush Memorial Park, where the bayou's banks are lined with black willow, sycamore, box elder, ash, and river birch, with an undergrowth of moss, ferns, verbena, dwarf palmetto, muscodyne vine, and mustang grape. Fauna sightings include the occasional alligator, opossum, or armadillo.

Canoeing is permitted along the bayou within Memorial Park and farther east in Cleveland Park; plans are underway to extend greenbelt areas along the bayou all the way from Cleveland Park to the ship channel. Canoe equipment can be rented or purchased from Canoesport (tel. 713-660-7000), 5630 Bellaire Boulevard.

The 14-acre gardens at **Bayou Bend** (tel. 713-529-8773) along Buffalo Bayou (at 1 Westcott St., off Memorial Dr.) are open for self-guided touring Wed.-Sat. 10-5, Sun. 1-5; admission is $2 for adults, free for children under 12; on the second Sun. of each month (March and August excepted) admission to the gardens is free for everyone.

Brazos Bend State Park

Less than 50 miles from the city is one of the state park system's largest parks, covering 4,897 acres of bayous, creeks, lakes, wetlands, coastal prairies, and hardwood forests. Migrating water-fowl, including ibis, grebes, egrets, and herons, are numerous here, as are white-tailed deer, feral hogs, Russian boars, gray foxes, bobcats, coyotes, and alligators.

Facilities: The 15 miles of hike-and-bike trails at Brazos Bend are some of the system's best maintained. Fishing is permitted on all of the park's six lakes; Elm Lake has seven piers, while both Forty Acre and Hale lakes have lighted piers for night fishing. Fish-cleaning tables are close at hand. Camping areas include primitive tentsites ($5 a night on weekdays, $7 on weekends), tent/camper sites with water ($7/9), multi-use sites with w/e ($10/12), and screened shelters ($15/18). For further information or campsite reservations, contact the Park Superintendent (tel. 409-553-3243), Brazos Bend State Park, 21901 FM 762, Needville, TX 77461.

Getting There: There are two routes from Houston, both about the same distance (45-50 miles). The scenic (and shorter) route is via State 288 south to Rosharon, then west on FM 1462. Slightly quicker because of the higher speed limit is US 59 south to Richmond, then east on FM 762.

Amusement Parks

AstroWorld (tel. 713-799-1234), opposite the Astrodome off Loop 610, covers 75 acres of concrete with over a hundred rides, including the Viper, a roller coaster that does a 360° loop inside the pitch-black "Viper Pit." Open Mon.-Fri. at 11 a.m., Sat. and Sun. at 10 a.m., late March to late May and Sept.-Nov.; closed at dusk. All-inclusive admission is $21 for adults, $15 children two years to 48 inches, $12 for seniors.

Next door is **WaterWorld** (tel. 713-799-8404) with various water rides and a wave pool. It's open the same hours as AstroWorld except that the season is May-September. Admission is $12.90 per person, free for children under three.

The complex also includes the **Southern Star Amphitheater** (tel. 713-799-1466), one of the city's main venues for large-scale concerts. The reserved area has 3,000 seats; beyond that it's general-admission grass seating.

SHOPPING

Shopping Areas

The Galleria at 5075 Westheimer is the city's premier mall. A three-level extravaganza centered around a skating rink with a vaulted-glass ceiling, its department-store pillars are Macy's, Marshall Fields, Neiman-Marcus, and Lord & Taylor. The nearby **Post Oak** area is thick with other high-end department stores and smaller boutiques.

Rice Village, near Rice University between Morningside, Kirby, University, and Bolsover, is a public-square-style shopping area frequented by students, faculty, medical center staff, tourists, and European expatriates. Clothing stores, arts and crafts shops, and bookstores sit side by side with bistros and neighborhood pubs. Even more idiosyncratic is the **Montrose** district, centered on Montrose Boulevard. This ever-changing area of small specialty stores near the museum district features designer clothing, jewelry, cards, and various art-oriented items.

Chinatown, bounded by St. Emanuel, Chartres, Lamar, and Rush in the downtown area offers a selection of shops dealing in Orientalia, including foods, jewelry, herbs, furniture, and clothing.

Antique Districts, Auction Houses, And Flea Markets

Junk-and-antiquity hunters will love Houston, which has more than its share in this category because of its huge port status. The **River Oaks Antiques Center** (tel. 713-520-8238) at 2119 Westheimer comprised of 25 antique dealers who mostly handle furniture, crystal, china, and jewelry. There are several other antique shops along Westheimer, from the 300 block out to Shepherd. Roughly parallel strips run along Washington and W. Gray farther north. **Norbert Antiques** (tel. 522-7300), 3607-3617 Main, specializes in French and English antiques, primarily furniture and objets d'art.

Bogan's Auction Barn (tel. 713-482-6983) at 15799 Telephone (one mile south of Pearland off State 35) auctions a broad selection of American antiques on Thurs. nights. **Falkirk Auction** (tel. 789-8883) at 8626 Westpark deals almost exclusively in Scottish antiques on Mon. and Thursday. **Webster's Auction Palace** holds its auctions of American antiques on Fri. and Sunday.

There are at least six flea markets in the city, all open on weekends only. The busiest is the outdoor **Houston Flea Market** (tel. 713-782-0391), also known as the Southwest Common Market, at 6616 Southwest Fwy. (Westpark exit). Booths cover 14 acres of pavement—very hot in the summertime. The **Coles Antique Village/Flea Market** (tel. 485-2277) at 1022 N. Main (off State 35 in Pearland) features 550 dealers in a 70,000-square-foot air-conditioned facility. Two more indoor places that beat the heat include the equally huge **Trade Mart** (tel. 467-2508) at 2121 W. Belt and **Trading Fair II** (tel. 731-1111) at 5515 S. Loop 610 near the Astrodome. The city has recently opened a new 100-acre flea market, **Trader's Village** (tel. 896-0017), with over 600 dealers, at 7979 N. Eldridge Parkway.

Western Wear

Several of Houston's western-wear stores have been around since the turn of the century. The city's oldest is **Stelzig's** (tel. 713-629-7779) at 3123 Post Oak, which has been a purveyor of boots, hats, saddles, and ranching supplies since 1870. Two venerable establishments specialize in hats (new and reconditioned): **Shudde Bros. Hatters** at 905 Trinity (est. 1907) and **Gary's Hat 'N' Boots** (tel. 227-2996) at 307 Louisiana (est. 1915). For custom-made boots, try the **Palace Boot Shop** (tel. 224-1411) at 1212 Prairie (est. 1919); they also carry factory-made boots. **Just Boots** (tel. 442-2617) at 11358 Eastex Fwy. is a chain outlet that sells several brands of Texas boots (and hats) at discount prices.

HOUSTON INFORMATION

Tourist Offices

The **Greater Houston Convention and Visitors Council** (tel. 713-523-5050 or 800-231-7799) at 3300 Main is open Mon.-Fri. 8:30-5, and has a wealth of free printed material on area attractions, services, and accommodations as well as a staffed information counter (French- and German-speaking specialists available).

Houston is the only Texas city outside of Laredo that has a **Mexican Government Tourist Office** (tel. 713-880-5253), at 2707 N. Loop 610 W, Suite 450.

Consulates

Houston has more foreign consulates than any other city in the state. If you're planning a trip outside the U.S. in the near future, this is a good place to collect the necessary visas. Most of the consulates are located in the city's west end. (See "Houston Consulates" chart.)

Telephone

The area code for Houston is 713.

TELEPHONE AND EMERGENCY INFORMATION

Emergency (police, fire, medical)	911
Travelers Aid	668-0911 or 223-8946
Coast Guard Air and Sea Rescue	481-0657
Time/Temperature	976-1122
Passport Office	653-3153 or 653-3159
Road Conditions	681-6187
Telephone Directory Assistance	1-411

Foreign Exchange

With all the international trade centered here, Houston is a good place to change foreign currency. **Thomas Cook Foreign Exchange** (tel. 713-782-8091) at 10777 Westheimer, Suite 105, is a full-service money-changing agency with good rates; they also sell travelers checks. **Texas Foreign Exchange** (tel. 654-0999) at 1130 Travis also handles foreign exchange, but the rates aren't quite as good as Thomas

Cook's. Some of the major banks offer foreign-exchange services for a limited number of currencies (German marks, Japanese yen, Mexican pesos), including **First Bank of Houston** (2824 Hillcroft), **First City Bancorporation of Texas** (1001 Main), and **Texas Commerce Bank** (712 Main).

TRANSPORT

Downtown Tunnel/Skywalk System

Dozens of buildings downtown are linked by a system of underground tunnels and suspended skywalks, open year-round. Maps are available at several junctions in the system.

City Buses

The **Metropolitan Transit Authority** (tel. 713-739-4000), called Metro for short, operates over 100 bus routes in the city and parts of surrounding Harris County (including the NASA/Clear Lake area). General fares are 85 cents. Two of the downtown routes are only 25 cents; the Texas Special Red runs along Lamar, McKinney, Smith, and Louisiana,while the Texas Special Blue runs on Franklin, Main, Travis, and short sections of Calhoun and Pierce.

On all routes, free transfers are available for bus changes and short stopovers. A free *Transit Map of Greater Houston* is available from the Greater Houston Convention and Visitors Council at 3300 Main.

Inter-city Buses

The **Greyhound-Trailways Bus Terminal** (tel. 713-759-6515) is at 2121 Main downtown, where buses are available to most major towns in the state and beyond. **Texas Bus Lines** (tel. 523-5694) departs from the same terminal to various regional destinations, including Galveston (seven departures a day, $9 one way).

Train

The Amtrak passenger station is at 902 Washington downtown. The *Sunset Limited* has thrice-weekly service, west to Los Angeles, east to New Orleans. Call 800-USA-RAIL for schedule information.

The *Texas Limited* (tel. 713-522-0574 or 800-522-0574) is a passenger excursion train that runs

between Houston's Amtrak station and the Galveston railway station (25th and The Strand) Fri.-Sun. for $45.50 1st class ($33.50 children 12 and under) and $27.50 excursion class ($20 children 12 and under) roundtrip. The trip takes two hours and 20 minutes each way. On Fri. and Sat. the train leaves Houston at 9:30 a.m. and returns from Galveston at 3 p.m.; on Sun. it leaves Houston at 11 a.m. and returns at 5 p.m.

The *Texas Limited* pulls five refurbished coaches from railroad yesteryear: the *Chimayo* (a 1938 Pullman originally built for Santa Fe's famous Super Chief), the *Hawkeye* (1941, from the Chicago, Rock Island, and Pacific Railroad's Rocket streamliners), the *Silver Stirrup* (1948, former service for the California Zephyr), the *Silver Queen* (1957, Minneapolis & St. Louis), and the *NYC 61* (late '40s, New York Central). Advance ticket purchase is required; tickets are available at any Ticketron outlet in Houston or in Galveston at the Railroad Museum (25th and The Strand).

Taxis

Houston has around 20 taxi companies. **Yellow Cab** (tel. 713-236-1111) is the largest; others include **United Cab** (tel. 699-0000) and **Liberty Cab** (tel. 999-0088). **Fiesta Cab** (tel. 255-2666) has Spanish bilingual drivers.

Airports

Houston Intercontinental Airport, 22 miles north of the city via Eastex Fwy. (US 59), is Houston's main air hub, with daily service to 101 U.S. destinations and 26 international destinations. Its four terminals and Marriott Hotel are connected by an efficient subway system but the airport is miserably lacking in restaurant quality and economy. Driving to the airport from the city takes a half-hour when the traffic's light, at least 45 minutes during rush hours. **Airport Express** (tel. 713-523-8888) operates a shuttle between the airport and three city terminals—the Hyatt Regency downtown, the Texas Medical Center, and the Galleria/Post Oaks/Greenway area (5000 Richmond)—every half-hour for $9.70 per person one way. A taxi from Intercontinental to downtown Houston costs a flat rate of $26.50.

Hobby Airport was the city's first commercial airport but is now relegated to secondary status, with daily flights to 72 U.S. cities. The food selection here is better than at Intercontinental; the **Food**

HOUSTON CONSULATES
Area code: 713

Argentina
(tel. 971-8935)
2000 Post Oak, Ste. 1810

Australia
(tel. 629-9131)
1990 Post Oak, Ste. 800

Austria
(tel. 623-2233)
4800 San Felipe, Ste. 1100

Belgium
(tel. 529-0775)
2929 Allen Pkwy., Ste. 2222

Brazil
(tel. 961-3063)
1333 W. Loop 610 S,
Ste. 1100

Canada
(tel. 627-7433)
3935 Westheimer, Ste. 301

Chile
(tel. 621-5853)
1360 Post Oak, Ste. 2300

China
(tel. 524-0780)
3417 Montrose

Colombia
(tel. 527-8919)
2990 Richmond, Ste. 544

Costa Rica
(tel. 785-1315)
3000 Wilcrest, Ste. 544

Denmark
(tel. 622-7514)
5 Post Oak, Ste. 2180

Ecuador
(tel. 622-1787)
4200 Westheimer

Egypt
(tel. 961-4915)
2000 W. Loop 610 S.,
Ste.1750

El Salvador
(tel. 270-6239)
6655 Hillcroft, Ste. 112

Finland
(tel. 627-9700)
1300 Post Oak, Ste. 1990

France
(tel. 528-2181)
2727 Allen Pkwy., Ste. 976

Germany
(tel. 627-7770)
1330 Post Oak, Ste. 1850

Indonesia
(tel. 785-1691)
5633 Richmond

Israel
(tel. 627-3780)
1 Greenway Plaza, Ste. 722

Italy
(tel. 850-7520)
1300 Post Oak, Ste. 660

Japan
(tel. 652-2977)
1000 Louisiana

Korea
(tel. 961-0186)
1990 Post Oak, Ste. 745

Mexico
(tel. 524-2300)
4200 Montrose, Ste. 120

Morocco
(tel. 963-9110)
5555 Del Monte #2405

Netherlands
(tel. 622-8000)
2200 Post Oak, Ste. 610

Norway
(tel. 521-2900)
2777 Allen Pkwy., Ste. 1185

Peru
(tel. 781-5000)
5847 San Felipe, Ste. 1481

Philippines
(tel. 621-8618)
5177 Richmond, Ste. 1100

Saudi Arabia
(tel. 785-5577)
5718 Westheimer, Ste. 1500

South Africa
(tel. 850-0150)
1980 Post Oak, Ste. 1520

Spain
(tel. 783-6200)
2411 Fountainview, Ste. 130

Switzerland
(tel. 650-0000)
1000 Louisiana, Ste. 5670

Turkey
(tel. 622-5849)
1990 Post Oak, Ste. 1300

United Kingdom
(tel. 659-6270)
2250 Dresser Tower,
601 Jefferson

Venezuela
(tel. 961-5141)
2700 Post Oak, Ste. 1500

Court allows travelers to choose from several fast-food outlets, including **Porras Mexican Food,** where a vegetarian burrito costs less than $2.

Hobby is only seven miles southeast of town, about 15-20 minutes during off-peak traffic periods, up to 45 minutes in rush hours. A **Hobby Airport Limousine Service** (tel. 713-644-8359) van is $5 to/from downtown (same city terminals as for Airport Express), $11.50 to/from Intercontinental. Continental Airlines's **Continental Express** flies turboprops between the two airports for $25 (or free if you're flying out of Intercontinental on a Continental ticket).

Taxi service between Hobby and downtown is $15-18.

Tours
Gray Line (tel. 713-223-8800) offers a four-hour tour of the city ($20 per person), a four-hour tour of Johnson Space Center ($20), an eight-hour city/space center/Port of Houston tour ($35), and a nighttime steakhouse/Gilley's tour ($39).

BEAUMONT-PORT ARTHUR-ORANGE

Beaumont (pop. 120,000), Port Arthur (pop. 59,000), and Orange (pop. 19,000) form a triangle that encompasses two counties in the southeastern corner of the state. This area borders southwestern Louisiana and is sometimes called the Cajun Triangle because of the predominance of Cajun culture on either side of the state boundaries here (see "The People," p. 37, for a description of the Cajuns). It has also been called the Golden Triangle for the abundance of oil that brought wealth to these communities during the 20th century.

All three cities have deep-water ports and oil refineries, though the surrounding counties are very rural; shipping, marine construction/repair, petrochemical production, agriculture (primarily rice cultivation), and crawfish farming are the primary sources of income. This variety of economic opportunities has drawn a multicultural melange of people from far and wide. The result is that, in terms of regional culture, this is one of the richest areas in the state.

The area code for all telephone numbers in the triangle area is 409.

BEAUMONT

History
The lower Neches River area was first settled by Spanish and French fur trappers in the early 1800s; the original Beaumont city charter was issued by the Republic of Texas in 1838. For the next six decades, the town supported itself almost exclusively by cutting the abundant local timber for lumber mills and growing (and milling) rice. The Neches River provided a convenient outlet to the Gulf of Mexico via Sabine Pass, so Beaumont products were able to reach a wide market.

Beaumont would probably have remained a sleepy agricultural town if it hadn't been for the gusher that blew in on January 10, 1901, at Spindletop, a salt-dome hill just south of town. It was the largest-producing oil field in America at the time and ushered in an era of cheap liquid fuel that ignited the petrochemical industry worldwide. Six hundred oil companies sprang up over the next year or two, including a few that became industry giants: the Texas Company (Texaco), Guffey Petroleum Company (Gulf, now Chevron), Magnolia Petroleum Company (Mobil), and Standard Oil (Exxon).

Today Beaumont is the state's fourth-largest port and the county seat for Jefferson County, which has one of the highest percentages of African-American residents in the state (32%, compared with 61% Caucasian and 2% Hispanic). Black culture has had a strong influence on Beaumont's cultural identity, from arts and music to cuisine (perhaps best experienced during Juneteenth festivities—see "Events" below). Beaumont is also known for its small, offbeat museums.

Sights
Spindletop/Gladys City Boomtown And Lucas Gusher Monument: This is a reproduction of the small boom towns that grew up practically overnight in the Spindletop area in 1901-02. Located on Lamar University campus (University Dr. and US 69/ 96/287), the exhibit consists of 15 clapboard buildings around a square—including replicas of oil company offices, a general store, post office, barbershop, saloon, and livery. The

BEAUMONT–PORT ARTHUR–ORANGE

© MOON PUBLICATIONS, INC.

complex is open Tues.-Sun. 1-5; admission is $2 adults, $1 cents children.

Nearby is a 58-foot granite monument to the gusher that changed East Texas history. It's named for Anthony Lucas, the Austrian engineer who drilled the first Spindletop well.

Art Museum of Southeast Texas: This well-designed facility (tel. 409-832-3432) at 500 Main St. houses permanent and traveling art exhibits by Texas artists. Besides the galleries, the museum has a sculpture courtyard and several rooms that host films, lectures, musical performances, and art classes. There's also a tea room that's open Tues.-Sun. for lunch (11:30-1:30). The galleries are open Tues.-Sat. 9-5, Sun. noon-5; free admission.

Edison Plaza Museum: The chief executive officer for Gulf States Utilities Co. from 1979 to 1982 donated the funds to restore the 1920s-vintage Travis St. Power Substation and convert it into this museum that celebrates the achievements of inventor Thomas Edison. Displays in-

clude several of Edison's original inventions, including an 1890s cylinder phonograph, the 1880 Mimeograph, the Ediphone, and "The Master Violet Ray Machine," which was once used to treat a wide variety of ailments. Other exhibits explain present energy technology and anticipate future developments. The museum (tel. 409-839-3089) is at 350 Pine, behind the Gulf State Utilities Building. Hours are Mon.-Fri. 8-5; free admission.

Fire Museum of Texas: Among the collection of antique firefighting equipment at this museum (tel. 409-880-3927), housed in the 1927 Beaumont Fire Dept. headquarters, are a 1779 Chinese hand pump, a horse-drawn fire wagon, an 1856 hand-drawn tub pumper, an 1879 steamer, and the country's first searchlight truck (which was developed in Beaumont in 1931). Also on display are collections of photos, newspaper clippings, and other memorabilia from famous fires. One of the fire poles in the museum is set up for children to slide down. The museum is open Mon.-Fri. 10-4; free admission.

Babe Didrikson Zaharias Memorial Museum: Beaumont native Zaharias was considered the greatest female athlete of the first half of the century. The Associate Press named her Woman Athlete of the Year six times—1931, 1945, 1946, 1947, 1950, and 1954. In track and field sports, she held or tied world records for four events and also gained All-American status in basketball. Later in her career she took up golf and eventually won every major golf championship at least once (most of them several times). In 1950 alone she won the All-American Open, World Championship, U.S. Women's Open, Titleholders, 144-hole Weathervane, and the Women's Western Open.

The round memorial building, located a mile off I-10 at the Gulf St. exit, contains a collection of trophies, awards, and other memorabilia tracing "The Babe's" career. Open daily 9-5; free admission.

John Jay French Museum: This simple Greek Revival-style house (tel. 409-898-3267) at 2985 French Rd. (Delaware exit, US 69/96/287 N) was the city's first two-story house and the first to be built of lumber rather than logs. Built in 1845 by merchant John Jay French, it is now operated as a museum by the Beaumont Heritage Society and has been refurbished in period style. Open Tues.-Sat. 10-4, Sun. 1-4; admission is $2 for adults, 50 cents for children under 18.

McFaddin-Ward House: This magnificent example of Beaux Arts Colonial architecture (tel. 409-832-2134), built in 1906, stayed in the McFaddin family until the 1982 death of Mamie McFaddin Ward, who had established a foundation before she died to provide for the preservation of the house as a museum. The rooms are decorated with antiques collected over a 75-year period, including noteworthy silver, porcelain, and Persian rug collections. The house is at 1906 McFaddin Ave. (from I-10 E exit at Calder, turn right to 3rd, then left to McFaddin). It's open Tues.-Sat. 10-4, Sun. 1-4 for one-hour guided tours (reservations suggested). Admission is $3; children under 12 aren't admitted.

Old Town: This 36-block area between Laurel, Harrison, 2nd, and 10th is noted for historic houses, many of which have been converted to shops selling jewelry, antiques, and clothing. The Babe Zaharias Visitor Center at I-10 W and Martin Luther King Pkwy. (exit 854) distributes a free map brochure of Old Town that lists all the shops and their locations.

Lamar University: This medium-sized university of 11,000 students offers a full range of undergraduate and graduate programs but is strongest in health sciences, engineering, and computer science. The Fine Arts and Theater Departments are also quite active. The central campus is off Martin Luther King Pkwy. in the southeast corner of town. Lamar has smaller branches in Port Arthur and Orange as well. For further information, call (409) 880-7011.

Port of Beaumont: At the east edge of town (end of Milam), on the Neches River, this is the state's fourth largest port (four million cargo tons per year) even though it's 40 miles from the Gulf of Mexico. You can get a good view of the port from the observation deck (tel. 409-832-1546) atop the Harbor Island Transit Warehouse (about a thousand feet from the main gate). The deck is open daily; free tours of the port are available during these hours as well (ask at the gate).

Hotels And Motels

See the "Beaumont Hotels And Motels" chart .

Food

The Golden Triangle is a great area for travelers seeking to taste authentic regional cuisines. Beaumont is particularly strong in down-home cooking and barbecue. Many restaurants will have a few Cajun or Creole dishes on the menu or a Cajun touch to the cooking as well.

If you're on a food pilgrimage or just want some of the best barbecue in the state, don't miss **Patillo's BBQ,** an informal over-the-counter place with two locations: 2775 Washington (tel. 409-833-3154) and 610 N. 11th (tel. 832-2572). The standard platter (choice of brisket, homemade links, or chicken) comes with extra southeast Texas-style sauce, beans, cole slaw, potato salad, and dirty rice (the Cajun touch). Another local favorite is **Dean's Bar-B-Que** (tel. 835-7956) at 805 Magnolia.

Two places that specialize in Cajun and Creole seafood are **Don's Seafood** (tel. 409-842-0686) at I-10 and Washington and the **French Quarter Restaurant** (tel. 835-9001) at 491 Fannin. The **Texas Crawfish Co. & Seafood Restaurant** (tel. 866-1625) on US 90 just west of I-10 also has a few Cajun dishes, plus all-you-can-eat buffets daily for lunch (boiled crawfish, barbecue crabs, fried shrimp, and étouffée) and dinner (the same, plus gumbo, frogs' legs, and oysters).

BEAUMONT HOTELS AND MOTELS

Add 13% hotel tax to all rates. Area code: 409

NAME	ADDRESS	PHONE	RATES	FEATURES
Alamo Plaza Hotel	1930 College	833-1437	$28	—
Beaumont Hilton	2355 I-10 S (Washington Ave. exit)	842-3600	$77-100	pool, airport shuttle weekly and monthly rates
Best Western Beaumont Inn	2155 N. 11th	898-8150	$37-43	pool, coin laundry
Best Western Jefferson Inn	1610 I-10 S (exit 851)	842-0037	$36-42	pool, cont. breakfast
Castle Motel	1125 N. 11th	892-5110	$19-24	—
Daystop	4085 I-10 S (exit 848)	842-9341	$25-30	coin laundry, cont. breakfast
HoJo Inn	I-10 and 11th	892-8111	$22-31	pool
Holiday Inn Midtown	2095 N. 11th	892-2222	$42-52	pool, YMCA privileges, airport shuttle, weekly rates
Holiday Inn Plaza	3950 I-10 S (College St. exit)	842-5995	$69-84	heated pool, airport weekly rates
La Quinta Motor Inn	220 I-10 (exit 852A/B)	838-9991	$43-49	pool, senior discount, cont. breakfast
Motel 6	2640 I-10 E (exit 853B/C)	898-7190	$21.95 + $6 ea. add.	pool
Quality Inn	1295 N. 11th	892-7722	$39-48	pool, senior discount
Ramada Hotel	2525 N. 11th	892-2111	$39-59	pool
Roadrunner Inn	3985 College at I-10	842-4420	$27-30	pool, 24-hour restaurant
Super 8	I-10 and 11th	899-3040	$27-33	pool

For down-home cooking, there are several choices: **The Black-Eyed Pea** (tel. 409-866-2617) at 6455 Phelan, **Shilo's Restaurant** (tel. 835-8018) at 2999 Goliad (at Washington), and **Texas Pig Stand** (tel. 835-5753) at 612 Washington or 1595 Calder in Old Town (tel. 835-9702); both Texas Pig Stands are open 24 hours.

For lighter fare, the **Green Beanery Café** (tel. 409-833-5913) at 2121 McFaddin in Old Town is a good alternative; the menu here includes salads, soups, sandwiches, crepes, and pasta. The **House of Chee** (tel. 898-8783) at 4414 Dowlen in the Crossroads Shopping Center is reputed to have the best Chinese food in town. If you're looking for Mexican, an interesting choice is **Chula Vista** (tel. 898-8855) at 1135 N. 11th, just off I-10, where Sonoran dishes are the specialty. And if you can't decide, **The Tamale Co.** (tel. 866-8033) at 6025 Phelan (behind Fertita's Grocery) offers Mexican and Cajun, including homemade tamales and chicken gumbo.

Entertainment
Boulevard (tel. 409-833-3271) at 3965 Phelan features live bands (usually R&B) Mon.-Sat. until 2 a.m. **Get Down Brown's** (tel. 892-1931) in the Holiday Inn Midtown on N. 11th is a change from the usual Holiday Inn disco-lounge; the DJs play

a gnarly mix of R&B, old rock 'n' roll, Cajun, and country. (The original Get Down Brown's was on State 347 near Port Arthur, where the DJ/owner invented the "funky chicken" dance.) On Wednesday evenings the club offers free barbecue (or, during the season, crawfish for $3/lb.) buffets.

If you happen to be passing through Beaumont (or anywhere in the vicinity) on a Sunday morning between 6 and 10:30 a.m., tune in "Tee Bruce's Cajun Jamboree" radio show on KLVI AM 560. Listening to Tee Bruce take requests and dedicate songs is as much fun as listening to the Cajun music; the show has been a Golden Triangle tradition for 25 years now. The signal is strong (on a clear day it can be heard all the way to Austin); during the rest of the week they play country.

Events

The city's biggest annual celebration is the **Neches River Festival,** held for 10 days near the end of April. Activities include a ball, parade, concerts, arts and crafts shows, flower shows, and boat races.

On Mother's Day weekend in May is **Kaleidoscope,** a juried art show held outdoors in tents at the Art Museum of South Texas (tel. 409-832-3432). Entries from all over the U.S. are accepted and all of the art is for sale at the close of the show. Entertainment and food are also on hand, culminating in a Saturday night dance.

Juneteenth (June 19th, the date that news of the Emancipation Proclamation reached Texas) is celebrated with fervor by Beaumont's black population. Three events mark the celebration on the nearest weekend to the 19th. On Saturday at Riverfront Park (near the junction of Main and Cypress) the city sponsors an outdoor program of gospel, R&B, rap, and zydeco music, along with food vendors and other activities. That same day and Sunday, the **Zydeco Creole Dust Fest** is held at the Fair Park Arena (at Gulf and Regent, north of I-10) from 11 a.m. till midnight both days. When this event was first held in 1989, it featured zydeco greats Boozoo Chavis and Lawrence Black Ardoin, along with a lineup of several other zydeco (and Cajun) bands. The food booths focus on Cajun and Creole food, including crawfish and boudin (rice-pork sausage, which in this area is spelled and pronounced "boudain"). In some years, the **Bill Picket Invitational Rodeo** is held at the Fair Park Coliseum. Bill Pickett was a famous African-American cowboy who invented the rodeo event called "bulldogging"—wrestling a steer to the ground.

For 10 days in the middle of October, the **South Texas State Fair** is held at Fair Park. Participants come from all over the Golden Triangle area and beyond to take part in rodeos, livestock shows, auctions, and music. (How the city feels justified in calling this area "South Texas" is difficult to understand.)

Beaumont Information

The **Beaumont Convention and Visitors Bureau** (tel. 409-880-3749 or 800-392-4401 in

Bill Picket Invitational Rodeo, Beaumont

Texas) is in the city hall at 801 Main; it's open Mon.-Fri. 8:30-5. They've got stacks of information on attractions, accommodations, and dining, and can answer other questions about the city. A visitor information center at the Babe Zaharias Museum (tel. 833-4622), I-10W and Martin Luther King Pkwy. (exit 854), distributes information on the Beaumont area daily 9-5.

PORT ARTHUR

This city got its start in 1895 when Arthur Stilwell selected the Sabine Lake as the terminal for his Kansas City, Pacific, and Gulf Railroad. He mod-

estly called the town Port Arthur and set about looking for investors and settlers. One of the investors was John "Bet-A-Million" Gates, who gained control of the railroad and changed it to the Kansas City and Southern. Also among the investors was a group of Dutch settlers who bought 42,000 acres of prairie from the Port Arthur Land Co. in 1897 and named it Nederland; there are now some 500 families in Nederland and Port Arthur descended from the original 51 settlers (the late country music star Tex Ritter was a Nederland descendant).

When the oil business took root following the nearby Spindletop oil discovery in 1901, thousands of Cajuns from Southwest Louisiana

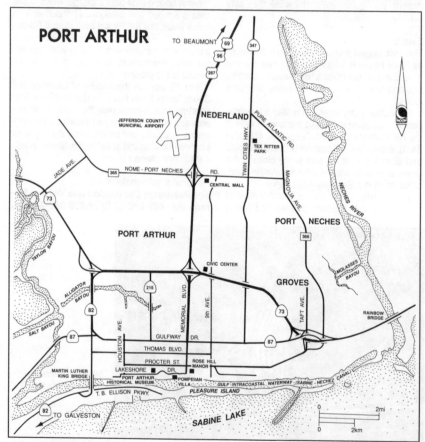

Pompeiian Villa,
Port Arthur

began migrating to Port Arthur to take jobs in oil exploration and later at the city's huge refineries. Port Arthur, or "Port Ar-tour" as it's pronounced by Cajuns, now has the largest concentration of Acadian descendants in Texas.

During the late 1970s Southeast Asian immigrants, particularly Vietnamese, began arriving in Port Arthur in some numbers. Many Vietnamese took jobs on shrimp boats and later started their own shrimping enterprises. They were so successful at it (many families had fished the South China Sea for generations) that at first there was some friction between the locals and the immigrants. Lately, though, the warring groups seem to have worked things out and the Vietnamese have been accepted as part of the multicultural community.

Sights
Museum of the Gulf Coast: This ambitiously named museum collection is comprised of artifacts and memorabilia that outline Port Arthur's history. One of the more rare items on display is the original painting by William McMasters that was used as the frontispiece in the first edition of Longfellow's 1895 *Evangeline,* a story about the migration of Acadians from Nova Scotia to Louisiana.

In an adjacent room is the recently established **Southeast Texas Musical Heritage Exhibit.** Perhaps because of all the cross-cultural influences (Cajun, Dutch, Anglo, Hispanic, and African-American), the triangle area has been an unusually fertile ground for American music. The area's most famous musical native is undoubtedly Janis Joplin (born in Port Arthur in 1943), who shot to stardom in the late '60s as a blues and rock singer and tragically died of a drug overdose in 1970. Part of the exhibit is devoted to Janis and includes photos, paintings, album covers, early childhood memorabilia donated by the Joplin family, and a large five-headed sculpture by Doug Clark.

Other exhibits chronicle the lives and music of Jivin' Gene (Gene Joseph Bourgeois, born in Port Arthur in 1940), a pioneer of "swamp music," Harry Choates, the "godfather of Cajun music" (who was born in Louisiana in 1922, worked in Port Arthur, and died in Austin in 1951), country singer George Jones (born in nearby Saratoga in 1931), blues singer Ivory Joe Hunter (born in nearby Kirbyville in 1911), Jerry LaCroix, a singer and saxophonist for the influential jazz/rock/R&B band Blood, Sweat, and Tears (Jerry still lives and performs in Port Arthur), mandolin and fiddle player Tiny Moore (born in Port Arthur in 1920), who played with Bob Wills and Merle Haggard, R&B singer Barbara Lynn (born in Beaumont in 1942), the Big Bopper (born Jules Richardson in Sabine Pass in 1930), Tex Ritter (born in Nederland in 1905), and the Winter brothers, Johnny and Edgar (born in 1944 and 1946 in Beaumont), who play blues, R&B, and rock.

The museum and musical heritage exhibit at 317 Stilwell, are open Mon.-Fri. 10-5; free admission.

Rose Hill Manor,
Port Arthur

Historic Buildings: Several of the homes along Lakeshore Dr. were built in the early 1900s as winter resorts for wealthy businessmen from the Midwest. When they were built, they commanded a view of Sabine Lake just a few hundred yards away. The dredging of the Gulf Intercoastal Waterway and the construction of levees for hurricane protection have obstructed the view, but the district has retained a quiet, antebellum atmosphere. The most unusual building in the district is the **Pompeian Villa** (tel. 409-983-5977) at 1953 Lakeshore, which was constructed in 1900 as an architectural replica of an A.D. 79 Pompeiian home (copied from the ruins at Pompeii). Accordingly, the house was built around a peristyle (three-sided courtyard), with a Roman fountain in the center; each room of the villa opens onto the peristyle. The house is painted according to Pompeiian color schemes—cerulean blue, pink, ivory, gray, almond green, and peach—and is furnished with 18th-century antiques (the preference of the original owner, Isaac Ellwood). The house is listed with the National Register of Historic Places and maintained by the Port Arthur Historical Society. It's open to the public Mon.-Fri. 9-4 (or by appointment); admission is $2 adults, $1 children.

White Haven (tel. 409-982-3068) at 2545 Lakeshore is a large Greek Revival-style home built in 1915 and furnished with Victorian antiques. Tours are conducted by a local chapter of the Daughters of the American Revolution on Mon., Wed., and Fri. 10-1 (or by appointment); admission is $2 per person. Similar in style but larger is **Rose Hill Manor** (tel. 985-7292) at 100 Woodworth (at the east end of Lakeshore). Built in 1906, it's listed with the NRHP and maintained by the Port Arthur Federated Women's Club. Open for guided tours Tues.-Fri. 9-5, Sat. 9-noon; free admission. During the summer, lemonade is sometimes served on the front lawn.

Area of Peace: This district along 9th Ave. (700-900 block) is mostly occupied by the residences and businesses of local Vietnamese, who have designated it Khu Vuc Hoa Binh or "Area of Peace." The center of the district is the **Queen of Peace Park** at 801 9th, which consists of flower gardens surrounding a huge statue of the Virgin Mary, built by the parishioners of the Queen of Vietnamese Martyrs' Catholic Church (across the street). About 10% of Port Arthur's current population is Vietnamese.

Buu Mon Buddhist Temple: Not all the Vietnamese in Port Arthur are Catholics. An old Baptist church at 2701 Proctor has been converted into a Buddhist temple, complete with a four-tiered pagoda outside and a seven-foot bronze Buddha from Thailand inside. The temple is open to non-worshipers Sun. 2-5. Buddhist meditation classes, open to all, are held Wed. 7:30-9:30 p.m.

Seawall Drive: Along the top of the levee between the Gulf Intracoastal Waterway (here called the Sabine-Neches Canal) and Lakeshore Dr. is a one-way street and walkway for sightseeing purposes. When ships pass, you can almost reach out and touch them.

Tex Ritter Park: This park in the little town of Nederland on Port Arthur's northern city limits commemorates hometown boy and country singer Tex Ritter. To make the most of this piece of real estate, the town added the **Dutch Windmill Museum**, which contains Tex Ritter mementos as well as artifacts pertaining to the original 1890s Dutch settlement. If that isn't enough, there's also **La Maison Acadienne Museum**, a replica of an early southern Louisiana Cajun home. The park is located at 1500 Boston, west of Twin Cities Hwy. (State 347) and is open Tues.-Sun. 1-5 through March 1 and Labor Day, Thurs.-Sun. 1-5 the rest of the year; free admission.

Port of Port Arthur: It sounds redundant but that's what it's called. Although not as large as the ports of Houston, Beaumont, or Galveston, this harbor (tel. 409-983-2011) can handle ships with a 40-foot draft and lengths up to a thousand feet. The port authorities offer free guided tours Mon.-Fri. 8-5. At West Lakeshore and Houston.

Rainbow Bridge: This amazing two-lane bridge was built over the Neches River in 1938 and arches to a height of 177 feet above the water. Nothing that passes beneath the bridge (between the Gulf and the Port of Beaumont) these days requires such clearance; the bridge was originally built to accommodate the USS *Patoka*, a U.S. Navy dirigible tender which sported an extremely tall mast for dirigible moorings. (Before the bridge was even completed, the Navy quit using dirigibles.) To drive over the bridge, an uplifting experience to say the least, take State 87 east out of town. A new bridge (133-foot clearance) is under construction parallel to the Rainbow Bridge; when finished, each bridge will carry traffic in different directions.

Martin Luther King Jr. Memorial Bridge: At a height of 138 feet above the water, this one's just about as impressive as the Rainbow Bridge. Constructed in 1970, it connects the city with Pleasure Island, a narrow barrier island on the south side of the Gulf Intracoastal Waterway.

Refineries: Touted as the world's largest petrochemical complex, the adjacent Texaco and Chevron refineries at the junction of State 82 and State 87 (southwest end of town) look like somebody's version of technological hell. You have to drive right through these monsters to get to Sabine Pass and the Bolivar Peninsula (see "Gulf Coast").

PORT ARTHUR GUMBO

Recipe: 1 cup cooking oil
1 cup flour
2 yellow onions, chopped
1 cup green onions, chopped
2 ribs celery, chopped
1 cup green pepper, chopped
2 lbs. shrimp, chicken, crawfish, or duck (or any combination)
4 quarts water
½ tablespoon red pepper (or more to taste)
1 tablespoon black pepper
2 tablespoons salt
1 teaspoon gumbo filé

Heat oil in heavy skillet with flour to make a roux. Cook until it turns medium brown, stirring constantly (about 4-5 minutes).

When roux is done, add to four quarts of water in saucepan on medium heat; stir until the roux is dissolved. Add yellow onions, celery, and green pepper; bring to a boil, reduce heat, and simmer for an hour.

Add seasonings, green onions, and shrimp (or chicken, etc.) and cook on medium heat until the shrimp (or chicken, etc.) is done. Serves at least six.

Port Arthur Hotels And Motels

If you're on a budget, Port Arthur is a good base from which to explore the Triangle area since hotel/motel rates are very reasonable. The basic **Sea Gull Motel** (tel. 409-962-4437) at 6828 Gulfway has rooms for $23 s, $30 d. At the **Seashell Motel** (tel. 736-1589), 2811 State 73, rooms are $25 s or $27 d and kitchenettes are available on request. In nearby Sabine Pass, the **Sabine Pass Motel** (tel. 971-2156) at 5623 Greenwich (first street past Broadway from Port Arthur) has rooms for $23-32. Other economical hotels include the **Holiday Motor Hotel** (tel. 985-2538), 3889 Gulfway, $28 s, $34 d, the **Imperial Inn** (tel. 985-9316) at 2811 Memorial, $23 s, $26 d, and **Percy's Motel** (tel. 736-1554) at State 73 and Jade, in the west end of town, $28-32. Percy's has the distinct advantage of being near Percy's Cafe (see "Food" below).

For more spacious rooms and lobbies, you can spend a bit more for the **Holiday Inn Park Central** (tel. 409-724-5000) at 2929 75th, where rooms are $50-52 s, $53-55 d, or the **Ramada Inn of Port Arthur** (tel. 962-9858) at 3801 State 73, $48 s, $56 d.

Campgrounds And RV Parks

The nearest public campground is at Sea Rim State Park on the Bolivar Peninsula, about nine miles southwest of Port Arthur via State 87 (see "Sea Rim State Park" under "Gulf Coast," p. 370). The **Lazy L Campground** (tel. 409-794-2985) at FM 365 at I-10, 18 miles west of Port Arthur (in Fannett), has tent/camper sites with w/e for $10 a night and RV sites with full hookups for $12.

Pleasure Island, the thin barrier island just across the Gulf Intracoastal Waterway, h•s two RV facilities. **Jep's RV Park** (tel. 409-983-3822) at 1900 Martin Luther King charges $12 a day, $45 on weekends. On the same road is **J&C RV Park** (tel. 985-3638) with similar rates.

Food

If you like Cajun, you'll like eating in Port Arthur. **Farm Royal** (tel. 409-982-6483) at 2701 Memorial specializes in Cajun-style seafood, including gumbo and étouffée. **The Jetty** (tel. 727-5465) at 8484 Central Mall Dr. (off US 69/96/287 N) also serves Cajun-style seafood. If the food at these two places isn't soulful enough for you, head for the **Boudain Hut** (tel. 962-5079) at 5714 Gulfway. Besides regular boudain and "boudain balls," they serve cracklins, hoghead cheese, and deep-fried turkey. Another down-home place is **Percy's Cafe** (tel. 736-3573) at 5891 Jade, just off State 73 W. House specialties are shrimp gumbo and chicken-fried steak and the decor features John Wayne collectibles. **Southern Kitchen** (tel. 983-2115) at 2749 Memorial is similar but with a heavier emphasis on Cajun dishes.

A little hard to find but worth the trip for the Cajun-style catfish is **Boondocks** (tel. 409-796-1482). To get there, take State 73 13 miles west to Jap Rd., then right about 1.3 miles; it's on the left, on Taylor Bayou (near Fannett). A window table will give you a view of the picturesque bayou, including alligators and raccoons who gather near the restaurant hoping for handouts.

Locals say the best seafood in the area is at two restaurants in nearby Sabine Pass, a small fishing town about nine miles southwest of town

via State 87. Both specialize in "barbecue crabs," which aren't really barbecued but are deep-fried in Cajun spices. They also serve catfish, frogs' legs, shrimp, stuffed crab, crab claws, oysters, and other fresh seafood broiled or fried. The advertised "platter service" means seafood is served family-style—a platter of barbecue crabs, a platter of fried shrimp, etc.—and the platters are refilled until you've had enough (three-person minimum). Of the two, **Sartin's** (tel. 409-892-6771) is the oldest and most well known (also the most crowded). The **Channel Inn** (tel. 971-2400) across the road is often a better choice, since the staff try harder and it's usually less crowded. Both restaurants are on State 87 at the entrance to Sabine Pass (the channel, not the town).

The Schooner (tel. 409-722-2323) at 1508 US 69/96/287, just north of Port Arthur in Nederland, has been in business for nearly 50 years, serving steak and a dependable variety of seafood dishes (the house specialty is red snapper Alexander—snapper stuffed with crab and shrimp and smothered in onions and artichoke hearts).

Entertainment

Live Music: The **Boudain Hut** (see "Food" above) features a variety of live bands Tues.-Sun. till 2 a.m. The Schooner Restaurant's **Blue Dolphin Club** (see "Food" above) has live folk and R&B music on weekends and sometimes during the week (Jerry LaCroix, formerly of Blood, Sweat, and Tears, plays here on occasion).

Frenchy's Lounge (tel. 962-9041) at 6630 Gulfway has live Cajun music on Sat. nights, country on Fri., and jukebox dancing the rest of the week (plus happy hour from 7 a.m. to 11 a.m.—that's right, a.m.). The long-established **Rodair Club** (tel. 736-9001) on FM 365, about four miles west of US 69/96/287, holds Cajun dances Fri. and Sat. nights as well as Sun. afternoons.

Radio: Local station KOLE AM 1340 broadcasts zydeco music Mon.-Fri. noon-3, Cajun music Mon.-Fri. 3-6 and Sat. 7-noon. For a wide selection of gospel, R&B, and blues, tune in KALO AM 1250.

Events

January: This on-again, off-again event celebrates Janis Joplin's birthday (Jan. 19) with a concert of local performers along with original members of Big Brother and the Holding Company. In previous years the concert has been held at the

Port Arthur Civic Center; contact the Port Arthur Convention and Visitors Bureau (tel. 409-985-7822) for the latest information.

March: On a weekend in mid-March, over a dozen Port Arthur restaurants compete in the **Taste of Gumbo** at the Port Arthur Civic Center on Cultural Center Dr. (off 9th, just north of the State 73 junction). Sponsored by the Rotary Club (tel. 409-724-7663 or 962-8448)

May: The **Pleasure Island Music Festival,** held the first weekend of the month at the Logan Music Park on Pleasure Island (off T.B. Ellison Pkwy.), brings together the best of the local music talent and a few national acts for three days of blues, gospel, jazz, country, Cajun, rock, and R&B music, plus food vendors, arts and crafts, and various family-oriented games. For information, call the Port Arthur Convention and Visitors Bureau (tel. 409-985-7822).

The last weekend of the month is reserved for the **Cajun Festival** at Bishop Byrne Stadium (9th and State 73), a three-day celebration of Cajun culture with food, music, and dancing.

September: The **Cayman Island Fest** is a joint effort with Port Arthur's sister community in the Caribbean, the Cayman Islands. A planeload of Cayman Islanders fly in for the festival, which features a soccer match between the Cayman national team and the Southeast Texas All-Stars, Caribbean music, and plenty of Cajun and Caribbean food. Held at the Civic Center on the second weekend of the month. For further information, call the Convention and Visitors Bureau (tel. 409-985-7822).

On either the last weekend of September or the first weekend of October, the small town of Winnie (30 miles east via State 73) hosts the **Texas Rice Festival,** featuring a beauty pageant, parade, carnival, music, farm equipment displays, and food booths emphasizing rice dishes.

Fishing

The Port Arthur area offers a combination of freshwater and saltwater fishing opportunities that is unparalleled along the Texas coast. Freshwater anglers have a choice of Taylor and Cow bayous (and several smaller bayous), and the Neches and Sabine rivers, where bass, bream, crappie, catfish, and gar are common. Saltwater fishing places include the Sabine Ship Channel (Sabine Pass), Sabine Lake, the lower reaches of the Neches River (east of Rainbow Bridge), the Tay-

lor Bayou Outfall (where Taylor Bayou joins the Gulf Intracoastal Waterway), and Cow Bayou south of I-10. Saltwater catches here generally include speckled trout, red drum, flounder, croaker, redfish, and sheepshead. Crabbing is excellent in the latter areas, too. The Gulf of Mexico is easily reached from Sabine Pass or the Bolivar Peninsula (see "Gulf Coast" chapter) for offshore and deep-sea fishing.

Boat-launching facilities are available at the Pleasure Island Marina on Sabine Lake and at the Rainbow Marina on the Neches River. Taylor Bayou has a few private landings on the west side of the State 73 bridge and one public landing on the east. For Cow Bayou, there's LeBlanc's Landing on the east side of the State 87 bridge at Round Bunch Road. In those sections of the bayous where saltwater fish can be caught, anglers must hold saltwater fishing permits (available at most bait shops or marinas).

Port Arthur Information

The **Port Arthur Convention and Visitors Bureau** (tel. 409-985-7822), in the Civic Center at 3401 Cultural Center Drive (off 9th and State 73), distributes printed information on Port Arthur and the vicinity and a free street map of the city (including the nearby towns of Nederland, Groves, and Port Neches). The helpful *Easy Driving Tour* pamphlet outlines an auto route for seeing the city's main attractions with a description of each and a simplified route map.

ORANGE

The eastern point of the triangle is only separated from Louisiana by the Sabine River. Pirate Jean Lafitte is reported to have used the Sabine River mouth here as a haven for ship repairs in the early 1800s. French traders and fur trappers settled along the river in the 18th century but it wasn't until the 1850s that the county was established (originally named Madison and changed to Orange in 1858). No one's quite sure whether the town and county's name originally referred to a small grove of wild orange trees on the river or was a reference to Holland's House of Orange (some of the 19th-century settlers in the area were Dutch).

Originally a lumber and rice town like Beaumont, Orange eventually became prominent in the marine construction and petrochemical industries (though rice and timber still play a role in the local economy).

Stark Museum Of Art

The collection in this imposing marble structure focuses on traditional American art, including works by Frederic Remington, Charles Russell, and the Taos Society of Artists, Audubon prints, and Amerindian art from the Plains and Southwest. The museum (tel. 409-993-6661) is at 712 Green, on the Civic Plaza. Open Wed.-Sat. 10-5, Sun. 1-5; free admission.

W.H. Stark House

Another legacy of the wealthy Stark family, this three-story Queen Anne-style Victorian (tel. 409-883-0971) at 610 W. Main was built in 1894 and has been restored and furnished to serve as a museum. It's open for one-hour guided tours Tues.-Sat. 10-3; admission is $2 (no one under 14 admitted) and reservations are required.

Heritage House Museum

This two-story colonial-style home was built in 1902 and now serves as a historical museum for Orange County. Like the Stark House, it's listed with the National Register of Historic Places; part of the house has been restored and furnished in period style.

Lutcher Memorial Church
(First Presbyterian)

Begun in 1908 and completed in 1912, this monumental church was financed by Frances Ann Lutcher in memory of her husband. Kansas City architect James Hogg used Texas granite and Italian marble for the walls and floor of the church building, and topped the center of the ceiling with the nation's only opalescent glass dome. The outside of the dome is protected by a copper outer dome; light fixtures throughout the building are bronze, other metalwork is brass, and the pews and paneling in the organ loft are mahogany. When the church opened in 1912, a private power plant had to be built to provide sufficient current to operate the lighting, cooling, and heating systems. The church is located at 902 W. Green Ave.; free tours of the building can be arranged by calling tel. (409) 883-2097.

Piney Woods Country Wines

One of the only wineries in East Texas, Piney Woods specializes in award-winning Muscadine and fruit wines (including blackberry, plum, pear, peach, "baked peach," and orange). The winery is at 3408 Willow Dr. off I-10 east (exit 875) and is usually open for tasting and sales Mon.-Sat. 9-6, Sun. noon-5. Call (409) 883-5408 before visiting to be sure it's open.

Super Gator Tours

Super Gator (tel. 409-883-7725) at 108 E. Lutcher Dr. (exit 878 off I-10) leads swamp-boat tours of Cypress Lake and vicinity to view waterfowl, alligators, and other wildlife native to East Texas swamps, lakes, and bayous. The hour-long tours cost $15 per adult, $10 for children 12 and under.

Delta Downs

Ten miles east of Orange via I-10 is this Louisiana horse track where parimutuel betting is legal; thoroughbred and quarter-horse racing are held year-round. General admission is $1.25 per person (plus $1 for parking); more expensive clubhouse seats are available for $4.50 and $8.

Events

The event of the year is the **International Gumbo Cookoff** held the first weekend in May at the old Navy base on the river (Simmons Dr.). Cajun chefs from Texas and Louisiana (and beyond) square off to see who can screw the best roux into a gumbo. Besides all the gumbo permutations available for tasting (which, as in chili cookoffs, may contain just about anything that moves), the celebration includes country and Cajun music, dancing, a mudbug-eating contest ("mudbug" is Cajun slang for "crawfish," itself a Southern corruption of crayfish), and a parade. Call the Orange Convention and Visitors Bureau at (409) 883-3536 for further information.

Accommodations

The **Best Western Inn** (tel. 409-883-6616) at 2630 I-10 (exit 877) and **Days Inn** (tel. 883-9981) at 2900 I-10 (exit 876) each have rooms for $34-36 s, $39-44 d.

PINEY WOODS

The vast Piney Woods form the heart of East Texas and have provided shelter and livelihood for its inhabitants for centuries. The name is a loose term for all the various forest communities stretching from Beaumont in the southeast all the way to the Texas-Arkansas border in the northeast. To the west, the pine-predominant forests give way to the Post Oak Belt and blackland prairies after a couple-hundred miles. They're bordered on the east by Louisiana—the forests continue past the state line, of course, but "Piney Woods" is primarily a Texas term.

The East Texas timber industry got its start in the 19th century and has increased steadily ever since, threatening to defoliate the entire landscape. Much has been lost forever (or at least for the foreseeable future); fortunately, the federal government has taken measures to ensure that at least some portions of the Piney Woods will be preserved by creating the Sabine, Davy Crockett, Angelina, and Sam Houston national forests and Big Thicket National Preserve (for a combined total of about 750,000 acres). Only Big Thicket National Preserve is completely protected, however, since the U.S. National Forest Service practices "timber management" in the four national forests, which allows planned harvesting of trees for the lumber industry. You can tell how important the industry is to the area by the small-town names—Woodville, Wildwood, Bleakwood, Lumberton, Forest, Pineland.

The area code for all phone numbers in the Piney Woods area is 409.

BIG THICKET NATIONAL PRESERVE

American Indians knew it as "the Big Woods," the Spanish called it "impenetrable," and to the Anglo-Americans who settled here in the early 1800s, it was "the Big Thicket." Nowadays, as complex forest environments are disappearing from the planet at an ever-increasing rate, it's being called "America's ark" and "the best-equipped ecological laboratory in North America."

Before the early 19th century, the Big Thicket covered an area of over 3.5 million acres and

successfully resisted all but the most tentative of human intrusion (draft dodgers and runaway slaves hid here during the Civil War). Since the arrival of the lumber and petroleum industries, however, human intervention has whittled Big Thicket's domain to approximately 300,000 acres, a figure that is undergoing further reduction at a current rate of about 50 acres a day. Congress established Big Thicket National Preserve in 1974 to protect 86,000 acres, which may soon be increased to 100,000 acres (if proposed legislation succeeds). In 1982, the United Nations added Big Thicket National Preserve to its select list of 250 International Biosphere Reserves worth protecting worldwide. (The Alabama-Coushatta Indians also act as guardians over about 4,000 acres of Big Thicket—see "Alabama-Coushatta Indian Reservation," p. 455).

The preserve currently encompasses 12 separate units, consisting of four river corridors and eight land tracts that range in size from the 550-acre Loblolly Unit to the 25,000-acre Lance Rosier Unit. Three of the units are connected by a 54-mile stretch of the Neches River, which is in turn linked to the Lance Rosier Unit via the Little Pine Island Bayou Corridor.

The Land

One of the main features that gives the Big Thicket its character is the Neches River, along with the bayous, creeks, and sloughs that feed into it and the swamps that form in its floodplains during rainy periods. Historically, this thickly forested, watery environment made it difficult for even the indigenous Caddo and Atakapa Indians to navigate the interior of the Big Thicket.

Five basic North American environments—Eastern and Appalachian forests, Southeastern swamps, Midwestern prairies, and Southwestern desert—meet here to produce an unusually high number of "ecotones," or ecological meeting zones. The result of this interweaving of ecotones is a mosaic of nearly a hundred different soil types, which, coupled with the abundant rainfall (55-60 inches a year), produce more plant communities than any other area of comparable size on the continent (a phenomenon called "the edge effect").

BIG THICKET

Climate

Because the forest environment acts as a natural insulator, temperatures are moderate throughout the year. The average temperature range in January is 42-61° F; in July it's 73-92° F. Rain and humidity are the key traits of the climate. The relative humidity reaches as high as 94% in July. You can expect rain at any time of year (an average of 4.5 inches a month), but the driest months are usually Feb., March, and October. During the late spring and summer, mosquitoes can be a problem; any time of year, be sure to bring insect repellent.

Flora

Eight vegetational zones (palmetto-hardwood flatlands, wetland savannahs, dry savannahs, pine uplands, sandhills or sandyland, mixed pine-hardwood slope forests, baygalls, and stream flood plains) are found within the preserve, harboring 85 tree species, over 60 shrubs, and nearly a thousand flowering plants, including rare ferns, orchids, and carnivorous plants.

Big Thicket forests are comprised of a six-layer canopy of trees in places. Dominant trees across several of the dryer plant communities include beech, magnolia, and shortleaf, longleaf, and loblolly pine; in the sandylands grow post oak, blackjack oak, and black hickory. Two trees—bald cypress and tupelo—predominate in the scenic cypress sloughs along the flood plains; both feature swollen bases, but cypress trunks are reddish and the base is fluted while the tupelo has a grayish trunk and smooth base. Sweetbay and gallberry holly trees thrive in baygalls or acid bogs, perpetually wet depressions where decaying vegetation create tea-colored, highly acidic pools of water.

The nine carnivorous plant species that grow in the preserve fall into four of the five known types found in the U.S.: pitcher plants, bladderworts, butterworts, and sundew. The pitcher plant is the largest and most common and can be seen growing mostly in wet savannahs. Like all carnivorous plants, it needs animal matter (mostly insects) to supplement the low mineral content of its native soil.

Fauna

The black bear, black panther, and red wolf that once roamed the Big Thicket haven't been sighted for years. Still plentiful, however, are deer, coyotes, bobcats, raccoons, beavers, otters, gray foxes, armadillos, feral hogs, squirrels, rabbits, alligators, turtles, and snakes. Over 300 bird species are permanent or migrating residents, including the endangered red-cockaded woodpecker and the large, somewhat rare pileated woodpecker. The ivory-bill woodpecker, once the largest woodpecker existent, unfortunately hasn't been sighted since 1904.

Visiting the Preserve

The **Big Thicket Information Station** is located at the southern end of the Turkey Creek Unit, which is off FM 420, about 30 miles north of Beaumont via US 69/287 N (the Park Service has plans to open a new visitors center at the US 69/FM 420 junction within two or three years). The information station is open daily 9-5 except Christmas Day. It's staffed by a park ranger and stocked with free printed information on the preserve. During spring and summer, the Park Service offers a range of free lectures, guided hikes, canoe trips, and overnight sandbar-camping trips. If you're new to the Big Thicket, participating in one or more of these activities is an excellent way to introduce yourself gradually to the preserve's complexities. In the Big Thicket, more than at any other national park facility in Texas, it pays to enter the area with a guide the first time out. All ranger-guided programs require reservations; call tel. (409) 246-2337.

Hiking

The preserve maintains eight established hiking trails, ranging from one to 18 miles in length. No permits are required for hiking these trails, but the Park Service asks that you register at the trailhead; upon registering, you'll receive a detailed trail map or trail guide booklet.

Besides the usual preparations—wearing comfortable shoes, carrying plenty of drinking water—Big Thicket hikers should bring a good insect repellent along, preferably one containing a high percentage of DEET (N,N-diethyl-metatoluamide), the most effective synthetic repellent (persons wishing to avoid synthetics should use lemongrass oil or citronella). For maximum protection, spread repellent on exposed skin and on your clothes. During the warmer, wetter months, mosquitoes can be ferocious—most people can't walk 10 yards without some kind of protection before they're forced to run for shelter.

It's also important to take the weather into consideration. During periods of heavy rain, trails may be flooded—always inquire at the information station about trail conditions before setting out.

Trails: The **Kirby Nature Trail** begins at the Big Thicket Visitor Information Station (Turkey Creek Unit) and forms a double loop (1.7 miles along the inner loop, 2.4 miles along the outer loop) through a mixture of hardwood and pine stands, cypress sloughs, and flood plains.

The 17-mile **Turkey Creek Trail** winds through the most diverse vegetation in the preserve. The main trailhead is 3.5 miles east of Warren on FM 1943 (about 18 miles north-northeast of the information station); two other trailheads begin at the south end of the trail and toward the middle of the trail via unnumbered gravel roads (inquire at the information station for exact directions to these trailheads). Starting from the north end, the trail passes through a pine-hardwood forest interspersed with sandy knolls, then into a forest of loblolly and short-leaf pines, red and white oak, beech, and magnolia. Next comes a flood plain forest of sweetgum, beech, and water and basket oak, with occasional sloughs supporting bald cypress and tupelo. Near the south end of the trail, a boardwalk leads across a baygall where sweetbay and gallberry predominate, along with black titi, red and white bay, blackgum, and azalea.

Running east off the Turkey Creek Trail, near its north end, is the quarter-mile-long **Pitcher Plant Trail.** You can choose to take this trail as an adjunct to the Turkey Creek Trail or drive 4.3 miles east of Warren on FM 1943, then 1.9 miles south along the east boundary road to the trailhead. From the trailhead, a surfaced trail leads through a mixed pine forest to the edge of a wetland savannah, where a boardwalk allows hikers to view a number of carnivorous plants (predominantly the pitcher plant) and wild orchids.

For a look at a wetland savannah that specializes in the more delicate sundew (a carnivorous plant that looks deceptively like a common wildflower), take the **Sundew Trail** in the **Hickory Creek Savannah Unit,** a half mile south of FM 2827, off US 69/287 (3.1 miles north of the road that leads to the information station). A one-mile loop leads through a longleaf pine wetland savannah full of perennial flowers, including the sundew. (Sticky globules at the base of the plant attract and trap insects until the plant can digest them.)

The **Beech Woods Trail,** a one-mile loop in the southwest corner of the **Beech Creek Unit,** winds through one of the preserve's best examples of a beech-loblolly-magnolia forest. To get to the trailhead, go 4.3 miles north of Warren on US 69/287 to Hillister, then east 10.2 miles on FM 1013 to FM 2992. The trail starts at the parking lot about two miles north off FM 2992.

The **Woodland Trail,** at the northwest edge of the **Big Sandy Creek Unit,** is a 5.4-mile loop through upland pine forests, overgrown pastures, and mature flood-plain forests. This unit is 21 miles east of Woodville via US 190, then 3.3 miles south on FM 1276. From the information station, a quicker way here is to take FM 1003 1.8 miles east off US 69/287, then FM 943 north 18.5 miles to the FM 1276 junction; from here it's about 10 miles to the trailhead.

In 1991 the NPS added two new trails to the preserve. The **Beaver Slide Trail** is in the southeast corner of the **Big Sandy Creek Unit,** off FM 943 about a quarter mile west of the FM 1276/943 intersection. This 1½-mile loop trail winds around a series of ponds formed by beaver dams. In the same vicinity is the new **Big Sandy Horse Trail,** an 18-mile (roundtrip) trail designed for horseback riding, hiking, and all-terrain bicycling. The trail is reached by proceeding west on Sunflower Rd. off FM 1276 a half mile north of Dallardsville; the trailhead is three miles west of this intersection.

Canoeing

The Big Thicket looks its best from water level and is a favorite destination for savvy canoeists. Even novices can easily handle most watercourses in the preserve since there are no rapids or strong currents to contend with. The main requirement is a good map; detailed topographical maps are for sale at the Turkey Creek Unit information station. Without a map, first-timers can easily lose their way in the dense array of rivers, sloughs, creeks, and bayous.

The main watercourses available for navigation in the preserve are the Neches River (93 miles from Steinhagen Lake near Woodville to Cooks Lake in the Beaumont Unit), Pine Island Bayou (49 miles from Saratoga to Beaumont), and Village Creek (37 miles from Village Mills to the Neches River below Silsbee). Detailed maps of each of these watercourses, showing put-in/take-out locations, are available at the information station.

Canoe Camping: Camping along riverbanks or on sandbars is permitted in designated backcountry camping areas within the preserve boundaries as long as you have a Backcountry Use Permit. The land along sections that are between preserve units (much of Pine Island Bayou and almost all of Village Creek) is privately owned but camping is usually permitted (on banks or sandbars only) unless otherwise posted. Open fires are not permitted within the preserve except on Neches River sandbars, so overnight canoeists should bring campstoves for cooking.

Overnight backcountry trips are limited to five days. During hunting season (Oct. to mid-Jan.), backcountry camping is suspended in all units of the preserve except the Turkey Creek Upper and Lower Neches, and Loblolly units.

Backcountry Use Permits are issued free at three locations: the Turkey Creek Unit information station; the preserve headquarters at 3785 Milam, Beaumont (Mon.-Fri. 8-4:30); the North District Ranger Office on US 287 in Woodville (open whenever a ranger is there).

Canoe Rentals: Several local businesses rent canoe equipment by the day; most provide drop-off and pick-up services to renters as well. Contact **Eastex Canoe Rentals** (tel. 409-892-3600, 5865 Cole, Beaumont; $15/day, shuttle service available), **H&H Boat Dock and Marina** (tel. 283-3257, US 190 near State 92 junction, Steinhagen Lake; $10/day, no shuttle service), **Piney Woods Canoe Rental** (tel. 246-4481, FM 418, Kountze; $17/day, shuttle service available), or **Canoe Rentals Silsbee** (tel. 385-6241, Old Beaumont Hwy.; Silsbee, shuttle service available).

Camping Outside The Preserve

The Big Thicket Museum (tel. 409-274-5000) in Saratoga allows tent camping on their grounds for a washroom charge of $5 per night and has full-hookup RV sites for $14.50. **Big Thicket RV Park & Campground** (tel. 246-3759 May-Aug. or 246-4488 Sept.-April), about nine miles west of Kountze on FM 1003 (just south of Honey Island), is a 12-acre facility with tent and RV sites (two-way hookups only) for $6 and $10. **Chain-O-Lakes Campground** (tel. 592-2150), farther northwest off FM 787 near Romayor, is a 271-acre area with tent facilities for $12, full RV hookups for $15. They also have cabins for $45-130 a night.

The U.S. Army Corps of Engineers (tel. 409-429-3491) maintains two campgrounds along the east side of Steinhagen Lake (**Sandy Park** and **East End Park**) and one on the west (**Magnolia Ridge Park**); rates are $6 for tent/camper sites without utilities, $8 with electricity. Also on the east side of Steinhagen Lake is **Martin Dies, Jr. State Park** (tel. 384-5231), a 705-acre park with tentsites for $6 weekdays, $8 weekends, tent/ camper sites with w/e for $9/11, RV sites with full hookups for $10/12, and screened shelters for $15/16.

The Alabama-Coushatta Indian Reservation, just north of the Big Sandy Creek Unit, also operates a full-service campground (see "Alabama-Coushatta Indian Reservation" below).

Food: There are grocery stores in Woodville and Beaumont, but not much in between. **Rice Grocery,** on the left side of US 69/287 a few miles north of the FM 420 junction, has groceries and gas (the proprietor also plays hot blues tapes on her boom box inside).

Information

Further information can be obtained by contacting the Superintendent (tel. 409-839-2689), Big Thicket National Preserve, 3785 Milam, Beaumont, TX 77701.

Big Thicket Museum

The nonprofit Big Thicket Association operates the **Big Thicket Museum** (tel. 409-274-2972) in Saratoga, 15.3 miles east of Kountze, at the northwest edge of the Lance Rosier Unit. This homespun affair includes slide presentations, taxidermic displays, plant exhibits, and displays pertaining to local culture and history. The museum is open Tues.-Sat. 9-5, Sun. 1-5; admission is $2 adults, 50 cents for students. Every Sat. during March, April, and May, the museum staff leads tours of the preserve (including an auto tour in the morning and a two-hour hike in the afternoon) for $3 per person. They can also arrange guides for longer trips.

ALABAMA-COUSHATTA INDIAN RESERVATION

The Alabama-Coushatta Indian tribe lives on 4,600 acres adjacent to Big Thicket National Preserve's Big Sandy Creek Unit. Had it not been for the tenacity and self-determination of this Amerindian group, they would probably have been run out of Texas and all but dispersed by now. This is one of America's few remaining for-

pine-needle baskets
crafted by the
Alabama-Coushatta
Indians

est Indian reservations; the Alabama-Coushattas have resisted all attempts by loggers and oil interests to buy them off, preferring to maintain their given homeland in its natural state.

History

Little is known of the Alabama-Coushattas' prehistoric past. Anthropologists have surmised that they are descendants of the Mississippian Temple-Mound Culture that flourished in the southeastern U.S. between A.D. 700 and 1300 (which had disappeared by 1700). By the early 18th century, there were two tribes left, the Alabama (Alibamo) clans who lived along the Alabama, lower Coosa, and Tallapoosa rivers, and the Coushatta (Koasati), who lived along the Tennessee River; both groups are members of the Muskogean Nation. Traditionally, their tribal economies were based on hunting and subsistence farming; Europeans who came into contact with them in their native lands called them "Creek" Indians because their villages were built along rivers and creeks.

The Alabamas and Coushattas began migrating westward into East Texas from Alabama to escape pressure from European immigrants in the late 1700s. When English and French colonists competed for their political affiliation, they decided to side with the French; when England gained control of French territories, their fear of Anglo vengeance hastened the migration flow. By 1809, the two tribes had several villages in the Big Thicket area with a combined population of around 1,650. During the Texan struggle for independence from Mexico, the tribes adopted a neutral position but harbored Texans who passed through their village in flight. In 1839, the Coushattas successfully turned back a Comanche raid at Long King Creek (named for Coushatta chief Long King), a decisive event in the struggle to hold onto their adopted homelands.

The future seemed fairly secure when Republic of Texas President Sam Houston granted two leagues of East Texas land to each tribe in 1840, but they never received title to the designated real estate because it was occupied by white settlers. After Texas became a state, the state legislators purchased 1,110 acres in Polk County for the Alabamas and approved a 640-acre land grant for the Coushattas; because the Coushattas never got their land, they moved onto the Alabama land in 1858. This same year, however, Governor H.R. Runnels tried to persuade both tribes to move to another reservation in Young County (northeast of Fort Worth), probably in acquiescence to pressure from the timber industry (Polk County was, and still is, the leading Texas county in lumber production), but they refused to move. As a gesture of solidarity, the two tribes elected one chief in common in 1871. In 1873, U.S. Congress approved a plan to move the tribes to Oklahoma (as was happening to many other Texas tribes at this time), but the Alabama-Coushattas again stood fast.

In a last attempt to shake their stance, the state abolished the post of Indian agent for Polk County Indians in 1879. After this, political conditions began improving and in 1928, following a lobbying trip to Washington, D.C., by Alabama-Coushatta Chief Charles Thompson and Second Chief McConnico Battise, the U.S. government purchased 3,701 Polk County acres to add to the Alabamas' original 1,110 acres.

Culture And Customs

Well before they left Alabama for Texas, the Alabama-Coushattas had replaced their stone implements with ones of steel as a result of contact with Europeans; they also began wearing European-style clothing and today they dress like just about anyone else in this part of the state (except during Indian ceremonies when they may wear traditional clothing). The traditional homes of the Alabama-Coushatta Indians were made of logs and branches but they now live in wood-frame or brick homes. Alabama-Coushatta children attend public schools in nearby Woodville, Livingston, and Big Sandy (a right granted them only since 1942).

Around 500 persons currently live on the reservation. The tribal government is organized around a first chief, second chief, and tribal council. The chiefs are elected for a lifetime term; the second chief takes over in the event of the first's death (in which case a new second chief is elected). The seven tribal council members are elected for three-year terms. Meetings of the council are conducted in the Alabama-Coushatta language (the separate Alabama and Coushatta dialects were always very close and have emerged as one language).

The tribe supports itself by employment outside the reservation (often with lumber mills) and a multifaceted visitor program that includes the sale of traditional arts and crafts items. Many feature a circular symbol with two waterfowls (head and stylized wings) facing in opposite directions. These are said to represent the dual aspects of day and night, earth and sky, life and death, male and female, strength and vulnerability, and the two tribes that have voluntarily affiliated. These waterfowls are joined at the center by a smaller circle that represents the cell, egg, or seed of creation. The wing feathers have seven points that symbolize the seven members of the tribal council, the seven sacred ceremonial fires, and the seven sacred pipes. There are two sets of feathers—seven times seven equals the age at which the tribe recognizes that a member has embarked on the final stage of wisdom and spiritual power (as proven through various deeds and tests).

One of the most outstanding examples of Alabama-Coushatta craftwork is pine-needle basketry. Since they are handwoven, no two baskets are alike; most are bowl-shaped but some are formed into animal shapes. The first step in the basket-weaving process is collecting longleaf pine needles and drying them for several weeks. When the needles are ready, the basket makers weave them into coils and bind them with fibers from the raffia palm (rainy or humid days, when the needles are more pliant, are preferred workdays); how long it takes to finish a basket depends on the size—a few hours for a smaller basket or a few days for a large one. A few pine-needle baskets are sometimes available for sale in the reservation gift shop, but demand often exceeds the supply.

Visitor Programs

A single admission price ($9 adults, $7.50 children 4-10 on weekdays in the spring and fall, $11 adults, $9 children on weekends and during the summer; senior, military, and AAA discounts available) to the tourist complex covers a Big Thicket nature bus tour, an Indian country historical tour, a living Indian village tour, a narrow-gauge train ride, and a tribal dance performance. The reservation also operates a gift shop and the **Inn of the Twelve Clans** restaurant, which serves burgers, burritos, frybread, Indian tacos, beverages, and snacks.

The tourist complex is open Mon.-Sat. 10-6, Sun. 12:30-6 between June and August. From mid-March to May and Sept. to late Nov., it's open Fri. and Sat. 10-5, Sun. 12:30-5 (the gift shop stays open year-round).

Camping

The campgrounds are situated around 26-acre Lake Tombigbee a bit beyond the tourist complex. Tentsites are $6 a night and trailer sites with w/e are $10, with full hookups $12. Fishing in the lake is permitted.

Information

For further information or campsite reservations, contact the Alabama-Coushatta Indian Reservation (tel. 409-563-4391 or 800-444-3507), Route 3, Box 640, Livingston, TX 77351.

Getting There

The main entrance to the reservation is about 17 miles west of Woodville (or 16 miles east of Livingston) via US 190.

NATIONAL FORESTS

The U.S. Forest Service administers 665,729 acres of the Piney Woods timberlands as national forests. This administration differs from U.S. Park Service efforts to preserve Texas woodlands in that it follows a "multiple-use" principle in which timber, wildlife, recreation, and other forest resources are consumed according to a master plan that accounts for replenishment rates. In other words, they're trying for the best of both worlds (preservation and consumption); outside opinions differ as to how prudent and effective such management is but it's definitely a compromise. Without the Forest Service presence, however, these forests would probably disappear by the end of the century.

Each of the four Piney Woods national forests features designated recreation areas with varying facilities. Many have tent and trailer camping facilities but none have RV hookups (except for Ratcliff Lake Recreation Area in Davy Crockett National Forest, which has electrical hookups); rates are generally $5 or less a night. Primitive camping is allowed anywhere within national forest boundaries except during hunting season (Oct. to mid-Jan.) and there's no charge. There are also designated wilderness areas where only primitive camping is allowed. It would require a hundred-page book in itself to describe in detail all the features of each of the numerous recreational areas (26 in all) in the national forests;

contact the relevant office (addresses and phone numbers below) for further information.

Angelina National Forest

This forest covers 156,153 acres surrounding Lake Sam Rayburn in Angelina, Jasper, Nacogdoches, and Augustine counties (tel. 409-639-8620, U.S. Forest Service, Box 756, Lufkin, TX 75901).

Bouton Lake Recreation Area: Picnicking, camping, boating (no motors), hiking trails; 15 miles southeast of Zavalla via State 63 and Forest Service Road (FSR) 303.

Boykin Springs Recreation Area: Picnicking, camping, swimming, boating (no motors), hiking trails; 14 miles southeast of Zavalla via State 63 and FSR 313.

Caney Creek Recreation Area: Picnicking, camping, swimming, boating, fishing, food concessions; on Lake Sam Rayburn 14 miles southeast of Zavalla via State 63 and FM 2390.

Harvey Creek Recreation Area: Picnicking, camping, boating, fishing, hiking trails; on Lake Sam Rayburn, east and south of Broaddus via FM 83 and FM 2390.

Sandy Creek Recreation Area: Picnicking, camping, swimming, boating, fishing, food concessions; on Lake Sam Rayburn, 21 miles southeast of Zavalla via State 63 and FSR 333.

Letney Recreation Area: Picnicking, camping, swimming, boating, fishing, food concessions, hiking trails; on Lake Sam Rayburn, 25 miles southeast of Zavalla via State 63, FM 225, and FSR 335.

Townsend Recreation Area: Picnicking, camping, swimming, boating, fishing, hiking trails; on Lake Sam Rayburn five miles northwest of Broaddus via State 147, FM 255, and FSR 335.

Sawmill Hiking Trail: Connects Boykin Springs Recreation Area and Bouton Lake Recreation area; 5.5 miles.

Turkey Hill Wilderness Area: Primitive camping only; five miles north of Broaddus via State 147 and east on FSR 300.

Upland Island Wilderness Area: Primitive camping only; 1.5 miles north of the Neches River via US 60 and east on FSR 314.

Davy Crockett National Forest

Covers 161,478 acres in Houston and Trinity counties (two ranger offices: Neches Ranger District, tel. (409) 544-2046, 1240 E. Loop 304, Crockett, TX 75835, and Trinity Ranger District, tel. 831-2246, Box 130, Apple Springs, TX 75926).

Big Slough Canoe Trail: Canoeing on Big Slough and the Neches River, primitive camping; two miles north of Ratcliff on FM 227, then east five miles on US 69 and east on FSR 314.

Ratcliff Lake Recreation Area: Picnicking, camping (including electrical hookups), swimming, boating (no motors), food concessions, hiking trails; between Kennard and Ratcliff on FSR 520.

4-C's Hiking Trail: 20-mile trail from Ratcliff Lake to the Neches Overlook; primitive camping.

Kickapoo Recreation Area: Picnicking, hiking trails; three miles southeast of Groveton via US 287.

Neches Bluff Recreation Area: Picnicking, hiking trails; on Neches River, seven miles southwest of Alto via State 21 and FSR 511.

Sabine National Forest

Covers 189,451 acres along Toledo Bend Reservoir in Jasper, Sabine, Newton, and Shelby counties (two ranger offices: Tenaha Ranger District, tel. 409-275-2632, 101 S. Bolivar, San Augustine, TX 75972, and Yellowpine Ranger District, tel. 787-2791, Box F, Hemphill, TX 75948).

Indian Mounds Recreation Site And Wilderness Area: Picnicking, camping, boating, fishing, hiking trails; on Toledo Bend Reservoir, five miles east of Hemphill via FM 93, then seven miles southeast on FSR 115 and FSR 115A.

Lakeview Recreation Area: Picnicking, camping; on Toledo Bend Reservoir, 16 miles southeast of Hemphill via State 87 and access road.

Ragtown Recreation Area: Picnicking, camping, boating, fishing, food concessions, hiking trails; on Toledo Bend Reservoir, 15 miles southeast of Shelbyville via State 87, FM 139, FSR 101, and FSR 1262.

Red Hills Lake Recreation Area: Picnicking, camping, swimming, boating (no motors), food concessions, hiking trails; on Toledo Bend Reservoir, three miles north of Milam via State 87.

Willow Oak Recreation Area: Picnicking, camping, boating, fishing; on Toledo Bend Reservoir, 14 miles southeast of Hemphill via State 87 and FSR 117.

Sam Houston National Forest

Covers 160,443 acres in Montgomery, San Jacinto, and Walker counties (two ranger offices:

Raven Ranger District, tel. 409-344-6205, Box 393, New Waverly, TX 77358, and San Jacinto Ranger District, tel. 592-6462, Box 1818, Cleveland, TX 77327).

Double Lake Recreation Area: Picnicking, camping, swimming, boating (no motors), food concessions, hiking trails; four miles south of Coldspring via State 150 and FM 2025.

Kelley Pond Recreation Area: Primitive camping, chemical toilets; 11 miles west of New Waverly via FM 1375, then one mile south on FSR 204 and FSR 271.

Little Lake Creek Wilderness Area: Primitive camping; 14 miles east of New Waverly via FM 1375, then four miles south on FM 149.

Lone Star Hiking Trail: A 126-mile trail that starts west of Lake Conroe off FM 149, then proceeds to Kelly Pond, Stubblefield Lake, Huntsville State Park, Double Lake, and finally ends at FM 1725 in Cleveland; primitive camping along the trail, drinking water at established campgrounds.

Stubblefield Lake Recreation Area: Picnicking, camping, boating, fishing, hiking trails; on West Fork of San Jacinto River, about 12 miles northwest of New Waverly via FM 1375 and FSR 208.

NACOGDOCHES

Touted as the oldest city in Texas (an honor easily contested by Ysleta and San Angelo in West Texas), Nacogdoches (pronounced Nack-a-DOE-chez) was once an important settlement of the Caddo Indian confederacy, which spread from here east into Louisiana. It later became a center for the Texas independence movement and the source for the first two newspapers printed in the state.

Today Nacogdoches is a mixture of early and modern East Texas. A number of older homes in town date back to the 19th and early 20th centuries but many of the historical sites are marked only by historical plaques.

History

Caddo legend says that an early Caddo chief who lived on the Sabine River had twin sons, one with fair hair and skin, the other with dark hair and skin. When they were old enough to lead their own clans, he sent one son east and one west with the orders that they stop after three days' journey and start a village. The light-haired son established Nacogdoches, the other Natchitoches (Louisiana)—each about 50 miles from the Sabine River in opposite directions (as the crow flies; 85 miles by today's highways).

The first Europeans probably came upon the village around 1541, when De Soto's men stopped here on their way to Mexico following De Soto's death. In 1716, Spain's Padre Margil established Misión de Nuestra Señora de Guadalupe de Nacogdoches as a counter to French claims on the area. Pressure from French colonists to the east (and the dissolution of the Caddo confederacy, caused by disease and social decline under missionary influence) forced the missionaries to leave around 1720; later in the century when the French were no longer in the picture, Spain ordered all Spanish colonists to move from East Texas to San Antonio. Some of the colonists negotiated for permission to resettle along East Texas's Trinity River, 60-70 miles west of Nacogdoches, but they weren't happy here (because of flooding and Comanche raids), so a few began moving back to Nacogdoches in 1770. One of the leaders of this movement was Gil Antonio Ybarbo (Ibarvo), who built a stone house that is considered to have been the town's first permanent structure.

By the early 19th century, Anglo-Americans were migrating into East Texas as the territory was transformed from a Spanish colony into part

NACOGDOCHES

MILLARD'S CROSSING

LOOP 224

NACOGDOCHES COUNTY EXPOSITION CENTER

OLD TYLER RD.

NORTH ST.

59
BUS

PARKER RD.
LAKEWOOD

PEARL

E. AUSTIN

BOWIE

RAGUET

E. COLLEGE

CHAMBER OF COMMERCE
(EUGENE BLOUNT HOUSE)

STEPHEN F.
AUSTIN STATE
UNIVERSITY

UNIVERSITY DR.

STALLINGS DR.

2609

1878

LOGANSPORT RD.

1411

RUSK

POWERS

KING

MOUND

HOUSTON

PARK

LANANA

LOOP 224

DURST

VIRGINIA AVE.

FREDONIA ST.

UNIVERSITY DR.

STERNE - HOYA HOUSE

SAN AUGUSTINE RD.

225

TO LAKE
NACOGDOCHES

7

59

2259

LOOP 224

21

21

59

i638

NOT TO SCALE

© MOON PUBLICATIONS, INC.

of the Republic of Mexico. Nacogdoches was an important way station along the migration route and many Anglo-American immigrants settled down here. Perhaps because the area was so far removed from the Coahuila y Texas state government in San Antonio, the growing dissatisfaction with Mexican authority was particularly intense here. In 1819 a group of Anglo-Americans tried unsuccessfully to claim Texas as part of the Louisiana Purchase, using Ybarbo's stone fort as a headquarters. The following year Haden Edwards, a man who had a grievance with the Mexican government over a land grant (he hadn't thoroughly understood the contract, which was of course in Spanish), gathered a group of sympathizers who raised a flag at the old stone fort and declared an independent "Republic of Fredonia." They were immediately dispersed by Mexican troops and Fredonia was never heard from again.

When Texas independence was finally declared in 1836, four of the signers were from Nacogdoches, which became one of the original counties (est. 1836). The state's first oil well was drilled a few miles from here by Lyne Tol Barret in 1866, but oil was not an important economic consideration in Nacogdoches County until the early 1900s. Timber, poultry, and cattle were the traditional livelihoods for the county until manufacturing, education (Stephen F. Austin State University), and tourism were added in the latter half of this century.

Sights
Walking Tour: The Nacogdoches Chamber of Commerce distributes the free, tourist-oriented *Nacogdoches Sampler* newspaper, which contains a map of the historic central part of town. Over 25 points of historic interest are marked on the map.

Old Stone Fort: This reconstruction of Gil Ybarbo's 1779 house (at Griffith and Clark on the Stephen F. Austin State University campus) originally stood at the corner of Main and Fredonia. In 1936 it was rebuilt using the original stones for the Texas centennial. Over its long history, the building has been used as a trading post, a jail, a fort, the state's first newspaper, the first district court in the state, the home of a judge and district attorney, and now a museum. Displays include guns, tools, Indian artifacts, and other early Nacogdoches memorabilia. Open Tues.-Sat. 9-5, Sun. 1-5; free admission.

Sterne-Hoya House: This East Texas colonial-style house (tel. 409-560-5426) at Pilar and Lanana is the oldest surviving, unreconstructed home in Nacogdoches. It was built around 1830 by German immigrant Nicolas Adolphus Sterne, who participated in the 1820 Fredonia episode (see "History" above) and invested in the Texas revolution in 1836. Many early Texas dignitaries visited the Sterne house; Sam Houston was baptized into the Catholic church here (to comply with Mexican law). After Sterne died, his widow sold the house to Prussian immigrant Joseph von der Hoya; it stayed in the Hoya family until the city acquired it in 1958. It now serves as a museum (a few of the rooms are furnished in period style) and historical library. Open Mon.-Sat. 9-noon and 2-5; free admission.

Millard's Crossing: Lera Millard Thomas, the first woman from Texas to have served in the U.S. House of Representatives (she finished out husband Albert Thomas's term when he died), has moved a number of early East Texas structures to Millard's Crossing for historical preservation. Included are an 1830 double corncrib, 1843 Methodist church, 1830 log cabin, 1837 two-story house (which contains a collection of early Texas maps and other historic documents), and several other 19th-century buildings. All are furnished with period antiques. Millard's Crossing (tel. 409-564-6631) is at 6020 North St. (US 59 N), on the north edge of town. Open Mon.-Wed. and Fri. and Sat. 9-4, Sun. 1-4; admission is $2.50 for adults, $1.50 for children 6-12.

Stephen F. Austin State University: This tertiary institution with an enrollment of around 13,000 (nearly half Nacogdoches's population of 28,000) offers a wide variety of baccalaureate and master's degree programs, plus a doctoral program in forestry. The 400-acre campus is in the center of town off North St. (at Griffith). A number of university film, theater, and musical events are open to the public. For information, call (409) 568-2011.

Hotels And Motels
Most of the city's hotels and motels are found along State 21 (San Augustine Rd.), US 59 Business (North or South streets), or Loop 224.

Less expensive places include the **Nacogdoches Continental Inn** (tel. 409-564-3726) at 2728 North, where rooms are $25 s, $28-35 d, and the **Heritage Motor Inn** (tel. 560-1906) at 4809 N.W. Stallings (Loop 224), $27 s, $31.50 d.

Millard's Crossing,
Nacogdoches

The **Econo Lodge** (tel. 569-0880) at 2020 N.W. Stallings and the **La Quinta Motor Inn** (tel. 560-5453) at 3215 South are both in the $35-45 range. Better in this range is the **Holiday Inn** (tel. 569-8100) at 3400 South, where rooms are $51 s, $61 d.

Well located for downtown exploration is the newly restored **Fredonia Hotel and Convention Center** (tel. 564-1234), 200 N. Fredonia (formerly the Hotel Fredonia). Rooms range from $50 s, $58 d to $78 for a suite.

Bed And Breakfast Inns

The **Haden-Edwards Inn** (tel. 409-564-9999) is an 1860 house within walking distance of the downtown area at 106 N. Lanana; rooms with private bath are $60 on weekdays, $72 on weekends while rooms without bath are $50 (all week long). All rates include a full breakfast. **The Little House** (tel. 564-2735) is a country cottage behind the 1880 Raguet House at 110 Sanders (also within walking distance of downtown); the cottage accommodates two guests for $45 a night with continental breakfast.

The **Llano Grande Plantation** (tel. 409-569-1249), three miles south of Loop 224 on FM 2863, has three separate houses with B&B accommodation. The 1848 East Texas-style **Tol Barret House**, listed with the National Register of Historic Places, is $70 for the first night, $60 each additional night, including a full breakfast of venison sausage, eggs, homemade bread, and homemade jam. The proprietors live downstairs in the **Sparks House** and offer the second floor at the same rates. The **Gate House**, a 50-year-old ranch-style farmhouse, is also available. The plantation's mailing address is Route 4, Box 9400, Nacogdoches, TX 75961.

Campgrounds And RV Parks

The closest campground to Nacogdoches is at **Mission San Francisco de los Tejas State Historical Park** (tel. 409-687-2394, mailing address Route 2, Box 108, Grapeland, TX 75844), about 37 miles southwest of the city off State 21 (just past Neches). Tent/camper sites with water are $6, with w/e $9, and with full hookups $10.

The **Ratcliff Lake Recreation Area** (Neches Ranger District, tel. 409-544-2046) in Davy Crockett National Forest is 36 miles southwest of Nacogdoches via State 7; rates are $5 for tent/camper sites, $8 with electricity.

Food

Catfish King of Nacogdoches (tel. 560-9470) at 3120 North is part of an East Texas chain that specializes in fresh catfish and other seafood at moderate prices. **Casa Tomas Mexican Restaurant** (tel. 560-2403) at 1514 North serves a variety of Tex-Mex, including fajitas and *pollo al carbon*. More upscale is **La Hacienda** (tel. 564-6487), a Mexican, steak, and seafood restaurant in a large converted house at 1411 North.

Events

The week-long **Heritage Festival** is held in early June to celebrate the city's glorious history and features an old-fashioned "barn dance," eight-km run through town, antique show and sale, "Tastes of Nacogdoches" restaurant sampler, beauty pageant and coronation of Heritage Queen, chili cook-off, old-timers hall of fame breakfast, and a charity ball. Most of the festival events are held at the Nacogdoches County Exposition Center on US 59, north of State 21 near the Old Tyler Rd. (FM 1638) junction.

The Expo Center is also the sight of October's **Piney Woods Fair,** which features agricultural and livestock exhibits, a carnival, music, arts and crafts, and food booths.

Lake Nacogdoches

This 2,210-acre impoundment of Bayo Loco Creek (12 miles southwest via FM 224) has two municipal parks with facilities for picnicking, boating, fishing, swimming, water-skiing, and hiking.

Caddoan Mounds State Historic Site

Known to archaeologists as the George C. Davis site, Caddoan Mounds was the westernmost center of the Mississippian Temple-Mound Culture (or Mound-Builder Culture) that once spanned the southeastern woodlands of North America from approximately 1000 B.C. to A.D. 1500. This particular site was inhabited by the most sophisticated of the Indian mound-builder tribes, the Early Caddos. Chosen for its fertile alluvial soil and proximity to the Neches River, the site remained active for over 500 years beginning around A.D. 800. The Caddos mysteriously abandoned the site in the late 13th or early 14th century; contemporary theory has it that the ruling elite here was losing influence over outlying Caddo villages, so its members left.

Current excavations consist of two temple mounds, a burial mound, and some village remnants. A visitor center offers interpretive exhibits and an audio-visual presentation about Caddo history and culture; a 3/4-mile self-guided trail leads visitors through the mound and village area. Many questions about the mounds and the people who built them remain unanswered; periodic excavation work continues (carried out by the University of Texas and Texas A&M University) and visitors are welcome to observe. The facilities

are open for day use only, Wed.-Sun. 8-5; admission is $3 per vehicle, $1 for pedestrians and cyclists.

The site is located on State 21 about 30 miles west of Nacogdoches. For more information, contact Caddoan Mounds State Historic Site (tel. 409-858-3218), Route 2, Box 85C, Alto, TX 75925.

Nacogdoches Information

The **Nacogdoches Chamber of Commerce** (tel. 409-564-7351), housed in the historic Eugene Blount House at 1801 North, distributes the *Nacogdoches Sampler,* maps, and brochures containing information on attractions, dining, and accommodations in and around Nacogdoches.

The area code for Nacogdoches and vicinity is 409 unless otherwise noted.

TEXAS STATE RAILROAD STATE HISTORICAL PARK

The only railroad park in the state system started out as a prison railroad that served an iron plant in Rusk in 1896. By 1913 the penitentiary and iron plant had closed and the line was operated by Southern Pacific until the Parks and Wildlife Dept. acquired it in 1969 (Missouri Pacific Railroad still leases a 3.7-mile stretch to serve a local meat-packing plant).

The 25-mile stretch between Rusk (40 miles northwest of Nacogdoches via State 21 W and US 175 N) and Palestine farther west is dedicated to the preservation and exhibition of steam locomotives. Steam trains take passengers on a 50-mile roundtrip excursion through pine and hardwood forests (including Fairchild State Forest) and across 30 bridges (including a 1,100-foot span across the Neches River). The six locomotives in use were built between 1896 and 1927 and range in weight from 71 to 224 tons each. Park facilities at Rusk include a small theater with a film and various exhibits that recount the railroad's history. Facilities at both ends include picnic grounds.

Trains run Thurs.-Mon. from May 30 to Oct. 30, Sat. and Sun. only the rest of the year. A train departs from each end of the line at 11 a.m.; return trips are at 3 p.m. (two hours each way, with a two-hour break between—time enough for a picnic). The fare is $6 one way, $8 roundtrip for

TODD CLARK

adults, $4 and $6 for children 3-12.

Camping: The park in Rusk offers tent/camper sites with w/e for $9, full hookups for $10.

Information: Contact Texas State Railroad State Historical Park (tel. 903-683-2581), P.O. Box 39, Rusk, TX 75785.

KILGORE

Kilgore was named after its founder C.B. "Buck" Kilgore, who started businesses here in 1871 to serve lumberjacks and sawmill workers. Cotton was the only other game in town until the massive East Texas Oil Field was discovered four miles south of Kilgore in December 1930. By August 1931 the National Guard had to be called in to restore law and order among the wildcatters, drillers, roughnecks, and camp followers that had descended on the little town. Since then, petroleum deposits here have produced 4.5 billion barrels of crude oil.

The city leadership had enough foresight to begin diversifying the economy before the bottom dropped out of the oil market in the 1980s. Kilgore is no longer solely reliant on local commodities; numerous manufacturing companies here produce everything from fiberglass fishing boats to toilet bowls.

Sights

Architecture: You can tell that the '30s were Kilgore's glory days by all the leftover art deco buildings in the downtown area. A few brick structures from the late 1800s are also still standing. The Kilgore Chamber of Commerce (tel. 903-984-5022, 1100 Stone) distributes two informative pamphlets for those interested in historic buildings: *Downtown Walking Tour: Historic Sites & Art Deco Architecture* and *Driving Tour of Historic Sites.*

East Texas Oil Museum: On the campus of Kilgore College at Henderson (US 59) and Ross, this museum (tel. 903-983-8295) features handpainted murals depicting early oil production, films on the Texas oil boom, and an indoor replica of Kilgore in the '30s, with vintage cars and horsedrawn carriages stuck in the mud street, a general store, barbershop, post office, feed store, and other boom-town businesses, all furnished with original period artifacts. Open Tues.-Sat. 9-4 (till 5 June-August), Sun. 2-5; admission is $2.50 adults, $1.50 children under 12.

Rangerette Showcase: The Kilgore College Rangerettes were organized in 1940 to "bring show business to the gridiron" and were the first to develop precision dancing for sports events. Today they're much in demand for half-time shows at national football bowls. The Rangerette Showcase (tel. 903-984-8531), at Broadway and Ross on the Kilgore College campus, displays a collection of Rangerette props, costumes (stylized white cowboy hats, white boots, blue skirts, and red blouses or jackets), photos, newspaper clippings, and other memorabilia. The facility also includes a theater where a 20-minute film about the Rangerettes is shown. Open Tues.-Fri. 10-noon and 1-4:30, Sat. and Sun. 2-5; free admission.

Accommodations

With a population of 12,000, Kilgore only has a few motels. The **Kilgore Community Inn** (tel. 903-984-5501) is well located at 801 US 259 N near Kilgore College and the downtown area. Rooms are $35 s, $42 d.

The **Ramada Inn** (tel. 903-983-3456) at 3501 US 259N has rooms for $42-52.

The **Hidden Valley Mobile Home & RV Park** (tel. 903-983-2760) is about two miles south of I-20 off FM 1249 at 1803 Roberts. Full hookups are $12 a night—lower for longer stays.

Food

The hickory-smoked barbecue (beef, ham, sausage, and turkey) at **Bodacious Bar-B-Q** (tel. 903-983-1421), State 42 N near I-20, is very popular—the wood is stacked out back and the meat's served on butcher paper, always a good sign. **Bert T's Bar B Que** (tel. 983-1125), five miles south of Kilgore on US 259, specializes in smoked Cajun boudain as well as the usual fare.

The most authentic Tex-Mex in town is at **Los Dos Mexican Restaurant** (tel. 903-984-4790) at 2612 US 259 N. Farther north in a huge 1935 mansion is the more upscale **La Hacienda** (tel. 983-1629). The inexpensive breakfast buffet at the Kilgore Community Inn (see "Accommodations" above) is a favorite local meeting spot.

Events

Kilgore College hosts the **Texas Shakespeare Festival** in its Van Cliburn Auditorium during the last week in June and first two weeks of July. Four Shakespeare plays are performed on an alternating basis. Ticket prices range $5-10; season tickets are available for $15-36. Call (903) 983-8120 or 983-8118 for more information.

Kilgore Information

Contact the **Kilgore Chamber of Commerce** (tel. 903-984-5022) at 100 Stone Road. The area code for Kilgore is 903.

LONGVIEW

Established as a rail terminal for the regional cotton and timber trade in 1870, Longview mushroomed overnight with the East Texas oil boom of the 1930s, centered at nearby Kilgore. It's now the Gregg County seat with a population of approximately 75,000 and is a headquarters for diverse manufacturing interests (Resistol Hats, the Stroh Brewery, Continental Can, and various oilfield equipment manufacturers).

Gregg County Historical Museum

This small museum, housed in a restored 1910 bank at 214 N. Fredonia, chronicles the county history with exhibits on early oil industry, lumber, farming, printing, and railroads. It also makes the most of its setting with a refurbished teller's cage, bank president's office, and bank vault. Other period rooms include a dentist's office, schoolroom, and a log cabin interior. Open Tues.-Sat. 10-4; admission is $2 adults, $1 seniors and persons under 18.

Longview Museum And Arts Center

The permanent collection in this museum (tel. 903-753-8103) at 102 W. College focuses on contemporary Texan artists. Temporary exhibits change six to eight times a year and feature a range of work by Texas and Southwestern artists (including occasional East Texas folk art). Open Tues.-Fri. 9-5, Sat. 10-4; free admission.

The Stroh Brewery Company

This is one of seven breweries operated by Stroh nationwide and is the largest brewery in Texas. On-line since 1966, this one produces Stroh's, Old Milwaukee, Schaefer, and Schlitz (plus "light" and malt liquor variations of these labels).

Visitors may join guided 40-minute tours of the brewing and packaging facilities that end in the Strohaus hospitality room for free samples. Tours are conducted Mon.-Fri. at 10 a.m., 11 a.m., 1 p.m., 2 p.m., and 3 p.m.; free admission. For further information, call (903) 753-0371.

Accommodations

Motel 6 (tel. 903-758-5256) at 110 I-20 W (exits 595/595A) has rooms for $24 s, plus $6 for each additional adult. Next up in price is the **Shilo Inn** (tel. 758-0711) at 3304 S. Eastman (I-20 and

State 149), where rooms are $34 s, $39 d. In the same range is the **Comfort Inn** (tel. 757-7858) at 203 N. Spur 63 (one block north of US 80).

La Quinta Motor Inn (tel. 903-757-3663) at Estes Pkwy. and I-20 has rooms for $45-51 s, $51-57 d (senior discount available). The nearby **Best Western Longview Inn** (tel. 753-0350) has similar rates. Also at Estes Pkwy. and I-20 is the **Holiday Inn** (tel. 758-0500), where rooms are $50-60 s, $57-66 d.

Annie's Bed & Breakfast (tel. 903-636-4355) is a three-story Queen Anne Victorian 23 miles west of Longview (via US 80 W and State 155 N) in the small town of Big Sandy; rates range from $38 for a cozy second-floor room with shared bath to $115 for a spacious, elegant third-floor room with private balcony. All 13 rooms are furnished with country antiques; a full breakfast is served in Annie's Tea Room, which is also open to non-guests.

Food

They say you haven't been to Longview if you haven't dined at **Johnny Cace's Seafood and Steak House** (tel. 903-753-7691), at 1501 E. Marshall (US 80 E), which has been serving Creole-style seafood since 1949. Kilgore's **Bodacious Bar-B-Q** has a branch in Longview (tel. 753-2714) at 904 Sixth downtown, with the same hickory-smoked ribs, brisket, ham, sausage, and turkey. **The Shed** (tel. 758-5866), on State 32 a half mile north of I-20, is famous for its moderately priced, custom-cut steaks. **Lupe's** is a local Tex-Mex chain specializing in *tacos al carbon, flautas,* fajitas, and *carne asada.* In Longview, there are two locations: 809 Pine Tree (tel. 297-6916) and 1015 E. Marshall (tel. 757-5940).

US 80 (Marshall Ave.) is good hunting grounds for fast-food outlets like Dairy Queen, Pizza Hut, and the like.

Entertainment

Longview has the oldest continually operating dance hall in the state (Gruene Dance Hall in the Hill Country is older but closed down for a while), the **Reo Palm Isle Ballroom** (tel. 903-753-4440) at the junction of State 31 and FM 1845 (between I-20 and US 80). Originally established as Mattie's Ballroom in the 1930s, the hall features a hardwood dance floor and serves only beer and setups; men must check their hats at the door. Live country bands generally appear Tues.-Sun. nights.

Annie's Tea Room (see "Accommodations" above) hosts occasional art shows, dinner theaters, and small country fairs.

Information

The **Longview Convention And Visitors Bureau** (tel. 903-753-3281) at 100 Grand Blvd. has printed information on the city and area, as does the larger **East Texas Tourism Association** (tel. 757-4444) at 400 N. Center.

The area code for Longview is 903.

JEFFERSON

This little town on Big Cypress Bayou between Lake O' The Pines and Caddo Lake is well worth visiting for those with an interest in Texas history. At one time it was the westernmost terminus for Mississippi, Ohio, and Tennessee river steamboats, which reached Jefferson via the Red River (which joined the Mississippi River at Shreveport, Louisiana), Caddo Lake, and the bayou. Second in importance only to the Port of Galveston, the docks in Jefferson offloaded westward passengers arriving from New Orleans (800 miles away) and shipped cotton and timber east.

During the Civil War, Trans-Mississippi Confederate troops were stationed here and the port served as an important supply point for textiles and munitions. After the war, the port continued to grow; in 1872, over 200 sternwheelers, each with a cargo capacity of 225 to 700 tons, called at Jefferson. The first refrigerator in the state arrived here in 1873, followed by the first ice factory and brewery. Later that same year, the U.S. Army Corps of Engineers irrevocably reversed the town's fortunes when they dynamited a 170-mile-long logjam in the Red River (the infamous "Red River Raft") which had until then diverted a great deal of water into Big Cypress Bayou. Once the logjam was cleared, the water level in Caddo Lake and Big Cypress Bayou lowered to such an extent that riverboat travel was no longer feasible; within a very short time the population dropped from 30,000 to 3,000.

Jefferson's loss was the historian's gain, however. "Progress" bypassed the little town in this forgotten corner of the state and instead of being torn down and replaced by glass-and-concrete blocks, old buildings were left standing. Today Jefferson has no skyscrapers, Holiday Inns, apartment buildings, or supermarkets, and in fact almost no modern buildings of any kind. Except for improved roads, it looks very much like it must have looked in the steamboat era. Nearly a hundred structures in a 20-block radius of downtown bear historical plaques of one kind or another.

The town's population hasn't increased at all since the blasting of the Red River Raft and is now only about 2,500 (though around 10,000 are buried in the cemetery!). Tourism keeps the town alive; nearly 25 local structures have been restored and converted into bed-and-breakfast inns while dozens of others have become antique shops, art studios, restaurants, and cafes. (Some residents are employed in Marshall, a manufacturing and petroleum center of 27,000 people, 16 miles south of Jefferson.)

Historic Buildings

Many Jefferson buildings are made of cypress heartwood gathered from the flood plains of Big Cypress Bayou or Caddo Lake. Such wood is well suited to construction since it's straight, strong, and impervious to termites; only cypress trees over 500 years old contain heartwood—very few are left today. Several homes are open year-round for public tours while others are open only during the annual Spring Pilgrimage (see "Events" below). For a complete list of historic buildings, contact the Marion County Chamber of Commerce (tel. 903-665-2672) at 115 W. Austin

(near Excelsior House).

The second-oldest hotel in Texas, the **Excelsior House** (tel. 903-665-2513) at 211 W. Austin, was built in 1858 in the New Orleans style and hosted such luminaries as railroad tycoon Jay Gould, Ulysses S. Grant, Rutherford B. Hayes, and Oscar Wilde. It was eventually purchased and restored by the local Jessie Allen Wise Garden Club, which has been responsible for a number of restoration projects in town. Inside, the ballroom and dining room are crowned by two French Sevres chandeliers; walls and ceilings are of pressed tin and all rooms are furnished in period antiques. A French cast-iron fountain sits in the center of the New Orleans-style courtyard in back and original guest registers are on view in the lobby. Tours of the building are conducted daily 1-2; admission is $2 adults, $1 children under 12.

The **House of the Seasons** (tel. 903-665-8880, 665-3141), at 409 S. Alley, was built at the peak of Jefferson's early glory in 1872 by Benjamin H. Epperson, a prominent lawyer and Sam Houston confidante. The two-story house shows a transition between Greek Revival and Victorian styles, with Italianate details superimposed on the basic colonial design. It's crowned by a four-sided cupola with stained-glass windows; each side represents a different season with a different color. Inside, a dome lined with frescoes can be viewed from the first floor through a banistered opening in the second floor. Guided tours are

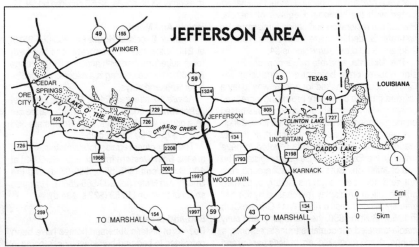

House of the Seasons,
Jefferson

conducted Mon.-Sat. at 10:30 a.m. and 1:30 p.m., Sun. at 1:30 p.m. (or by appointment); admission is $4 adults, $2.50 students, $1 children under 12.

The **Freeman Plantation** (tel. 903-665-2320), built in 1850, once sat in the middle of a thousand-acre sugar cane plantation (now about a mile west of town on State 49). The design is typical Louisiana/Greek Revival-style, with the main body of the house raised seven feet above the ground. The 14-inch-thick walls of the lower floor are made of clay brick that was hand-molded by slave labor; the upper walls are cypress, with framing timbers that were notched and pegged rather than nailed. Listed with the National Register of Historic Places, the restoration and period furnishings are first-rate. Guided tours are given Thurs.-Tues. at 2:30 and 3:30 p.m.; admission is $4.

The **Atalanta**, a private railcar opposite Excelsior House, once belonged to financier Jay Gould. Gould had asked for right of way to lay a railroad through Jefferson, promising increased prosperity for a town whose economy was based on the transportation industry. At the time, Jefferson was riding high as a riverboat port, so the city leadership declined. Gould is reputed to have written in the Excelsior House guest register, "The end of Jefferson." But the town's still around, he's not, and now they've got his plushly appointed private railcar on display (purchased by the historically minded Jessie Allen Wise Garden Club in 1953). Built in 1890, the mahogany- and curly maple-paneled car contains four staterooms, a lounge, dining room, kitchen, butler's pantry, and bathroom. Open for tours daily 9-4:30; admission is $1 adults, 50 cents children under 12.

Jefferson Historical Society Museum

Housed in the 1888 Federal Building at 223 W. Austin (tel. 903-665-8880), this four-story museum (including the basement and garret) contains 3,000 items pertaining to Jefferson history. Some of the more notable exhibits are the Caddo Indian artifacts, gun collection, and antique furniture on the second floor. Historic documents are displayed on the main floor. Open daily 9:30-5; admission is $3.50 adults, $2.50 children under 12.

Hotels And Motels

The historic **Excelsior House** (tel. 903-665-2513) at 211 Austin has 13 rooms and one two-bedroom suite furnished with antiques. Rates range $40-60; advance booking is a necessity, especially for weekend stays.

Across the street at 124 W. Austin is the **Hotel Jefferson** (tel. 903-665-2631), which started out as a cotton warehouse in 1851. Rooms are $65 s or d, $75-85 for four people.

The only other regular hotels/motels in town are the **Best Western Inn** (tel. 903-665-3983) at 400 S. Walcott ($45-55 s, $50-65 d) and the **Sherry Inn Motel** (tel. 903-665-2581), 1 1/2 miles south of town on US 59 ($22 s, $34 d).

Bed-and-breakfast Inns

Dozens of historic Jefferson homes have been converted to bed-and-breakfast inns, ranging in price from $35 to $115 a night including breakfast—sometimes "continental" (coffee, juice, and bread or pastries), sometimes "plantation" (eggs, sausage or bacon, rolls or cornbread, coffee, and juice) depending on the establishment. The Marion County Chamber of Commerce (tel. 903-665-2672), 115 W. Austin, Jefferson, TX 75657, can furnish visitors with a complete list.

Campgrounds And RV Parks
Jefferson sits between two of the state's most attractive waterways, Lake O' The Pines and Caddo Lake. Plenty of camping and RV facilities are available at each—see "Lake O' The Pines" and "Caddo Lake" below.

Food
Probably the top restaurant in town is **The Black Swan** (tel. 903-665-8922) at 210 Austin, which specializes in Cajun and Creole dishes. It's open Fri.-Mon. for lunch and dinner; prices are moderate. Also competing for first slot is the **Stillwater Inn** (tel. 665-8415), 203 E. Broadway at Owens, a converted home with a changing continental menu for dinner only, Wed.-Sun. (April-July they also serve Sunday brunch).

The Bakery (tel. 903-665-2253) at 201 W. Austin is a casual sit-down/takeout place that will please just about anybody, with a menu that includes gumbo, red beans and rice, dressed baked potatoes, Italian pasta, chili, and chicken-fried steak, plus assorted fresh-baked goods. Downhome or Southern-style cooking is available at the **Club Cafe** (tel. 665-2881), 109 N. Polk (breakfast and lunch), and the **Galley Pub** (tel. 665-3641), 121 W. Austin (lunch and dinner). **Auntie Skinner's Riverboat Club** (tel. 665-7121) at 107 W. Austin serves Mexican and down-home (lunch and dinner).

Entertainment
Most of Jefferson seems to be asleep by 9 p.m. Between May and Sept., **The Haywood House After Dinner Theatre** (tel. 903-665-2241) at Dallas and Market hosts "cowboy melodrama." On occasional weekend nights, Auntie Skinner's Riverboat Club (see "Food") features live music.

Events
On the first weekend of May, the Jessie Allen Wise Garden Club sponsors the **Spring Pilgrim-age** in which many historic homes that are closed to the public most of the year are open for tours. Another feature of this celebration is the annual performance of *The Diamond Bessie Murder Trial* at the Jefferson Playhouse, Delta and Henderson. Every year since 1955, local residents have presented this reenactment of an actual 1887 trial in which diamond heir Abe Rothschild was charged with the murder of his wife, an ex-prostitute called "Diamond Bessie" because of the abundance of diamonds she wore. (If you want to know what happened, go see the show.)

The **Jefferson Christmas Candlelight Tour** is held the first weekend of December and is the town's most popular event. Four historic homes are selected and bedecked with 19th-century Christmas decorations (with lots of candles); hostesses in Victorian gowns receive visitors and conduct the tours in each. Carolers and handbell choirs roam the streets and there are Christmas music concerts at the Jefferson Playhouse and at the First United Methodist Church (305 W. Henderson).

Canoeing The Bayou
Paddler's Post (tel. 903-665-3251, 938-3334), 101 Market St., and **Big Cypress Canoe Rental** (tel. 665-7163, 665-7288), 502 E. Watson, rent equipment for canoeing on Big Cypress Bayou, which runs along the southeast edge of town. Standard rates are around $5 an hour or $20 a day. These rental facilities can also provide shuttle service to a more remote seven-mile upper section of the bayou (west of Jefferson) that's popular for fishing and primitive camping—ask for maps and information. Put-in points are below Lake O' The Pines or closer to Jefferson just east of French Creek; popular takeouts are in Jefferson itself, farther east at Black Cypress Bayou, or at Long's Camp.

Lake O' The Pines
This 18,700-acre reservoir, an impoundment of Cypress Creek set among pine forests, is one of the most scenic lakes in the state and very popular for fishing, swimming, and boating. During most times of year, the best fishing (bass, bream, crappie, catfish) is at the north end of the lake near Willow Point and Cedar Springs. A wide variety of facilities—campgrounds, marinas, picnic areas, and boat ramps—encircle the lake, most of which are administered by the Army Corps of Engineers.

Alley Creek (open March-Sept. only), **Brushy Creek, Buckhorn Creek,** and **Johnson Creek** each have tent/camper sites with w/e for $10 a night or $6 for water only. The **Cedar Springs, Hurricane Creek,** and **Oak Valley** areas have no-fee primitive campsites with pit toilets and cooking grills only. The stay limit for all Corps-operated camping areas is 14 days.

Several commercial concessions operate campgrounds on the lake as well, including **Big Cypress Marina, Island View Landing, Lakeview Marina, Sunrise Cove,** and **Willow Point.** All offer two-way hookups, but only Lakeview Marina (off FM 729 and FM 1969 on the southeast side of the lake) has a trailer dump station. Rates are about the same as at the Corps facilities. Lakeview Marina and Willow Point also rent cabins for around $25 a night.

For further information, contact the Corps of Engineers (tel. 903-665-2336), Lake O' The Pines, Drawer W, Jefferson, TX 75657.

Caddo Lake

Before the dynamiting of the Red River Raft near Shreveport, Caddo Lake was an important waterway for steamboat traffic between New Orleans and Jefferson. Caddo Indian legend says that the 25,400-acre lake was created by powerful earth-shaking spirits who were angry with a Caddo chief. The story could be based on fact since it's possible the lake was formed by the great 1811 New Madrid earthquake (centered in Missouri); at any rate, this is the only natural lake of any size in the state (about a third of it is actually in Louisiana). It's also one of the most atmospheric, bending around coves and islands and fringed by lush flood-plain forests. Cypress trees and tupelo, hung with Spanish moss, dot the lake's surface and add to the primeval effect.

The only town on the lake is Uncertain (pop. 173), which is situated on the southwestern shore. Just north of town along the lake are several fishing camps where bait, tackle, and boats are available. Some of the townspeople have decided that the town's name sounds negative and are trying to change it to Certain, so it reads differently on some maps. (You might say they're uncertain about the name).

Canoeing: The lake and its adjoining bayous and creeks are a favorite destination among canoeists since they offer so many possibilities for exploration. Several private concessions along the lakeshore offer canoe rentals for around $20 a day. If you're new to the lake, be sure to get a map that shows the 40 miles of established boat lanes; channel markers on the lake help but it's easy to get lost. Several bait and tackle shops, lodges, and campgrounds can also arrange for boating/fishing guides at a rate of approximately $55 per half day, $75 for a full day.

Cabins: Big Pines Lodge (tel. 903-679-3466), **Johnson's Ranch** (tel. 789-3213), and **Pine Needle Lodge** (tel. 665-2911) offer cabins for rent along the south and southwest shores of the lake. Rates start at $30-45 a night for a one-bedroom cabin (two beds) with kitchenette and reach as high as $100 for a three-bedroom cabin (six beds) with a large kitchen; most cabins are air-conditioned. Caddo Lake State Park also has cabins (see below).

Camping: Caddo Lake State Park is on Big Cypress Bayou where it feeds into the lake's west end, just off FM 134 from Jefferson. Day-use facilities include picnic areas, a boat launch, fishing pier, boat rentals, and hiking trails. Camping facilities include tent/camper sites with water only ($6 a night on weekdays, $8 on weekends), with w/e ($9/11), RV sites with full hookups ($10/12), screened shelters ($15/16), and cabins ($35 for one to two persons, plus $5 for each additional adult, $2 for children 6-12). For information or reservations, contact Caddo Lake State Park (tel. 903-679-3351), Route 2, Box 15, Karnack, TX 75661.

Private camping areas are available at Uncertain's **Crip's Camp** (tel. 903-789-3233) and at **Long's Camp** (tel. 679-3427), which is northwest of Caddo Lake State Park near Baldwin (off FM 134), on Big Cypress Bayou. Tentsites run around $5 with water only, $8 with w/e (Long's also has full hookups for $10). Also in this area is **Shady Glade** (tel. 789-3295), where RV sites with full hookups are $10 and you can pitch a tent for $5.

Shopping

Jefferson has over 30 antique and collectibles shops, most of them along Polk, Austin, Lafayette, and Walnut. A map/brochure listing all of them is available from the chamber of commerce (tel. 665-2672) at 115 W. Austin. **Old Mill Antiques** (tel. 665-8601) houses 10 dealers under one roof at 210 E. Austin. **Three Rivers Antiques & Collectors Mall** (tel. 665-8721) at 116 Walnut also has several dealers. **Steamboat Warehouse Country Pottery Shop** (tel. 665-8481) at 113 E. Austin sells country-style crockery made on the premises.

Transport And Tours

Bicycles can be rented by the hour, half day, or day at **Crossroads Market** (tel. 903-665-2326), 101 S. Polk. Jefferson is small and fairly flat, so this is a good way to see the town.

Mullins Narrated Tours (tel. 903-665-2857) offers half-hour tours by horse-drawn surrey, departing from 302 Dallas; $5 adults, $3 children under 12. **Austin Street Transit** (tel. 665-2222) operates a one-hour narrated tour by open-air trolley-style bus, departing from Haywood House on Austin St.; $4 adults, $1.50 children under 12.

The same family operates one-hour boat tours of Big Cypress Bayou aboard the *Bayou Queen,* passing abandoned mills and a Confederate gunpowder magazine along the old steamboat route. The boat departs from **Jefferson Landing** from Austin St., go north to Polk, then south across the bridge and follow the sign to the landing (an easy walk).

In addition to surrey, bus, and boat tours, you can take a ride on the **Jefferson And Cypress Bayou Railroad** (tel. 903-665-8400), a narrow-gauge steam train that runs along Big Cypress Bayou. The five-mile, 45-minute trip runs through stands of cypress, pine, and dogwood to the Confederate powder magazine, then returns. The depot is at the end of E. Austin; May-Sept. departures are Thurs., Fri., and Sun. at 1:30 p.m. and 3:30 p.m., Sat. at 1:30 p.m., 3 p.m., and 4:30 p.m. During the remainder of the year the train runs Fri.-Sun. only. The company has plans to extend the railroad eventually; for the time being the fare is $6.50 adults, $4.50 children 3-12.

Jefferson Area Information

The **Marion County Chamber of Commerce** (tel. 903-665-2672) at 115 W. Austin distributes free information on Jefferson and vicinity; they can also arrange bed and breakfast bookings. Open daily 8:30-4:30 from May to Oct., Mon.-Fri. the remainder of the year.

The area code for Jefferson and vicinity is 903.

BOOKLIST

DESCRIPTION AND TRAVEL

American Automobile Association. *Texas Tour Book*. Published annually; 240 pages. A slim summary of things to see in the more popular tourist areas, including up-to-date hotel, motel, and restaurant information.

Brook, Stephen. *Honkytonk Gelato: Travels Through Texas*. New York: Paragon House, 1988; 283 pages. Brook is an Englishman who brings insight and humor to bear on his Texas travels; probably the best travelogue yet written about the state.

Rafferty, Robert R. *Texas*. The Texas Monthly Guidebooks series. Texas Monthly Press, 1989; 985 pages. Ambitious guide that covers a large number of Texas towns by region, in alphabetical order. Despite some organizational problems (Beaumont is placed in South Texas while Houston—farther south in reality—is put under East Texas), the completeness of the coverage is exemplary.

Ruff, Ann. *A Guide to Historic Texas Inns and Hotels*. Lone Star Books, 1985; 132 pages. A survey of hotels and inns mostly built between 1880 and 1950. Worth reading for the historical background, but quite out-of-date for practical information.

State Department of Highways and Public Transportation. *Texas Public Campgrounds.* * Published annually; page count varies. A free publication that lists the facilities and locations of virtually every city, county, state, Corps of Engineers, or National Park Service campground in the state. Keyed to the State Dept. of Highways' *Offipcial Highway Travel Map*.

State Department of Highways and Public Transportation. *Texas State Travel Guide.* * 1989; 248 pages. Another free publication; contains capsule descriptions of a wide range of state destinations, in alphabetic order.

Texas Almanac. Dallas Morning News, published annually; 600 + pages. Contains a wealth of information in the areas of politics, government, geography, culture, business, transportation, and education. Each year the book concentrates on the history of a different part of the state.

Works Projects Administration. *Texas: A Guide to the Lone Star State*. American Guide Series, 1940, reprinted by Texas Monthly Press, 1986; 718 pages. Part of the classic guide series that employed writers during the New Deal era. Contains some interesting historical tidbits.

NATURE

Bomar, George W. *Texas Weather*. Austin: University of Texas Press, 1985; 265 pages. An excellent summary of weather patterns throughout the state, including the physics of hurricanes and tornadoes. Contains charts with average temperatures, relative humidity, precipitation, and wind velocities for various points in all Texas regions.

Lane, James A., and John L. Tveten. *A Birder's Guide to the Texas Coast*. L & P Press, 1989; 119 pages. Detailed and comprehensive, covering the coastal area from Beaumont to Brownsville; includes sections on indigenous mammals, amphibians, and reptiles.

Phelan, Richard. *Texas Wild: The Land, Plants, and Animals of the Lone Star State*. This out-of-print book offers a wonderful synthesis of the state's geography and natural history; instead of isolating the animate and the inanimate, Phelan demonstrates their intricate connections; along the way he takes a few jabs at local, regional, and state environmental policies. Includes color plates and maps.

Tennant, Alan. *A Field Guide to Texas Snakes*. Texas Monthly Field Guide Series. Texas Monthly Press, 1985; 260 pages. A well-researched, well-written guide; includes an identification key, color plates, and a useful section on venom poisoning.

Texas Parks & Wildlife. *A Checklist of Texas Birds.*† Technical Series No. 32. 1989; 33 pages. A complete birder's checklist categorized by bird family, including extinct, hypothetical, accidental, introduced, historical, and extirpated species. Available free at many state parks.

Wauer, Roland H. *Naturalist's Big Bend.* College Station: Texas A&M University Press, 1980; 149 pages. A good introduction to the flora and fauna of the Big Bend area.

CULTURE

Govenar, Alan. *Meeting the Blues: The Rise of the Texas Sound.* Dallas:Taylor Publishing Co., 1988; 239 pages. An excellent combination of interviews, photos, and historical descriptions that trace the development of Texas musical styles (including R&B, swamp music, Cajun, and zydeco as well as blues) from the late 19th century to the present.

Hall, Douglas Kent. *The Border: Life on the Line.* New York: Abbeville Press; 1988; 251 pages. Part photo essay, part narrative that successfully evokes life along the Texas-Mexican border.

Linck, Ernestine Sewell, and Joyce Gibson Roach. *Eats: A Folk History of Texas Foods.* Fort Worth: Texas Christian University Press, 1989; 257 pages. A montage of recipes, history, regional food classification, and anecdotes.

Porterfield, Bill. *The Greatest Honky-Tonks in Texas.* Dallas: Taylor Publishing Co., 1981; 148 pages. Indispensable reading for anyone contemplating a serious journey along the honky-tonk circuit; not as out-of-date as its 1981 publication date might indicate, since the author attempted to select the tried and true. Humorously written, it includes charts and instructions for learning the dance hall waltz, polka, cotton-eyed Joe, sweetheart schottische, and two-step.

Stewart, Rick. *Lone Star Regionalism: The Dallas Nine and Their Circle.* Texas Monthly Press, 1985; 199 pages. Examines the work of a group of young Dallas artists (around 25 in all, led by an influential nine) who achieved nationwide recognition in the 1930s for their strong regional style, which combined elements of surrealism, American Indian design, and Italian quattrocento painting. Contains many color plates.

HISTORY

A Concise History of Texas. Dallas Morning News, 1988; 157 pages (formerly part of the *Texas Almanac).* Exactly what it claims to be; remarkably comprehensive and accurate.

Fehrenbach, T.R. *Lone Star.* American Legacy Press, 1988; 761 pages. This thick tome is considered the best history of the state available, but is sadly lacking in proportion and style.

Newcombe, W.W., Jr. *The Indians of Texas.* Austin: University of Texas Press, 1961; 404 pages. The definitive work on Texas Indians; well balanced.

RECREATION

Dunn, Barbara, and Stephan Myers. *Diving and Snorkeling Guide to Texas.* Houston: Pisces Books (Gulf Publishing), 1991.

Parent, Laurence. *The Hiker's Guide to Texas.* Helena: Falcon Press, 1991; 200 pages. Contains up-to-date descriptions of 75 trails throughout the state, noting length, elevation, difficulty, water availability, and special features of each.

Texas Parks & Wildlife. *Texas Hunting Guide.*† Published annually; page count varies. A free publication that contains a thorough listing of state hunting regulations.

Texas Parks & Wildlife. *Texas Recreational Fresh & Saltwater Fishing Guide.*† Published annually; page count varies. A free, complete account of all state fishing regulations, including those for shellfish.

*Can be ordered by writing the Texas Dept. of Highways and Public Transportation, Travel and Information Division, P.O. Box 5064, Austin, TX 78763.

†Can be ordered by writing the Texas Parks & Wildlife Dept., 4200 Smith School Rd., Austin, TX 78744.

INDEX

Boldface page numbers indicate the primary reference; *italicized* page numbers refer to information found in photos, illustrations, captions, or callouts.

THE METRIC SYSTEM

1 inch = 2.54 centimeters (cm)
1 foot = .304 meters (m)
1 mile = 1.6093 kilometers (km)
1 km = .6214 miles
1 fathom = 1.8288 m
1 chain = 20.1168 m
1 furlong = 201.168 m
1 acre = .4047 hectares (ha)
1 sq km = 100 ha
1 sq mile = 2.59 sq km
1 ounce = 28.35 grams
1 pound = .4536 kilograms (kg)
1 short ton = .90718 metric ton
1 short ton = 2000 pounds
1 long ton = 1.016 metric tons
1 long ton = 2240 pounds
1 metric ton = 1000 kg
1 quart = .94635 liters
1 US gallon = 3.7854 liters
1 Imperial gallon = 4.5459 liters
1 nautical mile = 1.852 km

To compute centigrade temperatures, subtract 32 from Fahrenheit and divide by 1.8. To go the other way, multiply centigrade by 1.8 and add 32.

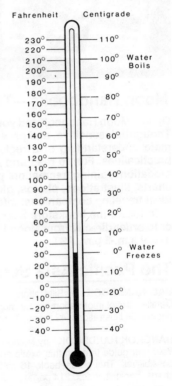

Moon Handbooks—The Ideal Traveling Companions

Open a Moon Handbook and you're opening your eyes and heart to the world. Thoughtful, sensitive, and provocative, Moon Handbooks encourage an intimate understanding of a region, from its culture and history to essential practicalities. Fun to read and packed with valuable information on accommodations, dining, recreation, plus indispensable travel tips, detailed maps, charts, illustrations, photos, glossaries, and indexes, Moon Handbooks are ideal traveling companions: informative, entertaining, and highly practical.

To locate the bookstore nearest you that carries Moon Travel Handbooks or to order directly from Moon Publications, call: (800) 345-5473, Monday-Friday, 9 a.m.-5 p.m. PST

The Pacific/Asia Series

BALI HANDBOOK   by Bill Dalton
Detailed travel information on the most famous island in the world. 12 color pages, 29 b/w photos, 68 illustrations, 42 maps, 7 charts, glossary, booklist, index. 428 pages.   **$12.95**

BANGKOK HANDBOOK   by Michael Buckley
Your tour guide through this exotic and dynamic city reveals the affordable and accessible possibilities. Thai phrasebook, 16 color pages, 55 b/w photos, 30 maps, 19 illustrations, 9 charts, booklist, index. 214 pages.   **$10.95**

BLUEPRINT FOR PARADISE: How to Live on a Tropic Island   by Ross Norgrove
This one-of-a-kind guide has everything you need to know about moving to and living comfortably on a tropical island. 8 color pages, 40 b/w photos, 3 maps, 14 charts, appendices, index. 212 pages.   **$14.95**

FIJI ISLANDS HANDBOOK by David Stanley
The first and still the best source of information on travel around this 322-island archipelago. 8 color pages, 35 b/w photos, 78 illustrations, 26 maps, 3 charts, Fijian glossary, booklist, index. 198 pages. **$8.95**

INDONESIA HANDBOOK by Bill Dalton
This one-volume encyclopedia explores island by island the many facets of this sprawling, kaleidoscopic island nation. 30 b/w photos, 143 illustrations, 250 maps, 17 charts, booklist, extensive Indonesian vocabulary, index. 1,000 pages. **$19.95**

MICRONESIA HANDBOOK:
Guide to the Caroline, Gilbert, Mariana, and Marshall Islands by David Stanley
Micronesia Handbook guides you on a real Pacific adventure all your own. 8 color pages, 77 b/w photos, 68 illustrations, 69 maps, 18 tables and charts, index. 300 pages. **$11.95**

NEW ZEALAND HANDBOOK by Jane King
Introduces you to the people, places, history, and culture of this extraordinary land. 8 color pages, 99 b/w photos, 146 illustrations, 82 maps, booklist, index. 546 pages. **$14.95**

OUTBACK AUSTRALIA HANDBOOK by Marael Johnson
Australia is an endlessly fascinating, vast land, and *Outback Australia Handbook* explores the cities and towns, sheep stations, and wilderness areas of the Northern Territory, Western, and South Australia. Full of travel tips and cultural information for adventuring, relaxing, or just getting away from it all. 8 color pages, 39 b/w photos, 63 illustrations, 51 maps, booklist, index. 355 pages. **$15.95**

PHILIPPINES HANDBOOK by Peter Harper and Evelyn Peplow
Crammed with detailed information, *Philippines Handbook* equips the escapist, hedonist, or business traveler with thorough coverage of the Philippines's colorful history, landscapes, and culture. 8 color pages, 2 b/w photos, 60 illustrations, 93 maps, 30 charts, index. 587 pages. **$12.95**

SOUTHEAST ASIA HANDBOOK by Carl Parkes
Helps the enlightened traveler discover the real Southeast Asia. 16 color pages, 75 b/w photos, 11 illustrations, 169 maps, 140 charts, vocabulary and suggested reading, index. 873 pages. **$16.95**

SOUTH KOREA HANDBOOK by Robert Nilsen
Whether you're visiting on business or searching for adventure, *South Korea Handbook* is an invaluable companion. 8 color pages, 78 b/w photos, 93 illustrations, 109 maps, 10 charts, Korean glossary with useful notes on speaking and reading the language, booklist, index. 548 pages. **$14.95**

SOUTH PACIFIC HANDBOOK by David Stanley
The original comprehensive guide to the 16 territories in the South Pacific. 20 color pages, 195 b/w photos, 121 illustrations, 35 charts, 138 maps, booklist, glossary, index. 740 pages. **$15.95**

TAHITI-POLYNESIA HANDBOOK by David Stanley
All five French-Polynesian archipelagoes are covered in this comprehensive guide by Oceania's best-known travel writer. 12 color pages, 45 b/w photos, 64 illustrations, 33 maps, 7 charts, booklist, glossary, index. 235 pages. **$11.95**

THAILAND HANDBOOK by Carl Parkes
Presents the richest source of information on travel in Thailand. Color and b/w photos, illustrations, maps, charts, booklist, glossary, index. 600 pages **$16.95**

TIBET HANDBOOK by Victor Chan
This remarkable book is both a comprehensive trekking guide and a pilgrimage guide that draws on Tibetan literature and religious history. Color and b/w photos, illustrations, maps, charts, booklist, glossary, index. 1,200 pages. **$24.95**

The Hawaiian Series

BIG ISLAND OF HAWAII HANDBOOK by J.D. Bisignani
An entertaining yet informative text packed with insider tips on accommodations, dining, sports and outdoor activities, natural attractions, and must-see sights. 12 color pages, 72 b/w photos, 73 illustrations, 22 maps, 5 charts, booklist, glossary, index. 347 pages. **$11.95**

HAWAII HANDBOOK by J.D. Bisignani
Winner of the 1989 Hawaii Visitors Bureau's Best Guide Book Award and the Grand Award for Excellence in Travel Journalism, this guide takes you beyond the glitz and high-priced hype and leads you to a genuine Hawaiian experience. 12 color pages, 86 b/w photos, 132 illustrations, 86 maps, 44 graphs and charts, Hawaiian and pidgin glossaries, appendix, booklist, index. 879 pages. **$15.95**

KAUAI HANDBOOK by J.D. Bisignani
Kauai Handbook is the perfect antidote to the workaday world. 8 color pages, 36 b/w photos, 48 illustrations, 19 maps, 10 tables and charts, Hawaiian and pidgin glossaries, booklist, index. 236 pages. **$9.95**

MAUI HANDBOOK: Including Molokai and Lanai by J.D. Bisignani
"No fool-'round" advice on accommodations, eateries, and recreation, plus a comprehensive introduction to island ways, geography, and history. 8 color pages, 60 b/w photos, 72 illustrations, 34 maps, 19 charts, booklist, glossary, index. 350 pages. **$11.95**

OAHU HANDBOOK by J.D. Bisignani
A handy guide to Honolulu, renowned surfing beaches, and Oahu's countless other diversions. 12 color pages, 93 b/w photos, 67 illustrations, 18 maps, 8 charts, booklist, glossary, index. 354 pages. **$11.95**

The Americas Series

ALASKA-YUKON HANDBOOK by Deke Castleman and Don Pitcher
Get the inside story, with plenty of well-seasoned advice to help you cover more miles on less money. 8 color pages, 26 b/w photos, 95 illustrations, 92 maps, 10 charts, booklist, glossary, index. 384 pages. **$13.95**

ARIZONA TRAVELER'S HANDBOOK by Bill Weir
This meticulously researched guide contains everything necessary to make Arizona accessible and enjoyable. 8 color pages, 194 b/w photos, 74 illustrations, 53 maps, 6 charts, booklist, index. 505 pages. **$14.95**

BAJA HANDBOOK by Joe Cummings
A comprehensive guide with all the travel information and background on the land, history, and culture of this untamed thousand-mile-long peninsula. 8 color pages, 40 b/w photos, 28 illustrations, 41 maps, 29 charts, booklist, index. 356 pages. **$13.95**

BELIZE HANDBOOK by Chicki Mallan
Complete with detailed maps, practical information, and an overview of the area's flamboyant history, culture, and geographical features, *Belize Handbook* is the only comprehensive guide of its kind to this spectacular region. 8 color pages, 65 b/w photos, 43 illustrations, 25 maps, 30 charts, booklist, index. 212 pages. **$11.95**

BRITISH COLUMBIA HANDBOOK by Jane King
With an emphasis on outdoor adventures, this guide covers mainland British Columbia, Vancouver Island, the Queen Charlotte Islands, and the Canadian Rockies. 8 color pages, 56 b/w photos, 45 illustrations, 66 maps, 4 charts, booklist, index. 381 pages. **$13.95**

CANCUN HANDBOOK and Mexico's Caribbean Coast by Chicki Mallan
Covers the city's luxury scene as well as more modest attractions, plus many side trips to unspoiled beaches and Mayan ruins. 12 color pages, 76 b/w photos, 25 illustrations, 24 maps, 12 charts, Spanish glossary, booklist, index. 257 pages. **$10.95**

CATALINA ISLAND HANDBOOK: A Guide to California's Channel Islands
by Chicki Mallan
A complete guide to these remarkable islands, from the windy solitude of the Channel Islands National Marine Sanctuary to bustling Avalon. 8 color pages, 105 b/w photos, 65 illustrations, 40 maps, 32 charts, booklist, index. 245 pages. **$10.95**

COLORADO HANDBOOK by Stephen Metzger
Essential details to the all-season possibilities in Colorado fill this guide. Practical travel tips combine with recreation—skiing, nightlife, and wilderness exploration—plus entertaining essays. 8 color pages, 92 b/w photos, 15 illustrations, 57 maps, 10 charts, booklist, index. 422 pages. **$15.95**

IDAHO HANDBOOK by Bill Loftus
A year-round guide to everything in this outdoor wonderland, from whitewater adventures to rural hideaways. 8 color pages, 35 b/w photos, 21 illustrations, 42 maps, booklist, index. 275 pages. **$12.95**

JAMAICA HANDBOOK by Karl Luntta
From the sun and surf of Montego Bay and Ocho Rios to the cool slopes of the Blue Mountains, author Karl Luntta offers island-seekers a perceptive, personal view of Jamaica. 8 color pages, 21 b/w photos, 35 illustrations, 16 maps, 7 charts, booklist, glossary, index. 213 pages. **$12.95**

MONTANA HANDBOOK by W.C. McRae and Judy Jewell
The wild West is yours with this extensive guide to the Treasure State, complete with travel practicalities, history, and lively essays on Montana life. 8 color pages, 62 b/w photos, 43 illustrations, 49 maps, 10 charts, booklist, index. 393 pages. **$13.95**

NEVADA HANDBOOK by Deke Castleman
Nevada Handbook puts the Silver State into perspective and makes it manageable and affordable. 34 b/w photos, 43 illustrations, 37 maps, 17 charts, booklist, index. 400 pages. **$12.95**

NEW MEXICO HANDBOOK by Stephen Metzger
A close-up and complete look at every aspect of this wondrous state. 8 color pages, 85 b/w photos, 63 illustrations, 50 maps, 10 charts, booklist, index. 375 pages.   **$13.95**

NORTHERN CALIFORNIA HANDBOOK by Kim Weir
An outstanding companion for imaginative travel in the territory north of the Tehachapis. 12 color pages, 200 b/w photos, 54 maps, 36 illustrations, booklist, index. 759 pages.   **$16.95**

OREGON HANDBOOK by Stuart Warren and Ted Long Ishikawa
Brimming with travel practicalities and insider views on Oregon's history, culture, arts, and activities. 8 color pages, 113 b/w photos, 26 illustrations, 28 maps, 20 charts, booklist, index. 422 pages.   **$12.95**

TEXAS HANDBOOK by Joe Cummings
Seasoned travel writer Joe Cummings brings an insider's perspective to his home state. 8 color pages, 79 b/w photos, 60 maps, 45 illustrations, 18 charts. booklist, index. 483 pages. **$13.95**

UTAH HANDBOOK by Bill Weir
Weir gives you all the carefully researched facts and background to make your visit a success. 8 color pages, 102 b/w photos, 61 illustrations, 30 maps, 9 charts, booklist, index. 452 pages. **$12.95**

WASHINGTON HANDBOOK by Dianne J. Boulerice Lyons and Archie Satterfield
Covers sights, shopping, services, transportation, and outdoor recreation, with complete listings for restaurants and accommodations. 8 color pages, 92 b/w photos, 24 illustrations, 81 maps, 8 charts, booklist, index. 433 pages.   **$13.95**

WYOMING HANDBOOK by Don Pitcher
All you need to know to open the doors to this wide and wild state. 16 color pages, 30 b/w photos, 42 illustrations, 64 maps, 19 charts, booklist, index. 427 pages.   **$12.95**

YUCATAN HANDBOOK by Chicki Mallan
All the information you'll need to guide you into every corner of this exotic land. 8 color pages, 154 b/w photos, 55 illustrations, 57 maps, 70 charts, appendix, booklist, Mayan and Spanish glossaries, index. 391 pages.   **$12.95**

The International Series

EGYPT HANDBOOK by Kathy Hansen
An invaluable resource for intelligent travel in Egypt. 8 color pages, 20 b/w photos, 150 illustrations, 80 detailed maps and plans to museums and archaeological sites, Arabic glossary, booklist, index. 510 pages.   **$14.95**

MOSCOW-LENINGRAD HANDBOOK by Masha Nordbye
Provides the visitor with an extensive introduction to the history, culture, and people of these two great cities, as well as practical information on where to stay, eat, and shop. 8 color pages, 36 b/w photos, 20 illustrations, 16 maps, 9 charts, booklist, index. 205 pages. **$12.95**

NEPAL HANDBOOK by Kerry Moran
Whether you're planning a week in Kathmandu or months out on the trail, *Nepal Handbook* will take you into the heart of this Himalayan jewel. 16 color pages, 76 b/w photos, 45 illustrations, 46 maps, 9 charts, booklist, glossary, index. 378 pages. **$12.95**

NEPALI AAMA by Broughton Coburn
A delightful photo-journey into the life of a Gurung tribeswoman of Central Nepal. Having lived with Aama (translated, "mother") for two years, first as an outsider and later as an adopted member of the family, Coburn presents an intimate glimpse into a culture alive with humor, folklore, religion, and ancient rituals. 67 b/w photos. 165 pages. **$13.95**

PAKISTAN HANDBOOK by Isobel Shaw
For armchair travelers and trekkers alike, the most detailed and authoritative guide to Pakistan ever published. 28 color pages, 86 maps, appendices, Urdu glossary, booklist, index. 478 pages. **$15.95**

Moonbelts

Made of heavy-duty Cordura nylon, the Moonbelt offers maximum protection for your money and important papers. This all-weather pouch slips under your shirt or waistband, rendering it virtually undetectable and inaccessible to pickpockets. One-inch-wide nylon webbing, heavy-duty zipper, one-inch quick release buckle. Accommodates traveler's checks, passport, cash, photos. Size 5 x 9 inches. Black. **$8.95**

Travel Matters

Travel Matters is a biannual newsletter for travelers, containing book reviews, practical travel news, articles, and humorous essays. For a free copy, call Moon Publications toll-free at (800) 345-5473.

New travel handbooks may be available that are not on this list.
To find out more about current or upcoming titles,
call us toll-free at (800) 345-5473.

IMPORTANT ORDERING INFORMATION

FOR FASTER SERVICE: Call to locate the bookstore nearest you that carries Moon Travel Handbooks or order directly from Moon Publications:

(800) 345-5473 · Monday-Friday · 9 a.m.-5 p.m. PST · fax (916) 345-6751

PRICES: All prices are subject to change. We always ship the most current edition. We will let you know if there is a price increase on the book you ordered.

SHIPPING & HANDLING OPTIONS:

1) Domestic UPS or USPS first class (allow 10 working days for delivery):
   $3.50 for the first item, 50 cents for each additional item.

Exceptions:

· **Moonbelt** shipping is $1.50 for one, 50 cents for each additional belt.

· Add $2.00 for same-day handling.

2) UPS 2nd Day Air or Printed Airmail requires a special quote.

3) International Surface Bookrate (8-12 weeks delivery):
   $3.00 for the first item, $1.00 for each additional item. Note: Moon Publications cannot guarantee international surface bookrate shipping.

FOREIGN ORDERS: All orders which originate outside the U.S.A. must be paid for with either an International Money Order or a check in U.S. currency drawn on a major U.S. bank based in the U.S.A.

TELEPHONE ORDERS: We accept Visa or MasterCard payments. Minimum order is US $15.00. Call in your order: 1 (800) 345-5473. 9 a.m.-5 p.m. Pacific Standard Time.

ORDER FORM

**Be sure to call (800) 345-5473 for current prices and editions or for the name of the bookstore nearest you that carries Moon Travel Handbooks · 9 a.m.-5 p.m. PST
(See important ordering information on preceding page)**

Name:_____Date:_____

Street:_____

City:_____Daytime Phone:_____

State or Country:_____Zip Code:_____

Quantity	Title	Price

	Taxable Total	
	Sales Tax (7.25%) for California Residents	
	Shipping & Handling	
	TOTAL	

Ship: ☐ 1st class   ☐ UPS (no P.O. Boxes)   ☐ International Surface

Ship to: ☐ address above   ☐ other_____

_____

_____

Make checks payable to:
Moon Publications Inc., 722 Wall Street, Chico, California 95928 U.S.A.
We Accept Visa and MasterCard
To Order: Call in your Visa or MasterCard number, or send a written order with your Visa or MasterCard number and expiration date clearly written.

Card Number: ☐ **Visa**   ☐ **MasterCard**

☐ ☐ ☐ ☐   ☐ ☐ ☐ ☐   ☐ ☐ ☐ ☐   ☐ ☐ ☐ ☐

Exact Name on Card: ☐ same as above   expiration date:_____

☐ other_____

signature_____

3-80-8

WHERE TO BUY THIS BOOK

Bookstores and Libraries:
Moon Publications Handbooks are sold worldwide. Please write our sales manager for a list of wholesalers and distributors in your area that stock our travel handbooks.

Travelers:
We would like to have Moon Publications Handbooks available throughout the world. Please ask your bookstore to write or call us for ordering information. If your bookstore will not order our guides for you, please write or call for a free catalog.

MOON PUBLICATIONS INC.
722 WALL STREET
CHICO, CA 95928 U.S.A.
tel: (800) 345-5473
fax: (916) 345-6751

ABOUT THE AUTHOR

Joe Cummings' Texas roots reach back to when his great-great-great grandfather emigrated to the state from "up north" in the 1840's. Another relative, David Lawhon, published the state's first bilingual newspaper, *The Texian and Emigrant's Guide,* which was printed in both Spanish and English and praised by the *New York Courier* as a publication "edited with intelligence and success." Lawhon was later appointed chief justice of Jefferson County.

With his Panhandle-born father in the Army, Joe moved in and out of Texas, California, Washington, D.C., and France before attending college and university in North Carolina and California. Attracted to geological extremes (a probable Texas legacy), his first in-depth journeys after college were in the river deltas and rainforests of Southeast Asia, where he worked as a Peace Corps volunteer (Thailand) and university lecturer (Malaysia) and later authored and co-authored popular guidebooks to Asian destinations for Australia's Lonely Planet Publications. Joe is also the author of Moon's *Baja Handbook.*

Joe criss-crosses Texas's freeways, ranch roads, plains, forests, mountains, and canyons for every edition of *Texas Handbook.*

Joe Cummings